Cardiac Rehabilitation
Programme.

Do NOT REMOVE

DR E. W. THORNTON

Anxiety and the Heart

Edited by

D. G. Byrne
The Australian National University
Canberra, Australia

Ray H. Rosenman
SRI International
Menlo Park, California

⬤HEMISPHERE PUBLISHING CORPORATION
A member of the Taylor & Francis Group

New York Washington Philadelphia London

ANXIETY AND THE HEART

1 2 3 4 5 6 7 8 9 0   B R B R   9 8 7 6 5 4 3 2 1 0

This book was set in Times Roman by Hemisphere Publishing Corporation. The editors were Nancy Niemann, Lisa Warren, and Deanna K. D'Errico; the production supervisor was Peggy M. Rote; and the typesetters were Linda Andros, Lori Knoernschild, and Sandra F. Watts.
Cover design by Sharon DePass.
Printing and binding by Braun-Brumfield, Inc.

A CIP catalog record for this book is available from the British Library.

Library of Congress Cataloging-in-Publication Data

Anxiety and the heart / edited by D. G. Byrne and Ray Rosenman.
    p. cm. — (The Series in health psychology and behavioral
  medicine)
    "Outgrowth of the Ninth World Congress of the International College of Psychosomatic Medicine held in Sydney, Australia, August
  30 to September 4, 1987"—Foreword.
    Includes bibliographical references.
    1. Heart—Diseases—Psychosomatic aspects—Congresses.
  2. Anxiety—Congresses. I. Byrne, D. G. (Donald Glenn)
  II. Rosenman, Ray H., date. III. International College of
  Psychosomatic Medicine. World Congress (9th : 1987 : Sydney,
  N.S.W.) IV. Series.
    RC682.A59 1990
  616.1'23071—dc20   89-26894
                                                                              CIP

ISBN 0-89116-860-5
ISSN 8756-467X

Contents

PART I
BASIC CONCEPTS OF ANXIETY

PART II
BIOLOGICAL APPROACHES TO ANXIETY

     and Denial   **259**
     Jerry Suls

     Empirical Studies on Chronic Psychological Distress and Type A Behavior   **260**
     The Role of Personal Beliefs, Uncertainty, and Avoidance in Type A Behavior   **265**
     Summary and Implications   **271**
     References   **272**

12 **Anxiety and Mitral Valve Prolapse**   **277**
     Stephen R. Dager and David L. Dunner

     Pathophysiology   **277**
     Epidemiology   **279**
     Etiology   **279**
     Anxiety Disorders and Mitral Valve Prolapse   **283**
     Diagnosis   **281**
     Medical Intervention   **286**
     Treatment of Mitral Valve Prolapse   **288**
     Summary   **288**
     References   **289**

13 **Pathogenesis of Mitral Valve Prolapse and Its Relationship to**
     Anxiety   **295**
     Ray H. Rosenman

     Variants of Mitral Valve Prolapse   **295**
     Pathologic Findings in MVP   **297**
     Idiopathic Mitral Valve Prolapse: A Normal Variant   **305**
     The Association Between Mitral Valve Prolapse and Underlying Conditions   **307**
     Anxiety and Mitral Valve Prolapse Syndrome   **319**
     The Possible Dominant Role of Salt   **324**
     Conclusion   **327**
     References   **329**

14 **The Relationship of Anxiety and Cardiovascular Reactivity**   **347**
     Marcia M. Ward

     Definitions   **347**
     Studies of Anxiety and Cardiovascular Reactivity in Normal Subjects   **348**
     Studies of Cardiovascular Reactivity in Patients with Generalized
         Anxiety Disorder   **352**
     Studies of Cardiovascular Reactivity in Patients with Panic Disorder   **355**
     Problems in Studies of Anxiety and Cardiovascular Reactivity   **357**
     Conclusion   **359**
     References   **362**

PART IV
RESPONSES TO CARDIOVASCULAR ILLNESS
AND PATIENT MANAGEMENT

PART V
CONCLUSIONS

Contributors

Ezra Amsterdam   University of California Davis Medical Center, Sacramento, California, USA

Gavin Andrews   St. Vincent's Hospital, Darlinghurst, Australia

D. G. Byrne   The National Australian University, Canberra, Australia

A. E. Byrne   Alcohol and Drug Foundation of Australia, Canberra, Australia

Stephen R. Dager   University of Washington, Seattle, Washington, USA

John E. Deanfield   The Hospital for Sick Children, London, England

Christian M. Delandsheere   University of Liege, Liege, Belgium

David L. Dunner   University of Washington, Seattle, Washington, USA

Murray Esler   Baker Medical Research Institute, Prahran Victoria, Australia

John H. Griest   University of Wisconsin, Madison, Wisconsin, USA

Paul Hjemdahl   Karolinska Hospital, Stockholm, Sweden

Eric Hollander   New York State Psychiatric Institute, New York, New York, USA

Peter Horlock   MRC Cyclotron Unit, London, England

Gail H. Ironson   Stanford University, Stanford, California, USA

James Jefferson   University Hospital, Madison, Wisconsin, USA

Ernest Johnson   University of Michigan Medical Center, Ann Arbor, Michigan, USA

Malcolm Kensett   MRC Cyclotron Unit, London, England

Michael R. Liebowitz   Columbia University, New York, New York, USA

Paul McReynolds   University of Nevada, Reno, Nevada, USA

Chandra Patel   University College and Middlesex School of Medicine, London, UK

Ray Rosenman   SRI International, Menlo Park, California, USA

Neil Schneiderman   University of Miami, Coral Gables, Florida, USA

Andrew P. Selwyn   Brigham and Women's Hospital, Boston, Massachusetts, USA

Michael Shea   University of Michigan Medical Center, Ann Arbor, Michigan, USA

Charles Spielberger   University of South Florida, Tampa, Florida, USA

Theodore Stern   Massachusetts General Hospital, Boston, Massachusetts, USA

Jerry Suls   State University of New York, Albany, New York, USA

Marcia Ward   SRI International, Menlo Park, California, USA

Richard A. Wilson   Oregon Health Sciences University, Portland, Oregon, USA

Contributors

Foreword

This book is an outgrowth of the Ninth World Congress of the International College of Psychosomatic Medicine held in Sydney, Australia, August 30 to September 4, 1987. Dr. Byrne of the Australian National University in Canberra organized a symposium on cardiovascular disorders and asked Dr. Rosenman of San Francisco to give the keynote address and to hold a full-day workshop on cardiovascular disorders. Instead, Rosenman and Byrne arranged a workshop on anxiety and the heart, aimed at discussing various aspects of the interface between brain and heart. A generous educational grant was given by The Upjohn Company of Kalamazoo, Michigan, to the college for support of this workshop, and lectures were given by several of the authors represented in this book, including Byrne, Dunner, Esler, Jefferson, Rosenman, Shea, and Spielberger. After the symposium, the organizers decided to use the nucleus of manuscripts as the basis for a comprehensive book on the issue of anxiety and the heart.

In today's science, inductive approaches are favored over deductive thinking, and methodology is increasingly reductionist. In medicine the old division of "organic" and "functional" has almost disappeared. These days everything is thought of as ultimately resolvable if just the right gene were to be found or the underlying molecular biological phenomena could be understood. Recently, I presented to some psychiatry residents data on personality patterns in patients with borderline hypertension. These individuals are sensitive to their surroundings, submissive to other people, and prone to hold in a considerable amount of unexpressed anger. My colleagues and I postulated that people with such personalities may be characterized behaviorally by increased vigilance. Could this behavior be responsible for an excessive sympathetic tone so often found in these individuals? And could that excessive sympathetic tone play a role in the pathophysiology of their hypertension? The psychiatry residents were not ready to join me in these musings. Clearly, they said, the behavior, sympathetic overactivity, hormonal imbalance, and high blood pressure must be expressions of the same underlying membrane or protein abnormality in the genetically inherited condition we call hypertension. Maybe they are right, but are humans really just complexes of DNA for which everything is predetermined and just waiting to happen, or do an individual's life experience, responses to challenges, and idiosyncrasies also count?

No one questions the fact that when you are acutely scared your heart beats wildly and your stomach feels as tight as a knot. Why is it no possible to extrapolate that, when repeated frequently, this behavior may have some health consequences? The answer is simple. Behavioral factors are hard to measure, and what cannot be measured is less likely to be investigated. Yet research continues, thanks to hard-working individuals who dare to explore a difficult, but intellectually challenging, area. The editors of this book undertook to survey the accumulated knowledge in the area of anxiety and the heart. As the reader will plainly see, much is known, and there is no doubt that the heart pays a price for chronic anxiety. It is also clear that some health conditions induce anxiety. Understanding of the physiology of chronic anxiety and of its neurohumoral correlates has greatly increased. This volume is proof that physiologic, integrative approaches to human conditions are important and that such research can be productive. I am glad that the editors nurtured this book from its design to publication.

Stevo Julius
University of Michigan Medical Center

Preface

The possibility that a link exists between anxiety and the heart has captured the attention of both physicians and their patients for as long as the history of medicine has been documented. In much more recent times, evidence has been brought to bear on the role that the emotions might play in the regulation of the cardiovascular system. The demonstration, in the psychophysiology laboratory, that the imposition of cognitive challenges could produce repeatable if not entirely consistent responses measured within the several modalities of cardiodynamic activity, gave rise to the view that patterns of individual behavioral and emotional function and dysfunction might be reflected in chronic alterations to levels of cardiovascular activation. The sheer volume of experimental work aimed at specifying the precise (or more often, the less than precise) relation between psychological and cardiovascular functioning has, over time, produced a conviction among many scientists, both medical and psychological, that although such relationships are as yet to be fully determined, persistence coupled with the increased sophistication of measurement will ultimately lead to a set of "biological laws" allowing the accurate prediction of cardiovascular responses to psychological events. The need to evaluate the present status of this evidence and of the expectations arising out of it produced the motivation for this book.

In order to cover the whole range of topics relevant to the broad issue of anxiety and the heart, we have arranged the chapters deliberately into five sections. The first section deals with basic concepts of anxiety from both the psychological and psychiatric perspectives. Its aim is to acquaint the reader, from whatever background, with contemporary thought on both normal and clinical anxiety. McReynolds's chapter on current conceptual issues serves as an orientation to the notion of anxiety and is followed by Andrews's chapter on the psychiatric view of anxiety. This theme is followed up in the chapter by Hollander and Liebowitz, in which the concept of "panicogenic syndrome" is introduced. The final chapter in this section, by Spielberger and Rickman, examines current trends in the measurement of anxiety as both a normal and an abnormal phenomenon. Section 1 therefore allows those readers quite naive in the areas of psychology and psychiatry to acquire a working knowledge of anxiety sufficient for a complete understanding of the material to follow.

The second section examines the biological bases and consequences of anxiety and is crucial to the theme of the book, to the extent that its material provides the possible link between anxiety and the heart. If there is a connection between the experience of emotion and both the regulation and dysfunction of the cardiovascular system, it is most likely to be found in the complex and intricate physiological and pharmacological mechanisms interposed between a psychological state and a physiological or a pathological condition. Hjemdahl's chapter details the possible neuropharmacological mechanisms linking imposed stress (laboratory stressors) with cardiovascular activity, whereas Esler examines the neurochemical mechanisms involved in the regulation of cardiovascular activity in both health and disease. Schneiderman's chapter provides a conceptual tie for this material by specifically considering the biochemical and neuroendocrinological determinants and consequences of anxiety.

With both the conceptual and biological evidence firmly in mind, the third section turns to the clinical and epidemiological accounts of the evidence linking anxiety to coronary disease in each of its several manifestations. The chapter by Byrne and Byrne presents the epidemiological evidence for the role of stress and anxiety in the onset of coronary heart disease (myocardial infarction), whereas Shea looks more particularly at the laboratory evidence linking stress with silent myocardial ischemia. Amsterdam considers anxiety in relation to the precipitation of potentially fatal cardiac arrhythmias, whereas Suls covers the controversial area of the relation between emotions and the Type A behavior pattern. The topic of mitral valve prolapse and anxiety is comprehensively discussed in chapters by Dager and Dunner and by Rosenman. Finally, Ward discusses the evidence linking anxiety with cardiovascular reactivity and the development of cardiovascular pathology.

In the fourth section, evidence arising from the laboratory and from epidemiological studies is translated for the purpose of patient management. Byrne discusses emotional and behavioral responses to myocardial infarction and the psychological procedures and strategies that have been put to use in the care of the survivor of this illness event. The pharmacological and psychological management of clinical anxiety is covered in some detail by Jefferson and Greist, whereas Stern extends this to the management of anxiety specifically in patients with coronary heart disease. Patel's chapter on the psychological management of anxiety in hypertensive patients concludes the section.

The final section, with concluding chapters by Rosenman and by Byrne, seeks to draw the material together and to present a balanced view of this complex and as yet unresolved area from the perspectives of both the cardiologist and the psychologist. The conclusions reached by the two authors, though arising from professional orientations that seem widely disparate, are remarkably similar. In essence, they hold that although much of the evidence, viewed without criticism, supports a relation between anxiety (sometimes synonymously referred to as stress) and one or other forms of cardiovascular disease, a more careful examination of the evidence, its methodology, and the strength of the results would recommend a more cautious view. Acute stress or anxiety, often imposed under laboratory conditions, can have a marked effect on levels of cardiovascular activation and on the pharmacological and endocrinological mechanisms underlying these; the associations between emotional states and pathological changes to the cardiovascular system in the longer term are far more equivocal.

Anxiety and the Heart had its beginnings in a symposium organized for the Ninth World Congress of the International College of Psychosomatic Medicine held in Sydney, Australia, in 1987. Support for this symposium came in the form of an educational grant from the Upjohn Company to the Congress for the purpose of supporting the satellite symposium. We are very grateful to the Upjohn Company for this invaluable assistance in sowing the seed for this book, and we are particularly grateful to Mr. Douglas E. McCarter of Upjohn for initiating the company's support. Following the symposium, the scope of the developing book was expanded, and further contributors were invited to provide additional chapters. Dr. Charles Spielberger provided considerable support in this process. Our thanks are also extended to him, not simply for providing useful contacts but also, and most important, for having enough faith in our efforts to accept the book for the health psychology and behavioral medicine series that he edits for the Hemisphere Publishing Corporation. Much of the final editorial work for the book was undertaken at the Australian National University, and we wish to thank Mrs. Monika Reinhart for her efforts in the process of putting the pieces together. In the latter stages of production, Mr. Ron Wilder of Hemisphere was instrumental in maintaining the pace of work, and we are grateful to him for his careful prompting of our activities.

The greatest acknowledgment that the editors of any composite work must make, however, is to their contributors, and we extend our sincere thanks to those scientists and clinicians, all eminent in their own fields, who have taken the time to prepare chapters for this book. Their knowledge and scholarship is reflected in each of the chapters, and it is this collected wisdom that give the substance to a work that attempts to bring together such a diverse but essentially interrelated set of themes and topics.

D. G. Byrne
Ray H. Rosenman

I

BASIC CONCEPTS OF ANXIETY

1

The Concept of Anxiety: Background and Current Issues

Paul McReynolds

INTRODUCTION

Anxiety is one of the most characteristic and most powerful of all human emotions. The influence that this strong negative affect exerts over the lives of people everywhere can hardly be overestimated. The decisions that individuals make, the ventures they undertake, and the actions they avoid are all partially determined by their motivations to avoid or diminish feelings of anxiety. There are a number of other terms—nervousness, tension, stress, worry, feeling upset, and the like—that people frequently employ to reflect an inner distress, but these numerous loose synonyms only emphasize the commonplaceness of the experience of anxiety.

In view of the ubiquity of anxiety in the human condition, it might be expected that this concept would play a significant role in scientific explanations of behavior, and this is definitely the case. Indeed, there is probably no other construct that has been so widely employed as a mediating variable in psychological theories. Thus, the concept of anxiety is central in conceptualizations of psychopathology, motivation, and personality. At the psychological level, approaches as diverse as psychoanalysis, behaviorism, cognitivism, and humanism all find the anxiety construct useful, if not actually essential. Currently, research on anxiety is the one of the most exciting and active areas in psychology (see, e.g., Barlow, 1988; Klein & Rabkin, 1981; Kleinknecht, 1986; Schwarzer, 1984; Spielberger & Sarason, 1986; Tuma & Maser, 1985). Anxiety is, of course, a biological as well as a psychological phenomenon, and is also the focus of extensive study from the genetic and physiological perspectives.

These introductory remarks lead naturally to the following questions: What is anxiety? What are its correlates, its effects, its origins? How is it to be conceptualized and explained? The purpose of this chapter is to provide a general introduction to the concept of anxiety and in so doing to offer at least some tentative answers to these questions. My focus is on contemporary research and theory, and my orientation is primarily psychological and behavioral. A later section of this volume will survey biological aspects of anxiety.

3

HISTORICAL BACKGROUND

Interest in the concept of anxiety has a long history, reaching back to the earliest periods of recorded thought (McReynolds, 1986). Thus, anxiety—in the form of concern over mortality—was a key theme in the earliest preserved narrative poem, the Sumerian *Epic of Gilgamesh*. A concern with inner anguish is also expressed in the earliest books of the Bible; thus we read in Isaiah 41:10: "Fear thou not, for I am with thee: be not dismayed; for I am thy God." By the time of the Hellenistic period, the notion of anxiety had been systematically articulated, as we see in this quotation from the Stoic philosopher Epictetus (1st century A.D./1944):

> When I see anyone anxious, I say, what does this man want? Unless he wanted something or other not in his own power, how could he still be anxious? A musician, for instance, feels no anxiety while he is singing by himself; but when he appears upon the stage he does, even if his voice be ever so good, or he plays ever so well. For what he wishes is not only to sing well but likewise to gain applause. But this is not in his own power. . . . When, therefore you see anyone pale with anxiety, just as the physician pronounces from the complexion that a patient is disordered in the spleen and another in the liver, so do you likewise say, this man is disordered in his desires and aversions; he cannot walk steadily; he is in a fever. For nothing else changes the complexion, or causes trembling, or sets the teeth chattering. (pp. 117–119)

Coming now to the modern era, we find an interesting conception of anxiety in John Locke's (1690/1959) *An Essay Concerning Human Understanding*. Locke was concerned with the development in an individual of *uneasiness*—a term then used to refer to mental distress and worry. He theorized that both unpleasant physical states and unsatisfied strivings lead to heightened uneasiness and that there is an inherent motivation to reduce one's uneasiness. Several decades later, Francis Hutcheson (cf. McReynolds, 1969, p. xiii), although he did not use the term *conditioning*, delineated what amounted to a conception of conditioned fears.

In 1758 William Battie, an English physician, published *A Treatise on Madness*. This innovative work included what I believe to have been the first technical discussion of anxiety by that name. Battie's conception, apparently influenced by the views of Locke, held that anxiety is the result of the extreme intensity of stimulation. Battie's work is memorable also for suggesting that anxiety can be adaptive. It is, he wrote, "absolutely necessary to our preservation, in such a manner, that without its severe but useful admonitions the several species of animals would speedily be destroyed" (p. 28). Another important contribution by Battie was the designation of extreme anxiety as a separate mental disorder.

In 1826 a Belgian psychiatrist, Joseph Guislain, posited that anxiety is influential in the development of psychopathology, and in 1859, in Germany, Heinrich Neumann proposed that anxiety arises when a person becomes aware of a threat to vital concerns and that it serves as a danger signal. In the same period, the philosopher Søren Kierkegaard, in his *Concept of Anxiety* (1844/1980), emphasized the relation between anxiety and personal choice, and in so doing laid the foundation for the existential interpretation of anxiety.

By the time Sigmund Freud published his first paper on anxiety (1895/1959a), the theme of anxiety was fairly common in technical works. Freud proposed a new diagnostic category, "anxiety-neurosis," which he posited to arise from the psyche's inability to discharge endogenous sexual excitation. More generally, Freud conceived that "the psyche develops the affect of anxiety when it feels itself incapable of dealing (by an adequate reaction) with a task (danger) approaching it externally" (pp. 101–102).

Freud later revised and elaborated his theory of anxiety, and his book, *The Problem of Anxiety* (1926/1936), remains one of the classics in the field. In this final formulation Freud attributed anxiety to an influx of stimuli too great for the individual to master. He conceived that the anticipation of a traumatic situation leads to signal anxiety, and he distinguished between normal (realistic) and pathological (neurotic) anxiety.

Since Freud's work, the concept of anxiety has played a major, even central, role in psychodynamic theories. This trend was particularly pronounced in the conceptions of Harry Stack Sullivan (1953), who conceived that anxiety at the adult level can be explained "as anticipated unfavorable appraisal of one's current activity by someone whose opinion is significant" (p. 113). He placed great emphasis on the direct spread of anxiety from a mothering person to an infant.

The concept of fear is closely related to that of anxiety, and fear was the operative term in early behaviorist approaches to the problem of anxiety. John B. Watson, founder of behaviorism, which held that certain fears in infants are innate and may be conditioned to yield an emotional response (Watson & Rayner, 1920). The learning theorist O. H. Mowrer, in 1939, proposed a stimulus–response analysis of anxiety. He considered fear as the anticipation of pain and suggested that fears are difficult to unlearn because the organism tends to avoid the situation that originally caused the fear, even when avoidance is no longer effective. Other prominent learning theorists in the 1950s and 1960s who focused on anxiety, primarily in its role as a motivational variable, were John Dollard and Neil Miller (1950) and Janet Taylor Spence and Kenneth Spence (1966).

This brief and heavily abridged historical survey is perhaps sufficient to demonstrate that recognition of the significance of anxiety and questions about its underlying nature have long been of scientific concern. It is interesting to note that many of the theories proposed to account for anxiety have recurred throughout history. For example, Sullivan's view that anxiety results from anticipation of a negative evaluation by others was augured by Epictetus's interpretation quoted earlier. The notion that anxiety has an adaptive value and that it may serve as a signal for possible danger has also been suggested more than once in the past. Another recurrent theme in speculations about anxiety is the idea that it is somehow related to an individual's feelings of control or mastery over relevant events. Still another question with a historical record is whether normal and pathological anxiety are qualitatively, or only quantitatively, different. All of these themes from the past are involved in contemporary research and theory.

THE STRUCTURE OF ANXIETY

Anxiety is an emotion characterized by intense feelings of inner distress and anguish, and by associated behavioral and physiological features. As with all emotions and feeling states, it is difficult to define anxiety—especially its phenomenal aspects—in a rigorous way. For this reason, investigators have sometimes sought to emphasize physiological and behavioral indices, which can be highly objective, in evaluating and studying anxiety. Such indices, however, invaluable as they are in increasing our understanding of anxiety, have a number of limitations and cannot replace or serve adequately as an index of phenomenal anxiety. Self-reports of felt anxiety do not give the whole story either. In short, anxiety is a complex phenomenon, the explanation of which must be approached from several different perspectives.

A number of authors have concerned themselves with the basic structure of anxiety. Hamilton (1959), working with psychiatric patients, derived two anxiety factors, which he interpreted as "psychic anxiety" and "somatic anxiety." This result was given further support in a study by Buss (1962), who related the two factors to Eysenck's (1961) posited factors of autonomic overreactivity and conditioned anxiety responses (restlessness, worry, and muscular tension). The two-faceted conception of anxiety—in terms of its psychological and physiological manifestations—continues to be central in anxiety research, but a number of more elaborate schematizations have been put forth.

Lang (1985) has proposed a tripartite classification, which includes verbal report of distress, fear-related behavioral acts (e.g., avoidance or hypervigilance), and visceral and somatic activity. In Lang's conceptualization the patient is not considered an observer of an inner state, but rather the verbal reports as such are considered part of the anxiety response. Lang emphasizes that the three data sources are only loosely coupled, with the implication that no one of them can adequately encompass anxiety. Lader (cf. Jablensky, 1985, p. 741) suggested four relevant aspects of anxiety: the subjective, cognitive, behavioral, and physiological. Akiskal (1985) proposed the following five dimensions: subjective experience, cognition, arousal and vigilance, autonomic hyperactivity, and observable behavior. I (McReynolds, 1976, p. 37) have identified four important facets of anxiety—the affective, motivational, behavioral, and physiological. Although these various ways of conceptualizing anxiety do not take us very far toward gaining a fundamental understanding of the emotion, they are important in emphasizing that anxiety is not a limited affective variable, but rather is involved in the entire functioning of the human organism.

Phenomenology of Anxiety

The experience of intense anxiety is exceedingly unpleasant. As is true with all feelings, moods, and emotions, however, the phenomenology of anxiety is difficult to describe in words—which, after all, are cognitive and informational in form. Terms like anguish, distress, uneasiness, tension, and apprehension come to mind. Vague as they are, such terms seem quite sufficient to make it possible for people to communicate meaningfully about the private experience of anxiety and to certify the general reality of the phenomenon. Arguments that verbal reports of anxiety should be treated simply as verbal data, without assuming that they refer to actual inner experience, are philosophically ill-founded and methodologically ill-advised. Only by assuming that there is a real experience behind the verbal report does it make sense to probe deeply to learn further details of an anxious experience and to judge if the verbal report is truthful.

Feelings of anxiety are sometimes so vague as to be almost formless—that is, devoid of specific content—and is termed free-floating anxiety. More frequently, however, the anxiety concerns—or, to put it metaphorically, is attached to—some particular topic, that is, the person is anxious about something. For example, a man may be anxious about his relations with his wife, or about an upcoming exam, or about an inappropriate behavior in the past. From having collected brief descriptions of personal anxiety over many years it is my conclusion that the contentual foci of anxiety are almost endless. Certain content themes, however, can be grouped into useful categories, such as separation anxiety, speech anxiety, social anxiety, and achievement anxiety.

Not only is there great diversity among the subjective concerns in different episodes of anxiety, but also there are marked individual differences in the extent and nature of the perceived physiological concomitants; that is, felt anxiety leads to, or is associated with, numerous autonomic and somatic changes, and not only does the pattern of these changes differ somewhat from person to person, but also individuals vary in the extent to which they are aware of such physiological processes (Blaskovich & Katkin, 1983; Scheier, Carver, & Matthews, 1983). It can be concluded, then, that both the idiosyncratic nature of the cognitive aspects of anxiety and individual variations in the perception of its physiological aspects contribute to the marked phenomenal heterogeneity of different episodes of anxiety.

Anxiety as a Motivator

The role of anxiety as a motivator is clearly expressed in statements such as "I'm anxious to get the job." Implicit in this statement are the propositions that (a) "I will be anxious if I fail to obtain the job" and (b) anxiety is extremely unpleasant, and thus to be avoided (this interpretation of course does not say that avoidance of anxiety is the only motivational factor involved). The use of the term *anxiety* in a motivational context in everyday life is probably almost as commonplace as is its use in an affective sense. Nor is the motivational usage of *anxiety* any less prominent in technical conceptions of motivation. Among the major theorists who have used anxiety avoidance as a motivational construct are S. Freud (1926/1936), A. Freud (1937/ 1966), Sullivan (1953), and Dollard and Miller (1950). Although anxiety is conceptualized differently by various theorists, the essential assumption in all such models is that felt anxiety is a state that organisms desperately seek to avoid or reduce, in a straightforward, hedonistic sense. There is ample empirical evidence for this assumption, and it is also supported by the great extent to which distraught individuals seek professional help or use pharmaceutical agents such as alcohol to relieve their anxieties.

As compared with other internal motivational states, such as hunger or physical pains, anxiety at the human level has a peculiar fluidity and modifiability. Because anxiety can arise from the way an individual perceives events (e.g., feeling that one cannot manage a given task), it can be reduced by perceiving things differently (e.g., deciding that he or she can manage the task). More generally, anxiety arises largely from the way in which an individual views and interprets events and experiences, and can be magnified and reduced, or attributed to alternate sources, by various internal cognitive maneuvers. It is the unique fluidity of anxiety as a motivatior that has made it so theoretically attractive to psychodynamic theorists.

The motivation to take steps to reduce anxiety can be very great, but it does not always prevail. A behavioral choice is usually the result of some combination of partially divergent motives, and when anxiety is involved, it is often a matter of balancing the negative pull of anxiety with the positive pull of some positive incentive (McReynolds, 1971). It is of course commonplace for individuals to deliberately choose to engage in activities that they are well aware will cause anxiety. For example, a person may deliver a speech, confront a supervisor, or explore a cave despite the anxiety involved. A major contributor to a person's feeling of stress is a continuing pattern of deliberate engagements in anxiety-provoking activities.

Anxiety as an Emotion

There is no doubt that anxiety is an emotion: It has all the characteristics commonly ascribed to that concept—strong affective feelings and motivational, physiological, and behavioral concomitants. Furthermore, like other emotions, anxiety applies to the entire organism and cannot be localized. Thus, with respect to pain, one might say, for example, "My tooth hurts," but in the case of an emotion, the whole person is involved. Similarly, we say "I am happy" or "I am anxious." Emotions tend to arise in situations that are highly significant or important to a person. The fact that anxiety—an emotion—is also a motivator is not a cause for confusion; many, perhaps all, emotions have motivational implications.

The ancient Stoics posited four basic *passions* (a term similar to the present *emotion*): joy, sadness, hope, and fear. Descartes proposed six primitive passions: joy, sadness, love, hatred, desire, and wonder. By the time of William James (1890), the emphasis had shifted to the process of emotion, rather than an enumeration of the types of emotion. James theorized that bodily visceral changes follow directly from one's perception of exciting stimuli, that one then perceives these bodily changes, and that emotion is the awareness of these physiological changes. This formulation, it may be noted, is quite the opposite of the common sense view that one first experiences emotion and then visceral changes. Although James's position (sometimes called the James–Lange theory, because a similar view was proposed by Carl Lange) has long been discredited in its original strong form, it continues to have considerable indirect influence on contemporary emotion theory. This influence is in the form of a renewed emphasis on the perception of somatic and visceral variables in emotion, including anxiety.

The study of emotion is currently a very active research field that includes several different strands. Perhaps the most prominent of these trends is a renaissance of interest in the question of basic emotions (e.g., Izard, 1979; Plutchik, 1980; Tomkins, 1984). The strongest evidence for the existence of fundamental human emotions is that gathered by Ekman (1984) and his colleagues in their investigations of facial expressions in different cultures. Their findings support the existence of six innate emotions: fear, surprise, anger, disgust, sadness (sometimes labeled distress), and happiness. Izard (1972; Izard & Buechler, 1980), who has specifically discussed anxiety, posits 10 basic emotions: interest, joy, surprise, sadness, anger, disgust, contempt, fear, shame/shyness, and guilt. Notably, anxiety is not on this list. This is because anxiety, in Izard's opinion (Izard, 1972; Izard & Blumberg, 1985), is not a fundamental emotion, but rather is a blend of fear with other emotions, including—on a variable basis—interest, anger, guilt, shame, and shyness. Thus, Izard and Blumberg stated that "The variable patterns of anxiety clearly show that anxiety is not a unitary phenomenon. Both within and between individuals there are neurophysiologically, phenomenologically, and motivationally different anxieties" (1985, p. 124).

Izard's interpretation of anxiety is ingenious, and not implausible. However, it would be extremely difficult to test the conception in a rigorous way, and considerable ambiguity remains about how the posited constituents of anxiety would blend together. The argument that the conception accounts for the variability in instances of anxiety is not particularly telling, because instances of fear and sadness, presumably basic emotions, also appear to show great heterogeneity. Furthermore, as I discuss later, it is not altogether clear that fear is involved in all experiences of anxiety.

Spielberger (1985), in contrast to Izard, considered anxiety a basic emotion. Mandler (1975) held that the distress manifested by infants—unarguably a fundamental emotion—is an early form of anxiety. Akiskal (1985) considered anxiety "to be a distinct emotion that has evolved over millions of years" (p. 796). In summary, it is clear that anxiety is properly considered an emotion, but whether it is a basic emotion in its own right, or a blend of other more fundamental affects, must for the present be considered moot. Regardless of this issue, however, it is evident that in terms of its effects and dynamics, anxiety typically appears to function as a relatively unitary variable.

Physiological Aspects of Anxiety

It is a commonplace observation that phenomenal anxiety, as already noted, is closely associated with various physiological manifestations. Later chapters in this volume examine the neurophysiological aspects of anxiety in detail, but a few introductory remarks are necessary at this point. The physiological indices of anxiety include autonomic variables, EEG activity, muscular tension, and biochemical processes. The most widely employed psychological measures in research on anxiety are probably heart rate and skin conductance. Both of these are typically employed in the sense of assessing general arousal, and the concept of arousal plays a central role in psychophysiological approaches to anxiety.

The notion of arousal is rather loose, because the intercorrelations among its various indices are typically fairly low. Nevertheless, it is generally considered that there is sufficient homogeneity among the indicants of arousal to justify conceptualizing it as a theoretical variable. Anxiety can thus to some extent be considered as a state of hyperarousal. There are, however, two important points that need to be made here: one, individuals differ markedly in the particular pattern of physiological variables in which their arousal is expressed; and two, there are conditions other than anxiety (e.g., exercise) that increase arousal.

To clarify the matter somewhat, I briefly examine the empirical relation between phenomenal anxiety and physiological arousal. Although the various facets of this relationship have not been fully clarified, there are several generalizations that can be made with some confidence. Looking first at normal subjects, the evidence indicates that there is little or no correlation between subjective estimates of general (trait) anxiety and autonomic variables (see, e.g., Calvin, McGuigan, Tyrrell, & Soyars, 1956; Spelman & Ley, 1966) or muscular tension (e.g., Balshan, 1962). However, under conditions of rapid increments in felt anxiety, occurring either naturalistically (e.g., when a person is facing surgery) or as induced in the laboratory (e.g., while performing mental tasks), there are marked physiological reactions (e.g., Katkin, 1965; McReynolds, 1976; Mainzer & Krause, 1940; Smith & Wenger, 1965).

Psychiatric patients reporting severe anxiety also show increased arousal in response to stressful stimuli (see, e.g., Kelly, 1966; Lader & Wing, 1966; Malmo, Shagass, & Davis, 1951). Furthermore, and in contrast to normal subjects, they tend to be in a relatively constant state of hyperarousal, as is indicated by significant differences between normal and anxious patients on relevant physiological indices (see, e.g., Kelly & Walter, 1968; Lader & Wing, 1966; Plutchik, Wasserman, & Mayer, 1975; White & Gildea, 1937). The overall picture, then, is of meaningful relations between phenomenal and physiological expressions of anxiety, although not in a simple one-to-one way.

It is also important to note that individuals differ in the extent to which they are sensitive to physiological feedback. To the degree that an individual is aware of physiological concomitants of felt anxiety and is threatened by these changes, felt anxiety will increase, thus leading to a self-perpetuating cycle. Finally, it should be noted that a person may experience certain physiological concomitants of anxiety while at the same time firmly denying any phenomenal anxiety.

Anxiety and Behavior

The effects of anxiety on behavior are manifold. Some of these are obvious: the anxious person tends, if possible, to avoid situations likely to accentuate the anxiety; the individual's mind typically is focused on the circumstances that seem to be causing the anxiety, and he or she finds it difficult to attend to or to concentrate on other topics; and a variety of defensive and coping mechanisms—frequently involving intensive rumination and worry—are called into service. On a less obvious, more subtle level a number of other cognitive and behavioral changes occur under high anxiety. One of the earliest researched areas is the relation of anxiety to conditioning and learning. There is considerable evidence that mildly high anxiety facilitates aversive conditioning (Taylor, 1951) and simple stimulus–response (paired associates) learning but hinders complex learning (Spence, Farber, & McFann, 1956; also see Crowne, 1979, chap. 2, for a review of this topic). A question with these generalizations, however, is that it is not clear whether the results were due to anxiety in its phenomenal meaning or simply to arousal. Thus, Lovaas (1960) obtained similar results by having subjects squeeze a dynamometer to create tension.

There is a well-established relation between arousal and quality of performance, and, in those instances in which arousal is due to anxiety, between anxiety and performance. In this relationship the quality of performance is best at moderate levels of arousal, with performance falling off when arousal is either below or above this optimal level. As early as 1908 Yerkes and Dodson performed an experiment indicating that there is an optimal level of motivation for task performance, with values above or below this level leading to poorer performance. In 1955 this concept was applied specifically to arousal in an important paper by Hebb, who posited an inverted U relation between arousal (on the abscissa) and performance (on the ordinate). Support for this relationship was afforded by two studies (Courts, 1939; Wood & Hokanson, 1965) in which arousal was induced by having the subjects grip a dynamometer.

Evidence that arousal induced by anxiety influences performance in the posited manner can also be inferred from research by Doerr and Hokanson (1965) and Samuel, Baynes, and Sabeh (1978). In the first of these studies, arousal, induced by different levels of frustration and assessed by heart rate in children, affected performance in a coding task in the predicted manner. In the Samuel et al. experiment, different conditions of stress yielded a clear inverted U relationship on anagram performance.

It should be emphasized, however, that it is the arousal associated with anxiety, not the felt negative affect as such, that establishes the optimal level for best performance. This relationship is clearly stated in the following words of Eddie Sutton, former University of Arkansas basketball coach:

> Fullerton has a gritty bunch of young men. Boy, do they play hard. They play with great intensity. There is just the right emotional level you want in basketball. You don't want to be above it and you don't want to be below it. ("Fullerton Earns," 1978)

For most of the tasks of living, of course, the optimal arousal level is less than in competitive sports, and for individuals suffering from uncomfortable levels of anxiety, with its hyperarousal, the problem is that of getting anxiety—and the accompanying arousal—down to a level suitable for adequate performance.

On an intuitive level one would predict that increases in anxiety would result in a narrowing of the range of attention. For example, one might predict that people who are fearful of a dentist would note and remember fewer objects than would unanxious individuals. Experimental evidence for this general proposition abounds (Bacon, 1974; Easterbrook, 1959; Mueller, 1976; Zaffy & Bruning, 1966). Easterbrook (1959) theorized that arousal effects a restriction in cues that are attended to, and this hypothesis was supported in a study by Zaffy and Bruning (1966) employing a self-report measure of anxiety. Bacon (1974) found that anxiety induced by threat of shock also reduced the range of cues utilized.

These examples refer to the effects of anxiety on the range of incidental stimuli perceived. It is another story with respect to the amount of attention given to anxiety-provoking stimuli. In these cases, highly anxious people tend to be especially attentive to threatening stimuli, and individuals with low anxiety, who give more of their input-processing capacity to neutral stimuli, tend to avoid such cues (Eysenck, 1988; Eysenck, MacLeod, & Mathews, 1987). This interpretation was also supported in a visual detection study by MacLeod, Mathews, and Tata (1986). Anxiety also reduces the efficiency of memory, especially short-term memory (reviewed by Eysenck, 1984b), and this fact—along with the effects of anxiety on attention—are doubtless among the reasons that anxiety typically attenuates performance on complex tasks.

Anxiety frequently arises from an internal, personal problem that an individual has been unable to resolve in a satisfactory manner. The ability to solve problems in a creative fashion is thus especially important for anxious individuals. But it is possible that a state of anxiety depresses creative thought, thus reducing a person's capacity to deal effectively with his or her problems at the very time when they are most pressing. Relevant research on this question includes not only studies on anxiety and creativity, but also work on the influence of anxiety on curiosity, which seems to be essential to the first phases of creativity. Empirical data on the effects of anxiety on curiosity are not definitive, although the general import of research (reviewed by Voss & Keller, 1983) indicates that in general anxiety inhibits curiosity. Thus, McReynolds, Acker, and Pietila (1961) and Penny (1965), in studies with children, reported data in support of this position. Although their results were correlational, it is most plausible to assume a casual direction from anxiety to curiosity.

Whereas some studies (e.g., Okebukola, 1986; Smith & Carlsson, 1983) provide limited support for a negative relation between anxiety and creativity, others (e.g., Kitay, 1986; Smith, 1984) are negative or equivocal. The matter is complex, and it may be that anxiety affects different phases of the creative process differentially. My own suggestion is that higher levels of anxiety significantly depress creative problem solving, but that this effect may frequently be compensated for by the increased motivation to solve the problems stimulated by the anxiety.

PERSPECTIVES ON ANXIETY

The Evolutionary Perspective

Although there are a number of provocative discussions concerning the evolution of the human emotions (see, e.g., Buss 1987; Izard, 1979; Plutchik, 1980), the area is inevitably quite speculative. This is particularly true in the case of anxiety, because the question of whether anxiety is a basic human emotion is itself unclear, as I noted earlier. There are, however, certain general trends that can be posited with considerable confidence. In the simplest animals, approach and avoidance reactions to various stimuli are evident, and these develop, in the course of evolution, into the flight or fight reaction (Cannon, 1929), coupled with the emotions of fear and anger, in reaction to certain situations causing distress. Although the emotion of distress is logically prior to those of fear and anger, one would not expect to find any living species exhibiting distress in the absence of fear and rage, because without these two emotions and their behavioral concomitants higher species would not have adapted sufficiently to survive.

In considering the evolutionary background of human anxiety, it is important to emphasize the role of cognitive functions. The tremendous advances in cognitive capacity in *Homo sapiens* have enlarged astronomically the kinds of matters about which people can become distressed. Thus, it is a commonplace that most of the issues about which people become anxious involve complex memories, anticipations of the future, or interpretations of personal relationships—or, more broadly, complex ideas and abstract concepts. Consider, for example, the existential anxiety arising for one's awareness of one's mortality—something that everyone experiences sooner or later. Instances such as this make it clear that human anxiety, despite its adumbrations in lower species, is quite unique and can only with great caution be reduced to animal models. Regardless of the cognitive content of human anxieties, however, such anxieties are served—as are the related emotions of fear and anger—by the same physiological arousal processes that were developed in the long-ago periods during which humans existed precariously among dangerous predators and had constantly to be prepared for physical flight or combat.

The Life-Span Perspective

The empirical literature on emotional development in infants and children, as compared with the analogous literature on cognitive development, is relatively sparse. There are, however, a number of very solid investigations (e.g., Lewis & Michalson, 1983; Sroufe, 1984; Trevarten, 1984) as well as numerous clinical and theoretical contributions. Do young infants experience anxiety? Freud (1926/1936) held that they do and suggested that the birth trauma is the first—and paradigmatic—instance of anxiety. Later psychodynamic theorists (e.g., Mahler, Pine, & Bergman, 1975; Sullivan, 1953) have also assumed the existence of anxiety in infants. Kagan (1984), a prominent developmental psychologist, has also accepted the meaningfulness of the term *anxiety* at the infant level. For the most part, however, investigators in this area have been reluctant to describe the manifest discomforts of infants as anxiety, and instead prefer the term *distress*.

There are two main positions concerning the ontogenesis of emotions. One position, first enunciated in a classic work by Bridges (1932), posits that the various emotions are differentiated out of a primitive emotion of excitement, which appears at or shortly after birth, with the first derived emotion, which appears very early, being distress, followed by delight and then others. Sroufe (1984), a contemporary theorist, has developed a somewhat similar conception in that he emphasized emotions as evolving systems. One of these is what he terms the "wariness–fear system," which involves the infant's reactions to distress.

A quite different perspective is afforded by the discrete emotions theorists, such as

Izard, whose conception of basic emotions I discussed earlier. In Izard's (1979) view, the different emotions are not derived from earlier emotions but rather emerge onto-genetically as the infant matures. Expressions indicative of distress are present in the neonate, with expressions of anger appearing at around 3 to 4 months and expressions of fear at around 5 to 7 months. It will be recalled that Izard considered anxiety to be a blend of several discrete emotions around the kernel of fear.

Neither of the two approaches posits the existence of anxiety in very young in-fants, and in this respect they differ from the more psychodynamically oriented posi-tions. All positions, however, emphasize the very early presence of the emotion of distress, and it will be recalled that Mandler (1975) considered distress to be an early form of anxiety. It seems to me that infant distress, if not actually the forerunner of later anxiety, at least plays a somewhat similar role in the sense that it is a strongly negative affect that the infant seeks to reduce. A relevant study, which so far as I know has not been performed, would determine whether there is a correlation, in an individual differences sense, between indications (fretting, crying, and disturbed sleep) of early distress and later assays of anxiety.

There are two well-documented instances of anxiety or fear—some authors use one term and some the other—in very young children. These are stranger anxiety and separation anxiety. Stranger anxiety (Bronson, 1972; Freud, 1926/1936; Ka-gan, 1984), which typically begins around the age of 7 to 9 months and may last for some time, is manifested when an unknown person approaches the child. Separation anxiety (Bowlby, 1973; Doris, McIntyre, & Tamaroff, 1980; Kagan, 1984) is de-fined as the distress that frequently arises when a child is separated from a familiar care-taking adult. By the time children reach their preschool years it is possible to rate their level of anxiety—according to the adult meaning of that term—with fair reliability (Neighbors, McReynolds, Essa, & Harrington, 1989). The contents of the anxiety, that is, the matters about which the child is anxious, are of course unique for each child's own world, and it can be taken as a general principle that as people mature and their life scenes change, so will the cognitive contents of their anxious concerns.

There have been a number of studies in which the foci of anxiety at the child and adolescent level were examined (e.g., Davis, 1987; Sarason, Davidson, Lighthall, Waite, & Ruebush, 1960). Davis, in her recent systematic survey of inner-city Black and White youth, found the most common anxiety theme to concern family problems, followed in order by peer relationships; break-up with a partner; death, illness, and injury; and academic problems. The nature of adult concerns has also been surveyed. Cantril (1965) carried out a large international study of the topics that reflect people's assumptions and hopes. Americans, he found, were most concerned about their health, next about a decent standard of living, and next about their children. An overall conclusion was that "the concerns of people are patterned largely according to the phases of development they are in both culturally and ontogenetically within their society" (p. 301). A study by White (1982), employing a sample of 107 college students, focused more directly on matters reported to be anxiety-provoking. Career and future plans were listed most frequently, followed in order by relationships with significant others, one's self-concept, and school performance. The common themes of anxiety continue to change throughout life, as they mirror the milestones that people pass through. The later stages of life typically bring anxieties centering on declining powers, loss of friends and family, and the imminence of death (Sobel, 1980).

Classification Perspectives

Anxiety is a very complex emotion, and in order to accurately describe it and to deal with it systematically in the clinic and in research, a number of qualifying terms have been adapted, and certain meaningful dimensions have been identified. First, it should be emphasized that different instances of anxiety may manifest considerable diversity in the clinical picture (McReynolds, 1965). Thus the indicants of anxiety may include behaviors such as nervous mannerisms, difficulties in concentrating, plaintive voice, excessive rumination, muscular tension, and moist palms. Furthermore, as I have already observed, there is extreme variation in the cognitive contents in different episodes of anxiety, and there is a tendency, when a particular content appears with sufficient frequency in clinical reports, for it to be referred to as a class of anxiety, for example, stranger anxiety, separation anxiety, test anxiety, achievement anxiety, and the like. Although in most instances felt anxiety includes certain focal contents—that is, the person is anxious about something—this is not always the case. As noted earlier in this chapter, feelings of anxiety may sometimes be essentially formless, vague, and free-floating, without any perceived cause.

As numerous studies (e.g., McReynolds, Acker, & Brackbill, 1966) have demonstrated, individuals' levels of anxiety are not constant over long periods but vary over time as a function of both internal and external stimulation. For example, a man might suddenly recall an important commitment that he had forgotten to keep and have resultant surge of anxiety, or a woman might suffer a disappointing turn of events at her office and similarly experience a drastic increase in anxiety. People reacting to a sudden traumatic event—for example, to an unexpected death in the family—may be said to suffer from acute anxiety. Individuals who are more or less continuously afflicted with severe anxiety can be described as being chronically anxious.

Our understanding of anxiety has been greatly clarified by the concepts of state anxiety and trait anxiety first proposed in 1961 by Cattell and Scheier and developed in systematic detail by Spielberger (1966, 1972, 1985, chap. 4, this volume). Both terms refer to the degree, or intensity, of anxiety. State anxiety is a person's level of anxiety at a given point in time, and trait anxiety is one's general level of anxiety. As already observed, people's levels of anxiety vary over time—frequently from day to day or even from moment to moment—as a function of changing circumstances, and the notion of state anxiety captures the importance of the here-and-now intensity of anxiety. In contrast, that anxiety is conceptualized, as the word *trait* implies, as the relatively enduring tendency of an individual to manifest anxiety in stressful situations. Trait anxiety can thus be thought of as a reflection of anxiety proneness, and the higher one's trait anxiety, the broader the range of situations that the person finds anxiety-provoking, and thus the more frequently he or she tends to experience elevated state anxiety. The distinction between state and trait anxiety has proved extremely useful in research (e.g., Auerbach, 1973). Thus, if one is interested in studying, say the long-term somatic effects of high levels of anxiety, then trait anxiety is the relevant construct, whereas if one is concerned, in contrast, with the effects of anxiety on mental performance, then state anxiety is probably a more appropriate concept.

Another important way of categorizing occurrences of anxiety is in terms of their most typical patterns. In this context, there is a history of identifying three primary categories, although not always with the same names. In the first pattern, which may be termed *cognitive anxiety,* the individual is struggling with seemingly intractable internalized personal problems, and his or her behavior is marked by intense rumination, worry, and attempts to resolve the problem. This is probably the most common type of anxiety and is what most people have in mind when the say that a person is anxious.

The second pattern can be termed *situational anxiety.* I am referring here to what is sometimes called conditioned anxiety or, in its extreme forms, phobic anxiety. The idea is that the anxiety is set off by a particular stimulus object, such as a spider or snake, or a particular activity, such as riding in an airplane or giving a speech. Anxieties of this type are usually referred to as fears. The third category is a sudden, generally unexpected, and extremely severe episode of anxiety. Sometimes referred to as anxiety attacks, these harrowing experiences are now usually designated by the term *panic.* The causes of panic states typically seem inexplicable to the person involved, and they frequently include very noticeable physiological symptoms, such as faintness, heart palpitations, and shortness of breath. The distinction between cognitive and situational anxiety has been elaborated by me and my associates (Baldo, 1986; McReynolds, 1976, 1989; McReynolds, Eyman, White, & Baldo, 1989). The study of panic has recently received concentrated attention (e.g., Barlow, 1988; chap. 3, this volume).

These three types of anxiety, as Barlow (1988, p. 89) has observed, were first distinguished by Freud (1935/1969, pp. 345–348). Although they are not mutually exclusive, and the borders among them are not always clear, they nevertheless represent a highly meaningful classification. And if to these three types we add the obsessive–impulsive category, then the four types reflect in substance the anxiety diagnoses in the DSM-III-R (American Psychiatric Association, 1987).

Episodes of intense anxiety are exceedingly unpleasant, and for this reason individuals who have experienced them tend to fear new episodes and to do what they can to avoid them. The study of the fear of anxiety, of the anxiety concerning the possibility of anxiety, also has a long history (Reiss, 1987). Ellis (1979) distinguished between two types of anxiety: *ego anxiety,* which arises from the feeling of threat to one's self-worth, and *discomfort anxiety,* which refers to the fear of aversive experiences, including fear of the discomfort that would be involved in an anticipated anxiety-provoking situation. The fear of fear has recently been analyzed into two components—*anxiety expectancy* and *anxiety sensitivity*—by Reiss and McNally (1985). The former concept refers to the anticipation that a given stimulus situation will result in anxiety, whereas the latter term designates the extent to which the person believes that the possible anxiety experience would have undesirable consequences in addition to the anxiety as such (e.g., that it might lead to a heart attack).

There are a number of other ways in which various authorities have conceptualized anxiety, but most of these are connected with specific theories of anxiety. I will consider only one other issue here: the question of whether there is a qualitative difference between normal and pathological anxiety. Freud (1935/1969) distinguished between what he conceived as *objective anxiety,* which he defined as reflecting the rational concerns that a person may have about external threats, and *neurotic anxiety,* which, in contrast, is considered to be based on internal, typically unconscious conflicts. Contemporary theorists are more likely to view normal and pathological anxieties as differing only quantitatively, but with the qualification that the latter are less realistic and are excessive reactions (American Psychiatric Association, 1987, p. 252).

The Related Concepts Perspective

In order to clarify a concept, not only is it necessary to indicate its range of application, but also it is helpful to show how it differs from other, closely related concepts. In this context, I now contrast the concept of anxiety with the notions of fear, stress, and depression.

Clearly, anxiety and fear have a great deal in common in that both refer to an unpleasant inner state about which something needs to be done. Some authors, particularly those working with animals and in the behavioral perspective, tend to use the two terms more or less interchangeably. Most authorities, however, although considering anxiety and fear to be closely related, have found it helpful to distinguish between them (e.g., Freud, 1935/1969; Kleinknecht, 1986; McReynolds, 1976; see also Fischer, 1970, for distinctions made by Goldstein, Heidegger, Kierkegaard, and Sullivan). The general theme of these various positions is that fear is a focal emotional response to a perception of external threat, whereas anxiety is a more diffuse and pervasive emotion involving an individual's complex cognitive concerns. As noted earlier, differential emotions theorists (Izard, 1972) hold that fear, but not anxiety, is a basic emotion and that anxiety always includes a kernel of fear. From their perspective, then, anxiety is a more complex emotion than fear, and the ways in which it differs from fear are determined by the particular additional basic emotions involved.

The contemporary psychoanalytic theorist Brenner (1982) has conceived that anxiety is an emotion evoked by the anticipation of danger. When the danger

> is perceived as acute or imminent, we may speak of fear; if the unpleasure is intense, of panic. If the unpleasure is mild and if the danger is perceived as slight, as uncertain, or as distant, we may well speak of worry or uneasiness. (p. 46)

The term *fear* refers by definition to abhorrence of a possible future event, and fear can be construed as an avoidance motive. A great deal—perhaps most—of the anxiety that people experience also arises from a concern with possible undesirable future occurrences, but it is not clear to me that anxiety always fits this pattern. Thus it appears that anxiety may also arise from an input overload. For example, it is a common observation that children may become anxious from an excess of stimulation.

I suggest that for pragmatic usage fear and anxiety can be conceptualized in the manner of two partially overlapping circles or, to put it differently, that the border between them is fuzzy and indistinct (Rosch & Lloyd, 1978). For example, what we ordinarily term phobic anxiety obviously involves strong fears, and conversely, a person's fear of death typically includes the worry and rumination that are characteristic of anxiety. Perhaps general linguistic usage provides a meaningful clue to the distinction between fear and anxiety: We ordinarily say that we are fearful *of* something but anxious *about* something.

Next I contrast anxiety and stress. Since its systematic formulation by Selye in 1956, the topic of stress—its nature and its effect on the human organism—has generated an extensive body of research (e.g., Appley & Trumbull, 1986; Dohrenwend & Dohrenwend, 1974; Goldberger & Breznitz, 1982; Lazarus & Folkman, 1984; Schwarzer, 1984; Spielberger & Sarason, 1986). The term *stress* is widely employed in everyday discourse, as when, say, a business man engaged in a continuing series of difficult negotiations that tax or perhaps overtax his capacity reports that he is under a great deal of stress. Grammatically, a person is anxious, but he or she is *under* stress. The causes of stress (stressors) are conceived to be in an individual's personal environment, that is, in the circumstances and events that he or she has to cope with—for example, a difficult academic or career task, a serious illness, a divorce, or a car that will not start. However, whether and to what degree particular events are stressful for an individual are ultimately a function of how the person appraises the situation. A situation is stressful for a person when he or she feels that something important is at stake, and feels some uncertainty about his or her ability to cope adequately with the situation. Life, unfortunately, is cluttered with such problematic situations.

How, then, is stress related to anxiety? The connection is that the affect aroused by a stressful situation, as just defined, is essentially the same as state anxiety (Spielberger, Pollans, & Worden, 1984), except that it is not construed as anxiety, but rather as stress. Stress thus represents that variety of anxiety that, from the subject's perspective, can plausibly be attributed in large part to trying circumstances more than to internal conflicts.

I turn now to the relations between the concepts of anxiety and depression. A distinction between these two unpleasant affects has long been assumed by diagnosticians and is, indeed, a part of our everyday cultural lexicon. Just as everyone knows in a general way the meaning of anxiety from having experienced it personally, at least in some degree, so likewise everyone intuitively recognizes the meaning of depression, from having experienced to some extent its low, blue feelings of disappointment and resignation. Furthermore, from such experiences one can readily appreciate that the two negative affects often verge into each other, or are so intermingled with each other that they seem inseparable.

The same close and somewhat ambiguous relationship between the concepts of anxiety and depression is also evident in the clinic, and it is not entirely clear whether anxiety and depression should be viewed a separate syndromes, with considerable overlap in symptomatology, or as a unitary syndrome with varied manifestations (Dobson, 1985). However, the weight of the evidence (Hershberg, Carlson, Cantwell, & Strober, 1982; Roth & Mountjoy, 1982) is in support of a conceptual and clinical distinction between anxiety and depression. Recent studies (Beck, Brown, Steer, Eidelson, & Riskind, 1987; Mitchell & Campbell, 1988) on the cognitions associated with anxiety and depression point up conceptions such as worthlessness and hopelessness in depression and concerns about performance in anxiety.

Considerable work has recently been done on the identification and elaboration of two broad affective dimensions—positive affect and negative affect (Tellegen, 1985; Watson & Clark, 1984; Watson, Clark, & Carey, 1988). The high correlations between self-report measures of anxiety and depression indicate that both states are high on negative affect, but anxiety is particularly high on negative affect, whereas depression is especially low on positive affect (Tellegen, 1985). Whereas both anxiety and depression reflect a person's strong dissatisfaction with his or her perceived reality, they differ in that a state of anxiety entails an unwillingness to accept that reality and a motivation to improve it, whereas a state of depression implies an acceptance of the unsatisfactory state, and a resignation to it.

THE ORIGINS OF ANXIETY

In this section I present an overview of the factors and circumstances that cause anxiety. This review is highly abridged, and it should also be noted that although advances in knowledge have been rapid in recent years there are still major gaps in our understanding of the etiology of anxiety. I first discuss some of the known predisposing or causal factors and then consider briefly several current theoretical interpretations. Except for a few comments on possible genetic influences, the discussion does not address biological determinants of anxiety, which are addressed in later chapters of this book.

Determinants of Anxiety

A logical first question about the etiology of anxiety concerns the possible influence of familial background. There is ample evidence (e.g., Turner, Beidel, & Costello, 1987) that children of highly anxious parents are at risk for the manifestation of marked anxiety. Because it is intuitively plausible that parents suffering from anxiety would create an environment inducing anxiety in their offspring, most of the research (e.g., Cloninger, Martin, Clayton, & Guze, 1981; Slater & Shields, 1969; Torgerson, 1983; see reviews by Barlow, 1988, and Carey & Gottesman, 1981) has focused on the question of a genetically based vulnerability to clinical levels of anxiety. The results, taken in their entirety, provide strong evidence for a genetic sensitivity to panic disorder, but only weak support for a genetically transmitted vulnerability to generalized anxiety. There is, however, extensive support (reviewed by Barlow, 1988) for the heritability of a broad trait of emotionality, or "nervousness," which presumably is related to anxiety.

Emotionality is also one of the three basic temperaments identified by Buss and Plomin (1984) and is one of the five robust personality factors currently being championed by personologists (e.g., McCrae & Costa, 1987). An impressive multivariate analysis by Kendler, Heath, Martin, and Eaves (1987), who used self-report data on 2,896 volunteer, same-sex twins, yielded a major genetic factor of vulnerability to distress. This factor was nonspecific with respect to anxiety and depression, with the implication that environmental factors determine whether nonclinical levels of distress will be felt as anxiety or depression. In summary, there appears to be a modest but significant tendency for symptoms of anxiety to run in families, with strong suggestive evidence for a genetic component.

Despite the probable influence of genetic factors, however, it is evident, simply on the basis of the uniqueness of the content of different anxiety experiences, that most anxieties involve significant learning. The nature of emotional learning, except in the case of specific fears, has not been studied adequately, yet the range of such learning, including presumably the learning of anxiety, is undoubtedly very broad. Sullivan (1953), for example, many years ago produced clinical evidence showing that anxiety in a mothering person induces anxiety in an infant.

Most of both theory and research on anxiety and learning concerns the role of conditioning in the acquisition of phobic anxieties. Formerly it was believed that such fears were always due to the traumatic association of a neutral stimulus with a highly aversive stimulus—for example, that a person's phobic fear of snakes could be traced to an earlier traumatic experience with a snake. This general paradigm, at least in its simple form, is, however, no longer considered adequate (McReynolds, 1989; Rachman, 1977), because many phobias appear to arise in the absence of relevant unconditioned stimuli (e.g., McNally & Steketee, 1985).

There is no doubt, however, that human aversive conditioning is a real phenomenon (Campbell, Sanderson, & Laverty, 1964), and many instances of phobic anxiety appear to be explicable on this basis (Ost & Hugdahl, 1981). Many—perhaps most—fears arise on the basis of observational and vicarious learning (Bandura, 1986; Mineka, 1985; Windheuser, 1977). Another ingredient in the understanding of intractable fears is the possibility (Ohman, 1986; Seligman, 1971), currently somewhat controversial (McNally, 1987), that human beings have been "prepared" by evolution to be particularly susceptible to the development of certain fears—for example, fears of snakes and animals.

The next factor in the causation of anxiety that I wish to consider is input overload. By input overload I refer to an ongoing sequence of sensory, perceptual, and cognitive experiences beyond an individual's capacity for adequate integration and resolution, with resultant feelings of tension and anxiety. Stimulus overload can be due either to an overly rapid rate of input data that require attention, or to the problematic nature of certain inputs, or to both. Although the idea of overstimulation as a basis of anxiety can be traced back to Freud (1926/1936) and has since been employed by certain theorists (McReynolds, 1976; Miller, 1960; Spitz, 1964), it has so far received relatively little experimental attention in relation to anxiety. Instead, the concept of overstimulation or overload has generally been studied under the rubric of environmental stress (Goldberger, 1982; Suedfeld, 1986).

Another important determinant of anxiety is the nature of the perceptual and cognitive input. I am referring here to the variables of uncertainty, unpredictability, and lack of personal control in one's ongoing experiencing. When these variables are at moderate levels, they stimulate attention and create interest, but when they reach extreme degrees the individual's world seems chaotic, unstable, and frightening (reviewed by Barlow, 1988). Weiss (1971) compared rats exposed to predictable and controllable stimuli with rats subjected to the same stimuli under unpredictable and uncontrollable conditions and found greatly increased ulceration in the latter animals. Experiments by Pervin (1963); Geer, Davison, and Gatchel (1970); and others on human subjects strongly substantiate a positive relation between the uncertainty variables and anxiety or stress.

The determinants discussed so far are more or less equally relevant at the human and infrahuman levels, but many—probably most—human anxieties are intimately related to the concept of the self (Schwarzer, 1984), a construct hardly meaningful in subhuman species. Many years ago, Goldstein (1951), on the basis of clinical data, conceptualized intense anxiety as the "*inner experience of castastrophe*" (p. 46), "of danger, of going to pieces, of losing one's existence" (p. 38). Similarly, May (1950) attributed anxiety to perceived threats to values that one considers essential to his or her existence as a self. Rogers (1959) conceived that anxiety results from incongruence between the self and one's experience, with the degree of anxiety depending on the extent of self-structure threatened. There is abundant empirical evidence for a relation between aspects of one's self-concept and anxiety. For example, Kawash (1982) reported substantial negative relations between measures of self-esteem and anxiety. In an experimental study, Bandura, Reese, and Adams (1982) obtained data indicating that the greater one's perceived coping inefficacy in a threatening situation the greater the fear.

It is probable that most of the anxieties that people are afflicted with, both of the run-of-the-mill variety and of the more serious kind, arise from personal problems that occur in the course of living. I indicated the nature of some of these concerns in my earlier comments on the contents of anxieties. Individual problems that cause anxiety can be generally conceptualized in terms of intrapsychic (intrapersonal) conflicts. For example, a person might be in conflict over whether to seek a divorce or whether to change jobs. Inner conflicts are typically conscious, but they may also involve unconscious needs and fears. The study of intrapsychic conflicts was pioneered by Freud (cited in Fenichel, 1945) and has recently been advanced in the psychoanalytic tradition by Brenner (1982). Empirical approaches, from a broadly cognitive perspective, have recently been developed by Lauterbach (1975) and myself (1987, 1989).

Current Theoretical Approaches

Although a great deal is now known about anxiety, there are still major gaps in our knowledge, and a number of theoretical proposals have been put forward to complete the picture and to suggest further research. A comprehensive review of these formulations is beyond the scope of this chapter; instead, I will indicate, in a selective and highly summary fashion, some of the current directions in psychological theories of anxiety (for a review of "classical" theories of anxiety, cf. Fischer, 1970).

Modern theories of anxiety began with Freud, but his conception has relatively little direct influence today. The most prominent current formulation in the psychoanalytic tradition is that of Brenner (1982), who defined anxiety as a feeling of displeasure plus the anticipation of danger. The possible dangers from which anxiety arises are fundamentally of four types: object loss (e.g., a child losing a parent), loss of love, castration (possibility of injury), and possibility of punishment. All four originate in childhood and are often represented unconsciously.

An interpretation of anxiety based on the concept of the self has been developed by Epstein (1986). In Epstein's view, each person develops an implicit conception of what he or she is like—a complex self-system. Anxiety arises from three sources: threats of injury or death, threats to the assimilative capacity of the self-system, and threats to the person's self-esteem.

As was noted earlier in this chapter, Mandler (1975) considered the distress manifested by infants to be an early form of anxiety. He conceived anxiety according to the following paradigm. The interruption of any action or task that a person is engaged in results in tension and arousal. If the person has no means available for completing the action or for a satisfactory alternate action, then the feeling is one of helplessness and disorganization, and this feeling is anxiety.

The anxiety model proposed by Spielberger (1966, 1972, 1985) emphasizes the concepts of state and trait anxiety, as discussed earlier. When either external stressors or internal stimuli (memories, thoughts, feelings) are appraised by an individual as personally threatening, the result is the arousal of state anxiety, the magnitude of which is a function of the degree of perceived threat. The concept of trait anxiety refers to the tendency to see the world as threatening, and to a proneness to experience state anxiety.

Barlow's (1988) recent theory of anxiety is one of the most detailed yet proposed. Barlow posited a variable of biological vulnerability for anxiety, which, when coupled with stressful life events, sets the stage for anxiety. Frequently, negative life events result in a frightening feeling of alarm, and the person becomes apprehensive lest such alarms or negative life events recur. States of anxious apprehension are accentuated to the extent that such recurrences are seen as unpredictable and as beyond the person's control. Furthermore, worry over these two factors contributes to the tendency of states of anxious apprehension to become self-perpetuating, in the sense of a vicious cycle of anxiety.

Several theorists have investigated anxiety from the cognitive perspective. Sarason (1985, 1988) has focused on the ruminative self-preoccupation that anxious people engage in and its deleterious effects on behavior, especially test-taking behavior. Borkovec and his associates (Borkovec, Robinson, Pruzinsky, & DePree, 1983) and Eysenck (1984a) have studied the nature and determinants of the worrying that typically accompanies anxiety. Beck and his colleagues (1985; Beck et al., 1987) have examined the cognitions that are characteristic of anxious people.

Bandura's (1986) social cognitive theory of behavior includes an interpretation of anxiety. The key concept in Bandura's position is self-efficacy, by which he means an individual's perceived capacity to deal adequately with a given situation. A person experiences anxiety when he or she feels ill-equipped to cope successfully with potentially aversive events. The important point here is the person's judgment of personal control, not the aversiveness of an impending event as such. Furthermore, individuals who feel ineffectual in dealing with threatening situations tend to ruminate and worry about them.

I (McReynolds, 1976, 1989) have proposed a cognitively oriented conceptualization of anxiety. The general theme of the model is that experiential contents highly incongruent with a person's overall cognitive structure are difficult to assimilate, and that their occurrence brings about a surge of anxiety. Furthermore, incongruent contents tend to accumulate in a kind of cognitive backlog, supporting a general high level of anxiety. Unassimilated contents—and thus anxiety—can result from an input overload, unassimilation of previously assimilated data, or the input of highly incongruent contents. The latter source can be rationalized in terms of intrapersonal conflicts (McReynolds, 1989) and the anticipation of problems beyond one's coping capacity. Finally, it is conceived that neutral stimuli may become conditioned arousers of anxiety.

It is clear from the preceding comments that considerable diversity exists among the various competing theories of anxiety. Nevertheless, it is important to emphasize the extent to which they include common assumptions. Thus all theorists appear to accept the complementary roles of phenomenal and autonomic factors in anxiety. Similarly, the significance of worry and rumination in chronic anxiety is central in all conceptions. Furthermore, many theories of anxiety emphasize the place in the origins of anxiety of an individual's uncertainty with respect to impending events, coupled with a personal concern of his or her ability to cope with those events.

REACTIONS TO ANXIETY

The reactions that individuals manifest in response to anxiety, particularly to chronic levels of high anxiety, can be divided into two groups: psychological reactions and somatic reactions. By psychological reactions I refer to the steps or changes that an individual performs in order to terminate or alleviate the anxiety or to prevent further anxiety. By somatic reactions I refer to the cumulative effects of anxiety on the various organ systems, including the cardiovascular system, which constitutes the main topic of this volume. I restrict my brief comments here to certain psychological reactions to anxiety.

It was the psychoanalysts, in particular, Anna Freud (1937/1966), who first addressed the question of how people deal with anxiety. This interest led to the identification of certain *defense mechanisms,* repression, projection, denial, and others, that people use to reduce and defend against feelings of anxiety. Defense mechanisms consist essentially of different ways of organizing one's cognitive contents in a way that is less anxiety-provoking; they are involuntary and unconscious (cf. McReynolds, 1987, regarding cognitive strategies that people employ to reduce anxiety).

In recent years there has been extensive research and theoretical development (e.g., Goldberger & Breznitz, 1982; Haan, 1977; Lazarus & Folkman, 1984) on the methods and techniques that individuals employ to cope with stress. The delineation of techniques for coping with stress can be applied rather directly to the problems of coping with anxiety. Lazarus and Folkman (1984) have distinguished between problem-focused coping and emotion-focused coping. The former category comprises techniques that an individual might deliberately employ to resolve or circumvent the problem situation that he or she feels is causing the anxiety. For example, a person anxious about relations with another individual might approach the other person directly, or might seek advice from a mutual friend, and so on. In emotion-focused coping the aim is to reduce the intensity of the negative affect as such, for example, by using alcohol or drugs or by trying to keep one's mind on other things.

I close with some comments on the psychodynamics of anxiety, in particular on the concept of unconscious anxiety as contrasted with manifest anxiety. If we think of anxiety as being a phenomenal feeling of anguish, then unconscious anxiety is, by definition, impossible. However, as was noted earlier in this chapter, people who find the recognition of anxiety too threatening may deny experiencing it, to themselves as well as to others. In such cases the physiological indicants of anxiety, as well as its behavioral and somatic effects, would still exist. What is sometimes labeled "unconscious anxiety" (Fenichel, 1945, pp. 238–239; Freud, 1915/1959b, pp. 109–111) refers to the situation in which the cognitive aspects of an intrapsychic conflict, which would cause anxiety if they were to become conscious, are firmly repressed. According to psychoanalytic theory, such a process, although it prevents or reduces felt anxiety, nevertheless creates a tension that has marked somatic and behavioral effects.

More typical is the situation in which a conflict is only partially repressed or suppressed, leading to the situation in which the person feels anxious, but is unclear as to a cause for the anxiety. Such a condition rarely lasts long; instead, the individual finds what seems to be a plausible cause, and attributes the anxiety to that; if this factor is shown to be groundless the person finds another cause, and so on. It is this dynamic process that I had in mind, in part, when I commented earlier on the unique fluidity of anxiety.

This is a very belief discussion of psychological reactions to anxiety, but it is perhaps sufficient to make the point that the degree of anxiety an individual experiences in a given situation depends on three factors: (a) the psychological and genetic vulnerability of the individual, (b) the amount of stress in that situation for that person, and (c) the influence of the individual's defensive and coping maneuvers.

REFERENCES

Akiskal, H. S. (1985). Anxiety: Definition, relationship to depression, and proposal for an integrative model. In A. H. Tuma & J. D. Maser (Eds.), *Anxiety and the anxiety disorders* (pp. 787–797). Hillsdale, NJ: Erlbaum.

American Psychiatric Association (1987). *Diagnostic and statistical manual of mental disorders* (3rd ed. rev.). Washington, DC: American Psychiatric Press.

Appley, M. H., & Trumbull, R. (1986). *Dynamics of stress.* New York: Plenum Press.

Auerbach, S. M. (1973). Trait–state anxiety and adjustment to surgery. *Journal of Consulting and Clinical Psychology, 40,* 264–271.

Bacon, S. J. (1974). Arousal and the range of cue utilization. *Journal of Experimental Psychology, 192,* 81–87.

Baldo, R. M. (1986). *The personal anxiety survey: A study of cognitive and conditioned anxiety in normals and psychiatric patients.* Unpublished doctoral dissertation, University of Nevada, Reno.

Balshan, I. D. (1962). Muscle tension and personality in women. *Archives of General Psychiatry, 7,* 436–448.

Bandura. A. (1986). *Social foundations of thought and action: A social cognitive theory.* Englewood Cliffs, NJ: Prentice-Hall.

Bandura, A., Reese, L., & Adams, N. E. (1982). Microanalysis of action and fear arousal as a function of differential levels of perceived self-efficacy. *Journal of Personality and Social Psychology, 43,* 5–21.

Barlow, D. H. (1988). *Anxiety and its disorders.* New York: Guilford Press.

Battie, W. (1969). *A treatise on madness.* New York: Brunner/Mazel. (Original work published 1758)

Beck, A. T. (1985). Theoretical perspectives on clinical anxiety. In A. H. Tuma & J. Maser (Eds.), *Anxiety and the anxiety disorders* (pp. 183–196). Hillsdale, NJ: Erlbaum.

Beck, A. T., Brown, G., Steer, R. A., Eidelson, J. I., & Riskind, J. H. (1987). Differentiating anxiety and depression: A test of the cognitive content-specificity hypothesis. *Journal of Abnormal Psychology, 96,* 179–183.

Blaskovich, J., & Katkin, E. S. (1983). Visceral perception and social behavior. In J. T. Cacioppo & R. E. Petty (Eds.), *Social psychophysiology* (pp. 493–509). New York: Guilford Press.

Borkovec, T. D., Robinson, E., Pruzinsky, T., & DePree, J. A. (1983). Preliminary exploration of worry: Some characteristics and processes. *Behaviour Research and Therapy, 21,* 9–16.

Bowlby, J. (1973). *Attachment and loss: Vol. 2. Separation.* New York: Basic Books.

Brenner, C. (1982). *The mind in conflict.* New York: International Universities Press.

Bridges, K. M. B. (1932). Emotional development in infancy. *Child Development, 3,* 324–341.

Bronson, G. (1972). Infant's reactions to unfamiliar persons and novel objects. *Monographs of the Society for Research in Child Development, 37* (3, Serial No. 148).

Buss, A. H. (1962). Two anxiety factors in psychiatric patients. *Journal of Abnormal and Social Psychology, 65,* 426–427.

Buss, A. H. (1987). Personality: Primate heritage and human distinctiveness. In J. Aronoff, A. I. Rabin, & R. A. Zucker (Eds.), *The emergence of personality* (pp. 13–48). New York: Springer.

Buss, A. H., & Plomin, R. (1984). *Temperament: Early developing personality traits.* Hillsdale, NJ: Erlbaum.

Calvin, A. D., McGuigan, F. J., Tyrrell, S., & Soyars, M. (1956). Manifest anxiety and the palmar perspiration index. *Journal of Consulting Psychology, 20,* 356.

Campbell, D., Sanderson, R., & Laverty, S. G. (1964). Characteristics of a conditioned response in human subjects during extinction trials following a single traumatic conditioning trial. *Journal of Abnormal and Social Psychology, 66,* 627–639.

Cannon, W. B. (1929). *Bodily changes in pain, hunger, fear and rage* (2nd ed.). New York: Appleton-Century-Crofts.

Cantril, H. (1965). *The patterns of human concerns.* New Brunswick, NJ: Rutgers University Press.

Carey, G., & Gottesman, I. I. (1981) Twin and family studies of anxiety, phobic, and obsessive disorders. In D. F. Klein & J. Rabkin (Eds.), *Anxiety: New research and changing concepts* (pp. 117–136). New York: Raven Press.

Cattell, R. B., & Scheier, I. H., (1961). *The meaning and measurement of neuroticism and anxiety.* New York: Ronald.

Cloninger, C. R., Martin, R. L., Clayton, P., & Guze, S. B. (1981). A blind follow-up and family study of anxiety neurosis: Preliminary analysis of the St. Louis 500. In D. F. Klein & J. Rabkin (Eds.), *Anxiety: New research and changing concepts* (pp. 137–154). New York: Raven Press.

Courts, F. A. (1939). Relations between experimentally induced muscular tension and memorization. *Journal of Experimental Psychology, 25,* 235–256.

Crowne, D. P. (1979). *The experimental study of personality.* Hillsdale, NJ: Erlbaum.

Davis, C. (1987). *A study of anxiety and coping in adolescents.* Unpublished doctoral dissertation, University of Nevada, Reno.

Dobson, K. S. (1985). The relationship between anxiety and depression. *Clinical Psychology Review, 5,* 307–324.

Doerr, H. O., & Hokanson, J. E. (1965). A relation between heart rate and performance in children. *Journal of Personality and Social Psychology, 2,* 70–76.

Dohrenwend, B. S., & Dohrenwend, B. P. (Eds.) (1974). *Stressful life events: Their nature and effects.* New York: Wiley.

Dollard, J., & Miller, N. E. (1950). *Personality and psychotherapy: An analysis in terms of learning, thinking and culture.* New York: McGraw-Hill.

Doris, J., McIntyre, A., & Tamaroff, M. (1980). In I. L Kutash, L. B. Schlesinger, & Associates. *Handbook of stress and anxiety* (pp. 298–316). San Francisco: Jossey-Bass.

Easterbrook, J. A. (1959). The effect of emotion on cue utilization and the organization of behavior. *Psychological Review, 66,* 183–201.

Ekman, P. (1984). Expression and the nature of emotion. In K. R. Scherer & P. Ekman (Eds.), *Approaches to emotion* (pp. 319–343). Hillsdale, NJ: Erlbaum.

Ellis, A. (1979). A note on the treatment of agoraphobics with cognitive modification versus prolonged exposure in vivo. *Behaviour Research and Therapy, 17,* 162–164.

Epictetus (1944). *Discourses* (T. W. Higginson, Trans.). Roslyn, NY: Walter J. Black. (Original work written 1st century A.D.)

Epstein, S. (1986). Anxiety, arousal, and the self-concept. In. C. D. Spielberger & I. G. Sarason (Eds.), *Stress and anxiety* (Vol. 10, pp. 265–305). Washington, DC: Hemisphere.

Eysenck, H. J. (1961). *The handbook of abnormal psychology.* New York: Basic Books.

Eysenck, M. W. (1984a). Anxiety and the worry process. *Bulletin of the Psychonomic Society, 22,* 545–548.

Eysenck, M. W. (1984b). *A handbook of cognitive psychology.* Hillsdale, NJ: Erlbaum.

Eysenck, M. W. (1988). Anxiety and attention. *Anxiety Research, 1,* 9–15.

Eysenck, M. W., MacLeod, C., & Mathews, A. (1987). Cognitive functioning and anxiety. *Psychological Research, 49,* 189–195.

Fenichel, O. (1945). *The psychoanalytic theory of neurosis.* New York: Norton.

Fischer, W. F. (1970). *Theories of anxiety.* New York: Harper & Row.

Freud, A. (1966). *The ego and the mechanisms of defense* (rev. ed.). New York: International Universities Press. (Original work published 1937)

Freud, S. (1936). *The problem of anxiety.* New York: Norton. (Original work published 1926)

Freud, S. (1959a). The justification for detaching from neurathenia a particular syndrome: The anxiety-neurosis. In *Sigmund Freud: Collected papers* (Vol. 1, pp. 76–106) New York: Basic Books. (Original work published 1895)

Freud, S. (1959b). The unconscious. In *Sigmund Freud: Collected papers* (Vol. 4, pp. 109–111). New York: Basic Books. (Original work published 1915)

Freud, S. (1969). *A general introduction to psychoanalysis.* New York: Simon & Schuster. (Original work published 1935)

Fullerton earns more respect. (1978, March 19). *Reno Gazette-Journal,* p. 21.

Geer, J. H., Davison, G. C., & Gatchel, R. I. (1970). Reduction of stress in humans through nonveridical perceived control of aversive stimulation. *Journal of Personality and Social Psychology, 16,* 731–738.

Goldberger, L. (1982). Sensory deprivation and overload. In L. Goldberger & S. Breznitz (Eds.), *Handbook of stress: Theoretical and clinical aspects* (pp. 410–418). New York: Free Press.

Goldberger, L., & Breznitz, S. (1982). *Handbook of stress: Theoretical and clinical aspects.* New York: Free Press.

Goldstein, K. (1951). On emotions. *Journal of Psychology, 31,* 37–46.

Guislain, J. (1826). *Traite sur L'aliénation mentale.* Amsterdam: Van der Hey et fils.

Haan, N. (1977). *Coping and defending: Processes of self-environment organization.* New York: Academic Press.

Hamilton, M. (1959). The assessment of anxiety by ratings. *British Journal of Medical Psychology, 32,* 50–55.

Hebb, D. O. (1955). Drives and the C.N.S. (conceptual nervous system). *Psychological Review, 62,* 243–254.

Hershberg, S. G., Carlson, G. A., Cantwell, D. P., & Strober, M. (1982). Anxiety and depressive disorders in psychiatrically disturbed children. *Journal of Clinical Psychiatry, 43,* 358–361.

Izard, C. E. (1972). Anxiety: A variable combination of interacting fundamental emotions. In C. D. Spielberger (Ed.), *Anxiety: Current trends and research* (Vol. 1, pp. 55–106). New York: Academic Press.

Izard, C. E. (1979). Emotions as motivations: An evolutionary–developmental perspective. In H. E. Howe (Ed.), *Current theory and research in motivation* (pp. 163–200). Lincoln: University of Nebraska Press.

Izard, C. E., & Blumberg, S. H. (1985). Emotion theory and the role of emotions in children and adults. In A. H. Tuma & J. D. Maser (Eds.), *Anxiety and the anxiety disorders* (pp. 109-129). Hillsdale, NJ: Erlbaum.

Izard, C. E., & Buechler, S. (1980). Aspects of consciousness and personality in terms of differential emotions theory. In R. Plutchik & H. Kelleran (Eds.), *Emotion: Theory, research and experience* (Vol. 1, pp. 165-187). New York: Academic Press.

Jablensky, A. (1985). Approaches to the definition and classification of anxiety and related disorders in European psychiatry. In A. H. Tuma & J. D. Maser (Eds.), *Anxiety and the anxiety disorders* (pp. 735-758). Hillsdale, NJ: Erlbaum.

James, W. (1890). *Principles of psychology* (Vol. 2). New York: Henry Holt.

Kagan, J. (1984). *The nature of the child.* New York: Basic Books.

Katkin, E. S. (1965). Relationship between manifest anxiety and two indices of automatic response to stress. *Journal of Personality and Social Psychology, 2,* 324-333.

Kawash, G. F. (1982). A structural analysis of self-esteem from pre-adolescence through young adulthood: Anxiety and extraversion as agents in the development of self-esteem. *Journal of Clinical Psychology, 38,* 301-311.

Kelly, D. H. W. (1966). Measurement of anxiety by forearm blood flow. *British Journal of Psychiatry, 112,* 789-798.

Kelly, D. H. W., & Walter, C. J. S. (1968). The relationship between clinical diagnosis and anxiety, assessed by forearm blood flow and other measurements. *British Journal of Psychiatry, 114,* 611-626.

Kendler, K. S., Heath, A. C., Martin, N. G., & Eaves, L. J. (1987). Symptoms of anxiety and depression: Same genes, different environments? *Archives of General Psychiatry, 44,* 451-457.

Kierkegaard, S. (1980). *The concept of anxiety* (R. Thomte, Ed. and Trans., with A. B. Anderson). Princeton, NJ: Princeton University Press (Original work published 1844)

Kitay, W. (1986). *The effects of state and trait anxiety on creativity.* Unpublished doctoral dissertation, Hofstra University, Hempstead, NY.

Klein, D. F., & Rabkin, J. G. (Eds.). (1981). *Anxiety: New research and changing concepts.* New York: Raven Press.

Kleinknecht, R. A. (1986). *The anxious self: Diagnosis and treatment of fears and phobias.* New York: Human Sciences Press.

Lader, M. H., & Wing, L. (1966). *Physiological measures, sedative drugs, and morbid anxiety.* London: Oxford University Press.

Lang, P. H. (1985). The cognitive psychophysiology of emotion: Fear and anxiety. In A. H. Tuma & J. D. Maser (Eds.), *Anxiety and the anxiety disorders* (pp. 131-170). Hillsdale, NJ: Erlbaum.

Lauterbach, W. (1975). Assessing psychological conflict. *British Journal of Social and Clinical Psychology, 14,* 43-47.

Lazarus, R. S., & Folkman, S. (1984). *Stress, appraisal, and coping.* New York: Springer.

Lewis, M., & Michalson, L. (1983). *Children's emotions and moods.* New York: Plenum Press.

Locke, J. (1959). *An essay concerning human understanding* (Vols. 1-2. New York: Dover. (Original work published 1690)

Lovaas, O. I. (1960). Supplementary report: The relationship of induced muscular tension to manifest anxiety in learning. *Journal of Experimental Psychology, 59,* 205-206.

MacLeod, C., Mathews, A., & Tata, P. (1986). Attentional bias in emotional disorders. *Journal of Abnormal Psychology, 95,* 15-20.

Mahler, M. S., Pine, F., & Bergman, A. (1975). *The psychological birth of the human infant.* New York: Basic Books.

Mainzer, F., & Krause, M. (1940). The influence of fear on the electrocardiogram. *British Heart Journal, 2,* 221-230.

Malmo, R. B., Shagass, C., & Davis, J. F. (1951). Electromyographic studies of muscular tension in psychiatric patients under stress. *Journal of Clinical and Experimental Psychopathology, 12,* 45-66.

Mandler, G. (1975). *Mind and emotion.* New York: Wiley.

May, R. (1950). *The meaning of anxiety.* New York: Ronald.

McCrae, R. R., & Costa, P. T. (1987). Validation of the five-factor model of personality across instruments and observers. *Journal of Personality and Social Psychology, 52,* 81-90.

McNally, R. J. (1987). Preparedness and phobias: A review. *Psychological Bulletin, 101,* 283-303.

McNally, R. J., & Steketee, G. S. (1985). The etiology and maintenance of severe animal phobias. *Behaviour Research and Therapy, 4,* 431-435.

McReynolds, P. (1965). On the assessment of anxiety: 1. By a behavior checklist. *Psychological Reports, 16,* 805–808.

McReynolds, P. (Ed.). (1969). *Four early works on motivation.* Gainesville, FL: Scholars' Facsimiles and Reprints.

McReynolds, P. (1971). Behavioral choice as a function of novelty-seeking and anxious-avoidance motivations. *Psychological Reports, 29,* 3–6.

McReynolds, P. (1976). Assimilation and anxiety. In M. Zuckerman & C. D. Spielberger (Eds.), *Emotions and anxiety* (pp. 35–86). New York: Wiley.

McReynolds, P. (1986). Changing conceptions of anxiety: A historical review and a proposed integration. In C. D. Spielberger & I. G. Sarason (Eds.), *Stress and anxiety* (Vol. 10, pp. 131–158). Washington, DC: Hemisphere.

McReynolds, P. (1987). Self-theory, anxiety and intrapsychic conflicts. In N. Cheshire & H. Thomae (Eds.). *Self, symptoms and psychotherapy* (pp. 197–223). New York: Wiley.

McReynolds, P. (1989). Toward a general theory of anxiety. In C. D. Spielberger, I. G. Sarason, & J. Strelau (Eds.), *Stress and anxiety* (Vol. 12, pp 5–14). Washington, DC: Hemisphere.

McReynolds, P., Acker, M., & Brackbill, G. (1966). On the assessment of anxiety: 4. By measures of basal conductance and palmar sweat. *Psychological Reports, 19,* 347–356.

McReynolds, P., Acker, M., & Pietla, C. (1961). Relation of object curiosity to psychological adjustment in children. *Child Development, 32,* 393–400.

McReynolds, P., Eyman, J., White, P., & Baldo, R. (1989). *An instrument for differentiating cognitive and conditioned anxiety.*

Miller, J. G. (1960). Information input overload and psychopathology. *American Journal of Psychiatry, 116,* 695–704.

Mineka, S. (1985). The frightful complexity of the origins of fears. In F. R. Brush & J. B. Overmier (Eds.), *Affect, conditioning, and cognition* (pp. 55–73). Hillsdale, NJ: Erlbaum.

Mitchell, S., & Campbell, E. A. (1988). Cognitions associated with anxiety and depression. *Personality and Individual Differences, 9,* 837–838.

Mowrer, O. H. (1939). A stimulus–response analysis of anxiety and its role as a reinforcing agent. *Psychological Review, 46,* 553–565.

Mueller, J. H. (1976). Anxiety and cue utilization in human learning and memory. In M. Zuckerman & C. D. Spielberger (Eds.), *Emotions and anxiety* (pp. 197–229). Hillsdale, NJ: Erlbaum.

Neighbors, B., McReynolds, P., Essa, E., & Harrington, M. (1989). *Personality structure in preschool children.*

Neumann, H. (1859). *Lehrbuch der Psychiatrie.* Erlanger, Germany: F. Enke.

Ohman, A. (1986). Face the beast and fear the face: Animal and social fears as prototypes for evolutionary analyses of emotion. *Psychophysiology, 23,* 123–145.

Okebukola, P. A. (1986). Relationships among anxiety, belief system, and creativity. *Journal of Social Psychology, 126,* 815–816.

Ost, L.-G., & Hugdahl, K. (1981). Acquisition of phobias and anxiety response patterns in clinical patients. *Behaviour Research and Therapy, 19,* 439–447.

Penny, R. K. (1965). Reactive curiosity and manifest anxiety. *Child Development, 36,* 697–702.

Pervin, L. A. (1963). The need to predict and control under conditions of threat. *Journal of Personality, 31,* 570–587.

Plutchik, R. (1980). *Emotion: A psychoevolutionary perspective.* New York: Harper & Row.

Plutchik, R., Wasserman, N., & Mayer, M. (1975). A comparison of muscle tension patterns in psychiatric patients and normals. *Journal of Clinical Psychology, 31,* 4–8.

Rachman, S. (1977). The conditioning theory of fear acquisition: A critical examination. *Behaviour Research and Therapy, 15,* 375–387.

Reiss, S. (1987). Theoretical perspectives on the fear of anxiety. *Clinical Psychology Review, 7,* 585–596.

Reiss, S., & McNally, R. J. (1985). The expectancy model of fear. In S. Reiss & R. R. Bootzin (Eds.), *Theoretical issues in behavior therapy* (pp. 107–121). New York: Academic Press.

Rogers, C. (1959). A theory of therapy, personality, and interpersonal relationships, as developed in the client-centered framework. In S. Koch (Ed.), *Psychology: A study of a science* (Vol. 3, pp. 184–256). New York: McGraw-Hill.

Rosch, E., & Lloyd, B. B. (Eds.). (1978). *Cognition and categorization.* Hillsdale, NJ: Erlbaum.

Roth, M., & Mountjoy, C. Q. (1982). The distinction between anxiety states and depressive disorders. In E. S. Paykel (Ed.), *Handbook of affective disorders* (pp. 70–92). New York: Guilford Press.

Samuel, W., Baynes, K., & Sabeh, C. (1978). Effects of initial success or failure in a stressful or relaxed environment on subsequent task performance. *Journal of Experimental Social Psychology, 14,* 205–216.

Sarason, I. G. (1985). Cognitive processes, anxiety, and the treatment of anxiety disorders. In A. H. Tuma & J. D. Maser (Eds.), *Anxiety and the anxiety disorders* (pp. 87–107). Hillsdale, NJ: Erlbaum.

Sarason, I. G. (1988). Anxiety, self-preoccupation and attention. *Anxiety Research, 1,* 3–8.

Sarason, S. B., Davidson, K. S., Lighthall, F. F., Waite, R. R., & Ruebush, B. K. (1960). *Anxiety in elementary school children.* New York: Wiley.

Scheier, M. F., Carver, C. S., & Matthews, K. A. (1983). Attentional factors in the perception of bodily states. In J. T. Cacioppo & R. E. Petty (Eds.), *Social psychophysiology* (pp. 510–542). New York: Guilford Press.

Schwarzer, R. (Ed.). (1984). *The self in anxiety, stress and depression.* Amsterdam: North-Holland.

Seligman, M. E. P. (1971). Phobias and preparedness. *Behavior Therapy, 2,* 307–320.

Selye, H. (1956). *The stress of life.* New York: McGraw-Hill.

Slater, E., & Shields, J. (1969). Genetical aspects of anxiety. *British Journal of Psychiatry, 3,* 62–71.

Smith, D. B. D., & Wenger, M. A. (1965). Changes in autonomic balance during phasic anxiety. *Psychophysiology, 1,* 267–271.

Smith, G. J. W., & Carlsson, J. (1983). Creativity and anxiety: An experimental study. *Scandanavian Journal of Psychology, 24,* 107–115.

Smith, K. L. (1984). *The relation of test anxiety to the manifestation of creativity in a group of adolescents.* Unpublished doctoral dissertation, University of Southern California.

Sobel, E. F. (1980). Anxiety and stress in later life. In I. L. Kutash, L. B. Schlesinger, & Associates (Eds.), *Handbook of stress and anxiety* (pp. 317–328). San Francisco: Jossey-Bass.

Spelman, M. S., & Ley, P. (1966). Psychological correlates of blood pressure. *Medical Journal of Australia, 2,* 1138–1140.

Spence, J. T., & Spence, K. W. (1966). The motivational components of manifest anxiety: Drive and drive stimuli. In C. D. Spielberger (Ed.), *Anxiety and behavior* (pp. 291–326). New York: Academic Press.

Spence, K. W., Farber, I. E., & McFann, H. H. (1956). The relation of anxiety (drive) level to performance in competitional and noncompetitional paired-associates learning. *Journal of Experimental Psychology, 52,* 296–305.

Spielberger, C. D. (1966). Theory and research on anxiety. In C. D. Spielberger (Ed.), *Anxiety and behavior* (pp. 3–20). New York: Academic Press.

Spielberger, C. D. (1972). Anxiety as an emotional state. In C. D. Spielberger (Ed.), *Anxiety: Current trends in theory and research* (Vol. 1, pp. 24–49). New York: Academic Press.

Spielberger, C. D. (1985). Anxiety, cognition and affect: A state–trait perspective. In A. H. Tuma & J. D. Maser (Eds.), *Anxiety and the anxiety disorders* (pp. 171–182). Hillsdale, NJ: Erlbaum.

Spielberger, C. D., Pollans, C. H., & Worden, T. J. (1984). Anxiety disorders. In S. M. Turner & M. Hersen (Eds.), *Adult psychopathology: A behavioral perspective* (pp. 263–303). New York: Wiley.

Spielberger, C. D., & Sarason, I. G. (Eds.). (1986). *Stress and anxiety* (Vol. 10). Washington, DC: Hemisphere.

Spitz, R. A. (1964). The derailment of dialogue. *Journal of the American Psychoanalytic Association, 12,* 752–775.

Sroufe, L. A. (1984). The organization of emotional development. In K. R. Scherer & P. Ekman (Eds.), *Approaches to emotion* (pp. 109–128). Hillsdale, NJ: Erlbaum.

Suedfeld, P. (1986). Stressful levels of environmental stimulation. In C. D. Spielberger & I. G. Sarason (Eds.), *Stress and anxiety* (Vol. 10, pp. 83–104). Washington, DC: Hemisphere.

Sullivan, H. S. (1953). *The interpersonal theory of psychiatry.* New York: Norton.

Taylor, J. A. (1951). The relationship of anxiety to the conditioned eyelid response. *Journal of Experimental Psychology, 41,* 81–92.

Tellegen, A. (1985). *Structures of mood and personality and their relevance to assessing anxiety, with an emphasis on self-report.* In A. H. Tuma & J. D. Maser (Eds.), *Anxiety and the anxiety disorders (pp. 681–706). Hillsdale, NJ: Erlbaum.*

Tomkins, S. S. (1984). Affect theory. In K. R. Scherer & P. Ekman (Eds.), Approaches to emotion (pp. 163–195). Hillsdale, NJ: Erlbaum.

Torgerson, S. (1983). Genetic factors in anxiety disorders. *Archives of General Psychiatry, 40,* 1085–1089.

Trevarten, C. (1984). Emotions in infancy: Regulators of contact and relationships with persons. In K. R. Scherer & P. Ekman (Eds.), *Approaches to emotion* (pp. 129–157). Hillsdale, NJ: Erlbaum.

Tuma, A. H., & Maser, J. D. (Eds.). (1985). *Anxiety and the anxiety disorders.* Hillsdale, NJ: Erlbaum.

Turner, S. M., Beidel, D. C., & Costello, A. (1987). Psychopathology in the offspring of anxiety disorder patients. *Journal of Consulting and Clinical Psychology, 55,* 229–235.

Voss, H.-G., & Keller, H. (1983). *Curiosity and exploration: Theories and results.* New York: Academic Press.

Watson, D., & Clark, L. A. (1984). Negative affectivity: The disposition to experience aversive emotional states. *Psychological Bulletin, 96,* 465–490.

Watson, D., Clark, L. A., & Carey, G. (1988). Positive and negative affectivity and their relation to anxiety and depressive disorders. *Journal of Abnormal Psychology, 97,* 346–353.

Watson, J. B., & Rayner, R. (1920). Conditioned emotional reactions. *Journal of Experimental Psychology, 3,* 1–14.

Weiss, J. M. (1971). Effects of coping behavior with and without a feedback signal on stress pathology in rats. *Journal of Comparative and Physiological Psychology, 77,* 1–13.

White, B. V., & Gildea, E. F. (1937). "Cold pressor test" in tension and anxiety. *Archives of Neurology and Psychiatry, 38,* 964–984

White, P. (1982). *A study of cognitive anxiety and mental conflicts.* Unpublished doctoral dissertation, University of Nevada, Reno.

Windheuser, H. J. (1977). Anxious mothers as models for coping with anxiety. *Behavioral Analysis and Modification, 2,* 39–58

Wood, G. C., & Hokanson, J. E. (1965). Effects of induced muscular tension on performance and the inverted U function. *Journal of Personality and Social Psychology, 1,* 506–510.

Yerkes, R. M., & Dodson, J. D. (1908). The relation of strength of stimulus to rapidity of habit formation. *Journal of Comparative and Neurological Psychology, 18,* 459–482.

Zaffy, D. J., & Bruning, J. L. (1966). Drive and the range of cue utilization. *Journal of Experimental Psychology, 71,* 382–384.

2

The Anxiety Disorders:
A Psychiatric Perspective

Gavin Andrews

The anxiety disorders are common causes of psychiatric morbidity. In any six-month period, about 1 person in 20 will be sufficiently troubled by anxiety to seek help from a doctor or other health professional. Patients with anxiety disorders constitute 15% of the workload of psychiatrists (Andrews & Hadzi-Pavlovic, 1988) and 10% of the patients seen in general practice, and they frequently visit cardiologists and neurologists. These patients are seldom admitted to the hospital with anxiety as the primary diagnosis; they usually gain admission to the cardiology service for investigation of palpitations or to the neurology service for investigation of headache. The urgency of their complaints seems to preclude ordinary office visits. Students who have been educated in hospital medicine often go out into practice believing that anxiety disorders are default diagnoses and of little consequence. However, people with agoraphobia often become totally housebound, people with social phobias can become hermits, people with obsessional illness can become incapacitated by their compulsions, and people with generalized anxiety disorder will usually have a long and continuing struggle to control their nervousness. With many anxiety disorders, chronic disability is the rule. In this chapter I first present a general discussion of pathological anxiety and then a description of the more common anxiety disorders that are of interest to psychiatrists.

USEFUL VERSUS DEBILITATING ANXIETY

The seriousness of the anxiety disorders is frequently underestimated because anxiety is a normal, useful, and protective affect. Depression is seldom undervalued because, although attacks are often of short duration, depression is seldom useful and is sometimes dangerous. This notion of the usefulness of anxiety is very important in the management of the anxiety neuroses, for many patients have learned to fear even their normal anxiety and so react to it as though it were abnormal, thus compounding their complaint.

In 1908 Yerkes and Dodson described a relation between anxiety and performance that can help patients to understand the nature of the facilitating and debilitating

This chapter is a revised and extended version of the chapter, "The Anxiety States," In P. Beumont and R. B. Hampshire (Eds.), *Textbook of Psychiatry*. Oxford: Blackwell Scientific Publications, 1989.

effects of anxiety. They showed that performance on skilled tasks improves as anxiety increases above baseline relaxation, and thus anxiety is initially facilitating. The performance increment plateaus when the person is tense and alert, and from then on further anxiety will debilitate, rapidly reducing the capacity for skilled motor movements, complex intellectual tasks, and personal relationships, and especially impairing the perception of new information. "He plays better if he is psyched-up" is a colloquial description of facilitating anxiety and "she lost her head" is an apt description of the effects of debilitating anxiety, a relationship that is discussed in chapter 1.

Patients with anxiety disorders suffer considerably from the debilitating effect of their excessive and prolonged anxiety, because it impairs self-esteem, work performance, and personal relationships. Aware that excess anxiety can lead them to make a mess of things, they tend to avoid difficult situations so as not to appear unnecessarily stupid and defer to others rather than assert themselves and run the risk of becoming unnecessarily upset. It is therefore not long before the threat of their own anxiety becomes a stressor in its own right, a stressor to which they react with additional symptoms.

THE ROLE OF PERSONALITY

The enduring characteristics of a person's nature are called personality. Some people, year after year, become more sensitive, more emotional, and more prone to anxiety than are their peers. The major attempts by Eysenck, by Cattell, and by Spielberger to use questionnaires to describe the variations in human personality traits have consistently shown that the trait of proneness to anxiety is a major component of personality that determines behavior. For example, consider the influence of trait anxiety on the experience of anxiety symptoms, called state anxiety, during an eventful car journey to work. Calm when leaving home, the average person becomes tense when stopped by the police for speeding, and panics only when threatened by a head-on collision. The person with low trait anxiety will not become anxious when stopped by the police, and when threatened by the collision will be able to use the resulting anxiety to facilitate skillful avoiding action. A person who has a high level of trait anxiety will panic when stopped by the police and cease to function at the threat of a collision. All three could have been equally calm when they began their journeys, but because the person with high trait anxiety will have experienced more anxiety and will have habituated to it more slowly, the whole experience will prove to be exhausting for that person.

Precisely because of this influence of trait anxiety on state anxiety, the anxiety disorders are often dismissed as being simply manifestations of personality. Although this may be somewhat true for generalized anxiety disorder, it is certainly not so for the other anxiety disorders, for which the symptoms of illness are very distinct from personality. Nevertheless, trait anxiety is probably the single most important determinant of neurotic symptoms. In a study of a Canberra population, Henderson, Byrne, and Duncan-Jones (1981) showed that a measure of trait anxiety accounted for half the variance in symptoms of anxiety and depression over the 12 months of the study. In a study of patients with anxiety disorders, Andrews, Pollock, and Stewart (in press) showed that all four patient groups showed trait anxiety scores 1.5 standard deviations above the population mean and that this was the personality measure most closely associated with symptom level. In a twin study, Jardine, Martin, and Henderson (1984) showed that heredity was the single most important determinant of trait anxiety. In theirs, as in other studies, genetic factors accounted for half the variance in trait anxiety scores. Thus people with high trait anxiety probably inherit a type of nervous system that in response to stress seems to arouse too quickly and habituate too slowly.

Everyone defines anxiety as a response to stress, so with the importance of trait anxiety established, I discuss the role of stress and coping. When threatened by loss of love, position, wealth, or safety, most people will become anxious, and the extent of the immediate anxiety reaction is controlled by two factors: the significance of the threat and the level of trait anxiety. Life event research, a technique for enumerating events of a stressful nature, has repeatedly demonstrated the relation between threat and state anxiety but has also shown that this relationship is time-limited (Andrews, 1981) and that people recover quite quickly. Most humans seem to be very good at coping with normal adversity. Loss of money or position can usually be accepted within a month or so; loss of a parent, spouse, or child no longer disables after a year or so; but some experiences, so severe that they would horrify everyone, continue to produce symptoms for a very long time.

A schema for integrating the effects of four factors on anxiety—adverse events, level of appraisal, trait anxiety, and coping style—is illustrated in Figure 1. According to this model, when an untoward event occurs one asks "Is this a threat to me?". The event is appraised in terms of one's prior experience with similar events or in terms of knowledge about the level of threat that such events usually pose. Two points are important: Some of this appraisal appears to be conducted independently of conscious or rational control, and second, because the full threat of an event may take time to become evident, appraisal and coping are dynamic and continuous processes that, for the purposes of this model, are discussed as though they were static. If the event is appraised as threatening then two things happen: The person becomes sufficiently aroused to feel anxious—somatically anxious in terms of palpitations, cold sweats, trembling, and indeed all the manifestations of the flight or fight response, and psychologically anxious in terms of tension, apprehension, and hypervigilance.

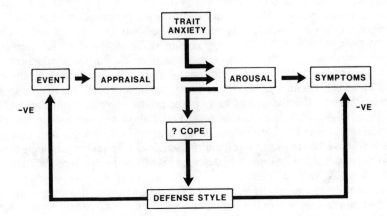

Figure 1   A model for anxiety that illustrates the relation between an adverse event and the consequent appraisal, arousal, and experienced anxiety and the exacerbating effect of trait anxiety and the moderating effects of coping and social support.

The magnitude of the response to a given event appraised as threatening will be heavily influenced by that individual's level of trait anxiety. Individuals respond to events that are identified as threatening by attempting to control the danger to themselves or to limit their anxiety, or both. Individuals who encounter considerable stresses over time yet have a successful adult adjustment have been shown to succeed by using one set of behaviors to cope with the reality threat (task orientation to neutralize the event, reappraisal and anticipation of possible solutions, and sublimation of energy into other activities if no solution is possible), and a second set of behaviors to regulate the disturbing emotions and debilitating anxiety (temporary suppression of the worrying thoughts, consolation through pleasurable or displacement activities, and minimization of the threat through humor, all these alternating with the reality-focused coping strategies, until a reality solution can be obtained or the threat subsides).

Both reality-focused and emotion-focused coping are believed to be potentiated if social support from others is available to provide help and advice in problem solving and to provide the opportunity to confide, ventilate, and be reassured. Only the most mature, and eventually most successful, individuals cope exclusively in this way. Under pressure most of us reduce the perceived salience of the threat by using more immature defenses such as denial and isolation of the significance of the threat or by overvaluing our own competence to deal with it. The intermittent use of these defenses does not seem to matter in the long term provided that the identity of the threat and the need to deal with it remain in consciousness. Persistent and habitual use of immature defenses such as blaming others (projection), solving the problem in fantasy only, or displacing the concern away from the threat to concern over physical symptoms or disease (somatization), prevent reality-focused coping and thus only worsen the situation. The use of immature defenses is characteristic of people who suffer from neuroses and personality disorders.

This model of anxiety, a model in which the relation between stress and anxiety is modulated by appraisal, trait anxiety, coping, and social support is based on research by Andrews, Tennant, Hewson, and Vaillant (1978). They showed that in one population sample, the percentage of people at risk for showing symptoms of anxiety and depression, which indicated their greater risk of being perceived as being psychologically impaired, varied considerably among those who experienced below-average adversity, those who had above-average coping skills and good social support, and those who experienced high adversity and had poor coping skills and poor social support (see Figure 2). When population samples are followed over time, the importance of life events declines so that trait anxiety and how people behave in response to this anxiety become the dominant factors in the production and maintenance of anxiety. Vaillant, who applied the ideas of Anna Freud about ego defenses to two Boston population samples and followed them for 30 years, has shown that a mature coping style is predictive of long-term work and personal success and psychological health, whereas the habitual use of immature defenses predicted the opposite (Vaillant, 1976; Vaillant, Bond, & Vaillant, 1986).

Two recent developments have advanced the measurement of coping style. Rotter (1966) had drawn attention to the importance of whether one perceived the problematic world as susceptible to one's own influence or not. His "locus of control" scale measured the extent to which people regarded problems as being within their own control (internals) or outside their own control (externals). This locus of control scale was subsequently redeveloped to measure control over personal difficulties (Craig,

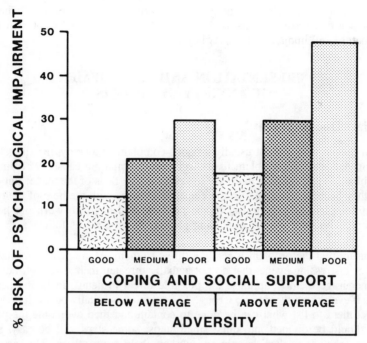

Figure 2 The percentage risk of being psychologically impaired in a Sydney population, the risk being associated with above and below median levels of adversity interacting with three levels of coping and social support. From Andrews et al. (1978). Adapted by permission.

Franklin, & Andrews, 1984). Patients with anxiety disorders, whatever their precise diagnosis, tend to score as externals and have scores one standard deviation above the mean of the general population (Andrews et al., in press). Both high trait anxiety and externalized locus of personal control were characteristic of patients with chronic anxiety disorders, irrespective of diagnosis.

The second advance in the measurement of coping was the development by Bond (1986) of the Defense Style Questionnaire that, when relabeled according to the draft glossary for the DSM-III-R (American Psychiatric Association, 1987), proved useful for distinguishing patients with anxiety from other patients and, more important, for showing different patterns of defenses to be used by patients with the different anxiety diagnoses (Andrews et al., in press; Pollock & Andrews, in press). On theoretical grounds, and from the factor structure in these studies, it appears that defenses can be described by three factors. Sublimation, humor, anticipation, and suppression characterize mature coping, whereby the threat is recognized but the anxiety is controlled until the threat can be dealt with. Undoing, pseudo-altruism, idealization, and reaction formation are characteristic of the neurotic or superego defenses wherein the event is recognized and responsibility is accepted but the meaning is inverted. Finally, projection, acting out, denial, passive aggression, somatization, displacement, and so forth are immature defenses whereby the very occurrence of the threat is denied or responsibility for the event transferred to another person or situation. Thus these three measures—trait anxiety, locus of personal control, and defensive style—allow one to characterize people according to how anxious they will become when faced with a standard stressor, how likely they are to try and cope, and what their habitual use of mature and immature defenses is likely to be.

PRESENTATION AND MANAGEMENT OF ANXIETY SYMPTOMS

Anxiety Due to Threat

When people who are not usually anxious complain of anxiety, the first step is to help them delineate the problem likely to be the precipating cause. Worrying about real problems is painful, and many try to keep the true facts of the matter out of mind in case they become too upset. In the consulting room, with the help of their doctor, they can complete their appraisal of the problem and begin to work out how they might cope. The steps to take in helping patients to cope are as follows:

1. Ensure that the problem is really a threat to them. Many people get needlessly upset over distressing events that do not actually threaten their own well-being.
2. Encourage them to appraise the possible threat in detail, including listing the outcome if everything were to go wrong. The situation is usually better than they fear.
3. Get them to list what can be done to contain and then overcome the problem. Coping should be divided into quite small steps; some steps will be easy, whereas others may require further thought and perhaps help from others. This process reduces a person's passivity in the face of stress and then encourages the adoption of mature or adaptive methods of coping.
4. Discuss how they plan to keep reasonably calm until the problem is resolved. Seeking comfort and support from sensible friends is helpful in encouraging good reappraisal of the situation and in the use of mature defenses such as anticipation, humor, and suppression. Putting energy into physical tasks or hobbies encourages the temporary use of sublimation, but remember that some level of tension is necessary if they are going to worry constructively until they find an acceptable solution. Long-acting benzodiazepines may be indicated for those who cannot sleep, whereas day-time sedation is rarely indicated and may well stop them from worrying appropriately.

Anxiety Secondary to Physical Factors

Some patients become acutely anxious whenever they experience unexpected physical symptoms for which there is no apparent cause. The prodrome of intercurrent illnesses like influenza; unexpected side effects from prescribed medication, street drugs, or alcohol; or even an excess of caffeine or nicotine can all precipitate acute anxiety that will be relieved by simple reassurance and education about the physiological changes responsible. Most doctors forget that their equanimity in the face of such symptoms is based on understanding the nature of autonomic arousal, knowledge that patients seldom have.

Some physical illnesses, like thyrotoxicosis and pheochromocytoma, can present with a primary anxiety that patients often try to understand in terms of intercurrent stressors in their lives. Effective management depends on the diagnosis and treatment of the underlying condition. Quite severe anxiety can be seen as a response to the threat posed by existing serious illness whether this be heart disease, asthma, or malignancy.

Anxiety Secondary to Psychiatric Illness

Patients who are severely depressed will be acutely anxious over what might happen to their families if their morbid fears become true, patients with schizophrenia often become very frightened by their bizarre hallucinations and delusions, and patients with acute organic brain syndromes experience severe anxiety as part of the symptomatology associated with the delerium. Treatment of the underlying disorder is imperative, and the use of anxiolytic drugs is seldom if ever called for. Nevertheless, patients with depression, schizophrenia, and dementia can also become anxious about the changes they note in themselves, and the management of this reactive anxiety is again a special case of anxiety due to threat. Anxiety is part of the presenting symptoms of neurotic depression and dysthymia, but in such cases antidepressant drugs and psychotherapy will be of more benefit than will anxiolytic drugs. Episodes of extreme anxiety are reported by patients with borderline, antisocial, and dependent personality disorders. Anxiolytics, especially benzodiazepines, are contraindicated for such patients because of the risk of dependence, or disinhibition leading to suicide attempts or other acting-out behavior. Most nonpsychiatrists think of an anxiety disorder when a patient with a psychiatric history complains of anxiety, but it is important to remember that quite severe anxiety is seen as a secondary symptom in most psychiatric disorders.

COMMON ANXIETY DISORDERS

The DSM-III-R (American Psychiatric Association, 1987) lists the following anxiety disorders: panic disorder with or without agoraphobia, social phobia and simple phobia, generalized anxiety disorder (GAD), obsessive–compulsive disorder, and posttraumatic stress disorder (PTSD). Adjustment disorder of an anxious type should be considered with these disorders. In the following sections, the diagnosis and management of each disorder is discussed separately, as though these disorders were mutually exclusive categories of illness. It must be remembered, however, that as these diagnoses describe dimensions of neurotic response, the various disorders can coexist and flow into each other.

In a study of two large samples, one from the community and one from the clinic, the experience of more than one anxiety disorder in their lifetimes to date was more frequent than would be expected from the individual prevalences of the diagnoses. The number of reported diagnoses was significantly associated with the extent of the underlying vulnerability factors as measured by the high neuroticism or trait anxiety and externalized locus of control (Andrews, Stewart, Morris-Yates, Holt, & Henderson, in press). Thus one patient may present a mixed social phobic and agoraphobic picture, whereas another, with a well-established obsessive–compulsive disorder, may from time to time experience periods of pervasive GAD or depression superimposed on the obsessive disorder. Despite this overlap, treatment is facilitated by careful diagnosis, for each disorder has a central issue that responds best to specific treatment.

Posttraumatic Stress Disorder

Posttraumatic stress disorder is a chronic syndrome that follows a terrifying calamity involving threatened or actual loss of life or severe bodily harm. The syndrome lasts for at least six months and can be distinguished from the period of distress that would be expected to follow the catastrophe. The traumatic event is persistently reexperienced through recurrent nightmares, recurrent intrusive thoughts about the event, or through distress in situations reminiscent of the event. The individual avoids such situations and tries to ignore the recurring memories and may become detached, remote, and emotionally numbed. Despite these efforts, the individual remains persistently aroused, irritable, and may sleep poorly.

Such symptoms have long been associated with war, but the present syndrome was first recognized in combat veterans of World War II and in concentration camp survivors from the same period. It was observed after the Korean and Vietnam wars and in survivors of Cambodian concentration camps, and it is now being described in survivors of natural disasters. In the latter case it has been recognized in victims of extreme personal violence, for example, after violent rape or assault, or following particularly harrowing motor vehicle accidents. It is not common, yet 1 person in 200 of the community report having or having had such symptoms. Even without treatment, symptoms do remit gradually in the years after the traumatic experience, so the prevalence in the community will depend on the occurrence of natural disasters, violence, and armed conflict during the previous 20 years.

In terms of the model of anxiety postulated earlier, the stressful event is a necessary and sufficient cause. Personality issues can be irrelevant and maturity of coping style seems inconsequential, for given sufficient horror even the most stable and the most mature will succumb. The question of interest is, "Why does the disorder become so chronic?" After all, one might think that after a few years the effects of even the worst trauma should begin to dissipate.

In part this chronicity occurs because the usual coping strategies are powerless: reality-focused coping appears to be irrelevant, the event is over, against all odds the individual survived, and there is now no threat to be coped with. Nothing can be done. Emotion-focused coping also seems to be powerless to control the memories, suppression does not work, humor is bitter, and consolation seems irrelevant. At best denial and isolation, at worst projection and inhibition, help the individual cope with the shame and the guilt, the anger and the outrage that follow the experience. These defenses fail repeatedly, and the flashbacks and nightmares constantly resensitize the person to the horror of the event.

Treatment is specific. One must bring stress-related information into consciousness so that the individual can relive the complete experience and so come to terms with it. After World War II, Pentothal abreaction was the means whereby anxiety was restrained sufficiently to allow the individual to recall all the memories. After Vietnam, discussion groups of veterans provided the support to allow the experiences to be recalled, whereas in civilian practice Horowitz (1974) has recommended that psychotherapy be used to permit a gradual cognitive and emotional working through, by repetitive recounting of the traumatic experience, so that the patient will be able to accommodate and assimilate the stressful memories. In short, there is a consensus between therapists of different theoretical positions about the need to incorporate exposure to memories of the traumatic event as an essential part of therapy.

Case Vignette

A 37-year-old veteran was admitted to the hospital for an elective orthopedic procedure and was noted to have recurrent and very disturbing nightmares. Questioned, he said they were usually about war service and had persisted for the five years since his return from Vietnam. His wife said that they occurred most nights and disturbed them both. She said her husband had been changed by Vietnam; he was now solemn and edgy much of the time, did not talk of the war, and seemed to be remote with her and the children. If he drank, he would become disturbed by his war memories.

During a series of psychotherapeutic interviews it transpired that he had regularly been on extended patrols behind Vietcong lines and that he and a friend were famous for the way they took care of and protected each other. On the last patrol he was the one to spot an ambush, but when he turned to warn his friend he could not call the warning out. He then saw his friend decapitated by a shot and the headless trunk spurt blood. Other members of the patrol were killed; the patient was wounded but was able to escape and return to base.

The key nightmare was about this event, but he always woke at the point when he was immobilized and unable to warn his friend. During a series of interviews, the details were gradually recalled, the guilt over the inability to call out worked through, and the grief over the death of his friend faced. The nightmares stopped, he became more relaxed with his family, and his performance at work improved.

Adjustment Disorder with Anxious Mood

The diagnosis of this disorder is a maladaptive reaction to an identifiable stressor so that function is impaired and symptoms of anxiety and worry abound. Adjustment disorder is one of the acute neurotic episodes that are called nervous breakdowns by lay people. Typically, after some moderately severe stressor has occurred (e.g., loss of a job, loss of money, or the end of a relationship), a person who would normally be expected to cope becomes persistently and irrationally anxious, nervous, jittery, and quite unable to cope in any rational way. Friends or family become alarmed, and the patient is brought to the doctor within a few days of the onset of the symptoms.

Reassurance that they are not going crazy, admission to the hospital if there is no one at home to care for them, and sedation with benzodiazepines (diazepam 10–20 mg at once and 5 mg every hour for eight hours thereafter) will produce a rapid drop in symptoms. These people become rational and task oriented and begin to ask, "How am I going to solve my problem?" Within days they are reacting appropriately and using their customary coping skills to cope with the stressor. Andreasen and Hoenk (1982) followed a group of these people after discharge and found that the majority suffered no further psychiatric illness.

Probably the condition should be conceptualized as the result of a stressor, particularly an unremembered past experience, which can cause such debilitating anxiety that all ability to cope is lost. Reassurance and sedation terminate this anxiety so that the person can begin to cope once again. The decompensation is so dramatic and the symptoms so marked that staff have difficulty in believing that recovery can be stable. They usually overtreat by continuing medication or advising psychotherapy after recovery. As a rule, neither are necessary for stable recovery, especially in those with stable premorbid personalities.

Case Vignette

A 20-year-old nurse who failed her final exams became acutely and irrationally preoccupied with worries about her professional future. After a full day's work on the ward she would stay up all night revising material for the next year's exams. She became exhausted and yet remained anxious and unable to sleep and was brought to the hospital. Within four days her anxiety had settled, she was embarrassed and puzzled by her breakdown, and she was determined to proceed in a more rational fashion. Follow-up at one year showed an excellent adjustment.

Generalized Anxiety Disorder

People with GAD may experience months of unrealistic and excessive worrying, usually about harm befalling a close family member or about future threats to finances, work, health, or personal relationships. This irrational worry is accompanied by problems with motor tension, with the physiological concomitants of anxiety, and with being keyed up and apprehensive all the time. Formerly, GAD and panic disorder were grouped together as anxiety neurosis. When panic disorder was recognized as a separate disorder, psychiatrists found that they seldom saw cases of GAD, although this disorder was commonly cited in surveys of the mental health of communities. There are several reasons for this.

People who are troubled by persistent, somewhat irrational worry and anxiety usually see this as an extension of their habitual nervousness. They do not identify it as evidence of illness, but rather see it as some further manifestation of their personality with which they will have to cope. They do not go to doctors. "How can I ask the doctor to fix my nature?" Instead they attend currently fashionable alternative therapies such as hypnosis, naturopathy, or meditation. Those who do go to doctors do so because of concern about the bodily symptoms of anxiety, and after physical disease has been excluded they are usually reassured that nothing is wrong and then placed on an anxiolytic drug.

Family practitioners can do much more than offer reassurance and drugs. The patient's assessment that the current worry is just another aspect of their personality is only partly right. In a statistical sense they are correct, for high trait anxiety is a necessary and sufficient cause for GAD. But because sufferers do not always have such symptoms, it is important to assess the influences of current adversity, life style, social predicament, and physical illness that could be contributing to the present symptoms. Because of the doctor's detailed knowledge of the patient's circumstances, he or she is in an ideal position to review what is being done to cope with these factors and to encourage reality and emotion-focused coping appropriate to the problems detected.

General practitioners seldom refer patients with GAD to psychiatrists, but there is another reason why psychiatrists make this diagnosis less often than would be expected. Psychiatric diagnosis is governed by the hierarchical notion that some diagnoses are more important than others. The symptom of anxiety can occur in all psychiatric disorders, yet the primary diagnosis of an anxiety disorder is made only if organic brain syndromes, schizophrenia, manic depression or other depressive illnesses, somatoform disorder, and dissociative disorder can be dismissed as causes for the anxiety. Furthermore, within the anxiety disorders, the diagnosis of GAD is made only if none of the other anxiety disorders account for the anxiety. GAD is therefore the default option, a diagnosis made only when no other primary diagnosis will account for the symptoms. It is not surprising that GAD, even though common in the community, is a relatively rare diagnosis in psychiatric practice.

Patients who are diagnosed as suffering from GAD realize the similarity of their symptoms to their normally anxious nature and have great difficulty knowing when they were first afflicted. Rapee (1985) confirmed that patients with GAD had difficulty putting a date to the first time they were troubled by such symptoms and that they tended to explain them as an extension of their usual anxiety. The age of onset was most frequently reported to be during childhood and adolescence, and onset became increasingly less likely with increasing age. Women were twice as likely as men to be diagnosed with this condition, and both sexes reported that other family members were also afflicted by nervousness, a finding that presumably reflects the genetic transmission of trait anxiety as a nonspecific vulnerability factor.

Because GAD is a default diagnosis, it is important to be familiar with the differential diagnosis. Differentiation from the psychoses should not prove difficult, but the overlap between neurotic anxiety and depression is common and does give rise to problems. Many people with GAD who complain of depression are clear that the depression is secondary to the anxiety. Yet unlike patients with neurotic depression, who often attribute the symptoms to external stressors, the GAD patient seems surprisingly blind to the salience of such stressors in the development of the disorder. Skilled psychotherapeutic interviewing will be necessary if the patient is to confront and deal with the relevant stressors and traumas.

Differentiating GAD from the other anxiety disorders sometimes proves difficult (Tyrer, 1984). In terms of severity, the anxiety fluctuates against a background of chronic anxiety in GAD, whereas in panic disorder, for instance, the anxiety is always episodic. GAD is a long-term, relapsing condition, whereas PTSD is a disorder in which relapse is rare once recovery has occurred. In GAD there is only a general diffuse relationship to the stressor, whereas in PTSD the relationship is clear and precise. Because of the dimensional nature of the neuroses, secondary symptoms of depression, phobia, or hypochondriasis are common in GAD, but they fluctuate and are not regarded by the patient as the central complaint. Conversely, anxiety is common in the phobic, depressive, obsessional, and hypochondriacal neuroses, but again, it is not the principal complaint.

Somatic symptoms of all types are seen in GAD but they fluctuate, are based on the physiological manifestations of anxiety, and patients respond, unlike patients with hypochondriasis, to reassurance that symptoms are caused by anxiety and not physical disease. In GAD a careful history will reveal that the symptoms are an extension of the underlying dependent or asthenic personality, whereas in the other anxiety disorders this is less likely to be the case. Some physical diseases can produce abnormal and persisting anxiety (e.g., thyrotoxicosis, pheochromocytoma, and insulinoma), but in patients with this type of anxiety, the more normal premorbid personality and lack of fluctuation of anxiety with intercurrent stressors will suggest the need for physical investigation.

Treatment for GAD should aim at relieving the present symptoms and reducing the vulnerability to anxiety. The benzodiazepine group of drugs are effective anxiolytics that are of value in the short-term management of anxiety, but there is increasing concern at the danger of dependence. A 5-mg dose of diazepam can be taken on occasions when the individual is faced with a particularly difficult situation, although many find it more helpful to take time to learn how to control their anxiety through the use of the relaxation response (Hellenberg & Collins, 1982). Stress management programs that include relaxation training, appraisal of external stressors, and training in mature styles of coping can produce symptomatic relief and a reduction in trait anxiety.

Case Vignette

A 30-year-old woman was referred because of somatic complaints, especially headaches, an irregular beating of her heart, and muscular tension that seemed to be worse when she was trying to relax. Always prone to worry and tension, she controlled this by eating and keeping compulsively busy caring for her husband, house, and children, and by working four nights a week. On Sundays, when there were no tasks, she would feel unwell and complain of the somatic symptoms. She was trained to relax and was taught more constructive ways of coping to replace her usual overeating and overworking. Her symptoms improved and she became calmer, more constructive, and more assertive. She no longer haunted her doctor because of her fears of disease.

Panic and Agoraphobia

Panic attacks are sudden spells of fear and anxiety that occur in situations where most people would not be afraid. The initial attacks take the person by surprise, and some people do continue to have spontaneous panic attacks that can wake them from sleep or occur when they are comfortable and relaxed. However, most soon discover the situations in which panic attacks are likely to occur and avoid some, or all, of those situations in an attempt to prevent the panic. The situations avoided are particularly those in which help would not be available, or escape possible, should a panic incapacitate—situations such as being on a train or bus, in a crowded shop, in a theater or church, on a lonely road or other open space, or even home alone and unable to call someone for help.

Panic attacks are more than just acute attacks of anxiety. They are accompanied by a range of symptoms due to autonomic arousal and hyperventilation; symptoms such as chest pain, choking, shortness of breath, palpitations, sweating, faintness, dizziness, or paresthesia, together with specific panic outcome fears such as a fear of dying, going crazy, or losing control. The attacks come on quickly, last less than 30 minutes, and clearly can be quite terrifying. Some people begin to avoid the range of situations after only a few attacks. They become anxious at the prospect of entering a feared situation and relieved whenever they decide to avoid the situation. In this way the fears are strengthened, and the fears and the disability soon become chronic. This is the disorder known as agoraphobia, or panic disorder with extensive phobic avoidance.

Other people, despite the panic attacks, continue to go about their daily tasks, often aware that it would be preferable to stay at home but determined not to let the fear of panic disable them. Panic disorder without phobic avoidance is the diagnosis reserved for these patients. It is not clear why, in the face of panic attacks, some people avoid and some do not. The severity of the panic attacks and the presence of predisposing personality characteristics are a factor, but avoidance related to ideas about the likely consequences of a panic attack and misattributions concerning the role of situations in precipitating panic attacks seem to be important.

Panic and agoraphobic afflict about 3% of the population, but because the condition is so often chronic, the lifetime risk is only double this rate. The disorder most commonly begins in the mid-20s (50% of cases between 20 and 35), but onsets in adolescence and in old age are also seen. The disorder is more common in women, with the sex ratio varying from 3:1 in the community to 8:1 among cases presenting for treatment. Most people visit their doctor soon after their first panic attack, but once the doctor and patient have assured themselves that there is no evidence of physical disease, treatment is often unsatisfactory. Many spend years being handi-capped by the disorder, restricted in their ability to travel, work, or be alone, depen-dent on others to take them places, dependent on benzodiazepines or alcohol to con-trol their anxiety, and often depressed and hostile when yet another ineffective treatment is suggested.

Panic and agoraphobia are disorders of considerable medical interest because it has been thought that these disorders were not simply another dimension of neurotic response but were a distinct and separate category of illness consistent with a medi-cal model, in that they are genetically determined (Crowe, Noyes, Wilson, Elston, & Ward, 1987), biochemically mediated (Pitts & McClure, 1967), and specifically responsive to pharmacological treatments (Klein, 1964). Both agoraphobia and panic disorder are three times more frequent among first-degree relatives of pa-tients than in the general population. Whether this increased risk is evidence of a specific genetic factor or best explained by the genetic transmission of high trait anxiety and cultural transmission of instructions to avoid anxiety-provoking situa-tions is currently being debated (Martin, Jardine, Andrews, & Heath, 1988; Moran & Andrews, 1985).

The second alternative seems most likely, particularly because the typical patient has a trait anxiety score in the top 5% of the population. The observation that people with panic disorder could be induced to panic in the laboratory by the infusion of lactate or by breathing 5% carbon dioxide whereas nonanxious control subjects could not lead to the strongest speculation that the disorder was associated with some physi-cal abnormality (Margraf, Ehlers, & Roth, 1986). Much more work needs to be done, particularly because it seems that the propensity to panic can be controlled when the patient is instructed about symptoms likely to follow the inhalation of carbon monoxide (Rapee, Mattick, & Murrell, 1986), and because the propensity to panic when provoked seems to be a graded characteristic of all patients with anxiety disorders and not specifically confined to those with panic disorder (Holt & Andrews, in press).

Klein's observation in 1964, however, that patients with panic disorder and ago-raphobia, unlike patients in other anxiety states, would respond to imipramine, a tricyclic antidepressant, really sparked interest in these disorders. Imipramine, pos-sibly phenelzine, a monoamine oxidase inhibitor antidepressant, and alprazolam, a triazolo benezodiazepine, have all been shown to have a specific effect on panic. At the present time, the evidence is probably best for imipramine, which has been considered the treatment of choice for panic disorder. Unfortunately there is no evidence that these disorders will remit after some months of drug-taking, and there is concern that in a disorder that is usually chronic, drugs may have to be taken for very many years.

A model for the development of agoraphobia is displayed in Figure 3. According to the model, a person with high trait anxiety who is subjected to a series of life stresses will become anxious, fail to cope with these threats in a mature way, and so remain chronically aroused. Sometimes the arousal can follow physical debility,

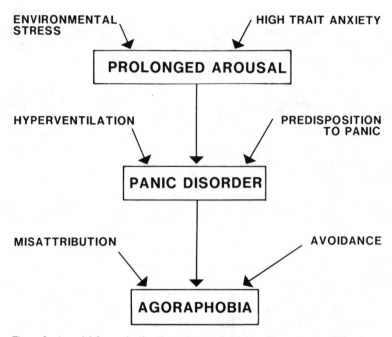

Figure 3   A model for panic disorder and agoraphobia that illustrates the effect of
stress and high trait anxiety in producing prolonged arousal;
hyperventilation and a genetic predisposition to panic in converting this
arousal to panic disorder; and the role of misattribution and avoidance in
the final development of agoraphobia from panic disorder.

such as after influenza or excessive alcohol. Whatever the cause, it seems that a
person who suddenly becomes aware of the physical symptoms of anxiety, but not
the psychological or physical antecedents, begins to hyperventilate, becomes terri-
fied of those symptoms, and experiences a panic attack. Any genetic predisposition
to panic would be manifested by either a sensitivity to the physical symptoms of
anxiety, or to those of hyperventilation, or both. If panic attacks continue to occur,
and individuals become sensitized to the early symptoms by a process of interocep-
tive conditioning, they then can begin to panic in response to these early symptoms
of anxiety alone.

When the cause of these panics is misattributed to the situations in which they
occur, and the patient then avoids the situation in the hope of avoiding the panic, then
agoraphobia has developed. In clinical practice, all agoraphobics say they avoid for
fear of panic, but in the community one finds some people who avoid crowded
situations, not because they might panic, but because they suffer from social phobia,
epilepsy, arrhythmia, diabetes, depression, paranoid schizophrenia, or other conditions that could make being in a crowd uncomfortable. These conditions therefore can
produce a secondary agoraphobia, and they must be considered in the differential
diagnosis of the condition.

Learning obviously plays a considerable role in the development of agoraphobia,
thus therapies based on learning to overcome the fears have been paramount with this
disorder. Conversely, panic attacks with their heavy emphasis on physical symptoms

have always seemed to call for a physical remedy, and drug therapy has been regarded as the treatment of choice for them. If panic and agoraphobia are but two aspects of the same disorder, then an integrated treatment plan would seem desirable. When patients present to their doctor complaints of the advent of panic attacks the doctor should

1. document the symptoms experienced during the worst attack;
2. explore in great detail the current environmental and physical stressors and help patients to find better ways of dealing with them;
3. arrange, both for the patient's and the doctor's peace of mind, referral to a cardiologist to ensure that no physical factors are contributing to the panics;
4. inform patients about the psychological nature of panic attacks, the importance of ideation in transforming the worry into marked anxiety, and the importance of hyperventilation in transforming marked anxiety into panic, and have them hyperventilate in the office and demonstrate the relation between this and the symptoms;
5. train patients in relaxation and in slow breathing techniques to control the development of the panic attack; and
6. counsel patients about the need to confront feared situations so that agoraphobia does not develop (medication should not be prescribed at this stage).

Should the panic attacks continue despite these measures, then the doctor should

1. decide if the complexity of the patient's predicament warrants more formal psychotherapeutic exploration by a psychiatrist;
2. decide whether this patient might warrant a therapeutic trial of imipramine (25 mg per day, increasing by one tablet every three days until the panics stop or a maximum dose of 200 mg per day is reached); and
3. decide whether this patient would be best referred to a behavior therapy clinic to learn how to control panics or overcome agoraphobic fears.

The actual choice of treatment will depend on the resources available in the area and on the preferences of the patient, but a cognitive behavior therapy that includes education about the disorder, control of hyperventilation, relaxation training to give control over debilitating anxiety and eventual reduction in trait anxiety, graded exposure to feared situations, and rational thinking and assertiveness training to aid effective appraisal of difficulties and more mature coping in general, is the treatment of choice when panic or agoraphobia has lasted longer than one year (Andrews & Moran, 1988; Barlow & Cerney, 1988). Imipramine is the treatment of choice in cases with a more recent onset. Benzodiazepines, regrettably even alprazolam, seem to be contraindicated because of the particular dangers of dependence in these patients.

Case Vignette, Panic Disorder

A 30-year-old sociologist, mother of two young children, married to an ambitious medical specialist, was busy finishing her thesis and arranging to lease her house and go to Boston to join her husband who had left earlier to do some postgraduate work, when she discovered that her mother had developed a fatal illness. While continuing to work on her thesis and arrange the trip, she made time to comfort her children and say goodbye to her mother. One day, while hurrying from her solicitors where she had reviewed their wills, she was caught in traffic and suffered a severe panic attack. The attacks recurred, and she consulted physicians who assured her that they were not evidence of physical disease, so she then consulted an expert on panic disorder. After discussing the various treatment options she elected to take imipramine "because I don't have time to learn to control the attacks." The imipramine was effective, and some time after settling her family in Boston she was able to come off the drug and the panics did not recur.

Case Vignette, Agoraphobia

A 40-year-old sensitive lady was referred with a 10-year history of agoraphobia that began after the birth of her second child, at a time of great financial difficulties and loneliness. She first panicked when out shopping and so quickly avoided shopping alone "in case I had an attack and couldn't look after the children." For the next 10 years she never became free of her fears of panic. At worst she would be housebound, depressed, and dependent on benzodiazepines, whereas during her better periods she would be able to travel locally within her own suburb. Her local doctor regarded her as incurably troubled by nerves, her family concurred, and there was no expectation that she could recover. Finally, a new doctor made the correct diagnosis and referred her for treatment. She was treated by being educated about her disorder, which included learning to control her panic and anxiety by hyperventilation control and by relaxation and learning to overcome her situational fears through a program of graded exposure. Finally her habitually inappropriate thoughts were dealt with through rational emotive therapy. She became confident, was able to travel freely, and went back to her job as a secretary. Perhaps best of all, both she and her family stopped thinking of her as nervous and neurotically ill.

Social Phobia

Social phobia is the fear and avoidance of situations in which one might be exposed to the scrutiny of others and in response become anxious, blush, shake, or otherwise behave in some way that will lead to humiliation. The irrational concern that social phobics have about the opinions of others leads them to avoid situations such as eating or drinking in public, talking in front of a small group of people, working while someone is watching (especially if work involves writing), and traveling on crowded public transport. Knowing their concern to be irrational and neurotic, they strive to keep the whole syndrome secret and make excuse after excuse to try to hide their disability.

Social phobia can be distinguished from the extremes of shyness, social skills deficit, or avoidant personality disorder (Nichols, 1974). The first symptoms usually appear during the teenage years and gradually worsen so that their education is impaired. Patients come for treatment in their mid-20s, by which time they are vocationally, socially, and educationally retarded; have used benzodiazepines and alcohol to blunt their sensitivity; and often have been sufficiently unhappy about their predicament to attempt suicide. Men are afflicted as often as women, and although the disorder seems to be rare in clinical practice, it is not so in the community (a six-month prevalence of about 1%) or in specialized phobia clinics. Sufferers are ashamed about their irrational beliefs, demoralized by the chronic unremitting course of the illness, and seldom go to general practitioners with this as their primary complaint. Doctors need to be on the alert for an unexpected withdrawal from college or job ("They wanted me to present my report orally in front of the whole team") or other signs of social withdrawal in young people.

The disorder is easily confused with schizophrenia, but social phobics are quite explicit about their reasons ("I couldn't stay there while they were all watching"), whereas schizophrenics give delusional explanations or are confused as to why they have withdrawn. The differentiation from agoraphobia is also not difficult. Even though both groups avoid crowded places and public transport, agoraphobics are usually clear that they avoid because of fear of panic and are helped by the presence of another, whereas social phobics know they are really avoiding the scrutiny of others and could enter the same situation if the place was deserted.

Social phobics are remarkably clever at hiding their disability. The journalist who tape-records everything rather than write notes in front of others, the intelligent and capable administrator who never says anything in meetings in case others turn to look, the efficient mother who says "I'm just not hungry" rather than eating in front of the family, and the university graduate who runs an office cleaning business by telephone so that he will never have to work in front of others are all examples of the ways in which social phobics hide their disability. Why do they do this? Most seem to have an extremely high fear of negative evaluation by others and feel that once others detect their nervousness they will be forever branded as being weak, inferior, or of no account.

Treatment with beta-blockers, which do improve performance anxiety in musicians, has been disappointing. Antidepressants do not help greatly, because the panics that social phobics experience are the consequence of being exposed to situations in which they fear humiliation and not the cause of the avoidance. Behavioral techniques that provide instruction in anxiety management, cognitive restructuring of the thoughts that form the basis for the fear of negative evaluation, and a program of graded exposure to the feared situations will result in substantial and long-lasting improvement (Mattick & Peters, 1988).

Case Vignette

A 27-year-old, highly skilled, farm machinery mechanic was brought to hospital because he had collapsed at the end of a day's work on a combine harvester that had broken down in the middle of the harvest. It transpired that he had avoided eating or drinking in front of others since he was at high school for fear that others would see his hand shake. When called to repair farm machinery, he would drink and eat in his truck just before entering the farm and would work without refreshment until the job was finished, apparently deaf to the farmer's offers of food or drink. On the day in question he had worked in midsummer heat from dawn to mid-afternoon before collapsing from dehydration. At family functions he would make excuses and leave before the food and drink were brought out. He was treated with a cognitive behavior therapy that emphasized the need to replace his faulty ideas with more rational thoughts and to replace his fear of negative evaluation with a more realistic view of what people thought of him. Now able to accept hospitality and go to the local hotel, he discovered that the townspeople respected his abilities and his hard work, and he was eventually elected to the local shire council.

Simple and Other Phobias

Fear and avoidance of circumscribed situations or things such as heights, insects, snakes, furry animals, dark or closed spaces, and still water are examples of other phobias. About 5% of the population fear one of these situations, a fear that they regard as irrational. The fear does not usually handicap them and such people very rarely present for treatment. These fears are common in childhood and may be atavistic in the sense that such fears were adaptive when we were primates who lived in trees and had to be aware of falling, being bitten by a poisonous spider or snake, taken by a carnivore or falling into water and drowning.

Parents usually take care to decondition their children to many of these fears. We learn to pat dogs, climb trees, swim, identify poisonous spiders, and maintain a healthy respect for snakes and dark closed spaces. Some people never learn to control these fears or, because of a traumatic experience with one of these situations, develop anew a persisting and irrational fear that does not extinguish through ordinary day-to-day encounters with the feared situations, as if these people were preprogrammed to develop such fears. The age of onset of these phobias is therefore in childhood with few cases developing after adulthood. The sex ratio is about 2:1, many have high trait anxiety scores, and most will become severely anxious and panic if forced to encounter their feared situation.

Treatment is relatively simple: exposure to the phobic stimulus in a graded hierarchy, or imaginal desensitization to the phobic stimulus if actual exposure is impossible. Simple training in relaxation and other anxiety management strategies makes the treatment easier. Insistence that one remains in the situation until anxiety abates ensures that the fear will extinguish. Blood and injury phobias that prevent people from going to the dentist or doctor or cause them to faint at the sight of blood or injury are probably similar. Certainly treatment is similar and equally successful.

Traumatic problems can follow a wide range of fear-provoking situations and are usually treated by graded exposure. In civilian life, the situations that most often give rise to traumatic phobias are motor vehicle and industrial accidents. Traumatic phobias can be distinguished from PTSD that follows similar accidents by the absence of nightmares, flashbacks, or emotional numbing.

Fear of flying is not a primary diagnosis. Agoraphobics, social phobics, and height phobics all avoid flying. People who have experienced a traumatic flight can also become acutely anxious at the prospect of flying. They actually have a fear of crashing and usually need specialized treatment to enable them to overcome their phobia.

If patients present with an atypical phobia that does not fit those described here, and is not due to obsessional illness or psychosis, then careful inquiry must be made about the circumstances in which the phobia first occurred and the secondary gain that has followed the phobia. Treatment for atypical phobias usually includes many sessions of exploratory psychotherapy to uncover the true meaning of the complaint.

Obsessive–Compulsive Disorder

Obsessions are recurrent thoughts or images, recognized by patients as their own, that persistently intrude into their minds despite their attempts to exclude them. The content of the obsession is usually limited to unpleasant aspects of dirt and contamination, aggression, orderliness of inanimate objects, sex, or religion. Compulsions are the most common, most disabling, and most noticeable of all the symptoms. Compulsions are repetitive behaviors that are performed in a stereotyped fashion to neutralize or prevent some dreaded but very unlikely happening.

The most common types of rituals are washing and checking. Washing is to prevent contamination. The washing is usually carried out in a ritualized way so that each part of the body is washed in a particular order, the unfortunate sufferer having to start the sequence again once there is doubt that the ritual has not been properly performed. Checking is done to prevent some future disaster, for example, checking electrical appliances repeatedly, laying out clean clothes in a certain way, or having to count or check objects repeatedly. Exactly as with the washing rituals, doubt that the checking has been properly done results in the need to begin the checking again. The individual realizes that the behavior is excessive and unreasonable but feels driven by a pressure to act that is felt as coming from within.

Obsessional ruminations also occur. The patient feels compelled to follow an endless sequence of thoughts about complex philosophical issues, about one's health, about the correctness of behavior, or about the importance of numbers. When the disorder is severe, the presenting symptoms are often concealed and the patient complains of the consequent depression, anxiety, or inability to get tasks done.

Obsessive–compulsive disorder (Beech, 1974) used to be regarded as rare, but recent epidemiological surveys have shown that the disorder afflicts 2.5% of adults and is a chronic condition beginning between the ages of 15 and 30 and in two out of three people after the age of 30. Severe cases are not common and most sufferers, because the disorder is so personal, try to keep the symptoms to themselves although the obsessions and compulsions slow their performance of everyday activities. About half of the patients will follow a constant or deteriorating course, and in the remainder symptoms will remit and recur. Both obsessions and compulsions are observed in some 70% of cases, obsessions occur alone in 25%, and the occasional patient seems to suffer only from compulsions. Anxiety is an important component of the disorder, and depression often complicates the course of the illness.

There are no clear data on the cause of the disorder, and views that it develops from a preexisting obsessive personality disorder, that it is inherited, or that it is evidence of regression to the anal phase of psychosexual development all lack empirical support. Obsessive–compulsive disorder is sometimes difficult to distinguish from other anxiety disorders, especially the phobias, but inquiry will reveal that the concern centers around fear of contamination and not fear of panic or fear of scrutiny. It can be confused with frightening delusions in schizophrenia, but the diagnostic point is the obsessional patient's recognition that the basic obsession is intense, unwanted, and comes from within. Obsessional and compulsive symptoms sometimes appear during a severe depressive illness, and it is very difficult to know, until the depression lifts, whether the patient has an independent obsessional illness. Obsessional symptoms can occasionally follow brain damage, but in these cases the need for orderliness is more a need to keep one's environment predictable and therefore easy to understand rather than being an unwanted preoccupation.

Despite the lack of information about etiology, treatment can be quite successful (Christensen, Hadzi-Pavlovic, Andrews, & Mattick, 1987). Short-term dynamic psychotherapy may be indicated for patients whose illness has lasted less than a year or in whom obsessions are the predominant symptom. Cognitive behavior therapy can also be used in cases of recent onset: relaxation to lower the general anxiety level, rational thinking to change the negative self-statements, and encouragement in resisting the compulsions. Once the compulsions are an established part of the syndrome, two other treatments should be utilized. Clomipramine, a tricyclic antidepressant, should be given first, up to 200 mg per day. If there is no improvement after six or eight weeks, then established compulsions should be treated by response prevention. This treatment involves exposing the patient to the situations or behaviors that characteristically produce the compulsions, and then by instruction or by persuasion prevent them from carrying out the rituals. This is repeated until the patient experiences, in situations in which symptoms would have been likely to occur, no recurrence of the intrusive obsession or pressure to carry out the ritual. Most patients, particularly those who have kept themselves working, can be substantially improved in the short- and long-term by these techniques. When patients remain incapacitated by their symptoms despite full and adequate courses of treatment, then they should be assessed as to their suitability for cingulotractomy, a cerebral surgical procedure that has been shown to produce substantial improvement in otherwise intractable illnesses.

Case Vignette

A 35-year-old homemaker with three children went to a new general practitioner complaining of depression. The doctor noticed that her hands were red and raw and on inquiry discovered that she spent so much time cleaning things that she was having difficulty looking after her family. Her problem began 10 years earlier, soon after the birth of her first child when she began to have intrusive thoughts that she might give germs to her baby. Gradually she found herself washing everything to guard against this possibility. Eventually even touching her daughter was too anxiety-provoking, and she sought help. She was treated with clomipramine and gradually improved.

She ceased taking the tablets and remained moderately improved for a few years, but she gradually deteriorated in the three years after the birth of her last child. She became disabled, felt compelled to wash her hands in an elaborate way at least 30 times per day, took all day to do the family laundry, and would not let packaged food into the house until each packet had been washed a prescribed number of times. An interview revealed that she was no more depressed than one would expect given her level of symptoms, and despite feeling compelled to act as though contamination was a real danger, she admitted that her actions were ridiculous and wished she could be different.

She was treated in a domiciliary day program, and the frequency of her rituals was observed so that a treatment plan could be constructed. Then she was placed on a response prevention schedule until she was able to handle soiled laundry or unpack groceries without her obsessions being activated. When followed up a year later, she had remained well, was managing the house adequately, and had returned to part-time work as a hairdresser.

CONCLUSION

Anxiety is a common symptom. People become anxious when threatened with physical harm or with loss of love, power, reputation, or property. People who are physically ill can become inordinately anxious about their illness and, in the case of some endocrine disorders, anxiety itself can stem directly from the hormonal imbalance. Anxiety symptoms can be a feature of other psychiatric disorders, and severe anxiety can confuse the clinical presentation of patients with marked depression, schizophrenia, and early dementia.

The anxiety disorders are quite distinct in presentation and natural history from the other diagnoses in which symptoms of anxiety occur. The anxiety disorders—PTSD, adjustment disorder with anxious mood, GAD, panic disorder and agoraphobia, social phobia, simple phobia, and obsessive–compulsive disorder—share a number of characteristics. The anxiety and the symptoms associated with each disorder often become severe and chronic if not correctly treated and can very easily result in considerable disability. The neuroses and the personality disorders are more frequent causes of a disability sufficient to warrant an invalid pension than are the disabilities that follow either the severe psychoses or heart disease. Yet despite the severity, chronicity, and disablement associated with the anxiety disorders, with treatment patients can lose their symptoms, even after years of illness, and remain well thereafter.

Permanent improvement requires a sophisticated treatment, usually through a planned behavioral, psychotherapeutic approach, but urgent instructions can produce temporary improvement that enables a housebound person to leave the home to attend to a sick child or a person incapacitated by washing rituals to work effectively at dirty tasks during a natural disaster. The issue seems to be that patients with anxiety disorders become afraid of their own symptoms and will avoid situations and forego opportunities rather than take the risk that (a) the panic will result in loss of control, (b) the general anxiety will debilitate, or (c) the flashback will produce guilty memories. Treatment by a specialist is indicated once an anxiety disorder has become chronic. The essential step in treatment is not to concentrate on reducing anxiety directly, but to teach people about the nature and meaning of their symptoms and of ways to control and reduce them. Once this has been achieved, then it is possible for patients to confront the difficult idea or situation and find that it no longer has the power to terrify them. Anxiety is then reduced.

There has been a very rapid growth in knowledge about the anxiety disorders in the last 20 years. It was probably sparked by the early behaviorists like Wolpe (1961), who introduced desensitization; by Marks (1969), who introduced exposure in vivo; and by Klein (1964), who raised the possibility that panic and agoraphobia might be categorically different from other anxiety disorders. The American Psychiatric Association, with the publication of the DSM-III-R, has been very influential in clarifying criteria for the individual diagnoses. Interest has recently been focused on the genetic and biological determinants of the various anxiety disorders. Knowledge is accumulating very rapidly, and some of the information in this chapter will soon need revision.

REFERENCES

American Psychiatric Association. (1987). *Diagnostic and statistical manual of mental disorders* (3rd ed., Rev.) Washington, DC: American Psychiatric Press.

Andreasen, N. C., & Hoenk, P. R. (1982). The predictive value of adjustment disorders: A follow-up study. *American Journal of Psychiatry, 139*, 584–590.

Andrews, G. (1981). A prospective study of life events and psychological symptoms. *Psychological Medicine, 77*, 795–801.

Andrews, G., & Hadzi-Pavlovic, D. (1988). The work of Australian psychiatrists, circa 1986. *Australian and New Zealand Journal of Psychiatrists, 22*, 153–165.

Andrews, G., & Moran, C. (1988). The treatment of agoraphobia with panic attacks: Are drugs essential? In I. Hand & H.-U. Wittchen (Eds.), *Panic and phobias: 2. Treatments and variables affecting course and outcome*. Heidelberg: Springer-Verlag.

Andrews, G., Pollock, C., & Stewart, G. (in press). The determination of defense style by questionnaire. *Archives of General Psychiatry*.

Andrews, G., Stewart, G. W., Morris-Yates, A., Holt, P. E., & Henderson, A. S. (in press). Evidence for a general neurotic syndrome. *British Journal of Psychiatry*.

Andrews, G., Tennant, C., Hewson, D., & Vaillant, G. (1978). Life event stress, social support, coping style, and risk of psychological impairment. *Journal of Nervous and Mental Disease, 16*, 307–316.

Barlow, D. H., & Cerney, J. A. (1988). *Psychological treatment of panic*. New York: Guilford Press.

Beech, H. R. (1974). *Obsessional states*. London: Methuen.

Bond, M. (1986). Defense Style Questionnaire. In G. E. Vaillant (Ed.), *Empirical studies of ego mechanisms of defense*. Washington, DC: American Psychiatric Press.

Christensen, H., Hadzi-Pavlovic, D., Andrews, G., & Mattick, R. P. (1987). Behaviour therapy and tricyclic medication in the treatment of obsessive compulsive disorder: A quantitative review. *Journal of Consulting and Clinical Psychology, 55*, 701–711.

Craig, A., Franklin, J., & Andrews, G. (1984). A scale to measure locus of control of behaviour. *British Journal of Medical Psychology, 57*, 173–180.

Crowe, R. R., Noyes, R., Wilson, A. F., Elston, R. C., & Ward, L. J. (1987). A linkage study of panic disorder. *Archives of General Psychiatry, 44*, 933–937.

Hellenberg, J. B., & Collins, F. L. (1982). A procedural analysis and review of relaxation training research. *Behaviour Research and Therapy, 20*, 251–260.

Henderson, A. S., Byrne, D. G., & Duncan-Jones, P. (1981). *Neurosis and the social environment*. London: Academic Press.

Holt, P. E., & Andrews, G. (in press). Provocation of panic: A comparison on three elements of the panic reaction in four anxiety disorders. *Behaviour Research and Therapy*.

Horowitz, M. J. (1974). Stress response syndromes. *Archives of General Psychiatry, 31*, 768–781.

Jardine, R., Martin, N. G., & Henderson, A. S. (1984). Genetic covariation between neuroticism and the symptoms of anxiety and depression. *Genetic Epidemiology, 1*, 89–107.

Klein, D. F. (1964). Delineation of two drug-responsive anxiety syndromes. *Psychopharmacologica, 5*, 397–408.

Margraf, J., Ehlers, A., & Roth, W. T. (1986). Biological models of panic disorder and agoraphobia: A review. *Behaviour Research and Therapy, 24*, 553–567.

Marks, I. (1969). *Fears and phobias*. London: Heinemann.

Martin, N. G., Jardine, R., Andrews, G., & Heath, A. C. (1988). Anxiety disorders: Are there genetic factors specific to panic? *Acta Psychiatrica Scandinavica, 77*, 698–706.

Mattick, R., & Peters, L. (1988). Treatment of severe social phobia: Effects of guided exposure with and without cognitive restructuring. *Journal of Consulting and Clinical Psychology, 56*, 251–260.

Moran, C., & Andrews, G. (1985). The familial occurrence of agoraphobia. *British Journal of Psychiatry, 146*, 262–267.

Nichols, K. A. (1974). Severe social anxiety. *British Journal of Medical Psychology, 47*, 301–306.

Pitts, F., & McClure, J. (1967). Lactate metabolism in anxiety neurosis. *New England Journal of Medicine, 277*, 1329–1336.

Pollock, C., & Andrews, G. (in press). The defensive style associated with specific anxiety disorders. *American Journal of Psychiatry*.

Rapee, R. (1985). Distinctions between panic disorder and generalized anxiety disorder. *Australian and New Zealand Journal of Psychiatry, 19*, 227–232.

Rapee, R., Mattick, R., & Murrell, E. (1986). Cognitive mediation in the affective component of spontaneous panic attacks. *Journal of Behaviour Therapy and Experimental Psychiatry, 17*, 245–253.

Rotter, J. B. (1966). Generalised expectancies for internal versus external control of reinforcement. *Psychological Monographs, 80*, 1–28.

Tyrer, P. (1984). Classification of anxiety. *British Journal of Psychiatry, 144*, 78–83.

Vaillant, G. E. (1976). Natural history of male psychological health. *Archives of General Psychiatry, 33*, 535–545.

Vaillant, G. E., Bond, M., & Vaillant, C. O. (1986). An empirically validated hierarchy of defense mechanisms. *Archives of General Psychiatry, 43*, 786–794.

Wolpe, J. (1961). The systematic desensitization treatment of neuroses. *Journal of Nervous and Mental Disease, 132*, 189–203.

3

Generalized Anxiety Disorders and Panicogenic Syndromes

Eric Hollander and Michael R. Liebowitz

Anxiety may manifest itself in various forms. If present in sufficient severity to cause distress or to interfere with functioning, an anxiety disorder may be present. Increased knowledge about anxiety disorders has led to the diagnostic classification of discrete anxiety disorders that differ in symptomatology, familial aggregation, pathophysiology, and response to specific treatments. In this chapter we define panic disorder and generalized anxiety disorder (GAD), describe clinical manifestations, and discuss similarities to and differences from other disorders in which anxiety is present. In addition, biological, psychosocial, and behavioral aspects of these disorders are described.

DIFFERENTIATING GENERALIZED ANXIETY DISORDER AND PANIC DISORDER

Definitions

The DSM-II (American Psychiatric Association, 1968) described an ill-defined condition of "anxiety neurosis" which included any patient suffering from chronic tension, excessive worry, frequent headaches, or recurrent anxiety attacks. However, subsequent findings suggested that discrete, spontaneous panic attacks may be qualitatively dissimilar from chronic anxiety states. Patients with panic attacks are unique in response to sodium lactate infusion, familial aggregation, development of agoraphobia, and response to tricyclic antidepressants. Thus the DSM-III-R (American Psychiatric Association, 1987) defined *panic disorder* as follows:

A. At some time during the disturbance, one or more panic attacks (discrete periods of intense fear or discomfort) have occurred that were (1) unexpected, ie, did not occur immediately before or on exposure to a situation that almost always caused anxiety, and (2) not triggered by situations in which the person was the focus of others' attention.

B. Either four attacks, as defined in criterion A, have occurred within a four-week

Preparation of this chapter was supported in part by Research Scientist Development Award MH-00750 from the National Institute of Mental Health to Eric Hollander.

period, or one or more attacks have been followed by a period of at least a month of persistent fear of having another attack.

C. At least four of the following symptoms developed during at least one of the attacks:

(1) shortness of breath (dyspnea) or smothering sensations
(2) dizziness, unsteady feelings, or faintness
(3) palpitations or accelerated heart rate (tachycardia)
(4) trembling or shaking
(5) sweating
(6) choking
(7) nausea or abdominal distress
(8) depersonalization or derealization
(9) numbness or tingling sensations (parethesia)
(10) flushes (hot flashes) or chills
(11) chest pain or discomfort
(12) fear of dying
(13) fear of going crazy or of doing something uncontrolled

NOTE: Attacks involving four or more symptoms are panic attacks; attacks involving fewer than four symptoms are limited symptom attacks.

D. During at least some of the attacks, at least four of the C symptoms developed suddenly and increased in intensity within ten minutes of the beginning of the first C symptoms noticed in the attack.

E. It cannot be established that an organic factor initiated and maintained the disturbance, e.g., Amphetamine or Caffeine Intoxication, hyperthyroidism.

The DSM-III-R further subdivided panic disorder into subtypes with agoraphobia and without agoraphobia, depending on whether there is any secondary phobic avoidance. Panic attacks are also further characterized according to level of severity.

The DSM-III-R defined GAD as follows:

A. Unrealistic or excessive anxiety and worry (apprehensive expectation) about two or more life circumstances, e.g., worry about possible misfortune to one's child (who is in no danger) and worry about finances (for no good reason), for a period of six months or longer, during which the person has been bothered more days than not by these concerns. In children and adolescents, this may take the form of anxiety and worry about academic, athletic, and social performance.

B. If another Axis I disorder is present, the focus of the anxiety and worry in A is unrelated to it, e.g., the anxiety or worry is not about having a panic attack (as in Panic Disorder), being embarrassed in public (as in social Phobia), being contaminated (as in Obsessive Compulsive Disorder), or gaining weight (as in Anorexia Nervosa).

C. The disturbance does not occur only during the course of a Mood Disorder or a psychotic disorder.

D. At least 6 of the following 18 symptoms are often present when anxious (do not include symptoms present only during panic attacks):

Motor tension
(1) trembling, twitching, or feeling shaky
(2) muscle tension, aches, or soreness

   (3) restlessness
   (4) easy fatigability

Autonomic hyperactivity
   (5) shortness of breath or smothering sensations
   (6) palpitations or accelerated heart rate (tachycardia)
   (7) sweating, or cold clammy hands
   (8) dry mouth
   (9) dizziness or light-headedness
  (10) nausea, diarrhea, or other abdominal distress
  (11) flushes (hot flashes) or chills
  (12) frequent urination
  (13) trouble swallowing or "lump in throat"

Vigilance and scanning
  (14) feeling keyed up or on edge
  (15) exaggerated startle response
  (16) difficulty concentrating or "mind going blank" because of anxiety
  (17) trouble falling or staying asleep
  (18) irritability

E. It cannot be established that an organic factor initiated and maintained the disturbance, e.g., hyperthyroidism, Caffeine Intoxication.

Thus, as currently defined, panic disorder consists of discrete panic episodes of anxiety plus physical symptoms of sufficient frequency and severity, which may be followed by anticipation or avoidance. In contrast, GAD consists of chronic anxiety and apprehension, accompanied by several physical and psychological symptoms, but not discrete panic attacks of the frequency found in panic disorder.

Differentiation Based on Drug Studies

Panic disorder and GAD patients differ in several important respects; however, the initial distinction between these disorders stemmed from pharmacological treatment studies. This differentiation of panic and GAD can be traced back to the early 1960s, when Klein and Fink (1962) and Klein (1964) demonstrated that patients with panic attacks improved most when treated with antidepressants, whereas patients with other anxiety neuroses responded better to minor tranquilizers. The original notion that tricyclics helped patients with panic disorder but not GAD and that benzodiazepines helped those with GAD but not panic disorder has been rendered more questionable by several findings. One is that several high potency benzodiazepines such as alprazolam and clonazepam have been shown to block panic attacks. Second, imipramine was found to be as helpful as chlordiazepoxide in a sample of anxious patients even after the panic subset was retrospectively removed (Kahn et al., 1986). GAD patients are rare in most anxiety research center, so this study is difficult to replicate. We have treated five GAD patients in an open imipramine protocol, and three significantly benefited, suggesting that tricyclics can be beneficial. The mechanism of this response is uncertain, however. Whereas major depression is an exclusion criteria, dysthymia is not, and is prevalent in the sample, so that the anti-anxiety and antidepressant effects of imipramine are difficult to disentangle.

What may distinguish imipramine and benzodiazepine effects in the various anxiety disorders is the dosage required. Imipramine and chlordiazepoxide appeared to be equipotent for GAD patients; in the same protocol imipramine was superior for panic patients (Kahn et al., 1986). Although early reports suggested that standard benzodiazepines such as diazepam and chlordiazepoxide were more potent for generalized anxiety than for panic, recent reports describe anti-panic efficacy for standard benzodiazepines in high doses. In our laboratory, diazepam pretreatment prior to lactate-induced panic induced a state of profound relaxation prior to the lactate (treating anticipatory anxiety) but did not significantly reduce the incidence of panic with subsequent lactate challenge. Thus drug response data still support some distinction between panic attacks and generalized anxiety.

Panic as Extreme Abnormal Anxiety

Some have proposed that panic is just an extreme form of anxiety. Others propose a two-stage model of panic. Extreme anxiety and physical arousal must be present in the initial stage. However, only if the cognitive appraisal of the episode includes the interpretation of catastrophe will panic result. Thus the whole process can be blocked with medication, or the secondary escalation can be blocked with breathing or cognitive training.

Some patients with GAD may have a history of infrequent panic attacks that do not meet criteria for panic disorder. Sodium-lactate infusions in GAD patients with a history of infrequent panic attacks caused panic at the same rate as they did in patients with panic disorder (Dager, Cowley, & Dunner, 1987). A recent lactate study compared GAD patients without a history of panic attacks to patients with panic disorder and normal control subjects (Cowley et al., 1988). Patients with GAD reacted more like patients with panic disorder than like normal control subjects in anxiety and symptom scores during lactate infusion and in the rate of positive responses to lactate. However, patients with panic disorder had a greater rate of full panic attacks in response to lactate compared to GAD patients. GAD patients do not have full panic attacks clinically or in the laboratory, which suggests biological or cognitive differences between the groups.

The Acute Panic Inventory (API) (Dillon et al., 1987) is a 17-item scale, which is a rating instrument designed to measure the severity of symptoms that typically occur during a spontaneous panic attack. The API appears to be robust in differentiating panic attacks from other forms of stress and anxiety (Dillon et al., 1987).

There is some recent neuroendocrine evidence for differences in anticipatory and panic anxiety. Normal individuals exposed to stress had increased cortisol levels (Berger et al.,1987; Meyerhoff, Oleshansky, & Mougey, 1988; Rose, 1980), although there was considerable individual variability (Berger et al., 1987). Neuroendocrine alterations with stress have not been consistently demonstrated in patients with anxiety disorder. Caffeine challenge (Charney, Heninger, & Jatlow, 1985), carbon dioxide challenge (Gorman et al., 1988; Woods, Charney, Goodman, & Heninger, 1988), and situational and spontaneous panic measurements (Cameron, Lee, Curtis, & McCann, 1987; Woods, Charney, McPherson, Gradman, & Heninger, 1987) did not find significant elevations in cortisol associated with panic. Administration of the reverse benzodiazepine receptor agonist beta carboline has produced significant rises in cortisol that correlate with increases in generalized anxiety (Dorow et al., 1983).

We have reported that patients who panic late in the course of sodium-lactate infusion (after 15 minutes) had elevated cortisol levels at baseline (Hollander et al., in press-a). However, there was no rise in cortisol with lactate-induced panic. Thus cortisol elevation occurred with moderate anxiety, but not with severe panic anxiety, and likewise with measures of prolactin in lactate-induced panic. Male panickers had significantly elevated baseline prolactin level, which supports a role for prolactin in anticipatory anxiety. There was a blunted rise in prolactin in the late panickers, suggesting a diminution of prolactin response in panic anxiety (Hollander et al., in press-b).

Family studies have supported a distinction between panic disorder and GAD. First-degree relatives of patients with panic disorder have a greater frequency of anxiety disorders, whereas relatives of patients with GAD do not (Cloninger et al., 1981). There are higher rates of panic disorder and agoraphobia among first-degree relatives of patients with panic disorder than among first-degree relatives of patients with GAD (Crowe et al., 1983; Harris et al., 1983). Twin studies have demonstrated that GAD is not influenced by genetic factors, but panic disorder seems to be influenced by heredity (Torgersen, 1983). Patients with GAD are more likely to have lost a parent before the age of 16, whereas relatives of patients with panic disorder have higher rates of affective disorders and alcohol abuse (Torgersen, 1986). Examination of demographic factors supports the discrete diagnostic entities of panic and GAD (Anderson, Noyes, & Crowe, 1984). Apparently patients with GAD have fewer autonomic symptoms, and the onset of the disorder occurs earlier and more gradually. The course of illness of GAD is more chronic, but the outcome more favorable.

Psychophysiological Differences

In one study patients with panic disorder were compared with normal control subjects after 24 hours of ambulatory monitoring of heart rate, finger temperature, ambient temperature, and self-rated anxiety (Freedman, Ianni, Ettedgui, & Puthezhath, 1985). No differences were found between the groups in tonic levels of any measure or in their patterns of variation throughout the day. However, substantial heart rate increases and finger temperature changes did occur in panic attacks but not during control periods having equally high anxiety ratings.

In another study agoraphobic patients and normal controls subjects were compared during structured exposure to phobic situations (Woods et al., 1987). Panicking patients displayed greater increases in heart rate but not blood pressure or plasma-free 3-methoxy-4-hydroxyphenylglycol (MHPG) or cortisol in comparison to control subjects. Growth hormone and prolactin responses tended to be smaller in the patients. Woods et al. suggested that chronically recurrent attacks may cause an adaptation of neuroendocrine mechanisms activated by anxiety or stress.

In our sodium-lactate study of panic patients and normal controls, physiological measures were recorded at baseline and during lactate infusion, and panickers were compared to nonpanickers and control subjects (Liebowitz et al., 1985). Both panickers and nonpanickers showed evidence at baseline of hyperventilation and autonomic arousal. However, patients who panicked had higher heart rates and diastolic blood pressure before receiving lactate, suggesting greater baseline autonomic arousal in subsequent panickers. Lactate-induced panic attacks were associated with heightened sympathetic arousal and hyperventilation. At the point of panic, patients had greater elevations in heart rate and greater decrements of PCO_2 and bicarbonate than did nonpanickers.

CLINICAL MANIFESTATIONS OF PANIC
AND GENERAL ANXIETY DISORDER

Panic Disorder

Onset

In the typical beginning of a case of panic disorder, the subject is engaged in some ordinary aspect of life when suddenly his or her heart begins to pound. The subject finds it difficult to breathe; feels dizzy, light-headed, and faint; and is convinced that death is imminent. This patient is usually a young adult, most likely in the third decade; however, we have seen cases that begin in the sixth decade.

Although the first attack generally strikes during some routine activity, there are several events that are often associated with the early presentation of panic disorder. Not uncommonly, the first panic attack occurs in the context of a life-threatening illness or accident, the loss of a close interpersonal relationship, or separation from family (starting college or a job out of town). Patients developing either hypothyroidism or hyperthyroidism may get the first flurry of attacks at this time. Attacks also begin in the immediate postpartum period. Finally, many patients have reported experiencing their first attacks while taking mind-altering drugs, especially marijuana, LSD, sedatives, cocaine, and amphetamines. However, even when these concomitant conditions are resolved, attacks often continue unabated. This situation gives the impression that some stressors may act as triggers to provoke the beginning of panic attacks in patients who are already predisposed.

A person experiencing a first panic attack generally fears that he or she is having a heart attack or going crazy. Such patients often rush to the nearest emergency room where routine laboratory tests, electrocardiography, and physical examination are performed. All that is found is an occasional case of sinus tachycardia, and the patient is reassured and sent home. The patient may indeed feel reassured, and at this point the diagnosis of panic disorder would be premature. However, perhaps a few days or even weeks later the patient again has the sudden onset of severe anxiety with all the associated physical symptoms. Again, the patient seeks emergency medical treatment. At this point, he or she may either be told the problem is psychological, be given a prescription for a benzodiazepine tranquilizer, or be referred for extensive medical workup.

Symptoms

Typically, during a panic attack, a person will be engaged in a routine activity—perhaps reading a book, eating in a restaurant, driving a car, or attending a concert—when he or she will experience the sudden onset of overwhelming fear, terror, apprehension, and a sense of impending doom. Several of a group of associated symptoms, mostly physical, are also experienced: dyspnea, palpitations, chest pain or discomfort, choking or smothering sensations, dizziness, or unsteady feelings, feelings of unreality (derealization or depersonalization), paresthesia, hot and cold flashes, sweating, faintness, trembling and shaking, and a fear of dying, going crazy, or losing control of oneself. It is clear that most of the physical sensations of a panic attack represent massive over stimulation of the autonomic nervous system.

Attacks usually last from 5 to 20 minutes, and rarely as long as an hour. Patients who claim they have attacks that last a whole day may fall into one of three categories. Some patients continue to feel agitated and fatigued for several hours after the main portion of the attack has subsided. At times attacks occur, subside, and occur again in a wave-like manner. Alternatively, the patient with so-called long panic attacks is often suffering from some other form of pathologic anxiety, such as agitated depression or obsessional tension states.

Many people experience an occasional spontaneous attack, and the diagnosis of panic disorder is made only when the attacks occur with some regularity and frequency or when strong anticipatory anxiety develops very quickly. However, patients with occasional, spontaneous panics may be genetically similar to patients with panic disorder. A twin study found best results for genetic linkage when patients with regular panic attacks were included together with patients who had only occasional panics (Torgersen, 1983).

Some patients do not progress in their illness beyond the point of continuing to have spontaneous panic attacks. Most patients develop some degree of anticipatory anxiety consequent to the experience of repetitive panic attacks. The patient comes to dread experiencing an attack and starts worrying about them in the intervals between attacks. This can progress until the level of fearfulness and autonomic hyperactivity in the interval between panic attacks almost approximates the level during the actual attack itself. Such patients may be mistaken for patients with GAD.

Symptoms of Generalized Anxiety Disorder

GAD is a residual category for anxiety disorders other than panic disorder. The essential feature of this syndrome, according to the DSM-III-R, is persistent anxiety lasting at least six months. The symptoms of this type of anxiety usually fall within four broad categories: motor tension, autonomic hyperactivity, apprehensive expectation, and vigilance and scanning.

Motor tension involves feelings of shakiness, trembling, inability to relax, and being easily startled. Autonomic hyperactivity is characterized by sweating, heart pounding, dry mouth, light-headedness, stomach upset, frequent urination, and diarrhea. Patients are constantly worried over trivial matters, fearful, and anticipating the worst. Difficulty concentrating, insomnia, irritability, and impatience are signs of vigilance and scanning.

Again it must be emphasized that the patient with GAD does not have discrete episodes of panic and terror; the illness is a more constant and insidious syndrome. Some patients are misdiagnosed as having GAD. The DSM-III-R sets a minimum duration of symptoms at six months, and many patients actually have depressive symptoms. The DSM-III (American Psychiatric Association, 1980) set a one-month minimum duration, and many patients had adjustment reactions.

Hyperventilation

A number of lines of research evidence have indicated that hyperventilation is a central feature in the pathophysiology of panic attacks and panic disorder. Patients with panic disorder have been shown to be chronic hyperventilators who also acutely hyperventilate during lactate-induced panic. Signs and symptoms of hyperventilation seem to disappear once a patient with panic disorder has been successfully treated with anti-panic medication or behavioral treatment. During the carbon dioxide induction procedure, patients with panic disorder who experience panic attacks while breathing 5% carbon dioxide demonstrated a much faster increase in both minute ventilation and inspiratory drive than did nonpanicking patients or normal control subjects (Gorman et al., 1988). It is not yet known whether hyperventilation-induced hypocapnia and respiratory alkalosis, which dramatically decrease cerebral blood flow, are causes or consequences of acute panic. Nevertheless, there are reports that treatments aimed at teaching the patient not to hyperventilate may be successful in decreasing the frequency of panic attack (Clark, Salkovskis, & Chalkly, 1985; Lum, 1981).

Life Events and Psychosocial Precipitants

Many studies have demonstrated that depressed patients have a greater frequency of life events before the onset of a depressive episode than do control subjects or other psychiatric populations. Some studies have also suggested that there may be a greater frequency of life events before the onset of panic disorder (Faravelli, 1985; Finlay-Jones & Brown, 1981). Several researchers examined a small number panic patients who had experienced a major loss or separation in the year before they had their first panic attack (Roy-Byrne, Geraci, & Uhde, 1986). The occurrence of severe loss before the onset of panic attacks was not related to the subsequent severity of anxiety symptoms, but it was related to the subsequent occurrence of a major depression.

In the early 1960s, Klein (1964) advanced an etiologic theory that agoraphobia with panic attacks represents an aberrant function of the biological substrate that underlies normal human separation anxiety. Based on work by Bowlby, Klein (1981) advanced the notion that the attachment of an infant animal or human to its mother is not simply a learned response but is genetically programmed and biologically determined. It is of great importance to this theory that 20% to 50% of adults with agoraphobia with panic disorder recall manifesting symptoms of pathologic separation anxiety, often taking the form of school phobia, when they were children. Furthermore, the initial panic attack in the history of a patient who goes on a develop panic disorder is sometimes preceded by the real or threatened loss of a significant relationship.

Infant animals demonstrate their anxiety when separated from the mother by a series of high-pitched cries called distress vocalizations. Imipramine has been found to be effective in blocking distress vocalizations in dogs by Scott (1974) and in monkeys by Suomi et al. (1978). Imipramine, as will be discussed, is a highly effective anti-panic drug in adult humans. Hypothesizing a link between adult panic attacks and childhood separation anxiety, Klein and Gittelman conducted a study of imipramine treatment for children with school phobia. In these children, fear of separation from their mothers was usually the cause underlying the refusal to go to school. The drug proved to be successful in getting the children to return to school.

Hence, there is good evidence that the same drug that diminishes protest anxiety in higher mammals also reduces separation anxiety in children and blocks panic attacks in adults. This is further confirmation of the link between separation anxiety and human panic attacks. It is still unclear whether early separation anxiety is linked to agoraphobia or to the panic attacks. If imipramine affects panic attacks, and separation anxiety is linked to agoraphobia, then why is imipramine effective in school phobia? However, school phobics do not have spontaneous panic attacks. Perhaps both panic disorder and panic disorder with agoraphobia are linked to a disordered separation mechanism that is responsive to imipramine. This may occur if the retrospective histories of a lesser degree of separation anxiety in patients with panic attacks alone are misremembered. We have seen a number of children, now grown up, who had massive separation anxiety as children and just did not remember it as adults (D. F. Klein, personal communication 1989).

Panic with Other Conditions

Phobias

In social phobia the individual's central fear is that he or she will act in such a way as to be humiliated or embarrassed in front of others. Social phobics fear or avoid a variety of situations in which they would be required to perform a task while in the presence of other people. Typical social phobias are of speaking, eating, or writing in public; using public lavatories; and attending parties or interviews. The anxiety is stimulus bound. When forced or surprised into the phobic situation, the individual experiences profound anxiety accompanied by a variety of physiologic anxiety symptoms (e.g., palpitations, sweating, tremor, stuttering, and faintness).

Somatic anxiety symptoms reported by social phobics may also show differences from those of agoraphobics and patients with panic disorder. Although further investigations are needed, in one study the social phobics reported more blushing and muscle twitching and less limb weakness, breathing difficulty, dizziness or faintness, actual fainting, and buzzing or ringing in the ears than did agoraphobics (Aimes, Gelder, & Shaw, 1983). Social phobics were also found to have lower extroversion scores on the Eysenck Personality Inventory than did agoraphobics, whose scores were similar to those of normal control subjects (Aimes et al., 1983). Simple phobias are circumscribed fears of specific objects, situations, or activities. This syndrome has three components: an anticipatory anxiety that is brought on by the possibility of confrontation with the phobic stimulus, the central fear, and the avoidance behavior by which the phobic minimizes anxieties.

Depression

Patients who suffer from depression often manifest signs of anxiety and agitation and may even have frank panic attacks. Patients with GAD or panic disorder, if untreated for significant amounts of time, routinely become demoralized as the impact of the illness progressively restricts the ability to enjoy a normal life. Further complicating the picture is the fact that some, but not all, studies have shown that patients with anxiety disorder have increased family history of affective disorder.

Although the differentiation of anxiety from depression can at times strain even the most experienced clinician, several points are helpful. Patients with GAD or panic disorder generally do not demonstrate the full range of vegetative symptoms that are seen in depression. Hence, anxious patients usually have trouble falling asleep but not awakening in early morning and do not lose their appetite or ability to concentrate. Diurnal mood fluctuation is uncommon in anxiety disorder. Perhaps of greatest importance is the fact that most anxious patients do not lose the capacity to enjoy things or be cheered up as do endogenously depressed patients.

The distinction between atypical depression and anxiety disorders is even more difficult, because of the lack of typical endogenous features in atypical depression. However, although atypical depressives can also be cheered up, they tend to slump faster than do patients with anxiety disorder. Panic attacks and atypical depression frequently coexist, and coexisting panic attacks may increase the monoamine oxidase inhibitor responsivity of atypical depressives (Liebowitz, Quitkin et al., 1984).

The order of developing symptoms also differentiates depression from anxiety. In cases of panic disorder or GAD, anxiety symptoms usually precede any seriously altered mood. Patients can generally recall having anxiety attacks first, then becoming gradually more disgusted with life, and then feeling depressed. In depression, patients usually experience dysphoria first, with anxiety symptoms coming later. However, panic disorder can be complicated by secondary major depression or vice versa. Results of the dexamethasone suppression test, which some consider useful in diagnosing depression, are generally normal in panic disorder. The test has not been systematically studied in patients with GAD.

Psychiatric Conditions

A few other psychiatric conditions often need to be differentiated from panic disorder and GAD. Patients with somatization disorder complain of a variety of physical ailments and discomforts, none of which are substantiated by physical or laboratory findings. They can appear to be like GAD patients because of their constant worry but are distinguished by their almost exclusive preoccupation with physical complaints. Unlike patients with panic disorder, their physical problems do not usually occur in episodic attacks but are virtually constant. However, Sheehan et al. (1980) has claimed that many patients diagnosed as having somatization disorder really have panic disorder.

Patients with depersonalization disorder have episodes of derealization or depersonalization without the other symptoms of a panic attack. Panic attacks not infrequently involve depersonalization and derealization as prominent symptoms. Although patients with panic disorder often fear they will lose their minds or go crazy, psychotic illness is not an outcome of anxiety disorder. Reassuring the patient on this point is often the first step in a successful treatment.

Substance Use

There is no question that some patients with anxiety disorder abuse alcohol and illicit drugs such as sedatives in attempts at self-medication (Quitkin & Rabkin, 1982). In one study, after successful detoxification, a group of alcoholics with a prior history of panic disorder was treated with medication to block spontaneous panic attacks (Quitkin & Rabkin, 1982). These patients did not resume alcohol consumption once their panic attacks were eliminated. Therefore, in evaluating any patient with substance abuse, the possibility that their illness began with spontaneous panic attacks or chronic anxiety should be considered. As is discussed later, social phobia also is frequently associated with alcoholism and may contribute to its onset, continuation, or relapse.

Lactate sensitivity may also help to differentiate panic disorder from other anxiety disorders. It has been well documented that sodium lactate induces panic attacks that closely resemble spontaneous panic attacks in many patients with panic disorder but not in normal control subjects (Liebowitz, Fyer et al., 1984). It has been shown that lactate does not cause panic attacks in social phobics (Liebowitz,Fyer et al., 1985) or in obsessive–compulsive patients (Gorman et al., 1985). However, it has been shown to induce panic in atypical depression patients with a history of panic (McGrath et al., 1988) and in GAD patients with a history of panic (Dager et al., 1987). GAD patients without a history of panic showed increases in anxiety and a positive response to lactate but not full panic attacks (Cowley et al., 1988).

BIOCHEMICAL THEORIES OF PANIC

Catecholamine Theory

Some investigators have found anxiety reactions to be associated with increases in urinary catecholamine levels, especially epinephrine. Studies of normal subjects exposed to novel stress have also demonstrated elevations in plasma catecholamine levels (Dimsdale & Moss, 1980). Elevated plasma epinephrine is not a regular accompaniment of panic attacks induced in the laboratory, however (Liebowitz et al., 1985). Levels of the enzyme that catabolizes catecholamines, monoamine oxidase, have also been found to be elevated in patients with anxiety disorder but do not resolve the question of whether the role is etiologic or simply a reaction to the anxiety state.

It is not clear whether administration of catecholamines can actually provoke anxiety reactions and whether, if they can, the reaction is specific only to patients with anxiety disorder. Researchers in the 1930s and 1940s did show that epinephrine infusion caused the physical, but not necessarily the emotional, symptoms of anxiety in human subjects, but methodologic and diagnostic issues limit the applicability of these studies to patients with GAD and panic disorder.

For many years the possibility that panic attacks are manifestations of massive discharge from the beta-adrenergic nervous system has been considered. During a panic attack the patient complains of palpitation, tremulousness, and excessive sweating, all symptoms that are characteristic of massive stimulation of beta-adrenergic receptors. Frohlich and colleagues (Frohlich, Tarazi, & Duston, 1969) gave intravenous isoproterenol infusions to patients with "hyper-dynamic beta-adrenergic circulatory state" and produced "hysterical outbursts" that were similar to panic attacks. Whereas some researchers have also shown that patients with spontaneous anxiety attacks are more sensitive to the effects of isoproterenol than are normal control subjects (Rainey, 1984), others have reported mixed results or lack of panic in panic disorder patients with alcoholism following isoprotenol (D. Nutt, personal communication 1988).

The beta-adrenergic hypothesis receives further support from innumerable studies claiming that beta-blocking drugs, such as propranolol, have an ameliorative effect on panic attacks and anxiety. When the properly designed and controlled studies of beta-adrenergic blockers used in specific, well-diagnosed anxiety disorders are reviewed, however, only modest anti-anxiety effects can actually be demonstrated. No study has ever shown that beta-adrenergic blockers are specifically effective in blocking spontaneous panic attacks. For example, intravenously administered propranolol, in doses sufficient to achieve full peripheral beta-adrenergic blockade, was not able to block a sodium lactate-induced panic attack in patients with panic disorder (Gorman et al., 1983).

Locus Ceruleus Theory

Another prominent hypothesis for the etiology of panic attacks involves the locus ceruleus. This nucleus is located in the pons and contains more than 50% of all noradrenergic neurons in the entire central nervous system and sends afferent projections to a wide area of the brain, including the hippocampus, amygdala, limbic lobe, and cerebral cortex. Support for this complex hypothesis comes from Redmond (1979), who showed that electrical stimulation of the animal locus ceruleus produced marked fear and anxiety response, whereas ablation of the animal locus ceruleus rendered an animal less susceptible to fear response in the face of threatening stimuli. Also, drugs known to be capable of increasing locus ceruleus discharge in animals are anxiogenic in humans, whereas many drugs that curtail locus ceruleus firing and decrease central noradrenergic turnover are anti-anxiety agents in humans. Yohimbine is an example of a drug that increases locus ceruleus discharge and has been shown to provoke anxiety in humans, whereas clonidine, propranolol, benzodiazepines, morphine, endorphin, and tricyclic antidepressants curtail locus ceruleus firing. In the latter group, there is obviously a range of drugs, from those clearly effective in blocking human panic attacks, like the tricyclic antidepressants, to those of more dubious efficacy, like clonidine, propranolol, and standard benzodiazepines. The effect on locus ceruleus firing of the benzodiazepine analog drugs alprazolam and clonazepam, which have definite anti-panic effects, are not yet known.

A controversy exists about the relevance of these animal models. Redmond (1979) has produced abundant evidence that situations that provoke fear and anxiety in laboratory animals are associated with increases in locus ceruleus discharge and in central noradrenergic turnover. This would, of course, support the idea that the locus ceruleus is a kind of generator for anxiety attacks. However, Mason and Fibiger (1979) stated that there is no consistent pattern of increased locus ceruleus discharge associated with anxiety in animals. Aston-Jones, Foote, and Bloom (1984) believed that the locus ceruleus is involved in our response to novel stimuli in general rather than in anxiety.

Carbon Dioxide Hypersensitivity

We have found that controlled hyperventilation and respiratory alkalosis do not routinely provoke panic attacks in most patients with panic disorder. Surprisingly, however, giving these patients a mixture of 5% carbon dioxide in room air to breathe causes panic almost as often as does a sodium lactate infusion (Gorman et al., 1984). This finding may be partially explained by the findings of Elam, Yoat, and Svensson (1981), which showed that carbon dioxide, when added to inspired air, causes a reliable dose-dependent increase in rat locus ceruleus firing. Alternatively, patients with panic disorder may have brain stem chemoreceptors that are hypersensitive to carbon dioxide. This could cause chronic hyperventilation (an attempt to keep carbon dioxide levels low) or be secondary to hyperventilation ("denervation" supersensitivity).

Lactate Panicogenic Metabolic Theory

Of all the biological theories of panic disorder, those involving the sodium lactate provocation of panic attacks have captured the most attention. Cohen and White (1950) first noted that patients with neurocirculatory asthenia, a condition closely related to anxiety disorder, developed higher levels of blood lactate while exercising than did normal control subjects. This finding stimulated Pitts and McClure (1967) to administer intravenous infusions of sodium lactate to patients with anxiety disorder; they found that most of the patients suffered an anxiety attack during the infusion. The subjects all believed these attacks were quite typical of their naturally occurring attacks; normal control subjects did not experience panic attacks during the infusion.

Having been replicated on numerous occasions under proper experimental conditions, the finding that 10 ml/kg of 0.5 molar sodium lactate infused over 20 minutes will provoke a panic attack in most patients with panic disorder but not in normal subjects is now a well-accepted fact. The mechanism by which this occurs, however, is not well understood. Theories include induction of metabolic alkalosis, hypocalcemia, or alteration of the NAD-NADH ratio; conversion of lactate to bicarbonate and then to carbon dioxide, producing a transient intracerebral hypercapnia (because carbon dioxide, but not bicarbonate, crosses the blood–brain barrier); and nonspecific arousal that frightens panic-prone patients. Patients with clinical panic attacks who panic with lactate are more anxious at baseline than are those who do not, suggesting an interaction of initial level of arousal and the effects of lactate to produce panic (Liebowitz, Fyer et al., 1984). Reiman and Robins (1986) have found subsequent lactate panickers to have a parahippocampal blood flow asymmetry on position emission tomography scans when tested just before the lactate infusion.

Benzodiazepine Receptor Theory

One area of inquiry that may relate specifically to the biological etiology of GAD is the study of the recently discovered brain benzodiazapine receptor. This receptor is linked to a receptor for the inhibitory neurotransmitter gamma-aminobutyric acid (GABA). Binding of a benzodiazepine to the benzodiazepine receptor facilitates the action of GABA, effectively slowing neural transmission. The receptor is found in gray matter throughout the human brain. One series of compounds, the beta-carbolines, specifically blocked the binding of benzodiazepines to the benzodiazepine receptor and, when administered to laboratory animals, produced an acute anxiety syndrome (Skolnick & Paul, 1982). This raises the possibility that some substance is produced by GAD patients that actually interferes with proper benzodiazepine receptor function and is the cause of their symptoms.

Genetic Basis of Panic Disorder

The final line of evidence for the biological etiology of anxiety are studies indicating their possible familial nature. Several family history studies of panic disorder have found a higher rate in relatives of probands with panic disorder than in relatives of normal subjects. Crowe et al. (1983) found a morbidity risk for panic disorder of 24.7% among relatives of patients with panic disorder, compared with only 2.3% among normal control subjects.

This kind of study cannot, of course, rule out the possibility that environmental rather than genetic influences are operant. Although studies comparing rates of illness in monozygotic and dizygotic twins are best for distinguishing these two components of familial transmission of a psychiatric illness, simple adoption studies of family members are also sufficient to dissect nature from nurture. Early twin studies done on patients with anxiety disorder included a mixed group of anxiety patients. These studies showed a higher concordance rate for anxiety disorder among monozygotic twins than among dizygotic twins, a finding that indicates that genetic influence predominates over environmental influence. More recently, Torgersen (1983) completed a study of 32 monozygotic and 53 dizygotic twins. Anxiety disorders with panic attacks were five times more frequent in monozygotic than in dizygotic twins. There was no such difference for GAD.

Even twin studies are open to question because they assume that parents treat identical twins in the same way that they treat fraternal twins. More definitive proof of a genetic component to a psychiatric illness can come from studies comparing concordance rates in identical and fraternal twins adopted away from their biological parents and raised in separate homes. No such studies have been reported for anxiety disorder. Genetic studies looking for DNA markers that are associated with the illness are now underway in large multigenerationally affected panic disorder pedigrees. No family or twin studies specifically investigating patients with GAD have been reported.

BEHAVIORAL CHARACTERISTICS OF PANIC

Behavior or learning theorists hold that anxiety is conditioned by the fear of certain environmental stimuli. If every time a laboratory animal presses a bar it receives a noxious electric shock, the pressing of the lever becomes a conditioned stimulus that precedes the unconditioned stimulus—the shock. The conditioned stimulus releases a conditioned response in the animal—anxiety—which leads the animal to avoid contact with the lever, thereby avoiding the shock. Successful avoidance of the unconditioned stimulus—the shock—reinforces the avoidant behavior. This leads to a decrease in anxiety level.

By analogy with this animal model, we might say that anxiety attacks are conditioned responses to fearful situations. For example, an infant learns that if his or her mother is not present (the conditioned stimulus), he or she will suffer hunger (the unconditioned stimulus), and the infant learns to become anxious automatically whenever the mother is absent (the conditioned response). The anxiety may persist even after the child is old enough to feed him- or herself. Or, to give another example, a life-threatening situation in someone's life, for example, skidding in a car during a snowstorm, is paired with the experience of rapid heart beat (the conditioned stimulus) and tremendous anxiety. Long after the accident, rapid heart beat alone, whether during vigorous exercise or minor emotional upset, becomes capable by itself of provoking the conditioned response of an anxiety attack.

There are clearly multiple problems with such a theory. First, although we have pointed out some traumatic situations, such as thyroid disease, cocaine intoxication, or life-threatening event, that do seem paired with the onset of panic disorder, for many patients no such traumatic event can ever be located. For patients with GAD, attempting to find a precipitating event that makes sense as an unconditioned stimulus is even more difficult. It is also the case that most conditioned responses ultimately extinguish in laboratory animals if they are not at least intermittently reinforced. Presumably, patients with panic disorder or GAD do not undergo repeat traumatic events and therefore should be able to unlearn their anxiety and panic attacks. This has no basis in clinical fact. Hence, even though learning theories have a powerful basis in experimental animal research they do not seem to explain adequately the pathogenesis of human anxiety disorders. They do, however, explain the development and maintenance of agoraphobia once a sequence of panic attacks has begun.

Table 1 Comparison of symptoms of mitral valve prolapse and panic disorder

Symptoms	Mitral valve prolapse	Panic disorder
Fatigue	+	−
Dyspnea	+	+ +
Palpitations	+ +	+ +
Chest pain	+ +	+
Syncope	+	−
Choking	−	+ +
Dizziness	−	+ +
Derealization	−	+ +
Hot and cold flashes	−	+ +
Sweating	−	+ +
Fainting	−	+ +
Trembling	−	+ +
Fear of dying, going crazy, losing control	−	+ +

+, Occasionally; + +, often present; —, rarely present.

PANIC ATTACKS AND MITRAL VALVE PROLAPSE

The relationship of mitral valve prolapse and panic disorder has attracted a great deal of attention recently. (For a comprehensive discussion of anxiety and mitral valve prolapse, see chap. 12, this volume.) This usually benign condition has been shown by a number of investigators to occur more frequently in patients with panic disorder than in normal subjects. However, screening of patients known to have mitral valve prolapse reveals no greater frequency of panic disorder than is found in the overall population.

Although patients with mitral valve prolapse occasionally complain of palpitations, chest pain, light-headedness, and fatigue, symptoms of a full-blown panic attack are rare (see Table 1). Panic patients with and without mitral valve prolapse are similar in several important ways. Treatment for panic attacks works regardless of the presence of the prolapsed valve, and patients with both mitral valve prolapse and panic disorder are just as sensitive to sodium lactate as are those with panic disorder alone. Some have speculated that mitral valve prolapse and panic disorder may represent manifestations of the same underlying disorder of autonomic nervous system function (Gorman et al., 1981). Others have suggested that panic disorder, by creating states of intermittent high-circulating catecholamine levels and tachyardia, actually causes mitral valve prolapse (Mattes, 1981). There are reports that mitral valve prolapse might go away if the panic disorder is maintained under control (Gorman et al., 1981). In any event, it is clear that the presence of mitral valve prolapse in patients with panic disorder has little clinical or prognostic importance in the management of spontaneous panic attacks. What it may tell us about the underlying etiology of panic disorder is a question currently under vigorous investigation.

PHOBIAS AND PANIC

Agoraphobia

The clinical picture in agoraphobia consists of multiple and varied fears and avoidance behaviors that center around three main themes: fear of leaving home, fear of being alone, and fear of being way from home in a place where one cannot suddenly leave or where help is not easily available in case of incapacitation. Typical fears are of using public transportation (buses, trains, subways, and planes); being in crowds, theaters, elevators, restaurants, supermarkets, or department stores; waiting in line; or traveling a distance from home. In severe cases, patients may be completely housebound, fearful of leaving home without a companion or even of staying home alone.

Most cases of agoraphobia begin with a series of spontaneous panic attacks. If the attacks continue, the patient usually develops a constant anticipatory anxiety characterized by continued apprehension about the possible occasion and consequences of the next attack. Agoraphobic symptoms represent a tertiary phase in the illness. Many patients will causally relate their panic attacks to the particular situation in which the attacks occurred. They then avoid these situations in an attempt to prevent further panic attacks. For example, a man who has had several attacks while taking the train to work may attribute the attacks to the train and, in order to avoid the train, starts driving to work. If he still experiences panic attacks in the morning while driving to work rather than on the train, he interprets this as a sign that the attacks have spread to driving situations rather than as an indication that they were not, in the first place, caused by the train.

Agoraphobics also fear situations in which they feel they cannot leave abruptly if an attack occurs, such as crowded rooms, front row seats, tunnels, bridges, airplanes, and so forth some individuals continue to have spontaneous panic attacks throughout the course of the illness. In other cases, after the initial phase of the illness, attacks may occur rarely or only (but not always) when the patient ventures into a phobic situation.

One interesting aspect of agoraphobia is the effect of a trusted companion on phobic behavior. Many patients who are unable to leave the house alone can travel long distances and partake in most activities if accompanied by a spouse, family member, or close friend. It is unclear if vulnerability to panic attacks is actually decreased in this situation, or whether the patient feels less helpless and isolated. In addition to panic attacks, multiple phobias, and chronic anxiety, these patients frequently exhibit symptoms of demoralization or secondary depression, multiple somatic complaints, and alcohol or sedative drug abuse.

Social Phobia

In social phobia, the individual's central fear is that he or she will act in such a way as to become humiliated or embarrassed in front of others (Liebowitz, Fyer, & Klein, 1985). Social phobics fear or avoid a variety of situations in which they would be required to perform a task while in the presence of other people. Typical social phobias are of speaking, eating, or writing in public; using public lavatories; and attending parties or interviews. An individual may have one social phobia or many.

As in simple phobia, the anxiety is stimulus-bound. When forced or surprised into the phobic situation, the individual experiences profound anxiety accompanied by a variety of physiologic anxiety symptoms (e.g., palpitations, sweating, tremor, stuttering, and faintness). Spontaneous panic attacks, which occur in situations unrelated to feeling scrutinized or evaluated by others, are symptomatically distinct from social phobia (Aimes et al., 1983). For example, blushing is frequent in social phobia but not in spontaneous panic, whereas the reverse is true for chest pain or pressure.

Individuals who have only one social phobia may be relatively a symptomatic unless confronted with the necessity of entering their phobic situation. When faced with this necessity they are often subject to intense anticipatory anxiety. A common fear of socially phobic individuals is that other people will detect and ridicule their anxiety in social situations. Multiple phobias of this type can lead to social isolation. Such patients may be chronically demoralized. Alcohol and sedative drugs are often utilized to alleviate at least the anticipatory component of this anxiety disorder, leading to abuse. Vocational as well as social impairment can at times be extreme.

Simple Phobia

Simple phobias are circumscribed fears of specific objects, situations, or activities. This syndrome has three components: an anticipatory anxiety that is brought on by the possibility of confrontation with the phobic stimulus, the central fear, and the avoidance behavior by which the patient minimizes anxieties. In simple phobia the fear is usually not of the object itself but of some dire outcome that the individual believes may result from contact with that object. For example, driving phobics are afraid of accidents; snake phobics, that they will be bitten; and claustrophobes, that they will suffocate or be trapped in an enclosed space. Although most simple phobics will readily acknowledge that they know "there is really nothing to be afraid of," reassuring them of this does not diminish their fear.

CONCLUSION

Clinical manifestations of panic disorder and GAD have been described in this chapter. The initial distinction between these two anxiety disorders stems from pharmacological dissection studies. However, there are important differences between these disorders in clinical symptoms, familial aggregation, response to biological challenges, course of illness, and complications. The hallmark of the panicogenic syndrome is the discrete panic attack, characterized by sudden onset and crescendo of anxiety, accompanied by various physical symptoms. Anticipatory anxiety and phobic avoidance are frequent complications of panic. In contrast, GAD involves chronic apprehension and arousal. Similarities and differences among these disorders and related disorders such as agoraphobia, social phobia, obsessive–compulsive disorder and affective disorders were also described.

Physiological and neuroendocrine manifestations of panic were discussed. Various biological models of panic have been proposed. These involve the role of catecholamines, noradrenergic mechanisms, carbon dioxide hypersensitivity, lactate metabolic activity, GABA-benzodiazepine receptors, and genetic inheritance in the production of panic. Psychosocial precipitants, hyperventilation, and cognitive interpretations may also play a role in initiating and escalating the panic attack.

A more comprehensive understanding of panic disorder and generalized anxiety disorder may help to clarify the relationship between anxiety and the heart.

REFERENCES

Aimes, P. L., Gelder, M. G., & Shaw, P. M. (1983). Social phobia: A comparative clinical study. *British Journal of Psychiatry, 142*, 174–179.

American Psychiatric Association. (1968). *Diagnostic and statistical manual of mental disorders* (2nd ed.). Washington, DC: Author.

American Psychiatric Association. (1980). *Diagnostic and statistical manual of mental disorders* (3rd ed.). Washington, DC: Author.

American Psychiatric Association. (1987). *Diagnostic and statistical manual of mental disorders* (3rd ed. rev.). Washington, DC: Author.

Anderson, D. J., Noyes, R., & Crowe, R. R. (1984). A comparison of panic disorder and generalized anxiety. *American Journal of Psychiatry, 141*, 572–575.

Aston-Jones, S. L., Foote, F. E., & Bloom, F. E. (1984). Norepinephrine. In M. G. Ziegler & C. R. Lake (Eds.), *Frontiers of clinical neuroscience* (Vol. 2, pp. 92–116). Baltimore: Williams & Wilkins.

Berger, M., Bossert, S., Krieg, J. C., et al. (1987). Interindividual differences in the susceptibility of the cortisol system: An important factor for the degree of hypercortisolism in stress situations? *Biological Psychiatry, 22*, 1327–1339.

Cameron, O. G., Lee, M. A., Curtis, G. C., & McCann, D. S. (1987). Endocrine and physiological changes during "spontaneous" panic attacks. *Psychoneuroendocrinology, 12*, 321–331.

Charney, D., Heninger, G., & Jatlow, P. (1985). Increased anxiogenic effects of caffeine in panic disorders. *Archives of General Psychiatry, 42*, 223–243.

Clark, D. M., Salkovskis, P. M., & Chalkly, A. J. (1985). Respiratory control as a treatment for panic attacks. *Journal of Behavior Therapy and Experimental Psychiatry, 16*, 23–30.

Cloninger, C. R., Martin, R. L., Clayton, P., et al. (1981). A blind follow-up and family study of anxiety neurosis: Preliminary analysis of the St. Louis 500. In D. F. Klein & J. G. Rabkin (Eds.), *Anxiety: New research and changing concepts* (pp. 137–154). New York: Raven Press.

Cohen, M. E., & White, I. D. (1950). Life situation, emotions, and neurocirculatory asthenia. *Research in Nervous and Mental Disorders Proceedings, 29*, 832–869.

Cowley, D. S., Dager, S. R., McClellan, J., et al. (1988). Response to lactate infusion in generalized anxiety disorder. *Biological Psychiatry, 24*, 409–414.

Crowe, R. R., Noyes, R., Pauls, D. L., et al. (1983). A family study of panic disorder. *Archives of General Psychiatry, 40*, 1065–1069.

Dager, S. R., Cowley, D. S., & Dunner, D. L. (1987). Biological markers in panic states: Lactate-induced panic and mitral valve prolapse. *Biological Psychiatry, 22*, 339–359.

Dillon, D. J., Gorman, J. M., Liebowitz, M. R., et al. (1987). Measurement of lactate-induced apnia and anxiety. *Psychiatry Research, 20*, 97–105.

Dimsdale, J. E., & Moss, J. (1980). Plasma catecholamines in stress and exercise. *Journal of the American Medical Association, 243*, 340–342.

Dorow, R., Horowski, R., Pschelke, G., et al. (1983, July 9). Severe anxiety induced by FG 7142, a beta-carboline ligand for banzodiazepine receptors. *Lancet*, p. 98.

Elam, M., Yoat, T. P., & Svensson, T. H. (1981). Hypercapnia and hypoxia: Chemo-receptor-mediated control of locus ceruleus neurons and splanchnic, sympathetic nerves. *Brain Research, 222*, 373–381.

Faravelli, C. (1985) Life events preceding the onset of panic disorder. *Journal of Affective Disorders, 9*, 103–105.

Finlay-Jones, R., & Brown, G. W. (1981). Types of stressful life events and the onset of anxiety and depressive disorders. *Psychological Medicine, 11*, 803–815.

Freedman, R. R., Ianni, P., Ettedgui, E., & Puthezhath, N. (1985). Ambulatory monitoring of panic disorder. *Archives of General Psychiatry, 42*, 244–248.

Frohlich, E. D., Tarazi, K. C., & Duston, H. P. (1969). Hyperdynamic beta-adrenergic circulatory state. *Archives of Internal Medicine, 123*, 1–7.

Gorman, J. M., Askanazi, J., Liebowitz, M. R., et al. (1984). Response to hyperventilation in a group of patients with panic disorder. *American Journal of Psychiatry, 141*(7), 857–861.

Gorman, J. M., Fyer, A. F., Gliklich, J., et al. (1981). Effect of imipramine on prolapsed mitral valves of patients with panic disorder. *American Journal of Psychiatry, 138*, 977–978.

Gorman, J. M., Fyer, M. R., Goetz, R., et al. (1988). Ventilatory physiology of patients with panic disorder. *Archives of General Psychiatry, 45*, 31–39.

Gorman, J. M., Levy, G. F., Liebowitz, M. R., et al. (1983). Effect of acute beta-adrenergic blockade on lactate induced panic. *Archives of General Psychiatry, 40*, 1079–1083.

Gorman, J. M., Liebowitz, M. R., Fyer, A. J., et al. (1985). Lactate infusions in obsessive–compulsive disorder. *American Journal of Psychiatry, 142*, 864–866.

Harris, E. L., Noyes, R., Crowe, R. R., et al. (1983). Family study of agoraphobia: Report of a pilot study. *Archives of General Psychiatry, 40,* 1061-1064.

Hollander, E., Liebowitz, M. R., Cohen, B., et al. (in press a). Cortisol and sodium lactate-induced panic. *Archives of General Psychiatry.*

Hollander, E., Liebowitz, M. R., Cohen, B., et al. (in press b). Prolactin and sodium lactate-induced panic. *Psychiatry Research.*

Kahn, R. J., McNair, D. M., Lipman, R. S., et al. (1986). Imipramine and chlordiazepoxide in depression and anxiety disorders. *Archives of General Psychiatry, 43,* 79-85.

Klein, D. F. (1964). Delineation of two drug-responsive anxiety syndromes. *Psychopharmocologia, 5,* 397-408.

Klein, D. F. (1981). Anxiety reconceptualized. In D. F. Klein & J. G. Rabkin (Eds.), *Anxiety: New research and changing concepts* (pp. 235-263). New York: Raven Press.

Klein, D. F., & Fink, M. (1962). Psychiatric reaction patterns to imipramine. *American Journal of Psychiatry, 119,* 431-438.

Liebowitz, M. R., Fyer, A. J., Gorman, J. M., et al (1984). Lactate provocation of panic attacks: 1. Clinical and behavioral findings. *Archives of General Psychiatry, 41,* 764-770.

Liebowitz, M. R., Gorman, J. M., Fyer, A. J., Levitt, M., Dillon, D., Levy, G., Appleby, I. L., Anderson, S., Palij, M., Davies, S. O., & Klein, D. F. (1985). Lactate provocation of panic attacks: 2. Biochemical and physiological findings. *Archives of General Psychiatry, 42,* 709-719.

Liebowitz, M. R., Quitkin, F., Stewart, J. W., et al (1984). Phenelzine versus imipramine in atypical depression: A preliminary report. *Archives of General Psychiatry, 120,* 669-667.

Liebowitz, M. R., Gorman, J. M., Fyer, A. J., & Klein, D. F. (1985). Social phobia: Review of a neglected anxiety disorder. *Archives of General Psychiatry, 42,* 729-736.

Liebowitz, M. R., Fyer, A. J., Gorman, J. M. et al. (1985). Specificity of lactate infusions in social phobia vs panic disorders. *American Journal of Psychiatry,* 142-947.

Lum, L. C. (1981). Hyperventilation and anxiety states. *Journal of the Royal Society of Medicine, 74,* 1-4.

Mason, S. T., & Fibiger, H. C. (1979). Anxiety: The locus ceruleus disconnection. *Life Science, 25,* 2141-2147.

Mattes, J. (1981). More on panic disorder and mitral valve prolapse. *American Journal of Psychiatry, 138,* 1130.

McGrath, P. J., Stewart, J. W., Liebowitz, M. R., et al. (1988). Lactate provocation of panic attacks in depressed outpatients. *Psychiatry Research, 25,* 41-48.

Meyerhoff, J. L., Oleshansky, M. A., & Mougey, M. S. (1988). Psychological stress increases plasma levels of prolactin, cortisol, and POMC-derived peptides in man. *Psychosomatic Medicine, 50,* 25.

Pitts, F. N., & McClure, J. N. (1967). Lactate metabolism in anxiety neurosis. *New England Journal of Medicine, 277,* 1329-1336.

Quitkin, F., & Rabkin, J. (1982). Hidden psychiatric diagnosis in the alcoholic. In J. Solomon (Ed.), *Alcoholism and clinical psychiatry* (pp. 129-140). New York: Plenum Press.

Rainey, J. M., Pohl, R. B., Williams, M., et al. (1984). A comparison of lactate and isoproternol anxiety states. *Psychopathology, 17* (Suppl. 1), 74-82.

Raskin, M., Peeke, H. V. S., Dickman, W., (1982). Panic and generalized anxiety disorder. *Archives of General Psychiatry, 39,* 687-689.

Redmond, D. E. (1979). New and old evidence for the involvement of a brain norepinephrine system in anxiety. In W. E. Fann, I. Karacan, A. D. Pokoiny, et al. (Eds.), *Phenomenology and treatment of anxiety.* New York: Spectrum.

Reiman, E. M., & Robins, E. (1986). *The lactate and pCO^2 story and P. E. T. scan evaluation.* Paper presented at the Panic Disorder Biological Research Workshop, Washington, DC.

Rose, R. M. (1980). Endocrine responses to stressful psychological events. In E. J. Sacher (Ed.), *The psychiatric clinics of North America: Advances in psychoendocrinology* (Vol. 3).

Roy-Byrne, P. P., Geraci, M., & Uhde, T. W. (1986). Life events and course of illness in patients with panic disorder. *American Journal of Psychiatry, 143,* 1033-1035.

Scott, J. P. (1974). Effects of psychotropic drugs on separation distress in dogs. *Proceedings of the IX Congress on Neuropsychopharmacology.* Amsterdam: Exerpta Medica.

Skolnick, P., & Paul, S. M. (1982). Benzodiazepine receptors in the central nervous system. *International Review of Neurobiology, 23,* 103-140.

Suomi, S. T., Seaman, S. F., Lewis, J. K., et al. (1978). Effects of imipramine treatment of separation-induced social disorders in Rhesus monkeys. *Archives of General Psychiatry, 35,* 321-325.

Torgersen, S. (1983). Genetic factors in anxiety disorders. *Archives of General Psychiatry, 40,* 1085-1089.

Torgersen, S. (1986). Childhood and family characteristics in panic and generalized anxiety disorders. *American Journal of Psychiatry, 143,* 630–632.

Woods, S. W., Charney, D. S., Goodman, W. K., & Heninger, G. R. (1988). Carbon dioxide-induced anxiety: Behavioral, physiologic, and biochemical effects of carbon dioxide in patients with panic disorder and healthy controls. *Archives of General Psychiatry, 45,* 43–52.

Woods, S. W., Charney, D. S., McPherson, C. A., Gradman, A. H., & Heninger, G. R. (1987). Situational panic attacks. *Archives of General Psychiatry, 44,* 365–375.

4

Assessment of State and Trait Anxiety in Cardiovascular Disorders

Charles D. Spielberger and Richard L. Rickman

Anxiety is generally defined as a psychobiological emotional state or reaction that can be distinguished most clearly from other emotions such as anger or sadness by its unique experiential qualities (Spielberger, 1972, 1979). An anxiety state consists of unpleasant feelings of tension, apprehension, nervousness, and worry, and activation of the autonomic nervous system. The physiological manifestations in anxiety generally include increased blood pressure; rapid heart rate (palpitations or tachycardia); sweating; dryness of the mouth; nausea; vertigo (dizziness); irregularities in breathing (hyperventilation); muscle tension; and muscular–skeletal disturbances such as restlessness, tremors, and feelings of weakness.

Anxiety also refers to relatively stable individual differences in anxiety-proneness as a personality trait. People who have high trait anxiety are more likely to perceive stressful situations as being personally dangerous or threatening and to respond to such situations with elevations in state anxiety. Individual differences in trait anxiety also reflect the frequency and intensity with which anxiety states have been manifested in the past and the probability that state anxiety will be experienced in the future. The stronger the anxiety trait, the more often the individual has experienced state anxiety in the past, and the greater the probability that intense elevations in state anxiety will be experienced in threatening situations in the future.

The major goals of this chapter are to describe and evaluate psychometric procedures for the assessment of state and trait anxiety and to examine research on anxiety in cardiovascular disorders. Because assessment methods typically follow conceptual advances, the evolution of anxiety as a scientific construct is reviewed briefly, and relations between the concepts of stress, threat, and anxiety are examined. Widely used psychometric approaches to the assessment of state and trait anxiety are then discussed, and the construction and validation of an objective self-report measure of anxiety, the State–Trait Anxiety Inventory (STAI), are described in some detail. Finally, applications of the STAI to the study of the Type A behavior pattern, hypertension, and cardiovascular disorders are presented.

EVOLUTION OF ANXIETY AS A SCIENTIFIC CONSTRUCT

In his classic book, *The Meaning of Anxiety,* May (1950/1977) noted that the historical roots of contemporary scientific conceptions of fear and anxiety reside in the philosophical and theological views of Pascal in the 17th century and Kierkegaard in the 19th century. The emergence of fear (anxiety) as a scientific construct is reflected in the writings of Darwin (1872/1965), who considered fear to be an inherent and adaptive characteristic of both humans and animals that has evolved over countless generations through a process of natural selection. Darwin observed that fear varied in intensity from mild apprehension or surprise, to an extreme "agony of terror" and that manifestations of fear included trembling, dilation of the pupils, increased perspiration, changes in voice quality, erection of the hair, and peculiar facial expression.

Sigmund Freud (1895/1924) described anxiety as "something felt"—an unpleasant affective (emotional) state or condition that was characterized by subjective feelings of chronic apprehension and "all that is covered by the word 'nervousness'" (1895/ 1924, p. 79). According to Freud, anxiety consisted of a unique combination of phenomenological and physiological qualities, with behavioral manifestations similar to those that Darwin attributed to fear. Although the physiological properties of anxiety were essential characteristics of this emotional reaction, Freud emphasized the subjective experiential qualities—the feelings of tension, apprehension, nervousness, and dread—in his theoretical formulations. Freud was concerned primarily with identifying the sources of stimulation that precipitated anxiety reactions rather than with analyzing the properties of such states. He sought to discover in prior experience "the historical element . . . which binds the afferent and efferent elements of anxiety firmly together" (1936, p. 70).

Initially, Freud believed that anxiety resulted from the discharge of repressed, somatic sexual tensions (libido). When blocked from normal expression, libidinal energy accumulated and was automatically discharged as free-floating anxiety. He subsequently modified this view in favor of a more general conception of anxiety as a signal indicating the presence of a danger situation. The perceived presence of danger evokes an unpleasant emotional state that serves to warn the individual that some form of adjustment is necessary. Thus Freud's danger signal theory, which emphasized the adaptive utility of anxiety as a motivater of behavior that helped an individual to avoid or cope with danger, was consistent with Darwin's evolutionary perspective.

Freud's danger signal theory also called attention to two potential sources of danger: the external world and one's own internal impulses. When the source of danger was external, this evoked an *objective anxiety* reaction, that was synonymous with fear. Objective anxiety, or fear, was defined as an unpleasant emotional state that was aroused when injury or harm from an external danger was anticipated. In objective anxiety, the emotional reaction was proportional in intensity to the magnitude of the external danger that caused it.

Freud's concept of objective anxiety (fear) may be interpreted as referring to a complex psychobiological process. This process can be broken down into three interrelated components: (a) a real danger in the external world (stressor); (b) the accurate perception of an external danger as potentially harmful (threat); and (c) an unpleasant emotional reaction (anxiety state), which varies in intensity as a function of the magnitude of the objective danger. The temporal relation among these components is illustrated in Figure 1.

Neurotic anxiety as conceptualized by Freud also implies a complex psychobiological process. But the source of the danger in neurotic anxiety resides in the derivatives of unacceptable internal impulses that were punished in childhood and subsequently repressed (see Spielberger, 1972, 1979). Consistent with Freud's conception,

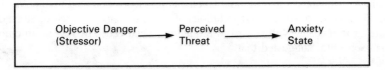

Figure 1 The temporal relation of the three components of objective anxiety as a psychobiological process.

Basowitz, Persky, Korchin, and Grinker (1955) defined neurotic anxiety as "the conscious and reportable experience of intense dread and foreboding, conceptualized as internally derived and unrelated to external threat" (p. 3). Thus in both objective and neurotic anxiety, the anxious individual can observe and describe her or his unpleasant feelings and can report the intensity and duration of these feelings.

In neurotic anxiety, as in objective anxiety, the unpleasant emotional reaction is characterized by feelings of tension, apprehension, and nervousness, and physiological arousal. However, because most of the cues associated with previously punished impulses remain repressed, neurotic anxiety is experienced as "objectless" or, as in the case of phobias, the relation between the feared object and the original danger situation is not recognized. Consequently, one of the most important characteristics of neurotic anxiety is that the anxiety state is proportional in intensity to the perceived (subjective) threat and disproportionately greater than would be warranted by the real (objective) danger.

State and Trait Anxiety

Research on anxiety as an emotional state has focused on delineating the particular properties of anxiety states (state anxiety) and identifying the specific conditions that evoke them. Definitions of state anxiety are comparable to the descriptions of fear reactions originally suggested by Darwin (1872/1965) and to objective anxiety as conceptualized by Freud (1936). On the basis of an extensive review of the research literature in psychology and psychiatry, Krause (1961) concluded that anxiety states are typically inferred from "clinical intuition" and five types of observable responses: introspective verbal reports, physiological signs, "molar" behavior (i.e., body posture, restlessness, and distortions in speech), task performance, and the response to stress. Of these, introspective reports, according to Krause, provide the most useful and widely accepted basis for defining transitory or state anxiety.

In contrast to Krause, Martin (1961) viewed anxiety as a complex neurophysiological reaction. Focusing on the observable physiological and behavioral response patterns associated with anxiety states, Martin differentiated between state anxiety and other emotional reactions on the basis of qualitative differences in these patterns. He also distinguished between anxiety reactions, the external or internal stimuli that evoke these reactions, and "defenses" against anxiety, that is, responses that have been learned because they were effective in reducing the intensity of anxiety. Taken together, the views of Krause and Martin suggest that state anxiety in humans can be most meaningfully and unambiguously defined and measured by some combination of introspective reports and physiological and behavioral signs.

Schachter (1964) presented impressive evidence that emotional states consist of two major components: physiological arousal and socially determined cognitions.

According to Schachter, an individual labels the feelings associated with physiological arousal on the basis of social interpretations of the situations in which these emotional states are experienced. With regard to the natural occurrence of fear as an emotional reaction, Schachter suggested that

> *cognitive or situational factors trigger physiological processes, and the triggering stimulus usually imposes the label we attach to our feelings. We see the threatening object; this perception-cognition initiates a state of sympathetic arousal and the joint cognitive-physiological experience is labeled "fear." (1967, p. 124)*

Cattell and Scheier (1963) pioneered the application of multivariate techniques to defining and measuring anxiety. Both phenomenological (self-report) and physiological measures of anxiety were included in their factor-analytic investigations of the covariation of different anxiety measures over time (Cattell, 1966). Relatively independent state and trait anxiety factors were consistently identified in this research. Measures that fluctuated over time, covarying over occasions of measurement, had high loadings on the state anxiety factor, whereas measures with high loadings on the trait anxiety factor were relatively stable over time. Thus state anxiety was defined as a transitory state or condition that was influenced by situational stress, and trait anxiety was defined in terms of individual differences in personality characteristics that were relatively stable over time.

Although many of the same variables loaded Cattell's (1966) state and trait anxiety factors, the pattern of loadings was quite different. A number of physiological variables, such as respiration rate and systolic blood pressure, fluctuated over time and had strong loadings on the state anxiety factor but only slight loadings on trait anxiety. Variables loading the relatively stable trait anxiety factor included personality characteristics such as "ego weakness," "guilt-proneness," and "tendency to embarrassment." Anxiety neurotics scored high on Cattell and Scheier's (1961) trait anxiety factor.

Stress, Threat, and Anxiety

In order to clarify the meaning of state and trait anxiety as scientific constructs, the relation of these constructs to stress and threat must be specified. In popular usage and in engineering and the physical sciences, *stress* generally refers to the external forces or pressures acting on an object. Severe or persistent stress results in *strain* that may permanently alter the internal structure of an object. In contrast, *stress* was used by Cannon (1929) to describe a disturbance in homeostasis in animals and people that results from noxious stimulation. The complex physiological and biochemical changes associated with disturbed homeostasis stimulate and motivate a person to engage in emergency "fight or flight" reactions. Similarly, Selye (1956) defined stress in terms of the stereotyped physiological and biochemical reactions associated with activation of the "hypothalamus-pituitary-adrenocortical axis." Thus Cannon and Selye equated stress with internal reactions (strains) evoked by external forces or pressures.

In keeping with the popular meaning of the term, stress was defined by Lazarus (1966; Lazarus & Folkman, 1984) as a special kind of transaction between a person and his or her environment. In describing stress transactions, Lazarus used the terms *stressor* and *threat* to denote different aspects of a temporal sequence of events that culminates in the evocation of an emotional state. Stressors are situations or events that are characterized by some degree of objective danger, whereas threat refers to a person's appraisal of a specific stressor as potentially harmful. Lazarus emphasized the importance of cognitive appraisal of a particular circumstance as threatening (i.e., harmful or dangerous) as the mediator of the arousal of an emotional state in a stress transaction.

Figure 2 presents a conceptual model of stress as a transactional process. This model provides a cross-sectional analysis of stress as a complex psychobiological process and includes the major variables that have been identified in research on stress and anxiety. Thus the model may be used as a theoretical framework for evaluating relations among external and internal stressors, cognitive appraisals of threat, state and trait anxiety, coping behavior, and psychological defenses.

Situations that involve physical dangers are generally interpreted as threatening by most people. Circumstances in which personal adequacy is evaluated are more likely to be perceived as threatening by individuals who are high in trait anxiety than by people low in trait anxiety (Spielberger, 1972). The origins of individual differences in trait anxiety may be due in part to genetic factors, but childhood experiences and early parent–child relationships that involve withdrawal of love or negative evaluations by parents, teachers, or peers appear to be extremely important (Perdue & Spielberger, 1966). Research has shown that people who are high in trait anxiety tend to be low in self-esteem, lack confidence in themselves, and are generally more vulnerable to being evaluated by others.

ASSESSMENT OF STATE AND TRAIT ANXIETY

Given the centrality of anxiety as a construct in theory and research in personality and psychopathology, there are many different approaches to its measurement. Projective techniques such as the Rorschach inkblots and the Thematic Apperception Test are used extensively in the clinical evaluation of anxiety. However, these tests do not readily lend themselves to quantification and are therefore limited in the extent to which they can be used in research. Rating scales and psychometric self-report inventories and questionnaires are by far the most popular procedures for assessing anxiety in research and clinical practice. An advantage of such instruments is that they are easily administered and scored and do not require a great deal of expensive professional time. The Hamilton Anxiety Rating Scale and six self-report psychometric inventories that are widely used in the measurement of anxiety are described in the following sections.

Hamilton Anxiety Rating Scale

The Hamilton Anxiety Rating Scale (HARS—Hamilton, 1959) was designed to be used as part of a clinical interview to facilitate quantifying anxiety symptoms in psychoneurotic patients. A total of 100 symptoms that are aggregated to define 13 scale variables are rated by the clinical examiner. These variables include subjective feelings of anxious mood, tension, a variety of fears and somatic symptoms, and autonomic complaints. Examples of HARS symptoms that appear to be most directly related to anxiety are anxious mood—worries, apprehension, and irritability;

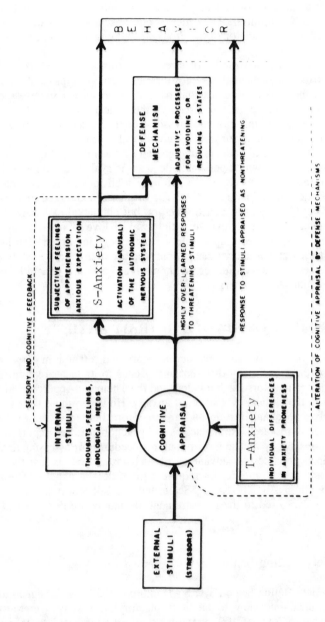

Figure 2 A cross-sectional model of anxiety as a complex psychobiological process. The model specifies the relations among the constructs of state anxiety and trait anxiety, external and internal stressors, cognitive appraisal of threat, coping behavior, and psychological defense mechanisms. From Spielberger (1966). Adapted by permission of publisher and author.

tension—inability to relax, trembling, and restlessness; and fears—of dark, crowds, strangers, and being left alone.

Patients are rated for the severity of each symptom on a scale of 0 to 4, using the following scale points: (0) none, (1) mild, (2) moderate, (3) severe, and (4) very severe to grossly disabling. Factor analysis of the responses of psychiatric patients identified a general anxiety factor and a bipolar factor, on which psychic symptoms (anxious moods and depression) had positive loadings and somatic complaints (cardiovascular and respiratory symptoms) had negative loadings.

Taylor Manifest Anxiety Scale

The Taylor Manifest Anxiety Scale (MAS—Taylor, 1953), one of the earliest self-report inventories, has been used extensively in experimental research. The MAS consists of 50 items from the Minnesota Multiphasic Personality Inventory (MMPI), with item content reflecting symptoms of manifest anxiety. These items were selected on the basis of consensual agreement of five clinical psychologists. In responding to the MAS, subjects report how they generally feel by checking either true or false for each item. A true response to the representative MAS items listed as follows signifies the presence of anxiety.

1. I often find myself worrying about something.
2. I cry easily.
3. At times I lose sleep over worry.
4. I am a nervous person.
5. I certainly feel useless at times.

An explicit reference to the frequency of occurrence of a symptom may be noted in three of the MAS items, for example, "often" in item 1 and "at times" in items 2 and 5. Thus the MAS can be considered a measure of trait anxiety. However, the content of several items appear to be more closely related to depression than to anxiety—for example, feeling useless and crying easily. Factor analyses of a large pool of anxiety items indicated that items such as "I feel like crying" and "I feel blue" have relatively low loadings on a trait anxiety factor (Spielberger, 1983).

Cattell's Trait and State Anxiety Measures

Cattell and Scheier (1963) developed the Anxiety Scale Questionnaire (ASQ) to provide a rapid, standardized clinical assessment of anxiety. Several ASQ items are listed as follows; the high anxiety alternatives are italicized.

1. As a child I was afraid of the dark: (a) *often* (b) sometimes (c) never
2. In discussions with most people, I get so annoyed that I can hardly trust myself to speak: (a) *sometimes* (b) rarely (c) never
3. Often I get angry with people too quickly. (a) *true* (b) in between (c) false

Whereas Taylor used a true–false format and selected her items on the basis of content validity and internal consistency, Cattell and Scheier used multiple-choice items and employed factor-analytic procedures as the primary basis for item selection. Despite major differences in the authors' conceptions of anxiety, item format, and the method of test construction, correlations between the ASQ and the MAS are typically .80 or higher. Because these correlations approach the reliabilities of the individual scales, the MAS and the ASQ may be considered to be equivalent measures of anxiety.

In terms of content of the ASQ items, it may be noted that items 2 and 3 seem to be conceptually more closely related to anger than they are to anxiety, reflecting what seems to be a critical limitation in the empirical procedures that were used in item selection. When only empirical procedures are used in scale construction, it is very difficult to differentiate between items that measure the same construct and those that assess closely related constructs. A similar problem in item content was noted for the MAS in which a rational selection procedure resulted in items with content more closely related to depression than anxiety. Typically, measures of anxiety, anger, and depression are moderately to highly correlated, especially in clinical populations. Therefore, a combination of rational and empirical procedures is generally more effective for assessing such related constructs.

Although the MAS and the ASQ were constructed before the importance of the state–trait distinction was established, these scales seem to measure trait anxiety. In responding to both inventories, subjects report how they generally feel or behave. Moreover, a number of items on both scales explicitly inquire about the frequency of occurrence of a particular symptom or experience. This was the case for all three of the ASQ items listed and for three of the five MAS items.

Following the conceptual distinction between anxiety as an emotional state and individual differences in anxiety as a personality trait, Scheier and Cattell (1960) constructed the 8-Parallel Form (8-PF) Anxiety Battery to assess repeated measurement of changes in anxiety level over time. The 8-PF consists of subtests with high loadings on a state anxiety factor that were identified in differential-R and P-technique factor analysis. But subtests from the Objective-Analytic (O-A) Anxiety Battery (Cattell & Scheier, 1960), which measures trait anxiety, were also included in the 8-PF.

Four O-A subtests (Susceptibility to Common Annoyances, Lack of Confidence in Untried Skills, Honesty in Admitting Common Frailties, and Susceptibility to Embarrassment) appear to reflect personality traits that are associated with trait anxiety rather than a transitory emotional state that varies in intensity. Another subtest, Questions, which requires subjects to report the frequency with which a given symptom has been experienced in the past ("often," "sometimes," or "never"), is also conceptually much more closely related to trait than state anxiety. Thus, at best, the 8-PF appears to be a confounded measure of state and trait anxiety. Moreover, although this scale was published commercially more than 25 years ago, there is little evidence of the construct validity of the 8-PF as a measure of state anxiety.

Affect Adjective Check List

Zuckerman (1960) and his associates (Zuckerman & Biase, 1962; Zuckerman & Lubin, 1965) developed the Affect Adjective Check List (AACL) to measure both state and trait anxiety. The Today Scale of the AACL, which requires subjects to check adjectives that describe how they feel on the day the scale is given, is used to assess state anxiety. Trait anxiety is assessed by the General Form of the AACL to which subjects respond by checking adjectives that describe how they generally feel. A unique feature of the AACL is that it comprises items (adjectives) that describe the absence of anxiety (e.g., "calm"), as well as its presence ("tense" or "nervous").

Evidence of the validity of the AACL as a measure of state anxiety is impressive. However, the AACL Today Scale would be more sensitive if instead of simply checking each adjective, subjects rated the level of intensity of the specified condition—for example, "I feel afraid: not at all, somewhat, moderately so, or very much so." Relatively low correlations of the AACL General Form with other trait anxiety measures such as the MAS and the ASQ raise questions about the concurrent validity of this scale. Here again, however, the sensitivity of the scale could be improved if subjects were required to report the frequency of occurrence of the condition described by each adjective.

SCL-90 Symptom Check List

This 90-item symptom check list (SCL-90) was originally designed by Derogatis and his colleagues (Derogatis, Lipman, & Covi, 1973) to serve as a criterion measure for evaluating the efficacy of psychotherapeutic agents in clinical drug trials. The scale was subsequently revised to assess psychiatric outpatients along nine major symptom dimensions (Derogatis, 1975). Scales to measure high manifest anxiety and phobic anxiety are included among these dimensions. The anxiety dimensions include general signs and symptoms such as nervousness and tension, as well as feelings of terror and panic. The phobic anxiety dimension focuses on symptoms that have been frequently observed in agoraphobia and other phobic anxiety states.

The instructions for the revised SCL-90 (SCL-90-R) require the patient to rate each of 90 complaints on the extent to which he or she has been "distressed or bothered" by a particular symptom or problem during the past seven days, including the day of testing. Each complaint is rated on the following 5-point scale: (0) not at all, (1) a little bit, (2) moderately, (3) quite a bit, and (4) extremely. The weighted score for each response alternative is the number in the parentheses. Thus, the scores for each item may vary from 0 to 4.

The Anxiety and Phobic Anxiety subscales comprise 10 and 7 items, respectively. Examples of anxiety items are nervousness or shakiness inside, feeling fearful, and heart pounding or racing. Examples of phobic anxiety are feeling afraid in open spaces on the streets, feeling afraid to go out of your house alone, and feeling nervous when you are left alone. The internal consistency of the SCL-90-R Anxiety and Phobic Anxiety subtests are relatively high as reflected by alpha coefficients of .85 and .82, respectively, for symptomatic nonpatient volunteers. The manual also reports 1-week test–retest correlations for a heterogeneous group of 94 psychiatric outpatients of .80 for the Anxiety Scale and .90 for Phobic Anxiety. Thus the internal consistency and short-term stability of the SCL-90-R appear to be well established.

Numerous studies are reported in the SCL-90-R test manual that demonstrate the utility of this scale for measuring mood changes in psychopharmacologic research. In a recent evaluation of the SCL-90-R, Payne (1985) stated that "the SCL-90-R is an interesting and reliable self-administered psychiatric symptom check list which can be very useful in research studies" (p. 1329). Similarly, Pauker (1985) observed that the internal consistency and test–retest stability of the SCL-90-R were satisfactory and that the factor structure was reasonably stable. However, the SCL-90-R has been criticized because the discriminant validity of its nine dimensions is questionable.

Gotlib (1984) reported that the average intercorrelation among the nine SCL-90-R subtests was .58, leading him to conclude that they measure a single factor of "psychiatric disturbance" or "complaining." Payne (1985) has also raised questions about the usefulness of the SCL-90-R for the purpose of differential psychiatric diagnosis. Because the scale was developed to measure how much a patient has been "bothered" by specific symptoms during the past week, this criticism seems justified in that a psychiatric diagnosis generally implies a condition of longer standing. But it is also unclear whether the SCL-90-R measures the intensity of disturbing states during the past week or the frequency with which such states were experienced, or is a confounded measure of both.

Profile of Mood States

The Profile of Mood States (POMS) was developed to measure the respondent's mood state at the time of testing (McNair, Lorr & Droppleman, 1971). The POMS is an adjective-rating form that was designed to assess the following six affective dimensions that were derived by factor analysis: tension–anxiety, depression–dejection, anger–hostility, vigor–activity, fatigue–inertia, and confusion–bewilderment. Unlike the scales previously described, the measurement of anxiety with the POMS focuses exclusively on physical or muscular–skeletal tension rather than on subjective feelings of tension, apprehension, or worry.

The POMS instructions, which require the subject to "respond as you have felt within the past week including today," are similar to the instructions for the SCL-90-R. However, the scale has also been used with instructions that emphasize more immediate mood states, for example, "rate your feelings during the last half hour." "Tense" and "shaky" are examples of POMS items (adjectives) that measure tension–anxiety. However, in contrast to the AACL, the intensity of each adjective "tense" is rated on a 5-point scale: (0) not at all, (1) a little, (2) moderately, (3) quite a bit , and (4) extremely. There is also one item on the Tension–Anxiety scale ("relaxed") that is negatively weighted in calculating the Tension–Anxiety score.

In a comprehensive review of the POMS, Eichman (1978) stated that the scale "appears to be optimally reliable and sensitive to change" (p. 1018). Weckowicz (1978) agreed and added: "It is particularly useful for an evaluation of the effects of psychotherapy and medication" (p. 1019). Although Peterson and Headen (1985) have also stated that the POMS is useful for assessing mood change, they noted a lack of specificity in the factor patterns obtained with the test. For example, Peterson, Calamari, Greenberg, Gifford, and Schiers (1983) found that the Depression–Dejection subtest was highly correlated with tension ($r = .90$) and anxiety ($r = .75$). On the basis of such findings, Peterson and Headen (1985) concluded that the POMS appears to measure only "two independent mood components, depression and vigor" (p. 527).

A number of additional questionnaires, inventories, and other types of measures that have been used to assess state and trait anxiety have been described by Levitt (1980), including the Rorschach inkblots (Auerbach & Spielberger, 1972), psychometric scales such as the S-R Inventory of Anxiousness (Endler & Okada, 1975), and a variety of physiological measures (e.g., heart rate, blood pressure, and skin resistance). Many of these scales and procedures have also been critically evaluated by McReynolds (1968) and Borkovec, Weerts, and Bernstein (1977), and Hodges (1976) has reviewed psychophysiological measures of anxiety.

THE STATE–TRAIT ANXIETY INVENTORY

The State–Trait Anxiety Inventory (STAI—Spielberger, Gorsuch, & Lushene, 1970) was developed to provide reliable, relatively brief, self-support scales for assessing state anxiety and trait anxiety in research and clinical practice. Freud's (1936) danger signal theory and Cattell and Scheier's (1961) concepts of state and trait anxiety, as refined and elaborated by Spielberger (1966, 1972, 1976, 1977, 1979), provided the conceptual framework that guided the construction of the test. For this test, state anxiety was defined as a temporal cross-section in the emotional stream-of-life of a person, consisting of subjective feelings of tension, apprehension, nervousness, and worry, and activation (arousal) of the autonomic nervous system (Spielberger et al., 1970). It was further assumed that state anxiety varies in intensity and fluctuates over time as a function of perceived threat. Trait anxiety was defined in terms of relatively stable individual differences in anxiety-proneness, that is, differences between people in the frequency with which anxiety states have been experienced in the past and in the probability that state anxiety reactions will be manifested in the future.

The initial item pool for the STAI comprised items adapted from existing anxiety measures with content consistent with the preceding definitions. When test construction began in 1964, the goal was to develop an inventory consisting of a single set of items that could be administered with appropriate instructions to asess both state and trait anxiety. Therefore, the essential psychological content of the adapted items was retained, but the format was modified so that the same item could gauge either state or trait anxiety. For example, the state anxiety instructions required subjects to report the intensity of their feelings of anxiety "right now, at this moment." Instructions for trait anxiety asked subjects to indicate how they generally feel by reporting the frequency of occurrence of anxiety-related feelings and symptoms. A number of new items for assessing state anxiety were also written, using anxiety-absent adjectives from the AACL.

The criterion measures for selecting items with demonstrable anxiety content were the MAS and the ASQ, the two most widely used anxiety scales at the time test construction was begun. The Welsh Anxiety Scale (Welsh, 1956), which was derived by factor analysis of the 566 MMPI items, also served as a criterion measure. Items from the initial pool that correlated significantly with scores on all three scales were identified for further study. The internal consistency and concurrent and construct validity of each item when given with state and trait instructions were then evaluated. Items with weak psychometric properties or that were considered redundant, ambiguous, or offensive, were eliminated. The final set of 20 items for the preliminary version (Form A) of the STAI were selected on a basis of extensive item-validity research with 10 independent samples, comprising more than 2,000 college students (Spielberger et al., 1970).

The test construction strategy resulted in the exclusion of some of the best items from the STAI (Form A) because the psycholinguistic connotations of key words in these items inteferred with using them to measure *both* state and trait anxiety. For example, when given with trait instructions, "I worry too much" correlated highly with other trait anxiety items, but scores on this item did not reliably increase under stressful conditions, nor did they decrease after relaxation training, as was required for a valid measure of state anxiety. Conversely, "I feel upset" was a sensitive measure of state anxiety but not trait anxiety. Scores on this item increased markedly under stressful conditions and were significantly lower under relaxed conditions. However, when given with trait instructions, the correlations of the scores on this item with other trait anxiety items were relatively low, and these scores were unstable over time.

STAI Form X

Because of the difficulties encountered in measuring state and trait anxiety with the same items, the test construction strategy for the STAI was modified, and separate sets of items were selected for the state and trait anxiety scales. The 20 items with the best concurrent validity as measures of trait anxiety, that is, the items with the highest correlations with the MAS, the ASQ, and the Welsh Anxiety Scale, and that were internally consistent and stable over time, were selected for the STAI (Form X) Trait Anxiety Scale. The 20 items with the best construct validity as measures of state anxiety (i.e., sensitivity to stress) were selected for the STAI (Form X) State Anxiety Scale. Only five items met the validity criteria for both scales. The remaining items were sufficiently different in content to be regarded as unique measures of state or trait anxiety.

The STAI (Form X) scales comprise both anxiety-present and anxiety-absent items. Representatiave trait anxiety present and absent items are "I worry too much over something that really doesn't matter," "I get in a state of tension or turmoil as I think over my recent concerns and interest," "I am content," and "I feel pleasant." In responding to these items, subjects report how they generally feel by rating themselves on the following 4-point frequency scale: (1) almost never, (2) sometimes, (3) often, and (4) almost always. The weighted scores for the anxiety-present items are 1, 2, 3, or 4; the anxiety-absent items are scored 4, 3, 2, or 1.

Correlations between the STAI (Form X) Trait Anxiety Scale, the ASQ, and the MAS were relatively high in several large samples, ranging from .73 to .85 for men and women. Because these correlations approach the reliabilities of the respective scales, the three inventories can be considered as essentially equivalent measures of trait anxiety. A major advantage of the STAI Trait Anxiety Scale, however, is that it consists of only 20 items, as compared to the 43-item ASQ and the 50-item MAS. Consequently, the STAI Trait Anxiety Scale requires less than half as much time to administer and score as the MAS and the ASQ.

In constructing the STAI State Anxiety Scale, the main goal was to assess a continuum of increasing intensity on which low scores indicated feeling calm and serene, intermediate scores were associated with moderate levels of tension and nervousness, and high scores reflected intense fear, approaching terror and panic. The following are representative state anxiety present and absent items: "I am tense," "I feel upset," "I am worried," "I feel calm," and "I feel secure." In responding to these items, subjects report the intensity of their feelings at a particular time by rating themselves on a 4-point scale: (1) not at all, (2) somewhat, (3) moderately so, and (4) very much so. The state anxiety present and absent items are scored in the same manner as the trait anxiety items. To demonstrate construct validity, the scores for each state anxiety item had to increase significantly in an a priori stressful situation and decrease significantly in a relaxing situation when compared with a neutral situation.

The procedures employed in the construction, standardization, and validation of the STAI (Form X) are described in the original test manual (Spielberger et al., 1970). More than 6,000 high school and college students and approximately 600 neuropsychiatric, medical, and surgical patients were tested in developing Form X and earlier versions of the inventory. Because the STAI state and trait anxiety scales were designed to assess unidimensional constructs, internal consistency, as measured by item-remainder correlations and factor loadings, was a major criterion in selecting items for both scales. Distinctive state and trait anxiety factors have been identified in six studies in which all 40 STAI items were factored simultaneously (Barker, Barker, & Wadsworth, 1977; Gaudry & Poole, 1975; Gaudry, Vagg, & Spielberger, 1975; Kendall, Finch, Auerbach, Hooke, & Mikulka, 1976; Spielberger, Vagg, Barker, Donham, & Westberry, 1980; Vagg, Spielberger, & O'Hearn, 1980).

The STAI has been used extensively in experimental investigations and clinical practice since it was introduced more than 20 years ago (Spielberger & Gorsuch, 1966). The inventory has also been used increasingly to assess anxiety in investigations of stress-related psychiatric, psychosomatic, and medical disorders, and as an outcome measure in research on the effectiveness of biofeedback, psychotherapy, and various forms of behavioral treatment. This research has been stimulated by a growing acceptance among behavioral and medical scientists of the critical need to differentiate between anxiety as a transitory emotional state and individual differences in anxiety-proneness as a relatively stable personality trait.

STAI Form Y

On the basis of insights gained from a decade of intensive research with the STAI (Form X), a major revision was undertaken in 1979. The main goal of this revision was to develop a "purer" measure of anxiety in order to provide a firmer basis for the differential clinical diagnosis of patients suffering from anxiety disorders and depressive reactions. In the construction and standardization of the revised STAI (Form Y), more than 5,000 additional subjects were tested. Of the 40 STAI (Form X) items, 12 of them (30%) were replaced.

The STAI (Form X) items that were replaced included several with content more closely related to depression than anxiety (e.g., "I feel blue" or "I feel like crying"). Other replaced items contained idioms whose meaning had apparently shifted over the past decade, possibly as a consequence of expanded drug use by adolescents and young adults (e.g., "I feel 'high strung'"). Also replaced were several ambiguous items with marginal psychometric properties for high school students; for example, "I feel anxious" was interpreted by many of these students to mean "eager."

The item replacement procedures, described in detail in the revised STAI (Form Y) Test Manual (Spielberger, 1983), resulted in a better balance between anxiety-present and anxiety-absent items in the trait anxiety scale and improved psychometric properties for both the state and trait anxiety scales. Studies of Form Y's factor structure have consistently yielded clear-cut state and trait anxiety factors (Spielberger et al., 1980; Vagg et al., 1980). Norms for high school and college students, working adults, military personnel, prison inmates, and psychiatric, medical, and surgical patients are reported in the revised STAI (Form Y) Test Manual (Spielberger, 1983).

Items from the STAI have been incorporated into the 60-item State–Trait Personality Inventory (STPI—Spielberger et al., 1979), which also measures state and trait anger and curiosity. The 30-item STPI state scale includes the 10 STAI state anxiety items with the best psychometric properties. The 10 best STAI (Form Y) trait items are included in the STPI trait anxiety subscale. The internal consistency of the STPI subscales are relatively high, as reflected in alpha coefficients ranging from .80 to .92, and the correlations of these scales with the corresponding STAI (Form Y) scales are .90 or higher for both men and women.

Table 1 Mean STAI state and trait anxiety scores of people classified as Type A

		Mean STAI scores	
Study	Description of Type A subjects[a]	State anxiety	Trait anxiety
Roskies et al. (1978, 1979)	36 men, assessed by SI; mean age 40	36.1	35.0
Jenni & Wollersheim (1979)	16 adults assessed by the Bortner scale; mean age 42	38.5	39.4
Suinn & Bloom (1978)	14 adults assessed by JAS; mean age 38	49.0	48.0
Hart (1980)	9 college students assessed by JAS; mean age 20	40.5	NA
Lobitz & Brammel (1981)	17 adults assessed by JAS; mean age 36	36.5	40.8
Levenkron et al. (1982)	38 men assessed by JAS	35.2	35.9
Southern & Smith (1982)	25 men assessed by JAS	37.8	36.5
Group mean	Men and women (*n* = 155)	37.9	37.9
Working adults (STAI Manual)	Men (*n* = 410) Women (*n* = 210)	36.5 36.2	35.5 36.2

[a]The Type A behavior pattern was assessed by the Rosenman et al. (1964) Structured Interview (SI), the Jenkins Activity Survey (JAS; Jenkins, Zyzanski, & Rosenman, 1979), the Bortner (1969) scale, or a combination of these measures.

ANXIETY, TYPE A BEHAVIOR, AND CARDIOVASCULAR DISORDERS

The role of anxiety and other emotional and behavioral factors in the etiology of cardiovascular disorders has received significant attention over the past 20 yeras, which is not surprising considering the crucial contribution of the autonomic nervous system in regulating cardiovascular function. The STAI has been used to assess state and trait anxiety in a number of studies in which relations between anxiety and the Type A behavior pattern, essential hypertension, and coronary heart disease have been investigated.

The Type A behavior pattern has been demonstrated to be a powerful predictor of coronary heart disease (e.g., Rosenman, Brand, Jenkins, Friedman, Straus, & Wurm, 1975; Rosenman & Friedman, 1974). Although emotional factors such as anger and hostility have been identified as the key coronary-prone elements of the Type A behavior pattern (Matthews, Glass, Rosenman, & Bortner, 1977), no such relations have been shown for anxiety. Table 1 presents the mean STAI state and trait anxiety scores obtained in seven different studies for people who were assessed as being Type A. The overall group means based on the combined samples for all seven studies are also reported.

With the exception of the study by Suinn and Bloom (1978), the anxiety scores of Type A individuals were not substantially different from those of normative samples of working adults (Spielberger, 1983). The elevated anxiety means in the Suinn and Bloom (1978) study probably resulted from the fact that the subjects were recruited by newspaper ads that invited people with Type A characteristics to volunteer for an anxiety management program. When the data from the Suinn and Bloom study are excluded, the overall group means for the combined data of the six remaining studies were 36.4 for state anxiety and 36.8 for trait anxiety, which are only slightly higher than the means for the normative samples. Because similar recruiting strategies were employed in several of the studies listed in Table 1, the anxiety scores of the self-selected samples of Type A individuals in these studies might be expected to be somewhat higher than those in the general Type A population.

Anxiety, Elevated Blood Pressure, and Essential Hypertension

Significant positive correlations of systolic blood pressure with state anxiety have been consistently found for hypertensive individuals (Banahan, Sharpe, Baker, Liao, & Smith, 1979; Whitehead, Blackwell, DeSilva, & Robinson, 1977). Johnson (1984) also reported a significant positive correlation between state anxiety and systolic blood pressure for healthy high school students. However, findings with regard to the relation between trait anxiety and systolic blood pressure are inconsistent. Some researchers have reported negative correlations (e.g., Johnson, 1984), whereas others have reported essentially zero correlations (Banahan et al., 1979). There is little evidence that either trait or state anxiety is related to diastolic blood pressure.

The mean state and trait anxiety scores obtained in four studies of the relation between anxiety and essential hypertension are reported in Table 2. van der Ploeg, van Buuren, and van Brummelen (1985) and Elias, Robbins, and Schulz (1987) found that hypertensives scored higher in state anxiety than did patients with normal blood pressure. Although van der Ploeg et al. (1985) also reported that hypertensives scored

Table 2 Mean STAI state and trait anxiety scores of hypertensive individuals

Study	Description of hypertensives	Mean STAI scores	
		State anxiety	Trait anxiety
Steptoe et al. (1982)	16 male English factory workers identified in worksite screening; mean age 46	29.1	34.1
Van der Ploeg et al. (1985)	69 male and 35 female hypertensive patients; mean age 49	39.3 39.6	39.8 38.6
Rudd et al. (1986)	687 employees identified in worksite screening (77% males); mean age 46	37.1* 34.5**	—
Elias et al. (1987)	153 hypertensive patients; mean age 40	37.7	—
Group mean	State anxiety (n = 960) Trait anxiety (n = 120)	36.3	38.7
Working adults	Men (n = 559) Women (n = 135)	35.9 36.0	35.1 35.0

*Subjects previously aware of their hypertension (n = 325).
**Subjects previously unaware of hypertensive status (n = 362).

Table 3 Mean STAI state and trait anxiety scores of patients with a documented history of myocardial infarction

		Mean STAI scores	
Study	Description of patients	State anxiety	Trait anxiety
Spielberger (1976)	84 male VA outpatients with history of infarction; mean age 59	39.4	38.31
Roskies et al. (1979)	6 male with EKG evidence of infarction; mean age 49	36.2	32.8
Hiland (1979)	40 VA outpatients with history of infarction; mean age 53	39.6	39.7
Group mean	Men and women (*n* = 130)	39.3	38.5
Working adults	Men (*n* = 559)	35.9	35.1
	Women (*n* = 135)	36.0	35.0

higher than control subjects in trait anxiety, the difference between these groups only approached statistical significance ($p < .10$). In a study that used the STPI to measure anxiety, Crane (1981) reported that hypertensives scored significantly higher in both state and trait anxiety than did patient control subjects.

The findings of Steptoe, Melville, and Ross (1982) are unusual in that the mean state anxiety score for the hypertensives in this study was substantially lower than the mean for the normative sample of working adults. As might be expected, Rudd et al. (1986) found that industrial workers who were aware of their hypertension had higher state anxiety scores than did workers who were unaware of their elevated blood pressure. It is unfortunate that Rudd et al. (1986) did not report correlations of state anxiety with blood pressure, or compare the state anxiety scores of their hypertensive subjects with those of people with normal blood pressure. The results for such a large sample would have provided considerable insight into the relation between anxiety and blood pressure.

Anxiety and Coronary Heart Disease

The importance of emotional and behavioral factors in the etiology of heart disease has been suggested by a number of investigators, but inconsistency in the definition of coronary heart disease has resulted in equivocal and sometimes contradictory findings. The diagnosis of coronary heart disease is based on clinical events that are evidenced in several ways. For myocardial infarction, direct evidence of the event is reflected in specific physical symptoms and laboratory signs such as the electrocardigram. For events such as angina pectoris, evidence of coronary artery disease is not directly observable and must be inferred from the patient's presenting chest complaints, or by invasive techniques such as coronary angiography.

The mean STAI state and trait anxiety scores obtained in three studies of patients with a documented history of myocardial infarction are presented in Table 3. It may be noted that the group means based on the combined data for all three studies were somewhat higher than the means for the normative sample of working adults of similar age (Spielberger, 1983). Although the anxiety scores of these patients did not differ significantly from a control group in two of the three studies (Roskies et al., 1979; Spielberger, 1976), the scores of these patients were substantially lower than those of a normative sample of general medical and surgical patients (42.38 for state anxiety; 44.63 for trait anxiety) reported in the STAI test manual (Spielberger, 1983).

In the Hiland (1979) study, the myocardial infarction patients scored significantly higher in anxiety than did a control group matched in socioeconomic status. In general, these patients tend to be relatively higher in socioeconomic status which is inversely related to trait anxiety (Spielberger, 1983). Although the anxiety scores of the patients in the Hiland study were not elevated as compared with the general population, these patients were higher in trait anxiety than would be expected on the basis of their socioeconomic status. Byrne (1979) reported interesting findings for state and trait anxiety in patients with acute chest pains who were admitted to a coronary care unit. State anxiety was assessed in this study with visual analog scales; trait anxiety was measured with *Eysenck's Neuroticism scale*. The results indicated that patients with documented myocardial infarction were higher in state anxiety than were patients for whom an infarction could not be confirmed.

The STAI and the STPI were used in several recent investigations of relations between anxiety, angina pectoris, and coronary artery disease. The results in several studies have been remarkably consistent in demonstrating that people with angina pectoris but no angiographically documented coronary artery disease scored higher on state and trait anxiety than did persons with both conditions (Elias, Robbins, Blow, Rice, & Edgecomb, 1982; Greene, 1988; Schocken, Greene, Worden, Harrison, & Spielberger, 1987). Schocken et al. (1987) and Greene (1988) have reported higher trait anxiety in younger males with chest pain, but no angiographic evidence of a prior infarction, than in patients with angina and coronary artery disease. Thus, high trait anxiety was not associated with coronary artery disease, but seems to be a risk factor for referral for angiography in younger males.

Taken together, these research findings suggest that individuals with hypertension, or with a documented history of myocardial infarction, are slightly higher in anxiety than people of similar socioeconomic status who do not have cardiovascular problems. Anxiety appears to be unrelated to the Type A behavior pattern, except in self-selected Type As who volunteer for special anxiety-reduction intervention programs. The finding that anxiety was more predictive of angina pectoris than coronary artery disease suggests that younger males with chest pains who are referred for coronary angiography and found to have clean arteries are likely to be higher in trait anxiety than patients whose chest pain is caused by coronary artery disease.

SUMMARY

This chapter reviewed the evolution of anxiety as a scientific construct, from Darwin and Freud to the present, and discussed implications for the measurement of anxiety of Freud's danger signal theory and his concepts of objective and neurotic anxiety. The distinction between anxiety as an emotional state and individual differences in anxiety proneness as a personality trait was considered in the context of empirical research on the assessment of anxiety. A transactional process model for examining relations between stress, threat, and state and trait anxiety was also presented. Six frequently used measures of anxiety—the Hamilton Rating Scale, the Taylor Manifest Anxiety Scale, Cattell's ASQ and 8-PF anxiety scales, the Affect Adjective Check List, the SCL-90-R Symptom Checklist, and the Profile of Mood States—were briefly described, and the construction and validation of State-Trait Anxiety Inventory was considered in some detail. Finally, the findings of research on the relationship between state and trait anxiety, Type-A Behavior, hypertension, and cardiovascular disorders were briefly examined.

REFERENCES

Auerbach, S. M., & Spielberger, C. D. (1972). The assessment of state and trait anxiety with the Rorschach test. *Journal of Personality Assessment, 36,* 314–335.

Banahan, B. F., Sharpe, T. R., Baker, J. A., Liao, W. C., & Smith, M. C. (1979). Hypertension and stress: A preventive approach. *Journal of Psychosomatic Research, 23,* 69–75.

Barker, B. M., Barker, H. R., Jr., & Wadsworth, A. P. (1977). Factor analysis of the State–Trait Anxiety Inventory. *Journal of Clinical Psychology, 32,* 450–455.

Basowitz, H., Persky, H., Korchin, S. J., & Grinker, R. R. (1955). *Anxiety and stress.* New York: McGraw-Hill.

Borkovec, T. D., Weerts, T. C., & Bernstein, D. A. (1977). Assessment of anxiety. In A. R. Ciminero, K. S. Calhoun, & H. E. Adams (Eds.), *Handbook of behavioral assessment.* New York: Wiley.

Bortner, R. W. (1969). A short rating scale as a potential measure of pattern A behavior. *Journal of Chronic Diseases, 22,* 87–91.

Byrne, D. G. (1979). Anxiety as state and trait following survived myocardial infarction. *British Journal of Social and Clinical Psychology, 18,* 417–423.

Cannon, W. B. (1929). *Bodily changes in pain, hunger, fear, and rage.* New York: Appleton.

Cattell, R. B. (1966). Patterns of change: Measurement in relation to state dimension, trait change, lability, and process concepts. *Handbook of multivariate experimental psychology.* Chicago, IL: Rand McNally.

Cattell, R. B., & Scheier, I. H. (1960). Stimuli related stress, neuroticism, excitation, and anxiety response patterns. *Journal of Abnormal and Social Psychology, 60,* 195–204.

Cattell, R. B., & Scheier, I. H. (1961). *The meaning and measurement of neuroticism and anxiety.* New York: Ronald Press.

Cattell, R. B., & Scheier, I. H. (1963). *Handbook for the IPAT Anxiety Scale* (2nd ed.). Champaign, IL: Institute for Personality and Ability Testing.

Crane, R. S. (1981). The role of anger, hostility, and aggression in essential hypertension (Doctoral dissertation, University of South Florida, 1981). *Dissertation Abstracts International, 42,* 2982B.

Darwin, C. (1965). *Expression of emotions in man and animals.* Chicago: University of Chicago Press. (Original work published 1872)

Derogatis, L. R. (1975). *The SCL-90-R.* Baltimore: Clinical Psychometrics Research.

Derogatis, L. R., Lipman, R. S., & Covi, L. (1973). SCL-90: An outpatient psychiatric rating scale: Preliminary report. *Psychopharmacology Bulletin, 9,* 13–27.

Eichman, W. J. (1978). Profile and mood states. In O. K. Buros (Ed.), *The eighth mental measurements yearbook* (Vol. 1, pp. 1015–1018). Highland Park, NJ: Gryphon Press.

Elias, M. F., Robbins, M. A., Blow, F. C., Rice, A. P., & Edgecomb, J. L. (1982). A behavioral study of middle-aged chest pain patients' physical symptoms reporting, anxiety, and depression. *Experimental Aging Research, 8,* 45–51.

Elias, M. F., Robbins, M. A., & Schulz, N. C. (1987). Influence of essential hypertension on intellectual performance: Causation or speculation? In J. W. Elias & P. H. Marshall (Eds.), *Cardiovascular disease and behavior.* Washington, DC: Hemisphere/Wiley.

Endler, N. S., & Okada, M. (1975). A multidimensional meaure of trait anxiety: The S-R inventory of general trait anxiousness. *Journal of Consulting and Clinical Psychology, 43,* 319–329.

Freud, S. (1924). *Collected papers* (Vol. 1). London: Hogarth Press. (Original work published 1895)

Freud, S. (1936). *The problem of anxiety.* New York: Norton.

Gaudry, E., & Poole, C. (1975). A further validation of the state–trait distinction in anxiety research. *Australian Journal of Psychology, 27,* 119–125.

Gaudry, E., Vagg, P. R., & Spielberger, C. D. (1975). Validation of the state–trait distinction in anxiety research. *Multivariate Behavior Research, 10,* 331–341.

Greene, A. F. (1988). *Coronary heart disease in anxious angry hearts.* Unpublished doctoral dissertation, University of South Florida, Tampa.

Gotlib, I. H. (1984). Depression and general psychopathology in university students. *Journal of Abnormal Psychology, 93,* 19–30.

Hamilton, M. (1959). The assessment of anxiety states by rating. *British Journal of Medical Psychology, 32,* 50-55.

Hart, K. (1980). *Stress management training for Type A individuals.* Unpublished manuscript.

Hiland, D. N. (1979). Type A behavior, anxiety, job-satisfaction and life stress as risk factors in myocardial infarction (Doctoral dissertation, University of South Florida, 1978). *Dissertation Abstracts International, 39,* 3516B.

Hodges, W. F. (1976). The psychophysiology of anxiety. In M. Zuckerman & C. D. Spielberger (Eds.), *Emotions and anixety: New concepts, methods, and applications.* Hillsdale, NJ: Erlbaum.

Jenkins, C. D., Zyzanski, S. J., & Rosenman, R. H. (1979). *Jenkins Activity Survey manual.* New York: Harcourt Brace Jovanovich.

Jenni, M., & Wollersheim, J. (1979). Cognitive therapy, stress management training and Type A behavior pattern. *Cognitive Therapy and Research, 3,* 61-73.

Johnson, E. H. (1984). *Anger and anxiety as determinants of elevated blood pressure in adolescents.* Unpublished doctoral dissertation, University of South Florida, Tampa.

Kendall, P. C., Finch, A. J., Jr., Auerbach, S. M., Hooke, J. F., & Mikulka, P. J. (1976). The State–Trait Anxiety Inventory: A systematic evaluation. *Journal of Consulting and Clinical Psychology, 44,* 406-412.

Krause, M. S. (1961). The measurement of transitory anxiety. *Psychological Review, 68,* 178.

Lazarus, R. S. (1966). *Psychological stress and the coping process.* New York: McGraw-Hill.

Lazarus, R. S., & Folkman, S. (1984). *Stress appraisal, and coping.* New York: Springer.

Levenkron, J., Cohen, J., Mueller, H., & Fisher, E. (1982). *Modifying the Type A coronary-prone behavior pattern.* Unpublished manuscript.

Levitt, E. E. (1980). *The psychology of anxiety* (2nd ed.). Hillsdale, NJ: Erlbaum.

Lobitz, W., & Brammel, H. (1981, August). *Anxiety management training versus aerobic conditioning for cardiac stress management.* Paper presented at the annual meeting of the American Psychological Association, Los Angeles.

Martin, B. (1961). The assessment of anxiety by physiological behavioral measures. *Psychological Bulletin, 58,* 234.

Matthews, K. A., Glass, D. C., Rosenman, R. H., & Bortner, R. W. (1977). Competitive drive, pattern A, and coronary disease: A further analysis of some data from the Western Collaborative Group Study. *Journal of Chronic Diseases, 30,* 489-498.

May, R. (1977). *The meaning of anxiety.* New York: Norton. (Original work published 1950)

McNair, D. M., Lorr, M., & Droppleman, L. F. (1971). *Profile of Mood States.* San Diego: Educational and Industrial Testing Service.

McReynolds, P. (1968). The assessment of anxiety: A survey of available techniques. In P. McReynolds (Ed.), *Advances in psychological assessment* (Vol. 1). Palo Alto, CA: Science and Behavior Books.

Pauker, J. D. (1985). The SCL-90-R. In J. V. Mitchell, Jr. (Ed.), *The ninth mental measurements yearbook* (Vol. 12, pp. 1325-1326). Highland Park, NJ: Gryphon Press.

Payne, R. W. (1985). Review of the SCL-90-R. In J. V. Mitchell, Jr. (Ed.), *The ninth mental measurements yearbook* (Vol. 12, pp. 1326-1328). Highland Park, NJ: Gryphon Press.

Perdue, O. R., & Spielberger, C. D. (1966). Anxiety and the perception of punishment. *Mental Hygiene, 50,* 390-397.

Peterson, R., & Headen, S. (1985). Profile of Mood States. In D. Keyser & R. Sweetland (Eds.), *Test critiques* (Vol. 1, pp. 522-528). Kansas City, MO: Testing Corporation of America.

Peterson, R. A., Calamari, J., Greenberg, G., Gifford, D., & Schiers, B. (1983, August). *Evaluation of two strategies to reduce stress and supervisory staff in a residential facility for the DD.* Paper presented at the meeting of the American Association in Mental Deficiency, Homewood, IL.

Rosenman, R. H., Brand, R., Jenkins, C. D., Friedman, M., Straus, R., & Wurm, M. (1975). Coronary heart disease in Western Collaborative Group Study: Final follow-up experience of 8 1/2 years. *Journal of the American Medical Association, 233,* 872-877.

Rosenman, R. H., & Friedman, M. (1974). Neurogenic factors in pathogenesis of coronary heart disease. *Medical Clinics of North America, 58,* 269-279.

Rosenman, R. H., Friedman, M., Strauss, R., Wurm, M., Kositchek, R., Hahn, W., & Werthessen, N. T. A predictive study of coronary heart disease. The Western Collaborative Group Study. *Journal of the American Medical Association, 189,* 103-110.

Roskies, E., et al. (1979). Generalizability and durability of treatment effects in an intervention program for coronary-prone (Type A) managers. *Journal of Behavioral Medicine, 2,* 195-208.

Roskies, E., Spevack, M., Surkis, A., Cohen, C., & Gilman, S. (1978). Changing the coronary prone (Type A) behavior pattern in a nonclinical population. *Journal of Behavioral Medicine, 1,* 201-216.

Rudd, P., Price, M. G., Graham, L. E., Beilstein, B. A., Tarbell, S. J. H., Bachetti, P., & Fortmann, S. P. (1986). Consequences of worksite hypertension screening. *American Journal of Medicine, 80,* 853–860.

Schachter, S. (1964). The interaction of cognitive and physiological determinants of emotional state. In L. Berkowitz (Ed.), *Advances in experimental social psychology* (Vol. 1, pp. 49–80). New York: Academic Press.

Schachter, S. (1967). Cognitive effects on bodily functioning: Studies of obesity and eating. In D. C. Glass (Ed.), *Neurophysiology and emotion* (pp. 49–80). New York: Rockefeller University Press.

Scheier, I. H., & Cattell, R. B. (1960). *Handbook and test kit for the IPAT 8 Parallel Form Battery.* Champaign, IL: Institute for Personality and Ability Testing.

Schocken, D. D., Greene, A. G., Worden, T. J., Harrison, E. E., & Spielberger, C. D. (1987). Effects of age and gender on the relationship between anxiety and coronary artery disease. *Psychosomatic Medicine, 49,* 119–126.

Selye, H. (1956). *The stress of life.* New York: McGraw-Hill.

Southern, S., & Smith, R. (1982). *Behavioral self-management counseling for Type A coronary prone university students.* Unpublished manuscript.

Spielberger, C. D. (1966). Theory and research on anxiety. In C. D. Spielberger (Ed.), *Anxiety and behavior* (pp. 3–20). New York: Academic Press.

Spielberger, C. D. (1972). Anxiety as an emotional state. In C. D. Spielberger (Ed.), *Anxiety: Current trends in theory and research* (Vol. 1, pp. 24–49). New York: Academic Press.

Spielberger, C. D. (1976). Stress and anxiety and cardiovascular disease. *Journal of the South Carolina Medical Association* (Suppl., February), 15–22.

Spielberger, C. D. (1977). Anxiety: Theory and research. In B. B. Wolman (Ed.), *International encyclopedia of neurology, psychiatry, psychoanalysis, and psychology.* New York: Human Sciences Press.

Spielberger, C. D. (1979). *Understanding stress and anxiety.* London: Harper & Row.

Spielberger, C. D. (1983). *Manual for the State–Trait Anxiety Inventory* (rev. ed.). Palo Alto, CA: Consulting Psychologists Press.

Spielberger, C. D., & Gorsuch, R. L. (1966). *Mediating process in verbal conditioning.* Final report to the National Institutes of Health, U.S. Public Health Service on Grants MH 7229, MH 7446, and HD 947.

Spielberger, C. D., Gorsuch, R. L., & Lushene, R. D. (1970). *Manual for the State–Trait Anxiety Inventory.* Palo Alto, CA: Consulting Psychologists Press.

Spielberger, C. D., Jacobs, G., Crane, R., Russell, S., Westberry, L., Barker, L., Johnson, E., Knight, J., & Marks, E. (1979). *Preliminary manual for the State–Trait Personality Inventory (STPI).* Tampa: University of South Florida, Human Resources Institute.

Spielberger, C. D., Vagg, P. R., Barker, L. R., Donham, G. W., & Westberry, L. G. (1980). The factor structure of the State–Trait Anxiety Inventory. In I. G. Sarason & C. D. Spielberger (Eds.), *Stress and anxiety* (Vol. 7). Washington, DC: Hemisphere.

Steptoe, A., Melville, D., & Ross, A. (1982). Essential hypertension and psychological functioning: A study of factor workers. *British Journal of Clinical Psychology, 21,* 303–311.

Suinn, R., & Bloom, L. (1978). Anxiety management training for pattern A behavior. *Journal of Behavioral Medicine, 1,* 25–35.

Taylor, J. A. (1953). A personality scale of manifest anxiety. *Journal of Abnormal and Social Psychology, 48,* 285–290.

Vagg, P. R., Spielberger, C. D., & O'Hearn, T. P., Jr. (1980). Is the State–Trait Anxiety Inventory multidimensional? *Personality and Individual Differences, 1,* 202–214.

van der Ploeg, H. M., van Buuren, E. T., & van Brummelen, P. (1985). The role of anger in hypertension. *Psychotherapy and Psychosomatics, 43,* 186–193.

Weckowicz, T. E. (1978). Profile of Mood States. In O. K. Buros (Ed.), *The eighth mental measurements yearbook* (Vol. 1, pp. 1018–1019). Highland Park, NJ: Gryphon Press.

Welsh, G. S. (1956). Factor dimensions A and R. In G. S. Welsh & W. G. Dahlstrom (Eds.), *Basic readings on the MMPI in psychology and medicine* (pp. 264–281). Minneapolis: University of Minnesota Press.

Whitehead, W. E., Blackwell, B., DeSilva, H., & Robinson, A. (1977). Anxiety and anger in hypertension. *Journal of Psychosomatic Research, 21,* 383–389.

Zuckerman, M. (1960). Development of an affect adjective check list for the measurement of anxiety. *Journal of Consulting Psychology, 24,* 457–462.

Zuckerman, M., & Biase, D. V. (1962). Replication and further data on the Affect Adjective Check List measures of anxiety. *Journal of Consulting Psychology, 26,* 291.

Zuckerman, M., & Lubin, B. (1965). *Manual for the Multiple Affect Adjective Check List.* San Diego, CA: Educational and Industrial Testing Service.

II

BIOLOGICAL APPROACHES TO ANXIETY

5

Physiology of the Autonomic Nervous System as Related to Cardiovascular Function: Implications for Stress Research

Paul Hjemdahl

INTRODUCTION

Cardiovascular adaptation to various stressful conditions and alterations of cardiovascular function in various disease states are often mediated by the autonomic nervous system. In addition, local factors can modulate cardiovascular function, especially blood flow to the myocardium and skeletal muscle. Aspects to be considered in the context of autonomic function include sympathetic nerve activity, the circulating "stress hormone" epinephrine mainly released from the adrenal medullae, parasympathetic (mainly vagal) nerve activity, and the various receptors mediating the effects of autonomic activation. Sympathetic nerves release norpinephrine as their primary transmitter. Norepinephrine may, under some conditions, also act as a circulating hormone. Recently interest has also focused on the possibility that co-stored agents such as neuropeptide Y and adenosine triphosphate may be involved in sympathetic neurotransmission. Finally, there are hypotheses that epinephrine may be co-stored with norepinephrine in sympathetic nerves and that some organs, notably the kidneys, may have a subset of nerves using dopamine as their main transmitter also in the periphery. Parasympathetic nerves release acetylcholine, which is rapidly broken down by cholinesterase and therefore acts primarily as a neurotransmitter. No hormonal link seems to exist in the parasympathetic nervous system.

Sympathetic nerve activity can be evaluated by nerve activity recordings, by measurements of norepinephrine release, or by studying effects of drugs influencing sympathetic function. The relation between plasma norepinephrine and nerve activity is an important topic, as plasma norepinephrine analyses are a frequently used and often misunderstood tool to assess sympathetic nerve activity in humans. The importance of epinephrine as a circulating stress hormone will be discussed. Possible physiological functions of pre- and postjunctional receptors and how these can be assessed will be commented on, as this field in my opinion sometimes is rather uncritical when

Preparation of studies from our laboratory presented in this chapter have been supported mainly by grants from the Swedish Heart Lung Foundation, the Swedish Medical Research Council (Grant #5930), and the Karolinska Institute.

it comes to human studies. Practical examples will be taken mainly from studies of autonomic mechanisms in mental stress, as this example illustrates how differentiated the patterns of activity of the autonomic nervous system may be. This overview of autonomic receptors and autonomic nerve activity in relation to circulating epinephrine, as well as how these systems can be studied in humans, will by necessity be brief in relation to the immense literature in the field.

Many examples will be taken from my own studies, which may give a limited outlook on the vast literature in the field, but which has the advantage that the studies have been performed under similar conditions and that catecholamines have been determined with the same and well-validated plasma catecholamine assay. This facilitates comparisons of studies. (For further information regarding sympathetic mechanisms and stress research, see, e.g., Christensen, Henriksen, & Lassen, 1986; and a Workshop Summary by Steptoe, 1987.) Methodological issues involved in studies of autonomic mechanisms will be emphasized in this chapter, which will mainly concern data obtained in humans; relevant animal data will also be mentioned.

PERIPHERAL AUTONOMIC RECEPTORS

Autonomic receptors may be situated either *prejunctionally* ("presynaptic" is best applied to the central nervous system), that is, on nerves and influencing neurotransmitter release, or *postjunctionally* on effector cells. Schematic outlines of neurotransmission and autonomic receptors in the heart and blood vessels are shown in Figures

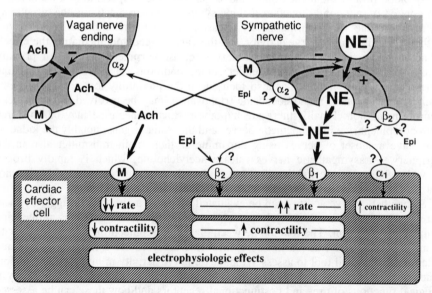

Figure 1 Schematic overview of pre- and postjunctional adrenergic and muscarinic receptors (M) involved in sympathetic and parasympathetic neurotransmission in the heart. Plus or minus signs refer to enhancement or inhibition of the release of norepinephrine (NE) or acetylcholine (Ach) per nerve impulse. Question marks refer to some doubt concerning the physiological importance of a mechanism, not the existence of it. A bold arrow indicates that the mechanism probably is more important than if it is indicated by a thin arrow.

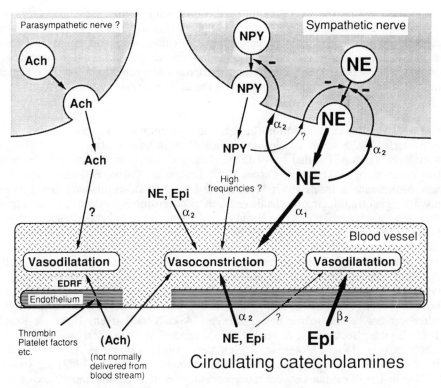

Figure 2   Schematic overview of sympathetic and parasympathetic regulation of vascular smooth muscle. Other prejunctional mechanisms than those involving α_2- and NPY-mediated mechanisms in sympathetic nerves are indicated in Fig. 1. A few factors evoking the release of endothelium derived relaxing factor (EDRF) are indicated.

1 and 2. Adrenergic receptors may be differentially activated by catecholamines because of intrinsic characteristics of the receptors (e.g., the subclass of a beta-receptor), intrinsic properties of the agonist (norepinephrine or epinephrine), and their accessibility from the neuroeffector junction or from the bloodstream. It will be argued that adrenergic receptors may be *innervated* or noninnervated, that is, *humoral*, and that functional differentiation of sympathoadrenal responses in part may be related to the anatomical localization of the receptors involved. Cholinergic receptors are believed to be innervated due to rapid inactivation of acetylcholine.

Adrenergic Receptors

Ahlquist (1948) categorized adrenergic receptors into alpha- and beta-adrenoceptors on the basis of functional responses to a series of adrenergic agonists. Alpha-adrenoceptors had stimulatory effects on smooth muscle, whereas beta-adrenoceptors relaxed smooth muscle and stimulated the heart. Later, these receptors were further subdivided into beta-1 and beta-2 adrenoceptors (Lands, Arnold, McAuliff, 1967) and alpha-1 and alpha-2 adrenoceptors (Berthelsen & Pettinger,

1977). There are specific dopamine receptors, which may be subdivided into dopamine-1 and dopamine-2, also in the periphery (Lokhandwala, 1988). In addition, atypical receptors activated by norepinephrine, or gamma-receptors (Hirst, DeGleria, & van Helden, 1985), and noncatecholamine-related neurotransmitter mechanisms (mainly neuropeptide Y and adenosine triphosphate, according to present knowledge) may be involved in sympathetic control of the cardiovascular system.

Beta-adrenoceptors

The structure and function of beta-adrenoceptors have been quite well-characterized in a series of elegant studies of their biochemistry and coupling to transducer mechanisms that translate receptor occupancy into junctional responses (for reviews see Lefkowitz & Caron, 1987; Lefkowitz, Caron, & Stiles, 1984; Mahan, McKernan, & Insel, 1987; Motulsky & Insel, 1982). In this overview I do not discuss signal transducing mechanisms, such as adenosine-3,5-cyclic monophosphate formation and inositol phospate-related events. With regard to beta-adrenoceptor subtypes, it is important to realize that the initial classification of cardiac and adipose tissue receptors as being beta-1 adrenoceptors and bronchial and vascular smooth muscle receptors as beta-2 adrenoceptors has not stood the test of time. Initially, Carlsson, Åblad, Brändström, and Carlsson (1972) showed that both receptor subtypes coexist in isolated cat hearts and mediate increases in heart rate. This observation has been extended to show that about one-third of human cardiac beta-adrenoceptors belong to the beta-2 subtype (Ask, Stene-Larsen, Helle, & Resch, 1985; Brodde, Beckeringh, & Michel, 1987; Brodde, O'Hara, Zerkowski, & Rohm, 1984; Buxton, Jones, Molenaar, & Summers, 1987; Kauman & Lemoine, 1987; Waelbroeck et al., 1983; Watanabe, Jones, Manalan, & Besch, 1982; Zerkowski, 1986). Studies of cardiac beta-adrenoceptor subtypes illustrate the importance of verifying results from animal studies in humans as, for example, the rat heart has a greater predominance of beta-1 adrenoceptors (e.g., Ask et al., 1985). Cardiac beta-2 adrenoceptors are coupled to adenylate cyclase and are functionally operative (Ask et al., 1985; Brodde et al., 1987; Kauman & Lemoine, 1987; Waelbroeck et al., 1983; Zerkowski et al., 1986). In fact, one study showed that as many as 50% of the human cardiac beta-adrenoceptors were of the beta-2 subtype and that only these receptors were coupled to adenylate cyclase in human heart tissue (Waelbroeck et al., 1983). Interestingly, Kaumann and Lemoine (1987) reported that almost all of the adenylate cyclase stimulation afforded by epinephrine and two-thirds of that produced by norepinephrine was mediated through beta-2 adrenoceptors. Thus in humans there may well be situations in which cardiac beta-2 adrenoceptors are functionally important.

As in the heart, both beta-adrenoceptor subtypes seem to coexist and mediate the same effects in several organs, including the lungs (Furchgott, Wakade, Sorace, & Stollack, 1975) and adipose tissue (Hjemdahl & Linde, 1985). Other important beta-2-mediated responses include relaxation of smooth muscle other than vascular and bronchial smooth muscle, increased glycogenolysis (liver and skeletal muscle), tremor, uterine relaxation, and electrolyte shifts (epinephrine-induced hypokalemia is well known, but magnesium and calcium also decrease). Renin release seems to be enhanced via beta-1 adrenoceptors. Lymphocytes and neutrophils have beta-2 adrenoceptors often used to assess beta-adrenoceptor status in clinical studies, but their functional importance is somewhat unclear. Platelets have beta-2 adrenoceptors that are capable of stimulating cyclic AMP accumulation and reducing aggregability (Kerry & Scrutton, 1985), but their functional importance under in vivo conditions seems unclear because beta-blockade may reduce rather than enhance platelet aggregability (Frishman, Christodoulou, & Weksler, 1978).

Pharmacological tools used to assess beta-adrenoceptors include the nonselective agonist isoprenaline, beta-1 selective agonists (e.g., the partial agonist prenalterol or dobutamine; the latter also possesses weak alpha-agonistic properties), and beta-2 selective agonists (e.g., partial agonists used as bronchodilators, such as terbutaline and salbutamol). Antagonists may be beta-1 selective (e.g., atenolol, betaxolol, or metoprolol), beta-2 selective (ICI 118,551, which unfortunately now is unavailable for human use because of its toxicity in animals), nonselective and without intrinsic activity (e.g., propranolol, timolol, or sotalol), or nonselective with intrinsic sympathomimetic activity (e.g., pindolol). The latter are interesting from a therapeutic point of view, but are often unsuited for studies of beta-adrenergic mechanisms because of the complexity of mechanisms involved. (For reviews of the various drugs, see e.g., Benfield, Clissold, & Brogden, 1986; Beresford & Heel, 1986; Bilski, Halliday, Fitzgerald, & Wale, 1983; Brogden, Speight, & Avery, 1975; Frishman, 1981; Gilman, Goodman, Rall, & Murad, 1985; Heel, Brogden, Speight, & Avery, 1979; Man in't Veld & Schalekamp, 1983; Riddel, Harron, & Shanks, 1987; Singh, Deedwania, Nademanee et al., 1987.) It should be remembered that the selectivity of an agonist or antagonist for a certain receptor subtype is concentration-dependent, as is illustrated by studies with the beta-1 selective antagonist practolol (Lertora, Mark, & Johannses, 1975) and the beta-2 selective antagonist ICI 118,551 (Harry, Norris, Percival, & Young, 1988).

The endogenous beta-agonists have different effects on the two beta-adrenoceptor subtypes, as norepinephrine is quite beta-1 selective (Ariëns & Simonis, 1983; Bristow, Ginsburg, Gilbert, & Herschberger, 1987; Brodde, 1988; Lands et al., 1967) and epinephrine is *functionally* beta-2 selective when reaching tissues from the blood stream (e.g. Ariëns & Simonis, 1983; Hjemdahl, Akerstedt, Pollare, & Gillberg, 1983). The latter statement is at variance with some opinions in the literature. Thus some in vitro studies, especially receptor binding studies, indicate that epinephrine is not very selective for beta-2 adrenoceptors (Lefkowitz et al., 1984). However, it is important to distinguish responses evoked by physiological concentrations of epinephrine delivered from the lumen of a blood vessel from those occurring when epinephrine is artificially introduced (most often in supraphysiologic concentrations) to cell membrane or tissue preparations, in which receptors may be reached and activated independently of their functional anatomical localization. As is outlined in Figures 1 and 2 there is evidence that beta-1 adrenoceptors are innervated, whereas vascular beta-2 adrenoceptors seem to be humoral, that is, located at some distance from the neuroeffector junction (e.g., Rosell & Belfrage, 1979; Rusell & Moran, 1980). This forms the basis for the functional differentiation discussed later.

Alpha-adrenoceptors

The initial classification of alpha-1 adrenoceptors as postjunctional and alpha-2 adrenoceptors as prejunctional receptors was soon modified, as it was shown that both alpha-adrenoceptor subtypes may coexist and mediate the same effect in a given tissue (Alabaster & Davey, 1984; Davey, 1986; Hoffman & Lefkowitz, 1980; Langer & Shepperson, 1982; Starke & Docherty, 1980). Norepinephrine and epinephrine display no striking selectivities for either alpha-adrenoceptor subtype, even if epinephrine may have a certain degree of alpha-2 selectivity in some systems (Hjemdahl & Linde, 1985). Vasoconstriction is mediated via both alpha-adrenoceptor subtypes, as has been shown in several different animal models (Alabaster & Davey, 1984; Davey, 1986b; Langer & Shepperson, 1982) and also in humans (Goldberg & Robertson, 1984; Jie, van Brummelen, Bermey et al., 1987b). There is some evidence that alpha-1 adrenoceptors are innervated and alpha-2 adrenoceptors noninnervated (Alabaster & Davey, 1984; Davey, 1986b; Goldberg & Robertson, 1984; Langer, & Shepperson, 1982; Jie et al., 1987). Cardiac alpha-1 adrenoceptor stimulation can evoke an inotropic response (Aas, Skomedal, Osnes et al., 1986; Davey, 1986a; Endoh, 1986; Schümann, 1980), but the physiological importance of this mechanism has been questioned (Jakob, Nawrath, & Rupp, 1988). The subdivision of alpha-adrenoceptors may progress even further, as prejunctional alpha-2 adrenoceptors may have two different recognition sites (Hicks, Langer, & MaCrae, 1985). Other alpha-adrenoceptor mediated events of interest include enhanced platelet aggregation (Kerry & Scrutton, 1985), enhanced glycogenolysis in the liver, and modulation of smooth muscle tone in other organs, including the uterus (Gilman et al., 1985).

Pharmacological tools used to selectively stimulate or inhibit alpha-1 adrenoceptors include agonists, such as methoxamine or phenylephrine (the latter also has weak beta-stimulating properties), and antagonists such as prazosin or doxazosin. Alpha-2 adrenoceptors may be selectively stimulated by alpha-methylnoradrenaline or clonidine (a partial agonist that mainly acts at the central nervous system level) and selectively antagonized by the competitive antagonists yohimbine, rauwolscine, or idazoxan. (For reviews of these drugs, see, e.g., Alabaster & Davey, 1984; Cubbeddu, 1988; Davey, 1986b; Gilman et al., 1985; Goldberg & Robertson, 1983; Hoffman & Lefkowitz, 1980; Langer & Shepperson, 1982; Starke & Docherty, 1980; van Zwieten, 1985.) It should be remembered that some responses to alpha-blockade may be related to central nervous system effects (Cubbeddu, 1988; Goldberg et al., 1983) and that the noncompetitive (irreversible) antagonist phenoxybenzamine (often used to abolish alpha-adrenergic influences) has some alpha-1 selectivity and may leave alpha-2 adrenoceptors unblocked (Constantine & Lebel, 1980).

Functional and Anatomical Arrangement of Alpha- and Beta-Adrenoceptors

Beta-1 adrenoceptors may be innervated and beta-2 adrenoceptors located more distantly from the neuroeffector junction. The functional implication of this concept is that beta-adrenergic responses to increases in sympathetic nerve activity will be beta-1 mediated for two reasons: the beta-1 selectivity of the neurotransmitter norepinephrine and the anatomical localization of this subclass of receptors in relation to the nerves. Beta-mediated responses to circulating epinephrine, conversely, will be mainly beta-2 mediated, as epinephrine is an efficient beta-2 agonist and these receptors are noninnervated (humoral) receptors. Similarly, if alpha-1 adrenoceptors are innervated and alpha-2 adrenoceptors are humoral (Alabaster & Davey, 1984; Davey, 1986b; Goldberg & Robertson, 1984; Jie et al., 1987b; Langer & Shepperson, 1982) effects of neurally released norpinephrine will be alpha-1 mediated and those of circulation catecholamines will be alpha-2 mediated (Alabaster & Davey; 1984; Davey, 1986b; Goldberg & Robertson, 1984; Langer, & Shepperson, 1982; Jie et al., 1987). This concept has been questioned, but one must also remember that neurally released norepinephrine diffuses rather easily from the neuroeffector junction and may also influence noninnervated alpha- and beta-adrenoceptors.

The importance of the concept is clearly illustrated by vascular responses to increased sympathetic nerve activity and to elevations of circulating epinephrine. Sympathetic nerve activity almost invariably evokes vasoconstriction, whereas physiological increments of epinephrine in plasma (less than 10 nM) cause vasodilatation in most tissues. In tissues with few vascular beta-adrenoceptors (e.g., in skin), epinephrine produces alpha-mediated vasoconstriction. Circulating norepinephrine evokes alpha-mediated vasoconstriction also in the presence of vascular beta-adrenoceptors, as norepinephrine is beta-1 selective. Following nonselective beta-blockade by propranolol, the vasoconstrictor response to norepinephrine is little influenced, whereas the vasodilator epinephrine is converted into an even more potent vasoconstrictor than norepinephrine. Indeed, epinephrine is a more potent alpha-agonist that norepinephrine in several in vitro systems (Gilman et al., 1985). Thus the abundance and accessibility of introluminal vascular beta-2 adrenoceptors confer functional beta-2 selectivity to the mixed agonist epinephrine under normal physiological circumstances in most tissues.

The mixed responses to norepinephrine and epinephrine are illustrated in Figure 3 by some simple measurements. Responses to the nonselective beta-agonist isoprenaline and effects of nonselective beta-blockade by propranolol on responses to norepinephrine and epinephrine are shown. Beta-blockade reduced resting heart rate and systolic blood pressure, indicating significant cardiac sympathetic stimulation at rest. Without beta-blockade, norepinephrine increased systolic and diastolic blood pressure, whereas epinephrine and isoprenaline increased systolic blood pressure and decreased diastolic blood pressure. Heart rate increased little with epinephrine, but markedly with isoprenaline (less than 2 nM in plasma evoked an increase of 50 bpm). The reduction of diastolic blood pressure evoked by 4 nM epinephrine was similar to that evoked by 0.6 nM isoprenaline. Epinephrine was almost as efficient as isoprenaline with regard to beta-2 mediated (see Hjemdahl et al., 1983) elevations of cyclic AMP in plasma, indicating that epinephrine is quite active on beta-2 adrenoceptors and that the diastolic blood pressure response to epinephrine was modified by simultaneous alpha-effects. The modest increase in heart rate during epinephrine infusion (see Figure 3) does not mean that circulating epinephrine does not influence cardiac function at low physiological concentrations, as there are pronounced increases in stroke volume (Freyschuss, Hjemdahl, Juhlin-Dannfeldt, & Linde, 1986), which are reflected by the widening of pulse pressure. Following beta-blockade the heart rate responses to epinephrine and norepinephrine became similar, that is, concentration- and blood pressure-dependent (reflexogenic) bradycardia; systolic and diastolic blood pressure responses in relation to the plasma concentrations of norepinephrine and epinephrine after beta-blockade indicate that epinephrine is a potent alpha-adrenoceptor agonist. Thus, responses to the mixed agonist epinephrine are complicated, but beta-2 adrenoceptor stimulation is clearly a prominent feature when epinephrine is delivered via the circulation, in the normal physiological fashion.

Dynamic Regulation of Adrenergic Receptors

It is well established that beta-adrenoceptors may be dynamically regulated (Harden, 1983; Lefkowitz et al., 1984; Motulsky & Insel, 1982). Thus, downregulation occurs with beta-2 agonist treatment (i.e., antiasthmatic and tocolytic drugs). This seems to be confined to various beta-2 adrenoceptor mediated events (see, e.g., Martinsson, Larsson, & Hjemdahl, 1987). Similarly, chronic beta-1 adrenoceptor stimulation results in reduced cardiac beta-1 adrenoceptor responsiveness,

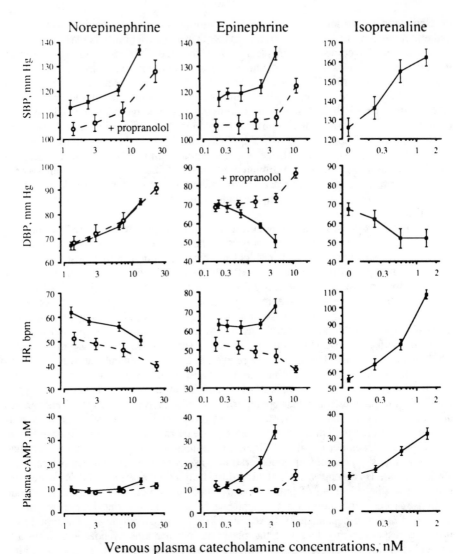

Venous plasma catecholamine concentrations, nM

Figure 3 A comparison of concentration–response curves for intravenously infused
norepinephrine, epinephrine, and isoprenaline with regard to systolic (SBP) and
diastolic (DBP) blood pressure, heart rate (HR), and plasma cyclic AMP (cAMP) in
healthy volunteers. Catecholamine concentrations were determined in antecubital
venous plasma. Responses to norepinephrine and epinephrine following nonselective
beta-blockade by propranolol (at a dose markedly inhibiting beta-2-mediated
enhancement of plasma cAMP by epinephrine) are also shown. It should be noted that
isoprenaline evokes marked beta-mediated responses at less than 1 nM and that
epinephrine influences heart rate relatively little before beta-blockade. After
beta-blockade, reflexogenic reductions of heart rate are similar for norepinephrine and
epinephrine, as are blood pressure responses. Data were derived from Hjemdahl et al.
(1983) and Martinsson et al. (1987).

whether induced pharmacologically (Leier, Nelson, Magorien, 1983) or by chronic cardiac sympathetic activation, such as in heart failure. Cardiac beta-2 adrenoceptor, however, are not downregulated in heart failure (Bristow et al., 1987; Brodde, 1988). This illustrates the beta-1 selectivity of norepinephrine and that circulating epinephrine has minor influences on cardiac beta-adrenoceptors in heart failure.

Conversely, upregulation and increased beta-adrenoceptor sensitivity occur when receptors are not stimulated, such as in diseases with sympathetic degeneration (Bannister, Boylston, Davies et al., 1981; Robertson, Hollister, Carey et al., 1984), in patients with heart transplants (Bjønerheim, Simonsen, & Golf, 1987; Yusuf, Theodoropoulos, Mathias et al., 1987), or during chronic beta-blockade (Frishman, 1987; Lefkowitz & Caron, 1987; Lefkowitz et al., 1984; Mahan et al., 1987). The latter phenomenon is of clinical significance when beta-blockade is rapidly discontinued in patients with ischemic heart disease, as supersensitivity may cause withdrawal phenomena with increased symptoms. This supersensitivity can be demonstrated by infusions of isoprenaline in vivo (Nattel, Rangno, & Van Loon, 1979). My colleagues and I have compared somatic and mental provocations following metoprolol withdrawal (Olsson, Hjemdahl, & Rehnqvist, 1984, 1986) and found that the supersensitivity is peripheral in origin, as heart rate responses to mental stress are normal in the withdrawal phase (Olsson et al., 1986). Beta-blockers with intrinsic sympathomimetic activity do not upregulate beta-adrenoceptors on lymphocytes, probably because the receptors are occupied by the drug but not deprived of stimulation (Brodde, Daul, & Stuka, 1985). Findings of dynamic receptor regulation on lymphocytes entail some methodological problems.

Platelet alpha-2 adrenoceptors may also be up- or downregulated by changes in stimulation (Davies, Sudera, Sagnella et al., 1982; Egan, Neubig, & Julius, 1985; Hollister, FitzGerald, Nadeau, & Robertson, 1983; Onrot, Goldberg, Biaggioni et al., 1987), but changes do not seem to be related to alpha-adrenoceptor responsiveness in vivo (Egan et al., 1985). Phenylephrine sensitivity in vivo (alpha-1 sensitivity) is increased in patients with autonomic dysfunction (Onrot et al., 1987). Denervation by 6-hydroxydopamine showed upregulation of beta-adrenoceptors but not of alpha-1 adrenoceptors in the heart (Chess-Williams, Broadley, & Sheridan, 1987). Tolerance to prazosin, which produces clear-cut arterial and venous dilator responses after the first dose (e.g., Awan, Miller, Maxwell, & Mason, 1977), may result in diminished hemodynamic changes and signs of reduced alpha-1 blockade in the long term (Eklund, Hjemdahl, Seideman, & Atterhög, 1983; Izzo, Horwitz, & Keiser, 1981; Mancia, Ferrari, Gregorini et al., 1980). This may involve several complex physiologic mechanisms of adaptation (sodium retention, etc.), but may also involve receptor adaptation (Hamilton & Reid, 1982; von Bahr, Lindström, & Seideman, 1982). Dynamic receptor regulation is less well established with regard to alpha-adrenoceptors than it is with beta-adrenoceptors.

Dopamine Receptors

Dopamine is a complex agonist with concentration-dependent actions. Thus, low-dose dopamine infusion causes dopamine-receptor mediated vasodilatation in certain vascular beds, particularly in the kidney, and increases natriuresis. Intermediate doses increase cardiac output via beta-1 adrenoceptor stimulation, and high doses elevate peripheral vascular resistance by activating alpha-adrenoceptors (Goldberg, 1972). The complicated dose–response relationships for various effects of dopamines are utilized in intensive care. Dopamine receptors may also inhibit norepinephrine release from postganglionic sympathetic nerves or ganglionic transmission and may influence aldoserone secretion (Lokhandwala & Barrett, 1982).

With regard to dopamine receptor subtypes, dopamine-1 receptors mediate mainly postjunctional effects, whereas dopamine-2 receptor stimulation reduces norepinephrine release (Goldberg, 1972; van Zwieten, 1985). However, as with alpha- and beta-adrenoceptors, this subdivision should not be viewed too categorically (Goldberg, 1972). Selective dopamine-1 agonists (e.g., fenoldopam) cause hypotension, renal vasodilatation, diuresis, and natriuresis. Dopamine-2 selective agonists (bromocriptine and certain ergot compounds, such as lergotrile and pergolide) reduce blood pressure, heart rate, and vascular resistance, presumably by reducing norepinephrine release. Bromocriptine readily passes the blood–brain barrier (it is mainly used to treat Parkinson's disease). Dopamine-1 selective and dopamine-2 selective antagonists (e.g., SCH-23390 and domperidone, respectively) may be used to block dopamine receptor subtypes differentially. The conventional neuroleptic dopamine receptor antagonists (e.g., haloperidol or chlorpromazine) often have other effects besides dopamine receptor blockade (Gilman et al., 1985).

Cholinergic Receptors

Cholinergic receptors are divided into *nicotinic* receptors (with one subclass acting at the skeletal muscle end plate and another subclass acting at the ganglionic level and in the adrenal medullae to enhance postganglionic sympathetic and parasympathetic nerve activity and epinephrine release, respectively), and *muscarinic* receptors (Gilman et al., 1985). This discussion concerns only muscarinic receptors. They may be activated by acetylcholine or synthetic agonists, such as methacholine or carbachol, and inhibited by anticholinergic agents, such as atropine. Prominent effects of muscarinic receptor stimulation in the cardiovascular system may be vasodilatation, bradycardia, and reduced cardiac contractile force. In addition, muscarinic receptor stimulation can reduce transmitter overflow from sympathetic and parasympathetic nerves (Gilman et al., 1985; Löffelholz & Pappano, 1985).

It has become increasingly evident that also muscarinic receptors are heterogenous and can be subdivided into at least two classes: M_1, with a high affinity for the atypical antagonist pirenzipine and apparently linked to phosphoinositide turnover, and M_2, with a low affinity for pirenzipine and inhibiting adenylate cyclase (Birdsall & Hulme, 1983; Hammer & Giachetti, 1982; Noronha-Blob, Lowe, Hanson, & U, Prichard, 1987; Woodcock, Leung, & Mcleod, 1987). M_2 receptors seem to predominate in the cardiovascular system, and M_1 receptors in the central nervous system and in ganglia (Birdsall & Hulme, 1983; Hammer & Giachetti, 1982). It may be possible to differentiate cardiac and smooth muscle M_2 receptors (Birdsall & Hulme, 1983) and to develop cardioselective muscarinic antagonists (Anwar-ul, Gilani, & Cobbin, 1986). However, the most frequently used muscarinic antagonist, atropine, is nonselective for muscarinic receptor subtypes.

Thus there is a basis for pharmacological differentiation of muscarinic receptor-mediated events, and further developments can be expected in the near future. The complexity of muscarinic receptor regulation is illustrated by findings that cholinergic agonists may have negative or positive inotropic effects, depending on their concentrations and on the state of stimulation of the cardiac preparation (Korth & Kühlkamp, 1987; Loffelholz & Pappano, 1985). In analogy with adrenergic receptors muscarinic receptors may also be dynamically regulated by the degree of stimulation (El-

Fakahany & Lee, 1986). Given the possibilities for complicated regulation of human cardiovascular muscarinic receptors and the sparsity of studies in that field, more knowledge is needed. (For an update on muscarinic receptor physiology and biochemistry, see Hirschowitz, Hammer, Giachetti et al., 1984; Levine, Birdsall, Giachetti et al., 1986.). Even if animal research has provided interesting information on muscarinic receptors and tools to study them, atropine remains the main tool for studies of cholinergic cardiovascular mechanisms in human.

Purinergic Receptors

Because sympathetic nerves store and release adenosine triphosphate (norepinephrine is bound to it in the storage granules) and because adenosine triphosphate evokes postjunctional events, so-called purinergic mechanisms may also be involved in sympathetic neurotransmission. Purinergic receptors may be subdivided into several subclasses. For example, P_2 receptors are stimulated by, and mediate postjunctional effects of, adenosine triphosphate (Burnstock, 1986), whereas P_1 receptors (adenosine A_1 subtype) are stimulated by adenosine, a breakdown product (Burnstock, 1986; Fredholm, Gustafsson, Hedqvist, & Sollevi, 1982). P_2 receptors may be inhibited by an antagonist, $ANPP_3$, or desensitized by a stable analogue, alpha/beta methylene adenosine triphosphate (Burnstock, 1986). The desensitization technique is the one most frequently used to study the role of adenosine triphosphate. Adenosine A_1 receptors are frequently implicated in prejunctional modulation of neurotransmission; these receptors are blocked by methylxanthines, such as theophylline or caffeine (Fredholm et al., 1982).

Other Receptors

Apart from the conventional adrenergic receptors, it is possible that sympathetic nerves may activate other receptors. It has been proposed that norepinephrine might act on a third type of receptor, called gamma-receptors (Hirst et al., 1985). This is mainly based on findings that competitive alpha-adrenoceptor blockade fails to abolish effects of iontophoretically applied norepinephrine at certain intrasynaptic locations but does so at other sites. However, noncompetitive blockade may be needed to overcome such effects, and the theory has not gained wide acceptance. Peptides also exert their effects via receptors. For example, specific and saturable binding of a certain portion of neuropeptide Y to tissue preparations has been demonstrated (Edvinsson, Håkanson, Wahlestedt, & Uddman, 1987; Haynes, 1986; Lundberg, Pernow, Franco-Cereceda, & Rudehill, 1987). However, the lack of specific antagonists for these receptors makes their evaluation difficult.

Techniques Frequently Used to Study Autonomic Receptors

Adrenergic and cholinergic receptors can be studied by quantitation of receptors by radioligand binding studies in tissues or membrane preparations in vitro or by stimulating or inhibiting various responses to autonomic stimulation in vivo or in vitro. By use of selective agonists or antagonists, the various subclasses of adrenergic and muscarinic receptors can be identified and effects they mediate can be characterized. Dose-response studies with agonists can identify a certain response and give an idea of the dynamic range of receptor-mediated control of this function, but it is important to keep in mind that they do not prove its functional significance. Inhibition of the response to a relevant physiological stimulus in vivo (e.g., exercise or mental stress) by an appropriate antagonist is indicative of a physiologically operating mechanism, but results may be complicated by other events (such as reflexogenic mechanisms) occurring in the complex in vivo system. This may be circumvented by local (intra-arterial) administration of the drug, which, however, seldom is done in humans because of practical limitations.

In vitro full–dose–response curves for agonists and high concentrations of antagonists, which fully block the receptor in question (but that may have nonspecific effects as well), can be studied. In vitro conditions also allow "cleaner" assessments of responses, which may be influenced by the endogenous environment or reflexogenic activity under in vivo condition. In vitro, a combination of functional response studies (e.g., heart rate or contractility responses to isoprenaline in a cardiac preparation) and radioligand binding studies (e.g., ^{125}I-labeled beta-blockers) will establish the presence of a receptor in the tissue. However, the receptor may not be activated in proportion to its occurrence in the in vivo setting, as the nature of endogenuous stimulus will be of paramount importance. For example, if moderately elevated epinephrine levels acting on beta-2 adrenoceptor compete with high levels of the beta-1 selective agonist norepinephrine in the neuroeffector junction (e.g., during exercise), the resulting response will be beta-1 mediated. The question of when epinephrine may become important is discussed subsequently.

One way of differentiating subtypes of receptors is to study responses to provocations or exogenously given agonists after administration of a subtype-selective antagonist. For example, effects of neuronal activation of beta-adrenoceptors by norepinephrine and humoral activation by epinephrine can be distinguished by comparing effects of beta-1 and beta-2 selective or nonselective beta-blockade (Brodde, Daul, Wellstein et al., 1988; Hjemdahl et al., 1983; McLeod, Brown, Kuhn et al., 1983). Responses thus attributable to beta-2 adrenoceptors are probably caused by epinephrine. As was mentioned, however, selectivity is dose-related (Lertora et al., 1975), and too high a dose of a beta-1 selective antagonist may also block beta-2 mediated effects of epinephrine.

Many in vitro studies are performed with supraphysiological doses of agonists, which leaves room to doubt their physiological significance. For example, isoprenaline is often used at concentrations of 10^{-6} M or even higher in vitro, whereas 10^{-9} M in plasma evokes marked cardiovascular and metabolic effects in vivo (see Figure 3). Similarly, epinephrine is often studied in vitro at concentration that are 3 to 4 orders of magnitude above those actually occurring in vivo. Findings with high agonist concentrations in vitro should be verified under in vivo conditions before the proposed mechanism is accepted as being physiologically relevant; it may prove to be a redundant, although experimentally demonstrable mechanism. Appropriate antagonists should also inhibit responses to physiological stimuli. Thus several lines of evidence are usually needed to prove the importance of a sympathoadrenal or cholinergic regulatory mechanism.

Even if it is important to verify in vitro findings in vivo, it should be realized that in vivo studies are performed under complex circumstances. Important problems when interpretating in vivo data are that responses often are mixed, that is, caused by the concerted action of the exogenous agonist or antagonist and endogenous influences, such as reflex activation or inhibition of autonomic nerves, release of hormones, or other changes (e.g., electrolyte shifts) influencing the target organ, and that full dose–response curves for obvious reasons seldom can be constructed in human. The complexity of the in vivo setting is often disregarded when results are favorable to the hypothesis, as is illustrated for example by the overinterpretation of plasma norepinephrine responses to beta-adrenergic stimulation in humans. Practical limitations may be even greater on the cholinergic side (inhibition of vagal influences on the heart may cause profound changes not related to cholinergic receptor function—see below), but in vitro findings regarding muscarinic receptor mechanisms should nonetheless be verified in relevant in vivo models. All demonstrable effects of muscarinic stimulation in vitro or in vivo may not be relevant, if acetylcholine is a locally acting neurotransmitter and cholinergic innervation is sparse or distant from the target site of interest. One example is if endogenous acetylcholine influences the endothelium and/or other aspects of vascular control.

Relevance of Adrenergic Receptor Studies on Blood Cells

Most studies of human adrenergic receptor physiology are performed on white blood cells endowed with beta-2 adrenoceptors or platelets endowed with alpha-2 and beta-2 adrenoceptors, because it is difficult to obtain tissue specimens for studies of adrenoceptor function in humans. Elaborate hypotheses concerning abnormalities of peripheral (or even central nervous system) adrenoceptor function in disease states may be based on studies performed only on blood cells. For example, a claim that alpha-2 adrenoceptor function is altered in Type A behavior (Kahn, Perumal, Gully et al., 1987) was based on such radioligand binding data and even lacked primary results from the binding assay (only ratios of alpha-2 to beta-2 adrenoceptors on the blood cells were reported). Receptors on blood cells are, by definition, noninnervated and may reflect innervated solid tissue receptors poorly. Even if they do reflect receptors in a certain solid tissue under some circumstances, this may not always be the case. It is therefore pertinent to give serious consideration to the possibility of differences in receptor regulation between blood cells and different solid tissues, even though they may be endowed with seemingly similar receptors.

Cardiac beta-2 adrenoceptors (but not beta-1 adrenoceptors) have been shown to correlate well with lymphocyte beta-2 adrenoceptors (Brodde et al., 1987; Michel, Beckeringh, Ikezono et al., 1986), as have pulmonary beta-2 adrenoceptors do not reflect pulmonary alpha-1 adrenoceptors (Liggett, Marker, Shah et al., 1988). Whether changes in these beta-2 adrenoceptors evoked by treatment or disease mirror each other has not been adequately studied. Platelet alpha-2 adrenoceptors (Liggett et al., 1988). Whether they reflect alpha-2 adrenoceptors in solid tissues does not seem to have been established. Upregulation of beta-adrenoceptors by beta-blockade has been shown to be similar in lymphocytes, cardiac tissue, and lung tissue in rats (Aarons & Molinoff, 1982). Downregulation may influence tissues differently (Hasegawa & Townley, 1983); beta-2 agonist treatment reduces several responses to beta-2 stimulation in vivo (see, e.g., Harvey, Baldwin, Wood et al., 1981; Martinsson et al., 1987). Thus there is some evidence that blood cell beta-receptors may reflect other receptors, but caution is advisable when extrapolating from in vitro results.

An interesting observation is that lymphocyte beta-2 adrenoceptors seem to be biphasically regulated by adrenergic stimulation. Thus infusions of epinephrine or isoprenaline initially increase and subsequently (during prolonged infusions) decrease receptor density (Tohmeh & Cryer, 1980). Results have, however, differed (DeBlasei, Maisel, Feldman et al., 1986). My colleagues and I have found initial upregulation of lymphocyte beta-2 adrenoceptors (and increased responsiveness) during epinephrine infusion, but not during mental stress. With regard to the subsequent downregulation, however, we found that responsiveness (isoprenaline-induced cyclic AMP accumulation) was clearly reduced, but that receptor numbers only returned to baseline after 3 hours of epinephrine infusion (Larsson, Martinsson, Olsson, &Hjemdahl, 1990). These changes of lymphocyte beta-2 adrenoceptors were not accompanied by changes of platelet alpha-adrenoceptors (Larsson et al., 1987). Changes in posture may (Feldman, Limbird, Nadeau et al., 1983) or may not (DeBlasei et al., 1986) alter lymphocyte receptors. Exercise increases lymphocyte beta-2 adrenoceptors in most studies (Brodde, Daul, & O'Hara, 1984; Brodde, Daul, Wang et al., 1989; Landmann, Poertenier, Staehlin et al., 1988; Middeke, Remien, & Holzgreve, 1984), but receptor density may also decrease with physical activity (Krawietz, Klein, Unterberg, & Ackenheil, 1985). Thus, beta-adrenoceptors may be dynamically regulated in the short term, because adrenergic stimulation may result in either enhanced or reduced responsiveness.

One important point to keep in mind when interpreting studies of dynamic receptor regulation in blood cells is that white blood cell counts and the relative proportions of subsets of lymphocytes may vary (Griese, Körholz, Körholz et al., 1988; Postma, Kreyzer, Meurs et al., 1985). Recruitment of cells with different characteristics into the circulation may well explain findings of altered receptor function after sympatho-adrenal stimulation. In particular, it is difficult to reconciliate changes in lymphocyte receptors during a mild stimulus such as standing with agonist-promoted receptor regulation (Feldman et al., 1988), because standing causes very modest elevations of the endogenous beta-2 agonist epinephrine in plasma. The effect of exercise on lymphocyte beta-adrenoceptors may be explained by an altered T- to B-cell ratio in peripheral blood (Landmann et al., 1988). Catecholamine infusions do not appear to alter circulating T- to B-cell ratios (Tohmeh & Cryer, 1980), but changes in the cell population may nonetheless have been of importance. The hypothesis of dynamic receptor regulation (initial upregulation followed by downregulation) should be verified in solid tissues, in which the receptor population remains stable.

A trend during recent years has been to study autonomic receptors (both adrenergic and cholinergic) from the standpoint of radioligand binding characteristics only, and to overlook the functional point of view. This is questionable when one considers that beta-adrenoceptor desensitization involves functional changes before changes in binding characteristics (Kassis, Olasma, Sullivan, & Fishman, 1986; Terasaki, Linden, & Brooker, 1979). Thus receptor studies should preferably include some relevant response, and not only radioligand binding characteristics.

Adrenergic Agonist Infusion Tests
as Measures of Receptor Function In Vivo

Adrenoceptor function is often assessed in vivo by giving catecholamines or other adrenergic agonists as bolus injections or as continuous infusions. Epinephrine sensitivity is of physiological interest, but the mixed nature of responses complicates receptor studies. Some responses to exogenously administered norepinephrine may, for practical purposes, be considered to be alpha-mediated (see Figure 3), but norepinephrine is also a beta-1 agonist. Beta-blockade is therefore advisable when using norepinephrine to study alpha-adrenergic mechanisms, if it is not contraindicated, for example, by asthma.

Isoprenaline sensitivity testing. The nonselective agonist isoprenaline is frequently used to study beta-adrenoceptor sensitivity in humans. The classical test is based on bolus injections of isoprenaline recordings of doses that elevate heart rate (peak responses recorded by electrocardiogram [ECG] by 25 beats/minute (Cleaveland, Rangno, & Shand, 1972; George, Conolly, Fenyvesi et al., 1972; Wood, 1987). Such heart rate responsiveness has been found to correlate with lymphocyte responsiveness in vitro (FitzGerald, Doyle, Kelly, & O'Malley, 1984; Jennings, Bobik, Esler, & Korner, 1980). Alternatively, isoprenaline may be infused, and heart rate (Frohlich, Tarazi, & Dustan, 1969) or beta-mediated vasodilatation, finger tremor or hypokalemia may be studied (Wood, 1987). Heart rate responses to injected (Brown, McLeod, & Shand, 1983) or infused (Arnold, O'Connor, Riddell et al., 1985; Brodde, Daul, Wellstein et al., 1988; McGibney, Singleton, Like, & Taylor, 1983) isoprenaline also appear to be beta-2 mediated. Elevation of cAMP in plasma is another sensitive humoral beta-2 mediated response to infused isoprenaline (Hjemdahl et al., 1983; Martinsson, Larsson, & Hjemdahl, 1985, 1987; Martinsson, Lindvall, Melcher, & Hjemdahl, 1989) and epinephrine (see Figure 3).

The two major problems with isoprenaline sensitivity testing in vivo are that reflexogenic mechanisms may be involved and that studies usually are performed as dose–response studies not taking pharmacokinetic variation into account. Reflexogenic activation must be considered when an agent causes marked vasodilatation, as is the case with isoprenaline. Bolus injections of isoprenaline seem to cause reflex withdrawal of vagal tone (Arnold & McDevitt, 1986; Jennings, Bobik, Esler, & Korner, 1981; Martinsson et al., 1989), whereas vagal activity has been claimed to increase during continuous infusions of isoprenaline (Arnold & McDevitt, 1984, 1986). My colleagues and I found a methodological explanation for the latter finding. It is difficult to evaluate if and to what extent cardiac sympathetic nerve activity is altered by isoprenaline. The best way to avoid confounding reflexogenic mechanisms when evaluating beta-adrenoceptor is to administer the drug locally, that is, intra-arterially. Such techniques have been used to evaluate vasodilator responsiveness to isoprenaline (Van Brummelen, Bühler, Kiowski, & Amann, 1984) and cardiac responsiveness to dobutamine (Colucci, Leatherman, Ludmer, & Gauthier, 1987). Another way is to pretreat subjects with drugs that inhibit reflexes without influencing beta-adrenoceptors. A combination of atropine (inhibiting vagal influences) and clonidine (inhibiting sympathetic outflow at the central nervous system level) provides a useful alternative (Jennings et al., 1981; Martinsson et al., 1989). Such treatment enhances the vasodepressor response and attenuates increases in plasma norepinephrine (Martinsson et al., 1989), indicating that a counterregulatory sympathetic vasoconstrictor reflex is activated by isoprenaline.

The interindividual variation of isoprenaline kinetics in plasma is quite large (see Figure 4); up to sixfold differences of plasma isoprenaline concentrations are achieved during standardized infusions (Hjemdahl, Martinsson, & Larsson, 1986). At the group level, patients and controls may differ with regard to concentrations (Martinsson et al., 1985). Isoprenaline kinetics in plasma may also vary within individuals, as exemplified by higher plasma levels after atropine and clonidine (Martinsson et al., 1989). In fact, heart rate responsiveness to infused isoprenaline influenced by autonomic reflexes if results were related to concentrations in plasma. Thus studies of plasma concentration–effect curves improve the precision of isoprenaline sensitivity testing in vivo. In addition, continuous infusions allow concentration–effect studies of responses other than heart rate, as well as measurements under "semi" steady-state.

Phenylephrine sensitivity testing. Phenylephrine may be used to assess alpha-1 adrenoceptor sensitivity in vivo in animals and humans. Also phenylephrine can be given as bolus injections or as constant infusions; dose–response curves for pressor effects (usually a blood pressure increase of 20 mm Hg) are constructed. There is pharmacokinetic variation also for phenylephrine in plasma, albeit smaller than for

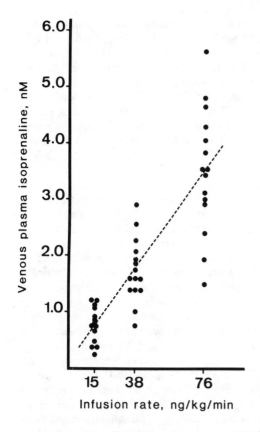

Figure 4 Individual venous plasma isoprenaline concentrations determined after 8 min of infusion at three dose levels in 15 subjects. Note the up to sixfold interindividual variation of isoprenaline concentrations achieved in response to standardized doses (per kg body weight). Within individuals, increases in plasma isoprenaline are strictly dose-related. From Hjemdahl et al. (1986) by permission of publisher and author.

isoprenaline (Martinsson, Bevegard, & Hjemdahl, 1986). Reflexogenic mechanisms are important for responses to phenylephrine. Reductions of plasma norepinephrine (Eckberg, Rea, Andersson et al., 1988; Martinsson et al., 1986) and muscle sympathetic nerve activity (Eckberg et al., 1988) concomitantly with blood pressure elevations suggest that withdrawal of vasoconstrictor nerve activity buffers pressor responses. It should be kept in mind that heart period changes in response to injected phenylephrine form the basis for the well-known Oxford test for baroreceptor sensitivity and that blood pressure is influenced also by cardiac output. Phenylephrine sensitivity correlates with baroreceptor sensitivity, but there also seems to be an independent component to the response, which reflects alpha-1 adrenoceptor sensitivity (Martinsson et al, unpublished).

SYMPATHETIC NEUROTRANSMISSION

Catecholamine Synthesis, Release, and Inactivation

Norepinephrine is the primary transmitter of sympathetic nerves, as was demonstrated by von Euler in 1946. (For reviews of sympathetic neurotransmission see Gilman et al., 1985; Kopin, 1985; Langer & Hicks, 1984.) A schematic presentation is given in Figure 5. Norepinephrine is synthesized from tyrosine by a series of

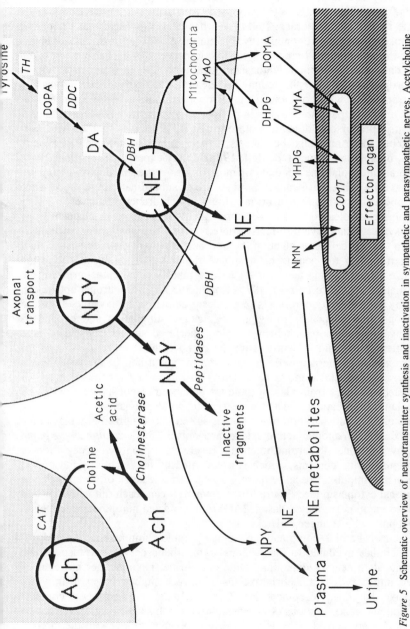

Figure 5 Schematic overview of neurotransmitter synthesis and inactivation in sympathetic and parasympathetic nerves. Acetylcholine (Ach), norepinephrine (NE), neuropeptide Y (NPY), dopamine (DA), 3,4-dihydroxyphenylglycol (DHPG), 3,4-dihydroxymandelic acid (DOMA), 3-methoxy-4-hydroxyphenylethyleneglycol (MHPG), 3-methoxy-4-hydroxy-mandelic acid (VMA), normetanephrine (NMN). Enzymes: tyrosine hydroxylase (TH), 1-aromatic amino acid decarboxylase or DOPA decarboxylase (DDC), dopamine-beta-hydroxylase (DBH), monoamine oxidase (MAO—acts on an intermediate aldehyde formed from NE), catechol-O-methyltransferase (COMT), choline acetyltransferase (CAT). Not shown are the formations of conjugates with sulfate and glucuronide that catecholamines and their metabolites undergo. Epinephrine forms metanephrine via COMT and subsequently VMA or MHPG. The end metabolites of DA (mainly formed in the central nervous system) are homovanillic acid (HVA) and conjugates of DA and HVA.

111

enzymatic steps: hydroxylation to form DOPA, decarboxylation of DOPA to form dopamine, and hydroxylation of dopamine to form norepinephrine. In adrenal medullary cells, norepinephrine is methylated to form epinephrine (phenylethanolamine-N-methyl transferase; PNMT). It has been suggested that peripheral sympathetic nerves also might contain PNMT, but the evidence for this is not clearcut. Most of the epinephrine found in sympathetic nerves has probably been taken up from the circulation. Whether synthesized locally or derived from the adrenals, it has been proposed that epinephrine may be released from sympathetic nerves and act as a co-transmitter with norepinephrine (Brown & Dollery, 1984; Rand & Majewski, 1984). Also dopamine is found in peripheral sympathetic nerves. This usually represents "precursor" dopamine stored in small amounts together with norepinephrine, but there may also be subsets of peripheral dopaminergic nerves in some organs, notably the kidney (see Bell, 1988). In my experience less than 2% to 3% of the total catecholamine contents of most tissues represent dopamine or epinephrine, suggesting that these catecholamines are of subordinate importance when compared to norepinephrine as neurotransmitters in noradrenergic nerves.

Norepinephrine is released by an exocytotic calcium-dependent mechanism upon excitation of sympathetic nerve terminals. There is active neuronal uptake of norepinephrine from the neuroeffector junction (by an "amine pump"), which has the dual function of terminating the neurogenic response rather rapidly and conserving the transmitter (i.e., reducing the need for *de novo* synthesis of norepinephrine in the nerves) (Gilman et al., 1985; Iversen, 1975; Kopin, 1985). This neuronal uptake can be inhibited by tricyclic antidepressants (e.g., desipramine) or by cocaine. Figure 6 shows vasoconstrictor responses to sympathetic nerve stimulation and exogenous (intra-arterially injected) norepinephrine in blood perfused skeletal muscle in vivo before and after desipramine. Neuronal uptake of norepinephrine is the major removal mechanism from the neuroeffector junction, as about half of the norepinephrine released is reaccumulated in the nerve but is also important for the clearance of circulating catecholamines from plasma (note the enhanced responsiveness to exogenous catecholamines in patients treated with tricyclic antidepressants).

After synthesis or reuptake, norepinephrine is stored in specialized granules in the nerve, which depend on another active uptake mechanism. This *granular amine pump* is inhibited by reserpine. Reserpine treatment results in a progressive depletion of granular norepinephrine contents, which is accelerated by nerve activity but occurs also without nerve impulses, because there is spontaneous leakage of norepinephrine into the neuronal cytoplasm (see Figure 5) from where it can reach mitochondria and be metabolized via monoamine oxidase (MAO) to deaminated norepinephrine metabolites (see Kopin, 1985; Langer & Hicks, 1984).

Both the neuronal amine pump and the storage granule pump take up the endogenous catecholamines available to them. Thus, sympathetic nerves may accumulate norepinephrine, its precursor dopamine, and epinephrine. Isoprenaline, however, is not taken up into nerves. Epinephrine seems to have a slightly lower affinity for neuronal uptake than does norepinephrine (Iversen, 1975) and also has to compete with high junctional concentrations of norepinephrine for this uptake system. Because epinephrine levels are considerably lower than norepinephrine levels in the circulation and norepinephrine is synthesized in large amounts in the neuron, it is quite logical that neuronal epinephrine concentrations should be very low in relation to norepinephrine concentrations. This is relevant to consider in relation to the proposed co-transmitter role for epinephrine.

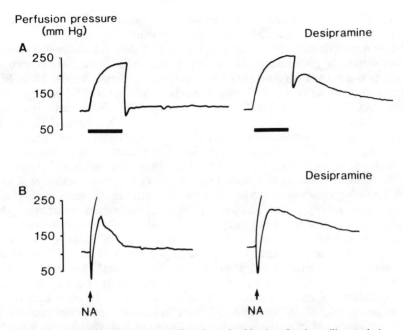

Figure 6 A: Perfusion pressure recordings in canine blood perfused gracilis muscle in connection with sympathetic nerve stimulation (2 Hz, 2 min; indicated by horizontal bars) before and after neuronal uptake inhibition by the tricyclic antidepressant desipramine. Note the rapid return toward basal perfusion pressure upon termination of sympathetic nerve stimulation in the absence of uptake inhibition. Desipramine doubles the norepinephrine overflow in this model and enhances the duration but not the magnitude of the vasoconstrictor response. Data from Kahan et al. (1984). B: Responses to intraarterial bolus doses of norepinephrine evoking similar peak vasoconstriction as in A (the initial upstroke of the pressure tracing is an artifact caused by the injection). Note the slow return toward basal perfusion pressure under control conditions (indicating the importance of neuronal uptake in the termination of responses to nerve stimulation in A) and the marked prolongation of vasoconstriction following desipramine.

Norepinephrine is also removed from the neuroeffector junction by diffusion (eventually into plasma) and by extraneuronal uptake followed by enzymatic conversion to the inactive metabolite normetanephrine (see Figure 5). Isoprenaline is also O-methylated. Intraneuronal deamination of norepinephrine via MAO results in the metabolites 3,4-dihydroxyphenylglycol (DHPG) and 3,4-dihydroxymandelic acid (DOMA). Metabolism via both MAO and catechol-O-methyltransferase (COMT) results in the end stage metabolites 3-methoxy-4-hydroxphenylethyleneglycol (MHPG) and 3-methoxy-4-hydroxy-mandelic acid (VMA) (see Gilman et al., 1985; Kopin, 1985). Inhibition of extraneuronal uptake and metabolism influences responses to neurally released norepinephrine less than does inhibition of neuronal uptake, but it enhances responses to circulating catecholamines more markedly (Iversen, 1975; Kopin, 1985; Rusell & Moran, 1980). This would be expected if neuronal uptake influences norepinephrine concentrations mainly at receptors in the vicinity of the neuroeffector junction and extraneuronal uptake influences norepinephrine and epinephrine levels at noninnervated receptors more markedly.

Another metabolic pathway for catecholamines (and their metabolites) is conjugation with sulfate or glucoronide. The catecholamine most extensively studied and discussed in this respect is dopamine (Ackerman, Hiebe, Sarau, & Jain, 1984; Bradley, Hjemdahl, DiBona et al., 1985; Buu & Kuchel, 1979; Cuche, Prinseau, Ruget et al., 1982; DeChamplain, Bovuier, Cleroux, & Farley, 1984; Demassieux, Bordeleau, Gravel, & Carriere, 1987; Joyce, Beilin, Vandongen, & Davidson, 1982; Kuchel, Buu, & Hamet, 1984; Kuchel, Buu, Racz et al., 1986; Michel, Lenz, Lernhardt et al., 1987; Ratge, Knoll, & Wisser, 1986; Romain, Demassieux, D'Angelo et al., 1986; Snider & Kuchel, 1983; Vandongen, 1984). Dopamine sulfate represents more than 98% of total dopamine in plasma (e.g., Ratge et al., 1986; Snider & Kuchel, 1983). Dopamine sulfation occurs in tissues and in platelets; it seems as if platelet sulfotransferase activity cannot account for the dopamine sulfation that takes place endogenously (e.g., Kuchel et al., 1984; Romain et al., 1986). Dopamine sulfate has been suggested to be biologically active (Buu & Kuchel, 1979; Snider & Kuchel, 1983), but there is little evidence is support that suggestion (Kopin, 1985). In fact, several studies (Ackerman et al., 1984; Bradley et al., 1985; Demassieux et al., 1987; Michel et al., 1987) have failed to find relevant effects of dopamine sulfates, even though deconjugation (formation of norepinephrine has even been demonstrated in vitro; Buu & Kuchel, 1979) might take place in tissues. Norepinephrine and epinephrine are much less extensively conjugated (Ratge et al., 1986; Snider & Kuchel, 1983). It is important to note that catecholamine conjugates may have a dietary origin (Vandongen, 1984). The overflow of conjugated dopamine to plasma is a less reliable indicator of dopamine release, at least from renal nerves (Bradley & Hjemdahl, 1984), than is the overflow of free dopamine. Thus, I do not agree with the opinion that conjugated catecholamines provide more reliable information on sympathetic activity than do the free catecholamines in plasma (Kuchel et al., 1986; Snider & Kuchel, 1983).

Catecholamines in plasma may also be taken up and stored in platelets and in red blood cells (DeChamplain et al., 1984). The catecholamines and their metabolites are excreted in urine in proportion to their concentrations in plasma. Urinary catecholamine excretion is influenced by glomerular filtration and by tubular uptake and secretion (Kopin, 1985). Urinary excretion is not important for the clearance of catecholamines from plasma; neuronal and extraneuronal mechanisms are of greater importance than urinary excretion for the removal of catecholamines from plasma even in the kidney (Kopp, Bradley, & Hjemdahl, 1983).

Nonadrenergic Sympathetic Neurotransmission: Possible Co-transmitters

There is a nonadrenergic vasoconstrictor component in several experimental models of sympathetic vascular control. Transmitters thought to mediate nonadrenergic vasoconstriction are mainly neuropeptide Y and adenosine phosphate (Burnstock, 1986, 1987; Edvinsson et al., 1987; Haynes, 1986; Lundberg et al., 1987; Potter, 1988; Stjärne, 1986). In addition, a number of other peptides and neuromodulators may influence vascular tone (see, e.g., Burnstock, 1987; Ganten, Lang, Archelos, & Unger, 1984; Pernow, 1984). Neuropeptide Y is stored in large dense-cored vesicles, which are recruited mainly at high stimulation frequencies, suggesting that release of this peptide might occur preferentially at high impulse frequencies (Haynes, 1986; Lundberg et al., 1987; Potter, 1988; Wharton, Gulbekian, Merighi et al., 1988). Norepinephrine is stored in both small and large vesicles. Neuropeptide Y is apparently inactivated by peptidases that produce more or less active peptide fragments, and it is not taken up into nerves (see Figure 5). Replenishment of neuropeptide Y stores in nerve terminals requires axonal transport from the nerve cell body where it is synthesized (Lundberg et al., 1987; Potter, 1988). Neuropeptide Y is released both from the adrenal glands and from sympathetic nerves (Edvinsson et al., 1987; Lundberg et al., 1987). Neuropeptide Y may have both pre- and postjunctional effects, resulting in reduced transmitter release (Lundberg et al., 1987; Edvinsson et al., 1987), construction of most blood vessels in vitro (Edvinsson et al., 1987; Lundberg et al., 1987; Potter, 1988; Waeber, Aubert, Corder et al., 1988) and vasoconstriction in several vascular beds in vivo (Lundberg et al., 1987; Wharton et al., 1988). However, not all blood vessels respond to neuropeptide Y (Lundberg et al., 1987). It is found in nerves close to blood vessles and myocytes in humans (Wharton et al., 1988). Cardiac effects have varied depending on the experimental model (Edvinsson et al., 1987; Potter, 1988). Perhaps coronary vascular responses (Tseng et al., 1988; Waeber et al., 1988) were more important than the direct effects of neuropeptide Y on the heart. Pre- and postjunctional neuropeptide Y receptors may differ (Haynes, 1986), but elucidation of these receptor mechanisms is hampered by the lack of specific antagonists.

Based on studies in isolated blood vessels, it has been suggested that low concentrations of neuropeptide Y might potentiate responses to norepinephrine, providing the possibility of synergistic dual transmission (e.g., Edvinsson et al., 1987; Potter, 1988). However, synergism is not seen in vivo in organs with normal vascular tone (Lundberg et al., 1987). The phenomenon has also been reported for several other vasoactive substances (e.g., serotonin) and may merely reflect a nonspecific subthreshold increase of tone by the potentiating agent in an atonic in vitro preparation.

How can the importance of neuropeptide Y be demonstrated without access to specific antagonists? Two interesting experimental models emerge—first, to examine responses after noncompetitive alpha-adrenoceptor blockade and, second, to deplete the sympathetic nerves of norepinephrine without depleting them of neuropeptide Y. Combined blockade of adrenergic receptors by the irreversible alpha-blocker phenoxybenzamine and propranolol (to remove beta-mediated vasodilator components in the response) failed to abolish vasoconstrictor responses to sympathetic stimulation in several in vivo models; norepinephrine is depleted and substantial amounts of neuropeptide Y are retained in the nerve if reserpine is given and nerve impulse activity is inhibited (Lundberg et al., 1987). There are substantial residual vasoconstrictor responses also in this model. Together with demonstrations of neuropeptide Y overflow from tissues in connection with sympathetic nerve stimulation, these results suggest that neuropeptide Y may mediate nonadrenergic sympathetic vasoconstriction (Lundberg et al., 1987; Pernow, 1988).

There is some evidence that neuropeptide Y may be preferentially released (relative to norepinephrine) at high nerve impulse frequencies, in accordance with its predominant localization in large dense-cored storage granules. This has been shown in models rich in neuropeptide Y, such as the pig spleen (Lundberg et al., 1987), but may also be seen in skeletal muscle where the release of neuropeptide Y is difficult to detect at a lower stimulation frequencies (Pernow, 1988; Pernow, Kahan, Hjemdahl, & Lundberg, 1988). Figure 7 illustrates that most of the vasoconstrictor response to sympathetic nerve stimulation can be blocked at a low frequency, but that substantial phenoxybenzamine resistant vasoconstriction can be seen at a high frequency. The protracted time course of the nonadrenergic vasoconstrictor response to high-frequency sympathetic nerve stimulation suggests involvement of neuropeptide Y at high frequencies and when norepinephrine-related mechanisms have been blocked. Figure 8, however, illustrates responses to intermediate-frequency sympathetic nerve stimulation (2 Hz) delivered either as regular impulses or burst activity (high-frequency bursts should release more neuropeptide Y) in the dog muscle model (Kahan, Pernow, Schwieler at al., 1988). Rapid fluctuations of perfusion pressure are abolished (because of neuropeptide Y or markedly enhanced norepinephrine release?), but the post-stimulatory decline of vascular tone remains rapid after alpha-blockade. Residual responses can therefore not unequivocally be attributed to neuropeptide Y.

Some caution when interpreting results concerning nonadrenergic vasoconstriction in animal models may be advisable. The alpha-1 selectivity of phenoxybenzamine (Constantine & Lebel, 1980) and the very large amounts of norepinephrine released with high frequency stimulation after alpha-blockade (see Figure 7) open the possibility of residual alpha-2 mediated responses. Norepinephrine depletion by reserpine may not abolish norepinephrine effects: As little as 10^{-5} to 10^{-6} of the neuronal norepinephrine stores are released per nerve impulse normally, and the releasable pool of norepinephrine may change after reserpine. Neuropeptide Y-mediated nonadrenergic vasocontriction is an interesting hypothesis, which is being tested in several

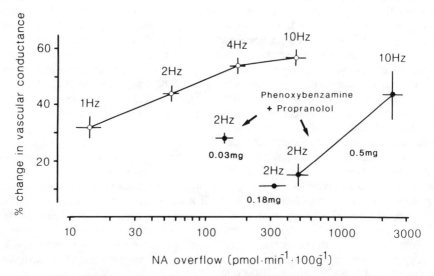

Figure 7 Vasoconstrictor responses (decreases in vascular conductance) in relation to norepinephrine (NA) overflow from canine blood perfused gracilis muscle during sympathetic nerve stimulation at 1–10 Hz before (open circles) and after propranolol (to block beta-mediated vasodilatation) and increasing doses of the noncompetitive alpha-blocker phenoxybenzamine. Note that alpha-blockade increases norepinephrine overflow almost tenfold at 2 Hz (removal of prejunctional inhibition—the tissues were pretreated with desipramine) and reduces the vasoconstrictor response markedly at 2 Hz but not at 10 Hz. From Pernow et al. (1988), by permission of publisher and author.

Perfusion pressure, mmHg

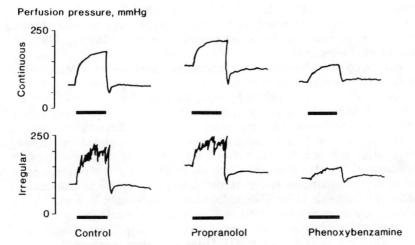

Figure 8   Comparison of vasoconstrictor responses to sympathetic nerve stimulation at the same average frequency (2 Hz), but delivered as continuous or irregular burst activity (governed by a microneurographic recording of human skeletal muscle nerve activity). Propranolol increased basal perfusion pressure but did not alter the response to sympathetic nerve stimulation. Phenoxybenzamine abolished the rapid alterations of vascular tone during irregular stimulation and reduced the vasoconstrictor response independently of impulse pattern (by about 75% in this experiment). Return to basal tone following stimulation is too fast to be compatible with neuropeptide-mediated vasoconstriction after phenoxybenzamine at this intermediate impulse frequency. At higher frequencies a slower poststimulatory waning of the response is seen (Pernow, 1988; Pernow et al., 1988). From (Kahan et al., 1988).

laboratories. Confirmation of its importance by use of specific antagonists (presently unavailable) is needed. Neuropeptide Y may constitute a reserve system causing vasoconstriction mainly at high frequencies of sympathetic nerve activity, when norepinephrine normally causes profound effects. Adenosine triphosphate, which is costored with norepinephrine in the reserpine-sensitive storage vesicles, may contribute to nonadrenergic responses to sympathetic stimulation (Burnstock, 1986, 1987; Stjärner, 1986). However, the ability of α,β-methylene-ATP to antagonize vasoconstrictor responses to sympathetic nerve stimulation varies with the experimental model; in the in vivo model of blood perfused gracilis muscle this procedure had no effect (Pernow, 1988; Pernow et al., 1988). The case for adenosine triphosphate as an important modulator of sympathetic vascular control appears to be weaker than that for neuropeptide Y.

Prejunctional Modulation of Norepinephrine Release

Norepinephrine release can be inhibited by stimulation of prejunctional alpha-adrenergic or muscarinic receptors (Alabaster & Davey, 1984; Davey, 1986b; Kahan, 1987; Starke, 1981; Starke & Docherty, 1980; Vanhoutte, Verbeuren, & Webb, 1981; Vizi, 1979). These alpha-adrenoceptors are mainly of the alpha-2 subtype, but a subset of prejunctional alpha-1 adrenoceptors may exist (Davey, 1986a, 1986b; Kahan, 1987). Prejunctional beta-adrenoceptors can facilitate norepinephrine release

(Dahlöf, 1981; Kahan, 1987; Langer, 1981; Misu & Kubo, 1986; Rand & Majewski, 1984). These receptors are mainly of the beta-2 subtype, but it has been proposed that there may be prejunctional beta-1 adrenoceptors as well (Dahlöf, 1981; Misu & Kubo, 1986).

Alpha-2 mediated inhibition of norepinephrine release seems to operate efficiently over the entire frequency range of nerve activity and is quite potent a modulator of norepinephrine release, as judged by overflow data after alpha-blockade in many systems. It is interesting to note that alpha-2 mediated modulation of norepinephrine overflow has been demonstrated also in humans (Jie, van Brummelen, Verney et al., 1987a). Prejunctional beta-2 mediated facilitation of norepinephrine release, conversely, seems to have a much narrower dynamic range of regulation. In the skeletal muscle model, for example, norepinephrine overflow can be increased more than fivefold by alpha-blockade and markedly reduced by additional exogenous alpha-stimulation, whereas beta-blockade reduces overflow by only 10% to 25% and beta stimulation enhances norepinephrine overflow very moderately (by about 30%) when marked vasodilator responses are evoked (Kahan, 1987; Kahan, Dahlöf, & Hjemdahl, 1987; Kahan & Hjemdahl, 1987). Using a different approach (studies of DBH release in norepinephrine-depleted tissues) Dixon, Mosimann, and Weiner (1979) reached a similar conclusion. Thus prejunctional beta-adrenoceptors are probably less important than prejunctional alpha-adrenoceptors in the control of norepinephrine release in vivo (Dixon et al., 1979; Kahan, 1987; Kahan & Hjemdahl, 1987).

The endogenous ligand for prejunctional beta-adrenoceptors should be epinephrine, because norepinephrine is a poor agonist at beta-2 adrenoceptors. However, at high junctional concentrations the selectivity of norepinephrine (which is about 1:100 for beta-2:beta-1) may disappear. Norepinephrine is, of course, the logical candidate as agonist for the prejunctional alpha-adrenoceptor. Prejunctional beta-2 mediated facilitation of norepinephrine release is often invoked as an important mechanism of action for epinephrine, be it as a circulating hormone or as the putative co-transmitter described earlier. However, circulating epinephrine has not clearly been shown to influence norepinephrine release importantly in vivo under conditions allowing conclusions regarding prejunctional mechanisms (i.e., under conditions where nerve activity is known). In the aforementioned skeletal muscle model, circulating epinephrine does not influence norepinephrine overflow in the relevant arterial plasma concentration range, that is, up to 6 nM (Kahan et al., 1987). Also other models have failed to demonstrate an effect of physiological epinephrine concentrations, unless alpha-blockade had been given (Steenburg, Ekas, & Lokhandwala, 1983). Even then the effect was small. Thus either epinephrine levels in plasma are too low or alpha effects counterbalance the beta-mediated facilitatory effect. Epinephrine may act prejunctionally only in some tissues or in some species. Many studies claiming that epinephrine modulates sympathetic neurotransmission have, however, been performed under conditions that can be debated from a methodological point of view.

Neuropeptide Y can inhibit norepinephrine release. However, intra-arterial infusion of neuropeptide Y requires extremely high concentrations for a modest effect (a 25% reduction of norepinephrine overflow when plasma neuropeptide Y is elevated from about 10^{-11} to 10^{-6} M) in the aforementioned dog model (Pernow et al., 1988). It may be argued that neuropeptide Y diffuses poorly into the tissue. However, overflows of norepinephrine and neuropeptide Y into the blood upon nerve stimulation are similar when expressed in relation to their tissue contents (Pernow et al., 1988), which is inconsistent with major diffusion limitation. Thus prejunctional inhibition of norepinephrine release mediated by neuropeptide Y is not strongly supported. Prejunctional alpha-mediated inhibition of neuropeptide Y release is more likely to occur, because alpha-blockade (Lundberg et al., 1987; Pernow, 1988; Pernow et al., 1988) or norepinephrine depletion (Lundberg et al., 1987; Pernow, 1988) markedly enhances neuropeptide Y overflow.

Prejunctional cholinergic (muscarinic) inhibition of norepinephrine release may occur in the heart, which has the prerequisite of dual autonomic innervation (Löffelholz & Pappano, 1985; Vizi, 1979) but is not likely to be of importance in most blood vessels. Thus acetylcholine is a locally acting neurotransmitter, and cholinergic innervation of blood vessels is a debatable subject. Also dopamine receptor stimulation may reduce norepinephrine release (Lokhandwala & Barrett, 1982) but this mechanism has not been shown to be of physiological importance in the periphery. On the whole, it is advisable to be cautious with regard to conclusions concerning the physiological importance of the many presynaptic regulatory mechanisms that can be demonstrated, usually in various in vitro models and with pharmacological doses of agonists. Very little is known about prejunctional modulation of sympathetic neurotransmission in humans, as is discussed in following sections.

Is Epinephrine a Prejunctional Modulator of Norepinephrine Release in Humans?

It is difficult to ascertain whether epinephrine enhances sympathetic neurotransmission under physiological conditions in humans, because definite conclusions regarding any neuromodulatory mechanism require data on the release of norepinephrine per nerve impulse from a tissue in vivo. It is not sufficient to demonstrate the effect in vitro. A common finding interpreted as evidence for prejunctional beta-adrenoceptors in humans is that beta-agonist infusion elevates plasma norepinephrine (e.g., Brown & Dollery, 1984; Musgrave et al., 1985; Vincent, Man In't Veld, Boomsma et al., 1982). However, this experimental situation does not allow such conclusions (merely speculation); nerve impulse activity may increase because of reflexogenic activation caused by the vasodilatation elicited by epinephrine or isoprenaline. In fact, increases of muscle sympathetic nerve activity during intravenous epinephrine infusion (Persson, Anderson, Hjemdahl et al., 1989) and attenuation of the plasma norepinephrine response to isoprenaline when autonomic reflexes are counteracted (Martinsson et al., 1989) have been demonstrated.

It has been proposed that epinephrine may be co-stored with neorepinephrine (following uptake from the circulation or local synthesis) and enhance norepinephrine release via a local action in the neuroeffector junction. This has been invoked as a possible cause of hypertension (Brown & Dollery, 1984; Rand & Majewski, 1984). Findings interpreted to support this hypothesis include (a) elevations of blood pressure following prolonged infusions of epinephrine (but not norepinephrine) in animals (Rand & Majewski, 1984) and humans (Blankestijn, Man In't Veld, Tulen et al., 1988); (b) long-lasting post-infusion tachycardia after epinephrine infusion in humans (Brown & Dollery, 1984); and (c) enhanced forearm vasoconstrictor responses to orthostatic stress during and after local intra-arterial infusions of epinephrine (Floras, Aylward, Victor et al., 1988). These observations are compatible with the co-transmitter hypothesis, but alternative explanations may be considered. Space does not allow detailed arguments. Post-infusion tachycardia may, for example, also be seen after infusions of isoprenaline, which is not taken up into sympathetic nerves.

Epinephrine may produce more marked such effects but does not stimulate the same receptors as does isoprenaline. Furthermore, epinephrine infusion is followed by a reduction of central venous pressure, resulting in an increase in vasoconstrictor nerve activity and, most likely, also reflexogenic cardiac effects (Persson et al., 1989). Alterations of postjunctional responsiveness during and after epinephrine infusion must also be seriously considered. One should not invoke effects of beta-blockade on responses of plasma norepinephrine to epinephrine infusion as indicative of a prejunctional site of action (Nezu, Miura, Adachi et al., 1983), as all beta-mediated effects of epinephrine (whether primary or secondary) will be altered by beta-blockade. Thus the physiological importance of prejunctional modulation of norepinephrine release by epinephrine (acting as a co-transmitter or as a hormone) is, in my opinion, still a matter of speculation. An important point to consider in relation to the epinephrine co-transmitter hypothesis is how facilitation of norepinephrine release at peripheral nerves would offset all homeostatic mechanisms (e.g., baroreceptors) and lead to hypertension. In my opinion, it is more likely that the sites of action are the blood pressure controlling centers of the central nervous system (for a derangement of transmitter release per nerve impulse) or the central command of peripheral nerve activity.

Methods of Assessing Sympathetic Neurotransmission in Humans

Nerve Activity Recordings

In animal experiments, nerve impulse activity to several different organs can be recorded by implantation of recording electrodes. In humans, however, neurographic recordings of nerve activity are possible only in sympathetic nerves supplying skeletal muscle and skin. These two regions have been studied extensively, and data concerning several physiological and pathophysiological states, as well as the effects of some drugs on nerve impulse activity are now at hand (Wallin & Fagius, 1988). Such studies have elegantly demonstrated the importance of baroreflex control of skeletal muscle sympathetic nerve activity and how it responds to a variety of different physiological stimuli. Despite its elegance, some drawbacks with the neurographic technique, as it is applied in human studies, may be kept in mind:

- Data usually represent "burst" activity in multi-unit recordings. Thus the exact frequency of impulses in a sympathetic axon cannot be determined. The amplitude of a recorded burst probably reflects the average impulse frequency of the burst, but recruitment of additional nerve fibers in the vicinity of the recording electrode is always a possibility to be considered.
- Nerve activity in other hemodynamically more important organs, such as the heart, kidneys, and splanchnic organs, cannot be recorded in humans. Sympathetic activity in one region may differ markedly from that in another region, even when the nerves supply similar tissues.
- Transmitter release at the effector organ level may not parallel axonal nerve impulse activity. This aspect is important to consider, because it has been shown that only a very small fraction (less than 1/100) of nerve impulses invading a sympathetic nerve varicosity actually evokes transmitter release from that varicosity (Brock & Cunnane, 1987). Prejunctional modulation may alter the relation between

electrical activity and transmitter release and recruitment of nerve varicosities may be frequency dependent (Brock & Cunnane, 1987), even when prejunctional receptors are blocked (e.g., Kahan, Hjemdahl, & Dahlöf, 1984). Thus the relation between nerve impulse activity and the efficiency of transmission at the neuroeffector junction may be complex, and the elegant neurographic technique is only one of several ways to evaluate sympathetic neurotransmission.

Plasma Norepinephrine Determinations

Because part of the norepinephrine released from sympathetic nerves diffuses into the bloodstream and modern analytical techniques allow the quantitation of small amounts of norepinephrine in plasma, it has become quite popular to measure plasma norepinephrine as a marker for sympathetic nerve activity in humans. There are numerous reports on sympathetic activity in normal physiology, in various disease states, during drug treatment, and so forth, whereby the evaluation of sympathetic nerve activity is based on antecubital venous plasma norepinephrine concentrations (see, e.g., Cryer, 1980; Goldstein, 1981, 1983). However, several methodological problems are often overlooked when using plasma norepinephrine levels as markers for sympathetic nerve activity.

Accuracy of catecholamine assays. The first requirement for the use of plasma norepinephrine as a marker for sympathetic nerve activity is, of course, that the assay is dependable. This is far from always the case, as is illustrated by a comparison of analytical results obtained in a number of laboratories considered to be experienced in the field (see Figure 9; Hjemdahl, 1984). Most assays are validated only with regard to sensitivity and reproducibility, which is essential for good results but does not prove accuracy. Analytical results should also be validated by comparing assays (to prove specificity). Plasma catecholamine data from the studies conducted by my colleagues and I have all been obtained with the same well-validated assay (Hjemdahl, 1987). Basal supine plasma norepinephrine levels should, on the average, be about 1–2 nM (170–350 pg/ml) in arterial and antecubital venous samples. Epinephrine levels should be 0.2–0.4 nM (35–70 pg/ml) in arterial plasma (half of that in venous plasma) and free dopamine levels below 0.1–0.2 nM (20–30 pg/ml). If basal plasma catecholamine levels are higher, either poor assay results or the conditions of the experiment (i.e., the basality or posture of the subject) may have influenced the results.

Time courses of changes. Circulating norepinephrine has a relatively short duration of action because of efficient elimination processes resulting in a plasma half-life of 1–2 min (Esler, Jennings, Korner et al., 1988). The half-life of epinephrine is at least as short, as is evidenced by the rapid return to basal levels following infusion (see, e.g., Hjemdahl & Linde, 1983). Thus changes in plasma catecholamine levels can occur rather rapidly, and it is important to standardize conditions closely when performing basal measurements. It is, in my opinion, not satisfactory to use acute venipunctures or arterial punctures for plasma catecholamine sampling, as this procedure may evoke different feelings of anticipation (anxiety) or pain in different individuals, and the time required to obtain the sample may differ between individuals. It is preferable to insert in-dwelling catheters and to allow at least 20–30 min of undisturbed rest before performing basal measurements. Some physiological variables, such as plasma renin activity (see Tidgren & Hjemdahl, 1989) or plasma beta-thromboglobulin (Larsson, Hjemdahl, Olsson et al., 1989), may require even longer resting periods to reach basal levels. It may also be advisable to take more than one

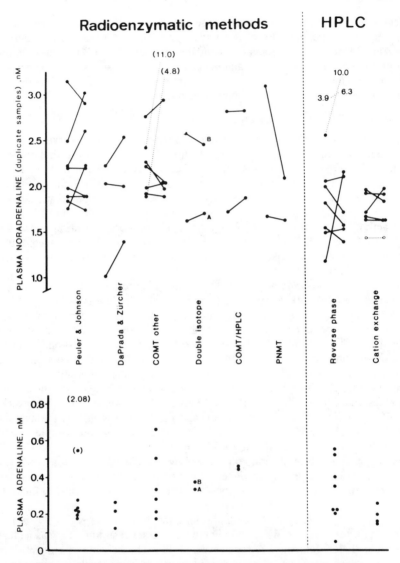

Figure 9 Comparison of duplicate determinations of basal plasma norepinephrine
with 41 assays in 34 different laboratories (top panel) and simultaneous
determinations of basal venous plasma epinephrine levels in one of the
samples (bottom panel). Results have been grouped according to type of
method used. All laboratories asked to participate were considered to be
experienced in the field. From Hjemdahl (1984).

basal sample and to average the results to eliminate baseline fluctuations of plasma
norepinephrine and epinephrine (Åkerstedt, Gillberg, Hjemdahl et al., 1983).

Plasma catecholamine levels increase rapidly during physiological provocations,
as would be expected from their short half-lives. During orthostatic testing, for example, arterial plasma norepinephrine increases within 1–2 minutes and steady-state

levels are achieved within 5–6 minutes (Linde & Hjemdahl, 1982). There is a lag phase of 1–2 min between increases in nerve activity and increases in norepinephrine in the venous effluent from the forearm during various stimuli. Thus, if a provocation increasing peripheral nerve activity is of short duration and vasoconstriction is produced, the peak response of plasma norepinephrine may even occur *after* the test, as is seen in connection with short-lasting isometric exercise (Wallin, Mörlin, & Hjemdahl, 1987) or cold pressor testing. Thus in studies of plasma catecholamine levels of responses to stress, attention has to be paid to the time courses involved.

Relations to sympathetic nerve activity. Does norepinephrine overflow to plasma reflect norepinephrine release? Animal studies have shown that neurotransmitter overflow to plasma can reflect nerve activity in several individual organs well. Thus there are frequency-dependent overflows of norepinephrine from the heart (Blombery & Heinzow, 1983), kidney (Bradley & Hjemdahl, 1984; Kopp et al., 1983), skeletal muscle (Kahan et al., 1984; Pernow et al., 1988) and several other organs in vivo upon sympathetic nerve stimulation. Thus, plasma norepinephrine can reflect sympathetic nerve activity well under certain conditions. In humans, however, plasma norepinephrine studies are usually performed by measuring antecubital venous norepinephrine levels, rather than individual organ overflow or arterial norepinephrine. It is becoming increasingly evident that there is no generalized "sympathetic tone" that allows indiscriminate extrapolation from one organ to another (Christensen et al., 1986; Folkow, DiBona, Hjemdahl et al., 1983; Hjemdahl, 1987; Steptoe, 1987). On the contrary, the sympathetic system seems to operate in a highly differentiated fashion, which necessitates studies of individual organ norepinephrine release. For studies of whole-body norepinephrine release (overall sympathetic activity), arterial sampling should be preferred, because antecubital venous norepinephrine levels overemphasize nerve activity in the forearm.

Importance of sampling site. An important but often overlooked requirement is that the norepinephrine measured in a plasma sample is derived from sympathetic nerves in the region of interest. Plasma norepinephrine is usually sampled from an antecubital venous catheter, which means that arterial blood containing norepinephrine from the whole body has passed the forearm before reaching the catheter. Because the forearm tissues extract about half of the norepinephrine in arterial plasma during one passage and arterial and venous norepinephrine levels usually are similar at rest (Chang, van der Krogt, & van Brummelen, 1987; Goldstein, Zimlichman, Stull et al., 1985; Hjemdahl, Freyschuss, Juhlin-Dannfelt, & Linde, 1984), it can be assumed that about half of the norepinephrine in antecubital venous plasma represents local release and that only half is derived from arterial blood plasma, that is, the rest of the body (Hjemdahl, 1987; Hjemdahl et al., 1984). The sources of norepinephrine in antecubital venous plasma are outlined in Figure 10. The marked dependence of venous plasma norepinephrine on local sympathetic nerve activity implies that conventionally sampled plasma norepinephrine primarily reflects sympathetic nerve activity in the forearm, which may behave quite differently from other regions (Hjemdahl, 1987, 1988).

Nonetheless, plasma norepinephrine studies based on antecubital venous sampling are frequently interpreted in terms of sympathetic nerve activity target organs controlling blood pressure (e.g., Goldstein, 1983; Izzo, Smith, Larrabee, & Kallay, 1987; Trimarco, Ricciardelli, De Luca et al., 1985) cardiac function (e.g., Goldstein, 1981; Izzo et al., 1987; Morady, DiCarlo, Halter et al., 1986; Sokoloff, Spielman, Greenspan et al., 1986) or other physiological functions of interest. If relations are poor,

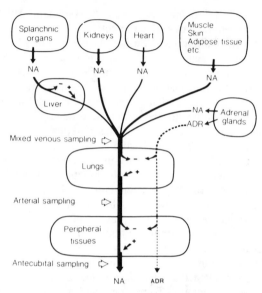

Figure 10   Schematic overview of norepinephrine release
and removal in different organs. Removal of
norepinephrine from arterial plasma varies
between organs from 40% to 50% at rest
over the forearm and kidneys (more over the
liver) to 0% over the heart during exercise.
Thus simple venoarterial concentration
differences for norepinephrine over an organ
cannot be multiplied by organ plasma flow to
assess overflow from the organ. About half
of antecubital venous norepinephrine is
derived from the forearm at rest. The
contributions of various organs to
norepinephrine in arterial plasma vary with
organ size, density of innervation, blood
flow, and nerve activity. Extraction of
norepinephrine (and epinephrine) over the
lungs is small. Thus arterial norepinephrine
and epinephrine levels reflect whole body
sympathetic nerve activity and the levels of
epinephrine to which organs are exposed,
respectively, whereas forearm levels do not.
From Hjemdahl (pp. 17–32 in Christensen et
al., 1986) by permission of publisher.

norepinephrine is said to reflect sympathetic nerve activity poorly (e.g., Thomas, Fouad, Tarazi, & Bravo, 1983) when, in fact, examination of methodological issues addressed here would have been appropriate. The pitfalls that can arise with the conventional approach are demonstrated by studies of mental stress (see below).

Kinetic alterations as a confounding factor. The third requirement for the use of plasma norepinephrine levels as markers for sympathetic nerve activity is that the levels are determined by the rate of overflow or spillover to plasma, rather than the rate of clearance from plasma. This problem can be solved by studying the kinetics of norepinephrine in plasma by radiotracer infusion methodology, as was introduced by Esler (see, e.g., Esler et al., 1988) and discussed in detail in a chapter of this book. He has argued that there are several situations where an elevation of norepinephrine in plasma may be caused by reduced clearance of norepinephrine from plasma. Often, however, concentrations correlate well with spillover to plasma, and the influence of norepinephrine clearance is less important. In key experiments it may be advisable to study kinetics to obtain an accurate evaluation of the factors determining norepinephrine concentrations in plasma, but in many situations one can do well with concentration measurements. The radiotracer technique is expensive and time-consuming and involves the administration of radioactivity to patients or volunteers, which may have ethical implications if the motives for its use are weak.

Regional overflow studies. One of the goals of this chapter is to point out that more studies of norepinephrine overflow from individual organs are needed to increase our knowledge of sympathetic nervous mechanisms in humans. When studying overflow from an organ, it is important to realize that a simple venoarterial step-up of norepinephrine over a tissue, as previously used (Goldstein, McCarty, Polinsky, & Kopin, 1983) does not give a correct estimate of norepinephrine release even if it is multiplied by the plasma flow through the organ. Because of marked and sometimes variable extraction of norepinephrine from arterial plasma, one must assess how much of the norepinephrine determined in the venous effluent was derived from the tissue and how much had simply passed through the tissue from arterial plasma.

The fractional extraction of norepinephrine by a tissue can be assessed by radiotracer methodology (^{3}H-norepinephrine infusions); or by use of endogenous epinephrine (Brown, Jenner, Allison, & Dollery, 1981; Hjemdahl, 1987), which is also a substrate for neuronal and extraneuronal removal mechanisms (Iversen, 1975; Kopin, 1985). In my experience (using data from skeletal muscle, kidneys, and the heart) epinephrine extraction differs little from ^{3}H-norepinephrine extraction. Changes of epinephrine and ^{3}H-norepinephrine extraction during provocations are also similar. Thus endogenous epinephrine may be used to calculate "corrected" venoarterial concentration differences for norepinephrine over a tissue. This may be multiplied by plasma flow to give good estimates of norepinephrine overflow from the tissue. Regional norepinephrine overflow studies provide valuable information on sympathetic nerve activity in individual organ during stress and in various pathophysiological states.

Urinary Catecholamine Excretion

Measurements of catecholamine excretion into urine have been used during many years to assess sympathoadrenal activity in stress research (Frankenhaeuser, 1986) and in clinical medicine. Urinary measurements are still preferable to plasma determinations for the diagnosis of pheochromocytoma, because norepinephrine and epinephrine have such short half-lives in plasma that tumors are missed if they are not constantly secreting or if samples are not taken during an attack. Furthermore, urinary sampling has the advantage of being more suitable for field studies. Often overlooked, however, is that factors such as posture and physical activity may provide greater differences in norepinephrine and epinephrine excretion than those one would expect to find because of stress or disease had the conditions been closely standardized.

Even if it is not possible to assess small interindividual differences in sympathoadrenal activity by urinary catecholamine measurements, the excretion of catechol-

KIDNEY

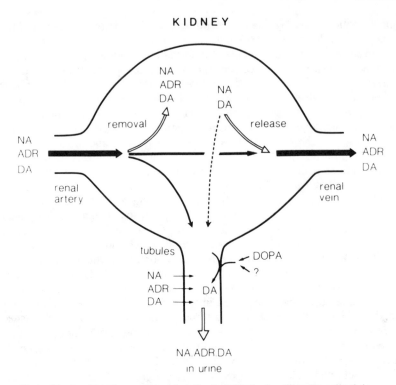

Figure 11   A schematic overview of renal catecholamine handling. Norepinephrine
(NA), Epinephrine (ADR), and dopamine (DA) are removed from
arterial plasma by neuronal and extraneuronal mechanisms and by
excretion (the minor elimination route). Norepinephrine and dopamine
released from nerves in the kidney are mainly recovered in the renal
venous effluent. Dopamine is also produced by nonneural mechanisms
and excreted in large amounts in urine. To estimate norepinephrine and
dopamine release from renal nerves venoarterial concentration
differences are calculated by correcting for catecholamine removal by
means of ^{3}H norepinephrine or endogenous epinephrine (both yield a
basal fractional extraction of 40%–45% in the human kidney). This
corrected venoarterial difference is multiplied by plasma flow.
Norepinephrine overflow thus calculated is approximately 200–250
pmol/min (35–40 ng/minute) from one kidney, and dopamine overflow is
about 10%–15% of norepinephrine overflow at rest. From Hjemdahl et
al. (1988) by permission of publisher.

amines into urine may reflect changes in circulating catecholamine levels within the
individual well if conditions are standardized. Figure 11 summarizes renal catecholamine handling. Norepinephrine excreted into urine reflects arterial norepinephrine
levels and not norepinephrine released from renal nerves (Kopp et al., 1983; Overy,
Pfister, & Chidsey, 1967). Changes in the urinary excretion of epinephrine seem to
reflect its secretion during stress well (Frankenhaeuser, 1986) and correlate with
simultaneously determined changes of epinephrine levels in plasma (Åkerstedt et al.,
1983). Thus, urinary measurements may still provide useful information on sympathoadrenal activity in humans.

Urinary dopamine, which has attracted considerable attention as it is related to salt excretion, appears to be nonneural in origin. The very large amounts excreted into urine do not reflect dopamine released from renal nerves, as is sometimes believed (e.g., Iimura, Yamaji, Kikuchi et al., 1987). Dopamine released from renal nerves appears mainly in renal venous plasma (for a more extensive discussion of renal dopamine, see Hjemdahl, Bradley, & Tidgren, 1988). Thus, urinary dopamine is formed mainly in nonneural elements in the kidney and influences salt excretion. The importance of neurally released renal dopamine is uncertain.

Platelet Catecholamine Determinations

Platelets take up catecholamines from plasma by an active uptake process. Short-lasting physiological stimuli, such as an exercise test, do not influence platelet catecholamine levels (McCulloch, Vandongen, Tunney et al., 1987), whereas more longlasting elevations of epinephrine produced by intravenous infusion elicit concentration-dependent (Rosen, Sanfield, Morrow, & Zweifler, 1987) and time-dependent (Joborn, Hjemdahl, Larsson et al., 1990) elevations of platelet epinephrine contents. Following infusion the decline of platelet epinephrine levels was considerably slower than that seen in plasma, but the levels were not maintained as if epinephrine were permanently stored by the platelets (Rosen et al., 1987). Thus platelet catecholamine levels reflect levels in plasma and may provide a rear-view image of sympathoadrenal activity during a certain (as yet not very well-defined) period of time before sampling. For example, platelet catecholamines are elevated in pheochromocytoma (Zweifler & Julius, 1982) and following myocardial infarction (Joborn et al., 1990). Interestingly, platelet epinephrine has also been found to be elevated in some individuals with Type A behavior (Schneider, Julius, Moss et al., 1987).

Platelet catecholamine determinations represent an analytical challenge (in my experience problems are greater than with plasma, as epinephrine levels are low and interferences more troublesome), which necessitates validation of assay results. Examination of published methods for platelet catecholamine determinations reveals up to tenfold differences in reported levels, which calls for caution. Platelet catecholamine levels may have functional implications, in addition to serving as markers for sympatho-adrenal activity. Thus, aggregating platelets release catecholamines and their ability to aggregate upon stimulation with several pro-aggregatory substances appears to be related to their norepinephrine contents (Wilson, Smith, Prichard, & Betteridge, 1987). Thus catecholamines stored in the platelets may further enhance aggregation. In addition, vascular and other effects of catecholamines and serotonin stored in them may occur in the vicinity of aggregating platelets.

Catecholamine Metabolite Determinations

The various catecholamine metabolites formed can be measured in plasma or urine as alternative indices of sympathetic function. Initial beliefs that MHPG levels in plasma or excretion in urine reflected noradrenergic activity in the central nervous system (Maas, Hattox, Greene, & Landis, 1979) did not stand the test of time (Kopin, 1985; Kpin et al., 1984; Wilson, Smith, Prichard, & Betteridge, 1987). Thus most of the MHPG in plasma is produced in the periphery and, indeed, MHPG levels correlate with norpeinephrine levels in plasma (Hjemdahl, Sjöqvist, Daleskog, & Eliasson, 1982), as well as with spillover to plasma and MSA (Hjemdahl, Wallin, Daleskog et al., 1985). Thus, MHPG levels in plasma or urine probably reflect peripheral sympathetic activity. MHPG is not an end-stage metabolite, as is illustrated by studies using stable isotopes (Mårdh, Sjöqvist, & Änggård, 1981). The half-life for MHPG in plasma is much longer than for norepinephrine, which may be an advantage under some circumstances, but its relation to nerve activity is less well established than that of norepinephrine.

DHPG levels in plasma are somewhat higher than norepinephrine levels and may increase upon sympathetic stimulation in humans (Goldstein, Eisenhofer, Stull et al., 1988; Halbrügge, Gerhardt, Ludwig et al., 1988; Howes, Hawksby, & Reid, 1986). DHPG measurements may provide information on the neuronal handling of norepinephrine in humans (Goldstein et al., 1988) and may improve the diagnostic power of plasma norepinephrine determinations in phaeochromocytoma (Brown, 1984; Duncan, Compton, Lazarus, & Smythe, 1988; Howes et al., 1986). The latter condition may, however, be better diagnosed by urinary catecholamine measurements (Duncan et al., 1988). Information on the relationships between DHPG levels and sympathetic activity is not extensive, and such measurements cannot replace norepinephrine measurements. The same goes for normetanephrine, the other primary metabolite of norepinephrine that also has been determined in plasma. Dopamine-beta-hydroxylase (DBH) is also exocytotically released from sympathetic nerves when they are stimulated. Early studies used DBH levels in plasma to reflect sympathetic nerve activity. However, the turnover of this large molecule is dependent on other factors, such as lymph flow, and this measure of sympathetic activity has been abandoned in favor of norepinephrine measurements.

Neuropeptide-like Immunoreactivity in Plasma

Neuropeptide-like immunoreactivity (NPY-LI) can be measured in plasma and seems to reflect neuropeptide Y release from sympathetic nerves (Lundberg et al., 1987; Pernow, 1988; Potter, 1988; Waeber et al., 1988). Thus animal experiments have shown that neuropeptide Y-LI overflow to plasma is enhanced by sympathetic nerve stimulation, particularly at high stimulation frequencies. Pronounced sympathetic activation in vivo, such as that caused by dynamic exercise, elevates plasma neuropeptide Y-LI in humans (Lundberg, Martinsson, Hemsé et al., 1985; Morris, Russel, Kapoor et al., 1986; Pernow, Lundberg, Kaijser et al., 1986). Effects of milder stimuli have varied. Thus, orthostatic stress (Morris et al., 1986; Pernow et al., 1986), isometric exercise (Pernow et al., 1986), and mental stress (Tidgren, Theodorsson, & Hjemdahl, 1990) fail to elevate plasma neuropeptide Y-LI. Cold pressor testing has been shown to do so (Maisel, Scott, Motulsky et al., 1989) even though it does not cause marked elevations of plasma norepinephrine. Hypoglycemia elevates plasma neuropeptide Y-LI (Takahashi, Mouri, Murakami et al., 1988), suggesting that neuropeptide Y may be released from the adrenal medullae in humans. Pathophysiological alterations of plasma neuropeptide Y-LI are subject to investigation in several laboratories. For example, congestive heart failure associated with elevated antecubital norepinephrine levels is also associated with elevated plasma neuropeptide Y-LI (Maisel, Scott, Motulsky et al., 1989). Whether this has any pathophysiological significance remains to be established.

Because neuropeptide Y has a longer half-life in plasma than norepinephrine, it is more difficult to detect neuropeptide Y-LI (compared to norepinephrine) release from individual tissues. For example, no clear-cut evidence of neuropeptide Y release was obtained when measuring neuropeptide Y-LI overflow from the arm during dynamic exercise (Pernow et al., 1986) or from the kidney during mental stress (Tidgren, 1990), despite marked effects on renal norepinephrine overflow. This may reflect either technical problems with the assay or the correctness of the aforementioned theory that neuropeptide Y is released mainly at high frequencies of nerve activity. One problem with plasma neuropeptide Y-LI measurements is that levels obtained with different assays differ markedly, suggesting important problems with the specificities of the antibodies used or the sample handling techniques. Thus basal levels of plasma neuropeptide Y-LI may be less than 5 pM (Watson, Sury, Corder et al., 1988), 20–30 pM (e.g., Lundberg et al., 1985, 1987; Pernow et al., 1986), approximately 40 pM (Takahashi et al., 1988), or 80–100 pM which equals 300–400 pg/ml (Maisel et al., 1989; Morris et al., 1986). In the absence of comparative evaluations it is difficult to judge which levels are correct, but differences in assay results are too large to be acceptable.

Another problem is that plasma neuropeptide Y-LI may be influenced by factors other than release, as is the case for norepinephrine in plasma. The turnover of neuropeptide Y appears to be slow, with an initial half-life of about 4 minutes and a half-life in the elimination phase of about 20 minutes following iv infusions (Pernow, 1988). Inter- and intra-individual variation of neuropeptide Y turnover in plasma have not been worked out. Neither has the possible influence of changes in distribution volume (caused, e.g., by vasoconstriction). The elevation of neuropeptide Y-LI during exercise, however, does not seem to be related to nonspecific changes of peptide distribution or clearance, because the levels of a couple of other peptides did not show similar changes during exercise in an earlier study (Lundberg et al., 1985). More information on the relations between neuropeptide Y-LI levels in plasma and nerve activity is needed.

PARASYMPATHETIC NEUROTRANSMISSION

Acetylcholine is the primary transmitter of parasympathetic postganglionic nerves. Figure 5 outlines cholinergic neurotransmission. Acetylcholine is synthesized by acetylation of choline and subsequently stored in specific storage granules (Gilman et al., 1985; Whittaker, 1986). The enzyme responsible for its synthesis, choline acetyl transferase, can be used to identify cholinergic nerves histochemically (e.g., Whittaker, 1986). After synthesis, acetylcholine is taken up into the storage granules by an active process that is not homogeneous among different granules—some granules take up and release newly synthesized acetylcholine more easily than others, in analogy with the situation in adrenergic nerves. Thus transmitter labeling procedures used to study acetylcholine release may not fully reflect endogenous events. Following quantal release, which occurs by calcium-dependent exocytosis also in cholinergic nerves, acetylcholine is rapidly broken down by choline esterases. Choline thus formed may be taken up and reutilized, but there is no neuronal uptake of acetylcholine. Even if overflow can be demonstrated, for example, from isolated hearts in vitro (Löffelholz, Brehm, & Lindmar, 1984), the efficiency of cholinesterases is probably so great that acetylcholine should be a locally acting neurotransmitter.

There appear to be multiple chemical messengers also in the parasympathetic nervous system, as peptides (e.g., vasoactive intestinal peptide, VIP), may be co-stored with acetylcholine (Lundberg, 1981; Whittaker, 1986). Functionally important cotransmitter interactions have, for example, been demonstrated between acetylcholine and VIP in salivary glands, where VIP induces an atropine resistant vasodilatation that enhances the secretory response (Lundberg, 1981). Recently, neuropeptide Y, which usually is localized in sympathetic nerves, has been shown to be released from parasympathetic nerves in the pancreas (Sheikh, Holst, Skak-Nielsen et al., 1988). Adenosine triphosphate has also been invoked as a co-transmitter in cholinergic neurons (Burnstock, 1986).

Acetylcholine release may be modulated by prejunctional receptors, in analogy with the regulation of norepinephrine release from sympathetic nerves. Muscarinic receptor stimulation reduces acetylcholine release (Levy, 1984; Vizi, 1979; Wetzel & Brown, 1985), as does alpha-2 adrenoceptor stimulation (Loiacono & Story, 1986; Vizi, 1979; Wetzel & Brown, 1985). In the heart, with its close proximity between sympathetic and parasympathetic nerves, there is probably "cross-talk" between these nerves (see Figure 1). Circulating catecholamines are not likely to influence acetylcholine release, as the concentrations of norepinephrine and epinephrine required for a reduction of acetylcholine release seem to be some 10,000 times above those actually occurring (Wetzel & Brown, 1985). The idea of physiologically important alpha-2 adrenergic modulation of acetylcholine release has been contested (e.g., Lew & Angus, 1983). Experimental designs may, however, influence the outcome of studies, because there may be a time-dependent factor in this interaction (Furukawa, Ogiwara, Saegusa et al., 1987). With regard to sympathetic-parasympathetic interactions in the heart it has been suggested that cardiac vagal actions may be inhibited by two mechanisms, one short-lasting and beta-mediated and another more long-lasting one related to neuropeptide Y release from sympathetic nerves following more intense stimulation (Potter, 1988). There are several possibilities for nonautonomic prejunctional modulation of transmitter release (such as purines) also from parasympathetic nerves.

Methods of Studying Parasympathetic Nerve Activity

Transmitter Release

Because of its rapid breakdown, it is difficult to evaluate the release of endogenous acetylcholine under in vivo conditions. Release can be demonstrated under some in vitro conditions, using bioassay techniques (this was how chemical neurotransmission was first demonstrated by Loewi, cited in Gilman et al., 1985) or other methods (Löffelholz & Pappano, 1985). After inhibition of choline esterase, the overflow of endogenous or radiolabeled acetylcholine is markedly enhanced. This, however, causes such marked alterations of cholinergic neuroeffector function that the data probably bear little relevance to the normal physiological regulation of cholinergic transmission. A radiolabeling technique can be used to assess acetylcholine release in animal experiments. Thus preincubation of tissues with ^{3}H-choline labels the neuronal acetylcholine pool and allows estimation of transmitter release in terms of radioactivity overflow (see, e.g., Loiacono & Story, 1986). The radiolabeling technique may provide valuable information on acetylcholine release when coupled with data on effector responses. The two need not necessarily go hand in hand.

Pharmacological Studies

Responses to exogenous administration of muscarinic agonists may demonstrate the existence of muscarinic receptor-mediated events, but not their physiological importance. Muscarinic receptor antagonists (such as atropine) or inhibition of cholinesterase (e.g., by edrophonium), which elevates acetylcholine concentrations at the receptors, may provide more information on their importance, However, cholinesterase inhibition can be expected to influence ganglionic transmission and postganglionic sympathetic activity as well. Atropine readily passes the blood–brain barrier, which creates the possibility of mixed central and peripheral changes. Initial bradycardia in response to atropine injection is attributed to a central effect (Gilman et al., 1985). Central effects may be minimized by use of a quarternary anticholinergic agent (e.g., methscopolamine), but atropine remains the most commonly used pharmacological tool in cardiovascular research, for example, on vagal mechanisms.

Atropine increases heart rate substantially, indicating considerable vagal nerve activity in the resting state. The cardiovascular system may, however, also influence the cardiovascular system in ways not directly related to parasympathetic mechanisms, as is indicated by reductions of plasma norepinephrine (Atterhög, Eliasson, & Hjemdahl, 1981). When studying the possibility of cholinergic vasodilator nerves it is important to give atropine locally, in order to avoid cardiac effects and reflexogenic alterations of sympathetic vasoconstrictor nerve activity. Cardiac sympathetic nerve activity may also be influenced by atropine, in analogy with the effects of isoprenaline on vagal activity. Atropine testing alone may not provide adequate information (e.g., Cappato, Alboni, Paperella et al., 1987) but is useful as one of several tools in the evaluation of cardiac parasympathetic nerve activity.

Physiological Studies

One way to assess vagal activity is to study heart rate variability in relation to respiratory movements (e.g., Akselrod, Gordon, Madwed et al., 1985; Eckberg, Harkins, Fritsch et al., 1986; Ewing, 1978) or in response to deep breathing or facial immersion (Kaijser, 1986). These tests may not, however, selectively reflect vagal function. Animal experiments have demonstrated a sympathetic component in respiratory arrhythmia (Koizumi, Terui, & Kollai, 1983), and the diving reflex elicits marked peripheral sympathetic activation that precedes the bradycardia (Fagius & Sundlöf, 1986). Respiratory variation of heart rate may provide a better index of vagal function after beta-blockade (Pfeifer, Weinberg, Cook et al., 1983). The Valsalva maneuver evokes mixed sympathetic and parasympathetic activation; the various components of responses to this test are often used to assess cardiac autonomic function (Ewing, 1978; Hoshino, Blaustein, & Gaasch, 1988; Kaijser, 1986). Interestingly, a battery of tests of vagal activity have shown vagal influences on ventricular electrophysiology in humans (Rardon & Bailey, 1983; Waxman, Cupps, & Cameron, 1988). Thus a combination of physiological tests may give valuable information on cardiac parasympathetic nerve activity in health and disease, but a single test may be inadequate (Ewing, 1978; Kaijser, 1986).

TOTAL AUTONOMIC BLOCKADE

To study autonomic influences on the circulation, one may wish to eliminate both sympathetic and parasympathetic influences in order to evaluate, for example, the autonomic component of hypertension. This can be done by administering a ganglionic blocker or combined autonomic receptor blockade by phentolamine, propranolol, and atropine. The techniques have been used to study neural mechanisms in hypertension (e.g., Julius & Esler, 1975; Korner, Shaw, Uther et al., 1973; Murphy, Brown, Causon, & Dollery, 1983). However, it is difficult to abolish autonomic influences with these drugs, as most of them are competitive antagonists and the organism may respond to autonomic blockade by marked increases in nerve activity in an attempt to overcome the lack of responsiveness. Dosages are limited by side effects. For example, the atropine and clonidine regimen causes marked sedation, and ganglionic blockade produces a plethora of side effects (see Gilman et al., 1985).

ENDOTHELIAL MODULATION OF VASCULAR TONE

Recently, considerable interest has focused on endothelial modulation of vascular function. Thus some comments on possible autonomic involvement may be of interest because the endothelium is involved in local modulation of vascular tone, as well as in protection against blood clots and in the development of atherosclerosis. Acetylcholine relaxes isolated arteries in the presence of endothelium but constricts them after removal of the endothelium. One mediator of this dilating influence, termed endothelium-derived relaxing factor (EDRF; Furchgott & Zawadski, 1980) has been shown to be nitric oxide (Moncada, Herman, & Vanhoutte, 1987), but there appear to be several EDRFs (Ignarro, 1989). Other vasoactive factors, including prostacyclin and lipoxygenase products, are also produced by the endothelium (Vane, Gryglewski, & Botting, 1987). Several vasoactive agents, as well as aggregating platelets and thrombin, may cause endothelium-dependent relaxation (Vanhoutte, 1988). EDRF-related relaxation has also been demonstrated in human vessels (Lüscher, Diederich, Siebenmann et al., 1988; Thom, Hughes, Martin, & Sever, 1987). EDRF may also reduce platelet adherence and aggregation (see Lüscher et al., 1988). There are also endothelium-derived constricting factors, such as the recently isolated peptide endothelin (Yanagisawa, Kurihara, Kimura et al., 1988), but this field is less advanced than that of the relaxing factors.

The role of autonomic mechanisms in endothelial control of vascular tone is not clear. Acetylcholine is rapidly broken down and probably does not diffuse into the lumen of the vessel and is probably not an endogenous stimulus for EDRF release. Whether sympathetic nerves or circulating catecholamines influence endothelium-dependent vascular control has not been established, even if norepinephrine is mentioned in this context (Vane et al., 1987; Vanhoutte, 1988). Norepinephrine may evoke alpha-2 mediated EDRF release in some blood vessels in vitro (Angus, Cocks, & Satoh, 1986), but responses are highly variable. Conversely, norepinephrine may counteract endothelial-relaxing influences in isolated vessels (Rubanyi, Lorenz, & Vanhoutte, 1985). Neuropeptide Y has been reported to cause endothelium-dependent enhancement of arterial constrictor responses to field stimulation in vitro but the lowest concentration to demonstrate such an effect was far above the levels seen in plasma (Daly & Hiebler, 1987). Thus the physiological importance of this observation is doubtful, again illustrating the importance of quantitative evaluation when assessing findings observed with pharmacological doses of physiological agonists. In vivo, slight endothelium-dependent relaxation has been found in large arteries in the dog (Young & Vatner, 1987). Interestingly, evidence compatible with EDRF release induced by acetylcholine has been found in the human coronary circulation (Ludmer, Selwyn, Shook et al., 1986). However, in isolated human coronary arteries, acetylcholine does not seem to evoke EDRF-dependent vasodilatation (Thom et al., 1987). Clearly, more information regarding direct interactions between endothelial function and autonomic vascular control in vivo is needed. Little is known regarding autonomic mechanisms in this context.

Sympathetic activity may influence endothelium-dependent vascular control indirectly by modifying platelet function and the coagulation system. Thus stress has been suspected of influencing platelet function and blood coagulation. Recently, mental stress or epinephrine infusion has been shown to enhance an in vivo measure of platelet aggregability (Larsson et al., 1989). Many factors influence platelet aggregability; interactions with the endothelium are clearly important (Steen & Holmsen, 1987). Norepinephrine has been shown to evoke alpha-1 mediated release of protein S and to influence receptors mediating the effects of this anticoagulant system on endothelial cells (Brett, Steinberg, deGroot et al., 1988). Mental stress also appears to influence other aspects of endothelial cell function in vivo (Musumeci, Baroni, Cardillo et al., 1987). Possible links between sympatho-adrenal activation, platelet function, the coagulation system, and the endothelium are of considerable interest and deserve further study.

PHYSIOLOGICAL ROLE
OF CIRCULATING CATECHOLAMINES

Circulating Catecholamine Levels

Catecholamines in blood are to some extent (about 20%–40%) bound to plasma proteins; the resulting reduction of the free (active) fraction of catecholamines in plasma is rather small and is usually disregarded. The circulating catecholamine of greatest interest is epinephrine which has a long-standing reputation as a stress hormone. However, norepinephrine may also act as a circulating hormone. Epinephrine levels in antecubital venous plasma and threshold levels for various effects of exogenously administered epinephrine have been reviewed by Cryer (1980). He has also proposed that part of circulating epinephrine may be nonadrenal in origin (derived from chromaffin cells) and has suggested the term sympathochromaffin rather than sympathoadrenal activity (Shah, Tse, Clutter, & Cryer, 1984). In my experience average resting arterial epinephrine levels are usually about 0.2–0.4 nM, venous levels being about half of that due to tissue extraction (see Figure 12).

Several authors have pointed out the importance of arterial sampling to obtain correct estimates of epinephrine responses to various stimuli (e.g., Best & Halter, 1982; Christensen et al., 1986; Hjemdahl, 1987; Hjemdahl et al., 1984; Jörgensen, Bönlökke, & Christensen, 1985; Kjeldsen, Westheim, Aakesson et al., 1986). The extraction of epinephrine tissues varies and may, in fact, increase so much during peripheral vasoconstriction (evoked by, e.g., lower body negative pressure) that a clear-cut increase in arterial epinephrine is absent in venous plasma (Hjemdahl, Eklund, & Kaijser, 1982). Conversely, epinephrine extraction over the heart may disappear during exercise, presumably due to the marked increase in coronary flow (Pehrsson, Hjemdahl, Nordlander, & Åtröm, 1988). There is also a flow dependence of peripheral catecholamine extraction from arterial plasma (Goldstein, Eisenhofer, Sax et al., 1987; Hjemdahl, Fagius, Freyschuss et al., 1989). Arterial epinephrine determinations are preferable to venous determinations for two reasons: (a) They give correct estimates of plasma epinephrine, and (b) they provide data on the levels of epinephrine to which the tissues were actually exposed.

My experience with regard to plasma epinephrine responses to physiological stimuli indicates that mild stimuli, such as orthostatic testing (standing, tilting, and lower body negative pressure), cold pressor testing, isometric exercise, various kinds of

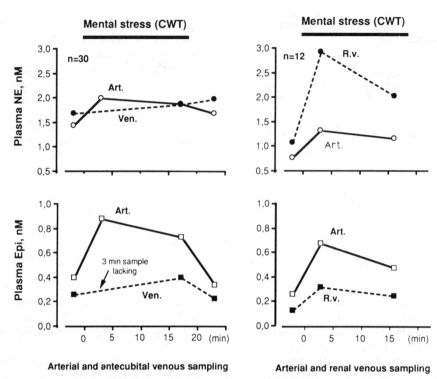

Figure 12 Arterial and antecubital venous (Freyschuss et al., 1988) and arterial and renal venous (Tidgren & Hjemdahl, 1989) norepinephrine and epinephrine in connection with the Stroop test (CWT). Note the lack of antecubital venous norepinephrine response and the marked renal venous norepinephrine response to the test. Arterial norepinephrine increased 50%–80% in both studies.

mental stress, and mild-moderate dynamic exercise, rarely elevate arterial epinephrine levels above 1 nM or venous levels above 0.5 nM. During so-called vaso-vagal (fainting) reactions, epinephrine levels may increase markedly (Tidgren & Hjemdahl, 1988, and unpublished further observations). Exhaustive exercise may elevate epinephrine to more than 5 nM (and norepinephrine to considerably more than 30 nM), but lower level exercise has rather modest effects on plasma epinephrine (see Lundberg et al., 1985). Hypoglycemia (neuroglycopenia) is a potent stimulus for epinephrine secretion (see Cryer, 1980). Surprisingly, a stimulus as strong as myocardial infarction evokes marked elevations of epinephrine in relatively few patients (Bertel, Bühler, Baitsch et al., 1982; Joborn et al., 1990; Karlsberg, Cryer, & Roberts, 1981). The substantial stimuli required to elevate epinephrine above 1–2 nM suggest that the importance of circulating epinephrine as a mediator of physiological responses under various conditions should be examined critically.

The Role of Epinephrine as a Mediator of Responses to Stress

The importance of epinephrine as a mediator of responses to stress is often taken for granted and exaggerated. Observations that elevations of plasma epinephrine may correlate to responses to various stimuli (e.g., tachycardia during mental stress) are sometimes taken too literally (e.g., Eisenhofer, Lambie, & Johnson, 1985; Krakoff, Dziedzic, Mann et al., 1985). A closer examination of mechanisms involved may show that epinephrine could not have mediated the response. To evaluate the importance of epinephrine as a mediator of responses, at least two lines of investigation may be followed:

1. Establish whether the levels of epinephrine attained in plasma actually are capable of producing the response in question when administered exogenously. If the response requires plasma epinephrine concentrations much higher than those seen during the stimulus (as is the case with mental stress and heart rate), there is little room for causality of correlations.

2. Establish whether the response is beta-2 mediated. Epinephrine seems to be the endogenous beta-2 ligand (see above). Norepinephrine levels in the neuroeffector junction are much higher than epinephrine levels, and beta-1 adrenoceptors seem to be more easily accessible to norepinephrine. Therefore, predominance of beta-1 mechanisms in a response favors neurogenic activation rather than circulating epinephrine, as is illustrated by exercise (Brodde et al., 1988; McLeod et al., 1983) and mental stress (Freyschuss, Hjemdahl, Juhlin-Dannfelt, & Linde, 1988).

Epinephrine is indeed a potent circulating hormone, as is illustrated by threshold levels in plasma required for various effects. As is illustrated in Figure 13, during intravenous infusion epinephrine elicits vasodilatation in the systemic circulation and several tissues, including skeletal muscle and adipose tissue (Freyschuss et al., 1986; Hjemdahl & Linde, 1983; Stratton, Pfeifer, Ritchie, & Halter, 1985). Effects are seen at about 1 nM in arterial plasma (half of that in venous plasma). The skin responds to low-dose epinephrine infusion with vasoconstriction (Östergren et al., unpublished), as it is endowed with alpha-adrenoceptors only. At high concentrations the alpha-agonistic properties of epinephrine may cause vasoconstriction in organs responding with vasodilatation to low concentrations of epinephrine, as its alpha-effect takes over. Epinephrine has been thought to elicit vasoconstriction in the kidney, but a closer examination of renal blood flow responses to epinephrine in humans reveals no changes at arterial levels up to 6 nM (Tidgren & Hjemdahl, 1989).

Tachycardia is not a prominent feature of the cardiovascular response to infused epinephrine, as is illustrated in Figures 3 and 13 (Freyschuss et al., 1986; Hjemdahl et al., 1983; Stratton et al., 1985). The increase in cardiac output (which balances peripheral vasodilatation to maintain an essentially unchanged mean arterial pressure) is mainly caused by increased stroke volume (Freyschuss et al., 1986; Stratton et al., 1985), as is illustrated in Figure 13. Other cardiac effects of epinephrine include ECG changes (Morady, Nelson, Kou et al., 1988; Taggart, Donaldson, Green et al., 1982; Struthers, Reid, Whitesmith, & Rodger, 1983) and echocardiographic signs of increased contractility at relatively low epinephrine levels (Leenen, Chan, Smith, & Reeves, 1988; Lindvall et al., unpublished). Leenen et al. (1988) concluded that epinephrine increased heart rate via beta-2 stimulation and contractility via beta-1 stimulation, but the dose of atenolol chosen also abolished the diastolic blood pressure reduction, indicating beta-2 blockade. In our hands, use of a more beta-1 selective antagonist, patenolol, provided no support for that claim (Freyschuss et al., unpublished). Thus mechanisms responsible for cardiac effects of epinephrine in humans have not been unequivocally delineated.

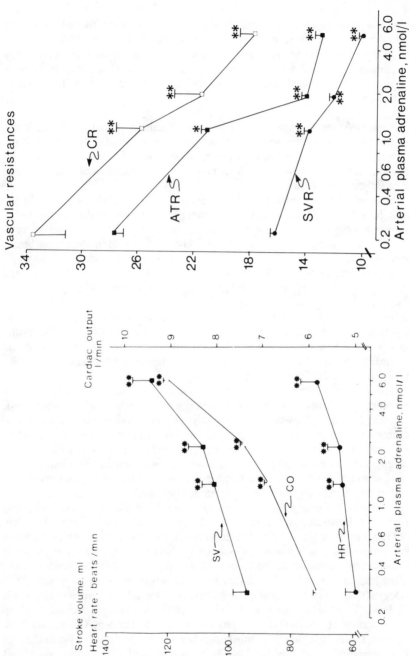

Figure 13 Cardiac (left) and vascular (right) responses to intravenously, infused epinephrine in relation to arterial plasma epinephrine concentrations. SV = stroke volume, CO = cardiac output, HR = heart rate, CR = calf resistance, ATR = adipose tissue resistance, SVR = systemic vascular resistance. Note that especially cardiac changes at the peak plasma epinephrine concentration attained during the Stroop color word test (approximately 0.8 nM) are relatively small. From Freyschuss et al. (1986, used by permission of publisher).

Metabolic responses to small elevations of circulating epinephrine include enhanced lipolysis (Freyschuss et al., 1986; Hilsted, Richter, Madsbad et al., 1987; Staten, Matthews, Cryer, & Bier, 1987) and metabolic rate (Staten et al., 1987). The hyperglycemic effect requires higher (e.g., Cryer, 1980; Freyschuss et al., 1986; Hilsted et al., 1987; Staten et al., 1987) and elevations of plasma lactate still higher epinephrine concentrations (Freyschuss et al., 1986; Staten et al., 1987). Epinephrine also influences electrolyte metabolism, causing reductions of potassium (e.g., Smithers et al., 1983), magnesium and free calcium in plasma (Joborn, Hjemdahl, Larsson et al., 1989). Electrolyte responses, however, seem to require relatively high levels of epinephrine and, in the case of magnesium and calcium, also relatively long-lasting stimulation (Joborn et al., in press). Platelet aggregability seems to be enhanced by high levels of circulating epinephrine (Larsson et al., 1989). Plasma epinephrine may correlate to heart rate under some circumstances simply because it is a marker of arousal and thus reflects neurogenic (vagal and sympathetic) cardiac activity (Eliasson, Hjemdahl, & Kahan, 1983; Hjemdahl, 1987, 1988). In fact, my colleagues and I have found relations between increases of arterial epinephrine and cardiac norepinephrine overflow, which, if it is true, suggests that epinephrine may be a marker for cardiac nerve activity during stress.

Circulating Norepinephrine Levels

Plasma levels of norepinephrine are usually less than 5 nM in connection with mild to moderate sympathetic activation (e.g., mental stress, cold pressor testing, orthostatic provocations, isometric exercise, etc.). Levels exceeding 10 nM (1700 pg/ml) are attained during relatively intense or longlasting dynamic exercise, and in some patients with myocardial infarction or surgical stress (Cryer, 1980). It should be remembered that arterial levels are considerably higher than venous levels during intravenous infusions of norepinephrine but that arteriovenous differences may be smaller or reversed when norepinephrine is endogenously released.

Norepinephrine was long thought to be inefficient as a circulating hormone (Cryer, 1980). Indeed, its main actions are those of a neurotransmitter. However, my colleagues and I have found increases in blood pressure (Hjemdahl & Linde, 1983; Hjemdahl et al., 1983; Nisell, Hjemdahl, & Linde, 1985), systemic vascular resistance (Nisell et al., 1985) and vasoconstriction in adipose tissue at reasonably low levels of norepinephrine, that is, at about 8–10 nM or less in arterial plasma. Lipolysis is also stimulated by these low levels of circulating norepinephrine (Hjemdahl & Linde, 1983). Small increments of norepinephrine in plasma have also been shown to increase sodium retention in the kidney (McMurray, Seidelin, Balfour, & Struthers, 1988); 4–8 nM of norepinephrine has been shown to depress sodium pump activity in leucocytes by a beta-mediated mechanisms (Riozzi, Heagerty, Bing et al., 1984). Thus norepinephrine may also act as a circulating hormone.

When considering the concept of innervated and noninnervated adrenoceptors, it should be borne in mind that norepinephrine diffuses rather freely from the neuroeffector junction. Even alpha-adrenoceptors situated at some distance from the neuroeffector junction can thus be activated either by circulating catecholamines (norepinephrine and epinephrine) in the true sense, or by norepinephrine released at some distance from the receptor but diffusing within the tissue (a "paracrine" effect). Thus, norepinephrine may act as a circulating hormone under some conditions, but the neurotransmitter may also influence noninnervated adrenoceptors in other ways.

AUTONOMIC RESPONSES TO MENTAL STRESS

Cardiovascular and other physiological responses to mental stress illustrate the diversity of mechanisms potentially involved in autonomic physiology. It has long been known that mental stress may cause cardiac stimulation, combined with peripheral vasodilatation and vasoconstriction in the kidneys (Brod, 1963; Folkow et al., 1983). Psychophysiologists have evaluated sympathoadrenal activation in terms of catecholamine excretion into urine (Frankenhaeuser, 1986) and frequently found increases of norepinephrine and, in particular, epinephrine excretion in response to stress. However, in studies of plasma catecholamine responses to mental stress, my colleagues and I found no clear-cut elevations of antecubital plasma norepinephrine and small increases of epinephrine, despite signs of marked cardiovascular activation (Åkerstedt et al., 1983; Atterhög et al., 1981; Eliasson et al., 1983; Hjemdahl & Eliasson, 1979). These findings stimulated us to perform detailed studies of sympatho-adrenal responses to mental stress and to attempt to delineate the mechanisms involved in individual organ responses in humans. The test we have used most frequently is a modified Stroop color word test (Frankenhaeuser, Mellis, Rissler et al., 1968). We have studied other mental tasks as well, but other tests tend to be less potent as stressors. Some of our results obtained with the Stroop test will illustrate sympathoadrenal response patterns for the purpose of this chapter.

Catecholamine and Nerve Activity Responses to the Stroop Test

The modified Stroop color word test evokes marked increases of heart rate and blood pressure, but modest increases of plasma epinephrine and no or very small increases (0%–20% in various studies) of antecubital plasma norepinephrine (Åkerstedt et al., 1983; Atterhög et al., 1981; Eliasson et al., 1983; Freyschuss et al., 1988; Hjemdahl et al., 1984). Arterial norepinephrine, on the other hand, increases by 50%–80% (Freyschuss et al., 1988; Tidgren & Hjemdahl, 1989) and renal venous norepinephrine increases considerably more (Tidgren & Hjemdahl, 1989), as is illustrated in Figure 12. This suggests that significant sympathetic activation occurs during the color word test, but that the activation is inhomogeneous and does not include the forearm region. The tissue of the forearm most likely to be the major contributor to antecubital venous norepinephrine is skeletal muscle, as skin sympathetic activity is very low at comfortable ambient temperatures (Wallin & Fagius, 1988). Furthermore, skin responds to arithmetics with vasoconstriction (Brod, 1963; Östergren et al., unpublished) which, presumably, would increase norepinephrine release to antecubital venous plasma during mental stress.

To test our proposal that MSA would not increase during a stimulus such as the color word test (Åkerstedt et al., 1983; Eliasson et al., 1983) my colleagues and I undertook a study comparing neurographically recorded MSA and plasma norepinephrine (both levels and kinetics in plasma). The closest possible relations were sought, so femoral venous blood was sampled and MSA was determined in the peroneal nerve of the leg. To my surprise, we found equally large increases of arterial and femoral venous norepinephrine and that MSA in the leg increased accordingly (Hjemdahl et al., 1989). A recent comparison of MSA in the arm and leg (the two are closely correlated at rest; Wallin & Fagius, 1988) seems to explain the discrepancy with our previous results as mental arithmetic stress was found to increase MSA in the leg, but not in the arm, as is illustrated in Figure 14 (Anderson, Wallin, & Mark, 1987). Thus mental stress influences sympathetic activity to skeletal muscle in different regions of the body differently—a truly inhomogenous reaction pattern. If this marked differentiation is true also for stimuli other than mental stress, one cannot safely extrapolate antecubital venous norepinephrine data (or peroneal MSA data) obtained during stimuli even to sympathetic activity in skeletal muscle in other regions of the body.

The elevation of arterial norepinephrine during mental stress is due to an increased spillover from tissues and not to reduced clearance from plasma, as was shown with the color word test (Hjemdahl et al., 1989) and other stressors (Goldstein et al., 1987). Goldstein et al. also confirmed the lack of elevation of antecubital norepinephrine during stress. Both studies found relations between blood flow and norepinephrine removal from plasma. Interestingly, this leads to increased recovery of norepinephrine derived from arterial plasma in venous plasma during stress. Thus norepinephrine determined in a sample may not have the same origin at rest and during stress. The release of norepinephrine from the kidney was markedly enhanced (Tidgren & Hjemdahl, 1989). Thus a substantial part of the increment in arterial norepinephrine may be due to release from the kidneys (more than 20% is derived from the kidneys at rest—see Esler et al., 1985). The lungs, on the other hand, do not seem to contribute (Freyschuss et al., 1988; Hjemdahl et al., 1989). Antecubital venous epinephrine levels increased little (by about 50%–80% from low basal levels) in the aforementioned studies. Arterial epinephrine levels (see Figure 12) were approximately doubled.

Hemodynamic Responses to the Stroop Test

The color word test usually increases heart rate by 25–30 beats/minute and blood pressure by 30–40/20–30 mm Hg (Atterhög et al., 1981; Eliasson et al., 1983; Freyschuss et al., 1988; Tidgren & Hjemdal, 1989). Stroke volume increases by 20% and systemic vascular resistance decreases by 25%, as is illustrated in Figure 15 (Freyschuss et al., 1988). These marked cardiovascular responses are accompanied by feelings of stress and palpitations (Eliasson et al., 1983; Freyschuss et al., 1988). Despite the biochemical and neurographic evidence for increased nerve activity to the leg muscles, we found vasocilatation also in the entire calf (plethysmography) and in muscle tissue (radiotracer clearance) during the color word test; adipose tissue responded similarly (Linde, Hjemdahl, Freyschuss, & Juhlin-Dannfelt, 1989). The kidney responded with a 50% increase in renal vascular resistance and increased renin secretion during (Tidgren & Hjemdahl, 1989). Also the splanchnic circulation responds with vasoconstriction during the color word test (Juhlin-Dannfelt, Freyschuss, & Linde, 1986). Thus the hemodynamic response pattern elicited by the color word test suggests that blood pressure increases because of cardio-renal and splanchnic sympathetic activation, whereas peripheral tissues dilate either with or without increases in sympathetic nerve activity.

How can this pattern, which resembles the defense reaction and is schematically illustrated in Figure 16, be explained? Experiments with beta-blockade and epinephrine infusions give some clues. The increase in cardiac output during the color word

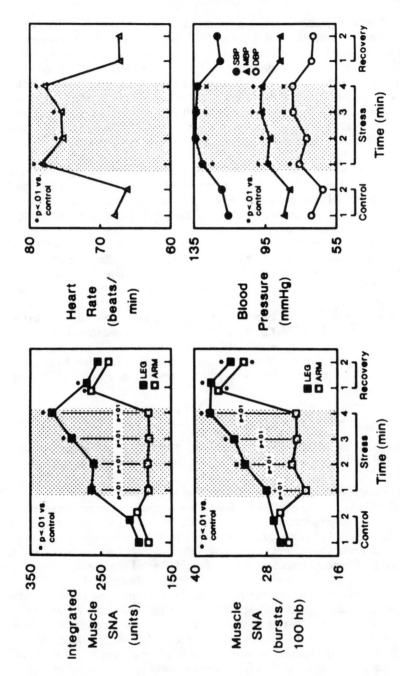

Figure 14 Muscle sympathetic nerve activity in the arm and leg (left; same data presented in two ways) and heart rate and blood pressure (right) during mental arithmetic stress. Note the increase in leg MSA during stress and in arm MSA after stress. This corresponds to venous plasma norepinephrine responses in the two regions. From Anderson et al. (1987) by permission of publisher and author.

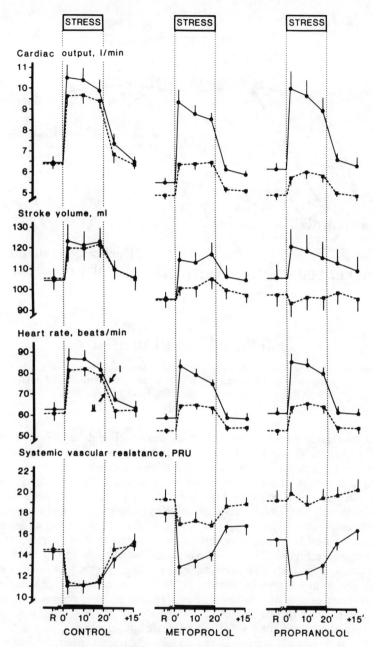

Figure 15 Cardiac responses to the Stroop test before and after placebo (control), beta-1 selective blockade by metoprolol and nonselective beta-blockade by propranolol in 3 × 10 healthy male subjects. Responses are quite reproducible after placebo. Vascular resistance and stroke volume responses are attenuated by metoprolol and abolished by propranolol. Heart rate responses are similarly inhibited. Adapted from Freyschuss et al., (1988) by permission of publisher.

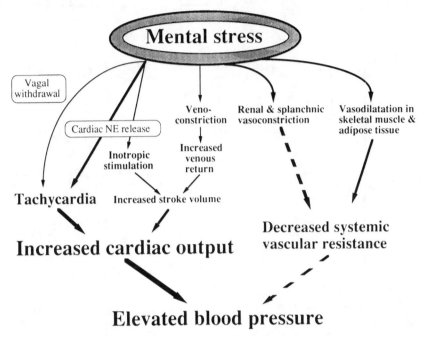

Figure 16 Schematic representation of cardiovascular responses to mental stress, based on
studies with the Stroop test (our results; see text for references) and mental
arithmetic (Brod, 1963; Brod et al., 1976; Barcroft et al., 1960).

test was two-thirds dependent on increased heart rate and one-third on increased
stroke volume (see Figure 15). The increase in heart rate during the test was equally
inhibited by propranolol and the beta-1 selective antagonist metoprolol, suggesting
that epinephrine was of minor importance (Freyschuss et al., 1988). Residual responses after beta-blockade may have been related to incomplete beta-blockade or
vagal withdrawal. The stroke volume response to the color word test showed a beta-2
mediated component, as propranolol abolished it and metoprolol had an intermediate
effect (see Figure 15). Epinephrine influences heart rate little in the relevant concentration range (see Figure 13) but may have contributed about half of the increase in
stroke volume as judged by intravenous infusion data (Freyschuss et al., 1986) and
effects of metoprolol (Freyschuss et al., 1988). The increase in stroke volume may in
part have been caused by increased venous return, because venous tone increases
during mental stress (Brod, Cachovan, Bahlman et al., 1976). Thus, with regard to
cardiac responses to the color word test, increases in heart rate appear to be entirely
neurogenic (sympathetic activation and vagal withdrawal), whereas stroke volume
responses may be more complex (that is, as well as increased contractility due to
sympathetic activation or epinephrine, such as increased venous return, and decreased impedance due to vasodilatation).

Vasodilator responses to the word test also showed a mixture of beta-1 and beta-2
mediated components, as propranolol abolished vasodilatation in skeletal muscle and
the systemic circulation (see Figure 14) and resulted in vasoconstriction in adipose
tissue—again metroprolol had intermediate effects (Freyschuss et al., 1988; Linde et

al., 1989). Based on infusion data (Freyschuss et al., 1986) and effects of beta-blockade (Freyschuss et al., 1988; Linde et al., 1989) epinephrine could only explain vasodilator responses to the color word test in part. Interestingly, pressor responses to the test seem to remain similarly intact after beta-1 selective and nonselective beta-blockade, whether given acutely (Freyschuss et al., 1988) or chronically (Eliasson, Kahan, Hylander, & Hjemdahl, 1987; Olsson et al., 1986). Furthermore, increases in cardiac output and decreases in systemic vascular resistance were almost identically related to each other with and without treatment (Freyschuss et al., 1988). Thus it is possible that the cardiovascular variable primarily regulated during mental stress is blood pressure, in agreement with ideas recently put forward by Julius (1988) in a broader scope.

The effects of beta-1 blockade by metoprolol and nonselective beta-blockade by propranolol on vasodilator responses to the color word test may thus reflect two vasodilating mechanisms: an active component related to epinephrine (which, according to infusion data, explains only part of the response) and a passive baroreceptor mediated component aimed at buffering the increase in cardiac output (partially inhibited by blockade) in order to maintain the centrally determined blood pressure response. Metoprolol may have been inadequately beta-1 selective, but the elevation of circulating epinephrine nonetheless seems to have been inadequate to explain test-induced vasodilatation. Cholinergic neurogenic vasodilatation may be elicited by mental stress (Barcroft, Brod, Hejl et al., 1960; Blair, Glover, Greenfield, & Roddie, 1959; Brod et al., 1976). Such a dilating influence could explain why the color word test did not evoke vasoconstriction in skeletal muscle, despite enhanced sympathetic nerve activity (Hjemdahl et al., 1989), even after propranolol (Freyschuss et al., 1988). The possibility of cholinergic vasodilatation during the test has not been evaluated yet. Thus vascular responses to mental stress are complex and probably involve several mechanisms, including increased sympathetic nerve activity (vasoconstriction in the kidney and splanchnic region and in adipose tissue after propranolol), cholinergic vasodilator nerves (speculative), circulating epinephrine (mostly skeletal muscle and adipose tissue), and, possibly, unidentified factors such as peptides.

Other Responses to the Stroop Test

The modified Stroop color word test also enhances lipolysis (Joborn et al., 1989; Linde et al., in press)—both nerve activity and circulating epinephrine may be involved in this response (Linde et al., 1989). The renin secretion response could not be accounted for by epinephrine, even though higher plasma concentrations of epinephrine had pronounced effects on renal renin release (Tidgren & Hemdahl, 1989). A measure of platelet aggregability in vivo increased during the color test (Larsson et al., 1989), but this apparently cannot be related to the modest elevation of circulating epinephrine (Larsson et al., submitted for publication). Plasma potassium and unionized calcium, both of which are reduced by epinephrine infusion, increased in response to the word test (Joborn et al., 1989). Thus the test is a potent stressor that elicits a wide range of physiological responses. Closer examination of the various mechanisms likely to be involved suggests that most responses are related to neurogenic mechanisms rather than to elevations of the classical stress hormone, epinephrine.

CONCLUSION

This overview has mainly dealt with basic autonomic physiology and methodological issues involved in studies of autonomic mechanisms in humans. I have tried to illustrate that the sympathetic nervous system does not operate in a synchronized fashion and that many, if not most, studies are performed in a manner not taking the concept of sympathetic differentiation into account. In fact, I believe the term "sympathetic tone" should be abandoned because it is misleading. The described effects of mental stress illustrate that different organs may respond quite differently to the same stimulus and that even the same tissue (skeletal muscle) in two different locations (arm and leg) may respond differently. This is not unique to mental stress, as forearm and calf vascular responses to other stimuli may differ as well (Rusch, Shepherd, Webb, & Vanhoutte, 1981). The concept of highly localized changes in the activity of the autonomic nervous system is not new—it has been pointed out by, for example, Brod et al. (1976), Wolf (1970), and Folkow (1982); Folkow et al., 1983—but it has not had an adequate impact on the way modern biochemical tools such as plasma catecholamine analyses have been (and often still are) used.

For example, numerous studies of plasma catecholamine levels in hypertension have been performed with antecubital venous plasma sampling. This sampling site introduces errors with regard to circulating epinephrine levels (variable tissue extraction) and distorts the image of sympathetic activity provided by plasma norepinephrine (this sampling site reflects forearm nerve activity). The possible sympathetic contribution to the etiology of essential hypertension should probably be sought in the heart, kidneys, and splanchnic region and not in skeletal muscle (Folkow, 1982). Therefore, regional norepinephrine overflow studies reflecting these target organs both at rest and during stress would seem most appropriate. Very few such studies have been published (see Esler et al., 1988; Hjemdahl, 1988). If regional studies are not feasible for technical reasons, overall sympathetic function should preferably be studied in terms of noreprinephrine levels in and spillover to arterial plasma, which will reflect all organs in proportion to their size, innervation, and nerve activity. Again, very few such studies have been performed (Hjemdahl, 1988). Thus a good marker for sympathetic nerve activity, norepinephrine in plasma, has very often been used in a manner not yielding optimal information.

Studies of sympathetic activity using plasma norepinephrine determinations should be aimed at the target organ also in other contexts, if possible. In cardiology conventional plasma norepinephrine (antecubital sampling) may give an indirect reflection of cardiac function, for example, in terms of the compensatory increase in nerve activity needed to elevate peripheral vascular resistance when cardiac output falls. Possible correlations between plasma norepinephrine and cardiac function merely reflect this indirect relation; less than 2% of antecubital norepinephrine probably derives from the heart (Esler et al., 1988). The most marked changes of nerve activity occur in the target organ, as is illustrated for example by the acute adaptation to exercise during different modes of pacing—a doubled cardiac norepinephrine overflow when ventricular rate is kept constant as compared to variable (Pehrsson et al., 1988). In that case less pronounced changes occur in the periphery. In the heart one must also consider the complex interplay between sympathetic and vagal nerves and baroreceptor reflexes controlling these nerves.

The importance of epinephrine as a mediator of various cardiovascular and other responses to stress is sometimes exaggerated. Several lines of evidence are needed to prove causality between epinephrine responses and physiological effects. I have argued that epinephrine may contribute, but that neurogenic mechanisms probably are more important for several responses to mental stress. The complex interplay between sympathetic and parasympathetic mechanisms, between cardiac and vascular responses, and between central command and local regulation in the in vivo setting make interpretations uncertain under several circumstances. I have tried to caution against indiscriminate interpretation of data according to current trends, such as prejunctional modulation of transmitter release, extrapolation of adrenoceptor data from blood cells to other cells, or invoking peptidergic mechanisms as being physiologically important because they can be demonstrated. Putative regulatory mechanisms should be examined critically until adequate evidence is at hand.

Available techniques allow us to obtain a fairly good idea of autonomic mechanisms involved in physiological responses to various provocations and in disease states, provided that they are used in an adequate manner and that limitations with the different techniques are appreciated. Several lines of evidence may be needed to delineate mechanisms behind a certain response. I have not attempted to describe mechanisms behind various physiological or pathophysiological states. Rather, I intended to give some background with which to critically assess various proposed mechanisms.

REFERENCES

Aarons, R. D., & Molinoff, P. B. (1982). Changes in the density of beta adrenergic receptors in rat lymphocytes, heart and lung after chronic treatment with propranolol. *Journal of Pharmacology and Experimental Therapeutics, 221,* 439–443.

Aas, H., Skomedal, T., Osnes, J. B., et al. (1986). Noradrenaline evokes an alpha-adrenoceptor-mediated inotropic effect in human ventricular myocardium. *Acta Pharmacologica et Toxicologica, 58,* 88–90.

Ackerman, D. M., Hiebe, J. P., Sarau, H. M., & Jain, T. C. (1984). Pharmacological characterization of dopamine-4-sulfate. *Archives Internationales de Pharmacodynamie et de Therapie, 267,* 241–248.

Ahlquist, R. P. (1948). Study of adrenotropic receptors. *American Journal of Physiology, 153,* 586–600.

Åkerstedt, T., Gillberg, M., Hjemdahl, P., et al. (1983). Comparison of urinary and plasma catecholamine responses to mental stress. *Acta Physiologica Scandinavica, 117,* 19–26.

Akselrod, S., Gordon, D., Madwed, J. B., et al. (1985). Hemodynamic regulation: Investigation by spectral analysis. *American Journal of Physiology, 249,* H867–H875.

Alabaster, V., & Davey, M. (1984). Precapillary vessels: Effects of the sympathetic nervous system and catecholamines. *Journal of Cardiovascular Pharmacology, 6,* S365–S376.

Anderson, E. A., Wallin, B. G., & Mark, A. L. (1987). Dissociation of sympathetic nerve activity in arm and leg muscle during mental stress. *Hypertension, 9* (Suppl. 3), 114–119.

Angus, J. A., Cocks, T. M., & Satoh, K. (1986). The α-adrenoceptor on endothelial cells. *Federation Proceedings: Federation of American Societies for Experimental Biology, 45,* 2355–2359.

Anwar-ul, S., Gilani, H., & Cobbin, L. B. (1986). The cardioselectivity of himbacine: A muscarine receptor antagonist. *Naunyn-Schmiedeberg's Archives of Pharmacology, 332,* 16–20.

Ariens, E. J., & Simonis, A. M. (1983). Physiological and pharmacological aspects of adrenergic receptor classification. *Biochemical Pharmacology, 32,* 1539–1545.

Arnold, J. M. O., & McDevitt, D. G. (1984). Vagal activity is increased during intravenous isoprenaline infusion in man. *British Journal of Clinical Pharmacology, 18,* 311–316.

Arnold, J. M. O., & McDevitt, D. G. (1986). Reflex vagal withdrawal and the hemodynamic response to intravenous isoproterenol in the presence of beta-antagonists. *Clinical Pharmacology and Therapeutics, 40,* 199–208.

Arnold, J. M. O., O'Connor, P. C., Riddell, J. G., et al. (1985). Effects of the β2-adrenoceptor antagonist ICI 118,551 on exercise tachycardia and isoprenaline-induced β-adrenoceptor responses in man. *British Journal of Clinical Pharmacology, 19,* 619–630.

Ask, J. A., Stene-Larsen, G., Helle, K. B., & Resch, F. (1985). Functional β1- and β2-adrenoceptors in the human myocardium. *Acta Physiologica Scandinavica, 123,* 81–88.

Atterhög, H. J., Eliasson, K., & Hjemdahl, P. (1981). Sympatho-adrenal and cardiovascular responses to mental stress, isometric handgrip and cold pressor test in asymptomatic young men with primary T wave abnormalities in the electrocardiograms. *British Heart Journal, 46,* 311–319.

Awan, N. A., Miller, R. R., Maxwell, K., & Mason, D. T. (1977). Effects of prazosin on forearm resistance and capacitance vessels. *Clinical Pharmacology and Therapeutics, 22,* 79–84.

Bannister, R., Boylston, A. W., Davies, I. B., et al. (1981). β-receptor numbers and thermodynamics in denervation supersensitivity. *Journal of Physiology, 319,* 369–377.

Barcroft, H., Brod, J., Hejl, Z., et al. (1960). The mechanism of the vasodilation in the forearm muscle during stress (mental arithmetic). *Clinical Science, 19,* 577–586.

Bell, C. (1988). Dopamine release from sympathetic nerve terminals. *Progress in Neurobiology, 30,* 193–208.

Benfield, P., Clissold, S. P., & Brogden, R. N. (1986). Metoprolol: An updated review of its pharmacodynamic and pharmacokinetic properties, in therapeutic efficacy, in hypertension, ischaemic heart disease and related cardiovascular disorders. *Drugs, 31,* 376–429.

Beresford, R., & Heel, R. C. (1986). Betaxolol: A review of its pharmacodynamic and pharmacokinetic properties and therapeutic efficacy in hypertension. *Drugs, 31,* 6–28.

Bertel, O., Bühler, F. R., Baitsch, G., et al. (1982). Plasma adrenaline and noradrenaline in patients with acute myocardial infarction: Relationship to ventricular arrhythmias of varying severity. *Chest, 82,* 64–68.

Berthelsen, S., & Pettinger, W. A. (1977). A functional basis for classification of α-adrenergic receptors. *Life Sciences, 21,* 595–606.

Best, J. D., & Halter, J. B. (1982). Release and clearance rates of epinephrine in man: Importance of arterial measurements. *Journal of Clinical Endocrinology and Metabolism, 55,* 263–268.

Bilski, A. J., Halliday, S. E., Fitzgerald, J. D., & Wale, J. L. (1983). The pharmacology of a $\beta2$-selective adrenoceptor antagonist (ICI 118,551). *Journal of Cardiovascular Pharmacology, 5,* 430–437.

Birdsall, N. J. M., & Hulme, E. C. (1983). Muscarinic receptor subclasses. *Trends in Pharmacological Sciences, 4,* 459–463.

Bjornerheim, R., Simonsen, S., & Golf, S. (1987). Increased β-adrenoceptor-coupled adenylate cyclase response in transplanted human hearts. *Scandinavian Journal of Clinical and Laboratory Investigation, 47,* 661–665.

Blair, D. A., Glover, W. E., Greenfield, A. D. M., & Roddie, I. C. (1959). Excitation of cholinergic vasodilator nerves to human skeletal muscles during emotional stress. *Journal of Physiology, 148,* 633–647.

Blankestijn, P. J., Man In't Veld, A. J., Tulen, J., et al. (1988). Support for adrenaline–hypertension hypothesis: 18 hour pressor effect after 6 hours adrenaline infusion. *Lancet, 2,* 1386–1389.

Blombery, P. A., & Heinzow, B. G. J. (1983). Cardiac and pulmonary norepinephrine release and removal in the dog. *Circulation Research, 53,* 688–694.

Bradley, T., & Hjemdahl, P. (1984). Further studies on renal nerve stimulation induced release of noradrenaline and dopamine from the canine kidney in situ. *Acta Physiologica Scandinavica, 122,* 369–379.

Bradley, T., Hjemdahl, P., DiBona, G. F., et al. (1985). Evidence against a functional role for dopamine-4-sulphate in the kidney. *Acta Physiologica Scandinavica, 125,* 739–741.

Brett, J. G., Steinberg, S. F., deGroot, P. G., et al. (1988). Norepinephrine down-regulates the activity of protein S on endothelial cells. *Journal of Cell Biology, 106,* 2109–2118.

Bristow, M. R., Ginsburg, R., Gilbert, E. M., & Herschberger, (1987). Heterogeneous regulatory changes in cell surface membrane receptors coupled to a positive inotropic response in the failing human heart. *Basic Research in Cardiology, 82*(Suppl 2), 369–376.

Brocke, J. A., & Cunnane, T. C. (1987). Relationship between the nerve action potential and transmitter release from sympathetic postganglionic nerve terminals. *Nature, 326,* 605–607.

Brod, J. (1963). Haemodynamic basis of acute pressor reactions and hypertension. *British Heart Journal, 25,* 227–245.

Brod, J., Cachovan, M., Bahlman, J., et al. (1976). Haemodynamic response to an acute emotional stress (mental arithmetic) with special reference to the venous side. *Australian and New Zealand Journal of Medicine, 6*(Suppl. 2), 19–25.

Brodde, O. E. (1988). The functional importance of $\beta1$- and $\beta2$-adrenoceptors in the human heart. *American Journal of Cardiology, 62,* 24C–29C.

Brodde, O. E., Beckeringh, J. J., & Michel, M. C. (1987). Human heart β-adrenoceptors: A fair comparison with lymphocyte β-adrenoceptors? *Trends in Pharmacological Sciences, 8,* 403–407.

Brodde, O. E., Daul, A., & O'Hara, N. (1984). β-adrenoceptor changes in human lymphocytes, induced by exercise. *Naunyn-Schmiedeberg's Archiv fur Pharmakologie, 325,* 190–192.

Brodde, O. E., Daul, A., Stuka, N., et al. (1985). Effects of β-adrenoceptor antagonist administration on β2-adrenoceptor density in human lymphocytes: The role of "intrinsic sympathomimetic activity." *Naunyn-Schmiedeberg's Archiv fur Pharmakologie, 328,* 417–422.

Brodde, O. E., Daul, A. E., Wang, X. L., et al. (1987). Dynamic exercise-induced increase in lymphocyte β2-adrenoceptors: Abnormality in essential hypertension and its correction by antihypertensives. *Clinical Pharmacology and Therapeutics, 41,* 371–379.

Brodde, O. E., Daul, A., Wellstein, A., et al. (1988). Differentiation of β1- and β2-adrenoceptor mediated effects in humans. *American Journal of Physiology, 254,* H199–H206.

Brodde, O. E., O'Hara, N., Zerkowski, H. R., & Rohm, N. (1984). Human cardiac β-adrenoceptors: Both β1- and β2-adrenoceptors are functionally coupled to the adenylate cyclase in right atrium. *Journal of Cardiovascular Pharmacology, 6,* 1184–1191.

Brogden, R. N., Speight, T. M., & Avery, G. S. (1975). Timolol: A preliminary report of its pharmacological properties and therapeutic efficacy in angina and hypertension. *Drugs, 9,* 164–177.

Brown, J. E., McLeod, A. A., & Shand, D. G. (1983). Evidence for cardiac β2-adrenoceptors in man. *Clinical Pharmacology and Therapeutics, 33,* 424–428.

Brown, M. J. (1984). Simultaneous assay of noradrenaline and its deaminated metabolite, dihydroxyphenglycol, in plasma: A simplified approach to the exclusion of phaeochromocytoma in patients with borderline elevation of plasma noradrenaline concentration. *European Journal of Clinical Investigation, 14,* 67–72.

Brown, M. J., & Dollery, C. T. (1984). Adrenaline and hypertension. *Clinical and Experimental Hypertension, A6,* 539–549.

Brown, M. J., Jenner, D. A., Allison, D. J., & Dollery, C. T. (1981). Variations in individual organ release of noradrenaline measured by an improved radioenzymatic technique: Limitations of peripheral venous measurements in the assessment of sympathetic nervous activity. *Clinical Science, 61,* 585–590.

Burnstock, G. (1986). Purines as cotransmitters in adrenergic and cholinergic neurones. *Progress in Brain Research, 68,* 193–203.

Burnstock, G. (1987). Mechanisms of interaction of peptide and nonpeptide vascular neurotransmitter systems. *Journal of Cardiovascular Pharmacology, 10*(Suppl. 12), 74–81.

Buu, N. T., & Kuchel, O. (1979). Dopamine-4-sulfate: A possible precursor of free norepinephrine. *Canadian Journal of Biochemistry, 57,* 1159–1162.

Buxton, B. F., Jones, C. R., Molenaar, P., & Summers, R. J. (1987). Characterization and autoradiographic localizations of β-adrenoceptor subtypes in human cardiac tissues. *British Journal of Pharmacology, 92,* 299–310.

Cappato, R., Alboni, P., Paparella, N., et al. (1987). Bedside evaluation of sinus bradycardia: Usefulness of atropine test in discriminating organic from autonomic involvement of sinus automaticity. *American Heart Journal, 114,* 1384–1388.

Carlsson, E., Åblad, B., Brändström, A., & Carlsson, B. (1972). Differentiated blockade of the chronotropic effects of various adrenergic stimuli in the cat. *Life Sciences, 11,* 953–958.

Chang, P. C., van der Krogt, J. A., & van Brummelen, P. (1987). Demonstration of neuronal and extraneuronal uptake of circulating norepinephrine in the forearm. *Hypertension, 9,* 647–653.

Chess-Williams, R. G., Broadley, K. J., & Sheridan, D. J. (1987). Cardiac post-junctional α1- and β-adrenoceptors: Effects of chronic chemical sympathectomy with 6-hydroxydopamine. *Journal of Receptor Research, 7,* 713–728.

Christensen, N. J., Henriksen, O., & Lassen, N. A. (Eds.). (1986). *The sympatho-adrenal system: Adrenergic physiology and pathophysiology.* Copenhagen: Munksgaard; New York: Raven Press; Tokyo: Nankodo.

Cleaveland, C. R., Rangno, R. E., & Shand, D. G. (1972). A standardized isoproterenol sensitivity test. *Archives of Internal Medicine, 130,* 47–52.

Colucci, W. S., Leatherman, G. F., Ludmer, P. L., & Gauthier, D. F. (1987). β-adrenergic inotropic responsiveness of patients with heart failure: Studies with intracoronary dobutamine infusion. *Circulation Research, 61*(Suppl. 1), 82–86.

Constantine, J. W., & Lebel, W. (1980). Complete blockade by phenoxybenzamine of α1- but not of α2-vascular receptors in dogs and the effects of propranolol. *Naunyn-Schmiedeberg's Archiv fur Pharmakologie, 314,* 149–156.

Cryer, P. E. (1980). Physiology and pathophysiology of the human sympathoadrenal neuroendocrine system. *New England Journal of Medicine , 303,* 436–444.

Cubbeddu, L. X. (1988). New α1-adrenergic receptor antagonists for the treatment of hypertension: Role of vascular α-receptors in the control of peripheral resistance. *American Heart Journal, 116,* 133–162.

Cuche, J. L., Prinseau, J., Ruget, G., et al. (1982). Plasma free and sulfoconjugated catecholamines in healthy men. *European Heart Journal, 3*(Suppl. C), 3–8.

Dahlöf, C. (1981). Studies on β-adrenoceptor mediated facilitation of sympathetic neurotransmission. *Acta Physiologica Scandinavica,* (Suppl. 500), 1–147.

Daly, R. N., & Hieble, J. P. (1987). Neuropeptide Y modulates adrenergic neurotransmission by an endothelium dependent mechanism. *European Journal of Pharmacology, 138,* 445–446.

Davey, M. J. (1986a). Alpha adrenoceptors: An overview. *Journal of Molecular and Cellular Cardiology, 18*(Suppl. 5), 1–15.

Davey, M. J. (1986b). Overview of α-adrenoceptors. *Clinical Science, 70*(Suppl. 14), 33s–39s.

Davies, B., Sudera, D., Sagnella, G., et al. (1982). Increased numbers of alpha adrenoceptors in sympathetic denervation supersensitivity in man. *Journal of Clinical Investigation, 69,* 779–784.

DeBlasei, A., Maisel, A. S., Feldman, R. D., et al. (1986). In vivo regulation of β-adrenergic receptors on human mononuclear leukocytes: Assessment of receptor number, location, and function after posture change, exercise, and isoproterenol infusion. *Journal of Clinical Endocrinology and Metabolism, 63,* 847–853.

DeChamplain, J., Bouvier, M., Cléroux, J., & Farley, L. (1984). Free and conjugated catecholamines in plasma and red blood cells of normotensive and hypertensive patients. *Clinical and Experimental Hypertension, A6,* 523–537.

Demassieux, S., Bordeleau, L., Gravel, D., & Carrière, S. (1987). Catecholamine sulfates: End products or metabolic intermediates? *Life Sciences, 40,* 183–191.

Dixon, W. R., Mosimann, W. F., & Weiner, N. (1979). The role of presynaptic feedback mechanisms in regulation of norepinephrine release by nerve stimulation. *Journal of Pharmacology and Experimental Therapeutics, 209,* 196–204.

Duncan, M. W., Compton, P., Lazarus, L., & Smythe, G. A. (1988). Measurement of norepinephrine and 3,4-disydroxyphenylglycol in urine and plasma for the diagnosis of pheochromocytoma. *New England Journal of Medicine, 319,* 136–142.

Eckberg, D. L., Harkins, S. W., Fritsch, J. M., et al. (1986). Baroreflex control of plasma norepinephrine and heart period in healthy subjects of diabetic patients. *Journal of Clinical Investigation, 78,* 366–374.

Eckberg, D. L., Rea, R. F., Andersson, O. K., et al. (1988). Baroreflex modulation of sympathetic neurotransmitters in humans. *Acta Physiologica Scandinavica, 133,* 221–231.

Edvinsson, L., Håkanson, R., Wahlestedt, C., & Uddman, R. (1987). Effects of neuropeptide Y on the cardiovascular system. *Trends in Pharmacological Sciences, 8,* 231–235.

Egan, B., Neubig, R., & Julius, S. (1985). Pharmacologic reduction of sympathetic drive increases platelet α2-receptor number. *Clinical Pharmacology and Therapeutics, 38,* 519–524.

Eisenhofer, G., Lambie, D. G., & Johnson, R. H. (1985). β-adrenoceptor responsiveness and plasma catecholamines as determinants of cardiovascular reactivity to mental stress. *Clinical Science, 69,* 483–492.

Eklund, B., Hjemdahl, P., Seideman, P., & Atterhög, J. H. (1983). Effects of prazosin on hemodynamics and sympatho-adrenal activity in hypertensive patients. *Journal of Cardiovascular Pharmacology, 5,* 384–391.

El-Fakahany, E. E., & Lee, J. H. (1986). Agonist-induced muscarinic acetylcholine receptor down-regulation in intact rat brain cells. *European Journal of Pharmacology, 132,* 21–30.

Eliasson, K., Hjemdahl, P., & Kahan, T. (1983). Circulatory and sympatho-adrenal responses to stress in borderline and established hypertension. *Journal of Hypertension, 1,* 131–139.

Eliasson, K., Kahan, T., Hylander, B., & Hjemdahl, P. (1987). Responses to mental stress and physical provocations before and during long-term treatment of hypertensive patients with β-adrenoceptor blockers or hydrochlorothiazide. *British Journal of Clinical Pharmacology, 24,* 1–14.

Endoh, M. (1986). Regulation of myocardial contractility via adrenoceptors: Differential mechanisms of α- and β-adrenoceptor mediated actions. In Grobecker et al. (Eds.), *New aspects of the role of adrenoceptors in the cardiovascular system* (pp. 78–105). Berlin: Springer Verlag.

Esler, M., Jennings, G., Korner, P. et al. (1988). Assessment of human sympathetic nervous system activity from measurements of norepinephrine turnover. *Hypertension, 11,* 3–20.

Ewing, D. J. (1978). Cardiovascular reflexes and autonomic neuropathy. *Clinical Science and Molecular Medicine, 55,* 321–327.

Fagius, J., & Sundlöf, G. (1986). The diving response in man: Effects on sympathetic activity in muscle and skin nerve fascicles. *Journal of Physiology, 377,* 429–443.

Feldman, R. D., Limbird, L. E., Nadeau, J., et al. (1983). Dynamic regulation of leukocyte beta adrenergic receptor agonist interactions by physiological changes in circulating catecholamines. *Journal of Clinical Investigation, 72,* 164–170.

FitzGerald, D., Doyle, V., Kelly, J. G., & O'Malley, K. (1984). Cardiac sensitivity to isoprenaline, lymphocyte β-adrenoceptors and age. *Clinical Science, 66,* 697–699.

Floras, J. S., Aylward, P. E., Victor, R. G., et al. (1988). Epinephrine facilitates neurogenic vasoconstriction in humans. *Journal of Clinical Investigation, 81,* 1265–1274.

Folkow, B. (1982). Physiological aspects of primary hypertension. *Physiological Reviews, 62,* 347–504.

Folkow, B., DiBona, G. F., Hjemdahl, P., et al. (1983). Measurements of plasma norepinephrine concentrations in human primary hypertension: A word of caution on their applicability for assessing neurogenic contributions. *Hypertension, 5,* 399–403.

Frankenhaeuser, M. (1986). In M. H. Appley & R. A. Turnbull (Eds.), *Dynamics of stress* (p. 101). New York: Plenum Press.

Frankenhaeuser, M., Mellis, I., Rissler, A., et al. (1968). Catecholamine excretion as related to cognitive and emotional reaction patterns. *Psychosomatic Medicine, 30,* 109–120.

Fredholm, B. B., Gustafsson, L. E., Hedqvist, P., & Sollevi, A. (1982). Adenosine in the regulation of neurotransmitter release in the peripheral nervous system. In R. M. Berne, T. W. Rall, & R. Rubio (Eds.), *Regulatory function of adenosine* (pp. 479–495). The Hague; Boston; London: Martinus Nijhoff Publishers.

Freyschuss, U., Hjemdahl, P., Juhlin-Dannfelt, A., & Linde, B. (1986). Cardiovascular and metabolic responses to low dose adrenaline infusion: An invasive study in humans. *Clinical Science, 70,* 199–206.

Freyschuss, U., Hjemdahl, P., Juhlin-Dannfelt, A., & Linde, B. (1988). Cardiovascular and sympathoadrenal responses to mental stress: Influence of β-blockade. *American Journal of Physiology, 255,* H1443–H1451.

Frishman, W. H. (1981). Nadolol: A new β-adrenoceptor antagonist. *New England Journal of Medicine, 305,* 678–682.

Frishman, W. H. (1987). Beta-adrenergic blocker withdrawal. *American Journal of Cardiology, 59,* 26F–32F.

Frishman, W. H., Christodoulou, J., Weksler, B. et al. (1978). Abrupt propanolol withdrawal in angina pectoris: Effects on platelet aggregation and exercise tolerance. *American Heart Journal, 95,* 169–179.

Frohlich, E. D., Tarazi, R. C., & Dustan, H. P. (1969). Hyperadrenergic β-adrenergic circulatory state. *Archives of Internal Medicine, 123,* 1–7.

Furchgott, R. F., Wakade, T. D., Sorace, R. A., & Stollack, J. S. (1975). Occurrence of both β1- and β2-adrenoceptors in guinea-pig tracheal smooth muscle, and variation of the β1-:β2-ratio in different animals. *Federation Proceedings: Federation of American Societies for Experimental Biology, 34,* 794.

Furchgott, R. F., & Zawadski, J. V. (1980). The obligatory role of endothelial cells in the relaxation of arterial smooth muscle by acetylcholine. *Nature, 288,* 373–376.

Furukawa, Y., Ogiwara, Y., Saegusa, K., et al. (1987). Time dependent impairment of vagally mediated inhibition of noradrenaline release in the dog heart. *Cardiovascular Research, 21,* 717–724.

Ganten, D., Lang, R. E., Archelos, J., & Unger, T. (1984). Peptidergic systems: Effects on blood vessels. *Journal of Cardiovascular Pharmacology, 6* (Suppl. 3), 598–606.

George, C. F., Conolly, M. E., Fenyvesi, T., et al. (1972). Intravenously administered isoproterenol sulfate dose–response curves in man. *Archives of Internal Medicine, 130,* 361–364.

Gilman, A. G., Goodman, L. S., Rall, T. W., & Murad, F. (Eds.). (1985). *Goodman and Gilman's the pharmacological basis of therapeutics.* New York: Macmillan.

Goldberg, L. I. (1972). Cardiovascular and renal actions of dopamine: Potential clinical applications. *Pharmacological Reviews, 24,* 1–29.

Goldberg, M. R., & Robertson, D. (1983). Yohimbine: A pharmacological probe for study of the α2-adrenoceptor. *Pharmacological Reviews, 35,* 143–180.

Goldberg, M. R., & Robertson, D. (1984). Evidence for the existence of vascular α2-adrenergic receptors in humans. *Hypertension, 6,* 551–556.

Goldstein, D. S. (1981). Plasma norepinephrine as an indicator of sympathetic neural activity in clinical cardiology. *American Journal of Cardiology, 48,* 1147–1154.

Goldstein, D. S. (1983). Plasma catecholamines and essential hypertension: An analytical review. *Hypertension, 5,* 86–89.

Goldstein, D. S., Eisenhofer, G., Sax, F. L., et al. (1987). Plasma norepinephrine pharmacokinetics during mental challenge. *Psychosomatic Medicine, 49,* 591–605.

Goldstein, D. S., Eisenhofer, G., Stull, R., et al. (1988). Plasma dihydroxyphenylglycol and the intraneuronal disposition of norepinephrine in humans. *Journal of Clinical Investigation, 81,* 213–220.

Goldstein, D. S., McCarty, R., Polinsky, R. J., & Kopin, I. J. (1983). Relationship between plasma norepinephrine and sympathetic neural activity. *Hypertension, 5,* 552–559.

Goldstein, D. S., Zimlichman, R., Stull, R., et al. (1985). Measurement of regional neuronal removal of norepinephrine in man. *Journal of Clinical Investigation, 76,* 15–21.

Griese, M., Körholz, U., Körholz, D., et al. (1988). Density and agonist-promoted high and low affinity states of the β-adrenoceptor on human B- and T-cells. *European Journal of Clinical Investigation, 18,* 213–217.

Halbrügge, T., Gerhardt, T., Ludwig, J., et al. (1988). Assay of catecholamines and dihydroxyphenylethyleneglycol in human plasma and its application in orthostasis and mental stress. *Life Sciences, 43,* 19–26.

Hamilton, C. A., & Reid, J. L. (1982). Changes in α-adrenoceptors during long-term treatment of rabbits with prazosin. *Journal of Cardiovascular Pharmacology, 3,* 977–985.

Hammer, G., & Giachetti, A. (1982). Muscarinic receptor substypes: M1 and M2 biochemical and functional characterization. *Life Sciences, 31,* 2991–2998.

Harden, T. K. (1983). Agonist-induced desensitization of the β-adrenergic receptor-linked adenylate cyclase. *Pharmacological Reviews, 35,* 5–32.

Harry, J. D., Norris, S. C., Percival, G. C., & Young, J. (1988). The dose in humans at which ICI 118,551 (a selective β2-adrenoceptor blocking agent) demonstrates blockade of β1-adrenoceptors. *Clinical Pharmacology and Therapeutics, 43,* 492–498.

Harvey, J. E., Baldwin, C. J., Wood, P. J., et al. (1981). Airway and metabolic responsiveness to intravenous salbutamol in asthma: Effect of regular inhaled salbutamol. *Clinical Science, 60,* 579–585.

Hasegawa, M., & Townley, R. G. (1983). Difference between lung and spleen susceptibility of beta-adrenergic receptors to desensitization by terbutaline. *Journal of Allergy and Clinical Immunology, 71,* 230–238.

Haynes, L. W. (1986). Peptide neuroregulation of vascular tone by the sympathetic nervous system. *Trends in Pharmacological Sciences, 7,* 383–384.

Heel, R. C., Brogden, R. N., Speight, T. M., & Avery, G. S. (1979). Atenolol: A review of its pharmacological properties and therapeutic efficacy in angina pectoris and hypertension. *Drugs, 17,* 425–460.

Hicks, P. E., Langer, S. Z., & MaCrae, A. D. (1985). Differential blocking actions of idazoxan against the inhibitory effects of 6-flouronoradrenaline and clonidine in the rat vas deferens. *British Journal of Clinical Pharmacology, 86,* 141–150.

Hilsted, J., Richter, E., Madsbad, S., et al. (1987). Metabolic and cardiovascular responses to epinephrine in diabetic autonomic neuropathy. *New England Journal of Medicine, 317,* 421–426.

Hirschowitz, B. I., Hammer, R., & Giachetti, A., et al. (Eds.). (1984). Subtypes of muscarinic receptors. *Trends in Pharmacological Sciences,* (Suppl.), 1–103.

Hirst, G. D. S., DeGleria, S., & van Helden, D. F. (1985). Neuromuscular transmission in arterioles. *Experientia, 41,* 874–879.

Hjemdahl, P. (1984). Inter-laboratory comparison of plasma catecholamine determinations using several different essays. *Acta Physiologica Scandinavica,* (Suppl. 527), 43–54.

Hjemdahl, P. (1987a). Catecholamine measurements in plasma by high-performance liquid chromatography with electrochemical detection. *Methods in Enzymology, 142,* 521–534.

Hjemdahl, P. (1987b). Physiological aspects on catecholamine sampling. *Life Sciences, 41,* 841–844.

Hjemdahl, P. (1988). Plasma catecholamines as markers for sympatho-adrenal activity in human primary hypertension. *Pharmacology Toxicology, 63,* (Suppl. 1), 27–31.

Hjemdahl, P., Åkerstedt, T., Pollare, T., & Gillberg, M. (1983). Influence of beta-adrenoceptor blockade by metoprolol and propranolol on lasma concentrations and effects of noradrenaline and adrenaline during i.v. infusion. *Acta Physiologica Scandinavica,* (Suppl. 515), 45–53.

Hjemdahl, P., Bradley, T., & Tidgren, B. (1988). Release of dopamine from canine and human kidneys in vivo. In C. Bell & B. McGrath (Eds.), *Peripheral actions of dopamine* (pp. 56–74). New York: Macmillan.

Hjemdahl, P., Eklund, B., & Kaijser, L. (1982). Catecholamine handling by the human forearm at rest and during isometric exercise and lower body negative pressure. *British Journal of Clinical Pharmacology, 77,* 324P.

Hjemdahl, P., & Eliasson, K. (1979). Sympatho-adrenal and cardiovascular response to mental stress and orthostatic provocation in latent hypertension. *Clinical Science, 57,* 189s–191s.

Hjemdahl, P., Fagius, J., Freyschuss, U., et al. (1989). *Sympathetic nerve activity and norepinephrine release during mental challenge.* Manuscript submitted for publication.

Hjemdahl, P., Freyschuss, U., Juhlin-Dannfelt, A., & Linde, B. (1984). Differentiated sympathetic activation during mental stress evoked by the Stroop test. *Acta Physiologica Scandinavica* (Suppl. 527), 25–29.

Hjemdahl, P., & Linde, B. (1983). Influence of circulating NE and Epi on adipose tissue vascular resistance and lipolysis in humans. *American Journal of Physiology, 245*, H447–H452.

Hjemdahl, P., & Linde, B. (1985). Adrenergic control of blood flow and lipolysis in human adipose tissue. In H. Refsum & O. D. Mjøs (Eds.), *Alpha-adrenoceptor blockers in cardiovascular disease* (pp. 151–164). London: Churchill Livingstone.

Hjemdahl, P., Martinsson, A., & Larsson, K. (1986). Improvement of the isoprenaline infusion test by plasma concentration measurements. *Life Sciences, 39*, 629–635.

Hjemdahl, P., Sjöqvist, B., Daleskog, M., & Eliasson, K. (1982). A comparison of noradrenaline, HMPG and VMA in plasma as indicators of sympathetic nerve activity in man. *Acta Physiologica Scandinavica, 115*, 507–509.

Hjemdahl, P., Wallin, B. G., Daleskog, M., et al. (1985). Biochemical and neurophysiological assessment of sympathetic activity in hypertension. *Journal of Hypertension, 3*(Suppl. 3), 550.

Hoffman, B. B., & Lefkowitz, R. J. (1980). Alpha-adrenergic receptor subtypes. *New England Journal of Medicine, 302*, 1390–1396.

Hollister, A. S., FitzGerald, G. A., Nadeau, J. H. J., & Robertson, D. (1983). Acute reduction in human platelet α2-adrenoceptor affinity for agonist by endogenous and exogenous catecholamines. *Journal of Clinical Investigation, 72*, 1498–1505.

Hoshino, P. K., Blaustein, A. S., & Gaasch, W. H. (1988). Effect of propranolol on the left ventricular response to the Valsalva maneuver in normal subjects. *American Journal of Cardiology, 61*, 400–404.

Howes, L. G., Hawksby, C. C., & Reid, J. L. (1986). Comparison of plasma 3,4-dihydroxyphenylethylene glycol (DHPG) and norepinephrine levels as indices of sympathetic activity in man. *European Journal of Clinical Investigation, 16*, 18–21.

Ignarro, L. J. (1989). Endothelium derived nitric oxide: Actions and properties. *FASEB Journal, 3*, 31–36.

Iimura, O., Yamaji, I., Kikuchi, K., et al. (1987). The pathophysiological role of renal dopaminergic activity in patients with essential hypertension. *Japanese Circulation Journal, 51*, 1232–1240.

Iversen, L. L. (1975). Uptake processes for biogenic amines. In L. L. Iversen, S. D. Iversen, & S. H. Snyder (Eds.), *Handbook of psychopharmacology* (Vol. 3, pp. 381–442). New York: Plenum Press.

Izzo, J. L., Horwitz, D., & Keiser, H. R. (1981). Physiologic mechanisms opposing the hemodynamic effects of prazosin. *Clinical Pharmacology and Therapeutics, 29*, 7–11.

Izzo, J. L., Jr., Smith, R. J., Larrabee, P. S., & Kallay, M. C. (1987). Plasma norepinephrine and age as determinants of systemic hemodynamics in men with established essential hypertension. *Hypertension, 9*, 415–419.

Jakob, H., Nawrath, H., & Rupp, J. (1988). Adrenoceptor-mediated changes of action potential and force of contraction in human isolated ventricular heart muscle. *British Journal of Pharmacology, 94*, 584–590.

Jennings, G. L., Bobik, A., Esler, M. D., & Korner, P. I. (1980). Relationship between maximum chronotropic response to isoproterenol in man and generation of cyclic adenosine monophosphate by lymphocytes. *Circulation Research, 46*(Suppl. 1), 49–50.

Jennings, G., Bobik, A., Esler, M., & Korner, P. (1981). Contribution of cardiovascular reflexes to differences in β-adrenoceptor mediated responses in essential hypertension. *Clinical Science, 61*, 177–180.

Jie, K., van Brummelen, P., Vermey, P. et al. (1987a). Modulation of noradrenaline release by peripheral presynaptic α2-adrenoceptors in humans. *Journal of Cardiovascular Pharmacology, 9*, 407–413.

Jie, K., van Brummelen, P., Vermey, P., et al. (1987b). Postsynaptic α1- and α2-adrenoceptors in human blood vessels: Interactions with exogenous and endogenous catecholamines. *European Journal of Clinical Investigation, 17*, 174–181.

Joborn, H., Hjemdahl, P., Larsson, P. T., et al. (1989). Effects of prolonged adrenaline infusion and of mental stress on plasma minerals and parathyroid hormone. *Clinical Physiology.*

Joborn, H., Hjemdahl, P., Larsson, P. T., et al. (in press). Platelet and plasma catecholamines in relation to plasm minerals and parathyroid hormone following acute myocardial infarction. *Chest.*

Jörgensen, L. S., Bönløkke, L., & Christensen, N. J. (1985). Plasma adrenaline and noradrenaline during mental stress and isometric exercise in man: Role of arterial sampling. *Scandinavian Journal of Clinical and Laboratory Investigation, 45*, 447–452.

Joyce, D. A., Beilin, L. J., Vandongen, R., & Davidson, L. (1982). Epinephrine sulfation in the forearm: Differences in free and conjugated catecholamines. *Life Sciences, 31*, 2513–2517.

Julius, S. (1988). The blood pressure seeking properties of the central nervous system. *Journal of Hypertension, 6*, 177–185.

Juhlin-Dannfelt, A., Freyschuss, U., & Linde, B. (1986). Splanchnic circulatory and metabolic responses to metnal stress—the importance of circulatory adrenaline. *Acta Pharmacologica et Toxicologica*, 59(Suppl. V), 62.

Julius, S., & Esler, M. (1975). Autonomic nervous control of cardiovascular regulation in borderline hypertension. *American Journal of Cardiology, 36*, 685–696.

Kahan, T. (1987). Prejunctional adrenergic receptors and sympathetic neurotransmission: Studies in canine skeletal muscle vasculature in situ. *Acta Physiologica Scandinavica*, (Suppl. 560), 1–38.

Kahan, T., Dahlöf, C., & Hjemdahl, P. (1987). Facilitation of nerve stimulation evoked noradrenaline overflow by isoprenaline but not by circulating adrenaline in the dog in vivo. *Life Sciences, 40*, 1811–1818.

Kahan, T., & Hjemdahl, P. (1987). Prejunctional B2-adrenoceptor-mediated enhancement of noradrenaline release in skeletal muscle vasculature in situ. *Journal of Cardiovascular Pharmacology, 10*, 433–438.

Kahan, T., Hjemdahl, P., & Dahlöf, C. (1984). Relationship between the overflow of endogenous and radiolabelled noradrenaline from canine blood perfused gracilis muscle. *Acta Physiologica Scandinavica, 122*, 571–582.

Kahan, T., Pernow, J., Schwieler, J. et al. (1988). Noradrenaline release evoked by physiological irregular sympathetic discharge pattern is modulated by prejunctional α- and β-adrenoceptors in vivo. *British Journal of Clinical Pharmacology, 95*, 1101–1108.

Kahn, J. P., Perumal, A. S., Gully, R. J., et al. (1987). Correlation of Type A behaviour with adrenergic receptor density: Implications for coronary artery disease pathogenesis. *Lancet, 2*, 937–939.

Kaijser, L. (1986). Autonomic nerve function tests: Need for standardization. *Clinical Physiology, 6*, 475–479.

Karlsberg, R. P., Cryer, P. E., & Roberts, R. (1981). Serial plasma catecholamine response early in the course of clinical acute myocardial infarction: Relationship to infarct extent and mortality. *American Heart Journal, 102*, 24–29.

Kassis, S., Olasmaa, M., Sullivan, M., & Fishman, P. H. (1986). Desensitization of the β-adrenergic receptor-coupled adenylate cyclase in cultured mammalizan cells: Receptor sequestration versus receptor function. *Journal of Biological Chemistry, 261*, 12233–12237.

Kauman, A. J., & Lemoine, H. (1987). β2-Adrenoceptor-mediated positive inotropic effect of adrenaline in human ventricular myocardium: Quantitative discrepancies between binding and adenylate cyclase stimulation. *Naunyn-Schmiedeberg's Archives of Pharmacology, 335*, 403–411.

Kerry, R., & Scrutton, M. C. (1985). Platelet adrenoceptors. In G. L. Longenecker (Ed.), *The platelets: Physiology and pharmacology* (pp. 113–157). New York: Academic Press.

Kjeldsen, S. E., Westheim, A., Aakesson, I. et al. (1986). Plasma adrenaline and noradrenaline during orthostasis in man: The importance of aterial sampling. *Scandinavian Journal of Clinical and Laboratory Investigation, 46*, 397–401.

Koizumi, K., Terui, N., & Kollai, M. (1983). Neural control of the heart: Significance of double innervation re-examined. *Journal of the Autonomic Nervous System, 7*, 279–294.

Kopin, I. J. (1985). Catecholamine metabolism: Basic aspects and clinical significance. *Pharmacological Reviews, 37*, 333–364.

Kopin, I. J., Jimerson, D. C., Markey, M. H. et al. (1984). Disposition and metabolism of MHPG in humans: Application to studies in depression. *Pharmacopsychiatry, 17*, 3–8.

Kopp, U., Bradley, T., & Hjemdahl, P. (1983). Renal venous outflow and urinary excretion of norepinephrine, epinephrine and dopamine during graded renal nerve stimulation. *American Journal of Physiology, 244*, E52–E60.

Korner, P. I., Shaw, J., Uther, J. B. et al. (1973). Autonomic and non-autonomic circulatory components in essential hypertension in man. *Circulation, 48*, 107–117.

Korth, M., & Kühlkamp, V. (1987). Muscarinic receptors mediate negative and positive inotropic effects in mammalian ventricular myocardium: Differentiation by agonists. *British Journal of Pharmacology, 90*, 81–90.

Krakoff, L. R., Dziedzic, S., Mann, S. J. et al. (1985). Plasma epinephrine concentration in healthy men: Correlation with systolic pressure and rate-pressure product. *Journal of the American College of Cardiology, 5*, 352–356.

Krawietz, W., Klein, E. M., Unterberg, C., & Ackenheil, M. (1985). Physical activity decreases the number of β-adrenergic receptors on human lymphocytes. *Klinische Wochenschrift, 63*, 73–78.

Kuchel, O., Buu, N. T., & Hamet, P. (1984). Catecholamine sulfates and platelet sulfotransferase activity in essential hypertension. *Journal of Laboratory and Clinical Medicine, 104*, 238–244.

Kuchel, O., Buu, N. T., Rasz, K., et al. (1986). Role of sulfate conjugation of catecholamines in blood pressure regulation. *Federation Proceedings: Federation of American Societies for Experimental Biology, 45*, 2254–2259.

Landmann, R., Poertenier, M., Staehlin, M., et al. (1988). Changes in β-adrenoceptors and leukocyte subpopulations after physical exercise in normal subjects. *Naunyn-Schmiedeberg's Archiv fur Pharmakologie, 337,* 261–266.

Lands, A. M., Arnold, A., McAuliff, J. P., et al. (1967). Differentiation of receptor systems by sympathomimetic amines. *Nature, 214,* 597–598.

Langer, S. Z. (1974). Presynaptic regulation of catecholamine release. *Biochemical Pharmacology, 23,* 1793–1800.

Langer, S. Z. (1981). Presynaptic regulation of the release of catecholamines. *Pharmacological Reviews, 23,* 1793–1800.

Langer, S. Z., & Hicks, P. E. (1984). Physiology of the sympathetic nerve ending. *British Journal of Anaesthesiology, 56,* 689–700.

Langer, S. Z., & Shepperson, N. B. (1982). Recent developments in vascular smooth muscle pharmacology: The post-synaptic α2-adrenoceptor. *Trends in Pharmacological Sciences, 3,* 440–444.

Larsson, P. T., Martinsson, A., Olsson, G., & Hjemdahl, P. (1990). Altered adrenoceptor responsiveness during adrenaline infusion but not during mental stress: Differences between receptor subtypes and tissues. *British Journal of Clinical Pharmacology, 29,* in press.

Larsson, P. T., Hjemdahl, P., Olsson, G., et al. (1989). Altered platelet function during mental stress and adrenaline infusion in humans: Evidence for an increased in vivo aggregability as measured by filtragometry. *Clinical Science, 76,* 369–376.

Larsson, P. T., Hjemdahl, P., Olsson, G., et al. (1990). Platelet aggregability in humans: Contrasting in vovo and in vitro findings during sympatho-adrenal activation and relationship to serum lipids. Submitted to *European Journal of Clinical Investigation.*

Leenen, F. H. H., Chan, Y. K., Smith, D. L., & Reeves, R. A. (1988). Epinephrine and left ventricular function in humans: Effects of β1- vs. non-selective β-blockade. *Clinical Pharmacology and Therapeutics, 43,* 519–528.

Lefkowitz, R. J., & Caron, M. G. (1987). Molecular and regulatory properties of adrenergic receptors. *Recent Progress in Hormone Research, 43,* 469–493.

Lefkowitz, R. J., Caron, M. G., & Stiles, G. L. (1984). Mechanisms of membrane-receptor regulation: Biochemical, physiological and clinical insights derived from studies of the adrenergic receptors, *New England Journal of Medicine, 310,* 1570–1579.

Leier, C. V., Nelson, S., Magorien, R. D., et al. (1983). Heart rate responsiveness after sustained chronotropic stimulation with a β1-adrenergic receptor agonist. *Journal of Laboratory and Clinical Medicine, 101,* 955–963.

Lertora, J. J. L., Mark, A. L., Johannses, U. J., et al. (1975). Selective beta-1 receptor blockade with oral practolol in man. *Journal of Clinical Investigation, 56,* 719–724.

Levine, R. R., Birdsall, N. J. M., & Giachetti, A. (Eds.). (1986). Subtypes of muscarinic receptors: 2. *Trends in Pharmacological Sciences,* (Suppl.), 1–97.

Levy, M. N. (1984). Cardiac sympathetic–parasympathetic interactions. *Federal Proceedings: Federation of American Societies for Experimental Biology, 43,* 2598–2602.

Lew, M. J., & Angus, J. A. (1983). Clonidine and noradrenaline fail to inhibit vagal induced bradycardia: Evidence against prejunctional alpha-adrenoceptors on vagal varcosities in guinea-pig right atria. *Naunyn-Schmiedeberg's Archiv fur Pharmakologie, 323,* 228–232.

Liggett, S. B., Marker, J. C., Shah, S. D., et al. (1988). Dirct relationship between momonuclear leukocyte and lung β-adrenergic receptors and apparent reciprocal regulation of extravascular, but not intrravascular, α- and β-adrenergic receptors by the sympathochromaffin system in humans. *Journal of Clinical Investigation, 82,* 48–56.

Linde, B., & Hjemdahl, P. (1982). Effect of tilting on adipose tissue vascular resistance and sympathetic activity in humans. *American Journal of Physiology, 242,* H161–H167.

Linde, B., Hjemdahl, P., Freyschuss, U., & Juhlin-Dannfelt, A. (in press). Adipose tissue and skeletal muscle blood flow during mental stress. *American Journal of Physiology.*

Löffelholz, K., Brehm, R., & Lindmar, R. (1984). Hydrolysis, synthesis, and release of acetylcholine in the isolated heart. *Federal Proceedings: Federation of American Societies for Experimental Biology, 43,* 2603–2606.

Löffelholz, K., & Pappano, A. J. (1985). The parasympathetic neuroeffector junction of the heart. *Pharmacology Review, 37,* 1–24.

Loiacono, R. E., & Story, D. F. (1986). Effect of α-adrenoceptor agonists and antagonists on cholinergic transmission in guinea-pig isolated atria. *Naunyn-Schmiedeberg's Archives of Pharmacology, 334,* 40–47.

Lokhandwala, M. F. (1988). Cardiovascular and renal effects of dopamine receptor agonists. *ISI Atlas of Science: Pharmacology,* 261–266.

Lokhandwala, M. F., & Barrett, R. J. (1982). Cardiovascular dopamine receptors: Physiological, pharmacological and therapeutic implications. *Journal of Autonomic Pharmacology, 3,* 189–215.

Ludmer, P. L., Selwyn, A. P., Shook, T. L. et al. (1986). Paradoxical vasoconstriction induced by acetylcholine in atherosclerotic coronary arteries. *New England Journal of Medicine, 315,* 1046–1051.

Lundberg, J. M. (1981). Evidence for coexistence of vasoactive intestinal polypeptide (VIP) and acetylcholine in neurons of cat exocrine glands. *Acta Physiologica Scandinavica,* (Suppl. 496), 1–57.

Lundberg, J. M., Martinsson, A., Hemsén, A. et al. (1985). Co-release of neuropeptide Y and catecholamines during physical exercise in man. *Biochemical and Biophysical Research and Communications, 133,* 30–36.

Lundberg, J. M., Pernow, J., Franco-Cereceda, A., & Rudehill, A. (1987). Effects of antihypertensive drugs on sympathetic vascular control in relation to neuropeptide Y. *Journal of Cardiovascular Pharmacology, 10*(Suppl. 12), 51–68.

Lüscher, T. F., Diederich, D., Siebenmann, R. et al. (1988). Difference between endothelium-dependent relaxation in arterial and venous coronary bypass grafts. *New England Journal of Medicine, 319,* 462–467.

Maas, J. W., Hattox, S. E., Greene, N. M., & Landis, D. H. (1979). 3-Methoxy-4-hydroxyphenylethyleneglycol production by human brain in vivo. *Science, 205,* 1025–1027.

Mahan, L. C., McKernan, R. M., & Insel, P. A. (1987). Metabolism of alpha- and beta-adrenergic receptors in vitro and in vivo. *Annual Review of Pharmacology and Toxicology, 27,* 215–235.

Maisel, A. S., Scott, N. A., Motulsky, H. J. et al. (1989). Elevation of plasma neuropeptide Y levels in congestive heart failture. *American Journal of Medicine, 86,* 43–48.

Man in't Veld, A. J., & Schalekamp, M. A. D. H. (1983). Effects of 10 different β-adrenoceptor antaonists on hemodynamics, plasma renin activity, and plasma norepinephrine in hypertension: The key role of vascular resistance changes in relation to partial agonist activity. *Journal of Cardiovascular Pharmacology, 5*(Suppl.), S30–S45.

Mancia, G., Ferrari, A., Gregorini, L. et al. (1980). Effects of prazosin on autonomic control of circulation in essential hypertension. *Hypertension, 2,* 700–707.

Mårdh, G., Sjöqvist, B., & Änggård. (1981). Norepinephrine metabolism in man using deuterium labelling: The conversion of 4-hydroxy-3-methoxyphenylglycol to 4-hydroxy-3-methoxymandelic acid. *Journal of Neurochemistry, 36,* 1181–1185.

Martinsson, A., Bevegård, S., & Hjemdahl, P. (1986). Analysis of phenylephrine in plasma: Initial data about the concentration–effect relationship. *European Journal of Clinical Pharmacology, 30,* 427–431.

Martinsson, A., Larsson, K., & Hjemdahl, P. (1985). Reduced β2-adrenoceptor sensitivity in exercise induced asthma. *Chest, 88,* 594–600.

Martinsson, A., Larsson, K., & Hjemdahl, P. (1987). Studies in vivo and in vitro of terbutaline-induced β-adrenoceptor desensitization in healthy subjects. *Clinical Science, 72,* 47–54.

Martinsson, A., Lindvall, K., Melcher, A., & Hjemdahl, P. (1989). β-adrenergic responsiveness to isoprenaline in humans before and after autonomic blockade: Concentration–effect, as compared to dose-effect evaluation. *British Journal of Clinical Pharmacology, 28,* 83–94.

McCulloch, R. K., Vandongen, R., Tunney, A. M. et al. (1987). Distribution of free and sulfate-conjugated catecholamines in human platelets. *American Journal of Physiology, 253,* E312–E316.

McGibney, D., Singleton, W., Like, B., & Taylor, S. H. (1983). Observations on the mechanism underlying the differences in exercise and isoprenaline tachycardia after cardioselective and non-selective β-adrenoceptor antagonists. *British Journal of Clinical Pharmacology, 15,* 15–19.

McLeod, A. A., Brown, J. E., Kuhn, C. et al. (1983). Differentiation of hemodynamic, humoral and metabolic responses to β1- and β2-adrenergic stimulation in man using atenolol and propranolol. *Circulation, 67,* 1076–1984.

McMurray, J. J., Seidelin, P. H., Balfour, D. J. K., & Struthers, A. D. (1988). Physiological increases in circulating noradrenaline are antinatriuretic in man. *Journal of Hypertension, 6,* 757–761.

Michel, G. L. A., Lenz, T., Lernhardt, U. et al. (1987). Sulfoconjugated catecholamines: Lack of β-adrenoceptor binding and adenylate cyclase stimulation in human mononuclear leukocytes. *European Journal of Pharmacology, 142,* 179–188.

Michel, M. C., Beckeringh, J. J., Ikezono, K., et al. (1986). Lymphocyte β2-adrenoceptors mirror precisely β2-adrenoceptor, but poorly β1-adrenoceptor changes in the human heart. *Journal of Hypertension, 4*(Suppl. 6), S215–S218.

Middeke, M., Remien, J., & Holzgreve, H. (1984). The influence of sex, age, blood pressure and physical stress on β2-adrenoceptor density of mononuclear cells. *Journal of Hypertension, 2,* 261–264.

Misu, Y., & Kubo, T. (1986). Presynaptic β-adrenoceptors. *Medicine Research Reviews, 6,* 197–225.

Moncada, S., Herman, A. G., & Vanhoutte, P. (1987). Endothelium-derived relaxing factor is identified as nitric oxide. *Trends in Pharmacological Sciences, 8,* 365–368.

Morady, F., DiCarlo, L. A., Jr., Halter, J. B. et al. (1986). The plasma catecholamine response to ventricular tachycardia induction and external countershock during electrophysiologic testing. *Journal of the American College of Cardiology, 8,* 584–591.

Morady, F., Nelson, S. D., Kou, W. H. et al. (1988). Electrophysiologic effects of epinephrine in humans. *Journal of the American College of Cardiology, 11,* 1235–1244.

Morris, M. J., Russel, A. E., Kapoor, V. et al. (1986). Increases in plasma neuropeptide Y concentrations during sympathetic activation in man. *Journal of the Autonomic Nervous System, 17,* 143–149.

Motulsky, H. J., & Insel, P. A. (1982). Adrenergic receptors in man: Direct identification, physiologic regulation, and clinical alterations. *New England Journal of Medicine, 307,* 18–29.

Murphy, M. B., Brown, M. J., Causon, R. C., & Dollery, C. T. (1983). The effects of pentolinium ion sympathetic activity in hypertensives and normotensive controls. *International Journal of Pharmacological Research, 3,* 227–232.

Musgrave, I. F., Bachmann, A. W., Jackson, R. V., & Gordon, R. D. (1985). Increased plasma noradrenaline during low dose adrenaline infusion in resting man and during sympathetic stimulation. *Clinical and Experimental Pharmacology and Physiology, 12,* 285–289.

Musumeci, V., Baroni, S., Cardiollo, C. et al. (1987). Cardiovascular reactivity, plasma markers of endothelial and platelet activity and plasma renin activity after mental stress in normals and hypertensives. *Journal of Hypertension, 5*(Suppl. 5), 1–4.

Nattel, S., Rangno, R. E., & Van Loon, G. (1979). Mechanism of propranolol withdrawal phenomena. *Circulation, 59,* 1158–1164.

Nezu, M., Miura, Y., Adachi, M., et al. (1983). The role of epinephrine in essential hypertension. *Japanese Circulation Journal, 47,* 1242–1246.

Nisell, H., Hjemdahl, P., & Linde, B. (1985). Cardiovascular responses to circulating catecholamines in normal pregnancy and in pregnancy-induced hypertension. *Clinical Physiology, 5,* 479–493.

Noronha-Blob, L., Lowe, V. C., Hanson, R. C., & U'Prichard, D. C. (1987). Heterogeneity of muscarinic receptors coupled to phosphoinositide breakdown in guinea pig brain and peripheral tissues. *Life Sciences, 41,* 967–975.

Olsson, G., Hjemdahl, P., & Rehnqvist, N. (1984). Rebound phenomena following gradual withdrawal of chronic metoprolol treatment in patients with ischemic heart disease. *American Heart Journal, 108,* 454–462.

Olsson, G., Hjemdahl, P., & Rehnqvist, N. (1986). Cardiovascular reactivity to mental stress during gradual withdrawal of chronic post-infarction treatment with metoprolol. *European Heart Journal, 7,* 765–772.

Onrot, J., Goldberg, M. R., Biaggioni, I., et al. (1987). Postjunctional vascular smooth muscle α2-adrenoceptors in human autonomic failure. *Clinical Investigations in Medicine, 10,* 26–31.

Overy, H. R., Pfister, R., & Chidsey, C. A. (1967). Studies on the renal excretion of norepinephrine. *Journal of Clinical Investigation, 46,* 482–489.

Pehrsson, S. K., Hjemdahl, P., Nordlander, R., & Åström, H. (1988). A comparison of sympathoadrenal activity and cardiac performance at rest and during exercise in patients with ventricular demand or atrial synchronous pacing. *British Heart Journal, 60,* 212–220.

Pernow, B. (1984). Interaction of neuropeptides and classical transmitters in the regulation of circulation. *Clinical Physiology, 3,* 195–199.

Perow, J. (1988). Co-release and functional interactions of neuropeptide Y and noradrenaline in peripheral sympathetic vascular control. *Acta Physiologica Scandinavica, 133*(Suppl. 568), 1–56.

Pernow, J., Kahan, T., Hjemdahl, P., & Lundberg, J. M. (1988). Possible involvement of neuropeptide Y in sympathetic vascular control of canine skeletal muscle. *Acta Physiologica Scandinavica, 132,* 43–50.

Pernow, J., Lundberg, J. M., Kaijser, L., et al. (1986). Plasma neuropeptide Y-like immunoreactivity and catecholamines during various degrees of sympathetic activation in man. *Clinical Physiology, 6,* 561–578.

Persson, B., Andersson, O. K., Hjemdahl, P. et al. (1989). Adrenaline infusion in man increases muscle sympathetic nerve activity and noradrenaline overflow to plasma. *Journal of Hypertension, 7,* 747–756.

Pfeifer, M. A., Weinberg, C. R., Cook, D. et al. (1983). Differential changes of autonomic nervous system function with age in man. *American Journal of Medicine, 75,* 249–258.

Postma, D. S., Kreyzer, J. J., Meurs, H. et al. (1985). Effect of beta-adrenergic stimulation on the circulatory lymphocyte count: Studies in normals and in patients with chronic airflow obstruction. *Chronobiology International, 2,* 290–215.

Potter, E. K. (1988). Neuropeptide Y as an autonomic neurotransmitter. *Pharmacology Therapy, 37,* 251–273.

Rand, M. J., & Majewski, H. (1984). Adrenaline mediates a positive feedback loop in noradrenergic transmission: Possible role in development of hypertension. *Clinical and Experimental Hypertension, A6,* 347–370.

Rardon, D. P., & Bailey, J. C. (1983). Parasympathetic effects on electrophysiologic properties of cardiac ventricular tissue. *Journal of the American College of Cardiology, 2,* 1200–1209.

Ratge, D., Knoll, E., & Wisser, H. (1986). Plasma free and conjugated catecholamines in clinical disorders. *Life Sciences, 39,* 557–564.

Riddel, J. G., Harron, D. W. G., & Shanks, R. G. (1987). Clinical pharmacokinetics of β-adrenoceptor antagonists. *Clinical Pharmacokinetics, 12,* 305–320.

Riozzi, A., Heagerty, A. M., Bing, R. F. et al. (1984). Noradrenaline: A circulating inhibitor of sodium transport. *British Medical Journal, 289,* 1025–1027.

Robertson, D., Hollister, A. S., Carey, E. L., et al. (1984). Increased vascular $\beta2$-adrenoceptor responsiveness in autonomic dysfunction. *Journal of the American College of Cardiology, 3,* 850–856.

Romain, Y., Demassieux, S., D'Angelo, G., et al. (1986). Is the platelet phenolsulfotransferase involved in the sulfoconjugation of plasma catecholamines? *Canadian Journal of Physiology and Pharmacology, 64,* 1197–1201.

Rosell, S., & Belfrage, E. (1979). Blood circulation in adipose tissue. *Physiological Reviews, 59,* 1078–1104.

Rosen, S. G., Sanfield, J. A., Morrow, L. A., & Zweifler, A. J. (1987). Relationship between plasma and platelet epinephrine concentrations in humans. *American Journal of Physiology, 252,* E334–E339.

Rubanyi, G. M., Lorenz, R. R., & Vanhoutte, P. M. (1985). Bioassay of endothelium-derived relaxing factor(s): Inactivation by catecholamines. *American Journal of Physiology, 249,* H95–H101.

Rusch, N. J., Shepherd, J. T., Webb, R. C., & Vanhoutte, P. M. (1981). Different behavior of the resistance vessels of the human calf and forearm during contralateral isometric exercise, mental stress, and abnormal respiratory movements. *Circulation Research, 48*(Suppl. 1), 118–130.

Rusell, M. P., & Moran, N. C. (1980). Evidence for lack of innervation of $\beta2$-adrenoceptors in the blood vessels of the gracilis muscle of the dog. *Circulation Research, 46,* 344–352.

Schneider, R. H., Julius, S., Moss, G. E. et al. (1987). New markers for Type A behavior: Pupil size and platelet epinephrine. *Psychosomatic Medicine, 49,* 579–590.

Schümann, H. J. (1980). Are there α-adrenoceptors in the mammalian heart? *Trends in Pharmacological Sciences, 1,* 195–197.

Shah, S. D., Tse, T. F., Clutter, W. E., & Cryer, P. E. (1984). The human sympathochromaffin system. *American Journal of Physiology, 247,* E380–E384.

Sheikh, S. P., Holst, J. J., Skak-Nielsen, T., et al. (1988). Release of NPY in pig pancreas: Dual parasympathetic and sympathetic regulation. *American Journal of Physiology, 255,* G46–G54.

Singh, B. N., Deedwania, P., Nademanee, K., et al. (1987). Sotalol: A review of its pharmacodynamic and pharmacokinetic properties, and therapeutic use. *Drugs, 34,* 311–349.

Snider, S. R., & Kuchel, O. (1983). Dopamine: An important neurohormone of the sympathoadrenal system. Significance of increased peripheral dopamine release for the human stress response and hypertension. *Endocrine Reviews, 4,* 291–309.

Sokoloff, N. M., Spielman, S. R., Greenspan, A. M., et al. (1986). Plasma norepinephrine in exercise induced ventricular tachycardia. *Journal of the American College of Cardiology, 8,* 11–17.

Starke, K. (1981). Presynaptic receptors. *Annual Review of Pharmacology and Toxicology, 21,* 7–30.

Starke, K., & Docherty, J. R. (1980). Recent developments in α-adrenoceptor research. *Journal of Cardiovascular Pharmacology, 2*(Suppl. 3), S269–S286.

Staten, M. A., Matthews, D. E., Cryer, P. E., & Bier, D. M. (1987). Physiological increments in epinephrine stimulate metabolic rate in humans. *American Journal of Physiology, 253,* E322–E330.

Steen, V. M., & Holmsen, H. (1987). Current aspects on human platelet activation and responses. *European Journal of Hematology, 38,* 383–399.

Steenberg, M. L., Ekas, R. D., & Lokhandwala, M. F. (1983). Effect of epinephrine on norepinephrine release from rat kidney during sympathetic nerve stimulation. *European Journal of Pharmacology, 93,* 137–148.

Steptoe, A. (1987). The assessment of sympathetic nervous function in human stress research. *Journal of Psychosomatic Research, 31,* 141–152.

Stjärne, L. (1986). New paradigm: Sympathetic transmission by multiple messengers and lateral interaction between monoquantal release sites? *Trends in Pharmacological Sciences, 6,* 547–548.

Stratton, J. R., Pfeifer, M. A., Ritchie, J. L., & Halter, J. B. (1985). Hemodynamic effects of epinephrine: Concentration–effects study in humans. *Journal of Applied Physiology, 58,* 1199–1206.

Struthers, A. D., Reid, J. L., Whitesmith, R., & Rodger, J. C. (1983). Effect of intravenous adrenaline on electrocardiogram, blood pressure, and serum potassium. *British Heart Journal, 49,* 90–93.

Taggart, P., Donaldson, R., Green, J. et al. (1982). Interrelation of heart rate and autonomic activity in asymptomatic men with unobstructed coronary arteries: Studies with atrial pacing, adrenaline infusion, and autonomic blockade. *British Heart Journal, 47,* 19–25.

Takahashi, K., Mouri, T., Murakami, O. et al. (1988). Increases of neuropeptide Y-like immunoreactivity in plasma during insulin-induced hypoglycemia in man. *Peptides, 9,* 433–435.

Terasaki, W. L., Linden, J., & Brooker, G. (1979). Quantitative relationship between β-adrenergic receptor number and physiologic responses as studied with long-lasting β-adrenergic antagonist. *Proceedings of the National Academy of Sciences, 76,* 6401–6405.

Thom, S., Hughes, A., Martin, G., & Sever, P. S. (1987). Endothelium-dependent relaxation of isolated human arteries and veins. *Clinical Science, 73,* 547–552.

Thomas, J., Fouad, F. M., Tarazi, R. C., & Bravo, E. L. (1983). Evaluation of plasma catecholamines in humans: Correlation of resting levels with cardiac responses to beta-blocking and sympatholytic drugs. *Hypertension, 5,* 858–863.

Tidgren, B., & Hjemdahl, P. (1988). Reflex activation of renal nerves in humans: Differential effects on noradrenaline, dopamine and renin overflow to renal venous plasma. *Acta Physiologica Scandinavica, 134,* 23–34.

Tidgren, B., & Hjemdahl, P. (1989). Renal responses to mental stress and epinephrine in man. *American Journal of Physiology, 257,* F682–F689.

Tidgren, B., Theodorsson, E., & Hjemdahl, P. (1990). Renal and systemic plasma neuropeptide Y and calcitonin gene-related peptide responses to stress and adrenaline in humans. *Clinical Psychology* (submitted for publication).

Tohmeh, J. F., & Cryer, P. E. (1980). Biphasic adrenergic modulation of β-adrenergic receptors in man. *Journal of Clinical Investigation, 65,* 836–840.

Trimarco, B., Ricciardelli, B., De Luca, N., et al. (1985). Participation of endogenous catecholamines in the regulation of left ventricular mass in progeny of hypertensive parents. *Circulation, 72,* 38–46.

Tseng, C. J., Robertson, D., Light, R. T., et al. (1988). Neuropeptide Y is a vasoconstrictor of human coronary arteries. *American Journal of Medical Science, 296,* 11–16.

Van Brummelen, P., Bühler, F. R., Kioswki, W., & Amann, F. W. (1984). Age-related decrease in cardiac and peripheral vascular responsiveness to isoprenaline: Studies in normal subjects. *Clinical Science, 60,* 571–577.

van Zwieten, P. A. (1985). Receptors involved in the regulation of vascular tone. *Arzneimittel-Forschung Drug Research, 35*(2), 1904–1909.

Vandongen, R. (1984). The significance of sulphate-conjugated catecholamines in man. *Netherlands Journal of Medicine, 129–135.*

Vane, J. R., Gryglewski, R. J., & Botting, R. M. (1987). The endothelial cell as a metabolic and endocrine organ. *Trends in Pharmacological Sciences, 8,* 491–496.

Vanhoutte, P. (1988). The endothelium: Modulator of vascular smooth-muscle tone. *New England Journal of Medicine, 319,* 512–513.

Vanhoutte, P. M., Verbeuren, T. J., & Webb, R. C. (1981). Local modulation of adrenergic neuroeffector interaction in the blood vessel wall. *Physiological Reviews, 61,* 151–247.

Vincent, H. H., Man In't Veld, A. J., Boomsma, F. et al. (1982). Elevated plasma noradrenaline in response to β-adrenoceptor stimulation in man. *British Journal of Clinical Pharmacology, 13,* 717–721.

Vizi, E. S. (1979). Presynaptic modulation of neurochemical transmission. *Progress in Neurobiology, 12,* 181–290.

von Bahr, C., Lindström, B., & Seideman, P. (1982). α-Adrenoceptor function changes after the first dose of prazosin. *Clinical Pharmacology and Therapeutics, 32,* 41–47.

Waeber, B., Aubert, J. F., Corder, R., et al. (1988). Cardiovascular effects of neuropeptide Y. *American Journal of Hypertension, 1,* 193–199.

Waelbroeck, M., Taton, G., Delhaye, M., et al. (1983). The human heart beta-adrenergic receptors: 2. Coupling of beta2-adrenergic receptors with the adenylate cyclase system. *Molecular Pharmacology, 24,* 174–182.

Wallin, B. G., & Fagius, J. (1988). Peripheral sympathetic neural activity in conscious humans. *Annual Review of Physiology, 50,* 565–576.

Wallin, B. G., Mörlin, C., & Hjemdahl, P. (1987). Muscle sympathetic activity and venous plasma noradrenaline concentrations during static exercise in normotensive and hypertensive subjects. *Acta Physiologica Scandinavica, 129,* 489–497.

Watanabe, A. M., Jones, L. R., Manalan, A. S., & Besch, H. R., Jr. (1982). Cardiac autonomic receptors: Recent concepts from radiolabelled ligand-binding studies. *Circulation Research, 50,* 161–174.

Watson, J. D., Sury, M. R. J., Corder, R., et al. (1988). Plasma levels of neuropeptide tyrosine Y (NPY) are increased in human sepsis but are unchanged during canine endotoxin shock despite raised catecholamine concentrations. *Journal of Endrocrinology, 116,* 421–426.

Waxman, M. B., Cupps, C. L., & Cameron, D. A. (1988). Modulation of idioventricular rhythm by vagal tone. *Journal of the American College of Cardiology, 11,* 1052–1060.

Wetzel, G. T., & Brown, J. H. (1985). Presynaptic modulation of acetylcholine release from cardiac parasympathetic neurons. *American Journal of Physiology, 248,* H33–H39.

Wharton, J., Gulbekian, S., Merighi, A., et al. (1988). Immunohistochemical and ultrastructural localization of peptide-containing nerves and myocardial cells in the human atrial appendage. *Cell Tissue Research, 254,* 155–166.

Whittaker, V. P. (1986). The storage and release of acetylcholine. *Trends in Pharmacological Sciences, 7,* 312–315.

Wilson, A. P., Smith, C. C. T., Prichard, B. N. C., & Betteridge, D. J. (1987). Platelet catecholamines and platelet function in normal human subjects. *Clinical Science, 73,* 99–103.

Wolf, S. (1970). Emotions and the autonomic nervous system. *Archives of Internal Medicine, 126,* 1024–1030.

Wood, A. J. J. (1987). Beta receptor sensitivity testing in humans. *Journal of Receptor Research, 7,* 523–526.

Woodcock, E. A., Leung, E., & McLeod, J. K. (1987). A comparison of muscarinic acetylcholine receptors coupled to phosphatidylinositol turnover and to adenylate cyclase in guinea-pig atria and venticles. *European Journal of Pharmacology, 133,* 283–289.

Yanagisawa, M., Kurihara, H., Kimura, S., et al. (1988). A novel potent vasoconstrictor peptide produced by vascular endothelial cells. *Nature, 332,* 411–415.

Young, M. A., & Vatner, S. F. (1987). Blood flow- and endothelium-mediated vasomotion of iliac arteries in conscious dogs. *Circulation Research, 61*(Suppl. 2), 88–93.

Yusuf, S., Theodoropoulos, S., Mathias, C. J., et al. (1987). Increased senstivity of the denervated transplanted human heart to isoprenaline both before and after β-adrenergic blockade. *Circulation, 75,* 696–704.

Zerkowski, H. R., Ikezono, K., Rohm, N., et al. (1986). Human myocardial β-adrenoceptors: Demonstration of both β1- and β2-adrenoceptors mediating contractile responses to β-agonists on the right atrium. *Nunyn-Schmiedeberg's Archives of Pharmacology, 332,* 142–147.

Zweifler, A. J., & Julius, S. (1982). Increased platelet catecholamine content in pheochromocytoma. *New England Journal of Medicine, 306,* 890–894.

6

Neural Regulation
of the Cardiovascular System

Murray Esler

The autonomic nervous system occupies a central position in the normal regulation of the cardiovascular system. This is achieved principally through the influence of the sympathetic nervous system on the function of the heart, large arteries, arterioles, veins, and the kidneys. The parasympathetic nervous system, through vagus nerve regulation of heart rate, plays a subsidiary role. These influences of the sympathetic nervous system on normal cardiovascular physiology are both short- and long-term. Long-term circulatory control involves the regulation of body salt and water balance, through sympathetic nervous regulation of renal function (especially renin secretion and renal tubular reabsorption of sodium (DiBona, 1982). Instances of short-term sympathetic nervous circulatory control include the regulation of regional blood flow (in parallel with metabolic and autoregulatory influences on flow), the neural modification of venous capacitance, and sympathetic nervous regulation of the rate, contractility, and overall pumping capacity of the heart (Korner, 1971). The integrated, second-by-second regulation of arterial blood pressure through several baroreceptor inputs and multiple autonomic outflows constitutes a good example of short-term cardiovascular control by the autonomic nervous system.

Because the autonomic nervous system plays such a pivotal role in circulatory adaptation, it is paradoxical that so little is known about the possible contribution of disturbed autonomic nervous function to the development of disease of the heart and circulation. Clinical tests of autonomic nervous system activity have, by and large, been routinely applied in one setting only: for the detection of sympathetic nervous failure in patients with postural hypotension. A range of candidate diseases for autonomic nervous system dysfunction exists. Such a list might include cardiac arrhythmias, cardiac failure, coronary artery spasm, essential hypertension, mitral valve prolapse, and Raynaud's syndrome. Until very recently, the picture of autonomic nervous pathophysiology that had emerged for conditions such as these was particularly sketchy because of the rudimentary nature of the tests of autonomic nervous system function available to investigative clinical medicine. Pertinent questions have gone incompletely answered, at best, such as the following. Is the autonomic nervous system directly involved in the early pathogenesis of essential hypertension (Julius, Pascal, & London, 1971)? Is increased renal sympathetic activity a common cause of sodium retention in edematous states (DiBona, 1982)? Are autonomic nervous system changes occurring in stress responses important in the production of cardiac arrhythmias in humans (Corley, Mauck, & Shiel, 1975; Verrier & Lown, 1984)?

In this chapter I review a variety of aspects of autonomic nervous system regulation of the circulation. The integrated nature of this cardiovascular control and the regional differentiation (patterning) of sympathetic nervous cardiovascular responses are highlighted. This leads to a discussion of abnormalities of autonomic nervous cardiovascular regulation in a range of circulatory disorders, with emphasis on the pathophysiology of the sympathetic nerves of the heart and their participation in stress responses.

THE ORGANIZATION OF AUTONOMIC NERVOUS SYSTEM CARDIOVASCULAR CONTROL

Schemes of the organization of circulatory control rightly emphasize the preeminence of reflex blood pressure homeostasis (see Figure 1). This is achieved, on the afferent side, through arterial and low-pressure baroreceptors, with reflex outputs to the heart, resistance vessels, capacitance vessels, and kidneys. The central nervous system integration of the high-pressure baroreceptor signal involves, in particular, the nucleus tractus solitarius of the brain stem. Sympathetic nervous outflows carry the principal burden of this circulatory adjustment, supplemented by vagal influences on heart rate, and cardiovascular effects of adrenal medullary catecholamines in some circumstances (Korner, 1971).

Another aspect of circulatory control is the organ-specific regulation of regional blood flow, which is achieved through an interplay of autoregulatory, metabolic vasodilator and neural mechanisms, an interaction that sometimes involves antagonisms. For example, the necessity for blood pressure homeostasis during aerobic exercise dictates that local neural vasoconstriction (in the exercising muscle) opposes regional metabolic vasodilatation. The postsynaptic receptor mechanisms underlying autonomic nervous cardiovascular control are listed in Table 1. In general, alpha-1 and beta-1 adrenergic receptors mediate neural circulatory responses; postsynaptic alpha-

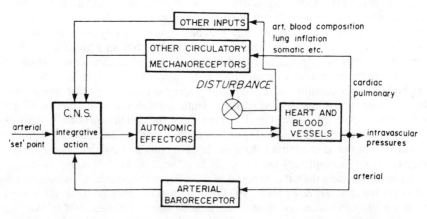

Figure 1 A neural circulatory control system, in which changes in the state of the circulation are signaled as intravascular pressures through various circulatory baroreceptors. From Korner (1971). Adapted by permission of publisher and author.

Table 1 Postsynaptic receptors mediating autonomic nervous circulatory adjustments

Site	Receptors	Minority receptor/subtypes
Heart	β_1, A Ch	β_2
Arteries	α_1	α_1, β_2
Arterioles	α_1	α_2, β_2, ?, A Ch
Veins	α_1	α_2, β_2
Kidneys		
tubules	α_1	—
renin	β_1	—
vessels	α_1	α_2

Alpha-(α) and beta-(β) adrenergic receptors and cholinergic muscarinic transmission (A Ch)) are indicated. The minority receptor subtypes listed do not subserve the principal control mechanism. Sympathetic transmission typically involves α_1- and β_1-receptor subtypes: Circulating catecholamines typically act on α_2- and β_2-postsynaptic receptors. The disputed and uncertain role of sympathetic cholinergic vasodilator mechanisms in resistance vessels is noted by a question mark. The physiological importance of purinergic and peptidergic receptors in autonomic nervous cardiovascular regulation at present is uncertain (Weiner & Taylor, 1985).

2 and beta-2 adrenoceptor stimulation seems to be more commonly due to the action of circulating catecholamines, these receptor subtypes typically being distributed at a distance from the sympathetic synaptic junction.

METHODS OF STUDYING CARDIOVASCULAR REGULATION

In principle, available methods for studying autonomic nervous system regulation of the circulation involve electrophysiological techniques for quantifying nerve discharge rates, biochemical methods for measuring neurotransmitter release, physiological techniques for studying the regulated circulatory variables, and pharmacological methods for antagonizing adrenergic and cholinergic receptors. In practice, the methodology for studying the two major divisions of the autonomic nervous system is much more precise for the sympathetic than for the parasympathetic system.

Clinical Tests of Sympathetic Nervous System Function

The various components in the sympathetic nervous control of the cardiovascular system (see Figure 2) have each served as a focus for the development of tests of sympathetic nervous system activity applicable to humans. (Esler, 1983; Esler, Hasking, Willett, et al., 1985). The principal clinical techniques that have been used for studying sympathetic nervous circulatory control are as follows:

- electrophysiological techniques for studying sympathetic nerve firing rates (e.g., Hagbarth & Vallbo, 1968; Wallin & Sundlof, 1982);
- the use of pharmacological blockers to quantify, by subtraction, the prevailing level of neural cardiovascular tone (e.g., Doyle & Smirk, 1955; Julius et al., 1971);
- the study of spontaneous circulatory rhythms, by spectral analysis (e.g., Akselrod et al., 1985; Hyndman, Kitney, & Sayers, 1971); and

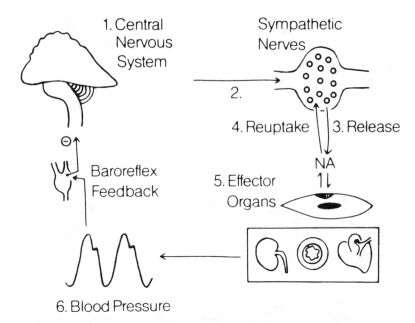

Figure 2 Individual elements in the sympathetic nervous control of the cardiovascular
system, and their clinical testing. (1) CNS control of BP: baroreflex
testing/psychometrics/mental stress responses. (2) Sympathetic nerve traffic:
electrophysiology of peripheral sympathetic nerves. (3) Transmitter release:
radiotracer measurement of noradrenaline spillover to plasma. (4) Transmitter
reuptake: clinical studies of the noradrenaline pump. (5) Receptor/effector
response: adrenergic receptor binding/cardiovascular responsiveness. (6)
Overall maintenance of adrenergic cardiovascular tone: hemodynamic response
to pharmacological autonomic blockade; spectral analysis of heart rate cyclical
rhythms. From Esler (1983). Reprinted by permission of publisher and author.

- biochemical methods for estimating rates of noradrenaline release (e.g., Cryer,
  1980; Esler et al., 1979).

Hagbarth and Vallbo (1968) devised clinical electrophysiological methods for
studying nerve firing (with multi-unit recording) in subcutaneous sympathetic nerves,
distributed to skeletal muscle and skin. The technique has since been imaginatively
applied by Wallin and Sundlof (1982) to the study of normal and abnormal sympathetic circulatory control. Doyle and Smirk (1955) introduced into clinical research
the technique of pharmacological autonomic blockade for the study of sympathetic
nervous maintenance of cardiovascular function, to estimate in particular the neurogenic component in essential hypertension. Sophisticated mathematical partitioning
(spectral analysis) of the individual, superimposed rhythms producing cyclical variation in heart rate can be used to study the properties of the sympathetic nerves of the
heart (Akselrod et al., 1985; Pagani et al, 1986).

Although these methods have proven valuable in the study of sympathetic nervous function in humans, each has its limitations. For example, with methods for
estimating the neural component in hypertension, based on the hemodynamic re-

sponse to pharmacological autonomic blockade, measured responses are influenced by both the level of sympathetic nerve firing and secondary hypertrophy in the heart and arteries through a "cardiovascular amplifier effect" (Folkow, 1982; Korner, 1982). This undermines attempts to estimate sympathetic nervous activity in hypertensive patients from hemodynamic responses. With microneurographic electrophysiological methods for studying nerve firing rates, only the sympathetic nerves to skin and skeletal muscle can be studied; an important limitation in cardiovascular diseases is that the nerves to internal organs are not accessible to testing.

Biochemical measurements might, perhaps, be more helpful in quantifying sympathetic nerve discharge rates in internal organs. Of the range of biochemical measures available, direct and indirect measures of neurotransmitter release have been most widely adopted as clinical tests of sympathetic nervous function (see Figure 3). Measurement of noradrenaline content and turnover in tissues, spillover of released noradrenaline to plasma, the concentration of noradrenaline in plasma, cerebrospinal fluid and blood platelets, and the excretion of noradrenaline have all been relied on. The general relationship that exists between sympathetic nerve firing rates and noradrenaline release, demonstrated for organs including the heart, lungs, spleen, and skeletal muscle (Esler et al., 1985, 1988), provides the experimental justification for using noradrenaline measurements in body fluids, especially blood plasma, as clinical indices of sympathetic activity.

Measurements of Noradrenaline in Plasma and Urine

Of the various clinical indices of sympathetic nervous function, measurements of the plasma concentration of noradrenaline have been used most extensively. Although plasma noradrenaline measurements are a sufficiently sensitive guide to sympathetic nerve function to identify patients with sympathetic failure in autonomic insufficiency syndromes, to demonstrate some effects of drugs action on the sympathetic nervous system, and sometimes to detect reflex sympathetic responses, to upright posture and exercise, for example (Robertson et al., 1979), the method has major limitations as a test of sympathetic nervous system activity. One important deficiency concerns the dependence of the plasma noradrenaline concentration on both noradrenaline plasma clearance and norepinephrine release. A variety of circumstances change the rate at which noradrenaline is removed from plasma in humans (Esler, 1982), rendering the plasma concentration invalid as an index of noradrenaline release and sympathetic nervous tone.

Urinary noradrenaline measurements suffer from the same limitations as plasma measurements (because urinary excretion of noradrenaline is dependent in particular on the plasma concentration) plus some additional ones. Interpretation of urinary noradrenaline measurements as an index of overall sympathetic nervous system activity is complicated by the dependence of urinary noradrenaline excretion on the glomerular filtration rate, renal noradrenaline production, and renal tubular secretion and reabsorption of noradrenaline (Esler, 1989). Despite these drawbacks, urinary noradrenaline measurements have provided a useful, although clearly somewhat ambiguous, qualitative index of overall sympathetic nervous tone. Until the availability of assays sufficiently sensitive to measure noradrenaline in plasma, urinary measurements remained the only available biochemical test of sympathetic activity.

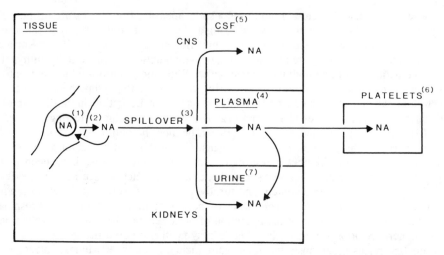

Figure 3 Measures of the tissue content of norepinephrine, (1) rates of norepinephrine release
(2) and spillover to plasma, (3) the concentration of norepinephrine in plasma and
(4) blood platelets, and (6) the urinary excretion of norepinephrine (7) have all been
developed as clinical indices of sympathetic nerve firing rates (sympathetic nervous
system activity) in humans. Measurements of norepinephrine metabolites have been
used similarly. Cerebrospinal fluid measurements (5) have been utilized in the study
of central nervous system norepinephrine release. From Esler (1987). Reprinted by
permission of publisher and author.

Measurements of the Overall Rate
of Release of Noradrenaline

Because plasma noradrenaline measurements provide a rather ambiguous guide
to sympathetic nervous activity, kinetic techniques for estimating the rate of release
of noradrenaline to plasma have been developed (Esler et al., 1979). These have the
important advantage over plasma noradrenaline measurements of avoiding the confounding influence of noradrenaline plasma clearance. The central features of these
methods is the determination of the clearance rate of plasma noradrenaline. Radiotracer methodology has been used extensively for studying noradrenaline kinetics in
human subjects (Esler, 1982; Esler et al., 1988), with noradrenaline overflow to
plasma being determined by isotope dilution. For infused tritiated noradrenaline
(NA),

$$\text{Overall NA spillover} = \frac{[^{3}\text{H}]\text{NA infusion rate}}{\text{plasma NA specific radioactivity}}$$

Rather than the rate of release of noradrenaline from sympathetic nerve variocosities,
the NA spillover rate represents the rate at which released noradrenaline enters
plasma. In humans this appears to be approximately 10%–20% of the release rate, for
the body as a whole (Hoeldtke et al., 1983).

It should be noted, however, that information conveyed by measurements of the
overall rate of release of noradrenaline to plasma is limited. There is an intrinsic
weakness in this and any other biochemical test of global sympathetic nervous activ-

ity: The sympathetic nervous system is not organized as an all-or-nothing system, because the sympathetic outflow to all organs is not uniform, and local, organ-specific increases or decreases in sympathetic activity can occur with different reflexes, and in different disease states (Esler et al., 1985; Folkow, 1982; Korner, 1971). A biochemical index of overall sympathetic activity represents the algebraic sum of the changes in regional noradrenaline release and has very restricted physiological meaning, because the pattern of sympathetic nervous activation is not delineated. For more penetrating analysis of sympathetic nervous pathophysiology in cardiovascular disorders, techniques allowing study of regional, organ-specific sympathetic nervous function are needed.

Measurements of Noradrenaline Release to Plasma by Individual Organs

Techniques measuring organ-specific noradrenaline release are available for studying regional patterns of sympathetic nervous activation in humans (Esler et al., 1985, 1988). The relation between the sympathetic nerve firing rate of an organ, with electrical stimulation in the physiological range, and the rate of noradrenaline spillover into its venous effluent provides the experimental justification for using measures of regional noradrenaline release as a clinical index of sympathetic nervous tone in individual organs. Measurement of the rate of spillover of released noradrenaline into the venous drainage is complicated by the fact that all organs release noradrenaline into and remove noradrenaline from the circulation simultaneously. Because noradrenaline flux is bidirectional, determination of noradrenaline spillover rates by the Fick principle requires an adjustment to be made for organ noradrenaline extraction. Noradrenaline extraction is probably best determined by using a constant rate infusion of isotope-labeled noradrenaline:

$$\text{Organ NA spillover} = [(C_V - C_A) + C_A(NA_E)] \times PF$$

where C_V = plasma noradrenaline (NA) concentration in draining vein, C_A = arterial plasma NA concentration, NA_E = fractional extraction of tritiated NA, and PF = organ plasma flow.

By measuring the regional release of noradrenaline throughout the body, it is possible to determine the relative contribution of individual organs to total noradrenaline release to plasma (Esler, Jennings, Leonard et al., 1984). The major sources of noradrenaline release to plasma are the sympathetic nerves of the lungs, kidneys, and skeletal muscle. Cardiac noradrenaline release (see Figure 4) accounts for only a few percent of the total (Esler, Jennings, Korner et al., 1984; Esler, Jennings, Leonard et al., 1984).

CLINICAL TESTS OF PARASYMPATHETIC NERVOUS SYSTEM FUNCTION

Tests of parasympathetic nervous system regulation of the circulation are less well developed than tests of sympathetic nervous system function, but also less pertinent. Vagal influences on heart rate and the electrical stability of the myocardium is the only area of relevance. There are no clinical tests based on measurement of neurotransmitter (acetylcholine) release, because survival of the transmitter in the synaptic

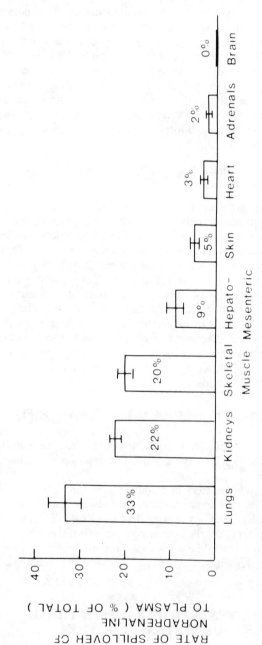

Figure 4 Spillover of noradrenaline to plasma from individual organs, expressed as a proportion of whole-body noradrenaline overflow. Only a few percent of the noradrenaline plasma pool is derived from the heart. From Esler et al. (1984). Adapted by permission of publisher and authors.

space and the circulation is so brief because of the speedy action of cholinesterases. Nor are there clinically applicable electrophysiological methods.

Vagal control of heart rate can be studied using spectral analysis of the superimposed rhythms producing cyclical variations in rate (Akselrod et al., 1985; Pagani et al., 1986). The high frequency component of approximately 0.3 Hz that is associated with respiratory rhythms is under vagal influence. Diminished spontaneous variation of heart rate with respiration is a clinically useful pointer to the presence of autonomic insufficiency involving parasympathetic efferents (Bannister et al., 1979). Pharmacological autonomic blockade of the parasympathetic system, with atropine, can be used to estimate vagal tone, from the changes produced in heart rate and cardiac output (Julius et al., 1971). For example, the lesser rise in heart rate and cardiac output noted with atropinization in patients with borderline hypertension than in normal subjects has been taken as evidence that vagal restraint on the heart is diminished in the phase of early development of essential hypertension. Atropinization has also been used to assess the degree to which vagal withdrawal contributes to the increase in heart rate with stimuli such as exercise, upright posture, and laboratory mental stress.

TESTS OF NONADRENERGIC, NONPARASYMPATHETIC AUTONOMIC FUNCTION

At present, few clinical methods are available for testing autonomic nervous function attributable to neurotransmitters other than noradrenaline and acetylcholine. Some autonomically mediated responses persist after cholinergic and combined alpha- and beta-adrenergic blockade and are thought to be mediated by dopaminergic, purinergic, or peptidergic mechanisms (Dinerstein et al., 1979; Pernow, Lundberg, & Kaijser, 1988). The plasma concentration of one presumed transmitter, the noradrenaline cotransmitter, neuropeptide Y, can be measured to estimate release and overflow to plasma (Pernow et al., 1988). From the effect of dopamine receptor antagonists, dopaminergic autonomic mechanisms can be inferred. Apart from these few examples, no clinical methods are available for testing nonadrenergic, nonparasympathetic autonomic nervous function.

AUTONOMIC NERVOUS SYSTEM REGULATION OF CARDIOVASCULAR RESPONSES

The autonomic nervous system can generate differentiated, integrated cardiovascular responses to a variety of challenges to circulatory homeostasis. In some instances, such as those involving high- and low-pressure receptors, the circulatory receptors, afferent connections, and central nervous system mechanisms have been well elucidated (Korner, 1971). In others, syncope being a case in point, the central nervous integration of the circulatory response remains uncertain. To illustrate some general principles of autonomic nervous cardiovascular regulation I describe the circulatory adjustments occurring with upright posture, fainting, and laboratory mental stress.

Upright Posture

With sitting and standing, translocation of blood occurs from the heart and lungs to the distensible veins of the abdomen and legs. The reduction in degree of distension

Table 2   Autonomic nervous system integration of cardiovascular responses

---

Upright posture
  • tachycardia (vagal withdrawal, sympathetics ↑)
  • neural increase in vascular resistance and venous tone
  • sympathetically mediated renal responses
Syncope
  • bradycardia (vagus ↑, cardiac sympathetics ↓)
  • vasodilatation from reduced firing of sympathetics
Laboratory mental stress
  • vagal withdrawal
  • sympathetics activated (but not uniformly)
  • adrenaline release

---

of cardiopulmonary volume receptors underlies the reflex circulatory response (see Table 2). High pressure arterial baroreceptors make little contribution. The elevation of heart rate is a consequence both of vagal withdrawal and increased sympathetic cardiac stimulation. Increases in vascular resistance and venous tone, and the renal responses (renin secretion, fall in glomerular filtration rate, and renal tubular retention of sodium) are mediated through the sympathetic nervous system. The small rise in plasma adrenaline concentration noted makes little contribution to the circulatory response (Cryer, 1980).

If the reflex adjustments to upright posture are defective, either blocked pharmacologically or deficient in patients with syndromes of autonomic nervous failure, postural hypotension results. With autonomic insufficiency, postural hypotension may be the most incapacitating symptom, patients in extreme cases being reduced to locomotion on hands and knees. In severe cases, the most effective form of treatment seems to be to increase blood volume with a salt-retaining steroid hormone (such as fludrocortisone) and to minimize venous pooling through prescription of the selective venoconstricting drug, dihydroergotamine, in a sufficient (rather high) dose (Jennings, Esler, & Holmes, 1979; Oliver et al., 1980).

The rise in plasma noradrenaline concentration with upright posture has been used extensively, and often uncritically, as a clinical index of reflex sympathetic nervous responsiveness. But noradrenaline plasma clearance falls with upright posture (Esler et al., 1988), presumably due to a reduction in cardiac output and organ blood flows, contributing to the rise in plasma noradrenaline concentration. The rise in plasma noradrenaline concentration, in fact, appears to be due at least as much to this fall in noradrenaline plasma clearance as to any increase in noradrenaline release (see Figure 5).

Syncope

The fainting reaction is a hypotensive circulatory response, often abrupt in onset, that may occur (particularly in young people) with prolonged standing or in response to unpleasant or threatening emotional experiences, such as venipuncture. The precise central nervous integration of the response is unclear. The hypotension is a consequence of bradycardia (presumed vagal) and falling vascular resistance, underlying use of the term *vasovagal reaction*. The fall in vascular resistance almost certainly results from withdrawal of sympathetic nervous vasoconstrictor tone and not the sympathetic cholinergic vasodilatation to which it was at one time attributed (see

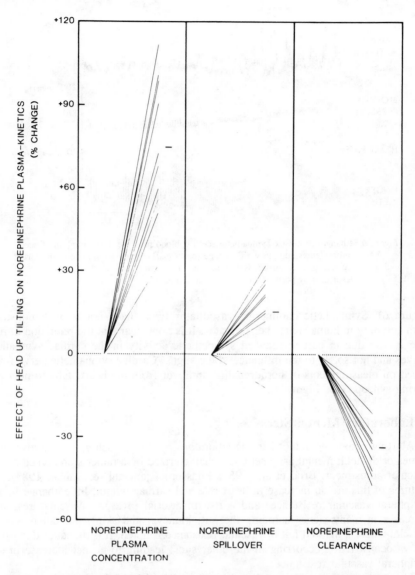

Figure 5 With 60 minutes of 40° head-up tilting in 10 patients with untreated essential hypertension the plasma concentration of noradrenaline (norepinephrine) rose, but this was due in part to a fall in the rate at which noradrenaline was removed from plasma. The increase in plasma noradrenaline concentration thus cannot be used to quantify the sympathetic nervous response. From Esler et al. (1988). Reprinted by permission of publisher and authors.

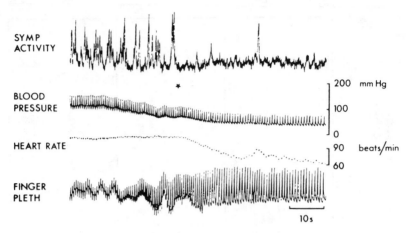

Figure 6 Changes in muscle sympathetic activity, blood pressure, heart rate, and finger pulse plethysmogram with syncope (onset marked by asterisk) occurring during the course of a nitroprusside infusion. From Wallin and Sundlof (1982). Reprinted by permission of publisher and authors.

Figure 6). Sympathetic cholinergic vasodilator fibers have not been demonstrated with certainty in humans or other primates. It is now clear that the reduction in heart rate is also due in part to reduced sympathetic activity in the cardiac sympathetic nerves and not solely to the influence of the vagus. Cardiac sympathetic nerve firing, based on measurements of noradrenaline spillover from the heart, falls to near zero during syncope (see Figure 7).

Laboratory Mental Stress

Alerting responses induced in the laboratory by things such as competitive video games or difficult mental arithmetic are characterized by a rather stereotyped cardiovascular adjustment (Brod et al., 1959; Eliasson, Hjemdahl, & Kahan, 1983). The features of this are an increase in heart rate and cardiac output, little change in total peripheral vascular resistance, and a rise in arterial pressure. Vascular resistance increases in many sites (including the gut, kidneys, and skin), but not in skeletal muscle, where a marked fall in vascular resistance is noted. It is the latter that offsets the vasoconstriction occurring in the other sites, leading to no net increase in total peripheral vascular resistance.

The sympathetic nervous system is activated in the "defense reaction," but not uniformly. The sympathetic nervous outflow to forearm skeletal muscle tends to fall with laboratory mental stress (Delius et al., 1972), underlying the reduction in regional vascular resistance. The heart rate increase is due to the combined influence of vagal withdrawal (Folkow, 1982) and increased cardiac sympathetic nerve firing (see Figure 8). The plasma concentration of adrenaline rises to a variable extent and contributes to an uncertain degree to the tachycardia, regional vasoconstriction, and skeletal muscle vasodilatation (Eliasson et al., 1983).

Note should be made here of a particular problem that arises if plasma noradrenaline measurements are used in an attempt to quantify stress responses, especially if antecubital venous sampling is used (Eliasson et al., 1983). Antecubital venous blood largely represents the venous drainage from skeletal muscle. Because sympathetic nervous activity in forearm muscle tends to fall with the defense reaction (Delius et al., 1972), peripheral venous plasma noradrenaline measurements are not well suited for monitoring stress responses. The plasma noradrenaline concentration in arterial blood more faithfully reflects rates of noradrenaline release from organs involved in the stress sympathetic nervous responses (such as the heart) than does peripheral venous blood. Failure to recognize this limitation of antecubital venous sampling for plasma noradrenaline measurements leads to popularization of the notion that mental stress causes an adrenergic rather than a noradrenergic response (Dimsdale & Moss, 1980). This is quite clearly not the case; the sympathetic outflow to the heart, for example, is intensely activated during laboratory mental stress reactions.

THE IMPORTANCE OF CIRCULATING CATECHOLAMINES TO CARDIOVASCULAR REGULATION

A variety of conditions cause sympathetic nervous activation and adrenal medullary secretion. These include exercise, anxiety, exposure to cold, pain, hypoglycemia, circulatory underfilling (from upright posture or hemorrhage), and numerous drug

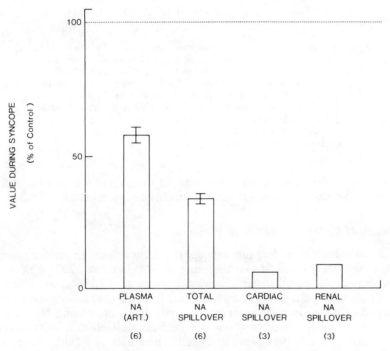

Figure 7 Catecholamine measurements, expressed as a fraction of baseline, are shown in five people experiencing a syncopal (vasovagal) reaction during insertion (under local anesthesia) of percutaneously placed cardiac catheters. The number of subjects for each measurement is shown in parentheses. Cardiac and renal noradrenaline spillover was decreased to near zero during syncope.

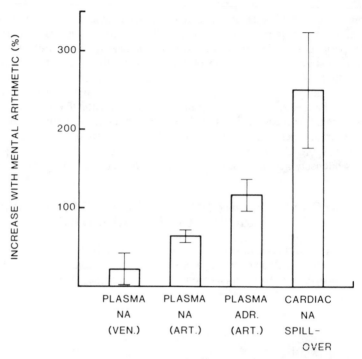

Figure 8 Plasma catecholamine measurements are influenced by the sampling
site in laboratory-induced mental stress. The increase above baseline
produced in 10 untreated patients with essential hypertension by 10
minutes of serial subtractions of 7 and 13 from a large number is
shown. The increase was greatest for cardiac noradrenaline
spillover, but inconsequential for antecubital venous blood. These
findings are dictated by the patterning of the sympathetic response,
which spares the sympathetic outflow to forearm skeletal muscle,
but preferentially involves the heart.

effects (Cryer, 1980). It is often a difficult matter to ascertain whether the observed
plasma catecholamine response has directly influenced cardiovascular function.

Sources of Catecholamines in Plasma

Mean concentrations of free (unconjugated) catecholamines in arterial plasma in
healthy, recumbent subjects are on the order of noradrenaline, 200 pg/ml (Cryer,
1980); dopamine, 30 pg/ml (Esler, Jennings, Leonard et al., 1984); and adrenaline,
50 pg/ml (Eliasson et al., 1983). Catecholamines from the central nervous system are
generally thought not to enter plasma directly (only after metabolism). Noradrenaline
in plasma, under unstimulated conditions, is almost exclusively derived from sympathetic nerves—only 2% from adrenal medulla (Brown et al., 1981; Planz et al.,
1978). Plasma adrenaline derives from the adrenal medulla, with traces from extra-
adrenal chromaffin tissue (Cryer, 1980). The source of plasma dopamine is unknown;
derivation from dopaminergic nerves, from the efflux of precursor dopamine in sympathetic nerves, and from decarboxylation of circulating DOPA by kidney have all

been suggested. A large fraction of the catecholamine plasma pool consists of the respective sulphoconjugates.

Effects of Plasma Catecholamine on the Cardiovascular System

Under most circumstances noradrenaline in plasma does not act as a circulating hormone. For noradrenaline the threshold plasma concentration for cardiovascular effects seems to be on the order of 1500 pg/ml, 5 times or more the plasma concentration in unstimulated, resting people (Cryer, 1980), although some would put the value lower (Izzo, 1983). Noradrenaline in plasma represents neurotransmitter spilling over into the circulation after release from sympathetic nerves. Only with extreme levels of sympathetic nervous stimulation (such as maximum aerobic exercise) are plasma concentrations sufficiently high to directly stimulate the heart and vasculature (Cryer, 1980).

Conversely, adrenaline functions as a circulating hormone, the threshold plasma concentration for discernible effects, 100–150 pg/ml, being readily exceeded (Cryer, 1980). The extent to which adrenaline in plasma in responsible for the cardiovascular changes accompanying mental stress, however, is still problematic. Evidence favors an overriding importance of the sympathetic nervous system (Eliasson et al., 1983), despite views to the contrary (Dimsdale & Moss, 1980). A particular metabolic effect of adrenaline, a capacity to lower serum potassium levels markedly by promoting the uptake of potassium into cells, is seen with plasma concentrations of adrenaline reached in experimental laboratory stress reaction (Struthers & Reid, 1984). The relation of stress-induced hypokalemia to psychogenic initiation of cardiac arrhythmias is an issue demanding further research attention.

DISTURBANCES OF AUTONOMIC NERVOUS SYSTEM FUNCTION IN CARDIOVASCULAR DISEASES

A number of disorders of the cardiovascular system have long been thought to result from the influence of disordered autonomic nervous system function on the circulation. These disorders are as follows.

- cardiac arrhythmias
- coronary artery spasm
- cardiac failure
- mitral valve prolapse
- essential hypertension
- Raynaud's disease

The development of tests of autonomic nervous function of greater sophistication and precision than was available previously has enabled this proposition to be put to the test. Central to any consideration such as this are the function and clinical testing of the cardiac sympathetic nerves.

The Cardiac Sympathetic Nerves

The sympathetic innervation of the heart passes from the spinal cord to the upper thoracic sympathetic ganglia. A proportion of these fibers travel along the sympathetic chain to the cervical ganglia. Post-ganglionic fibers aggregate into superior, middle, and inferior cardiac nerves and distribute to the heart. The sinoatrial node, atria, conducting system, and both ventricles are well innervated, although the density of innerveration differs from highest in sinoatrial node to lowest in apices of ventricles (Pierpont et al., 1985).

The activity (firing rate) of the cardiac sympathetic nerves may be inferred from the changes in heart rate and cardiac output producted by acute pharmacological beta-adrenergic blockade (Julius et al., 1971). The observed heart rate and cardiac output reductions, however, depend on factors other than the firing rate of the cardiac sympathetics. Altered adrenoreceptor number or affinity, or changed intracellular second messenger generation could underly different responses to beta-blockade. Measurement of the rate of overflow into plasma of noradrenaline released by the sympathetic nerves of the heart is an alternative technique that has been used to estimate cardiac sympathetic activity in humans (Esler et al., 1985, 1988). Typically this involves measuring the coronary sinus-arterial plasma noradrenaline concentration difference, the fractional extraction of radiolabeled noradrenaline across the heart, and the coronary sinus plasma flow, which is measured by thermodilution (Esler et al., 1984, 1985, 1988).

Cardiac noradrenaline spillover in healthy subjects at rest accounts for only 2%–3% of total body noradrenaline release to plasma (Esler, Jennings, Korner et al., 1984; Esler, Jennings, Leonard et al., 1984). Although the heart has a dense sympathetic innervation, density of innervation presumably is outranked by other determinants of noradrenaline spillover, by factors such as organ mass and blood flow, and mean width of the synaptic cleft (narrow in the heart) and the resultant level of neuronal noradrenaline reuptake. Neuronal reuptake of noradrenaline is in fact more complete in the heart than in other organs (Goldstein et al., 1988). Because the heart makes such a small contribution to the plasma noradrenaline pool, it follows that arterial or venous plasma noradrenaline measurements cannot validly be used to study cardiac sympathetic nerve responses. Despite views to the contrary (Goldstein et al., 1983), cardiac and overall sympathetic nervous stimulation commonly does not run in parallel (Esler, Jennings, & Lambert, 1989), as is illustrated in Figure 9.

Responses of the sympathetic nerves of the heart in a range of circumstances are shown in Figure 10, to illustrate the utility of noradrenaline overflow measurements in studying regional sympathetic nervous activity. Increases in cardiac noradrenaline release to plasma were noted during cognitive challenge (serial subtraction of 7 or 13 from large numbers) in 14 patients with untreated primary hypertension, and with supine bicycle exercise at 50% of maximum work capacity in 5 healthy subjects. Cardiac norepinephrine spillover fell to near zero in three patients in whom a syncopal attack occurred during the course of right heart catheterization. The increase in cardiac norepinephrine spillover with the norepinephrine uptake-blocker, desipramine, illustrates that norepinephrine overflow is influenced not only by norepinephrine release, but also by the adequacy of neuronal reuptake.

Two aspects of the influence of the sympathetic nerves of the heart on cardiac physiology are of special relevance to this chapter and volume, effects on coronary blood flow and on electrophysiological properties of cardiac muscle.

Neural Regulation of Coronary Blood Flow

Coronary blood flow is determined principally by the metabolic demands of the heart. Heart rate, which influences the available diastolic time for flow, is a second

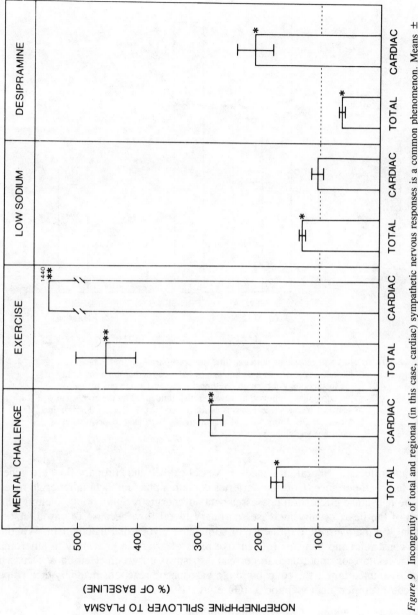

Figure 9 Incongruity of total and regional (in this case, cardiac) sympathetic nervous responses is a common phenomenon. Means ± SE. *p < 0.05, ** p < 0.01, paired *t*-test. From Esler et al. (1989). Reprinted by permission of publisher and authors.

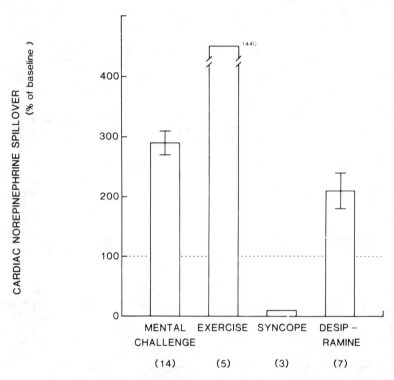

Figure 10 Rates of release of noradrenaline (norepinephrine) from the heart to
plasma, expressed as a percentage of baseline, demonstrate the utility of
the methodology for gauging regional sympathetic nervous responses.
Noradrenaline spillover, however, is also influenced by the competency of
neuronal reuptake mechanisms as illustrated by the effect of desipramine.
Means ± SE. From Esler et al. (in press). Reprinted by permission of
publisher and authors.

important influence. Neural influences on vessel caliber and coronary flow are generally of lesser importance. Coronary arteries contain alpha- and beta-adrenergic receptors; the resistance circulation possesses beta-adrenergic receptors only. Neural stimulation of the heart usually increases coronary blood flow because of vasodilatation
secondary to the overriding influence of stimulated myocardial metabolism. Whether
neural constrictor mechanisms (of reactive parts of artery in proximity to atheroma-
tous plaques) are of importance in coronary spasm is uncertain (Heusch & Deussen,
1983). Also uncertain is the contribution to vasospastic reactions made by the sympathetic cotransmitter, neuropeptide Y (Gu et al., 1983).

Neural Modification of Electrophysiological
Properties of Myocardial Cells

Cardiac muscle cells, to differing degrees, possess the properties of excitability
(can generate an action potential), automatically (able to initiate action potentials
spontaneously), and the capacity to conduct an impulse (propagation of an action
potential to a distance). The autonomic nervous system influences these phenom-

ena, in some instances by modifying the voltage threshold for firing of an action potential, by hyperpolarizing the cell membrane during diastole (an effect of the parasympathetic neurotransmitter, acetylcholine), or by modifying the rate of spontaneous diastolic depolarization of automatic (self-firing) cardiac muscle cells. Increased sympathetic nervous drive quickens diastolic depolarization. These effects of the vagus and cardiac sympathetic nerves on the electrophysiological properties of cardiac muscle may be manifested as influences on heart rate and the predisposition toward arrhythmia development (Verrier & Lown, 1984). Regional heterogeneity in cardiac sympathetic nervous activity and synaptic noradrenaline concentration, especially with myocardial ischemia, may also contribute to reentrant ventricular arrhythmias.

Essential Hypertension

The influential "mosaic theory" of Page (1949), with its central concept that essential hypertension is a multifactorial disease of disordered cardiovascular regulation, for 25 years dissuaded most researchers from seeking primary, initiating causes of hypertension. It came to be seen as a truism that any search for an isolated, primary cause of hypertension was futile. More recent studies, involving the renin-angiotensin system and membrane fluxes, have led to a changed viewpoint, namely that essential hypertension is a syndrome with multiple primary causes, differing from case to case, and that these discrete, initiating causes of the blood pressure elevation may possibly be identifiable in individual patients. Research on autonomic nervous system pathophysiology in essential hypertension has had similar implications. Biochemical evidence suggests that in certain instances the initiation of the blood pressure elevation in essential hypertension is primarily neurogenic.

Measurements of Noradrenaline Release

The turnover of noradrenaline in tissues has been used to quantify sympathetic nervous activity in various models of experimental hypertension in animals. The need for tissue sampling, after prior dosing with radiolabeled noradrenaline or its precursors, restricts the clinical applicability of the method. The radiotracer methods described earlier for studying noradrenaline turnover in plasma provide an alternative approach to estimating sympathetic nervous activity clinically. These methods show that the higher plasma noradrenaline concentration found in a proportion of patients with essential hypertension is due to an increased overall rate of spillover of noradrenaline, presumptive evidence of increased sympathetic nervous activity (see Figure 11). Noradrenaline plasma clearance is normal in hypertensive patients (Esler et al., 1985).

Measurements of the regional pattern of noradrenaline release to plasma give more precise information concerning sympathetic nervous pathophysiology in essential hypertension than do total noradrenaline spillover values. Noradrenaline spillover from the kidneys is increased in patients with essential hypertension, providing presumptive evidence of increased renal sympathetic activity (Esler et al., 1985, 1986, 1987). The finding cannot readily be accounted for by other factors possibly influencing noradrenaline spillover, such as altered renal blood flow and noradrenaline washout (renal blood flow is not increased in essential hypertension), or defective neuronal noradrenaline uptake (renal extraction of radiolabeled noradrenaline is normal in hypertensive patients). Renal noradrenaline spillover is increased particularly in young patients (see Figure 12), markedly so in some instances, to a level matching that seen in cardiac failure (Hasking et al., 1986). These measures of sympathetic neurotransmitter release complement rather less direct observations from several sources (Esler et al., 1977; Hollenberg, Williams, & Adams, 1981) which have previously suggested that renal sympathetic nervous activity is increased in young adults with essential hypertension.

Increased release of noradrenaline from the heart to plasma is also present in patients with essential hypertension. This is unlikely to be due to coexistent left ventricular hypertrophy, because cardiac noradrenaline content and turnover do not increase in parallel with the increase in ventricular mass in hypertensive hypertrophy of the heart. The cardiac noradrenaline spillover findings support earlier results, based on hemodynamic and pharmacological techniques, which suggest that cardiac sympathetic activity is increased in essential hypertension, especially in younger patients, contributing to higher heart rates and cardiac output (Esler et al., 1977; Julius et al., 1971).

Measurements of regional noradrenaline release to plasma suggest that selective activation of the sympathetic nervous system, confined to the outflows to the kidneys and heart, is present in essential hypertension, particularly in young patients. Sympathetic nervous activity in the lungs, and in the hepatomesenteric circulation, appears to be normal. The same conclusion can be tentatively reached, based on venoarterial plasma noradrenaline concentration gradients, for the sympathetic nerves to skin and

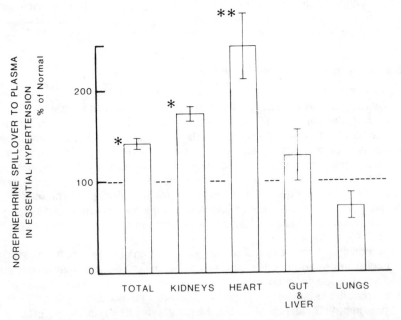

Figure 11 Total and regional spillover of noradrenaline in 50 patients with untreated essential hypertension. Cardiorenal noradrenaline overflow was increased, presumptive evidence of increased firing in the sympathetic outflows to the heart and kidneys. From Esler et al. (1986). Reprinted by permission of publisher and authors.

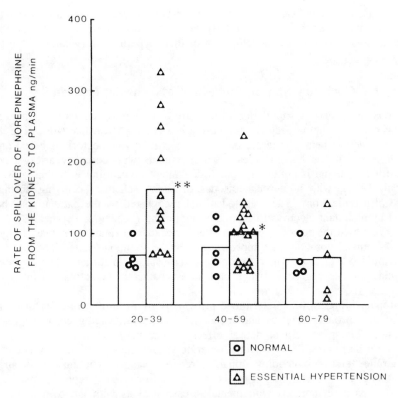

Figure 12 An influence of age on renal noradrenaline spillover was evident in
hypertensive patients, but not healthy subjects. Increased renal sympathetic
activity (based on measurements of noradrenaline overflow) was most
apparent in patients aged less than 40 years. *$p < 0.05$, **$p < 0.01$,
Mann-Whitney U-test. From Esler et al. (1988). Reprinted by permission of
publisher and authors.

skeletal muscle. How might this regional pattern of sympathetic nervous system activation in essential hypertension have originated?

Possible Causes of Sympathetic Nervous System Activation

The basis of a selective activation of renal and cardiac sympathetic nervous outflow in essential hypertension remains uncertain. Folkow (1982) has reviewed one
view of hypertension pathogenesis, which gives priority to psychosomatic mechanisms, emphasizing the importance of neurohumoral responses in the defense reaction. Could our research findings represent an accentuation of the stress response in
hypertensive patients? The increase in renal and cardiac sympathetic nervous activity
we describe, in the presence of what appears to be normal skeletal muscle sympathetic activity, is evocative of the defense reaction. Not consistent, however, is the
finding of apparently normal hepatomesenteric sympathetic activity. In short, the
precise cause of these changes in hypertensive patients is unclear. Mapping of the
regional pattern of sympathetic nervous system activity in patients with essential
hypertension has not pointed unequivocally to the primary cause of the hypertension.

The increased renal and cardiac sympathetic nervous activity present in some patients with essential hypertension, particularly younger ones, does, however, provide a plausible mechanism for the development of their hypertension, whatever the fundamental cause.

Angina, Coronary Spasm, and Silent Myocardial Ischemia

Sympathetic nervous stimulation of the cardiovascular system can be a direct and obvious cause of angina pectoris, increasing heart rate and cardiac work. The therapeutic efficacy of beta-adrenergic blocking drugs in angina pectoris is based on this fact. Recently it has become clear that in patients with coronary artery disease, myocardial ischemia is commonly painless, "silent myocardial ischemia" (Stern & Tzivoni, 1974), with numerous episodes of silent ischemia occurring during the course of a typical day. These episodes, not recognized by the patient, may be recorded by ambulant electrocardiographic monitoring (Schang & Pepine, 1977). The context in which the episodes occur is often other than at times of increased physical work; emotional upsets in fact appear to be a more common trigger. The unresolved issues are the extent to which coronary artery spasm underlies silent myocardial ischemia, and the degree to which cardiac sympathetic overactivity is involved in pathogenesis.

Coronary blood flow is determined principally by mean diastolic perfusion pressure of the coronary arteries and metabolic factors influencing coronary vascular resistance. The predominant neural effect on coronary vascular resistance, with healthy coronary arteries, is a beta-adrenergic vasodilatation. In the presence of atherosclerotic stenosis, overriding alpha-2 adrenergic vasoconstriction may occur with sympathetic nervous stimulation of the heart. The occasional reported instances of coronary spasm in humans with mental stress, such as with the pain of the cold pressor test, probably involve this mechanism.

The usual view is that mental stress does not commonly provoke coronary spasm. A pathological reduction in coronary blood flow with stress, however, may well be a common occurrence (Deanfield et al., 1984; Rozanski et al., 1988). The recent important study of Deanfield et al. (1984) showed that reduction in coronary blood flow and myocardial ischemia (studied with rubidium positron tomography) was very common indeed during experimental mental stress in patients with existing coronary artery disease (see Figure 13). It is not clear whether the increase in resistance to coronary blood flow seen here was in large arteries (coronary spasm) or in the microvasculature.

Myocardial Infarction

The extent to which autonomic nervous dysfunction and coronary spasm underlie myocardial infarction is disputed. In contrast, it is clear that profound disturbance of autonomic cardiovascular control may develop as a sequel to myocardial infarction. Vagal bradycardia and hypotension, promptly reversed by atropine, are particularly common with infarction of the inferior wall of the left ventricle. The reflex mechanism is uncertain. Another reflex response, a reflex increase in cardiac sympathetic nervous activity during myocardial ischemia, is well documented (Mallani & Lombardi, 1978). A different phenomenon, possibly very important in arrhythmia development, is the nonreflex leaching out of noradrenaline from sympathetic

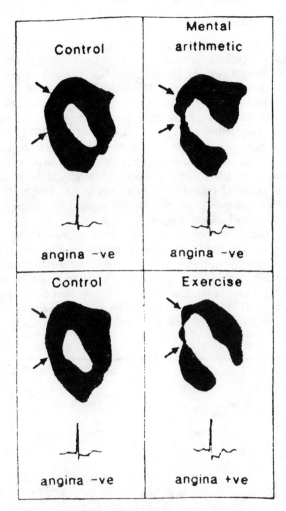

Figure 13 Changes in regional myocardial uptake of rubidium-82, in relation to the presence or absence of angina, before and after mental arithmetic or exercise. In the patient shown, arithmetic caused silent myocardial ischemia. Exercise caused ischemia, in a similar distribution, but accompanied by chest pain. From Deanfield et al. (1984). Reprinted by permission of publisher and authors.

nerves during prolonged ischemia, with or without infarction (Schomig et al., 1987). This process, which represents an inability of hypoxic cardiac sympathetic nerve fibers to provide the energy to maintain high intracellular concentration of noradrenaline in granular form, can produce very high tissue concentrations of noradrenaline at the periphery of ischemic myocardium. With circulatory collapse (cardiogenic shock) systemic sympathetic nervous system activation occurs.

Cardiac Arrhythmias

Neural mechanisms are undoubtedly very important in arrhythmia development. Increasing cardiac sympathetic nervous activity in dogs (through aversive conditioning or nerve stimulation) reduces the threshold for induced ventricular fibrillation (Verrier & Lown, 1984). The effect is abolished by sectioning the cardiac sympathetic nerves or by beta-adrenergic blockade. In fact, a variety of behavioral methods have been used in animals to alter (increase sympathetic, reduce vagal) neural tone in the heart, thereby potentiating arrhythmias (Corley et al., 1975; Verrier & Lown, 1984). The animal experiments appear to parallel experience in humans in which, in the view of many investigators, sudden cardiac death is an electrophysiological event that is often related to emotional stress and occurs typically in the absence of coronary thrombosis and myocardial infarction (Cobb, Werner, & Trobaugh, 1980; Eliot & Buell, 1985). Direct evidence exists that mental stress does increase cardiac sympathetic nervous activity in humans (Fig. 8).

In an ongoing study, my colleagues and I have observed that in patients with serious ventricular arrhythmias (e.g., ventricular tachycardia or resuscitated ventricular fibrillation) cardiac sympathetic activity was substantially increased when they were hemodynamically stable (see Figure 14). An extreme case of increased cardiac sympathetic nerve activity (a ten-fold increase) is provided by patients with cardiac failure (Hasking et al., 1986). Patients with heart failure have very reduced survival; death is often sudden, unexpected, and presumably due to ventricular fibrillation. It is

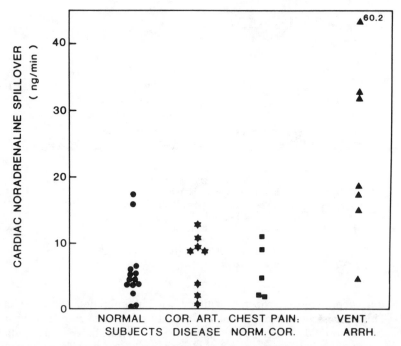

Figure 14   Cardiac sympathetic nervous activity was increased (based on measurements of neurotransmitter overflow) in patients with prior serious ventricular arrhythmias, compared with the reference populations.

not clear to date whether this propensity toward sudden death is a consequence of the extraordinary high level of cardiac sympathetic tone present. It may well be.

SUMMARY

Clinical study of autonomic nervous system control of circulation draws in particular on electrophysiological (measuring sympathetic nerve firing rates), biochemical (measuring noradrenaline turnover), and pharmacological (assessing cardiovascular response to adrenergic and cholinergic blockade) methods. Circulatory responses in a variety of circumstances are differentiated and appropriate to the stimulus, although their integration into the central nervous system in many instances is not well understood in humans. Disturbed autonomic nervous circulatory control can be demonstrated in a range of cardiovascular disorders, including essential hypertension and cardiac failure. The function of the cardiac sympathetic nerves is of paramount importance in these and allied circulatory disorders. A particular challenge for the future centers on the need to delineate the complex interrelation of emotional stress and cardiac sympathetic nerve activity to the pathogenesis of coronary spasm, silent myocardial ischemia, and sudden death.

REFERENCES

Akselrod, S., Gordon, D., Madwed, J. B., Sniderman, N. C., Shannon, D. C., & Cohen, R. J.: (1985). Hemodynamic regulation: Investigation by spectral analysis. *American Journal of Physiology, 249,* 867–875.

Bannister, R., Davies, B., Holley, E., Rosenthal, T., & Sever, P.: (1979). Defective cardiovascular reflexes and supersensitivity to sympathomimetic drugs in autonomic failure. *Brain, 102,* 163–176.

Brod, J., Fenal, V., Hejl, & Jirka, J.: (1959). Circulatory changes underlying blood pressure elevation during acute emotional stress (mental arithmetic) in normotensive and hypertensive subjects. *Clinical Science, 18,* 269–279.

Brown, M. J., Allison, D. J., Jenner, D. A., Lewis, P. J., & Dollery, C. T.: (1981). Increased sensitivity and accuracy of phaechromocytoma diagnosis achieved by use of plasma-adrenaline estimations and a pentolinium-suppression test. *Lancet, 1,* 174–177.

Cobb, L. A., Werner, J. A., & Trobaugh, G. (1980). Sudden cardiac death. *Modern Concepts of Cardiovascular Disease, 49,* 31–42.

Corley, K. C., Mauck, H. P., & Shiel, F. O'M. (1975). Cardiac responses associated with "yoked-chair" shock avoidance in squirrel monkeys. *Psychophysiology, 12,* 439–444.

Cryer, P. E. (1980). Physiology and pathophysiology of the human sympathoadrenal system. *New England Journal of Medicine, 303,* 436–444.

Deanfield, J. E., Shea, M., Kensett, M. (1984). Silent myocardial ischemia due to mental stress. *Lancet, 2,* 1001–1005.

Delius, W., Hagbarth, K.-E., Hongell, A. (1972). Manoeuvers affecting sympathetic outflow in human muscle nerves. *Acta Physiologica Scandinavica, 84,* 82–94.

DiBona, G. F. (1982). The function of the renal nerves. *Review of Physiological and Pharmacological Biochemistry, 94,* 76–181.

Dimsdale, J. E., & Moss, J. (1980). Short-term catecholamine response to psychological stress. *Psychosomomatic Medicine, 42,* 493–497.

Dinerstein, R. J., Vannice, J., Henderson, R. C., Roth, L. J., Goldberg, L. I., & Hofmann, P. C.: (1979). Histofluorescence techniques provide evidence for dopamine-containing neuronal elements in canine kidney. *Science, 205,* 497–499.

Doyle, A. E., & Smirk, F. H. (1955). The neurogenic component in hypertension. *Circulation, 12,* 543–552.

Eliasson, K., Hjemdahl, P., & Kahan, T. (1983). Circulatory and sympathoadrenal responses to stress in borderline and established hypertension. *Journal of Hypertension, 1,* 131–139.

Eliot, R. S., & Buell, J. C., (1985). Role of emotions and stress in the genesis of sudden death. *Journal of the American College of Cardiology, 5,* 95B–98B.

Esler, M. (1982). Assessment of sympathetic nervous function in humans from noradrenaline plasma kinetics. *Clinical Science, 62,* 247–254.

Esler, M. (1983). Neurogenic mechanisms in human hypertension. *Medicographia, 5,* 7–11.

Esler, M. (1987). Biochemical evidence for sympathetic overactivity in human hypertension. In S. Julius & D. R. Basset (Eds.), *Handbook of hypertension: Vol 9. Behavioural factors in hypertension (pp. 75–94). The Netherlands: Elsevier.*

Esler, M. (1989). Renal catecholamine metabolism. Mineral and Electrolyte Metabolism, 15, 16–23.

Esler, M. D., Hasking, G. J., Willett, I. R., Leonard P., & Jennings, G. (1985). Noradrenaline release and sympathetic nervous system activity. *Journal of Hypertension, 3,* 117–129.

Esler, M., Jackman, G., Bobik, A., Kelleher, D., Jennings, G., Leonard, P., Skews, H., & Korner, P. (1979). Determination of norepinephrine apparent release rate and clearance in humans. *Life Sciences, 25,* 1461–1470.

Esler, M., Jennings, G., Biviano, B., Lambert, G., & Hasking, G. (1986). Mechanism of elevated plasma noradrenaline in the course of essential hypertension. *Journal of Cardiovascular Pharmacology, 8*(Suppl. 5), 39–44.

Esler, M. Jennings, G., Korner, P., et al.(1984). Measurement of total, and organ-specific, noradrenaline kinetics in humans. *American Journal of Physiology, 247*(Suppl. 10), E21–E28.

Esler, M., Jennings, G., Korner, P., Willett, I., Dudley, F., Hasking, G., Anderson, W., & Lambert, G. (1988). Assessment of human sympathetic nervous system activity from measurements of norepinephrine turnover. *Hypertension, 11,* 3–20.

Esler, M., Jennings, G., & Lambert, G. (1989). Noradrenaline release and the pathophysiology of primary human hypertension. *American Journal of Hypertension, 2,* 140S–146S.

Esler, M., Jennings, G., Leonard, P., et al.(1984). Contribution of individual organs to total noradrenaline release in humans. *Acta Physiologica Scandinavica, 527*(Suppl.), 11–16.

Esler, M., Julius, S., Zweifler, A., Randall, O., Harburg, E., Gardiner, H., & DeQuattro, V. (1977). Mild high-renin essential hypertension: A neurogenic human hypertension? *New England Journal of Medicine, 296,* 405–411.

Folkow, B. (1982). Physiological aspects of primary hypertension. *Physiological Reviews, 62,* 347–504.

Goldstein, D. S., Brush, J. E., Eisenhofer, G., Stull, R., & Esler, M. (1988). In vivo measurement of neuronal uptake of norepinephrine in the human heart. *Circulation, 78,* 41–48.

Goldstein, D. S., McCarty, R., Polinsky, R. J., & Kopin, I. J. (1983). Relationship between plasma norepinephrine and sympathetic neural activity. *Hypertension, 5,* 552–559.

Gu, J., Polak, J. M., Adrian, T. E., Allen, J. M., Tatemoto, K., & Bloom, S. R. (1983). Neuropeptide tyrosine (NPY): A major cardiac neuropeptide. *Lancet, 1,* 1008–1010.

Hagbarth, K. D., & Vallbo, A. B. (1968). Pulse and respiratory grouping of sympathetic impulses in human muscle nerves. *Acta Physiologica Scandinavica, 74,* 96–108.

Hasking, G., Esler, M., Jennings, G., Burton, D., Johns, J., & Korner, P. Norepinephrine spillover to plasma in congestive heart failure: Evidence of increased overall and cardiorenal sympathetic nervous activity. *Circulation, 73,* 615–621.

Heusch, G., & Deussen, A. (1983). The effects of cardiac sympathetic nerve stimulation on perfusion of stenotic coronary arteries in the dog. *Circulation Research, 53,* 8–15.

Hoeldtke, R. D., Cilmi, K. M., Reichard, G. A., Jr., Boden, G., & Owen, O. (1983). Assessment of norepinephrine secretion and production. *Journal of Laboratory and Clinical Medicine, 101,* 772–782.

Hollenberg, N. K., Williams, G. W., Adams, D. F. (1981). Essential hypertension: Abnormal renal vascular and endocrine responses to a mild psychological stimulus. *Hypertension, 3,* 11–17.

Hyndman, B. W., Kitney, R. I., & Sayers, B. M. (1971). Spontaneous rhythms in physiological control systems. *Nature, 233,* 339–341.

Izzo, J. (1983). Cardiovascular hormonal effects of circulating norepinephrine. *Hypertension, 4,* 787–789.

Jennings, G., Esler, M., & Holmes, R. (1979). Treatment of orthostatic hypotension with dihydroergotamine. *British Medical Journal, 2,* 307–308.

Julius, S., Pascal, A., & London, R. (1971). Role of parasympathetic inhibition in the hyperkinetic type of borderline hypertension. *Circulation, 44,* 413–418.

Korner, P. I. (1971). Integrative neural cardiovascular control. *Physiological Reviews, 51,* 312–367.

Korner, P. I. (1982). Causal and homeostatic factors in hypertension. *Clinical Science, 63,* 5S–26S.

Malliani, A., & Lombardi, F. (1978). Neural reflexes associated with myocardial ischemia. In P. J. Schwartz, A. M. Brown, A. Maillani, & A. Zanchetti (Eds.), *Neural mechanisms in cardiac arrhythmias* (pp. 209–219). New York: Raven Press.

Olver, J., Jennings, G., Bobik, A., & Esler, M. (1980). Low bioavailability as a cause of apparent failure of dihydroergotamine in orthostatic hypotension. *British Medical Journal, 2,* 275.

Pagani, M., Lombardi, F. Guzzetti, S., Rimoldi, O., Furlan, R., Pizzinelli, P., Sandrone, G., Malfatto, G., Dell'Orto, S., Piccaluga, E., Turiel, M., Baselli, G., Cerutti, S., & Malliani, A. (1986). Power spectral analysis of heart rate and arterial pressure variabilities as a marker of sympathovagal interaction in man and conscious dog. *Circulation Research, 59,* 178–193.

Page, I. H. (1949). Pathogenesis of arterial hypertension. *Journal of the American Medical Association, 140,* 451–458.

Pernow, J., Lundberg, J. M., & Kaijser, L. (1988). Alpha-adrenoceptor influence on plasma levels of neuropeptide Y-like immunoreactivity and catecholamines during rest and sympathoadrenal activation in humans. *Journal of Cardiovascular Pharmacology, 12,* 593–599.

Pierpont, G. L., Master, E. G., Reynolds, S., Pederson, J., & Cohn, J. N. (1985). Ventricular myocardial catecholamines in primates. *Journal of Laboratory and Clinical Medicine, 106,* 205–210.

Planz, G., & Planz, R. (1979). Dopamine-β-hydroxylase, adrenaline, noradrenaline, and dopamine in the venous blood of adrenal gland in man: A comparison with levels in the periphery of the circulation. *Experientia, 35,* 207–208.

Robertson, D., Johnson, D. A. Robertson, R. M., Robertson, R. M., Nies, A. S., Shand, D. G., & Oates, J. A. (1979). Comparative assessment of stimuli that release neuronal and adrenomedullary catecholamines in man. *Circulation, 59,* 637–643.

Rozanski, A., Bairey, N., Krantz, D., Friedman, J., Resser, K. J., Morell, M., Hilton-Chalfen, S., Hestrin, L., Bietendorf, J., & Berman, D. S. (1988). Mental stress and the induction of silent myocardial ischemia in patients with coronary artery disease. *New England Journal of Medicine, 318,* 1055–1012.

Schang, S. J., Jr., & Pepine, C. J. (1977). Transient asymptomatic S-T segment depression during daily activity. *American Journal of Cardiology, 39,* 396–402.

Schömig, A., Fischer, S., Kurz, T., Richardt, G., & Schömig, E. (1987). Nonexocytic release of endogenous noradrenaline in the ischemic and anoxic rat heart: Mechanism and metabolic requirements. *Circulation Research, 60,* 194–205.

Stern, S., & Tzivoni, D. (1974). Early detection of silent ischemic heart disease by 24 hours electrocardiographic monitoring of active subjects. *British Heart Journal, 36,* 481–486.

Struthers, A. D., & Reid, J. L. (1984). The role of adrenal medullary catecholamines in potassium homeostasis. *Clinical Science, 66,* 377–382.

Verrier, R. L., & Lown, B. (1984). Behavioral stress and cardiac arrhythmias. *Annual Reviews of Physiology, 46,* 155–176.

Wallin, B. G., & Sundlof, G. (1982). Sympathetic outflow to muscle during vasovagal syncope. *Journal of the Autonomic Nervous System, 6,* 287–291.

Weiner, N., & Taylor, P. (1985). Neurohumoral transmission: The autonomic and somatic motor nervous systems. In A. F. Gilman, L. S. Goodman, T. W. Rall, & F. Murad (Eds.), *The pharmacological basis of therapeutics* (pp. 66–69). New York: Macmillan.

7

The Neurobiology of Anxiety

Ray W. Winters, Gail H. Ironson, and Neil Schneiderman

INTRODUCTION

Anxiety can be characterized as a state of the central nervous system associated with the anticipation of harm or vulnerability in response to perceived threat. When the stimuli that elicit this affective state can be identified, they usually fall into one of three categories: a signal for an aversive stimulus, a signal for the withholding of a positive reinforcer, or a novel stimulus (Gray, 1987). In instances in which the individual experiencing the affective state can identify the eliciting stimulus accurately, the state is referred to as fear or anticipatory anxiety. In many cases, however, the stimuli that elicit the affective state cannot be identified. These stimuli may be internal, as has been suggested for panic disorders (Uhde, Siever, & Poste, 1984) or the anxiety associated with withdrawal from an addicting substance. The conditioning history of the individual is particularly important in this regard. One may not be able to identify an anxiety-producing environmental stimulus, for example, in the anxious individual who has a conditioning history of frequent unpredictable aversive stimulation or the individual who has a history of negative feedback in response to attempts to implement control over the environment (i.e., helplessness).

The response profile of an individual in an anxious or fearful state includes the inhibition of ongoing activities (Charney, Menkes, & Heninger, 1981; Gray, 1987), hypervigilance (Beck, 1963; Dunner, Ishiki, Avery et al., 1986; Gray, 1987; Redmond, 1985), and escape or avoidance behaviors (Beck, 1963; Gray, 1987; Miller, 1982; Reiman, 1988). In addition, increases in forebrain arousal (Gray, 1987; Winters, 1985) and autonomic arousal (Lader, 1980) are usually associated with anxiety. Definitions of anxiety as an affective state focus upon conditioned fear (Bartlett & Izard, 1972; Costa, 1985; Gray, 1987; Miller, 1982) but may include feelings of helplessness (Epstein, 1972; Garber, Miller, & Abramson, 1980; Mandler, 1980; Seligman, 1975; Reiman, 1988; Weiss et al., 1982) and other emotions such as anger, guilt, and shame (Izard & Blumberg, 1985).

Continuity Versus Discontinuity

Anxiety can be a normal reaction to perceived risk or danger and serve as a positive motivating force in the production of adaptive coping responses. In such cases, the magnitude of the emotional response is roughly commensurate with the threat that is posed. In contrast, the emotional state associated with pathological anxiety may impair cognitive or motor functioning and lead to maladaptive, self-defeating behaviors. Because there are a variety of anxiety states, a question that naturally arises is whether these states are qualitatively different, constituting discrete entities and thus forming separate categories, or whether the various anxiety states represent quantitative variations along a single dimension involving normal neurophysiological and neurochemical systems. The issue of continuity versus discontinuity is particularly relevant to any discussion of the neurophysiological and neurochemical substrates of anxiety and will be addressed in this chapter.

Controllability

In recent years, theoretical discussions of anxiety have emphasized the importance of controllability in the etiology of anxiety disorders (Epstein, 1972; Garber et al., 1980; Lazarus & Averill, 1972; Mandler, 1980; Mandler & Watson, 1966; Mineka, 1985; Mineka & Kohlstrom, 1978; Seligman, 1975). According to this view, pathological anxiety occurs when an individual perceives a threat but believes that a clear coping response is not available or the coping response in ineffective. The symptoms of anxiety disorders are seen as inappropriate coping responses that mitigate the anxiety (e.g., obsessive–compulsive behavior) but do not eliminate it. Thus as an affective state, anxiety varies from one of tension and discomfort in situations in which effective coping responses are available, to a sense of helplessness and depression during situations in which no coping responses are available.

Although controllability appears to be an important factor in the understanding of anxiety and the relation it bears to depression, there are situations in which having a coping response available can be more stressful than not having one at all. Weiss (1968; 1971a; 1971b; 1971c) has reported that the ulceration rate of rats in a shock-avoidance paradigm is proportional to the rate of responding (or difficulty) as well as the type of feedback. Even animals that received positive feedback for avoidance responses showed ulceration rates higher than those of yoked controls, if the number of coping responses required was high. In situations in which feedback was inconsistent (i.e., an avoidance-avoidance conflict where negative feedback was given sometimes and positive feedback was given at other times), ulceration rate was higher than for yoked controls even when response rates were low. Tsuda and co-workers (Tsuda, Tanaka, Wishikawa, & Hirai, 1983) also have reported that the ulceration rate was highest in animals that had the most difficult task, that is, higher response rates. Similarly, Berger and colleagues (Berger, Starzec, & Mason, 1981) also found that animals that were required to respond at high rates to avoid electrical shock had higher corticosterone levels than did their yoked controls. Thus establishing relationships among controllability, anxiety, and pathophysiologic processes is of considerable importance, but task difficulty and conflict are factors that also must be considered in the assessment of anxiety states.

Comorbidity of Anxiety and Depression

The idea that the neuronal circuitries of anxiety and depression overlap is a belief shared by many investigators (e.g., Paul, 1988). The comorbidity between the two classes of disorders was noted as early as 1938 by Lewis and since that time has been discussed by a number of investigators (see Stein & Uhde, 1988). Anxiety is almost always a prominent symptom of patients with major affective illness and in fact is higher in patients with major depression than with some types of anxiety disorders

(Insel, Zahn, & Murphy, 1985). As was pointed out by Cole (1988), many of the items on two standard scales for anxiety and depression (Hamilton scales) overlap.

If controllability is an important factor in the etiology of anxiety, one would expect a high incidence of depression among patients with the more severe anxiety disorders. In this regard, panic disorders, agoraphobia (with panic attacks), and obsessive—compulsive disorders appear to be particularly debilitating because it is often not possible to identify accurately a stimulus in the environment that triggers the anxiety response. Attempts to cope with the anxiety are futile because response-initiated feedback does not include a safety signal. Responses that are under poor stimulus control, such as the rituals of an obsessive–compulsive, show extremely high response rates and are difficult to modify (Sidman, 1955).

Patients who suffer from panic disorder are most distressed by the random, unpredictable pattern associated with the attacks (Avonson & Logue, 1988). Uhde and co-workers (Uhde, Roy-Byrne, Vittone, Boulenger, & Post, 1985) have reported that agoraphobia was associated with panic disorder in 84% of their patients. Other investigators (e.g., Ost & Hugdahl, 1981, 1983) have reported similar rates. The high comorbidity of the two disorders has led many investigators (e.g., Ost & Hugdahl, 1981, 1983) to hypothesize that panic attacks play an important etiological role in the development of agoraphobia and that the behaviors associated with agoraphobia (e.g., not leaving the house) function as a means to cope with panic attacks.

The behaviors of patients with panic disorders, agoraphobia, and obsessive–compulsive disorders do not usually lead to safety signals from the environment, which suggests that feelings of helplessness and depression should be quite common in these patients. Indeed, this appears to be the case. Clinical observations of patients with agoraphobia (with panic attacks) and panic disorder reveal that depression often accompanies these disorders (Stein & Uhde, 1988). Uhde et al. (1985) have reported, for example, that 50% of the agoraphobic panic patients that they examined had a lifetime history of depression. These findings are consistent with those of other investigators, such as Van Valkinberg, Akiskal, Puzantian, and Rosenthal (1984) and Roth, Gurney, Garside, and Kerr (1972), who have observed that depression is the most frequent complication of panic disorder. In many cases the symptoms of depression are not secondary to panic disorder (Breier, Charney, & Heninger, 1986; Charney, Heninger, Price et al., 1986), but when depression does occur it is quite severe (Coryell, Endicott, Andreason et al., 1988). Stein and Uhde (1988) suggested that the depression that accompanies panic disorder is the result of disregulation in alpha-adrenergic mechanisms in the neuronal circuitry that is involved in both anxiety and depression. Welner, Reich, Robins, Fishman, and Van Doren (1976), in a study of 150 patients with obsessive–compulsive disorder, found that 120 patients presented depression as a major symptom. Goodwin, Guze, and Robins (1969), in their review of obsessive–compulsive treatment outcome studies, concluded that depression was the most common complication in obsessive–compulsive disorder.

The high comorbidity between some types of anxiety disorders and depressive disorders suggests an overlap in the neurochemical substrates of the two classes of disorders. Therefore, it comes as no surprise that many of the reactions of these patients to pharmacological agents are similar. The tricyclic compounds and the monoamine oxidase inhibitors have been found to be effective pharmacological agents for many depressed patients and are among the most effective drugs for the treatment of agoraphobia and panic attacks (Heninger & Charney, 1988; Klein, 1964; Klein & Fink, 1962; Klein, Gittelman, Quitkin, & Rifkin, 1980; Klein, Zitrin, & Woener,

1978; Sheehan, Ballenger, & Jacobson, 1980; Zitrin, Klein, Woerner, & Ross, 1983). Katz and co-workers (Katz, Robins, Croughan, Secunda, & Swann, 1982) have pointed out that the most reliable initial behavioral changes following the administration of tricyclic compounds and monoamine oxidase inhibitors in depressed patients are their anxiolytic effects. Several investigators (Klein, 1964; Klein & Fink, 1962; Ravaris et al., 1976) have reported that these two compounds are most effective when a patient shows symptoms of both anxiety and depression. A similarity in the underlying neurochemistry of depressed patients and patients with some types of anxiety disorders is also suggested by the observation that a marker for depression (Breier, Charney, & Heninger, 1984)—a blunted growth hormone response to clonidine—is also seen in patients with panic disorder (Charney & Heninger, 1986; Uhde et al., 1985; Uhde, Vittone, Siever et al., 1986) and obsessive–compulsive disorders (Siever et al., 1983). In this chapter we examine neurophysiological, neurochemical, and neuroendocrine systems that have been implicated in both anxiety and depressive disorders.

BASIC NEUROPHYSIOLOGY

Role of the Locus Coeruleus

The locus coeruleus is believed to be a nodal structure in both anxiety and depression (e.g., Gray, 1987; Redmond, 1985; Weiss et al., 1982). This nucleus, which is situated bilaterally in the most anterior portion of the rhomboid fossa is located near the cerebral aqueduct. It consists of approximately 20,000 melanin-pigmented noradrenergic neurons. The axons of these neurons have a remarkably wide distribution and project to the forebrain and to most of the structures that mediate the physiological response to pain and fear, including those involved in the control of blood pressure, heart rate, and mobilization of free fatty acids (see Grant & Redmond, 1981). High-intensity electrical stimulation of the locus coeruleus in monkeys produces fear-like behaviors that cannot be distinguished from the ones observed in conditioning experiments (Redmond, 1977; Redmond & Huang, 1979; Redmond, Huang, Snyder, Maas, & Baulu, 1976a). These responses can be blocked or diminished by lesions of this region (Redmond, Huang, Snyder, Maas, & Baulu (1976b) or by anxiolytics (Redmond, 1977; Redmond et al., 1976a). Attentiveness and vigilance in the awake monkey are associated with moderate levels of single cell activity in the locus coeruleus (Foote, Aston-Jones, & Bloom, 1980; Foote, Bloom, & Aston-Jones, 1983), whereas subnormal activity in this structure is associated with fearlessness and inattentiveness (Redmond, 1979). Fear-associated stimuli increase the level of activity in locus coeruleus neurons (Grant & Redmond, 1981), and increases in the activity of the sympathetic nervous system are associated with changes in locus coeruleus activity (Abercrombie & Jacobs, 1987a, 1987b). Locus coeruleus neurons do not habituate to noxious stimuli, even in anesthetized animals (Cedarbaum & Aghajanian, 1978). In general, drugs that reduce the activity of neurons in the locus coeruleus, including ethanol (Pohorecky & Brick, 1977), benzodiazepines (Redmond, 1977), and tricyclic antidepressants (Nyback, Walters, Aghajanian, & Roth, 1975) have anxiolytic effects.

If the level of neuronal activity in the locus coeruleus is proportional to the magnitude of anxiety, one would expect higher levels of activity with uncontrollable stress.

Indeed, there is evidence for this view from the work of Weiss and co-workers. When rats experience uncontrollable stress, they show many of the symptoms of helplessness and depression including anorexia, weight loss, loss of grooming and play behavior, sleep disturbances, and reduced aggressiveness (Weiss et al., 1982; Weiss & Goodman, 1985). The results of experiments (Weiss et al., 1982) in which the alpha-adrenergic agonist clonidine and the alpha-adrenergic antagonist piperoxane were infused into the ventricle near the locus coeruleus during uncontrollable stress, provided evidence that there was a reduction in amount of norepinephrine in this region during helplessness. These investigators hypothesized that this led to an increase in the activity of locus coeruleus neurons due to lowered alpha-adrenergic auto-receptor mediated inhibition of these neurons. Taken together, the results of experiments assessing the role of the locus coeruleus in anxiety and depression are consistent with the view that different forms of anxiety represent different degrees of severity along a single dimension, rather than forming separate discrete categories, and that controllability is a dimension that is essential to the prediction of the severity of the anxiety. Interestingly, a recent study by Breier and colleagues provides evidence that uncontrollable, but not controllable, stress in normal human subjects produces behavioral, neuroendocrine, and psychophysiological changes that are similar to those observed in depressed patients (Breier, Albus, Pickar et al., 1987).

Forebrain Structures

Gray (1979) and Petty and Sherman (1981) have emphasized the importance of the hippocampus in the mediation of learned responses to signals for aversive stimuli. Gray emphasizes the importance of the septum and the hippocampus in the mediation of the behavioral inhibition, the vigilance and increased arousal associated with anticipatory anxiety (see Gray, 1979, for a review) and the helplessness associated with uncontrollable stress (Gray, 1982, 1985). Petty and Sherman (1981) saw the hippocampus as a nodal structure in the development of helplessness. Both Gray (1985) and Petty and Sherman (1981) contended that the level of hippocampal activity is dependent on the level of noradrenergic input to it from the locus coeruleus.

Neuroendocrine Systems

SAM System

The focus of most research on neuroendocrine responses to stressful situations, such as those associated with anxiety, has been on two systems: the *sympathoadreno-medullary* (SAM) system and the *hypothalamic-pituitary-adrenocortical* (HPAC) system. An increase in the activity of the SAM system is known to be associated with "fight or flight" behaviors, but this neuroendocrine system is also activated during stressful situations that do not involve physical exertion. During behavioral situations perceived as threatening, the sympathetic nervous system releases norepinephrine from sympathetic nerve terminals and both norepinephrine and epinephrine from the adrenal medulla. During behavioral stress that elicits active coping (e.g., the defense reaction) or its anticipation, the heart increases its rate and force of contraction. The venous side of the circulation decreases its volume, thereby increasing the return of venous blood to the heart. Cardiac output is increased; arterioles in the gut and skin contract, increasing resistance to blood flow. Activation of the SAM system during fight or flight reactions also stimulates adipose tissue to mobilize free fatty acids, the liver to release glucose, and the kidney to release renin and to decrease the excretion of sodium and water.

In contrast to the pattern of SAM responses seen during acute fight, flight, or panic reactions, another pattern of sympathetic nervous system activation is often seen in more tonic stress reactions or in situations in which active coping is not perceived as being possible (McCabe & Schneiderman, 1985). In these cases, increases in blood pressure are related to an increase in peripheral resistance that is associated with vasoconstriction in the skin, gut, and skeletal muscles. Thus the activation of the SAM system would be associated with anxiety states in which a coping response is available, such as normal anticipatory anxiety and situations involving conflict, but would also be activated in pathological anxiety states in which a coping response may be inappropriate (e.g., obsessive–compulsive disorders) or the patient feels helpless (i.e., where depression occurs). The patterns of SAM responses in each of these two situations, however, is likely to differ.

There are a number of ways in which high levels of SAM activity may mediate relations between behavioral stress and cardiovascular pathology. Myocardial ischemia, for example, can occur as the result of an increased need for myocardial oxygenation in conjunction with a reduced blood supply caused by coronary atherosclerosis. In susceptible individuals, sudden violent episodes of SAM activity can provoke life-threatening arrhythmias. Elevated SAM activity can also lead to the deposition and incorporation into coronary artery plaques of thromboembolitic components of the blood, and can facilitate necrosis, calcification, and rupture of plaques, which in turn can produce thrombosis and myocardial infarction.

HPAC System

In addition to changes that occur in sympathetic nervous system activity, stressful situations in which an adequate coping response is not perceived as evident can lead to increases in HPAC activity (Henry & Meehan, 1981; Schneiderman, 1983). The resulting behaviors are characterized by extreme vigilance and an inhibition of movement. This "conservation-withdrawal pattern" (Seyle, 1946) has been associated with suppression of the immune system, clinical depression, and a variety of other disorders (Henry & Stephens, 1977). Activation of the HPAC system has also been associated with acute anxiety (Nesse et al., 1985) and with a number of anxiety disorders (Curtis & Glitz, 1988; Persky, 1975; Roy-Byrne et al., 1986).

The mechanism by which the HPAC system becomes activated has been traced to parvocellular neurons in the medial basal hypothalamus. In response to stimulation, the neurons in the medial basal hypothalamus secrete corticotropin-releasing hormone (CRH). This CRH is transported to the anterior pituitary via the hypothalamicohypophysial portal system. In the adenohypophysis, CRH stimulates secretion of adrenocorticotrophic hormone (ACTH) into the systemic circulation. The target organ, which is the adrenal cortex, is then activated by ACTH to release adrenocorticosteroids such as cortisol.

The HPAC system has several important negative feedback aspects. One of these is for the control of corticosteroid secretion. Activation of hypothalamic neurons by various stressors leads to the release of corticosteroids. In addition to their metabolic effects upon target organs, the corticosteroids have direct negative feedback effects upon (a) the hypothalamus to decrease formation of CRH and (b) the adrenohypophysis to decrease the formation of ACTH. This feedback serves to stabilize the concentration of corticosteroids in the circulation when the body is experiencing relatively low levels of stress. This stabilizing feedback, however, can be disrupted during periods of pronounced stress. In this case, dexamethasone suppression, which ordinarily suppresses cortisol release through negative feedback, is ineffective. Thus the extent of dexamethasone suppression can prove useful in assessing whether a particular condition (e.g., depression or anxiety) is capable of overriding the normal cortisol feedback mechanism. Indeed, an elevated level of cortisol is a marker for clinical depression.

Animal behavior experiments have provided evidence that increases in the release of the adrenocorticoids are closely associated with a lack of control over the environment. Rats receiving inescapable electric shock, for example, revealed significantly higher levels of corticosteroids than rats who were able to avoid shocks (Weiss, 1972). Also, monkeys subjected to unavoidable, intense noise, showed elevations in plasma cortisol, whereas this did not occur in monkeys who had control over the noise (Hanson, Larson, & Snowden, 1975).

Aside from its role in psychological states, cortisol hyperresponsivity may play a contributory role in the pathogenesis of both coronary atherosclerosis and acute coronary events. This may in turn be related to the synergistic relationship that exists between the HPAC and SAM systems under stressful conditions. Cortisol, for instance, has been demonstrated to (a) increase the sensitivity of adrenergic receptors to a given level of neurotransmitter, (b) stimulate the catecholamine-synthesizing enzyme tyrosine hydroxylase, and (c) inhibit catechol-O-methyltransferase, which is a major catecholamine-degrading enzyme (Kvetnansky, 1980). The view that cortisol hyperresponsivity may contribute to atherogenesis is supported by findings among air force personnel that elevated plasma cortisol levels during an oral glucose tolerance test are associated with increased severity of angiographically documented atherosclerosis (Troxler, Sprague, Albanese, Fuchs, & Thompson, 1977).

Neuroendocrine Changes and Anxiety

Normal Anxiety

Public speaking, which is considered to be anxiety-provoking in many people, is typically accompanied by increases in heart rate, blood pressure (Saab, Matthews, Stoney, & McDonald, in press), and catecholamines (Dimsdale & Moss, 1980; Taggart, Carruthers, & Somerville, 1973). Stutterers, who presumably would show more anxiety than nonstutterers during public speaking, have also shown greater increases in urinary epinephrine (Edgren, Leanderson, & Levi, 1970).

Simple Phobia

Neuroendocrine changes have been studied in various anxiety disorders. In simple phobia, patients have elevated levels of intense anxiety only when they are near a particular stimulus such as a snake, an elevator, or a needle. Exposure to phobic stimuli has been accompanied by significant increases in epinephrine (Nesse, Curtis, Thyer, McCann, Huber–Smith, & Knuff, 1985), norepinephrine (Nesse et al., 1985), plasma growth hormone (Nesse et al., 1985; Curtis, Nesse, Buxton et al., 1979), and plasma insulin (Nesse et al., 1985). Inconsistent results have been obtained for plasma cortisol; in two studies no significant increase was reported (Curtis et al., 1976; 1978), and in one a small but significant increase was reported (Nesse et al., 1985). No significant change during phobic exposure has been found for prolactin

(Nesse, Curtis, Brown, & Rubin, 1980), thyrotropin-secreting hormone (TSH—Nesse, Curtis, & Brown, 1982), or glucagon (Nesse et al., 1985). In a study using slides rather than exposure to the real phobic stimuli, patients having animal or blood injury phobias have displayed significant elevations in urinary free-cortisol excretion, greater distress, and skin conductance levels while viewing slides of phobic objects compared to neutral stimuli (Fredrikson, Sundin, & Frankenhaeuser, 1985).

Panic Disorder

Activation of the SAM system occurs during panic attacks. The increase in heart rate and the rapid, deep breathing that occurs during these attacks suggest an increase in beta-adrenergic activity. Tricyclic antidepressants, which prevent panic attacks, are known to down-regulate beta-adrenergic receptors (Sulser & Mobley, 1981; U'Prichard & Enna, 1979). In contrast, the beta-adrenergic agonist isoproterenol hydrochloride causes normal individuals to experience many somatic manifestations of panic including increases in breathing rate and heart rate (Weiner, 1980). The beta-blocker propranolol hydrochloride can block isoproterenol-induced anxiety as well as anxiety symptoms in patients (Carlsson, Engel, & Hansson, 1976; Kathol et al., 1980; Kielholz, 1977).

Patients with panic disorder experience acute symptoms of anxiety (usually lasting a short period of time) either spontaneously or in response to a specific stimulus on a fairly regular basis (more than three times a month). Researchers have examined differences between these patients and normal subjects with regard to resting or basal levels, as well as with patients' neuroendocrine levels during panic attacks. In interpreting differences in basal level, one must keep in mind that panic disorder patients may have higher levels of basal anxiety and anticipatory anxiety than do normal control subjects. Studies of urinary and plasma catecholamines show mixed results—with several studies showing higher levels in panic patients and some showing no difference (see Curtis & Glitz, 1988, for a review). A urinary metabolite of catecholamines, 3-methoxy-4-hydroxy-phenethyleneglycol (MHPG), which is an indicator of noradrenergic activity, has been reported to be the same or lower than in controls. However, platelet monoamine oxidase (MAO) levels are higher in panic disorder patients (Gorman, Liebowitz, Fryer et al., 1985; Yu, Bowen, Davis, & Boulton, 1983), a finding that has been interpreted as being caused by induction of MAO to facilitate degradation of catecholamines, possibly in response to earlier rises in those catecholamines. Basal cortisol levels have been found to be either elevated (particularly in the afternoon or evening) or normal (particularly in the morning or afternoon) in panic patients relative to control subjects (Curtis & Glitz, 1988). But even the largest differences have been small—11.1 mg/dl in patients versus 3.3 mg/dl in control subjects (Roy-Byrne et al., 1986). ACTH values were reported either to be higher (Roy-Byrne et al., 1986) or the same. Increased basal prolactin levels have been reported (Appleby, Klein, & Sachar, 1981; Liebowitz et al., 1985), as have increased growth hormone levels (Nesse, Cameron, Curtis, McCann, & Huber-Smith, 1984).

In an effort to capture neuroendocrine changes during spontaneous panic attacks, Cameron and co-workers (Cameron, Lee, Curtis, & McCann, 1987) followed neuroendocrine and Holter monitor observations during a 36-hour bedrest study period, which included non-panic and panic measurements in panic attack patients and normal control subjects. During panic attacks, the most consistent elevations were observed for plasma prolactin (this correlated with attack severity), with less consistent elevations occurring for plasma cortisol, growth hormone, and heart rate. Plasma norepinephrine showed small increases, whereas no significant changes were found for plasma epinephrine or MHPG. The authors interpreted these findings as being due to a gamma amino butyric acid (GABA) response. At predetermined (basal) levels, the only difference observed was a reduction in urinary conjugated epinephrine in patients. Some studies have examined hormonal changes during situational panic attacks (i.e., patients exposed to phobic situations). Although Ko and co-workers (Ko et al., 1983) found elevated MHPG levels suggestive of a central noradrenergic mechanism, Woods and colleagues (Woods, Charney, McPherson, Gradman, & Heninger, 1987) attributed this to walking (or possibly a too brief response or adaptation), because MHPG increased in both patients and control subjects. There were also no significant increases in cortisol in panic disorder patients versus healthy subjects, and the patients evidenced smaller growth hormone and prolactin responses than did normal subjects. The authors noted that these findings raise the question of adaptation of neuroendocrine response to stress in patients with chronically recurrent attacks.

Studies by Roy-Byrne et al. (1986) and Holsboer and co-workers (Holsboer, von Bardeleben, Buller, Heuser, & Streiger, 1987, 1988) suggest changes consistent with chronic stimulation and adaptation of the HPAC system including a blunted ACTH response to CRH and increased cortisol. The dexamethasone suppression test (DST) has been used as an indirect measure of HPAC function as well. Alteration of the HPAC system, for instance, has been suggested by higher cortisol plasma concentrations following a dexamethasone dose and higher 4:00 p.m. levels (17.7 vs. 5.0 μg per dl) in patients with panic disorder relative to normal control subjects (Carson, Halbreich, Ching-Ming, & Goldstein, 1988). Interestingly, changes in DST responses reflected clinical improvement among agoraphobics (Coryell, Noyes, Clancy et al., 1985), but baseline DST results did not predict subsequent outcome (Coryell & Noyes, 1988). In addition, although some studies have reported abnormal DST results in panic disorder or agoraphobic patients compared to normal subjects (Avery, Osgood, Ishiki, Wilson, Kenny, & Dunner, 1985; Grunhaus, Tionco, Haskett et al., 1987), suggesting some alteration in HPAC function, most differences have been small, and many studies have found no difference (Bridges, Yeragani, Rainey, & Pohl, 1986).

Several studies have suggested that the adrenergic mechanisms may be significantly involved in anxiety disorders. A series of studies have focused on changes in MHPG. The MHPG levels in response to yohimbine challenge (a presynaptic alpha-2 antagonist) have been correlated with anxiety. Furthermore, medications that blunt panic attacks (e.g., alprazolam and imipramine) attenuate the MHPG response to yohimbine (Edlund, Swann, & Davis, 1987) or directly decrease plasma levels of MHPG (Charney & Heninger, 1985). In addition, patients with panic attacks have exaggerated responses in the MHPG increase to yohimbine challenge, and exaggerated response in the MHPG decrease to clonidine challenge (a presynaptic alpha-2 agonist) (Charney & Heninger, 1986; Charney, Heninger, & Breier, 1984). This suggests increased presynaptic alpha-2 adrenergic receptor sensitivity. Studies showing a blunted response of growth hormone to clonidine challenge (Charney & Heninger, 1986; Uhde et al., 1986) in panic patients may be suggestive of reduced postsynaptic alpha-2 sensitivity, perhaps from overstimulation. Finally, studies of beta receptor function also suggest reduced responsiveness. For example, Nesse et al. (1984) found a lower heart rate response to isoproterenol challenge in panic patients (Lima & Turner, 1983) and found decreased cyclic AMP production in lymphocytes.

Alterations in the normal thyroid system have also been investigated in patients with panic disorder. In the typical challenge test, thyrotropin-releasing hormone (TRH) is injected at 9:00 a.m. and thyrotropin-secreting hormone (TSH) is collected for 45 min at 15-min intervals (Roy-Byrne, Mellman, & Uhde, 1988). The test is positive if TSH blunting occurs. Roughly 25% of depressed patients were reportedly positive. In panic disorder, increased frequency of TSH blunting has also occurred (Hamlin & Pottash, in press; Roy-Byrne et al., 1986), as has a decreased prolactin response to TRH.

Some interest has been generated in investigating serotonergic mechanisms in anxiety. Davis, Dunlop, Shea, Brittain, and Hendrie (1985) found increased serotonin during exam stress and a correlation between anxiety and serotonin levels. Serotonergic function, evaluated by the ability of tryptophan to increase prolactin release in panic patients versus healthy subjects both before and after treatment with alprazolam (Charney, Woods, & Goodman, 1986), however, has suggested that normal serotonin function occurs in panic patients.

Generalized Anxiety Disorder

Much less research has focused on patients with generalized anxiety disorder (GAD). In normal men, urinary epinephrine and norepinephrine correlate with anxiety (Faucheux, Baulon, & Poitrenaud, 1983). Elevated catecholamines have also been found in several studies of patients with GAD (Mathew, Ho, Kralik, Taylor, Semchuk, Weinman, & Claghorn, 1980; Mathew, Ho, Kralik, Taylor, & Claghorn, 1981; Mathew, Ho, Francis, Taylor, & Weinman, 1982) as have elevations of dopamine-beta-hydroxylase, which catalyzes the conversion of dopa to norepinephrine (Mathew, Ho, Taylor, & Semchuk, 1981). Disturbance of MAO activity has been found in activity of blood platelets in patients with affective disorders with marked anxiety (Coursey & Buchsbaum, 1981). In an intervention study with patients having GAD, relaxation therapy resulted in decreased MAO activity, epinephrine, and norepinephrine (Mathew et al., 1981). All of this research suggests involvement of the SAM system in chronic anxiety.

The HPAC system has also been examined. Patients with GAD have either normal or elevated basal urinary corticosteroid levels (Persky, Grinkel, & Hamburg, 1956; Rosenbaum, Schatzberg, Jost et al., 1983). The rate of positive DST in patients with GAD has been reported to be 23% to 27% (Avery et al., 1985; Schweitzer, Swenson, Winokur, Rickels, & Maislin, 1986; Tiller, Biddle, Maguire, & Davies, 1988), which is higher than the 5% found in normal control subjects and roughly comparable to that found for depressed outpatients. Both of these findings suggest HPAC associations with anxiety for patients with GAD. Other findings of interest include elevated melatonin in anxiety neurosis, which decreased to normal after therapy (Singh, Gupta, Prasad, & Udupa, 1980), and increased cortisol response and growth hormone response to a stressful task (Miyabo, Hisada, Asato, Mizushima, & Kiyomitsu, 1975).

Other Anxiety Disorders

Much less information has been obtained concerning neuroendocrine function in other anxiety disorders such as social phobia, obsessive–compulsive disorder, and posttraumatic stress disorder (PTSD). In the area of social phobia (public speaking), one study showed that stutterers had a much larger increase in urinary epinephrine during public speaking than did normal subjects (Edgren et al., 1970). Findings for patients with obsessive–compulsive disorder (see Curtis & Glitz, 1988, for a review) suggest abnormalities similar to those in depressed patients including adrenergic alterations in responsiveness, and high DST nonsuppression rates. Alterations in serotonergic function have also been suggested. Findings in subjects with PTSD have included decreased urinary free cortisol, increased basal plasma cortisol, blunted ACTH response to CRH, increased sympathetic nervous system activity (increased urinary epinephrine and norepinephrine), and blunted TSH response to TRH (Costa & Guidotti, 1979).

Endocrine Disorders

Endocrine disorders are often considered in the differential diagnosis of anxiety disorders. The endocrine disorder most frequently associated with anxiety is hyperthyroidism. Kathol, Turner, and Delahunt (1986) found that 23 of 29 patients with hyperthyroidism had symptoms of GAD. Furthermore, when antithyroid treatment was instituted, 21 of those patients had remission of their anxiety symptoms. In addition to use of thyroid function tests, hyperthyroidism can clinically be differentiated from GAD by a preference for cold room temperature (with sensitivity to heat) and increased appetite with weight loss and exopthalmus.

Pheochromocytoma is also included in the differential diagnosis of anxiety, especially panic disorder. It represents an abnormality of the chromaffin cells of the adrenal medulla and is associated with high levels of epinephrine and norepinephrine. It can be differentiated from anxiety disorders by urine laboratory tests, the greater presence of tachycardia and hypertension, and the absence of subjective anxiety, anticipatory anxiety, and phobic avoidance (Starkman, Zelnick, Nesse, & Cameron, 1985).

Other endocrine disorders having associated symptoms of anxiety include Cushings disease, in which there is an overproduction of ACTH and hyperplasia of the adrenal cortex, hypoglycemia (especially acute cerebral hypoglycemia), insulinoma (with associated hypoglycemia), hypoparathyroidism, electrolyte disturbances (potassium depletion and calcium excess), menopause, premenstrual syndrome, hypopituitarism, and carcinoid tumors (for reviews, see Curtis & Glitz, 1988; Lishman, 1987).

Anxiety, Endocrines, and Immune Function

Although there is much evidence suggesting that distress is associated with immune function decrement (Dorian & Garfinkel, 1987; Kiecolt-Glaser & Glaser, 1987) there is much less evidence directly associating anxiety with immune function (Linn, Linn, & Jensen, 1981). The stressors associated with immune decrement such as examinations, death of a spouse, divorce, noise, being a resident near the Three Mile Island nuclear accident, astronaut splash down phase, caretaking, and unemployment are likely to be associated with increased anxiety, but in most studies anxiety has not been directly measured. Possible mechanisms through which anxiety might influence immune function include increases in catecholamines and cortisol and are reviewed in Antoni et al. (in press). More direct evidence for an effort of anxiety has been provided by a recent study showing that beta-carboline, a compound promoting anxiety and acting at benzodiazepine receptors could induce a decrement in immune function (Arora, Hanna, Paul, & Skolnick, 1987). Increasingly, the presence of a peripheral type of benzodiazepine receptor on monocytes has been demonstrated and may be a possible mechanism for immunomodulation (Lenfant, Zavala, Haumont, & Potier, 1985; Ruff et al., 1985). In contrast, a study of patients with agoraphobia and panic attacks (Surman et al., 1986) showed normal in vitro lymphocyte function. Although this may represent chronic adaptation, further study is needed to clarify relevant issues.

Psychopharmacology, Neuropharmacology, and Anxiety

Benzodiazepines

Clinically, the benzodiazepines are used in a variety of anxiety disorders including GAD (Kahn, McNair, & Frankenthaler, 1987) and panic disorders (Blackwell, 1987; Pyke & Kraus, 1988; Sheehan, 1987) and for performance anxiety (Quitkin, Rabkin, & Klein, 1979). The benzodiazepines are particularly useful for the treatment of anticipatory anxiety (Edmondson, Roscoe, & Vickers, 1972; Ellison, 1979; Foreman, 1974; Weiner, 1979) and, as such, may be an aid in the treatment of certain types of phobias in that they would facilitate the patient in approaching the anxiety-inducing stimulus. There is a large body of literature that indicates that benzodiazepines attenuate or eliminate the behavioral inhibition elicited by the class of stimuli associated with anxiety, including the inhibition of behavior that occurs in (a) signaled punishment experiments, that is, passive avoidance (see Gray, 1979); (b) experiments in which there is a signal for the omission of reward, as is the case in experiments in which a learned response is extinguished (see Gray, 1979) and in partial reinforcement experiments (see Gray, 1979); (c) conflict paradigms such as approach–avoidance experiments (e.g., Aron, Simon, Larrouse, & Boisser, 1971; Corda, Blaker, Mendelson, Guidotti, & Costa, 1983; Geller & Seifter, 1960) and conditioned suppression experiments (see Gray, 1982); and (d) experiments in which a novel stimulus is presented (see Gray, 1979).

The anti-anxiety effects of benzodiazepines are believed to be mediated, at least in part, by the enhancement of GABA-ergic inhibition—particularly of GABA$_a$ receptors (Costa, 1983; Costa & Greengard, 1975; Costa & Guidotta, 1979; Majewska, Chuang, & Costa, 1983; Study & Barker, 1981). Activity at benzodiazepine recognition sites is thought to modulate GABA$_a$ effects on chloride channels (Paul, Crawley, & Skolnick, 1986; Schofield, Darlison, Fujita et al., 1987). In GAD, somatic symptoms and hyperarousal appear to respond better to medications acting on the GABA system, whereas cognitive symptoms appear to respond better to medications affecting noradrenergic or seratonergic systems (Hoehn-Saric, McLeod, & Zimmerli, 1988).

Although it is unlikely that activity at a single neuroanatomical site mediates the anxiolytic effects of benzodiazepines, the locus coeruleus has been implicated in a number of published reports (see Heninger & Charney, 1988). Intravenous (Grant, Huang, & Redmond, 1980) and microiontophoretic injections (Strahlendorf & Strahlendorf, 1981) of benzodiazepines into the locus coeruleus have been shown to decrease the activity of single cells in the locus coeruleus, and this effect probably results from the interaction of benzodiazepine receptors with GABA receptors located there. Benzodiazepines antagonize the effects of piperoxane and yohimbine (alpha-2 antagonists that increase the activity of norepinephrine neurons in the locus coeruleus) upon the cortical turnover rate of norepinephrine (Fuxe et al., 1975). High doses of benzodiazepine also decrease norepinephrine turnover rate (Taylor & Laverty, 1969). Norepinephrine systems have many inhibitory GABA inputs, and it is believed that benzodiazepines, which affect GABA neurons, decrease neuronal activity in norepinephrine systems (see Heninger & Charney, 1988).

Tricyclic Compounds and Monoamine Oxidase Inhibitors

These compounds increase the availability of monoamine neurotransmitters at synapses. The tricyclic compounds block monoamine reuptake, and the monoamine oxidase (MAO) inhibitors block enzymatic degradation of monoamines. Both compounds have been used in the treatment of some forms of depression, but they also are effective in the treatment of panic attacks and agoraphobia with panic disorder. The anti-panic effects of tricyclic compounds and MAO inhibitors are thought to be due, for the most part, to reduced noradrenergic activity. More specifically, effects of tricyclic compounds and MAO inhibitors, according to Charney and Heninger (1985), are to decrease locus coeruleus activity, norepinephrine turnover, MHPG plasma levels (a metabolite of norepinephrine), and postsynaptic beta-adrenergic function, and to increase postsynaptic alpha-1 adrenergic receptor function.

The observation that the tricyclic compounds, MAO inhibitors, and benzodiazepines are not equally effective in the treatment of different types or symptoms of anxiety could be interpreted as supporting the view that the various types of anxiety disorders (and nonclinical anxiety) form discontinuous, qualitatively different categories, and thus have different neural substrates. As Redmond (1985) pointed out, however, this may not be the case. Dose-response curves have rarely been determined in human pharmacological studies, and therapeutic effects are dose-dependent. As a case in point, Noyes et al. (1984) demonstrated in an anonymous crossover study that diazepam can be effective in the treatment of panic attacks when the appropriate dose of this benzodiazepine is used. Similar findings have been reported by other investigators (e.g., Dunner et al., 1986). Also, alprazolam, a benzodiazepine with a particularly high affinity for benzodiazepine receptors (and diminished sedative effects) is effective in the treatment of panic attacks and GAD (Charney, Woods, & Goodman, 1986; Chouinard, Annable, Fontaine, & Solyom, 1982; Coryell & Noyes, 1988; Woods, Charney, Loke, Goodman, Redmond, & Heninger, 1986).

The results of experiments concerning the neuropharmacological actions of the tricyclic compounds and the MAO inhibitors provide evidence that, although the mechanisms are different (see Poncelet, Martin, Danti, Simon, & Soubrie, 1987), they may have effects upon the locus coeruleus that are similar to those of the benzodiazepines. Because norepinephrine binds to alpha-1, alpha-2, and beta-adrenergic receptors, the increase in this neurotransmitter that results from administration of tricyclic compounds and MAO inhibitors could lead to a net increase, decrease, or no change in the output at locus coeruleus terminals in the forebrain and brainstem. A faciliatory effect would occur because of the effects on postsynaptic alpha-1 and beta-adrenergic receptors, but the inhibitory action of norepinephrine at alpha-2 sites due to inhibitory feedback (Simson & Weiss, 1987; Weiss, Simson, & Knight, 1987) would lead to a decrease in neuronal firing at the locus coeruleus. When these multiple effects have been tested on beta-adrenergic and alpha-2 receptors, both neurochemical and electrophysiological studies (Susler, Vetulani, & Mobley, 1978; Vetulani & Susler, 1975) have demonstrated that the inhibitory effects predominate both acutely (Huang, 1979) and chronically (Huang, Maas, & Hu, 1980; McMillen, Warnack, German, & Shore, 1980). These types of findings, coupled with the fact that chronic treatment with antidepressant compounds decreases postsynaptic receptor mechanisms, have led many investigators to adopt the position that tricyclic compounds and MAO inhibitors lead to a reduction in norepinephrine function (e.g., Koslow et al., 1983; Redmond, 1985).

Although the evidence is by no means conclusive (particularly with regard to faciliatory effects of tricyclic compounds and MAO inhibitors on alpha-1 receptors), the results of studies of benzodiazepines, tricyclic compounds, and MAO inhibitors are compatible with the view that the level of neuronal activity in norepinephrine-containing neurons in the locus coeruleus is associated with anxiety states ranging from vigilance and selective attention at low levels, to pathological states of anxiety at high levels (Redmond, 1985). Helplessness and depression would be, according to this view, associated with high levels of locus coeruleus activity. The mechanisms by which benzodiazepines, tricyclic compounds, and MAO inhibitors alleviate anxiety or depression are certainly different, particularly with regard to the receptor systems affected and the time course of action, but these differences do not warrant the rejection of the idea that anxiety states are discontinuous and form separate categories. One factor that is often overlooked in considering the effectiveness of pharmacological agents is the time course of the development of an anxiety disorder. As was pointed out by Gray (1985), Petty and Sherman (also see Drugan, Maier, Skolnick et al., 1985) have observed in animal experiments that benzodiazepines will prevent the development of helplessness if these drugs are given prior to exposure to uncontrollable stress but are of no benefit once helplessness has been induced. In contrast, tricyclic compounds chronically reverse helplessness after it is established.

Clonidine

Clonidine is an alpha-2 agonist that is typically used for the treatment of hypertension. An alpha-2 agonist would be expected to have dose-dependent anti-anxiety effects due to stimulation of alpha-2 auto-receptors in the locus coeruleus. Indeed, there is evidence that clonidine can be effective (on a short-term basis) for the treatment of panic attacks (Hoehn-Saric, Merchant, Keyser, & Smith, 1981; Ko et al., 1983), the anxiety associated with PTSD (Kolb, Burris, & Griffiths, 1983), and the anxiety associated with opiate withdrawal (Charney, Sternberg, Kleber, Heninger, & Redmond, 1981). There is a substantial amount of evidence that dysregulation of the alpha-2 adrenergic system underlies the symptoms of panic attack (Heninger & Charney, 1988).

Beta-Blockers

Beta-adrenergic antagonists appear to attentuate some components of the anxiety response, particularly somatic symptoms (Lader, 1988). Propranolol, a beta-antagonist, has been shown to block the peripheral physiological symptom of anxiety (Gottschalk, Stone, & Gleser, 1974; Granville-Grossman & Turner, 1966; Kielholz, 1977; Wheatley, 1969) and to a lesser extent the subjective experience of anxiety (Kellner, Collins, Shulman, & Pathak, 1974; Suzman, 1976; Tyrer & Lader, 1974). Similar results have been reported for other beta-blockers (Bonn, Turner, & Hicks, 1972; Gosling, 1977; Lader & Tyrer, 1972). The finding that practolol (Bonn et al., 1972), a beta-blocker that barely crosses the blood–brain barrier, has benefits that are similar to those produced by beta-blockers that have more pronounced effects upon the central nervous system suggests that the anti-anxiety effects of beta-blockers are due to the reduction in the magnitude of the peripheral physiological components of the anxiety response, or more specifically, the subsequent feedback to the central nervous system from peripheral structures. This finding does not preclude the possibility that some of the anti-anxiety effects of beta-blockers such as propranolol are the result of their effects on the central nervous system.

Anxiety Induction

The hypothesis that emerges from studies of the locus coeruleus and those involving the anti-anxiety effects of pharmacological agents is that the locus coeruleus and the forebrain structures to which it projects, including the hippocampus, are essential components of the circuitry that constitute the neuroanatomical substrates of anxiety. Moreover, the level of neuronal activity of norepinephrine-containing locus coeruleus neurons is proportional to the level of anxiety and, at extremely high levels of activity, correlates with feelings of helplessness and depression. Additional support for this hypothesis is provided by the results of experiments in which pharmacological agents or variations in PCO_2 have been used to induce anxiety states.

The anxiolytic effects of benzodiazepines are believed to result from the enhancement of GABA-ergic transmission that is a consequence of benzodiazepine receptor stimulation. This effect is believed to be mediated, at least in part, by benzodiazepine/GABA interaction at the locus coeruleus. As would be expected, the GABA antagonist pentylenetetrazol produces anxiety in humans (Rodin, 1958). The GABA antagonists also increase locus coeruleus activity (Grant et al., 1980). Administration of betacarbolines, which bind with high affinity to benzodiazepine receptor sites but reduce GABA transmission, leads to reports of severe fear or the perception of a threat of annihilation (Dorow, Horowski, Paschehke, Amin, & Braestrup, 1983). The alpha-2 antagonist yohimbine, which would cause an increase in locus coeruleus activity, produces anxiety (as measured by self-report) in normal subjects and patients with anxiety disorders and depression (Charney, Heninger, & Redmond, 1983; Charney, Woods, Goodman et al., 1987). In general, blocking alpha-2 receptors in the locus coeruleus leads to an increase in the sensitivity of these cells to stressful stimuli (Simson & Weiss, 1987; Weiss et al., 1987). High doses of methylxanthines lead to reports of anxiety in humans (Grant & Redmond, 1983) and increase locus coeruleus activity (Grant, Huang, & Redmond, 1980); both of these effects are reversed by the alpha-agonist clonidine (Grant & Redmond, 1983). In addition, increases in PCO_2 of 25% to 30% in inspired air produces anxiety in human subjects (Smith, Cooperman, & Wollman, 1980; Waeber, Adler, Schwank, & Galeazzi, 1982) and increases in locus coeruleus activity in rats (Hoehn-Saric et al., 1981).

SUMMARY AND CONCLUSIONS

The research reviewed in this chapter is consistent with the view that the neuronal circuitries of anxiety and depression overlap. The research discussed also underscores the importance of controllability in the etiology of anxiety. The level of neuronal activity of norepinephrine-containing locus coeruleus neurons appears to correlate with both the level of anxiety and the amount of control available, with extremely high levels of activity associated with helplessness and depression. Presumably, the rate of discharge of these neurons also correlates with the level of neuronal activity in forebrain structures to which they connect. One of these structures, the hippocampus, is thought to be an essential component of the neuronal circuitry involved in both anxiety and depression. Although controllability is an important factor in both anxiety and depression, conflict and task difficulty are also important variables. There are situations in which there is a higher level of stress associated with having a coping response available, such as an approach–avoidance conflict, than with not having one at all.

The literature reviewed also supports the hypothesis that the variety of anxiety states ranging from normal anticipatory anxiety to pathological anxiety, such as the one coupled with depression, represent quantitative variations along a single dimension, rather than categorically discrete entities involving different neurophysiological and neurochemical systems. According to this view, the high comorbidity between depression and some anxiety disorders such as panic disorder and obsessive–compulsive disorder results from a lower level of controllability in these disorders. The depression associated with panic disorder, however, may be due, at least in part, to disregulation in alpha-adrenergic mechanisms in the neuronal circuitry that is involved in both anxiety and depression.

Controllability also plays an important role in the neuroendocrine responses associated with anxiety. Animal experiments demonstrate that the SAM system and the HPAC system are activated when a coping response is available during stress, and that the HPAC system predominates during helplessness. Neuroendocrine studies of the anxiety associated with public speaking, simple phobias, and obsessive–compulsive disorders are consistent with these findings. Particularly noteworthy is the finding that the SAM and HPAC response abnormalities observed for obsessive–compulsive disorder are similar to those seen in clinically depressed patients; obsessive–compulsives and depressed patients also show a blunted growth hormone response to clonidine. The evidence regarding panic disorder is less clear. Tricyclic antidepressants and MAO inhibitors are effective for panic disorder patients and clinically depressed patients. In addition, both panic disorder patients and depressed patients show a blunted growth hormone response to clonidine and TSH blunting to TRH. However, one would expect that HPAC responsivity of the panic disorder patients would be similar to those of depressed patients, but it is not. As suggested earlier, this finding may be accounted for by the adaptation of neuroendocrine responses to stress in patients with chronically recurring attacks.

REFERENCES

Abercrombie, E. D., & Jacobs, B. L. (1987a). Single-unit response of noradrenergic neurons in locus coeruleus of freely moving cats: 1. Acutely presented stressful and nonstressful stimuli. *Journal of Neuroscience, 7*, 2837–2842.

Abercrombie, E. D., & Jacobs, B. L. (1987b). Single-unit response of noradrenergic neurons in locus coeruleus of freely moving cats: 2. Adaptation to chronically presented stressful stimuli. *Journal of Neuroscience, 7*, 2844–2849.

Antoni, M. H., Schneiderman, N., Fletcher, M. A., Goldstein, D. A., Laperriere, A., & Ironson, G. (in press). Psychoneuroimmunology and HIV-1. *Journal of Consulting and Clinical Psychology.*

Appleby, J. S., Klein, D. F., & Sachar, E. J. (1981). Anxiety: New research and changing concepts. In D. F. Klein & J. G. Rabkin (Eds.), *Biochemical indices of lactate-induced panic: A preliminary report* (pp. 411–428). New York: Raven Press.

Aron, C., Simon, P., Larousse, C., & Boissier, J. R. (1971). Evaluation of a rapid technique for detecting minor tranquilizers. *Neuropharmacology, 10*, 459–469.

Arora, P. K., Hanna, E. E., Paul, S. M., & Skolnick, P. (1987). Suppression of the immune response by benzodiazepine receptor inverse agonists. *Journal of Neuroimmunology, 15*, 1–9.

Avery, D. H., Osgood, T. B., Ishiki, D. M., Wilson, L. G., Kenny, M., & Dunner, D. L. (1985). The DST in psychiatric outpatients with generalized anxiety disorder, panic disorder, or primary affective disorder. *American Journal of Psychiatry, 142*, 844–848.

Avonson, T. A., & Logue, C. M. (1988). Phenomenology of panic attacks: A descriptive study of panic disorder patients' self-reports. *Journal of Clinical Psychiatry, 49*, 8–13.

Bartlett, E. S., & Izard, C. E. (1972). A dimensional and discrete investigation of the subjective experience of emotion. In C. E. Izard (Ed.), *Patterns of emotions: A new analysis of anxiety and depression* (pp. 218–252). New York: Academic Press.

Beck, A. T. (1963). Thinking and depression. *Archives of General Psychiatry, 1*, 324–333.

Berger, D. F., Starzec, J. J., & Mason, E. B. (1981). The relationship between plasma corticosterone levels and lever press avoidance and escape behavior in rats. *Psychological Psychology, 9*, 81–86.

Blackwell, B. (1987). Newer antidepressant drugs. In H. Y. Meltzer (Ed.), *Psychopharmacology: The third generation of progress* (pp. 1041–1049). New York: Raven Press.

Bonn, J. A., Turner, P., & Hicks, D. C. (1972). Beta-adrenergic receptor blockage with practolol in treatment of anxiety. *Lancet, 1*, 814–815.

Breier, A., Albus, M., Pickar, D., Zahn, T. P., Wolkowitz, O. M., & Paul, S. M. (1987). Controllable and uncontrollable stress in humans: Alterations in mood and neuroendocrine and psychophysiological functions. *American Journal of Psychiatry, 144*, 1419–1425.

Breier, A., Charney, D. S., & Heninger, G. R. (1984). Major depression in patients with agoraphobia and panic disorder. *Archives of General Psychiatry, 41*, 1129–1135.

Breier, A., Charney, D. S., & Heninger, G. R. (1986). Agoraphobia with panic attacks: Development, diagnostic stability, and course of illness. *Archives of General Psychiatry, 43*, 1029–1036.

Bridges, M., Yeragani, V. K., Rainey, J. M., & Pohl, R. (1986). Dexamethasone suppression test in patients with panic attacks. *Biological Psychiatry, 21*, 849–853.

Cameron, O. G., Lee, M. A., Curtis, G. C., & McCann, D. S. (1987). Endocrine and physiological changes during "spontaneous" panic attacks. *Psychoneuroendocrinology, 12*, 321–331.

Carlsson, C., Engel, J., & Hansson, L. (1976). Neuro-psychiatric effects of adrenergic beta-receptor blocking agents. H. P. Kuemmerle (Ed.), *Advances in clinical pharmacology* (Vol. 12, pp. 1–120). Munich: Urban & Schwarzenberg.

Carson, S. W., Halbreich, U., Ching-Ming, Y., & Goldstein, S. (1988). Altered plasma dexamethasone and cortisol suppressibility in patients with panic disorder. *Biological Psychiatry, 24*, 56–62.

Cedarbaum, J. M., & Aghajanian, G. K. (1978). Activation of locus coeruleus neurons by peripheral stimuli: Modulation by a collateral inhibitory mechanism. *Life Sciences, 23*, 1383–1392.

Charney, D. S., Menkes, D. B., & Heninger, G. R. (1981). Receptor sensitivity and the mechanism of action of anti-depressant treatment. *Archives of General Psychiatry, 38*, 1160–1180.

Charney, D. S., Heninger, G. R., & Breier, A. (1984). Noradrenergic function in panic anxiety. *Archives of General Psychiatry, 41*, 751–782.

Charney, D. S., & Heninger, G. R. (1985). Noradrenergic function and the mechanism of action of anti-anxiety treatment. *Archives of General Psychiatry, 42*, 473–481.

Charney, D. S., & Heninger, G. R. (1986). Abnormal regulation of noradrenergic function in panic disorders: Effects of clonidine in healthy subjects and patients with agoraphobia and panic disorders. *Archives of General Psychiatry, 43*, 1042–1054.

Charney, D. S., Heninger, G. R., Price, L. H., & Breier, A. (1986). Major depression and panic disorder: Diagnostic and neurobiological relationships. *Psychopharmacology Bulletin, 22*, 503–511.

Charney, D. S., Heninger, G. R., & Redmond, D. E. (1983). Yohimbine induced anxiety and increased noradrenergic function in humans: Effects of diazepam and clonidine. *Life Sciences, 33*, 19–29.

Charney, D. S., Sternberg, D. E., Kleber, H. D., Heninger, G. R., & Redmond, D. E. (1981). The clinical use of clonidine in abrupt withdrawal from methadone: Effects on blood pressure and specific signs and symptoms. *Archives of General Psychiatry, 38*, 1273–1277.

Charney, D. S., Woods, S. W., & Goodman, W. K. (1986). Drug treatment of panic disorder: The comparative efficacy of imipramine, alprazolam and trazodone. *Journal of Clinical Psychiatry, 47*, 580.

Charney, D. S., Woods, S. W., Goodman, W. K., et al. (1987). Neurobiological mechanisms of panic anxiety: Biochemical and behavioral correlates of yohimbine-induced panic attacks. *American Journal of Psychiatry, 144*, 1030.

Chouinard, G., Annable, L., Fontaine, R., & Solyom, L. (1982). Alprazolam in the treatment of generalized anxiety and panic disorders: A double-blind placebo-controlled study. *Psychopharmacology, 77*, 229–233.

Cole, J. O. (1988). The drug treatment of anxiety and depression. In E. Frazier (Ed.), *Medical clinics of North America* (pp. 815–830). London: W. B. Saunders.

Corda, M. G., Blaker, W. D., Mendelson, W. B., Guidotti, A., & Costa, E. (1983). β-carbolines enhance shock-induced suppression of drinking in rats. *Proceedings of the National Academy of Sciences, U.S.A., 80*, 2072–2076.

Coryell, W., Endicott, J., Andreason, N. C., et al. (1988). Depression and panic attacks. The significance of overlap as reflected in follow-up and family study data. *American Journal of Psychiatry, 145*, 293–300.

Coryell, W. R., & Noyes, R. (1988). HPA axis disturbance and treatment outcome in panic disorder. *Biological Psychiatry, 24*, 762–766.

Coryell, W., Noyes, R. J., Clancy, J., et al. (1985). Abnormal escape from dexamethasone suppression in agoraphobia with panic attacks. *Psychiatry Research, 15*, 301–311.

Costa, E. (1983). Are benzodiazepine recognition sites functional entities for the action of endogenous effectors or merely drug receptors? *Advances in Biochemistry and Psychopharmacology, 38*, 249–259.

Costa, E. (1985). Benzodiazepine/GABA interactions: A model to investigate the neurobiology of anxiety. In A. H. Tuma & J. D. Maser (Eds.), *Anxiety and anxiety disorders* (pp. 27–52). London: Erlbaum.

Costa, E., & Greengard, P. (1975). *Mechanism of action of benzodiazepines*. New York: Raven Press.

Costa, E., & Guidotta, A. (1979). Molecular mechanisms in the receptor action of benzodiazepines. In G. R. Okun & A. K. Cho (Eds.), *Annual review of pharmacology and toxicology* (Vol. 19, pp. 531–545). Palo Alto, CA: Annual Review.

Costa, E., Guidotti, A., & Mao, C. C. (1975). Evidence for involvement of GABA in the action of benzo-diazepines: Studies on rat cerebellum. In E. Costa & P. Greengard (Eds.), *Mechanism of action of benzodiazepines*. New York: Raven Press.

Coursey, R. D., & Buchsbaum, M. S. (1981). Biological high risk research strategy: A review of recent studies. In D. A. Regier & G. Allen (Eds.), *Risk factor research in the major mental disorders* (DHHS Publication No. ADM 81-1068). Washington, DC: U.S. Government Printing Office.

Curtis, G., Buxton, M., Lippman, D., Neese, R., & Wright, J. (1976). "Flooding in vivo" during the circadian phase of minimal cortisol secretion: Anxiety and therapeutic success without adrenal cortical activation. *Biological Psychiatry, 11*, 101–109.

Curtis, G. C., & Glitz, D. A. (1988a). Neuroendocrine findings in anxiety disorders. *Endocrinology and Metabolism Clinics of North America, 17*, 128–149.

Curtis, G. C., & Glitz, D. A. (1988b). Neuroendocrine findings in anxiety disorders. *Neurologic Clinics, 6*(1, February), 131–148.

Curtis, G. C., Nesse, R., Buxton, M., & Lippman, D. (1978). Anxiety and plasma cortisol at the crest of the circadian cycle: Reappraisal of a classical hypothesis. *Psychosomatic Medicine, 40*, 368–378.

Curtis, G. C., Nesse, R., Buxton, M., & Lippman, D. (1979). Plasma growth hormone: Effect of anxiety during flooding in vivo. *American Journal of Psychiatry, 136*, 410–416.

Davis, D. D., Dunlop, S. R., Shea, P., Brittain, H., & Hendrie, H. C. (1985). Biological stress responses in high and low trait anxious students. *Biological Psychiatry, 20*, 843–851.

Dimsdale, J. E., & Moss, T. M. (1980). Plasma catecholamines in stress and exercise. *Journal of the American Medical Association, 243*, 340–342.

Dorian, B., & Garfinkel, P. (1987). Stress, immunity, and illness: A review. *Psychological Medicine, 17*, 393–407.

Dorow, R., Horowski, R., Paschelke, G., Amin, M., & Braestrup, C. (1983). Severe anxiety induced by FG 7142, a β-carboline ligand for benzodiazepine receptors. *Lancet, 2*, 98–99.

Drugan, R. C., Maier, S. F., Skolnick, P., et al. (1985). An anxiogenic benzodiazepine receptor ligand induces learned helplessness. *European Journal of Pharmacology, 113*, 453–457.

Dunner, D. L., Ishiki, D., Avery, D. H., Wilson, L. G., & Hyde, T. S. (1986). Effect of alprazolam and diazepam on anxiety and panic attacks in panic disorder. A controlled study. *Journal of Clinical Psychiatry, 47*, 458–460.

Edgren, B., Leanderson, R., & Levi, L. (1970). A research programme on stuttering and stress. *Acta Otolaryngology, 263*, 113–120.

Edlund, M. J., Swann, A. C., & Davis, C. M. (1987). Plasma MHPG in untreated panic disorder. *Biological Psychiatry, 22*, 1488–1491.

Edmondson, E. D., Roscoe, B., & Vickers, M. D. (1972). Biochemical evidence of anxiety in dental patients. *British Medical Journal, 4*, 7–9.

Ellison, R. L. (1979). Pharmacologic control of anxiety, apprehension, and tension in dental practice. *General Dentistry, 27*, 23–27.

Epstein, S. (1972). The nature of anxiety with emphasis upon its relationship to expectancy. In C. M. Spielberger (Ed.), *Anxiety: Current trends in theory and research* (pp. 34–62). New York: Academic Press.

Faucheux, B. A., Baulon, A., & Poitrenaud, J. (1983). Heart rate, urinary catecholamines, and anxiety during mental stress in men. *Age and Aging, 12*, 144–150.

Foote, S. L., Aston-Jones, G., & Bloom, F. (1980). Impulse activity of locus coeruleus neurons in awake rats and monkeys is a function of sensory stimulation and arousal. *Proceedings of the National Academy of Sciences, U.S.A., 77*, 3033–3037.

Foote, S. L., Bloom, F. E., & Aston-Jones, G. (1983). Nucleus locus coeruleus: New evidence of anatomical and physiological specificity. *Psychological Reviews, 63*, 844–914.

Foreman, P. A. (1974). Control of the anxiety-pain complex in dentistry. Intravenous psychosedation with techniques using diazepam. *Oral Surgery, 37*, 337–349.

Fredrikson, M., & Sundin, O. (1985). Cortisol excretion during the defense reaction in humans. *Psychosomatic Medicine, 47*, 313–322.

Fredrikson, M., Sundin, O., Frankenhaevser, M. (1985). Cortisol excretion during the defense reaction in humans. *Psychosomatic Medicine, 47*, 313–319.

Fuxe, K., Agnati, L. F., Bolme, P., Hokfelt, T. I., Lidbrink, P., Ljungdahl, A., de la Mora, M. P., & Ogren, S. (1975). The possible involvement of GABA mechanisms in the action of benzodiazepines on central catecholamine neurons. In E. Costa & P. Greengard (Eds.), *The mechanism of action of benzodiazepines* (284–307). New York: Plenum Press.

Garber, J., Miller, S., & Abramson, L. (1980). On the distinction between anxiety and depression: Perceived control, certainty and probability of goal attainment. In J. Gabber & M. Seligman (Eds.), *Human helplessness: Theory and applications*. New York: Academic Press.

Geller, J., & Seifter, J. (1960). The effects of meprobamata, barbiturate, diamphetamine and promazine on experimentally induced conflict in the rat. *Psychopharmacologia, 1*, 482–492.

Goodwin, D., Guze, S., & Robins, E. (1969). Follow-up studies in obsessional neurosis. *Archives of General Psychiatry, 20*, 182–187.

Gorman, J., & Liebowitz, M. R. (1985). Platelet monoamine oxidase activity in patients with panic disorder. *Biological Psychiatry, 8*, 852–857.

Gorman, J. M., Liebowitz, M. R., Fyer, A. J., Dillon, D., Davies, S. O., Stein, J., & Klein, D. F. (1985). Lactate infusion in obsessive-compulsive disorder. *American Journal of Psychiatry, 142*, 864–866.

Gosling, R. H. (1977). Clinical anxiety with oxprenolol in treatment of anxiety in the United Kingdom. In P. Kielholz (Ed.), *Beta-blockers and the central nervous system* (114–148). Baltimore: University Park Press.

Gottschalk, L. A., Gleser, G. C., & Springer, K. J. (1974). Three hostility scales applicable to verbal samples. *Psychosomatic Medicine, 36*, 47–56.

Gottschalk, L. A., Stone, W. N., & Gleser, G. C. (1974). Peripheral versus central mechanisms accounting for antianxiety effects of propranolol. *Psychosomatic Medicine, 36*, 47–56.

Grant, S. J., Huang, Y. H., & Redmond, D. E. (1980). Benzodiazepines attenuate single unit activity in the locus coeruleus. *Life Sciences, 27*, 2231–2237.

Grant, S. J., & Redmond, D. E. (1981). The neuroanatomy and pharmacology of the nucleus locus coeruleus. In H. Lal & S. Fielding (Eds.), *The psychopharmacology of clonidine*. New York: Alan R. Liss.

Grant, S. J., & Redmond, D. E. (1983). Clonidine suppresses methylxanthine induced quasi-morphine withdrawal syndrome. *Journal of Pharmacology, Biochemistry, and Behavior, 17*, 655–658.

Granville-Grossman, K. L., & Turner, P. (1966). The effect of propranolol on anxiety. *Lancet, 1*, 788–790.

Gray, J. A. (1979). A neuropsychology of anxiety. In C. Izard (Ed.), *Emotions in personality and psychopathology*. New York: Plenum Press.

Gray, J. A. (1982). *The neuropsychology of anxiety: An enquiry into the functions of the septohippocampal system*. Oxford: Oxford University Press.

Gray, J. A. (1985). Issues in the neuropsychology of anxiety. In A. H. Tuma & J. D. Maser (Eds.), *Anxiety and anxiety disorders*. London: Erlbaum.

Gray, J. A. (1987). *The psychology of fear and stress*. New York: Cambridge University Press.

Grunhaus, L., Tionco, D., Haskett, R. F., et al. (1987). The dexamethasone suppression test in inpatients with panic disorder or agoraphobia with panic attacks. *Biological Psychiatry, 22*, 517–524.

Hamlin, C. L., & Pottash, A. L. C. (in press). Evaluation of anxiety disorders. In *Diagnostic and laboratory testing in psychiatry*. New York: Plenum Press.

Hanson, J. P., Larson, M. E., & Snowden, C. T. (1976). The effects of control over high intensity noise on plasma cortisol levels in rhesus monkeys. *Behavioral Biology, 16*, 333–340.

Heninger, G. R., & Charney, D. S. (1988). Monoamine receptor systems and anxiety disorders. In G. Winokur & W. Coryell (Eds.), *Psychiatric clinics of North America* (pp. 309–326). London: W. B. Saunders.

Henry, J. P., & Meehan, J. P. (1981). Psychosocial stimuli, physiological specificity, and cardiovascular disease. In H. Weiner, M. A. Hofer, & A. J. Stunkard (Eds.), *Brain behaivor and bodily diseases* (pp. 152–176). New York: Raven Press.

Hoehn-Saric, R., McLeod, D. R., & Zimmerli, W. D. (1988). Differential effects of alprazolam and imipramine in generalized anxiety disorder. Somatic versus psychic symptoms. *Journal of Clinical Psychiatry, 49*(8), 293–301.

Hoehn-Saric, R., Merchant, A. F., Keyser, M. L., & Smith, V. K. (1981). Effects of clonidine on anxiety disorders. *Archives of General Psychiatry, 38*, 1278–1282.

Holsboer, F., von Bardeleben, U., Buller, R., Heuser, I., & Steiger, A. (1987). Stimulation response to corticotropin-releasing hormone (CRH) in patients with depression, alcoholism and panic disorder. *Hormone and Metabolic Research, 16*, 80–88.

Huang, Y. H. (1979). Net effect of acute administration of desimipramine on the locus coeruleus-hippocampal system. *Life Sciences, 25*, 739–746.

Huang, Y. H., Maas, J. W., & Hu, G. H. (1980). The time course of noradrenergic pre- and postsynaptic activity during chronic desipramine treatment. *European Journal of Pharmacology, 68*, 41–47.

Insel, T. R., Zahn, T. A., & Murphy, D. L. (1985). Obsessive–compulsive disorder: An anxiety disorder? In A. H. Tuma & J. D. Maser (Eds.), *Anxiety and anxiety disorders*. London: Erlbaum.

Izard, C. E., & Blumberg. (1985). Emotions in anxiety. In A. H. Tuma & J. D. Maser (Eds.), *Anxiety and anxiety disorders*. London: Erlbaum.

Kahn, R. J., McNair, D. M., & Frankenthaler, L. M. (1987). Tricyclic treatment of generalized anxiety disorder. *Journal of Affective Disorders, 13*, 145–151.

Kathol, R. G., Noyes, R., Slymen, P. J., Crowe, R. R., Clancy, J., & Kerber, R. E. (1980). Propranolol in chronic anxiety disorders. *Archives of General Psychiatry, 37*, 1361–1365.

Kathol, R. G., Turner, R., & Delahunt, J. (1986). Depression and anxiety associated with hyperthyroidism: Response to antithyroid therapy. *Psychosomatics, 27*, 501.

Katz, M. M., Robins, E., Croughan, J., Secunda, S., & Swann, A. (1982). Behavioural measurement and drug response characteristics of unipolar and bipolar depression. *Psychological Medicine, 12*, 25–36.

Kauffman, C. D., Redist, C., Djenderedjian, A., Nelson, J. N., & Haier, R. J. (1987). Biological markers of affective disorders and posttraumatic stress disorder: A pilot study with desipramine. *Journal of Clinical Psychiatry, 48*, 366–367.

Kellner, R., Collins, C., Shulman, R. S., & Pathak, D. (1974). The short-term antianxiety effects of propranolol HCL. *Journal of Clinical Pharmacology, 14*, 301–304.

Kiecolt-Glaser, J. K., & Glaser, R. (1987). Psychosocial modulators of immune function. *Annals of Behavioral Medicine, 9*, 16–20.

Kielholz, P. (1977). *Beta-blockers and the central nervous system.* Baltimore: University Park Press.

Klein, D. F. (1964). Delineation of two drug-responsive anxiety syndromes. *Psychopharmacologia, 5*, 397–408.

Klein, D. F., & Fink, M. (1962). Psychiatric reaction patterns to imipramine. *American Journal of Psychiatry, 119*, 432–438.

Klein, D. F., Gittelman, R., Quitkin, F. M., & Rifkin, A. (1980). *Diagnosis and drug treatment of psychiatric disorders: Adults and children* (2nd ed.). Baltimore: Williams & Wilkins.

Klein, D. F., Zitrin, C. M., & Woerner, M. (1978). Antidepressants, anxiety, panic, and phobia. In M. A. Lipton, A. DiMascio, & R. F. Killam (Eds.), *Psychopharmacology: A generation of progress* (pp. 328–364). New York: Raven Press.

Ko, G. N., Elsworth, J. D., Roth, R. H., Rifkin, B. G., Leigh, H., & Redmond, D. E. (1983). Panic-induced elevation of plasma MHPG levels in phobic-anxious patients. *Archives of General Psychiatry, 40*, 425–430.

Kolb, L. C., Burris, B. C., & Griffiths, S. (1983, May). *Propranolol and clonidine in treatment of the chronic posttraumatic stress disorders of war.* Paper presented at the meeting of the American Psychiatric Association, New York, NY.

Koslow, S. H., Maas, J. W., Bowden, C. L., Davis, J. M., Hanin, I., & Javaid, J. (1983). CSF and urinary biogenic amines and metabolites in depression and mania: A controlled, univariate analysis. *Archives of General Psychiatry, 40*, 999–1010.

Kvetnansky, R. (1980). In E. Usdin, R. Kvetnansky, & I. J. Kolin (Eds.), *Catecholamines and stress: Recent advances.* North Holland: Elsevier.

Lader, M. H. (1980). Psychophysiological studies in anxiety. In G. D. Burrows & B. Davies (Eds.), *Handbook of studies in anxiety* (pp. 289–315). Amsterdam: Elsevier/North Holland.

Lader, M. (1988). Beta-adrenergic antagonists in neuropsychiatry: An update. *Journal of Clinical Psychiatry, 49*, 213–223.

Lader, M. H., & Tyrer, P. J. (1972). Central and peripheral effects of propranolol and solatol in normal human subjects. *British Journal of Pharmacology, 45*, 557–560.

Lazarus, R. S., & Averill, J. R. (1972). Emotion and cognition: With special reference to anxiety. In C. D. Spielberger (Ed.), *Anxiety: Current trends in theory and research* (Vol. 2, pp. 27–71). New York: Academic Press.

LeDoux, J. E. (1987). Emotion. In V. B. Mountcastle, F. Plum, & S. R. Geiger (Eds.), *Handbook of physiology: Section 1. The nervous system* (pp. 419–460). Baltimore: Williams & Wilkins.

Lenfant, M., Zavala, F., Haumont, J., & Potier, P. (1985). Presence of a peripheral type benzodiazepine binding site on the macrophage: Its possible role in immunomodulation. *C. R. Academy of Science, Paris t. 300, Serie III, 8*, 309–314.

Lewis, A. (1938). States of depression: Clinical and aetiologial differentiation. *British Medical Journal, 2*, 875–878.

Liebowitz, M. R., Gorman, J. M., Fyer, A. J., Levitt, M., Dillon, D., Levy, G., Appleby, I. L., Anderson, S., Palij, M., Davies, S. O., & Klein, D. F. (1985). Lactate provocation of panic attacks: 2. Biochemical and physiological findings. *Archives of General Psychiatry, 42*, 709–715.

Lima, D. R., & Turner, P. (1983). Propranolol increases reduced beta-receptor function in severely anxious patients. *Lancet, 2*, 1505–1514.

Linn, B., Linn, M., & Jensen, J. (1981). Anxiety and immune responsiveness. *Psychological Reports, 49*, 969–970.

Lishman, W. A. (1987). Organic psychiatry. In *Endocrine diseases and medical disorders* (2nd ed., pp. 428–482). Oxford: Blackwell.

Majewska, M. D., Chuang, D. M., & Costa, E. (1983). Stimulation by benzodiazepines of the prostaglandin D2 release in C6 glioma cells. *Society for Neuroscience Abstracts, 9*, 1042.

Mandler, G. (1980). The generation of emotion: A psychological theory. In R. Plutchik & H. Kellerman (Eds.), *Emotion: Theory, research, and experience* (pp. 185–205). New York: Academic Press.

Mandler, G., & Watson, D. L. (1966). Anxiety and the interruption of behavior. In C. D. Spielberger (Ed.), *Anxiety and behavior* (pp. 263–288). New York: Academic Press.

Mathew, R. J., Ho, B. T., Francis, D. J., Taylor, D. L., & Weinman, M. L. (1982). Catecholamines and anxiety. *Acta Psychiatrica Scandinavica, 65*, 142–148.

Mathew, R. J., Ho, B. T., Kralik, P., Taylor, D. L., Semehuk, K., Weinman, M., & Claghorn, J. L. (1980). Catecholamines and monoamine oxidase activity in anxiety. *Acta Psychiatrica Scandanavica, 63*, 245–271.

Mathew, R. J., Ho, B. T., Kralik, P., Taylor, D. L., & Claghorn, J. L. (1981). Catechol-O-methyltransferase and catecholamines in anxiety and relaxation. *Psychiatry Research, 3*, 85–89.

Mathew, R. J., Ho, B. T., Taylor, D. L., & Semchuk, K. M. (1981). Catecholamine and dopamine-beta-hydroxylase in anxiety. *Journal of Psychosomatic Research, 25*, 499–504.

McCabe, P. M., & Schneiderman, N. (1985). Biobehavioral responses to stress. In T. M. Field, P. M. McCabe, & N. Schneiderman (Eds.), *Stress and coping* (pp. 13–61). Hillsdale, NJ: Erlbaum.

McMillen, B. A., Warnack, W., German, D. C., & Shore, P. A. (1980). Effects of chronic desipramine treatment on rat brain noradrenergic responses to alpha-adrenergic drugs. *European Journal of Pharmacology, 61*, 239–246.

Miller, N. E. (1982). Motivation and psychological stress. In R. Pfaff (Ed.), *The physiological mechanism of motivation* (pp. 409–445). New York: Springer-Verlag.

Mineka, S. (1985). Animal models of anxiety-based disorders: Their usefulness and limitations. In A. H. Tuma & J. D. Maser (Eds.), *Anxiety and anxiety disorders* (pp. 199–259). London: Erlbaum.

Mineka, S., & Kohlstrom, J. (1978). Unpredictable and uncontrollable aversive events. *Journal of Abnormal Psychology, 87*, 256–271.

Miyabo, S., Hisada, T., Asato, T., Mizushima, N., & Kiyomitsu, U. (1975). Growth hormone and cortisol responses to psychological stress: Comparison of normal and neurotic subjects. *Journal of Clinical Endocrinology and Metabolism, 42*, 1158–1163.

Nesse, R. M., Cameron, O. G., Curtis, G. C., McCann, D. S., & Huber-Smith, M. J. (1984). Adrenergic function in patients with panic anxiety. *Archives of General Psychiatry, 41*, 771–776.

Nesse, R. M., Curtis, G. C., & Brown, G. M. (1982). Phobic anxiety does not affect plasma levels of thyroid stimulating hormone in man. *Psychoneuroendocrinology, 7*, 69–74.

Nesse, R. M., Curtis, G. C., Brown, G. M., & Rubin, R. T. (1980). Anxiety induced by flooding therapy for phobias does not elicit prolactin secretory response. *Psychosomatic Medicine, 42*, 25–37.

Nesse, R. M., Curtis, G. C., Thyer, B. A., McCann, D. S., Huber-Smith, M. J., & Knuff, R. F. (1985). Endocrine and cardiovascular responses during phobic anxiety. *Psychosomatic Medicine, 47*, 320–332.

Noyes, R. J., Anderson, D. J., Clancy, J., Crowe, R. R., Slymen, D. J., Ghoneim, M. M., & Hinrichs, J. V. (1984). Diazepam and propranolol in panic disorder and agoraphobia. *Archives of General Psychiatry, 41*, 287–292.

Nyback, H., Walters, J. R., & Aghajanian, G. K. (1975). Tricyclic antidepressants: Effects on the firing rate of brain noradrenergic neurons. *European Journal of Pharmacology, 32*, 302–312.

Ost, L., & Hughdahl, K. (1981). Acquisition of phobias and anxiety response patterns in clinical patients. *Behaviour Research and Therapy, 19*, 439–447.

Ost, L., & Hughdahl, K. (1983). Acquisition of agoraphobia, mode of onset and anxiety response patterns. *Behaviour Research and Therapy, 21*, 623–631.

Paul, S. M. (1988). Anxiety and depression: A common neurobiological substrate? *Journal of Clinical Psychiatry, 49*, 13–16.

Paul, S. M., Crawley, J. N., & Skolnick, P. (1986). The neurobiology of anxiety: The role of the GABA/benzodiazepine receptor complex. In P. A. Berger & K. H. Brodie (Eds.), *American Handbook of Psychiatry* (Vol. 8, pp. 581–596). New York: Basic Books.

Persky, H. (1975). Adrenocortical function and anxiety. *Psychoneuroendocrinology, 1*, 37–44.

Persky, H., Grinkel, R. K., & Hamburg, D. A. (1956). Adrenal cortical function on anxious human subjects. *Archives of Neurological Psychiatry, 76*, 549–553.

Petty, F., & Sherman, A. D. (1981). GABA-ergic modulation of learned helplessness. *Journal of Pharmacology, Biochemistry, and Behavior, 15*, 567–570.

Pohorecky, L. A., & Brick, J. (1977). Activity of neurons in the locus coeruleus of the rat: Inhibition by ethanol. *Brain Research, 131*, 174–179.

Poncelet, M., Martin, P., Danti, S., Simon, P., & Soubrie, P. (1987). Noradrenergic rather than GABA-ergic processes as the common mediation of the antidepressant profile of GABA agonists and imipramine-like drugs in animals. *Journal of Pharmacology, Biochemistry, and Behavior, 28*, 321–326.

Pyke, R. E., & Kraus, R. N. (1988). Alprazolam in the treatment of panic attack patients with and without major depression. *Journal of Clinical Psychiatry, 49*, 66–68.

Quitkin, F., Rabkin, A., & Klein, D. (1979). Monoamine oxidase inhibitors. *Archives of General Psychiatry, 36*, 749–760.

Ravaris, C. L., Nies, A., Robinson, D. S., Ives, J. O., Lamborn, K. R., & Korson, L. A. (1976). A multiple-dose, controlled study of phenelzine in depression-anxiety states. *Archives of General Psychiatry, 33*, 347–350.

Redmond, D. E. (1977). Alterations in the function of the nucleus locus coeruleus: A possible model for studies of anxiety. In I. Hanin & E. Usdin (Eds.), *Animal models in psychiatry and neurology* (pp. 278–295). New York: Pergamon Press.

Redmond, D. E. (1979). New and old evidence for the involvement of a brain norepinephrine system in anxiety. In W. E. Fann, I. Karacan, A. D. Pokorny, & R. L. Williams (Eds.), *Phenomenology and treatment of anxiety* (pp. 89–111). New York: Spectrum.

Redmond, D. E. (1985). Neurochemical basis of anxiety and anxiety disorders: Evidence from drugs which decrease human fear or anxiety. In A. H. Tuma & J. D. Maser (Eds.), *Anxiety and anxiety disorders* (pp. 533–576). London: Erlbaum.

Redmond, D. E., & Huang, Y. H. (1979). Current Concepts: 2. New evidence for a locus coeruleus-norepinephrine connection with anxiety. *Life Science, 25*, 2149–2162.

Redmond, D. E., Huang, Y. H., Snyder, D. R., Maas, J. W., & Baulu, J. (1976a). Behavioral effects of stimulation of the nucleus locus coeruleus in the stump-tailed monkey (Macaca arctoides). *Neuroscience Abstracts, 1*, 472.

Redmond, D. E., Huang, Y. H., Snyder, D. R., Maas, J. W., & Baulu, J. (1976b). Behavioral changes following lesions of the locus coeruleus in Macaca arctoides. *Brain Research, 116*, 502–510.

Reiman, E. M. (1988). The quest to establish the neural substrates of anxiety. In G. Winokur & W. Coryell (Eds.), *Psychiatric clinics of North America* (pp. 295–307). London: W. B. Saunders.

Rodin, E. (1958). Metrazol tolerance in a "normal" volunteer population. *Electroencephalography and Clinical Neurophysiology, 10*, 433–446.

Rosenbaum, A. H., Schatzberg, A. F., Jost, F. A., et al. (1983). Urinary free cortisol levels in anxiety. *Psychosomatics, 24*, 835–839.

Roth, M., Gurney, C., Garside, R. F., & Kerr, T. A. (1972). Studies in the classification of affective disorder: 1. The relationship between anxiety states and depressive illnesses. *British Journal of Psychiatry, 121*, 147–161.

Roy-Byrne, P. P., Mellman, T. A., & Uhde, T. W. (1988). Biological findings in panic disorder: Neuroendocrine and sleep-related abnormalities. *Journal of Anxiety Disorders, 2*, 17–29.

Roy-Byrne, P. P., Uhde, T. W., Post, R. M., Gallucci, W., Chrousos, G. P., & Gold, D. W. (1986). The corticotropin-releasing hormone stimulation test in patients with panic disorder. *American Journal of Psychiatry, 143*, 896–899.

Ruff, M. R., Pert, C. B., Weber, R. J., Wahl, L. M., Wahl, S. M., & Paul, S. M. (1985). Benzodiazepine receptor-mediated chemotaxis of human monocytes. *Science, 229*, 1281–1283.

Saab, P. G., Matthews, K. A., Stoney, C. M., & McDonald, R. H. (in press). Premenopausal and postmenopausal women differ in their cardiovascular and neuroendocrine response to behavioral stressors. *Psychophysiology*.

Schneiderman, N., & McCabe, P. M. (1985). Biobehavioral responses to stressors. In T. M. Field, P. M. McCabe, & N. Schneiderman (Eds.), *Stress and coping* (pp. 13–61). London: Lawrence Erlbaum Associates.

Schofield, P. R., Darlison, M. G., Fujita, N., et al. (1987). Sequence and functional expression of GABA receptor shows a ligand-gated receptor super-family. *Nature, 328*, 221–227.

Schweitzer, E. E., Swenson, C. M., Winokur, A., Rickels, K., & Maislin, G. (1986). The dexamethasone suppression test in generalized anxiety disorder. *British Journal of Psychiatry, 149*, 320–326.

Seligman, M. E. P. (1975). *Helplessness: On depression, development, and death*. San Francisco: W. H. Freeman.

Sheehan, D. V. (1987). Benzodiazepines in panic disorder and agoraphobia. *Journal of Affective Disorders, 13*, 169–181.

Sheehan, D. V., Ballenger, J., & Jacobson, G. (1980). Treatment of endogeneous anxiety with phobic, hysterial and hypochondriacal symptoms. *Archives of General Psychiatry, 37,* 51–59.

Sidman, M. (1955). Some properties of warning stimulus in avoidance behavior. *Journal of Comparative and Physiological Psychology, 48,* 444–450.

Siever, L. J., Insel, T. R., Jimerson, D. C., Lake, C. R., Uhde, T. W., Aloi, J., & Murphy, D. L. (1983). Growth hormone response to clonidine in obsessive–compulsive patients. *British Journal of Psychiatry, 142,* 184–187.

Simson, P. E., & Weiss, J. M. (1987). Alpha-2 receptor blockade increases responsiveness of locus coeruleus neurons to excitatory stimulation. *Journal of Neuroscience, 7,* 1732–1740.

Singh, P. M., Gupta, R. C., Prasad, G. C., & Udupa, K. N. (1980). Response of pineal gland in clinical cases of psychological stress. *Indian Journal of Psychiatry, 22,* 375–377.

Smith, T. C., Cooperman, L. H., & Wollman, H. (1980). The therapeutic gases: Oxygen, carbon dioxide, helium and water vapor. In A. G. Gilman, L. S. Goodman, A. Gilman, S. E. Mayer, & K. L. Melmon (Eds.), *Goodman and Gilman's the pharmacological basis of therapeutics* (6th ed.) (pp. 218–239). New York: Macmillan.

Starkman, M. N., Zelnik, T. C., Nesse, R. M., & Cameron, O. G. (1985). Anxiety in patients with pheochromocytomas. *Archives of Internal Medicine, 145,* 248.

Stein, M. B., & Uhde, T. W. (1988). Panic disorder and major depression: A tale of two syndromes. In G. Winokur & W. Coryell (Eds.), *Psychiatric clinics of North America* (pp. 441–461). London: W. B. Saunders.

Strahlendorf, H. K., & Strahlendorf, J. C. (1981). Iontophoretically applied benzodiazepines inhibit locus coeruleus unit activity. *Neuroscience Abstracts, 7,* 793.

Study, R. E., & Barker, J. L. (1981). Diazepam and (−)pentobarbital: Fluctuation analysis reveals different mechanisms for potentiation of gamma amino butyric acid responses in cultured central neurons. *Proceedings of the National Academy of Sciences, U.S.A., 78,* 7180–7184.

Sulser, F., Vetulani, J., & Mobley, P. L. (1978). Mode of action of anti-depressant drugs. *Biochemical Pharmacology, 27,* 257–261.

Sulser, F., & Mobley, P. L. (1981). Regulation of central noradrenergic receptor function: New vistas on the mode of action of antidepressant treatments. In E. Usdin, W. B. Bunney, & J. M. Davis (Eds.), *Neuroreceptors: Basic clinical aspects* (pp. 55–83). New York: Wiley.

Surman, O. S., Williams, J., Sheehan, D. V., Strom, T. B., Jones, K. J., & Coleman, J. (1986). Immunological response in agoraphobia and panic attacks. *Biological Psychiatry, 21,* 768–774.

Suzman, M. M. (1976). Propranolol in the treatment of anxiety. *Postgraduate Medicine Journal, 52,* 168–174.

Taggart, P., Carruthers, M., & Somerville, W. (1973). Electrocardiogram, plasma catecholamines and lipids, and their modification by oxprenolol when speaking before an audience. *Lancet, 2,* 341–346.

Taylor, K. M., & Laverty, R. (1969). The effect of chlordiazepoxide, diazepam and nitrazepam on catecholamine metabolism in regions of the rat brain. *European Journal of Pharmacology, 8,* 296–301.

Tiller, J. W. G., Biddle, K. P., Maguire, K. P., & Davies, B. M. (1988). The dexamethasone suppression test and plasma dexamethasone in generalized anxiety disorder. *Biological Psychiatry, 23,* 261–270.

Troxler, R. G., Sprague, E. A., Albanese, R. A., Fuchs, R., & Thompson, A. J. (1977). The associations of elevated plasma cortisol and early atherosclerosis as demonstrated by coronary angiography. *Atherosclerosis, 26,* 151–162.

Tsuda, A., Tanaka, M., Wishikawa, T., & Hirai, H. (1983). Effects of coping behavior on gastric lesions in rats as a function of the complexity of coping tasks. *Physiology and Behavior, 30,* 805–808.

Tyrer, P. J., & Lader, M. H. (1974). Response to propranolol and diazepam in somatic and psychic anxiety. *British Medical Journal, 2,* 14–16.

Uhde, T. W., Roy-Byrne, P. P., Vittone, B. J., Boulenger, J. P., & Post, R. M. (1985). Phenomenology and neurobiology of panic disorder. In A. H. Tuma & J. D. Maser (Eds.), *Anxiety and anxiety disorders* (pp. 557–576). London: Erlbaum.

Uhde, T. W., Siever, L. J., & Post, R. M. (1984). Clonidine: Acute challenge and clinical trial paradigms for the investigation and treatment of anxiety disorders effective illness and pain syndromes. In R. M. Post & J. C. Ballenger (Eds.), *Neurobiology of mood disorders* (pp. 314–334). Baltimore: Williams & Wilkins.

Uhde, T. W., Vittone, B. J., Siever, L. J., Kaye, W. H., & Post, R. M. (1986). Blunted growth hormone response to clonidine in panic disorder patients. *Biological Psychiatry, 21,* 1077–1081.

U'Prichard, D. C., & Enna, S. J. (1979). In vitro modulation of CNS beta-receptor number by antidepressants and beta-agonists. *European Journal of Pharmacology, 59,* 297–301.

Van Den Hout, M. A., & Greiz, E. (1984). Panic symptoms after inhalation of carbon dioxide. *British Journal of Psychiatry, 144,* 503.

Van Den Hout, M. A., van der Molen, G. M., Griez, E., Lousberg, H., & Nansen, A. (1987). Reduction of CO_2-induced anxiety in patients with panic attacks after repeated CO_2 exposure. *American Journal of Psychiatry, 144*, 788–791.

Van Valkenburg, C., Akiskal, H. S., Puzantian, V., & Rosenthal, T. (1984). Anxious depression: Clinical, family history, and naturalistic outcome comparisons with panic and major depressive disorders. *Journal of Affective Disorders, 6*, 67–82.

Vetulani, J., & Susler, F. (1975). Action of various antidepressant treatments reduces reactivity of noradrenergic cyclic AMP-generating system in limbic forebrain. *Nature, 257*, 495–496.

Waeber, R., Adler, R. H., Schwank, A., & Galeazzi, R. L. (1982). Dyspnea proneness to CO_2 stimulation and personality (neuroticism, extraversion, MMPI factors). *Psychotherapy and Psychosomatics, 37*, 119–123.

Weiner, A. A. (1979). Fear-anxiety: Rx. Intravenous diazepam sedation. *General Dentistry, 27*, 27–32.

Weiner, N. (1980). Norepinephrine, epinephrine, and the sympathomimetic amines. In A. G. Gilman, L. S. Goodman, & A. Gilman (Eds.), *The pharmacological basis of therapeutics* (6th ed., pp. 138–175). New York: Macmillan.

Weiss, J. M. (1968). Effects of coping responses on stress. *Journal of Comparative and Physiological Psychology, 65*, 251–260.

Weiss, J. M. (1970). Somatic effects of predictable and unpredictable shock. *Psychosomatic Medicine, 32*, 397–408.

Weiss, J. M. (1971). Effects of coping behavior in different warning signal conditions on stress pathology in rats. *Journal of Comparative and Physiological Psychology, 77*, 22–30. (a)

Weiss, J. M. (1971). Effects of coping behavior with and without a feedback signal on stress pathology in rats. *Journal of Comparative and Physiological Psychology, 77*, 1–13. (b)

Weiss, J. M. (1971). Effects of punishing the coping response (conflict) on stress pathology in rats. *Journal of Comparative and Physiological Psychology, 77*, 14–21. (c)

Weiss, J. M. (1972). Influence of psychological variables on stress-induced pathology. *Physiology, emotion and psychosomatic medicine, CIBA Foundation Symposium, 8*, 253–265.

Weiss, J. M., Bailey, W. H., Goodman, P. A., Hoffman, L. J., Ambrose, M. J., Salman, S., & Charney, J. M. (1982). A model for neurochemical study of depression. In M. Y. Spiegelstein & A. Levy (Eds.), *Behavioral models and the analysis of drug action* (pp. 195–223). Amsterdam: Elsevier.

Weiss, J. M., & Goodman, P. G. (1985). Neurochemical mechanisms underlying stress-induced depression. In T. M. Field, P. M. McCabe, & N. Schneiderman (Eds.), *Stress and coping* (pp. 93–116). Hillsdale, NJ: Erlbaum.

Weiss, J. M., Simson, P. E., & Knight, J. A. (1987). Hyperresponsivity of locus coeruleus is associated with stress-induced behavioral depression. *Society of Neuroscience Abstracts, 32*, 128.

Welner, A., Reich, T., Robins, E., Fishman, R., & Van Doren, T. (1976). Obsessive–compulsive neurosis: Record, family, and follow-up studies. *Comprehensive Psychiatry, 17*, 527–539.

Wheatley, D. (1969). Comparative effects of propanolol and chlordiazepoxide and anxiety states. *British Journal of Psychiatry, 115*, 1411–1412.

Winters, R. W. (1985). Arousal, sleep, and stress. In T. M. Field, P. M. McCabe, & N. Schneiderman (Eds.), *Stress and coping* (pp. 63–91). Hillsdale, NJ: Erlbaum.

Woods, S. W., Charney, D. S., Loke, J., Goodman, W. K., Redmond, D. E., Jr., & Heninger, G. R. (1986). Carbon dioxide sensitivity in panic anxiety: Ventilatory and anxiogenic response to carbon dioxide in healthy subjects and patients with panic anxiety before and after alprazolam treatment. *Archives of General Psychiatry, 43*, 900.

Woods, S. W., Charney, D. S., McPherson, C. A., Gradman, A. H., & Heninger, G. R. (1987). Situational panic attacks. *Archives of General Psychiatry, 44*, 365–375.

Yu, P. H., Bowen, R. C., Davis, B. A., & Boulton, A. A. (1983). Platelet monoamine oxidase activity and trace acid levels in plasma of agoraphobic patients. *Acta Psychiatrica Scandanavica, 67*, 188–194.

Zitrin, C. M., Klein, D. F., Woerner, M. G., & Ross, D. C. (1983). Treatment of phobias: 1. Comparison of imipramine hydrocholoride and placebo. *Archives of General Psychiatry, 40*, 125–138.

III

ANXIETY DISORDERS AND THE CARDIOVASCULAR SYSTEM

8

Anxiety and Coronary Heart Disease

D. G. Byrne and A. E. Byrne

INTRODUCTION

Anxiety is arguably the most widely experienced and universally distributed of all the emotional states. Its nature is recognized by most individuals, it is reported in the majority of cultures, and it has been the subject of intense and protracted investigation for many decades. Although anxiety has taken on a multitude of definitions and meanings, its clinical significance both in psychiatry and internal medicine is solidly established.

In the Greco-Roman tradition, the source of anxiety, and indeed of the other emotions, was clearly to be found in the heart. The physician Galen (A.D. 130–200) considered the "rational" functions of the individual, including imagination, judgment, and memory, to be the firm province of the brain. The "irrational" functions, however, among which emotions were prominent, claimed the heart as their regulatory organ. Although science has led to the adoption of other views in more recent times, poetry has continued to uphold the irrefutable connection between the heart and the experience of emotion. The heart has, in countless works of literature throughout history, been held responsible for greed and malice, sadness and joy, and, most pertinent to the present discussion, for fear.

Contemporary research on the biology of emotions has focused its attention firmly on the brain, and the regulation of emotional states is now seen to be very largely the result of neurohormonal factors (Mandler, 1984) that arise in response to a complex set of behavioral and cognitive triggers (Lazarus, 1982). Nonetheless, the heart continues to figure prominently in the discussion of emotions, nowadays as an "end-organ" or physiological system highly responsive to signals, specific or otherwise, emanating from the central nervous system (Surwit, Williams, & Shapiro, 1982).

Definitions of anxiety vary subtly one from another, and it is difficult to adopt any as standard. However, one element emerges with absolute consistency: The experience of anxiety involves both psychological and somatic distress. Thirty years ago, anxiety was defined somewhat graphically in the *American Handbook of Psychiatry* as

subjectively experienced uneasiness, apprehension, anticipation of danger, doom, disintegration and going to pieces, the source of which is unknown by the individual and toward which he feels helpless, with a characteristic somatic pattern. This somatic pattern shows evidence of increased tension in the skeletal muscles (stiffness, tremors, weakness, unsteadiness of voice, etc.); the cardio-vascular system (palpitations, blushing or pallor, faintness, rapid pulse, increased blood pressure, etc.); and the gastrointestinal system (nausea, vomiting, diarrhea, etc.). (Portnoy, 1959)

Less discursively and with a greater emphasis on the systematic specification of both the structural and functional components of anxiety, Rachman (1978) proposed that it was made up of four independent but integral parts, these being cognitive (expectations of impending harm), somatic (involving the body's emergency reaction to danger), emotional (seen in the form of distress, with panic at the extreme end), and behavioral (largely manifest as avoidance).

Focusing on the somatic component, Rosenhan and Seligman (1984) singled out cardiovascular responses for their universality and potency in the recognition of anxiety. They described the cardiovascular component of this emotional state to be manifest as paleness of the skin, increase in heart rate and blood pressure, acceleration and deepening of respiration, and an increase in blood levels of coagulants and lymphocytes. Although these changes can objectively be understood as arising from increases in sympathetic arousal, their subjective perception by the individual sufferer may be reported in terms of substantial discomfort and distress. Essentially, the experience of anxiety is associated in many, if not most individual sufferers, at least partly with somatic feelings of unease clearly identified with the heart and the circulation of the blood that it regulates. Anxiety, in other words, produces cardiovascular symptoms, if only transiently. Not surprisingly, therefore, it follows in the reasoning of most lay people and many in the medical and psychological professionals, that anxiety by whatever synonym it is described must be a contributory factor in diseases of the heart and circulation.

This view has been borne out in a number of surveys inquiring into public awareness of the causes of heart disease. In a national survey conducted in the United States in 1980, the large majority (67%) of a random sample of subjects nominated "stress and tension" as the major cause of heart attacks, ahead of smoking and diet (Roper Organization, 1980). The same survey found that most subjects (57%) nominated the same factor as the principal cause of high blood pressure. Public perceptions of heart disease therefore appear to reflect acceptance of a plausible causal link between anxiety and the signs, symptoms, and consequences of cardiovascular pathology. The relative importance of this finding is highlighted by the widespread nature of heart disease itself, which, at least in the form of acute myocardial infarction, accounts for sizable percentages both of morbidity and mortality in Western developed nations.

ANXIETY, STRESS, AND DISTRESS

The psychiatric connotations of anxiety are both clear-cut and widespread; they have been carefully reviewed earlier (see chap. 20), and in this chapter we clarify the nature of the phenomenon and the use of the term. However, with particular regard to cardiovascular disease, specific mention of anxiety is less common than is reference to the notion of stress. The bulk of the literature relating "emotional disequilibrium" in its broad and general sense to disruptions to the functional integrity of the cardiovascular system emphasize the more ambiguous concept of stress in preference to the more specific idea of an emotional state with distinct psychiatric implications. Prior to a discussion of anxiety and its effects on the heart, some conceptual reconciliation of the two ideas is therefore necessary.

In the theory of stress as a general factor in the formation of pathology and the precipitation of illness events (see Levi (1971) as a useful historical guide), anxiety is an integral component of the stress reaction. Stress, however, is a complex and multifaceted phenomenon, the nature of which is yet not completely understood. A dissection of the components of stress reveals a process involving several stages organized in an invariant sequence (Byrne, 1986).

The first of these stages focuses on the *stressor,* which may equate with a condition within the physical environment (heat, noise, proprioceptive discomfort, etc.), a discrete psychosocial or interpersonal event (loss of job, experience of an illness, etc.), or a protracted psychosocial or interpersonal difficulty (continuing poverty, progressive breakdown of a relationship, etc.). Lists of such stressors, also called life events or recent experiences, are typified by the seminal work of Holmes and Rahe (1967) on the construction of the Social Readjustment Rating Scale (SRRS), but more recent and comprehensive lists may be found in Brown and Harris (1978) and Henderson, Byrne, and Duncan-Jones (1981).

Mediating mechanisms form the second stage of this process. These mechanisms assume the role of determining, for each individual, the degree of personal significance placed on the occurrence of any given stressor. A variety of factors vie for inclusion in this list, among them patterns of individual personality (Byrne, 1983) and past experience with particular stressors (Lundberg, Theorell, & Lind, 1975). They are all subsumed, however, under the broad rubric of the cognitive interpretive filter (Lazarus, 1982), a mechanism whereby the sum of all such influences acts to impart an individual-specific interpretation to the experience of a given stressor in such a way as to direct the nature and magnitude of both psychological and physiological responses.

These responses, collectively termed the *stress reaction,* form the final stage of the process. They are to be seen both as physiological manifestations (primarily in the form of activation of the sympathetic nervous system) and as psychological distress or emotional discomfort. Whereas this latter mode of expression may be described by several terms of highly similar meaning (tension, nervousness, being on edge, and apprehensiveness are all common), the most salient descriptor is that of anxiety.

This is, of course, a simplistic account of a complex and controversial area. More comprehensive overviews may be found in a number of dedicated texts (see, for example, Mandler, 1984). Researchers who attempt to relate stress (or anxiety) to illness pose substantial conceptual and methodological difficulties and produce results that are often equivocal. It is important, therefore, to appreciate the complexity of the concept of stress if studies relating it to cardiovascular disease are to be refined to a point where they surpass simple and perhaps coincidental correlations between environmental events and illness episodes. Unfortunately, studies of anxiety, stress, and coronary heart disease (CHD) have, by and large, failed to recognize the essentially process nature of the concept of stress and have focused, instead, on data pertinent only to single stages of the sequence leading to the stress reaction. This does, however, provide a convenient structure for the discussion of these data. The evidence on stress, anxiety, and CHD is, therefore, considered in terms of whether the independent variables (stress and anxiety) have been viewed as largely environmental in nature, largely mediative, or largely as a response.

Cardiovascular disease covers a wide range of pathophysiological states. Most studies have been concerned with one particular sequence of pathoclinical events, that being the development of coronary atherosclerosis or coronary artery disease (CAD), which, in some individuals, proceeds via coronary occlusion, through thrombus formation, subintimal hemorrhage, or coronary vasospasm, to acute myocardial infarction or CHD. The myocardial infarction and CHD are often used interchangeably in the epidemiological evidence; we refer to all events involving coronary occlusion and subsequent infarction as CHD. Consideration of studies is limited largely to those in which this illness event forms the primary end-point of investigation.

STRESSORS AND CORONARY HEART DISEASE

The Link Between Life Events and Illness

The study of associations between exposure to stressful life events and illness in its multitude of forms has provided at one and the same time one of the most productive yet controversial contributions to psychosomatic medicine. Since the seminal work of Holmes in the 1950s, this area has been marked by considerable advances in the explanation of the impact of both social and interpersonal environments on human pathophysiology. Such progress has, however, been punctuated and at times greatly slowed by the emergence of very substantial difficulties to do with every aspect of the investigative process. Conceptual issues centering on the nature of stress, its origins, and its consequences have loomed large in constraining progress. So too has disagreement regarding the most appropriate means for the uncontaminated measurement of stress. The area has also generated a continuing and often vitriolic discussion concerning the merits of the particular kinds of research designs that might be put to use in establishing the life events–illness link; more specifically, the methodological superiority of prospective designs as opposed to the logistic convenience of retrospective ones has been the subject of many theoretical discourses. Despite this, the area continues to produce a steady flow of both conceptual and empirical material, most of which supports a quasi-causal association between exposure to stressful life events and illness.

The value of much of this work for explanations of illness in general and CHD in particular, rests with the development by Holmes and Rahe (1967) of the list of recent experiences and its associated metric for quantifying the impact of these experiences, the SRRS. The use of this instrument, or others deriving closely from it, has produced a substantial accumulation of empirical work documenting associations between stressful life events and illness, the bulk of which has supported the existence of such a link. Particularly for CHD, the consistency of support arising from studies in the 1960s and 1970s was sufficient to endow the association with a worthwhile credibility. Nonetheless, in more recent times such data have come up against a good deal of criticism, mostly stemming from methodological concerns to do with measurement or research design. These criticisms have promoted a careful reevaluation of the postulated link between life events and CHD and perhaps have led to a general slowing down of research activity in the area. Nonetheless, because stressors, that is, events or circumstances occurring in the environment external to the individual, form the initial stage of most models of stress, it is appropriate to begin any consideration of stress and CHD with an examination of the literature relating exposure to stressors to clinical onset of CHD.

Recent Catastrophic Stressors

The simplest, although crudest, methodology for establishing a link between exposure to stressors and CHD comes from work investigating individual encounters with single stressors of catastrophic proportions. Numerous examples of these stressors come to mind, although systematic research has focused on only three categories: some form of natural disaster, experience of bereavement of a close significant other, and experience of occupational disruption leading to economic hardship.

Elevations in coronary mortality in the weeks or months following a natural disaster have been reported for both the Civil War (Mackay, 1974) and the 1981 earthquake in Athens (Trichopoulos, Zavitsanos, Katsoyanni, Tzonou, & Dalla-Vorg, 1983), although in the former instance the prevailing conditions at the time do not allow any clear-cut inference regarding the possible influence of catastrophic life events on CHD. Moreover, a number of studies have shown no relation whatso-ever between experience of natural disaster situations and incidence of CHD (Byrne, 1987). The very nature of these studies with the absence of suitable control groups (comparison can often be made only on the basis of population averages) and the possible influence of innumerable unanticipated and therefore unmeasured variables on CHD limit very considerably the conclusions that can be drawn from such data.

The literature linking recent bereavement with onset of CHD provides somewhat more consistent and persuasive evidence for a link. Two uncontrolled studies (Cot-tington, Matthew, Talbott, & Kuller, 1980; Talbott, Kuller, & Perper, 1981) examined reports provided by relatives of women who had died suddenly of CHD and had been exposed to catastrophic stressors shortly beforehand. Relative to healthy women in the normal population, those who had recently succumbed to CHD appeared to have suffered an excess level of bereavement of a close significant other in the few months prior to their own deaths. Lack of an adequate control group does, however, preclude making useful conclusions from these findings. Parkes, Benjamin, and Fitzgerald's (1969) reanalysis of data collected six years earlier showed that widowed men had a significantly higher mortality from CHD in the first six months after their bereave-ment than did married men of the same age. A similar finding for men was reported by Chandra, Szklo, Goldberg, and Tonascia (1983), although their work suggested that mortality was highest later rather than sooner after bereavement. This raises the possibility that factors other than the stress of bereavement might exert significant influences on subsequent mortality.

Against this evidence, however, Clayton and Darvish (1979) reviewed nine studies of mortality following bereavement and concluded that there was no evidence to support a link between the stress of recent bereavement and death either from CHD or from any other cause. The evidence regarding death from all causes is certainly stronger in relation to recent bereavement than is death specifically from CHD (Rees & Lutkins, 1967), and there is sufficient evidence with specific regard to CHD to mark it as worthy of further study. However, the failure of existing experimental designs to control adequately for all factors that might influence CHD mortality (and many of these will of course be unanticipated and therefore unmeasured) suggests that very serious caution be placed on the interpretation of evidence of a causal or even an incidental link between the stress of recent bereavement and CHD.

Unemployment

One factor that might intrinsically be expected to be related to risk of CHD is the stress of unemployment. There is now substantial evidence to link the experience of unemployment with severe psychological disorder such as depression (Feather, 1982); however, very little evidence as yet to associate unemployment with risk of

CHD. Brenner (1979) examined the experience of unemployment together with its associated problems of financial difficulties and family disruption in relation to wide-ranging measures of morbidity and mortality. It was found that unemployment corre-lated with such things as psychiatric disorder and suicide within a year of the event taking place and also correlated, although less strongly, with cardiovascular disease incidence within two to three years of unemployment. Although the evidence to date is as yet rather preliminary, it does confirm, if only tentatively, an expected link between unemployment stress and CHD.

Past Exposure to Catastrophic Stressors

Long-term exposure to catastrophic stressors has been implicated as a risk factor for CHD in two broad groups of people: survivors of concentration camp experience during the second World War and survivors of prisoner-of-war (POW) camps during the same period. The rationale underlying this work involves the expectation that the traumatically stressful effects of either of these two experiences together with their long-term psychological sequelae would act by means of accepted stress and illness mechanisms to endow a greater risk of future CHD than would be expected in the general population. Only two studies (Eaton, Sigal, & Weinfeld, 1982; Levav & Abrahamson, 1984) have specifically addressed the issue of CHD mortality in essen-tially unselected groups of concentration camp survivors. In both studies, mortality from all causes was elevated significantly in relation to the general population. How-ever, although rates of CHD between 20 and 30 years after release from concentration camp were increased among concentration camp survivors relative to the general population, this increase was not statistically significant. It is worth noting, however, that rates of psychiatric morbidity were significantly higher in those who had gone through the concentration camp experience than in those who had avoided this trauma.

Data relating to survivors of POW camps show similar trends. Long-term psychi-atric morbidity in POW camp survivors is significantly elevated relative to the general population (Beebe, 1975; Tennant, Goulston, & Dent, 1986). Richardson (1965) found that survivors of POW camp experiences had in the long term similar rates of CHD mortality to their brothers (who had not undergone incarceration in POW camps), but in both cases, rates of CHD mortality were significantly elevated relative to the general population. Other studies among both British (Gill, 1983) and Austra-lian (Goulston et al., 1985) prisoners-of-war showed no elevation in CHD mortality in the long term relative to that of the general population. Once more, however, there is evidence of increased psychiatric morbidity in the 30 or 40 years following release from POW camps.

Therefore, although it is intuitively sensible to relate risk of CHD in the long term to the experience of single traumatic life events in the past, the evidence is by no means unequivocal in its support for this link, at least so far as survivors of concen-tration camps or POW camps are concerned. Moreover, there are many factors that might influence CHD mortality over and above the experience of such a traumatic life event. These include physical and nutritional hardship and exposure to conditions of poor hygiene, all of which would have been rampant in either situation. It is therefore difficult to say with any certainty whether or not such experiences increase risk of CHD.

Cumulative Life Events

Whereas studies of exposure to past life events allow for a quasi-prospective examination of the evidence, studies of exposure to cumulative life events are essentially limited to retrospective examinations of the data. This places substantial inferential constraints on conclusions that may be drawn from these data; however, the advent of the list of recent experiences (LRE) and its associated SRRS (Holmes & Rahe, 1967) has given rise to a number of systematic studies of cumulative life events in relation to CHD.

In what was perhaps the original study in this series, Theorell and Rahe (1971) showed that subjects who had experienced a first-documented myocardial infarction also reported a build-up of stressful life events in the two years prior to onset of illness. These life events produced high scores relative to those of control subjects on the Holmes and Rahe (1967) Life Change Index. Similar data from essentially the same population have been reported by Theorell (1974), Theorell and Rahe (1975), and Liljefors and Rahe (1970). Other work using the same Life Event Inventory (Defaire, 1975; Orth-Gomer, 1979; Theorell, Lind, Froberg, Karlsson, & Levi, 1972) have failed to establish convincing relations between life events demanding adjustment or life change and subsequent risk of CHD. Lundberg et al. (1975) have suggested that this may be due in part to the inappropriateness of the life change metric as an index of accumulated life events. Lundberg and his colleagues were unable to distinguish between patients with CHD and control subjects on the basis of a life change index, but the use of an index based on the extent to which subjects personally rated items in a life event inventory according to the dimension of "upsettingness," did significantly separate the CHD from control groups. This suggests that not accumulated life events per se but the ways in which individuals interpret these endows risk of CHD.

Moreover, the LRE has been criticized for its failure to address the full range of life events and experiences that an unselected individual may encounter in a given period of time and, therefore, to provide an adequate assessment of life event exposure (Henderson et al., 1981). Data from studies using instruments other than the original LRE have also established associations between cumulative life events and risk of CHD although these associations have not added up to unequivocal support for a link between life events and coronary risk. Studies by Siegrist (1984); Magni et al., (1983); and Bengtsson, Hallstrom, and Tibblin (1973) have all reported positive associations between accumulated life events measured by a variety of instruments and risk of CHD; however, no such association was evident in other studies (e.g., Byrne & Whyte, 1980; Connolly, 1976). Connolly (1976) attempted to distinguish between those life events that were unrelated to prodomal symptoms of CHD and those that may be associated with illness onset. Whereas the latter group of life events did relate to eventual onset of CHD, those events that were independent of the illness did not distinguish between patients who had experienced myocardial infarction and control subjects.

The evidence on accumulated life events and risk of CHD is therefore by no means clear-cut. Although there is some support for this link, which is intuitively sensible, the number of supportive studies is essentially balanced by those reporting neutral or negative associations between life events and CHD. Moreover, these studies are plagued by the problem of retrospectivity that distinctly limits the interpretations that may be placed on the data. The evidence is therefore suggestive, but it cannot be taken as strong support for an association between stress and CHD.

JUDGING THE IMPACT OF STRESSORS
ON CORONARY HEART DISEASE

The Meaning of Life Events

Whereas simple measures of accumulated life events do not correlate consistently with risk of CHD, stronger evidence for this link comes from the use of scales designed to reflect the impact of life events on the individual (Byrne, 1984). Lazarus (1966) introduced the notion that life events are not inherently stressful but become so only when interpreted as such within personal, cognitive frameworks. Lazarus and his colleagues were able to demonstrate in a series of sophisticated and persuasive laboratory studies that individual interpretation of the impact of environmental stressors rather than the objective nature of the stressors themselves formed the primary determinant of the magnitude of the stress reaction. The appearance of this work led to the view that measures of cumulative life events most likely to provide a reliable index of the impact of life events on the individual must derive from individual interpretations and not from estimates of average impact based on the judgments of unrepresentative samples. This idea is very much in accord with the work of Lundberg et al. (1975), which showed that the personal experience of a life event produces a markedly different rating of its impact when compared with ratings derived from individuals who had never experienced a given event.

Few studies of life events and CHD have taken up this challenge. In one study, life events in a sample of survivors of myocardial infarction were examined retrospectively and life event histories of the subjects were compared with those of patients hospitalized for other than life-threatening and cardiovascular illness (Byrne & Whyte, 1980). In addition to simply reporting life events and applying life change scaling to reported life events, these researchers undertook a clinical interview with each patient designed to estimate the individual impact of each reported life event as and when it was experienced. It was found that neither cumulative numbers of life events nor life change scales distinguished between survivors of myocardial infarction and control subjects. However, when subjects were allowed to judge for themselves the impact of personally experienced life events, it was found that patients with myocardial infarction estimated their own life events to have had significantly greater impact (controlled for the nature of life event) than did control subjects. This finding certainly confirms the importance of individual measures of life event impact but has not yet been replicated.

Moreover, the use of a methodology of this kind poses substantial questions regarding the reliability of measures of individual impact and the extent to which data deriving from them may be interpreted. Brown, Harris, and Peto, (1973) cautioned about the possible action of "effort and meaning" in which the report of life events within the context of existing symptomatology may produce contamination of life event recall as patients search for an explanation to account for their present symptoms. The use of retrospectively gathered data addressing the issue of individual impact is certainly prone to the operation of "effort after meaning," although the extent to which this casts doubt on the reliability of data is arguable. It has been shown, for example, that major life events are typically recalled with some accuracy and that the recall of life events either as a simple cumulative index or a measure of individual impact is essentially unrelated to measures of state or trait anxiety associated with the experience of cardiovascular symptoms (Byrne, 1983). Therefore, although the methodological limitations placed on data of this kind cannot be discounted, the conceptual attraction of an argument emphasizing measures of individual life event impact would suggest that if future studies of life events and CHD are to take place the role of individual interpretations of these life events must be addressed in such a way as to limit the potential contamination of life event recall that might arise from retrospective data collection.

THE STRESS REACTION AND CORONARY HEART DISEASE

Emotional Distress and Exposure to Stressors

There is now abundant evidence that even short-term exposure to environmental stressors causes the experience of symptoms of psychological distress (Henderson et al., 1981) that typically take the form of either anxiety or depression (Byrne, 1984). Although the experience of emotional distress may be short-lived, there is also evidence to support the view that chronic exposure to stressors may result in a more or less protracted state of emotional disturbance (Byrne, 1984). Theories of anxiety in particular extend well beyond those to do with exposure to environmental stressors (as has been discussed at great length in other chapters of this book), but it is also fair to say that environmental events form one very substantial source of explanation for the appearance of anxiety. Explanatory theories notwithstanding, there is no doubt whatsoever that anxiety is widespread as a form of psychological disorder in almost all populations. Given the hypothesized links between life events and CHD (Byrne, 1987), it is sensible to assume that those individuals afflicted with a chronic anxiety state in whatever psychiatric form this may take, and indeed whether it has been psychiatrically identified or not, will be at greater risk for CHD than will individuals whose emotional states are not characterized by the distress of anxiety. (The mechanisms through which this might take place have been discussed elsewhere in this book and will not be addressed here.)

Psychological Symptoms and Risk of Coronary Heart Disease

There is considerable anecdotal evidence (Kits van Heyningen & Treurniet, 1966) that psychiatric patients diagnosed with acute anxiety reactions suffer more CHD than do individuals with so-called normal emotional lives. Moreover, there are a number of systematic studies, albeit of a retrospective kind, that have shown consistent positive correlations between CHD and the experience of acute psychological symptoms (Bianchi, Fergusson, & Walshe, 1978; Spittle & James, 1977). The same association has been shown for chronic symptoms of emotional distress, typically anxiety (Gupta & Verma, 1983; Klein & Parsons, 1968; Thiel, Parker, & Bruce, 1973), although these studies have usually employed trait measures of psychological symptomatology and there is some debate as to whether such trait measures represent preexisting personality attributes or the immediate subjective experience of emotional distress.

Boman (1982) reviewed studies in this area and concluded that although they represented positive evidence of an association between psychological symptoms and CHD, they were marred by the characteristic of retrospective data collection (which places substantial constraints on causal interpretations from the data) and by variability and uncertainty regarding the nature of the measures of psychological symptomatology used.

Eastwood and Trevelyan (1971) were able to demonstrate statistically significant associations between neurotic illness identified psychiatrically and evidence of CHD from electrocardiograms (EKGs) in patients attending a general practice for reasons other than either emotional distress or cardiovascular discomfort. Few of these individuals had attracted a past diagnosis of CHD. Nonetheless, 30% of male subjects with diagnosed neurotic illness had abnormal EKGs indicating CHD, whereas only 11% of subjects without neurotic symptoms had this cardiovascular pattern. Rates of EKG abnormality were smaller for women, but the same trend was evident. The value of this study is that reports of neurotic symptoms could not have been contaminated by either preexisting knowledge of CHD or anxiety based on subjective perceptions of cardiovascular abnormality (because very few subjects either recognized or complained of this state). Although the epidemiological end-point of the study was not clinical CHD but only EKG changes indicating cardiac disorder, the design of the study does allow more comfortable conclusions regarding the possible association between psychiatrically identified anxiety and underlying cardiological disorder.

There is also evidence that symptoms of psychological distress are related to severity of CHD as evident on coronary angiography. Reports of associations between extent of coronary atherosclerosis and both acute situational anxiety (Zyzanski, Jenkins, Ryan, Flessas, & Everist, 1976) and hostility (Williams et al., 1980) have been reported; however, the results of these studies have been unconfirmed by further work (Blumenthal, Williams, Kong, Schanberg, & Thompson, 1978; Langeluddecke & Tennant, 1986). Although these studies contain important methodological differences from one another, the results are sufficiently intriguing to warrant further investigation regarding possible associations between emotional distress and extent of coronary artery disease as revealed by angiographic investigation. Recent work has also indicated an association between emotional distress measured in various ways and outcome following a documented episode of clinical CHD.

ANXIETY, STRESS, AND THE TYPE A BEHAVIOR PATTERN

Associations between anxiety, stress, and the Type A behavior pattern are somewhat contentious and not well understood. Traditional views of Type A behavior have sought to dissociate it from any notion of stress, neuroticism, or psychiatric impairment (Jenkins, 1978). Standard definitions of the pattern emphasize its essentially behavioral character (Rosenman & Chesney, 1980), whereas an early and perhaps broad overview portrays it, *inter alia*, as "an action-emotion complex," thus recognizing, at least in principle, the role of an affective element in the overall construct. More recent conceptualizations of Type A behavior are more explicit in their acceptance that insofar as the behavior confers coronary risk, both behavior and emotion (and particularly emotional distress) must bear conjoint responsibility (Price, 1983).

Support for this can be drawn from two interrelated sources. First, despite the opinion that those with Type A behavior are largely unaware of the character of their behaviors (Herman, Blumenthal, Black, & Chesney, 1981), there is mounting evidence that Type A behaviors are accompanied by significant emotional discomfort. Dimsdale, Hackett, Block, and Hutter (1978) reported associations between measures of Type A behavior and indices of subjective tension, depressive mood, and anger in a sample of patients awaiting cardiac catheterization, whereas Bass (1984) and Smith (1984) found significant relations between the pattern and both neuroticism and psychiatric symptomatology in similar groups of patients. In order to counter the very real argument that data obtained by self-report from samples of patients may be too prone to contamination, significant relationships between the Type A pattern and a range of measures of emotional distress (but not conspicuous psychiatric impairment) have also been found in several samples of healthy subjects free of coronary disease (Byrne & Rosenman, 1986; Chesney, Eagleston, & Rosenman, 1981; Francis, 1981; Wadden, Anderson, Foster, & Love, 1983). The most extreme interpretation of these data, based largely on correlations between measures of Type A behavior and those of both trait and state anxiety, holds that the Type A behavior and neuroticism are conceptually equivalent (Eysenck & Fulker, 1982; Irvine, Lyle, & Allon, 1982). Type A behavior is, however, strongly typified by overtly time-pressured behaviors (Haynes et al., 1980) and, under some conditions, induces a state of heightened autonomic arousal (Myrtek & Greenlee, 1984). In view of this, Byrne and Rosenman (1986) have argued that the subjective experience of these phenomena, either singly or in combination, can reasonably explain the emotional discomfort that many Type A individuals admit to.

Second, a little recent evidence has suggested that Type A behavior facilitates the accumulation of stressful life events. Following a close examination of the thematic character of the pattern, the claim has been made (Byrne, 1981) that individuals with Type A behaviors may act, albeit unwittingly, to place themselves in personal, social and occupational circumstances that increase the likelihood of their encountering stressful life events. Data from both patients (Byrne, 1981; Dimsdale et al., 1978; Falger, Bressors, & Dijkstra, 1980) and a sample of individuals free from CHD (Byrne & Rosenman, 1986) have all shown consistent significant correlations between measures of Type A behavior and self-reported frequency of stressful life event encounters. Moreover, it has been shown that Type A patients, at least, tend to interpret those life events that have occurred to them as being of greater emotional impact than control subjects free of coronary disease (Byrne, 1981). Interestingly, associations between Type A behavior and measures of life events have been strongest for those categories of life events independently judged to be under greatest personal control. This has led to the view that some part of the noxious character of the pattern has to do with the need by those with Type A behaviors to impose control not only on the environment but also on their responses to it (Vickers, Hervig, Rahe, & Rosenman, 1981; Vingerhoets & Flohr, 1984).

The definition of stress given by Tennant, Langeluddecke, and Byrne (1985) encompasses both external events and individual responses, whether emotional or physiological. Within the meaning of this definition, Type A behavior is clearly interconnected with the notion of stress, although the relationship might be situation-specific (Schwartz, 1983). A distinction must be made, however, between conceptual and empirical relationships. It may be argued that the nature of Type A behavior could create circumstances both within and outside of the individual that might facilitate the stress response, but some care must be taken lest the evidence presently at hand is extrapolated too far. Issues of measurement will dominate any criticism of this evidence (Byrne, Rosenman, Schiller, & Chesney, 1985). The debate surrounding the suitability of measures of Type A behavior continues but greater concern attaches to the measurement of stress whether as an environmental phenomenon or an individual response (Tennant et al., 1985). Some postulated interconnection between Type A behavior and stress provides an interesting explanatory model relating Type A behavior to CHD; however, the ultimate usefulness of this model must lie with the refinement both of concepts and measures of stress and their application in epidemiological designs minimizing the possibility of data contamination by self-report.

OCCUPATION, STRESS, AND CORONARY HEART DISEASE

Sources of Occupational Stress

A major source of occupational stress relates to the type of occupation engaged in. Some differences within (Russek, 1960) and between (French & Caplan, 1970) occupations are potentially important sources of stress. In addition, occupational stress may result from the source of remuneration, that is, self-paid versus salaried employment (Magnus, Matroos, & Strackee, 1983). In addition, employment status for women per se may be a source of occupational stress (Haynes & Feinleib, 1980). The nature of work demands (Haynes, Feinleib, Levine, Scotch, & Kannel, 1978), the nature of workload (Magnus et al., 1983), and the degree of satisfaction workers feel in their employment and situation (Sales & House, 1971) may also contribute significantly to stress in the work place. Further sources of occupational stress relate to the personality of workers and the amount of social support workers receive (e.g., Haynes & Feinleib, 1980) and the degree of personal control workers experience over the work demands that confront them (Karasek, Baker, Marxer, Ahlbom, & Theorell, 1981).

The Relation Between Occupational Stress and Coronary Heart Disease

Differences within particular occupational groups have been shown to link with the incidence of CHD. The exemplary work of Russek (1960) demonstrated that a group of general practitioners in the age range of 40 to 69 had a markedly higher prevalence of CHD than did a group of specialists working in the less stressful area of dermatology. In a further study (Russek, 1965), the CHD prevalence between specialties within the professions of medicine, law, and dentistry was investigated. As expected, there was a trend toward higher prevalence of CHD among the more stressful specialties within each of these occupational groups. Friedman and Hellerstein (1968), however, failed to replicate this finding in a study investigating stress ratings and their relation to CHD in a sample of individuals involved in a number of legal specialties. Working within the public versus the private sector for any single occupational group may also affect the rates of CHD experienced. In a longitudinal study (Kornitzer, Kittel, Debacker, & Dramlax, 1981; Kornitzer, Thilly, Van Roux, & Balthazar, 1975) involving samples of bank employees working either in the public or private sector, it was found that the incidence of CHD was greater in the sample of private basic employees; the explanation by the authors for this finding had to do with much greater pressure experienced by employees in private as compared to public banking institutions.

Apart from differences in the incidence of CHD within occupations, there is evidence that consistent differences between occupational groups exist in terms of CHD prevalence. The high rate of deaths from CHD in sea officers in Norway compared to the population average led Mundal, Erikssen, and Rodahl (1982) to conclude that occupational stress was the major cause of the inflated figure. Occupational stress was also given as a possible explanation for the high rates of death from CHD among sea officers in the United Kingdom and West Germany (Zorn, Harrington, & Goethe, 1977). In a study investigating occupational differences in cardiovascular disease prevalence, French and Caplan (1970) found that blue-collar trade employees and managers had a much higher incidence of cardiovascular disease than did engineers or scientists—irrespective of the age comparisons employed. The researchers argued that these differences were due to the higher levels of occupational stress in blue-collar workers and managerial staff compared with the engineers and scientists.

Other studies have shown that professions of roughly equal social status experience widely disparate rates of CHD (Kasl, 1978). For instance, the teaching profession was shown to have lower CHD rates as a group when compared to the total population, whereas other professional cohorts (e.g., lawyers and real estate agents) had a much higher incidence of CHD than did the population as a whole. Again, different levels of occupational stress would seem to be a likely explanation for these differences across occupational groups. In a major study of the occupational characteristics of patients who had experienced their first episode of acute myocardial infarction (Bolm-Audorff & Siegrist, 1983), it was found that blue-collar occupations were significantly overrepresented when compared with the incidence of myocardial infarction in the total population. Stress in the workplace was posited as the likely reason for this finding. Within the white-collar group, differences between the incidence of acute myocardial infarction were also evident. For example, pilots, air traffic controllers, and managers had a higher prevalence of myocardial infarction than did the total population. Stress in the workplace was posited as the likely reason for this finding.

Individuals who are self-employed have been found to have a much higher incidence of CHD than do those with employee status. More specifically, Magnus et al. (1983) concluded that self-employed people are at twice the risk for CHD than are people who are not self-employed. It is worth noting that very little work has been done with women, although the little that is available seems to corroborate the evidence for men. Certain groups of working women have been found to be at higher risk for CHD than other groups: In particular, clerical workers have been found to have a higher risk for CHD than do women generally (Haynes & Feinleib, 1980). The picture is more complicated for women than for men because a substantial percentage of women do not work, and the dual roles of working and raising a family may add additional stress that may not be evident in men.

The relation between work demands and CHD is far from clear. Early work (Liljefors & Rahe, 1970) supported a positive association between work demands (in this case, number of hours worked) and the incidence of myocardial infarction; later work has not, for the most part, confirmed this association. The Framingham study (Haynes et al., 1978; 1980) examined a relation between work demands (measured by an index and a work load) and CHD among a sample of older workers, but it failed to establish such an association for younger age groups. Moreover, the work demand measure did not make a significant independent contribution to the prediction of the prevalence of CHD. Magnus et al. (1983) failed to find a relationship between excessive working hours and time pressure and the incidence of CHD. In addition, Maschewsky (1982) found only equivocal support for the association between work demands (measured by items covering length of working hours, pressure on time, and responsibilities at work) and acute coronary events. Whereas workers experiencing myocardial infarction rated significantly higher on some measures of work demands, a control group (comprising healthy workers) was shown to rate significantly higher on other work demand indices.

Theorell and Rahe (1971) reported similar equivocal patterns in their comparison of the work demands experienced by a group of workers who had experienced an episode of myocardial infarction and a group of healthy workers; the former rated significantly higher on some measures of work demands, and the latter rated higher on other dimensions of this variable. Results from cross-cultural research have further confused the picture. In one study (Orth-Gomer, 1979), groups of Swedish and American people who had suffered from CHD were compared with healthy samples in each country. The Swedish sample of CHD victims reported higher rates of job demand than did the comparison sample; the opposite pattern emerged for the American sample. Overall, the linkages between work demands and the prevalence of acute coronary disorders seem tenuous at best and perhaps nonexistent.

One reason for the failure to find more consistent results in the study investigating the link between work demands and CHD may be the simplicity of the measures of work demand that have been employed. It has been suggested that composite measures of workload (including psychosocial as well as principal work stressors) are necessary to adequately assess the relations between work stressors and CHD. Composite measures of work stress have been found to be positively associated with CHD in samples of individuals recovering from CHD (Magnus et al., 1983) or myocardial infarction (Siegrist, 1984). In these studies, significant relations have been found between composite work stress indices and CHD and myocardial infarction, respectively. In a study employing a composite measure of workload, Theorell and Floderus-Myrhed (1977) found that frequency of workload was significantly higher for samples of people with myocardial infarction than for the population as a whole. Although it has been suggested that job satisfaction is positively associated with the occurrence of CHD (Sales & House, 1971), this interpretation is under review (cf. Frank & Weintraub, 1973). For the most part, no association has been found between job satisfaction and the incidence of CHD (Orth-Gomer, 1979; Theorell & Rahe, 1971).

The lack of control that an individual feels at work and the excessive demands that individuals feel control them in the workplace have both been found to be positively related to CHD. Alfredson, Karasek, and Theorell (1982) assessed whether high work demands and low opportunities for control at work were risk factors for CHD. Employing a large and representative sample of individuals engaged in a wide range of occupations in Sweden, it was found that the hectic nature of work coupled with a lack of control over work practices was significantly associated with the risk of myocardial infarction. Also it was found that shift-work (a high-demand characteristic) and monotony (a low-control characteristic) were significantly, albeit independently, related to the risk of myocardial infarction. It needs to be pointed out, however, that when physical job requirements and traditional risk factors (e.g., cigarette smoking and low education level) were taken into consideration, the relation between shift-work and CHD disappeared (Alfredson & Theorell, 1983). All other relations were maintained.

Karasek et al. (1981) investigated the relation between job characteristics and the risk of CHD. CHD was found to be predicted by high job demands and low intellectual discretion. By matching the characteristics of control subjects who had died from coronary heart or vascular disease, the same authors reported that the risk of coronary heart or vascular disease was significantly increased for individuals experiencing both high work demands and high work demands coupled with low personal freedom.

In a longitudinal study, Langosch, Brodner, and Borcherding (1983) investigated the association between job demand and control characteristics on the one hand, and the severity and progression of coronary disease on the other. It was reported that high work demands (including doing too many tasks at the same time) and lack of job control (uncontrollable job stress) were positively and significantly related to the severity of CHD as well as to the progression of that disease. Although it is believed that personality and social support variables are useful predictors of the incidence of CHD, there is, with one exception, little empirical support for this contention. In an attempt to explain the finding (reported earlier) that women holding clerical jobs were at greater risk of CHD than were other groups, Haynes and Feinleib (1980) provided evidence that personality factors and social support mechanisms were both significant contributors to CHD among clerical workers.

CONCLUSION

Both stress and anxiety, variously conceptualized, defined, and measured, and arising from a multitude of sources, have been statistically linked to risk of CHD in a large number of studies. This link is both intrinsically sensible (it is consistent with popular and scientific views of CHD) and empirically supported by a bulk of data purposefully addressing the issue of affect and CHD. This combination of circumstances, on the face of it, presents a compelling argument for the salience of stress and anxiety in the genesis or precipitation of CHD and its complications. Yet a careful examination of the evidence recommends that the understandable enthusiasm surrounding it be tempered with some necessary caution in its interpretation.

A number of methodological issues bear directly on the interpretation of much of the data, and due regard to these poses crucial questions about their acceptability. Many of the studies, particularly those examining life events in relation to CHD, were retrospective in design, and the potential for errors in life event recall when sought in the context of the experience of symptoms cannot be discounted (although the magnitude of this contaminating effect is largely unknown). Moreover, samples have frequently been poorly defined, seldom random, and not typically amenable to independent replication; this has been a particular problem when patients have been used. Extraneous variables almost certainly bearing on either the genesis or precipitation of CHD (physical condition, age, diet, etc.) have seldom been anticipated, measured, or included in analyses. Each of these broad categories of methodological concern may be found in the consideration of stress and anxiety as they related to CHD.

The very measurement of stress has been the focus of much discussion and controversy in examinations of the link between it and CHD. A concept capable of broad conceptualization and definition poses particular difficulties in this respect because the operationalization of a definition forms a necessary prelude to the measurement of any construct. Nonetheless, the adoption of an approach to stress that conceives of it as a sequence of events flowing from environmental occurrences, through individual interpretation of those occurrences to both psychological and physiological responses (as set out in the early part of this chapter), does allow at least a systematic approach to measurement that has been followed in many studies. Moreover, in a good percentage of these, results have affirmed a statistical link between measures of one or more parts of this sequence and risk or presence of CHD. The measurement of anxiety as an affective state, whether in isolation or as one component of the "stress reaction" is more clear-cut, at least from the psychometric point of view, and has been dealt with in great detail in an earlier chapter. Thus, although much of the work linking stress and anxiety with CHD may be criticized on grounds of inadequate, inappropriate, or erroneous measurement, this criticism cannot be taken to support a total denial of associations between stress or anxiety and CHD.

Matthews and Haynes (1986), in a comprehensive review of the evidence linking the Type A behavior pattern with CHD, provided a list of epidemiological criteria by which the acceptability of studies may be judged. This list includes the strength and consistency of associations emerging from empirical studies, the specificity of the relationship, the presence of a temporal lag between measurement of the risk factor and the appearance of the clinical event, the establishment of a biological gradient between the level of the risk factor and the severity or frequency of the clinical event, the biological plausibility of the association, and the capacity to demonstrate the association experimentally. Few studies on stress or anxiety and CHD have been prospective in design and thus the criterion regarding temporality has seldom been satisfied. Moreover, in view of the nature of the measurement of stress in particular, it would seem very difficult indeed to establish a biological gradient between it and the severity or frequency of clinical events of CHD (in fact, the irregular temporal course of the pathogenesis and precipitation of CHD may preclude the establishment of this index per se).

However, a number of studies have revealed quite strong statistical relationships (retrospectively established) between various measures of stress or anxiety and various manifestations of CHD, and there has been a notable consistency of findings across studies (although not, of course, a totally uniform set of results). Moreover, in view of the evidence presented in previous chapters bearing on biological associations between states of stress or anxiety and disruptions to cardiovascular regulation, there is a definite biological plausibility to the view that both stress and anxiety might, in principle, contribute to CHD in one or more ways along the complex pathways of its pathogenesis and precipitation. The present evidence does, therefore, satisfy at least some of the criteria necessary to justify the establishment of a coronary risk.

Clearly, the present evidence does not present a compelling case for the acceptance of stress or anxiety as primary risk factors for CHD. This field will, for some time, remain enigmatic; apparent enough to tantalize but lacking sufficiently in concept and substance to preclude definitive statements. Indeed, the definitive study is almost impossible to carry out. It is certain that whatever future evidence is presented, the links between stress, anxiety, and CHD will not be simple, straightforward or uniform across individuals or settings. Yet it would be foolhardy to dismiss it totally. This is one area for which it is not trite to say that further research, on a large scale and methodologically rigorous, is necessary.

REFERENCES

Alfredson, L., Karasek, R., & Theorell, T. (1982). Myocardial infarction risk and psychosocial work environment: An analysis of the male Swedish working force. *Social Science and Medicine, 16,* 463–467.

Alfredson, L., & Theorell, T. (1983). Job characteristics of occupations and myocardial infarction risk. *Social Science and Medicine, 17,* 1487–1503.

Bass, C. (1984). Test–retest reliability and psychometric correlates of Bortner scale. *Journal of Psychosomatic Research, 28,* 289–300.

Beebe, G. W. (1975). Follow-up studies of World War II and Korean war prisoners. *American Journal of Epidemiology, 101,* 400–422.

Bengsston, C., Hallstrom, T., & Tibblin, G. (1973). Social factors, stress experience, and personality traits in women with ischaemic heart disease, compared to a population sample of women. *Acta Medica Scandinavica, 549,* 82–127.

Bianchi, G., Fergusson, D., & Walshe, J. (1978). Psychiatric antecedents of myocardial infarction. *Medical Journal of Australia, 16,* 297–301.

Blumenthal, J. A., Williams, R., Kong, Y., Schanberg, S. M., & Thompson, L. W. (1978). Type A behavior and angiographically documented coronary disease. *Circulation, 58,* 634–639.

Bolm-Audorff, U., & Siegrist, J. (1983). Occupational morbidity data in myocardial infarction. *Journal of Occupational Medicine, 25,* 367–371.

Boman, B. (1978). Psychosocial stress and ischaemic heart disease: A response to Tennant. *Australian, New Zealand Journal of Psychiatry, 40,* 580–583.

Brenner, M. H. (1979, September). Mortality and the national economy: A review, and the experience of England and Wales. *Lancet,* 568–573.

Brown, G. W., & Harris, T. (1978). *Social origins of depression.* London: Tavistock.

Brown, G. W., Harris, T., & Peto, J. (1973). Life events and psychiatric illness: Nature of the causal link. *Psychological Medicine, 3,* 159–176.

Byrne, D. G. (1981). Type A behavior, life events and myocardial infarction: Independent or related risk factors? *British Journal of Medical Psychology, 54,* 371–377.

Byrne, D. G. (1983). Personal determinants of life-events stress and myocardial infarction. *Psychotherapy and Psychosomatics, 40,* 106–114.

Byrne, D. G. (1984). Personal assessments of life event stress and the near future onset of psychological symptoms. *British Journal of Medical Psychology, 57,* 241–248.

Byrne, D. G. (1986). Psychological factors and disease. In N. J. King & A. Remeyi (Eds.). *Health care: A behavioral approach* (pp. 33–38). Sydney: Grune & Stratton.

Byrne, D. G. (1987). *The behavioral management of the cardiac patient.* Norwood, NJ: Ablex.

Byrne, D. G., & Rosenman, R. H. (1986). The Type A behavior pattern as a precursor to stressful events: A confluence of coronary risks. *British Journal of Medical Psychology, 58,* 75–82.

Byrne, D. G., Rosenman, R. H., Schiller, E., & Chesney, M. A. (1985). Consistency and variation among instruments supporting to measure the Type A behavior pattern. *Psychosomatic Medicine, 47,* 242–261.

Byrne, D. G., & Whyte, H. M. (1980). Life events and myocardial infarction revisited: The role of measures of individual impact. *Psychosomatic Medicine, 42,* 1–10.

Chandra, V., Szklo, M., Goldbreg, R., & Tonascia, J. (1983). The impact of marital status on survival after an acute myocardial infarction: A population-based study. *American Journal of Epidemiology, 117,* 320–325.

Chesney, M. A., Eagleston, J. R., & Rosenman, R. H. (1981). Type A behavior: Assessment and intervention. In C. K. Prokop & L. A. Bradley (Eds.), *Medical psychology* (pp. 20–36). New York: Academic Press.

Clayton, P. J., & Darvish, H. S. (1979). Course of depressive symptoms following the stress of bereavement. In J. Barrett, R. M. Rose, & G. L. Klerman (Eds.), *Stress and mental disorder.* New York: Raven Press.

Connolly, J. (1976, December). Life events before myocardial infarction. *Journal of Human Stress,* 3–17.

Cottington, E. M., Mathew, K. A., Talbott, E., & Kuller, L. H. (1980). Environmental events preceding sudden death in women. *Psychosomatic Medicine, 42,* 567–574.

DeFaire, U. (1975). Life change patterns prior to death in ischaemic heart disease: A study on death-discordant twins. *Journal of Psychosomatic Medicine, 19,* 273–278.

Dimsdale, J. E., Hackett, T. P., Block, P. C., & Hutter, A. M. (1978). Emotional correlates of Type A behavior pattern. *Psychosomatic Medicine, 40,* 580–583.

Eastwood, M. R., & Trevelyan, H. (1971). Stress and coronary heart disease. *Journal of Psychosomatic Research, 15,* 289-292.

Eaton, W. W., Sigal, J. J., & Weinfeld, M. (1982). Impairment in Holocaust survivors after 33 years: Data from an unbiased community sample. *American Journal of Psychiatry, 139,* 773-777.

Eysenck, H. J., & Fulker, D. (1982). The components of Type A behavior and its genetic determinants. *Activitas Nervosa Superieur (Suppl. 3),* 111-125.

Falger, P., Bressors, I., & Dijkstra, P. (1980). Levensloop patronen van hartinfarct patienten en van controlegroepen: Enkele overeenkomsten en verschillen. *Gerontolgie, 11,* 240-257.

Feather, E. H. (1982). Unemployment and its psychological correlates: A study of depressive symptoms, self-esteem, Protestant ethic values, attributional style, and apathy. *Australian Journal of Psychology, 34,* 309-323.

Francis, K. T. (1981). Perceptions of anxiety, hostility and depression in subjects exhibiting the coronary-prone behavior pattern. *Journal of Psychiatric Research, 16,* 183-190.

Frank, F. D., & Weintraub, J. (1973). Job satisfaction and mortality from coronary heart disease: Critique of some of the research. *Journal of Chronic Diseases, 36,* 251-354.

French, J. R. P., & Caplan, R. D. (1970). Psychosocial factors in coronary heart disease: Critique of some of the research. *Industrial Medicine and Surgery, 39,* 31-45.

Friedman, E. H., & Hellerstein, H. K. (1968). Occupational stress, law school hierarchy and coronary artery disease in Cleveland attorneys. *Psychosomatic Medicine, 30,* 72-86.

Gill, G. (1983). Study of mortality and autopsy findings amongst former prisoners of the Japanese. *Journal of the Royal Army Medical Corps, 129,* 11-13.

Goulston, K. J., Dent, O. F., Chapuis, P. H., Chapman, G., Smith, C. I., Tait, A. D., & Tennant, C. C. (1985). Gastrointestinal morbidity among World War II prisoners of war: 40 years on. *Medical Journal of Australia, 143,* 6-10.

Gupta, L. N., & Verma, R. K. (1983). Psychosocial antecedents of myocardial infarction. *Indian Journal of Medical Research, 77,* 697-701.

Haynes, S. G., Feinleib, M., & Kannel, W. B. (1980a). The relationship of psychosocial factors to coronary heart disease in the Framingham study. *American Journal of Epidemiology, 111,* 37-58.

Haynes, S., & Feinleib, M. (1980b). Women, work and coronary disease: Prospective findings from the Framingham heart study. *American Journal of Public Health, 70,* 133-141.

Haynes, S. G., Feinleib, M., Levine, S., Scotch, N., & Kannel, W. B. (1978). The relationship of psychosocial factors to coronary heart disease in the Framingham study: 2. Prevalence of coronary heart disease. *American Journal of Epidemiology, 107,* 384-402.

Haynes, R. B., Taylor, D. W., Sackett, D. L., Gibson, E. S., Bernholz, C. D., & Mukherjee, J. (1980). Can simple clinical measurement detect patient noncompliance? *Hypertension, 2,* 757-764.

Henderson, A. S., Byrne, D. G., & Duncan-Jones, P. (1981). *Neurosis and the social environment.* Sydney: Academic Press.

Herman, S., Blumenthal, J. A., Black, G. M., & Chesney, M. A. (1981). Self-ratings of Type A (coronary prone) adults: Do Type A's know they are Type A's? *Psychosomatic Medicine, 43,* 405-413.

Holmes, T. H., & Rahe, R. H. (1967). The social readjustment rating scale. *Journal of Psychosomatic Research, 11,* 213-218.

Irvine, J., Lyle, R. C., & Allon, R. (1982). Type A personality as psychopathology: Personality correlates and an abbreviated scoring system. *Journal of Psychosomatic Research, 26,* 183-189.

Jenkins, C. D. (1978). A comparative review of the interview and questionnaire methods in the assessment of the coronary-prone behavior pattern. In T. M. Dembroski, S. M. Weiss, J. L. Shields, S. G. Haynes, & M. Feinleib (Eds.), *Coronary-prone behavior* (pp. 71-88). New York: Springer-Verlag.

Karasek, R., Baker, D., Marxer, F., Ahlbom, A., & Theorell, T. (1981). Job decision latitude, job demands, and cardiovascular disease. *American Journal of Public Health, 71,* 694-705.

Kasl, S. V. (1978). Epidemiological contributions to the study of work stress. In C. Cooper & R. Payne (Eds.), *Stress at work* (pp. 1-48). New York: Wiley.

Kits van Heyningen, H., & Treurniet, N. (1966). Psychodynamic factors in acute myocardial infarction. *International Journal of Psychoanalysis, 47,* 370.

Klein, H. P., & Parsons, O. A. (1968). Self-descriptions of patients with coronary disease. *Perceptual Motor Skills, 26,* 1099.

Kornitzer, M., Kittel, F., Debacker, G., & Dramlax, M. (1981). The Belgian heart disease prevention project: Type A behavior pattern and the prevalence or coronary heart disease. *Psychosomatic Medicine, 43,* 133-145.

Kornitzer, M., Thilly, C. H., Van Roux, A., & Balthazar, R. (1975). Incidence of ischaemic heart disease in two cohorts of Belgian clerks. *British Journal of Preventive and Social Medicine, 29,* 91-97.

Langeluddecke, P., & Tennant, C. (1986). Psychological correlates of the Type A behavior pattern in coronary angiography patients. *British Journal of Medical Psychology, 59,* 141–148.

Langosch, W., Brodner, G., & Borcherding, H. (1983). Psychological and vocational longterm outcomes of cardiac rehabilitation with post-infarction patients under the age of forty. *Psychotherapy and Psychosomatics, 40,* 115–128.

Lazarus, R. S. (1966). *Psychological stress and the coping process.* New York: McGraw-Hill.

Lazarus, R. S. (1982). Thoughts on the relations between emotion and cognition. *American Psychologist, 36,* 1019–1024.

Levav, I., & Abrahamson, J. H. (1984). Emotional distress among concentration camp survivors: A community study in Jerusalem. *Psychological Medicine, 14,* 215–218.

Liljefors, I., & Rahe, R. H. (1970). An identical twin study of psychosocial factors in coronary heart disease in Sweden. *Psychosomatic Medicine, 32,* 523–542.

Lundberg, U., Theorell, T., & Lind, E. (1975). Life changes and myocardial infarction revised: Individual differences in life change scaling. *Journal of Psychosomatic Research, 42,* 27–32.

MacKay, D. M. (1974). The effect of civil war on the health of a rural community in Bangladesh. *Journal of Tropical Medical Hygiene, 77,* 120–127.

Magni, G., Corfini, A., Berto, F., Rizzardo, R., Bombardelli, S., & Miraglia, G. (1983). Life events and myocardial infarction. *Australian, New Zealand Journal of Medicine, 13,* 257–260.

Magnus, K., Matroos, A. W., & Strackee, J. (1983). The self-employed and the self-driven: Two coronary prone sub-populations from the Zeist study. *American Journal of Epidemiology, 118,* 799–805.

Mandler, G. (1984). *Mind and body.* New York: Norton.

Maschewsky, W. (1982). The relation between stress and myocardial infarction: A general analysis. *Social Science and Medicine, 16,* 455–462.

Matthews, K. A., & Haynes, S. (1986). Type A behavior pattern and coronary disease risk: Update and critical evaluation. *American Journal of Epidemiology, 123,* 923–960.

Mundal, R., Erikssen, J., & Rodahl, K. (1982). Latent ischaemic heart disease in sea captains. *Scandinavian Journal of Work Environment and Health, 8,* 178–184.

Myrtek, M., & Greenlee, M. W. (1984). Psychophysiology of Type A behavior pattern: A critical analysis. *Journal of Psychosomatic Research, 28,* 455–466.

Orth-Gomer, K. (1979). Ischemic heart disease and psychological stress in Stockholm and New York. *Journal of Psychosomatic Research, 23,* 165–173.

Parkes, C. M., Benjamin, B., & Fitzgerald, R. G. (1969). Broken heart: A statistical study of increased mortality among widowers. *British Medical Journal, 1,* 740–743.

Portnoy, I. (1959). The anxiety states. In S. Ariete (Ed.), *American handbook of psychiatry* (pp. 73–96). New York: Basic Books.

Price, V. A. (1983). *Type A behavior pattern: A model for research and practice.* New York: Academic Press.

Rachman, S. (1978). *Fear and courage.* San Francisco: Freeman.

Rees, W. D., & Lutkins, S. G. (1967). Mortality of bereavement. *British Medical Journal, 4,* 13–16.

Richardson, H. J. (1965). Disabilities and problems of Hong Kong Veterans 1964–1965. *Repeat to Canadian Pensions Commission.* Ottawa, Canada: Author.

Roper Organization Incorporated. (1980). *Report to the US Federal Trade Commission on a survey conducted for the Commission.* New York: Author.

Rosenhan, D. L., & Seligman, M. E. P. (1984). *Abnormal psychology.* New York: Norton.

Rosenman, R. H., & Chesney, M. A. (1980). The relationship of Type A behavior pattern to coronary heart disease. *Activitas Nervosa Superieur, 22,* 1–45.

Russek, H. I. (1960). Emotional stress and coronary heart disease in American physicians. *American Journal of Medical Sciences, 39,* 711–721.

Russek, H. I. (1965). Stress, tobacco, and coronary heart disease in North American professional groups. *Journal of the American Medical Association, 192,* 89–94.

Sales, S. M., & House, J. (1971). Job dissatisfaction as a possible risk factor in coronary heart disease. *Journal of Chronic Diseases, 23,* 861–873.

Schwartz, P. J. (1984). Stress and sudden cardiac death: The role of the autonomic nervous system. *Journal of Psychology, 2,* 7–13.

Siegrist, J. (1984). Threat to social status and cardiovascular risk. *Psychotherapy and Psychosomatics, 42,* 90–96.

Smith, T. W. (1984). Type A behavior, anger and neuroticism: The discriminant validity of self-reports in a patient sample. *British Journal of Clinical Psychology, 23,* 147–148.

Spittle, B., & James, B. (1977). Psychosocial factors and myocardial infarction. *Australian, New Zealand Journal of Psychiatry, 11,* 37–43.

Surwit, R. S., Williams, R. B., & Shapiro, D. (1982). *Behavioral approaches to cardiovascular disease.* New York: Academic Press.

Talbott, E., Kuller, L. H., & Perper, J. (1981). Sudden unexpected death in women: Biologic and psychosocial origins. *American Journal of Epidemiology, 144,* 671–682.

Tennant, C., Goulston, K., & Dent, O. (1986). Clinical psychiatric illness in prisoners of war of the Japanese 40 years after release. *Psychological Medicine, 16,* 833–839.

Tennant, C., Langeluddecke, P., & Byrne, D. G. (1985). The concept of stress. *Australian, New Zealand Journal of Psychiatry, 19,* 113–118.

Theorell, T. (1974). Life events before and after the onset of a premature myocardial infarction. In B. S. Dohrenwend & B. P. Dohrenwend (Eds.), *Stressful life events: Their nature and effect* (pp. 101–118). New York: Wiley.

Theorell, J., & Floderus-Myrhed, B. (1977). "Workload" and risk of myocardial infarction: A prospective psychosocial analysis. *International Journal of Epidemiology, 6,* 17–21.

Theorell, T., Lind, E., Froberg, J., Karlsson, C. G., & Levi, L. (1972). A longitudinal study of 21 subjects with coronary heart disease: Life changes, catecholomine excretion and related biochemical reactions. *Psychosomatic Medicine, 34,* 505–516.

Theorell, T., & Rahe, R. H. (1971). Psychosocial factors and myocardial infarction: 1. An inpatient study in Sweden. *Journal of Psychosomatic Research, 15,* 25–31.

Theorell, T., & Rahe, R. H. (1975). Life change events, ballistocardiography and coronary death. *Journal of Human Stress, 3,* 18–25.

Thiel, H. G., Parker, D., & Bruce, T. A. (1973). Stress factors and the risk of myocardial infarction. *Journal of Psychosomatic Research, 17,* 43.

Trichopoulos, D., Zavitsanos, X., Katsouyanni, K., Tzonou, A., & Dalla-Vorg, I. P. (1983). Psychological stress and heart attack: The Athens (1981) Earthquake natural experiment. *Journal of Tropical Medical Hygiene, 77,* 120–127.

Vickers, R. R., Hervig, L. K., Rahe, R. H., & Rosenman, R. H. (1981). Type A behavior pattern and coping defense. *Psychosomatic Medicine, 43,* 381–396.

Vingerhoets, A. J. J. M., & Flohr, P. J. M. (1984). Type A behavior and self-reports of coping preferences. *British Journal of Medical Psychology, 47,* 15–21.

Wadden, T. A., Anderson, C. H., Foster, G. D., & Love, W. (1983). The Jenkins Activity Survey: Does it measure psychopathology? *Journal of Pschyosomatic Research, 27,* 321–325.

Williams, R. B., Haney, T. L., Lee, K. L., Kong, Y., Blumenthal, J. A., & Whalen, R. E. (1980). Type A behavior, hostility and coronary atherosclerosis. *Psychosomatic Medicine, 42,* 539–549.

Zorn, E. W., Harrington, J. M., & Goethe, H. (1977). Ischemic heart disease and work stress in West German sea pilots. *Journal of Occupational Medicine, 19,* 762–765.

Zyzanski, S. J., Jenkins, C. D., Ryan, T. J., Flessas, A., & Everist, M. (1976). Psychological correlates of coronary angiographic findings. *Archives of Internal Medicine, 136,* 1234–1237.

9

Silent Myocardial Ischemia in Patients with Angina Pectoris: The Effects of Mental Stress and the Role of Psychological Factors

Michael J. Shea, John E. Deanfield,
Christian M. DeLandsheere, Richard A. Wilson,
Malcolm Kensett, Peter Horlock, and Andrew P. Selwyn

Clinicians have long observed asymptomatic, transient episodes of (a) ST-segment depression on the electrocardiogram (EKG), (b) wall motion abnormalities during echocardiography and ventriculography, and (c) perfusion abnormalities during radio-nuclide scintigraphy. Only recently investigators have pursued systematic studies of this phenomenon of silent myocardial ischemia. However, the triggers of silent myocardial ischemia have been poorly understood. In this chapter we emphasize the effect of one trigger, mental arousal, in provoking both symptomatic and asymptomatic ischemia in patients with coronary disease. The objective measurements of ischemia include studies with electrocardiographic monitoring of ST-segments and the assessment of regional myocardial perfusion using positron emission tomography (PET) with rubidium-82 (Rb-82).

CONTINUOUS ELECTROCARDIOGRAPHIC MONITORING

A conventional indicator of myocardial ischemia is ST-segment depression on the EKG (Schamroth, 1984). Ambulant electrocardiographic recordings for 24–48 hours in patients with known ischemic heart disease suggest that ST-segment depression is surprisingly frequent (Deanfield et al., 1983; Schang & Pepine, 1977; Selwyn et al., 1978; Stern & Tzivoni, 1974). Also, the episodes of ST-segment depression accompanied by symptoms are far fewer than those episodes unaccompanied by symptoms.

Thirty patients with angina pectoris and arteriographically confirmed coronary artery disease were investigated extensively (Deanfield et al., 1983). The investigations included four days of continuous ambulant electrocardiographic recordings in

We thank Joan Stea for her excellent secretarial help. This work was supported by grants from the Medical Research Council of Great Britain, the British Heart Foundation, the American Heart Association and a private gift from Mr. and Mrs. Milford Boersma. The parent strontium-82 of the Sr-82/Rb-82 generator was a kind gift from the Clinton P. Anderson Meson Physics facility at the Los Alamos Scientific Laboratory, New Mexico.

each patient. In addition, 20 patients underwent serial electrocardiographic recording over 18 months. There were 1,934 episodes of ST-segment depression observed during 446 days of recording, but only 470 (20% of the total episodes) episodes were accompanied by angina pectoris (see Figure 1). The ischemia observed during ambulant recordings was more variable in frequency and considerably more prolonged than that observed during the conventional stimulus of exercise treadmill provocation. Thus the ambulant recordings gave a far different view of the ischemic events in a patient's life as compared to the traditional exercise treadmill test. Additional observations suggested that the heart rates at the onset of both symptomatic and asymptomatic episodes during the ambulant recordings were significantly lower than the heart rates at the onset of ST depression during exercise testing. This suggests that ischemia occurring out-of-hospital may be occurring because of a limitation of oxygen supply rather than oxygen demand.

The importance of ST-segment depression on electrocardiographic recordings has been questioned by some investigators who observed frequent ST-segment shifts in patients without clinical evidence for coronary artery disease (Armstrong, Jordan, Morris, & McHenry, 1982; Crawford et al., 1978), whereas others have found fewer problems with spurious ST-segment changes (Deanfield, Ribeiro, Oakley, Krikler, & Selwyn, 1985). The importance of electrocardiographic changes would be strengthened if an additional, independent measure of ischemia were employed. For this reason, we used PET to investigate symptomatic and asymptomatic myocardial ischemia in patients with coronary disease.

POSITRON EMISSION TOMOGRAPHY

Positron emission tomography is an analytical imaging technique that provides a noninvasive method for assessing regional organ physiology. Among the earliest advances using this technique have been studies of brain function and biochemistry (Phelps & Mazziotta, 1985). More recently, PET has been applied to cardiology (Shea, Wilson, Deanfield, DeLandsheere, & Selwyn, 1983; Wilson et al., 1984). The principal attractions of PET include its instrumentation and positron-emitting radiopharmaceuticals. Positrons that collide with electrons result in annihilation photons of 511 KeV traveling in opposite directions. A scanner will detect the annihilation event only if the two photons are detected simultaneously. Thus random photons are excluded. In this fashion, the density of positrons, which reflects the positron-emitting radiopharmaceuticals viewed by the scanning device, can be determined by computer reconstruction techniques. The resultant image reflects the concentration and distribution of tracer within the field of view. Positron emitters tend to be organic elements such as carbon-11 ($t^{1}/_{2}$ = 20.1 min), nitrogen-13 ($t^{1}/_{2}$ = 10 min), or oxygen-15 ($t^{1}/_{2}$ = 2.1 min). These positron emitters can be incorporated into naturally occurring substrates such as water or fatty acids and therefore can be utilized to investigate physiologic processes.

Measurement of Regional Myocardial Perfusion

The assessment of coronary blood flow and myocardial perfusion is of major clinical and research value because the physiologic importance of coronary stenoses can be determined. Thallium-201 scintigraphy is a single-photon technique that has found wide application in clinical and experimental cardiology to assess myocardial

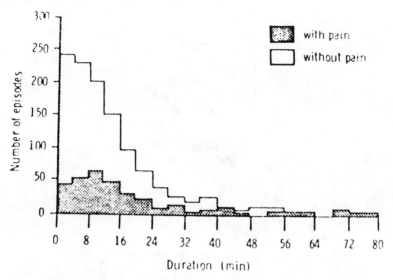

Figure 1 The distribution of symptomatic and asymptomatic episodes of ST-segment depression detected during 96 hours or more of ambulatory electrocardiographic monitoring in 30 patients with angina pectoris and coronary disease. From Deanfield et al. (1983). Reprinted by permission of publisher and authors.

perfusion (Pitt & Strauss, 1979). Unfortunately there are methodologic and technical drawbacks in using this tracer (Allan & Selwyn, 1982). A theoretically more appealing approach is to use a suitable flow tracer with PET to measure regional tissue perfusion.

Cations such as nitrogen-13 ammonia and Rb-82 have been used extensively as tracers for the study of myocardial perfusion (Selwyn et al., 1982; Shea, Deanfield, Wilson et al., 1987). Rb-82 is especially attractive because it is a generator-produced positron emitter. The convenient use of a generator enables the clinician to be free from the difficulties in scheduling when using a cyclotron-produced tracer. Also, the short half-life of the tracer (78 sec) allows the investigator to perform multiple scans of physiologic events of interest over a short time interval.

The use of Rb-82 as a flow tracer has been supported by both experimental and clinical investigations. In the open-chest, anesthetized dog, Rb-82 acts the same as other cations. The myocardial uptake of cation is related to blood flow and extraction (see Figure 2), although flow and extraction are inversely related so that at low flow rates extraction of cation is increased, but at higher flow rates cation extraction is diminished (Selwyn et al., 1982; Shea, Wilson et al., 1987; Wilson et al., 1987).

As Figure 3 shows, in patients with prior myocardial infarction, measurements of Rb-82 uptake were compared to regional myocardial blood flow as determined by carbon-11 labeled human albumin microspheres (Shea, Wilson et al., 1985). The distribution of cation uptake was directly related to myocardial blood flow as determined by the positron-labeled microspheres. In regions of infarcted myocardium, Rb-82 uptake was diminished, reflecting the decrease in blood flow. In normal, noninfarcted regions of myocardium, Rb-82 uptake and microsphere flow were normal.

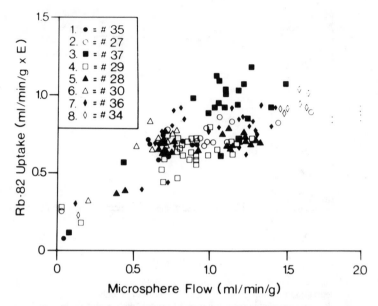

Figure 2 The results of several experimental canine studies relating microsphere
blood flow (abscissa) to Rb-82 uptake (ordinate). At high flow rates,
cation uptake underestimates flow, whereas at lower flow rates cation
uptake overestimates flow. These observations are explained by the
inverse relations between blood flow and extraction of cation. These
experimental observations support the use of rubidium-82 as a flow
tracer in humans. From Shea, Wilson et al., 1987. Reprinted by
permission of publisher and authors.

Thus the distribution of Rb-82 in the myocardium correlates well with regional
myocardial blood flow.

CLINICAL STUDIES WITH RUBIDIUM-82

Technique

A detailed description of the theory behind the equilibrium approach has been
previously published (Selwyn et al., 1982). A single mid-left ventricular slice is
identified for baseline and subsequent scanning with the ECAT II (made by Ortec,
Inc.). Rb-82 is eluted intermittently from an Sr-82/Rb-82 generator using an infusion
of 10 ml/min of saline. Tomography is then performed to record the arterial/left
ventricular concentration of cation delivered to the coronary arteries. The infusion is
stopped, and after clearing of the blood pool, a subsequent tomogram is performed to
record the regional myocardial activity of tracer. The second tomogram is normalized
to the arterial input function with the resultant tomogram representing Rb-82 uptake.

Following computer reconstruction, images are expressed in a matrix of 100 ×
100 pixels. The myocardium is identified by enclosing all the pixels with values >
50% of the peak value. In the first or baseline tomogram obtained for each patient,
five large anatomic regions of interest are identified for comparison to later tomo-

grams. These regions of interest include the interventricular septum, the anterior myocardium and the lateral wall of the left ventricle. Tomographic measurements are made at rest and following different provocations. Additional measures include heart rate, systolic blood pressure, the EKG, and assessment of the patients' symptoms. Patients are recruited for PET investigations after a complete clinical evaluation. Typically, these are outpatients with stable, effort angina pectoris who have positive exercise treadmill tests and arteriographic evidence of coronary artery disease.

Supine Bicycle Exercise

In the initial studies of PET with Rb-82, the ischemic provocation was supine bicycle exercise because exertional chest pain was the chief complaint in the outpatient clinics. Characteristically, patients developed increases in Rb-82 uptake in normal, nonischemic regions of myocardium, whereas Rb-82 uptake was decreased in the affected ischemic segments (see Figure 4). Angina pectoris and ST-segment depression usually accompanied the tomographic changes. These observations were

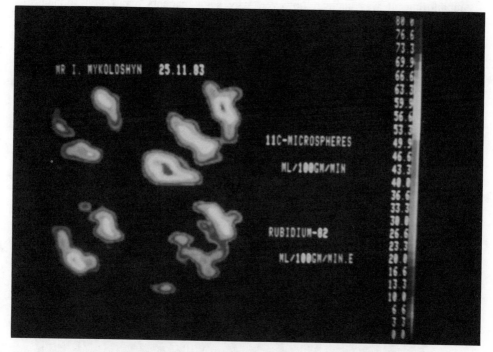

Figure 3 The distribution of regional myocardial blood flow (C^{11} labeled human serum albumin microspheres) is similar to regional myocardial Rb-82 uptake in a patient with a previous anterior myocardial infarction. Each image is a transaxial tomogram with the following orientation: 12:00–3:00 anteroseptal myocardium, 3:00–6:00 mitral orifice, 6:00–9:00 lateral myocardium, 9:00–12:00 anterolateral myocardium. The images in the upper half of the figure represent successive tomograms, rostrad and caudad, after microsphere injections. The bottom two images represent Rb-82 uptake in successive tomograms, rostrad and caudad. From Shea, Wilson et al. (1985). Reprinted by permission of publisher and authors.

reproducible when paired exercise tests were performed at the same visit, and they were also reproducible over time. In normal volunteers, Rb-82 uptake increased uniformly throughout the myocardium in response to exercise stress without evidence for regional inhomogeneities. Despite the inverse relationship between flow and extraction of cations, the physiologic response to an increase in internal work was to increase cation uptake throughout the myocardium.

"Spontaneous" Ischemia

Early in the course of the studies with exercise, it was noted that some patients developed apparent episodes of spontaneous ischemia (see Figure 5). These episodes were usually painless, often had associated ST-segment depression, and invariably revealed tomographic perfusion defects in the same regions of myocardium that were abnormal during previous exercise provocations (Shea, Deanfield, et al., 1985). The heart rates and systolic blood pressures during the spontaneous events were usually higher than during the baseline periods, yet the values never approached those observed during exercise. Of additional interest, several of these patients manifested asymptomatic episodes of ST-segment depression during continuous ambulatory monitoring. It was unclear, however, why some patients manifested spontaneous events and others did not. In comparing the clinical profiles of those who demonstrated spontaneous ischemia versus those who did not, there were no evident differ-

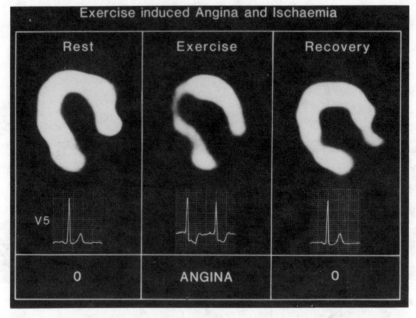

Figure 4   A set of tomograms for a patient with angina and coronary disease. At rest there is uniform uptake of Rb-82 with a normal electrocardiographic tracing and no symptoms. With exercise the patient develops a decrease in Rb-82 uptake to the free wall of the left ventricle. Along with the tomographic abnormality, the patient develops angina and ST-segment depression. In the third tomogram there is complete recovery.

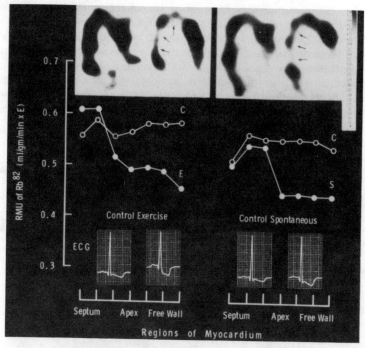

Figure 5 A patient with angina developed symptomatic ischemia in response to exercise and an apparent "spontaneous" ischemic event associated with electrocardiographic and tomographic abnormalities but no symptoms. The regional myocardial uptake of Rb-82 is graphed under each of the accompanying images. Note that the spontaneous event occurred in the same region of myocardium that was previously abnormal following exercise. From Shea et al. (1983). Reprinted by permission of publisher and authors.

ences, and none of the patients was felt to have Prinzmetal variant angina. Although the reasons for the spontaneous events were not readily apparent, these findings were important for subsequent investigations for two reasons. First, they supported and extended the observations that asymptomatic ST-depression in patients with known coronary disease was a likely manifestation of ischemia (Deanfield, Shea, Ribeiro et al., 1984). Also, the findings raised the potentiality that if the explanations for spontaneous ischemia were not related to demographic differences then possibly they were the results of some type of provocation.

Mental Stress

Among the classic precipitants of angina pectoris, emotion and mental arousal were well described by Hunter (1794) and Heberden (1818). More recently, stressful situations such as driving or public speaking have been shown to induce ST-segment depression in patients with coronary disease (Taggart, Carruthers, & Somerville, 1973; Taggart, Gibbons, & Somerville, 1969). Accordingly, we investigated the effect of a simple mental stress, subtraction of 7 from 100, and compared that to the traditional ischemic stimulus of exercise in 16 patients with angina and coronary disease and 13 normal volunteers (Deanfield, Shea, Kensett et al., 1984). Twelve of 16 patients developed tomographic evidence of ischemia, yet only 4 patients had angina with ST-depression and an additional 2 patients developed asymptomatic ST-segment depression (see Figures 6–8). Six patients had tomographic evidence of ischemia with no electrocardiographic or symptomatic abnormalities. In the entire group, all patients developed ST-segment depression and tomographic abnormalities during supine exercise that were regionally concordant with those observed during

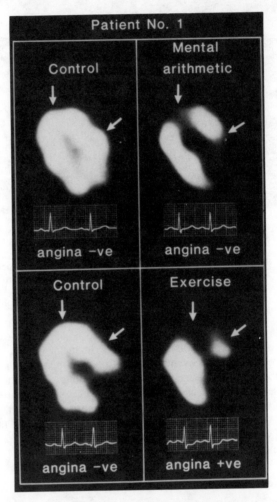

Figure 6 Control tomograms show homogeneous uptake of Rb-82. Following mental arithmetic and exercise there is anteroseptal ischemia, but only with exercise do symptoms and electrocardiographic changes occur. From Deanfield, Shea, Kensett et al. (1984). Reprinted by permission of publisher and authors.

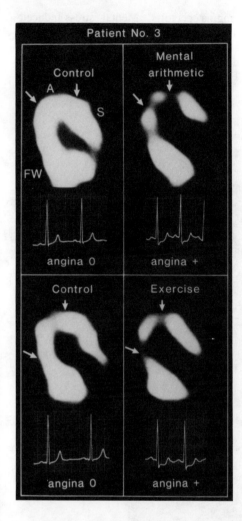

Figure 7 Control tomograms show homogeneous uptake of Rb-82. Following mental arithmetic and exercise the patient develops anterolateral ischemia with accompanying electrocardiographic changes and symptoms. From Deanfield, Shea, Kensett et al. (1984). Reprinted by permission of publisher and authors.

mental stress. Angina was present in all but one of the patients during exercise. In normal volunteers no symptoms or electrocardiographic changes developed, but regional myocardial perfusion did increase uniformly throughout the myocardium, more so with exercise than with mental stress.

An analysis of the hemodynamic changes revealed that mental stress-induced ischemia was occurring at a lower heart rate, 87 ± 10 beats/min, as compared to that during supine bicycle exercise, 108 ± 10 beats/min, whereas the blood pressure responses were identical. Furthermore, an analysis of Rb-82 uptake in the ischemic regions revealed similar decrements with both mental arithmetic and exercise. In view of the hemodynamic changes, it is interesting to speculate that the similar degrees of tomographic ischemia could be explained only by a more marked reduction in myocardial blood flow following mental stress, possibly owing to vasospasm. This speculation is also supported by the studies of Schiffer and colleagues (Schiffer, Hartley, Schulman, & Abelman, 1980), who used a stressful quiz to induce presumed coronary artery spasm in patients with angina pectoris. Mental stress-induced myocardial ischemia may also be an important trigger in another ischemic syndrome—sudden cardiac death. Specchia et al. (1984) described a patient who developed angina pectoris and ST-segment depression followed by ventricular tachycardia after a mental arithmetic stress (see Figure 9).

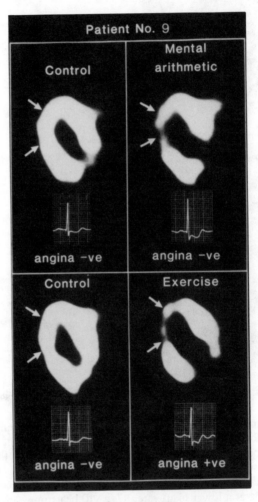

Figure 8 Control tomograms show homogeneous uptake of Rb-82. Following mental stress, lateral wall ischemia develops with accompanying electrocardiographic changes but no symptoms. Following exercise, lateral wall ischemia occurs along with electrocardiographic changes and angina pectoris. From Deanfield, Shea, Kensett et al. (1984). Reprinted by permission of publisher and authors.

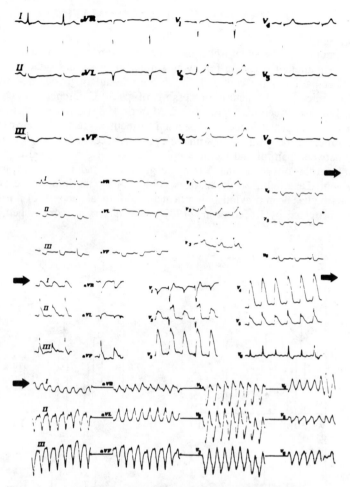

Figure 9 In A, the baseline electrocardiogram reveals nonspecific ST–T wave
changes. In B, a mental arithmetic stress test lends to anterior
ST-segment elevation followed by ventricular tachycardia that
required electrical defibrillation. From Specchia et al. (1984).
Reprinted by permission of publisher and authors.

These studies suggest that following a relatively simple provocation such as mental
arithmetic, patients with coronary disease manifest symptomatic and asymptomatic
myocardial ischemia. In selected patients the ischemia may prove to be a suitable
milieu for the development of life-threatening arrhythmias. Whereas mental stress is
one activity of daily life that can provoke myocardial ischemia, we also observed that
other activities such as smoking (Deanfield et al., 1986), mastication (Shea, Deanfield, Wilson, DeLandsheere, & Selwyn, 1987), or cold exposure (Shea, Deanfield,
DeLandsheere et al., 1987) could trigger the development of both symptomatic and
asymptomatic ischemia in similar types of patients.

MECHANISMS OF ASYMPTOMATIC
MYOCARDIAL ISCHEMIA

Why a patient manifests silent ischemia on one occasion and symptomatic myocardial ischemia on another occasion following similar or dissimilar ischemic stimuli is unknown. Speculations have centered on (a) the amount of myocardial tissue that becomes ischemic and (b) neural processing of pain. Chierchia and co-workers (Chierchia, Lazzari, Freedman, Brunelli, & Maseri, 1983) observed that symptomatic ischemic events lasted longer and seemed to incur a greater impairment in left ventricular function than did asymptomatic episodes (see Figure 10). Some of the differences between painful and painless episodes may also be related to the differences in myocardial oxygen demand that are generated under different physiologic stimuli (Selwyn, Deanfield, Shea, & Jones, 1986). Also, the importance of physiologic vasomotion has been previously implicated. Additional support for this hypothesis has been provided by Rocco et al. (1987), who observed more ischemic events

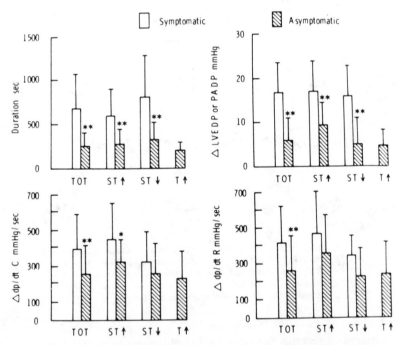

Figure 10 Comparison of symptomatic and asymptomatic episodes of ST-segment and T-wave changes in 14 patients with rest angina pectoris. The mean values and standard deviation are plotted for the duration in episodes, the increases in left ventricular end-diastolic pressure (LVEDP) or pulmonary artery diastolic pressure (PADP), and reduction of left ventricular peak contraction (C) and relaxation (R) dp/dt. *$p = <0.01$; **$p = 0.001$. Overall, asymptomatic ischemic episodes were shorter in duration and accompanied by lesser degrees of left ventricular impairment. ST ↑ or ↓ = transient ST elevation or depression; T ↑ = transient pseudonormalization or peaking of inverted or flat T waves; TOT = total events. From Chierchia et al. (1983). Reprinted by permission of publisher and authors.

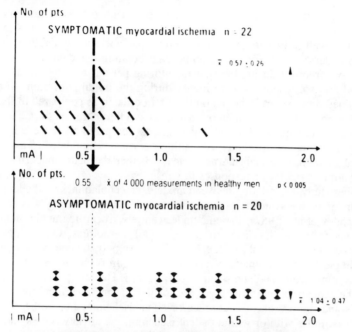

Figure 11 Electrical pain threshold in 22 patients with symptomatic
myocardial ischemia and 20 patients with asymptomatic
myocardial ischemia. Asymptomatic patients exhibited
significantly higher mean threshold of pain than symptomatic
patients on normal controls. From Droste and Roskamm (1983).
Reprinted by permission of publisher and authors.

occurring in the early morning hours after awakening instead of in the evening. This
may be explained by circadian variations in coronary vasomotor tone.

Differences in neural processing of pain have been emphasized by Droste and
Roskamm (1983). They studied 22 patients who had angina pectoris and ST-
depression during exercise electrocardiography and 20 patients who had asymptomatic ST-segment depression during exercise electrocardiography. No differences were
found between the patient groups in functional variables, coronary angiographic data
or risk factors for coronary disease (see Figure 11). When various experimental pain
measures were applied, the patients with asymptomatic myocardial ischemia had
higher pain thresholds to electrical, cold, and ischemic stimuli. The authors speculated that altered endorphinic mechanisms might be important to explain the observed
differences between the two groups of patients. However, a recent study from Austria
failed to show any effect of naloxone in patients with asymptomatic exertional ischemia (Weidinger et al., 1986).

The Role of Psychological Stress

Freeman, Nixon, and Sallabank (1987) investigated silent myocardial ischemia
and the role of psychological stress in patients who underwent cardiac catheterization
but who were not told of the results until 8 days later. Electrocardiographic monitor-

ing of ST-segments was performed at the time of catheterization and later after a discussion of results. All patients completed the General Health Questionnaire, a questionnaire well validated to screen medical patients for vulnerability to mental stress, and underwent urinary collection for catecholamines and cortisol. Silent ischemia was more frequent during the first monitoring period, and the urinary catecholamines and cortisol responses were higher during the initial collection. In those patients who had more silent ischemia on the first occasion as compared to the second, there were more diary entries of emotional upset and the scores on the General Health Questionnaire were higher for those patients as compared to those without silent ischemia. Therefore, in this study, psychological stress was related to asymptomatic myocardial ischemia although it was unclear whether the neuroendocrine responses were mediating variables or responses to stress.

In another study, the relation between anxiety, catecholamines, and silent ischemia in a group of patients undergoing aortocoronary bypass grafting was investigated (Shea, Sachdev et al., 1987). Patients underwent electrocardiographic monitoring of ST-segments from the day prior to surgery until sternotomy. On the day prior to surgery, patients also completed the State–Trait Anxiety Inventory and provided a venous sample for measurement of catecholamines. In 6 out of 18 patients, 37 episodes of asymptomatic ST-depression were observed. However, there was no relation between the acute or chronic anxiety scores or the plasma norepinephrine or epinephrine levels and the presence or absence of silent ischemia. For both groups of patients, that is, those with or without silent ischemia, the anxiety scores and catecholamine levels were higher than for general medical patients. The failure to observe a difference in anxiety scores or neuroendocrine variables may have been related to high levels of baseline stress in patients about to undergo a major surgical procedure.

Janne and co-workers (Janne, Reynaert, DeCoster, Cassiers, & Kremer, 1987) investigated the role of denial in two groups of patients: One group had angina, myocardial ischemia, and coronary disease and a second group had myocardial ischemia (confirmed by exercise thallium scintigraphy) and coronary disease but no anginal symptoms. Both groups were given descriptive self-rating scores in order to determine the tendency to acknowledge or deny: the Present Sickness Index, the Illness Assessment, and the Cardiac Disease Probability Assessment. Patients with silent ischemia had higher scores on all three denial scores than did the group with symptomatic ischemia. These studies suggest that psychological factors may be important in the genesis of silent ischemia. Clearly, further investigation is needed.

PROGNOSIS

Because the prognosis of asymptomatic ischemia requires some knowledge of its epidemiology, firm statements can be made only for limited populations. The majority of patients who have never had symptoms will probably go undetected until they present with one of the ischemic syndromes: stable angina pectoris, unstable angina pectoris, acute myocardial infarction, or sudden cardiac death. It is of interest that in a study of men given the Multiple Risk Factor Intervention Trial (MRFIT), those individuals with an ischemic response to exercise electrocardiographiy upon entry, who were in the usual care group, had an excess cardiovascular mortality as compared to (a) those who had negative exercise EKGs upon entry irrespective of usual care of special intervention or (b) those who had ischemic responses to exercise but who had special intervention (MRFIT Research Group, 1985). It should be noted that all men who entered this trial were asymptomatic at entry into the study. In the MRFIT trail, coronary artery arteriography was not performed; therefore, the presence or absence of coronary disease was unknown. In separate studies of patients with documented coronary artery disease who were totally asymptomatic but who manifested physiologic evidence of ischemia during functional testing, the yearly mortality appears to be 2%–3% (Cohn, 1986).

In patients with symptomatic and asymptomatic ischemia, prospective prognostic data is lacking. We have followed a single patient with serial ambulatory electrocardiographic recordings who developed more frequent episodes of silent ST-depression until an infarction occurred. This patient also had angina pectoris during the course of the electrocardiographic recordings, but the asymptomatic episodes of ischemia far outnumbered the symptomatic events. In patients with unstable angina pectoris, the presence of silent myocardial ischemia during electrocardiographic recordings predicts an unfavorable one-month outcome, with more patients needing revascularization or ending up with myocardial infarction (Gottlieb, Weisfeldt, Ouyang, Mellits, & Gerstenblith, 1986).

Since 1948 more than 5,000 patients have been followed and given a biennial cardiovascular examination including electrocardiography (the Framingham Study). Kannel and Abbott (1984) observed a 25% incidence of unrecognized myocardial infarctions out of 708 total infarcts detected during the study period. About half of the unrecognized infarcts were truly silent. Although plaque rupture and thrombotic occlusion may play a role in some patients who develop infarction without a preinfarction syndrome, it is likely that the majority of patients with silent myocardial infarction have increasingly frequent and prolonged episodes of silent ischemia preceding their infarctions. Kannel and Abbott (1984) also pointed out that the long-term outcome following infarction is no different whether the event is symptomatic or asymptomatic. This is a sobering observation considering that some clinicians have felt that asymptomatic infarcts are relatively benign.

MANAGEMENT

A retrospective assessment of the MRFIT (1985) suggested that if special interventions are applied to those patients with ischemic responses to exercise elecrocardiography, subsequent cardiovascular mortality is decreased and is similar to those who have negative exercise test responses. Therefore, it is reasonable to proceed with risk-factor modification in those individuals who have one or more coronary risk factors. The argument to use prophylactic drug therapy for the totally asymptomatic patient who has documented myocardial ischemia is a hotly debated issue for which there are inadequate prospective data. Our practice has been to make that determination case-by-case. The presence of hypertension or left ventricular hypetrophy on the EKG would lower our threshold to treat these patients with beta-blockers or calcium-channel blockers. For the patient with symptomatic myocardial ischemia who also has objective evidence of asymptomatic ischemia, our practice has been to treat the symptoms. Whether suppression of all ischemia will decrease morbidity and mortality is unknown at present.

Although the pathophysiology of silent ischemic events is uncertain, there is some suggestion that a primary reduction in blood flow may be important. If this is the case, one might expect that nitrates or calcium channel blockers would be the ideal agents because of their efficacy in treating coronary vasospasm. The evidence suggests that nitrates, beta-blockers, calcium-blockers, and possibly some anti-platelet agents are all effective in treating silent ischemia (Hill & Pepine, 1986). Based on the available data, no class of drugs seems to be superior.

For the patient with mental stress-induced silent ischemia, it is intriguing to speculate that sedative-hypnotics, biofeedback therapy, or some other neurobehavioral therapy might be effective. At present, this has not been rigorously investigated. However, in patients with documented myocardial ischemia who are totally asymptomatic, psychological counseling is worthwhile and often necessary, because these patients develop appropriate concerns regarding the future that may result in anxiety or depression.

SUMMARY

Silent myocardial ischemia, a phenomenon described most extensively in anginal patients with known coronary disease, is emerging as an important contributor to the morbidity and mortality of the ischemic heart syndromes. The traditional view that exercise provokes symptomatic ischemia has been supplemented with clinical observations that seemingly routine activities of daily life such as mental stress, exposure to cold, eating, and smoking can provoke both symptomatic and asymptomatic myocardial ischemia. These clinical observations have been explored more systematically and have led to ongoing epidemiologic and pathophysiologic investigations. In the next decade of progress, we can expect to see a characterization of the ischemic potential of specific stressors, which, coupled with the pathophysiologic investigations, will lead to firm management strategies.

REFERENCES

Allan, R. M., & Selwyn, A. P. (1982). Myocardial blood flow measurements in man. In R. T. Mathie (Ed.), *Blood flow measurement in man* (pp. 83–98), London: Castle House.

Armstrong, W. F., Jordan, J. W., Morris, S. N., & McHenry, P. L. (1982). Prevalence and magnitude of ST-segment and T-wave abnormalities in normal men during continuous ambulatory electrocardiography. *American Journal of Cardiology, 49*, 1638–1642.

Chierchia, S., Lazzari, M., Freedman, B., Brunelli, C., & Maseri, A. (1983). Impairment of myocardial perfusion and function during painless myocardial ischemia. *Journal of the American College of Cardiology, 1*, 924–930.

Cohn, P. (1986). Silent myocardial ischemia: Clinical significance and relation to sudden cardiac death. *Chest, 90*, 597–600.

Crawford, M. H., Mendoza, C. A., O'Rourke, R. A., White, D. H., Boucher, C. A., & Gorwit, J. (1978). Limitations of continuous ambulatory electrocardiogram monitoring for detecting coronary artery disease. *Annals of Internal Medicine, 89*, 1–5.

Deanfield, J. E., Maseri, A., Selwyn, A. P., Ribeiro, P., Cchierchia, S., Krikler, S., & Morgan, M. (1983). Myocardial ischemia during daily life in patients with stable angina: Its relation to symptoms and heart rate changes. *Lancet, 1*, 753.

Deanfield, J. E., Ribeiro, P., Oakley, K., Krikler, S., & Selwyn A. P. (1985). Analysis of ST-segment changes in normal subjects: Implications for ambulatory monitoring in angina pectoris. *American Journal of Cardiology, 54*, 1321–1325.

Deanfield, J. E., Shea, M. J., Kensett, M., Horlock, P., Wilson, R. A., DeLandsheere, C. M., & Selwyn, A. P. (1984). Silent myocardial ischemia due to mental stress. *Lancet, 2*, 1001–1005.

Deanfield, J. E., Shea, M. J., Ribeiro, P., DeLandsheere, C. M., Wilson, R. A., Horlock, P., & Selwyn, A. P. (1984). Transient ST-segment depression as a marker of myocardial ischemia during daily life. *American Journal of Cardiology, 54*, 1195–1200.

Deanfield, J. E. Shea, M. J. Wilson, R. A., Horlock, P., DeLandsheere, C. M., & Selwyn, A. P. (1986). Direct effects of smoking on the heart: Silent ischemic disturbances of coronary flow. *American Journal of Cardiology, 57*, 1005–1009.

Droste, C., & Roskamm, H. (1983). Experimental pain measurement in patients with asymptomatic myocardial ischemia. *Journal of American College of Cardiology, 1,* 940–945.

Freeman, L. J., Nixon, P. G. F., & Sallabank, P. (1987). Psychological stress and silent myocardial ischemia. *American Heart Journal, 114,* 477–482.

Gottlieb, S. O., Weisfeldt, M. L., Ouyang, P., Mellits, D., & Gerstenblith, G. (1986). Silent ischemia as a marker for early unfavorable outcomes in patients with unstable angina. *New England Journal of Medicine, 314,* 1214–1219.

Heberden, W. (1818). *Commentaries on the history and cure of diseases.* Boston: Wells and Lilly.

Hill, J. A., & Pepine, C. J. (1986). Clinical aspects of silent myocardial ischemia: Effects of treatment. *Chest, 90,* 906–911.

Hunter, J. (1794). *Treatise on the blood, inflammation and gun-shot wounds.* London: Richardson.

Janne, P., Reynaert, C., DeCoster, P., Cassiers, L., & Kremer, R. (1987). Denial and silent (asymptomatic) myocardial ischemia: A comparative study. *European Heart Journal, 8* (Suppl. G), 125–129.

Kannel, W. B., & Abbott, R. D. (1984). Incidence and prognosis of unrecognized myocardial infarction: An update on the Framingham study. *New England Journal of Medicine, 311,* 1144–1147.

Multiple Risk Factor Intervention Trial Research Group. (1985). Exercise electrocardiogram and coronary heart disease mortality in the Multiple Risk Factor Intervention Trial. *American Journal of Cardiology, 55,* 16–24

Phelps, M. E., & Mazziotta, J. C. (1985). Positron emission tomography: Human brain function and biochemistry. *Science, 228,* 799–809.

Pitt, B., & Strauss, H. W. (Eds.) (1979). *Cardiovascular nuclear medicine.* London: Mosby.

Rocco, M. B., Barry, J., Campbell, S., Nable, E. G., Rebecca, G. S., & Selwyn, A. P. (1987). Circadian variation of transient myocardial ischemia. *Circulation, 75,* 395–400.

Schamroth, L. (1984). *The electrocardiology of coronary artery disease.* Oxford: Blackwell.

Schang, S. J., & Pepine, C. J. (1977). Transient asymptomatic ST-segment depressing during daily activity. *American Journal of Cardiology, 39,* 396–402.

Schiffer, R., Hartley, L. H., Schulman, C. L., & Abelmann, W. H. (1980). Evidence for emotionally-induced coronary arterial spasm in patients with angina pectoris. *British Heart Journal, 44,* 62–66.

Selwyn, A. P., Allan, R. M., L'Abbate, A., Horlock, P., Camici, P., Clark, J., O'Brien, H. A., & Grant, P. M. (1982). Relation between regional myocardial uptake of rubidium-82 and perfusion: Absolute reduction of cation uptake in ischemia. *American Journal of Cardiology, 50,* 112–121.

Selwyn, A. P., Deanfield, J., Shea, M., & Jones, T. (1986). Different pathophysiology of painful and silent myocardial ischemia. *Circulation, 74,* II–57.

Selwyn, A. P., Fox., L., Eves, M., Oakley, D., Dargie, H., & Shillingford, J. (1978). Myocardial ischemia in patients with frequent angina pectoris. *British Medical Journal, 2,* 1594–1596.

Shea, M. J., Deanfield, J. E., DeLandsheere, C. M., Wilson, R., Kensett, M., & Selwyn, A. P. (1987). Asymptomatic myocardial ischemia following cold provocation. *American Heart Journal, 114,* 469–476.

Shea, M. J., Deanfield, J. E., Wilson, R., DeLandsheere, C., Jones, T., & Selwyn, A. P. (1985). Transient ischemia in angina pectoris: Frequent silent events with everyday activities. *American Journal of Cardiology, 56,* 34E–38E.

Shea, M. J., Deanfield, J. E., Wilson, R. A., DeLandsheere, C. M., Jones, T., & Selwyn, A. P. (1988). Silent myocardial ischemia: Studies with positron emission tomography. In D. D. Miller (Ed.), *Clinical cardiovascular imaging* (pp. 303–313). New York: McGraw-Hill.

Shea, M. J., Deanfield, J. E., Wilson, R. A., DeLandsheere, C. M., & Selwyn, A. P. (1987). Silent myocardial ischemia during mastication. *American Journal of Medicine, 82,* 357–360.

Shea, M., Sachdev, V., Luckoff, C., Wilson, N., Nicklas, J., & Kirsh, M. (1987). The relation between anxiety, catecholamines and perioperative myocardial ischemia. *Clinical Research, 35,* 326A.

Shea, M. J., Wilson, R. A., Deanfield, J., DeLandsheere, C. M., & Selwyn, A. P. (1983). Short-lived radionuclides in studies of coronary blood flow and myocardial metabolism. In M. D. Short, D. A. Pay, S. Leeman & R. M. Harrison (Eds.), *Physical techniques in cardiological imaging* (pp. 104–118). Bristol, England: Hilger Ltd.

Shea, M. J., Wilson, R. A., Deanfield, J. E., DeLandsheere, C. M., Turton, D. R., Brady, R., Pike, V. W., & Selwyn, A. P. (1985). Cation uptake as a measure of regional myocardial blood flow: Direct validation in patients with infarction. *Circulation, 72,* III–443.

Shea, M. J., Wilson, R. A., DeLandsheere, C. M., Deanfield, J. E., Watson, I. A., Kensett, M. J., Jones, T., & Selwyn, A. P. (1987). The use of short- and long-lived rubidium tracers for the study of transient ischemia. *Journal of Nuclear Medicine, 28,* 989–997.

Specchia, G., DeServi, G., Falcone, C., Gavazzi, A., Angoli, L., Bramucci, E., Ardissino, D., &

Mussini, A. (1984). Mental arithmetic stress testing in patients with coronary artery disease. *American Heart Journal, 108,* 56–62.

Stern, S., & Tzivoni, D. (1974). Early detection of silent ischemic heart disease by 24 hour electrocardiographic monitoring of active subjects. *British Heart Journal, 36* 481–486

Taggart, P., Carruthers, M., & Sommerville, W. (1973). Electrocardiogram, plasma catecholamines and lipids, and their modification by oxprenolol when speaking before an audience. *Lancet, 2,* 341–346.

Taggart, P., Gibbons, D., & Sommerville, W. (1969). Some effects of motor car driving on the normal and abnormal heart. *British Medical Journal, 4,* 130–134.

Weidinger, F., Hammerie, A., Sochor, H., Smetana, R., Frass, M., & Glogar, D. (1986). Role of beta-endorphins in silent myocardial ischemia. *American Journal of Cardiology, 58,* 428–430.

Wilson, R. A., Shea, M. J., DeLandsheere, C. M., Deanfield, J., Lammertsma, A. A., Jones, T., & Selwyn, A. P. (1987). Rubidium-82 myocardial uptake and extraction after transient ischemia: PET characteristics. *Journal of Computer Assisted Tomography, 11,* 60–66.

Wilson, R., Shea, M., DeLandsheere, C., Deanfield, J., Lammertsma, A., Terton, D., & Selwyn, A. (1984). Myocardial blood flow: Clinical application and recent advances. In M. L. Simoons & J. H. C. Reiber (Eds.), *Nuclear imaging in clinical cardiology* (pp. 39–64). Boston: Martinus Nijhoff.

10

Emotions, Cardiac Arrhythmias, and Sudden Death

Ezra A. Amsterdam

A 52-year-old woman happened upon two burglars when she returned to her place of business one night to check the office. The intruders, who fled upon her entry, were quickly apprehended by the police. A few hours later, while giving her statement to the police, she collapsed and died. We were consulted by the district attorney's office as to whether the victim's death could be attributed to the stress imposed by these events. At stake was a possible indictment for homicide.

The issues raised by the foregoing scenario are based on a general acceptance, deeply rooted in our culture, of the relation between sudden death and behavioral factors. However, convincing scientific evidence of such a link has only recently become available. Almost 20 years ago, Engel (1971) traced the historical notion, from Biblical to modern times, that psychological stress can induce sudden demise, generally through a cardiac catastrophe. From an extensive series of anecdotes of sudden deaths during acute emotional excitation, he provided a conceptual framework for understanding the interaction of somatic and psychological factors that might result in cardia perturbation, which, in certain settings, could produce serious or even lethal arrhythmias.

Sudden death is a problem of major magnitude in our society, causing more that 400,000 fatalities each year (Lown, 1987). This catastrophe usually, but not always, occurs in people who have serious cardiac conditions, the majority of which are overt coronary heart disease. The primary mechanism of sudden death (variably defined as a death occurring instantaneously or within six hours of the onset of symptoms) is a lethal tachyarrhythmia (ventricular tachycardia or fibrillation). Uncommonly, a severe bradyarrhythmia is the cause. These patients may be in an apparently stable state of their disease when the lethal event occurs. Furthermore, acute myocardial infarction is an unusual precipitating factor in most cases of fatal arrhythmia. Clarification of factors contributing to the onset of the fatal arrhythmia is thus not only of theoretical interest but also may provide insights leading to prevention.

Although the relation between psyche and soma had been previously suggested as an etiologic factor in a number of cardiovascular conditions, including hypertension, angina pectoris, myocardial infarction, arrhythmias, and sudden death (Cincirpini, 1986a, 1986b; Folkins & Amsterdam, 1977), progress in this field was impeded by theoretical and practical limitations. The past two decades, however, have witnessed major advances in our understanding of these complex problems. The basis for this progress has included an appreciation of the multifactorial concept of disease mechanisms and improved methods for pursuing laboratory and clinical investigation. Advances in studying mechanisms of cardiac arrhythmias, evaluating neurophysiological–cardiocirculatory interactions and monitoring cardiac rate and rhythm in humans have helped establish a scientific basis and biopsychological model for assessing data and testing hypotheses. The result has been an increasing body of objective evidence that the central nervous system can markedly affect cardiac function acutely and chronically. In terms of influencing cardiac rate and rhythm, the autonomic nervous system has been identified as a major mediator of the influence of higher cognitive function on the heart.

An important aspect of understanding the interactions of emotions and cardiac function is recognition that resultant pathogenesis, morbidity, and mortality in terms of arrhythmias are determined by the vulnerability of the substrate, that is, the myocardium, and the intensity of the provoking factor, in this case the stress emotions. Thus lethal arrhythmias rarely occur in individuals with normal hearts (Kuller, Talbott, & Robinson, 1987). Conversely, clinically significant arrhythmias related to behavioral factors are largely, but not completely, restricted to individuals with underlying heart disease, which may be overt or occult. However, in the continuum between normal and severely diseased myocardium and between mild and intense psychologic stress, a critical combination of these factors may produce a serious cardiac rhythm disturbance.

Thus, in the presence of severe cardiac disease, a relatively mild stress may induce dysfunction, whereas stress of great intensity would be required to provoke a derangement in a normal heart. In the latter case, the target organ is less vulnerable and its threshold for induction of arrhythmia by any provoking factor, physical or emotional, is high. The converse is true in the impaired heart and varies with the severity of disease. It is also important to emphasize that the emotional impact of a given external stimulus may differ among individuals and thereby provoke variable centrally triggered autonomic responses and cardiac manifestations.

PSYCHOPHYSIOLOGIC INFLUENCES ON CARDIAC FUNCTION

Emotional arousal has well-recognized effects on the heart and circulation, which are chiefly mediated by the autonomic nervous system. The emotions represent cognitive experiences (e.g., anxiety, anger, elation, and fear) processed by the frontal cortex, the output of which to lower centers such as the thalamus and medulla, influences autonomic nervous system control of the circulation. Increased activity of the sympathetic system produces cardioaccelerator effects through release of the catecholamines, norepinephrine and epinephrine, from cardiac sympathetic nerves and the adrenal medulla, respectively. Parasympathetic regulation, through the vagus nerve, provides an important inhibitory component in the autonomic control of the heart.

The cardiac manifestations of increased sympathetic stimulation are augmented mechanical, electrical, and metabolic activity in the form of increased heart rate, myocardial contractility, peripheral vascular resistance, blood pressure, and cardiac output. The propensity for myocardial ischemia rises when these effects are associated with flow-limiting coronary artery disease, which can result in an imbalance between myocardial oxygen supply and demand. Sympathetic stimulation to the heart can precipitate arrhythmias through its (a) direct effects on cardiac electrophysiogy—increased automaticity (through increased rate of rise of phase 4 of the cardiac action potential) and development of reentry mechanisms (through alterations in myocardial conductivity and refractory period)—and (b) indirect effects—by inducing ischemia-related alterations in cardiac electrical stability (Surawicz, 1985).

It is apparent from the foregoing that the effects of emotional arousal on the heart are similar to those of physical exercise, which follows from the fact that augmented sympathetic nervous system activity plays a major role in each state. It is of interest, in this regard, that emotional stress can be potentially more demanding than physical activity because metabolic vasodilation in working muscles reduces cardiac afterload, whereas vasoconstriction and increased afterload predominate when elevation of sympathetic stimulation is unassociated with physical activity.

STUDIES OF APPARENTLY HEALTHY SUBJECTS

Sinus Rate and Ectopic Beats

Cardiac rate and rhythm have been monitored by ambulatory recording systems during normal daily activities in subjects who have no evidence of heart disease. These studies demonstrate the high degree of cardiovascular reactivity of humans to stress states. The predominant response of apparently healthy individuals to excitatory situations is sinus tachycardia that may reach rates comparable to those achieved with moderate or even high levels of physical exertion. However, ventricular and atrial ectopic beats occasionally occur, usually in low density. Rare individuals who do not have heart disease develop potentially lethal ventricular arrhythmias when confronted with stressful life situations.

Taggart, Gibbons, and Somerville (1969) used telemetry to record the electrocardiograms of 32 subjects who had no evidence of heart disease (aged 21–55 years with average age of 29) during customary city automobile driving and of 10 healthy racing car drivers during competition. City driving was associated with a rise in sinus rate from a range of 55–100/min to a maximum of 75–155/min. Forty-one percent had maximum heart rates of 115/min or greater. No ectopic cardiac beats were induced by this activity in this group. In the racing drivers, sinus rate rose to 150–180 in the 15 min before the race and increased further to between 180 and 210/min during the race. No abnormal cardiac rhythms were reported in these subjects. The rise in cardiac rate in the racing drivers was associated with elevations of plasma catecholamines to as much as 20 times resting values, providing biochemical evidence of augmented sympathetic neurohumoral activity.

In a subsequent study of 23 normal adults (21–58 years, with an average age of 35), Taggart, Carruthers, and Somerville (1973) demonstrated similar, impressive rises in sinus rate (up to 180/min) and plasma catecholamines during public speaking. Six of the subjects developed ectopic beats (chamber of origin not specified) and no symptoms were reported. No comment was made in either of these studies of any relation between the degree of increase in catecholamines and the appearance of arrhythmias.

Medical residents have been studied by ambulatory electrocardiographic monitoring during case presentations at grand rounds (Moss, 1970). Group mean heart rate rose from 73/min before presentation to 154/min during this activity. There were no ectopic beats and no ST-segment or T-wave alterations, indicating absence of electrocardiographic evidence of myocardial ischemia. A group of 15 football coaches and

15 basketball coaches (age range 24–56 years), 27 of whom had negative cardiac histories, underwent electrocardiographic monitoring by telemetry throughout a game (Gazes, Sovell, & Dellastatious, 1969). Average heart rate for the group rose from 69/min before to a peak of 132/min during the event. Seven of the 27 normal subjects developed atrial ectopic beats, which were frequent in two and included a brief run of paroxysmal atrial tachycardia in one. None of the subjects experienced symptoms, and there was no electrocardiographic evidence of ischemia.

Life-Threatening Arrhythmias

Although it has been previously emphasized that serious arrhythmias are rarely induced by psychological stress in normal people, this phenomenon has been reported. It is difficult to document because an association between the stress emotion and the arrhythmia in such individuals is usually based on historical reconstruction rather than exclusively on objective evidence. However, in some cases of a very close temporal relation between acute emotional stress and the onset of the arrhythmia, the clinical picture is strongly suggestive. In one patient, provocation of the arrhythmia during a controlled stress interview confirmed the association.

Reich, DeSilva, Lown, and Murawski (1981) reported acute psychological disturbances preceding life-threatening arrhythmias (ventricular tachycardia or fibrillation unassociated with acute myocardial infarction) in 21 patients who had no demonstrable heart disease. More than half (11) of this group had suffered acute emotional distress in the preceding 24 hours and in some the arrhythmia occurred in the hospital, allowing documentation of the timing and details of the psychological event. The predominant affective state associated with the arrhythmia, which followed within an hour, was anger, but depression, fear, and excitement were also common. The situations producing these emotions included interpersonal conflicts, public humiliation, threat of or actual marital separation, bereavement, and nightmares. Because not all patients underwent invasive cardiac evaluation, absence of heart disease was not fully documented in this group. However, extensive clinical and noninvasive testing revealed no evidence of structural abnormality. These cases support the concept that intense psychological stress can provoke serious arrhythmias even in these individuals.

Independent findings consistent with the foregoing were provided by Brodsky, Sato, Iseria, Wolff, and Allen (1987). From a group of 80 patients referred for evaluation of cardiac arrest or syncope due to documented ventricular tachycardia, these investigators identified six patients through complete noninvasive and invasive studies who had no structural heart disease. All were women ranging in age from 22 to 60 years; the presenting arrhythmia, ventricular tachycardia in each, had induced cardiac arrest in one and syncope in the other five. Five of the six patients suffered from severe, chronic emotional distress with recurrent exacerbations, at the time of which the arrhythmias had occurred in several of the patients. Ambulatory monitoring in the hospital demonstrated recurrent ventricular tachycardia, reduction of ventricular ectopy during sleep, and diminution in the frequency of ventricular tachyardia runs by beta-adrenergic blocker therapy, findings that support a causal interaction between emotional stress, elevated sympathetic neural stimulation, and ventricular tachyarrhythmias in these patients.

Lown et al. (1976) presented a detailed study supporting psychologic factors and neurophysiologic mechanisms as the basis for recurrent ventricular fibrillation in a

39-year-old man who had no evidence of structural heart disease. The patient had had two episodes of ventricular fibrillation and had high frequency ventricular ectopic beats. He had a history of emotional disturbances, ventricular arrhythmias could be provoked by a controlled psychological stress, and they were reduced by meditation and beta-adrenergic blocker therapy. This carefully studied case further documents the potential for behavioral factors to induce lethal arrhythmias in individuals who have no evidence of structural heart disease.

Bradyarrhythmias

Although interest in the relation between emotional states and cardiac function has emphasized sympathetic excitatory phenomena, an imbalance in autonomic control resulting from increased parasympathetic stimulation can also cause deranged cardiac function. This is well demonstrated by vasodepressor syncope and presyncope, in which increased vagal tone results in reduced heart rate and blood pressure, the latter from decreased cardiac output and peripheral vasodilation. It has been postulated that in the presence of intense central nervous system stimulation that ordinarily elicits sympathetic responses, parasympathetic tone may become dominant, inhibiting cardiac activity (Engel, 1971). These concepts may pertain to the report of a 32-year-old man hospitalized for recurrent syncope (Schlesinger, Barzilay, Stryjer, & Almog, 1977). Emotional distress in this patient resulted in severe sinus bradycardia followed by complete heart block and Stokes-Adams attacks, and he required repeated resuscitations in the hospital. His condition was controlled by implantation of an artificial cardiac pacemaker.

STUDIES OF PATIENTS WITH CARDIAC DISEASE

Ventricular Ectopic Beats

The aforementioned studies of Taggart et al. (1969, 1973) on heart rate and rhythm during automobile driving and public speaking included individuals with coronary heart disease as well as normal subjects. In these and other investigations comparing the two populations in similar states of stress, coronary patients demonstrated a considerably greater propensity than normal subjects to develop ventricular arrhythmias, illustrating the increased vulnerability of their cardiac substrate. Thus, whereas comparable age-related elevations in heart rate occurred during driving and public speaking, 18 of 31 (58%) coronary patients developed ventricular extopic beats (VEBs) compared to 6 of 55 (11%) persons without heart disease. In addition, the ventricular ectopy was more often complex (high density, multifocal) in the coronary group. In the study of coaches (Gazes et al., 1969), only one had known coronary heart diseases, and he developed episodes of frequent (6 or more per min), multifocal ventricular ectopics during monitoring; 8 of the remaining 29 without overt disease had rare VEBs, and in 2 they were frequent.

My colleagues and I had the opportunity to perform a detailed psychophysiologic study in a 38-year-old man with a prior documented myocardial infarction who suffered from chronic anxiety, stormy interpersonal relations, and typical angina precipitated exclusively by emotional stress (Donlon, Meadow, & Amsterdam, 1979). Maximal exercise testing was unassociated with symptoms, ischemia, or arrhythmias. To determine the role of emotional factors in the etiology of his symptoms, we evaluated

Table 1   Number of ventricular ectopic beats (VEBs) during psychiatric interview

VEBs/min	Very relaxed	Mildly relaxed	Mildly stressful	Very stressful	Total minutes
5 or more	3	0	18	21	42
Less than 5	6	0	8	6	20
Total minutes	9	0	26	27	62

Note. From Donlon et al. (1979). Reprinted by permission of publisher and authors.

the patient through an in-depth, videotaped interview dealing with a spectrum of emotionally pleasurable, neutral, or arousing personal themes during which his EKG was continuously recorded. The videotape and electrocardiographic data were then independently analyzed for rating of stress and for electrocardiographic findings.

Correlation of these data revealed increases in VEBs during emotional distress variably consisting of grief, hostility, agitation, and depression, which were associated with pallor, diaphoresis, muscular rigidity, and tremor. By contrast, pleasurable themes induced relaxation, smiling, and smoother interaction with the interviewer, which were associated with reduction of ventricular ectopy to rare beats. As Table 1 shows, increased ventricular ectopy occurred during "very stressful" intervals (25 VEBs/min in 21 of 27 min), whereas the opposite effect was demonstrated during "very relaxed" periods (>5 VEBs/min in 6 of 9 min). There was no angina or evidence of myocardial ischemia during the interview. This patient with coronary disease is of considerable interest in demonstrating abnormalities of cardiac rhythm during emotional arousal that could not be replicated during maximal exercise testing. Systematic psychophysiologic evaluation yielded clinical evidence that the arrhythmia was associated with augmented sympathetic neural activity provoked by stress emotions.

Life-Threatening Tachyarrhythmias

In the Reich et al. (1981) study noted earlier, 104 of the patients presenting with life-threatening arrhythmias had organic heart disease, and in 14 of them an acute antecedent psychological disturbance could be identified, most commonly within one hour of the arrhythmia. A considerably higher proportion of the patients without structural heart disease had evidence of psychological precipitating factors with their arrhythmias (11 in 21 vs. 21 in 96 for people with heart disease). Although it is difficult to quantitate stress levels in these clinical situations, it would be expected that greater emotional arousal was required to provoke the arrhythmias in the nondiseased patients than for those with disease.

EXPERIMENTAL STUDIES

The development of experimental biobehavioral models and methods for quantitating arrhythmia threshold in animals has contributed significantly to our understanding of the relation of psychophysiological factors to arrhythmia induction. Lown, Verrier, Skinner, and others have quantitated the arrhythmogenic effects of behavioral stress and identified neurophysiologic mechanisms for these alterations. They have demonstrated that heightened sympathetic nervous system activity is a major arrhythmogenic factor in experimental animals and that these autonomic effects are related to output from the cerebral cortex, through which the organism experiences the external environment. Parasympathetic stimulation, through the vagus nerve, counteracts the deleterious influence of excessive adrenergic discharge. Thus higher central nervous system activity may contribute to an imbalance in autonomic regulation of the heart and circulation, one result of which can be induction of cardiac arrhythmias. This derangement is facilitated by abnormalities in the cardiac substrate, such as ischemia, which reduces myocardial electrical stability and promotes arrhythmogenesis.

Induction of stress in laboratory animals by several methods results in augmented vulnerability to ventricular arrhythmias. Thus aversive environment reduced the electrical threshold for inducing repetitive VEBs by 41% (Verrier, 1987). Similar results were obtained on arrhythmia threshold by eliciting an anger-like state in dogs denied access to food within view (Verrier, 1987). The latter situation was associated with consistent elevation of plasma catecholamines. In contrast to these studies, in which electrical stimuli to the heart were required to provoke ventricular arrhythmias, imposition of experimental myocardial ischemia during environmental stress increased the incidence of ventricular fibrillation by more than threefold over that occurring in the absence of stress (Verrier, 1987). (No external electrical stimuli to the heart were required to produce fibrillation in these animals.)

Experimental data support an important role for adrenergic factors in stress-induced arrhythmias. Interruption of sympathetic nervous system pathways by pharmacologic blockade with beta-adrenergic antagonists or surgical sympathectomy reduces the arrhythmogenic influence of stress states. Verrier also showed that parasympathetic stimulation can counteract the arrhythmogenic effects of stress factors. Thus, augmenting vagal tone can reduce the increased vulnerability to arrhythmias produced by environmental stress. Conversely, parasympathetic blockade considerably increased the propensity to develop arrhythmias in this setting.

The influence of the central nervous system in stress-induced arrhythmias via certain neural tracts has been elucidated by selective ablation of regions of the brain. Cold blockade of frontal cortical pathways to the brainstem via the thalamus inhibited stress-induced ventricular fibrillation (Skinner & Reed, 1981). In this regard, it is of interest that diazepam, an anxiolytic agent, had antiarrhythmic effects in this setting (Rosenfeld, Rosen, & Hoffman, 1978).

REFERENCES

Brodsky, M. A., Sato, D. A., Iseri, L. T., Wolff, L. J., & Allen, B. J. (1987). Ventricular tachyarrhythmia associated with psychological stress: The role of the sympathetic nervous system. *Journal of the American Medical Association, 257,* 2084.

Cincirpini, P. M. (1986a). Cognitive stress and cardiovascular reactivity: 1. Relationship to hypertension. *American Heart Journal, 112,*.

Cincirpini, P. M. (1986b). Cognitive stress and cardiovascular reactivity: 2. Relationship to atherosclerosis, arrhythmias, and cognitive control. *American Heart Journal, 112,* 1051.

Donlon, P. T., Meadow, A., & Amsterdam, E. A. (1979). Emotional stress as a factor in ventricular arrhythmias. *Psychosomatics, 20,* 233.

Engel, G. L. (1971). Sudden and rapid death during psychological stress: Folklore or folk wisdom? *Annals of Internal Medicine, 74,* 771.

Folkins, C. H., & Amsterdam, E. A. (1977). Control and modification of stress emotions through chronic exercise. In E. A. Amsterdam, H. H. Wilmore, & A. N. DeMaria (Eds.), *Exercise in cardiovascular health and disease* (pp. 280–294). New York: Yorke Medical Books.

Gazes, P. C., Sovell, B. F., & Dellastatious, J. W. (1969). Continuous radioelectrocardiographic monitoring of football and basketball coaches during games. *American Heart Journal, 78,* 509.

Kuller, L. H., Talbott, C. O., & Robinson, C. (1987). Environmental and psychosocial determinants of sudden death. *Circulation, 76*(Suppl. 1), 1–177.

Lown, B. (1987). Sudden cardiac death: Biobehavioral perspective. *Circulation, 76*(Suppl. 1), 186.

Lown, B., Temte, J. V., Reich, P., Gaughan, C., Regetein, Q., & Hai, H. (1976). Basis for recurring ventricular fibrillation in the absence of coronary heart disease and its management. *New England Journal of Medicine, 294,* 623.

Moss, A. J. (1970). Tachycardia in house officers presenting cases at grand rounds. *Annals of Internal Medicine, 72,* 255.

Reich, P., DeSilva, R. A., Lown, B., & Murawski, J. (1981). Acute psychological disturbances preceding life-threatening arrhythmias. *Journal of the American Medical Association, 246,* 233.

Rosenfeld, J., Rosen, M. R., & Hoffman, B. F. (1978). Pharmacologic and behavioral effects on arrhythmias that immediately follow abrupt coronary occlusion: A canine model of sudden coronary death. *American Journal of Cardiology, 41,* 1075.

Schlesinger, Z., Barzilay, J., Stryjer, D., & Almog, C. H. (1977). Life-threatening "vagal reaction" to emotional stimuli. *Israel Journal of Medical Sciences, 13,* 59.

Skinner, J. E., & Reed, J. C. (1981). Blockade of frontocortical–brain stem pathway prevents ventricular fibrillation of ischemic heart. *American Journal of Physiology, 240,* H156.

Surawicz, B. (1985). Ventricular fibrillation.

Taggart, P., Carruthers, M., & Somerville, W. (1973). Electrocardiogram, plasma catecholamines and lipids, and their modification by oxprenolol when speaking before an audience. *Lancet, 2,* 341.

Taggart, P., Gibbons, D., & Somerville, W. (1969). Some effects of motor car driving on the normal and abnormal heart. *British Medical Journal, 4,* 130.

Verrier, R. L. (1987). Mechanisms of behaviorally induced arrhythmias. *Circulation, 76*(Suppl. 1), 1–48.

11

Type A Behavior Pattern: The Role of Anxiety, Self-Awareness, and Denial

Jerry Suls

The Type A behavior pattern, consisting of extremes of competitive achievement-striving, hostility, aggressiveness, and time urgency, has been identified as a risk factor for coronary heart disease (Friedman & Rosenman, 1959). People who have many of these behavioral features are classified as Type A; those who show a relative absence of Type A behaviors are classified as Type B. Prospective research such as that conducted by the Western Collaborative Group, which followed a sample of more than 3,000 nominally healthy men at intake showed that Type As were twice as likely as Type Bs to develop coronary heart disease (CHD) at an 8-1/2 year follow-up (Rosenman et al., 1975). Although subsequent findings have been less consistent (see Booth-Kewley & Friedman, 1987; Matthews, 1988, for recent reviews), prospective investigations of population samples indicate that Type A and one of its subcomponents, potential for hostility—defined as the predisposition to respond to a broad range of frustrating situations with degrees of anger and irritation—are significant predictors of subsequent CHD after controlling for traditional CHD risk factors (Matthews, Glass, Rosenman, & Bortner, 1977; Williams, Barefoot, & Shekelle, 1985).

Because Type As lead extremely active, hurried lives, observers might expect such individuals to experience considerable upset much of the time. Friedman and Rosenman (1959) argued, however, that Type As exhibit little evidence of distress despite their hectic, ambitious life styles. To quote the famous 19th-century cardiologist, William Osler (1892), "It is not the neurotic, delicate person who is prone to angina, but the robust, the vigorous in mind and body, the keen and ambitious man, the indicator of whose engine is always at 'full speed ahead'" (p. 839). Rosenman (1978b) has also commented at length on this matter:

> Type A behavior [is] exhibited by an individual who is engaged in a relatively chronic and excessive struggle. . .to obtain a usually unlimited number of things in the shortest possible period of time and/or against the opposing efforts of other persons in the same environment. . . . Since Type A's rarely despair of losing the chronic struggle, such individuals differ sharply from those with fear, anxiety, or a garden variety of neuroses. (p. xv)

I wish to thank Glenn Sanders and Ray Rosenman for their helpful comments on earlier versions of this chapter. Preparation of this chapter was supported in part by National Institutes of Health Grant HL39118 to Jerry Suls.

259

These comments notwithstanding, the psychological dynamic that sets this chronic struggle in motion is unclear. Although Rosenman and Friedman may be correct that Type As evidence little distress, fear, or anxiety, descriptions also do not reveal them to be happy, self-accepting, or possessing peace of mind (Van Egeren, in press). It has been suggested that some deep-seated anxiety or uncertainty is responsible for the chronic competitiveness with time and other people that is characteristic of Type As, but they are reluctant to admit it even to themselves (Matthews, 1982; Strube, 1987; Gastorf, Suls, & Sanders, 1980; Rosenman, in press).

Following Friedman and Rosenman, I propose that a basic uncertainty and insecurity are at the root of Type A behavior. Some individuals exhibiting the Type A pattern, however, have awareness of their behavior and are conscious of its chronic affective consequences. In contrast, other Type As make extensive use of denial and show little self-awareness of their behavior or its affective consequences. The thesis of this chapter is that there are two kinds of Type As. One kind, the self-aware Type A, exhibits many of the behaviors commonly associated with the pattern, such as achievement-striving and impatience, and also reports moderate to high levels of upset. The other kind also exhibits achievement-striving and impatience but is not self-aware and reports little distress. Of special significance is that only the Type A that is not self-aware is coronary-prone. In essence, then, I propose that denial distinguishes the two kinds of Type As and also contributes to disease risk.

This line of thinking was suggested in part by prior research on the relation between the Type A pattern and psychological distress, so first I briefly review this literature. Following the review, the conceptual perspective on the two types of Type As is presented. Finally, I discuss the implications of this approach and its connections to related work on other psychological precursors of disease.

EMPIRICAL STUDIES ON CHRONIC PSYCHOLOGICAL DISTRESS AND TYPE A BEHAVIOR

In the last two decades, many researchers have examined the relationship between Type A behavior and psychological indicators of chronic distress, but this literature has not been systematically reviewed. To conduct such a review, my colleagues and I searched the PsychINFO and MEDLARS data bases. This search identified 37 appropriate studies involving men and women ranging in age from 18 to 65. The study sample varied widely in the kinds of measures used to assess Type A behavior and to evaluate chronic distress. As background for this review and the conceptual model, the measures are described in the following sections.

Measures of Type A Behavior

The most widely accepted measure of Pattern A is the Structured Interview (SI), actually a behavioral test in which voice and psychomotor mannerisms in response to the interviewer's questions are given more weight to classify subjects as Type A or B than are the contents of their answers. Examples of questions are "Do you get impatient when you are watching a slow co-worker?" and "Are you satisfied with your present job?" Characteristics classified as Type A include loud, explosive, rapid, and accelerated speech; verbal responses indicative of hostility; and facial bodily expressions indicating heightened tension or arousal (Rosenman, 1978a). Individuals who do not show a rushed pace or excessive competitiveness in the interview are classified as Type B.

Assessment with the SI into Type A, B, or X (neither one or the other style) successfully predicted CHD in the Western Collaborative Group Study (WCGS) at an 8 1/2-year follow-up even after adjusting for traditional risk factors such as serum cholesterol, age, education, smoking status, and blood pressure. Some subsequent studies failed to find that the SI-global Type A predicts CHD, but these involve CHD patients or individuals with high-risk status on factors such as serum cholesterol and blood pressure (e.g., Shekelle, Hulley, Neaton et al., 1985). A higher prevalence of Type As in the studies of high risk or deliberate efforts by subjects to change behavior may be partly responsible for the null findings (Matthews, 1988). There is also controversy about whether SI-Type A predicts CHD incidence but not mortality (Ragland & Brand, 1988). Noncomparability in the methods of analysis across studies makes drawing any conclusions premature and beyond the range of this chapter.

Several self-report questionnaires followed the development of the SI. The most popular is the Jenkins Activity Survey (JAS), which was specifically designed to mimic the interview and uses similar questions (Jenkins, Rosenman, & Friedman, 1967). The JAS is self-administered and was derived through discriminant function analysis with the SI as the criterion. Another self-report scale is the Framingham Type A scale, a 10-item questionnaire derived from a larger interview administered to participants in the Framingham Heart Study (Haynes, Feinleib, & Kannel, 1980). A panel of expert judges deemed 10 items to be an approximate index of Type A behavior. Several other self-report measures have been used less frequently; these include the Bortner inventory (Bortner, 1969), the Thurstone Temperament Schedule (TTS—Thurstone, 1949), the Vickers scale (Caplan, Cobb, French, Harrison, & Pinneau, 1975), and the Adjective Checklist (Gough & Heilbrun, 1975).

Although all Type A measures assess somewhat similar constructs, the associations among measures are unimpressive. The JAS and Framingham Scale agree with the classifications made from the SI in about 60% or less of the cases. Because by chance the agreement rates should be 50%, if one presumes that 50% of the population is Type A (the rate reported in the WCGS), the JAS and Framingham Scale concur with SI classification at 10%–20% above chance levels (Matthews, Krantz, Dembroski, & MacDougall, 1982). In a systematic assessment of intercorrelations among all Type A measures, Byrne, Rosenman, Schiller, and Chesney (1985) found low levels of agreement. These findings strongly suggest that the instruments are measuring different aspects of the Type A construct.

Given the low level of overlap among all instruments, the question of which Type A measure best predicts CHD is important. Recent epidemiological evidence suggests that the self-report measures of Pattern A are, at best, inconsistent, weak predictors of CHD—particularly of "hard" indicators such as clinically documented myocardial infarction. The JAS is not an independent predictor of CHD after controlling for traditional risk factors (Brand, Rosenman, Jenkins, Sholtz, & Zyzanski, 1978). Epidemiological results with the JAS show that it is primarily related to the angina endpoint (Haynes et al., 1980). Because of difficulties distinguishing between ischemic angina (where there is underlying disease) and functional chest pain, which may reflect neurotic somatic overconcern, these results have been questioned (Dembroski & Costa, 1988). Nonetheless, because the self-report measures do assess some aspects of what has been described as Type A behavior, they continue to be used. Moreover, the self-report measures have greater construct validity; probably because of their ease of administration, they have been used more in experimental studies and have been good predictors of aggressive, hard-driving, and impatient behavior in the laboratory (Glass, 1977). In light of the lack of concordance among the measures and with illness endpoints, evaluation of empirical studies on the relation between Type A and dysphoria requires that each study's findings be interpreted with the kind of Type A measure in mind. The distinction is doubly important for our purposes, because the questionnaire measures require that the subject be aware of the behavior pattern in order to score high in Type A, whereas the SI does not.

Measures of Dysphoria

A wide range of self-report measures of psychological distress were represented in the study sample including popular measures such as the Spielberger (Spielberger, Gorsuch, & Lushene, 1970) Trait–State Anxiety Inventory, the Derogatis (1977) Symptom Check List (SCL-90), and author-constructed scales. These measures exhibit high reliability so they can be considered as good indices of chronic as opposed to episodic dysphoria. Many self-report questionnaires commonly refer to themselves as measures of neuroticism, anxiety, depression, and so forth. However, recent research indicates that these measures exhibit considerable overlap and should not be considered as measures of specific clinical disorders in contrast to the diagnostic specificity provided by the Diagnostic and Statistical Manual-III-R (Gotlib, 1984). The self-report measures are best viewed as indices of general chronic dysphoria— referred to as "negative affectivity." This is defined as the tendency to report a general dissatisfaction and distress in virtually any situation (Gotlib, 1984; Watson & Clark, 1984). In light of these considerations, I have pooled the results across all of the psychological distress measures.

Meta-Analysis of Type A–Dysphoria Relationships

An effect size for each study that represents the magnitude of relation between Type A and psychological distress was calculated. The effect sizes from each study were then aggregated to evaluate the status of the relation between two or more variables across many studies. This method of research synthesis is known as meta-analysis (Rosenthal, 1984). To derive an effect size for the results of each study discussed in this chapter, my colleagues and I advised the difference between the means of the contrast groups by the variation (or error variance). Because we employed Hedges and Olkin's (1985) meta-analytic approach, the study effect size, equaled the difference between the means for psychological distress of the two groups (As vs. Bs) divided by the pooled within-group standard deviation:

$$g = \frac{M_a - M_b}{SD}$$

where g is the study effect size, M_a is the mean for the Type A group, M_b is the mean for the Type B group, and SD is the pooled within-group variation.

Dividing the difference between groups by the variation in each study provides an effect size that has a common metric across studies. Study effects were given a positive value if Type As exhibited more distress than Bs and a negative value if Bs

Table 1 Tests of Categorical Models for Kind of Type A Effect Sizes

Type A measure	n	Mean g	95% Confidence interval
SI	12	.06	0.00–.11
JAS	51	.24	.20–.28
Framingham	18	.58	.53–.64
Bortner	6	.44	.34–.54
TTS	5	.19	.11–.27
Vickers	4	.09	−.01–.19
Adjective Checklist	5	.28	.20–.35

Note. Mean effect sizes (*g*) are positive if people with more Type A behaviors exhibit more emotional stress than Type Bs and are negative if Type Bs exhibit more distress than Type As. A significant between-class effect (36.07) indicates that the variable accounted for a significant portion of the variability among study effect sizes. Confidence intervals that include 0.0 indicate that the mean effect size was not significantly different from 0.0, the null hypothesis.

exhibited more distress. If individual study effect sizes do not exhibit significant levels of variability, then averaging the values of the individual study effect sizes yields an overall index or study effect mean of the relative size and direction of the relation between Type A and dysphoria across studies. I used this formula cases in which As and Bs were categorized and then contrasted by *t* or *F* statistics. In contrast, some of the study samples treated Type A as a continuous variable and reported correlations between Type A behaviors and dysphoria. A statistical transformation permits the calculation of a study effect that is comparable to that coming from *t* or *F* tests and that can then be combined with study effects computed from categorical tests. In accord with Hedges and Olkin's (1982) procedures, study effect sizes were adjusted for small sample size bias and weighted by the reciprocal of their variances before being averaged with other study effect sizes. In cases when too little information was reported to derive an effect size (only four cases), they were assigned a value of 0.00 as a conservative strategy.

Many of the 37 studies included multiple measures of Type A behavior and hence reported several tests of the Type A–dysphoria association. Effect sizes were computed for each test of the relation between Type A and measure of dysphoria; there were 101 tests altogether. The individual effect sizes were then averaged for each Type A measure, and the grand average was computed. The results are shown in Table 1. Aggregated across studies, Type A behavior is moderately associated with psychological dysphoria (*g* = .27). More interesting are the average values associated with each Type A measure. A mean effect size falling outside the 95% confidence interval is statistically significant from 0.00, thus indicating a significant relation between chronic dysphoria and Type A behavior. Tendencies toward competitiveness, impatience, and achievement-striving assessed by the Framingham, Bortner, Adjective Checklist, and the Jenkins scales are significantly associated with chronic dysphoria. The SI, the "behavioroid" measure, is not, however, significantly correlated with psychological distress. (For a more comprehensive report of the results, see Suls & Wan, 1989.)

The meta-analytic results indicate that Type A is associated with chronic upset, but only if Type A behaviors are self-reported. When Type A behavior is assessed by overt behavior in the interview, it is essentially unrelated to upset. One explanation is that SI-Type As actually experience considerable subjective upset but deliberately conceal their dysphoria in self-report questionnaires. In fact, admitting despondency or anxiety might be a sign of defeat that Type As are reluctant to admit. This cannot be discounted, but if there were real mental health problems being concealed, one would expect that it would be reflected in a higher rate of suicides and mental health referrals. No such evidence has emerged thus far for SI-assessed Type As (Suls & Sanders, 1988; Zyzanski, 1978).

The reason for the difference in results for the SI versus the other measures may be that to score high on the JAS or Framingham Scale, one must be aware of one's competitiveness, impatience, and hostility. In contrast, the SI bases its assessment mainly on gestures and speech patterns; the individuals classified as Type A by SI lack self-awareness of their behavior or its causes. Thus, SI-Type As may not report distress because they force it out of awareness. Before elaborating on this notion, I examine the relation between a specific subcomponent of Type A and dysphoria, because it may provide some further clues concerning the differences in dysphoria across Type A measures.

Hostility and Chronic Dysphoria

It has long been recognized that Type A is not a unitary concept, but a collection of behaviors. In the first study of the contribution of component dimensions of the SI, Matthews et al. (1977) suggested that hostility and anger-related tendencies may be particularly important coronary-prone elements of the pattern. A relevant question, then, is whether hostility viewed as a subcomponent of pattern A is related to chronic dysphoria. Common sense might suggest that chronic hostility would be consistently associated with high levels of psychological distress, but it is important to recognize that hostility in the SI, referred to as "Potential for Hostility" (Costa, McCrae, & Dembroski, 1989; Dembroski & Costa, 1987), reflects an interpersonal style rather than intrapsychic affect (Dembroski & Costa, 1988). In coding for Potential for Hostility, argumentative responses, challenging remarks to the interviewer, and rudeness or condescension receive considerable weight. Interestingly, some portions of the population report or display this interpersonal style but may not exhibit another form of hostility characterized by feelings of resentment, annoyance, or rage. This latter form of hostility, sometimes called "neurotic hostility," is highly related to anxiety, depression, and guilt. Although some people exhibit both so-called neurotic hostility and the antagonistic interpersonal style, standing on the one dimension does not strongly predict standing on the other dimension (Costa et al., 1989); they are independent personality dimensions.

To evaluate the extent to which Potential for Hostility and dysphoria are associated, a meta-analysis similar to the one conducted with respect to global Type A would have been preferred, but such an analysis was unfeasible because there are relatively few relevant studies. Nonetheless, the available reports are highly consistent in their conclusions. Musante, MacDougall, Dembroski, and Costa (1989) found that scores of potential for hostility in a sample of nominally healthy men were positively correlated with high expression of hostile or angry *behavior,* but not with *feelings* of resentment, guilt, or mistrust. Thus these individuals behave callously, cynically, and manipulatively toward others in the absence of angry feelings or hostile attitudes. Dembroski and Costa (1988) characterized people scoring high in potential for hostility (or high in antagonism) as "cold-blooded." In contrast, people high in neuroticism report experiencing frequent and intense periods of angry experience and hostile attitudes toward others (Musante et al., 1989) but may not vent these feelings.

In a sample of patients referred for angiography, Siegman (1989) found similar results. Patients high in a measure of expressive hostility, which is strongly correlated with Potential for Hostility, showed low levels of chronic, negative affectivity. In contrast, patients scoring high on measures of hostile experience also reported other kinds of negative affect—resentment, mistrust, and suspicion (Siegman, 1989; Siegman, Dembroski, & Ringel, 1987). Of interest, too, is that degree of coronary occlusion was positively correlated with expression of hostility but negatively correlated with neurotic hostility. Thus the overt expression of anger was associated with coronary disease, but feelings of resentment and anxiety tended to be protective.

It seems paradoxical that people with chronic tendencies to act callously and manipulatively do not experience hostile, resentful feelings. After all, chronic anger is commonly conceived as stemming from basic beliefs that one has been or is being treated unjustly and wants restitution or revenge (Epstein, 1983). As in the case of global Type A, the clues lead to the conclusion that the chronic tendency toward antagonistic behavior is built on a strong foundation of denial or suppression among people who are coronary-prone.

THE ROLE OF PERSONAL BELIEFS, UNCERTAINTY, AND AVOIDANCE IN TYPE A BEHAVIOR

Friedman & Rosenman's (1959) original approach and more recent approaches (Price, 1982) propose that people characterized as high in Pattern A or the hostility subcomponent hold a set of implicit personal beliefs acquired as a function of early socialization and perhaps biological temperament. In addition to these beliefs, however, I propose that the coronary-prone person has a pervasive avoidant coping style that blocks from awareness the cognitive and emotional roots of the pattern and its behavioral consequences. My approach is unique in identifying an avoidant coping style as an integral part of global Type A and the hostility subcomponent (cf. Suls & Fletcher, 1985). In the past some investigators have suggested that Type As may deny physical symptoms caused by overexertion or illness because to acknowledge them would require taking time from work. I argue, however, that denial is not an offshoot of the coronary-prone pattern, but an essential element. Moreover, in the absence of denial, strong tendencies toward competition, achievement, and hostility do not incur increased coronary risk. To explain the rationale for these assertions. I outline the central Type A beliefs and then describe factors facilitating their development. Then I describe the critical role of denial in this account of the coronary-prone Type A person.

Type A Beliefs

The Type A has a set of beliefs that are different from those held by Type Bs. Actually, the term *belief* is probably a misnomer because these are preconscious assumptions or constructs that may be unacknowledged but that assimilate new experience and direct ongoing behavior. According to this view, borrowed from Lecky (1945), Kelly (1955), and Epstein (1983), personal constructs are usually implicit and rarely questioned because they provide the foundation for higher level postulates about the self and the world. The existence of particular postulates may be inferred, however, when emotions are aroused, because this signals that the person's theory of reality is implicated.

Price (1982) has provided a systematic discussion of the personal beliefs that underlie the behavior pattern; major beliefs having their origins in prevailing socio-cultural values of an achievement-oriented, materialistic society are seen to be at the core of Type A behavior. A primary belief is that personal esteem is a function of the number and quality of one's achievements. Hence, to think well of oneself and for others to do so as well, one must achieve a lot. But achievement is essentially relative and transitory. If one's sense of worth is tied to accomplishment, then it is a chronic struggle to stay ahead of the game.

A second belief is that no universal moral principles exist, which leads, in turn, to the fear that good may not prevail. "One of the effects of the fear that good does not prevail is that the principle of expediency comes to be seen as the law of survival" (Price, 1982, p. 118). This belief also has another consequence. If there is no universal or supreme justice, one must personally ensure justice for oneself, leading to vengeful behavior or the hostility observed in many Type As.

The third belief is that resources are scarce, thus necessitating ceaseless competitive striving ("your win is my loss"). It also engenders the fear that one does not have sufficient time so one rushes about and takes on multiple tasks. Believing that resources are scarce complements the other notions—that the law of survival governs and that one must always stay ahead of the game.

Beliefs that self-esteem is tied to personal achievements and that the world is unjust and scarce in resources are plausible personal constructs of the main elements of the Type A pattern. To Price's credit, these beliefs provide a framework for understanding the competitiveness, impatience, and hostility seen in Type A individuals. But I propose that there is a meta-belief that unites these constructs. A common thread running through these themes is a deep-seated anxiety or uncertainty about the self. Because the individual is uncertain, there are basic feelings of inadequate security and self-esteem, but my approach emphasizes the sense of uncertainty over the feeling of worthlessness. If the latter were the main mechanism then Type A behavior should not differ from the garden varieties of neuroses. Furthermore, if they suffered from low self-esteem, it is unclear why Type As should set their sights on superhuman goals and work tirelessly to attain them. Also, the antagonism and condescension exhibited by people high in Potential for Hostility are not suggestive of low self-esteem. This issue cannot be fully settled here; it is possible that low self-esteem and uncertainty are both underlying themes responsible for the beliefs described by Price and these personal beliefs, in turn, provide the "motor" for Type A behaviors.

The main point is that a deep-seated anxiety or uncertainty serves as the underlying preconscious assumption that drives the Type A action–behavior complex. Uncertainty or anxiety about the self as a central theme of Type A was explicit in earlier research showing that Type As exhibit a strong desire for social comparison information to evaluate their performance (Gastorf et al., 1980; Suls, Becker, & Mullen, 1981), in the developmental research of Matthews and Siegel (1983), and in the research of Strube (1987). By positing an underlying basic ontological anxiety or uncertainty, one is using the term *anxiety* differently from clinical diagnostic criteria such as the DSM-III-R. Contemporary diagnosis criteria place great weight on overt symptomatology, and patterns of behavioral avoidance, but none of these features is likely to be seen in Type As.

Why Does Uncertainty Lead to Type A?

Each of the core beliefs implicates a basic insecurity or uncertainty, but at the same time also provides a rationale and justification for Type A behaviors. But why should a basic uncertainty about the self lead to these particular beliefs and Type A behavior rather than to behavioral withdrawal or paralysis of efforts? Uncertainty would appear to be a necessary, but not sufficient, cause. A full explanation must acknowledge the influence of sociocultural, developmental, and biological factors, a subject to which I now turn.

First, it seems clear that Type A is a behavior pattern highly consistent with the goals of Western industrial society, which values hard work, perseverance, competition, and rugged individualism (Margolis, McLeroy, Runyan, & Kaplan, 1983; Van Egeren, in press). As a cultural prototype, this kind of behavior was glamorized in the last century as rugged individualism. To the degree that individuals are insecure or uncertain about their self-worth, this pattern of achievement provides an avenue for presumably finding and marking one's relative standing as a person. At other times and in other cultures, the Type A pattern would probably be characterized as pathological! Indeed, Van Egeren (in press) has suggested that the current reward environment, unlike the 1900s and the first half the 20th century, actually encourages the Type B person who is less hostile and competitive—Riesman's "other-directedness." Van Egeren views the Type A as entrapped between the modern and postmodern value systems.

Although societal values may channel a basic feeling of uncertainty into an individualistic competitive behavior pattern, societal values must be ingrained by early family socialization. Matthews (1977; Glass, 1977) has studied socialization processes in the families of children identified as high in competitiveness and impatience. A relevant finding from this research is that mothers of extreme Type A children showed higher levels of disapproval and of encouragement to try harder following a good performance than did mothers of extreme Type Bs. Mothers of the Type A children also made fewer positive evaluations of the children. Such practices do not communicate that the child is low in ability or unworthy of love, however. The message is more complex and breeds uncertainty; it suggests that more is expected and, by implication, that the children *may* be able to achieve the higher goal. The subtle "positive" message may prevent the child from disengaging from effort altogether. Practices that include infrequent positive rewards and frequent disapproval in combination with escalating performance standards may help to encourage the development of a basic sense of uncertainty while simultaneously encouraging Type A behaviors to reduce feeling of uncertainty about the self.

Biologically given temperamental differences may also channel feelings of uncertainty in the Type A direction. Evidence indicates that some components of Type A such as loudness of speech, competition for control of the interview, and hostility are heritable based on study of identical and fraternal male twins (Matthews, Rosenman, Dembroski, MacDougall, & Harris, 1984; Carmelli, Rosenman, & Swan, 1988). Similar findings have been found for questionnaire-rated Type As (Rahe, Hervig, & Rosenman, 1978). Thus some people may be genetically predisposed to Type A behaviors.

A complex set of temperamental variables may also be necessary to foster Type A behavior, otherwise uncertainty may be manifested behaviorally in another form (e.g., depression). In this regard, Steinberg (1985) examined the relation between early temperamental variables measured at ages 3–4 and Type A behaviors at approximately 21 years of age by using the classic New York Longitudinal Study sample. Mothers of 133 children were interviewed annually during the childrens' first five years. Ratings were made on nine dimensions of temperament: activity level, rhythmicity, approach/avoidance, adaptability, intensity of reaction, sensory threshold, quality of mood, persistence, and distractibility. Steinberg correlated the ratings made at 3–4 years with scores taken from an interview tapping basic Type A dimensions when the same subjects were young adults. For global Type A, a combination of low activity level coupled with high levels of approach to new situations and a low sensory threshold at age 3–4 was predictive of Type A behavior as adults.

The high level of approach makes good intuitive sense, but the childrens' low activity level is curious in light of their high level of activity as adults. Steinberg (1985) suggested that children exhibiting a low activity level may be actively encouraged by their parents to develop strong achievement-related motives in an effort to compensate for their passive nature. The basic uncertainty proposed as the underlying cause of pattern A makes some sense if Type As as children exhibited tendencies that would appear contradictory to their parents such as being low in general activity level but reacting intensely to low levels of stimulation. If a child presents "incongruent behavior," the parent may be uncertain about what to expect, leading to caretaking that, in turn, creates uncertainty for the child. Clearly, more research is needed, but even the available evidence provides a plausible scenario for how basic feelings of uncertainty about the self in combination with sociocultural, developmental, and biological factors lead to Type A beliefs and behaviors.

Denial: The Essential Mediator

Whereas uncertainty is at the root of Type A beliefs and behavior, it is denial that confers coronary risk when it co-occurs with Type A behaviors. Avoidant coping, such as denying anxiety, dysphoria, or resentment, is integral because the individual must not consciously acknowledge the fundamental uncertainty about the self. To acknowledge such feelings would reveal the ultimate uselessness of the chronic struggle to which the Type A is dedicated. For no matter how many material accomplishments have been achieved and how many competitors have been surpassed, future outcomes are not assured and the uncertainty about the self will persist. In fact, the companion beliefs concerning scarce resources and no moral justice ensure that success can be viewed only as transitory. The achievement-striving, multiphasic, and time-urgent behavior of Type As help to keep these thoughts out of awareness. In this way, Type A behaviors represent attempts to both reduce the uncertainty and to block from awareness the basic feeling of uncertainty and insecurity to which the Type A feels vulnerable.

In addition, the Type A probably also has developed sophisticated defenses such as suppression and fantasy. Suppression would account for the lack of psychological-mindedness observed in Type As. Use of fantasy or wish-fulfillment coping would further contribute to the undefined but ambitious goals for which the Type A strives. Avoidance is also suggested by the results described earlier by Musante et al. (in press). People who behave antagonistically and rudely toward others but report no hostile feelings are essentially denying the fact that other people have upset them.

Development of strong patterns of avoidance are suggested by the meta-analytic results described earlier. When Type A is assessed by self-report (which requires self-awareness of the behavior pattern), it is associated with feelings of anxiety, depression, and general dysphoria. To the degree that the behavior is recognized as contributing to distress and that no amount of accomplishment is satisfying, the individual should be prompted to "put the brakes" on and refrain from overexertion. In this way, the self-aware, dysphoric Type A may reduce the coronary risk conferred by a harried and impatient life style, which may account for the fact that self-report measures of Type A behavior do not reliably predict CHD risk. It does not follow that self-aware Type As are completely protected from physical disease, however, and they may be at somewhat greater risk than Type Bs (see Suls & Sanders, 1988). High levels of achievement-striving, impatience, and so forth, probably carry some cumulative effect just as accumulation of stressful life events increase general illness susceptibility (Rabkin & Struening, 1976). It would be more proper to consider the self-aware Type A to be at lower risk of physical disease than is the Type A who is not self-aware.

In contrast, people who paralinguistically exhibit behaviors of a competitive, antagonistic, and impatient nature (in the SI) but are not necessarily aware of their behavior report little dysphoria. These individuals are also at greater risk for subsequent CHD. A lack of self-awareness may be implicated. It is of no small interest that Type As tend to deny early signs of heart disease such as chest pains and thereby seek medical attention too late (Matthews, Siegel, Kuller, Thompson, & Varat, 1983; Weidner & Mattews, 1978). Furthermore, a substantial proportion of heart attack patients in coronary care wards tend to deny that they had an attack in the face of hard evidence to the contrary (Hackett, Cassem, & Wishnie, 1968).

Hence, my argument is that Type A behavior and the hostility subcomponent are directly related to a set of beliefs, stemming from a basic uncertainty and insecurity about the self and its relationship with the world. To reduce the uncertainty, the individual seeks to gain accomplishment via aggressive, competitive actions—the only behaviors that seem appropriate in a world scarce in resources and justice. The hurried, work-filled schedule provides both an attempted solution to reduce the uncertainty about the self and a distraction from the anxiety that would be produced by dwelling on feelings of insecurity. Similarly, for people who show potential for hostility, admission of anger would mean admitting that one has been mistreated. Acting rudely and condescendingly toward others serves as a defense or denial of feelings of insecurity. Of course, accomplishments cannot reduce the uncertainty because material accomplishments are transitory, thus inspiring a continuing spiral of efforts. Similarly, an antagonistic style may bring respect, but is unlikely to elicit affection. In this way, the behaviors do not resolve the basic problem, but they block from awareness the fundamental constructs of which they are a manifestation.

In addition to the evidence suggestive of denial from the meta-analysis described earlier, there is also evidence from laboratory studies. In an experiment in which Type A and B subjects were threatened with shock if they made errors on a task, Type As denied being afraid although their physiological arousal was higher than that exhibited by Type B subjects (Pittner & Houston, 1981). Schlegel, Wellwood, Copps, Gruchow, and Sharratt (1981) found that SI-Type As who adopted a pattern of intense and challenging activity in their daily living after having myocardial infarction reported fewer physical symptoms than Type Bs under similar circumstances. The researchers interpreted their results as indicative of suppression of physical symptoms or overexertion.

Perhaps the most interesting supportive evidence comes from studies of the effects of beta-adrenergic stimulation on Type A behavior. Krantz et al. (1987) examined the short-term effects of isoproterenol, which produces increases in sympathetic nervous system arousal. In two sessions, placebo (saline) was administered first, followed by the SI, a challenging mental arithmetic test, and completion of affect scales. The procedure was then repeated with the active drug. Not surprisingly, anxiety and hostility ratings increased as did heart rate and blood pressure when isoproterenol was administered. The interesting result was that global Type A and subcomponents such as hostility were lowered by isoproternol. Specifically, isoproterenol reduced rapid and accelerated speech and verbal competition.

In discussing these results, Krantz noted that the beta-agonist produces feelings of fear and tenseness resulting in self-perception of anxiety that are incompatible with Type A speech or behavioral characteristics. Carrying this reasoning a bit further, we might argue that Type As are able to maintain their hurried, antagonistic behavior only when they are not cognizant of intense subjective feelings. Administration of the isoproterenol disrupts the usual process of denial and in so doing restricts the Type A's usual manner of coping with stress.

There is also relevant evidence from the large literature devoted to comparing psychophysiological reactivity to stressors of individuals differing in Type A behavior. Although the results are mixed, some studies show that people classified as Type A by the SI show exaggerated blood pressure and heart rate responses to laboratory stressors when compared to Type Bs (Contrada & Krantz, 1988; Harbin, 1989; Houston, 1988). Hyperactivity has been suggested as a potential pathway through which Type A behavior promotes the development of CHD (but see Rosenman & Ward, 1988; Suls & Sanders, 1989). Interestingly, Type A behavior measured with self-report measures such as the JAS and the Framingham Scale is not consistently associated with reactivity. Some reviewers have suggested that reactivity differences fail to emerge because self-report measures do not tap "true" Type A behavior. As an alternative explanation, self-awareness of Type A behaviors (as measured by the JAS or the Framingham Scale may prompt people with competitive, impatient, and hostile tendencies to attenuate their vigorous concentration on the laboratory stressors. Hence, the physiological reactivity of self-aware Type As, in contrast to Type As who are not self-aware, does not strongly diverge from that exhibited by Type Bs.

The preceding comments have not addressed why some Type As are self-aware and others are not. Of course, level of self-awareness is a continuum that self-report measures probably only approximate. Several factors may be responsible for the fact that some people make greater use of denial and avoidant tactics. One possibility is that people with more intense feelings of uncertainty and insecurity have greater need of avoidance so the latter may be a "flag" for greater underlying uncertainty and insecurity. Patterns of avoidance may also be learned from parents (Bandura, 1986), and there may also be as yet undetermined biological dispositions that allow some people to block or avoid unsettling feelings more successfully than others. If my thesis is correct, however, the gains provided by chronic avoidance are offset by the long-term physical costs.

In brief, the available evidence lends support to the distinction between Type As who are and are not self-aware, and to the differential consequences of self-awareness for physical and psychological functioning. Of course, a final verdict requires an experimental study in which the effects of making Type As self-aware of their behavior reduces their coronary risk. The closest approximation to such a test is the Recurrent Coronary Prevention data (Friedman et al., 1986), which purportedly showed that cognitive–behavioral interventions that lessened Type A behavior reduced CHD recurrences. One important part of the intervention was teaching Type As to recognize and become aware of their behavior, but there were other components as well (e.g., relaxation), so it is not an unambiguous test of my thesis, although the data are broadly consistent with the thesis.

SUMMARY AND IMPLICATIONS

I began the chapter by asking whether chronic tendencies toward achievement-striving, impatience, and hostility, which have been implicated as risk factors for heart disease, are also associated with psychological distress. The best available evidence indicates that only self-reported Type A behavior is associated with chronic dysphoria. In contrast, individuals who are categorized on the basis of their behavior by the SI may show little awareness of the behavior pattern and little overt psychological upset. I suggest that there is an underlying uncertainty or insecurity about the self that seems to be common to all Type As, but some also exhibit cognitive avoidance and lack of self-awareness. Self-aware Type As show psychological distress, presumably as a consequence of their chronic struggle with time and other people, but these Type As are not at risk for CHD. In contrast, the Type A who is not self-aware exhibits no psychological sequelae but is at greater risk for CHD. The presence or absence of chronic denial appears to make the difference between whether Type A behaviors have coronary versus psychological sequelae.

The concept of denial also plays an important role in other areas of behavioral medicine is revealed. Avoidance or denial has been proposed as a primary mediator in disregulation (or control systems) accounts of the relation between stress and physical adaptation (Lazarus, 1983; Schwartz, 1983; Suls & Fletcher, 1985). The disregulation model proposes that experience of distress is a negative feedback process that serves as a prerequisite for engaging in appropriate cognitive or instrumental health-relevant behaviors. Individuals differ, however, in the degree to which they attend to or monitor distress or physical symptoms as a function of situational and personalogical factors. Chronic failure to monitor external or internal cues can result in a breakdown of the physical system. For example, ignoring symptoms of overexertion may lead to physical problems, or avoidance itself can consume considerable effort resulting in hyperactive physiological responding (Glass & Singer, 1972). This may help explain why chronic cognitive or behavioral avoidance has been found to be associated with long-term physical health consequences (Roth & Cohen, 1986; Suls & Fletcher, 1985).

In the case of the Type A who lacks self-awareness two explanations are plausible for his or her increased coronary risk. As noted earlier, by blocking awareness of subjective perceptions, the Type A may overexert him- or herself in face of a challenge. The resulting physiological hyperactivity may exacerbate the atherosclerotic process. Chronic denial or suppression may also lead the individual to engage in certain behaviors that are dangerous to health. These include poor health practices, overeating, and the consumption of high levels of alcohol in combination, and the seeking out of stressful situations (e.g., projects with short deadlines), all of which have been implicated as precursors of myocardial infarction and sudden cardiac death from cardiac arrhythmias (e.g., Myers & Dewar, 1975).

Currently, the specific mechanisms by which Type A behavior and the hostility subcomponent confer coronary risk are still unclear (Dimsdale, 1988; Rosenman &

Ward, 1988; Suls & Sanders, 1989). The self-awareness approach developed in this chapter suggests that a deep-seated anxiety or uncertainty leads to the competitiveness, impatience, and hostility characteristic of Type A individuals. The self-awareness approach also provides an explanation for why self-report and behavioroid measures of pattern A appear to predict different outcomes. It also holds some promise of resolving questions about the mechanisms by which a behavior pattern confers disease risk.

REFERENCES

Bandura, A. (1986). *Social learning theory.* Englewood Cliffs, NJ: Prentice-Hall.

Booth-Kewley, S., & Friedman, H. (1987). Psychological predictors of heart disease: A quantitative review. *Psychological Bulletin, 101,* 343–362.

Bortner, R. (1969). A short rating scale as a potential measure of pattern A behavior. *Journal of Chronic Diseases, 22,* 87–91.

Brand, R. J., Rosenman, R. H., Jenkins, C. D., Sholtz, R., & Zyzanski, S. J. (1978). Comparison of coronary heart disease prediction in the Western Collaborative Group Study using the structured interview and Jenkins Activity Survey assessments of the coronary-prone Type A behavior pattern. *American Heart Association CVD Epidemiology Newsletter, 24.*

Byrne, D. G., Rosenman, R. H., Shiller, E., & Chesney, M. (1985). Consistency and variation among instruments purporting to measure the Type A behavior pattern. *Psychosomatic Medicine, 47,* 242–261.

Caplan, R. D., Cobb, S., French, J., Harrison, & Pinneau, S. (1975). *Job demands and worker health* (DHEW Publication No. 75-160). Washington, DC: U. S. Government Printing Office.

Carmelli, D., Rosenman, R. H., & Swan, G. E. (1988). The Cook and Medley HO scale: A heritability analysis in adult male twins. *Psychosomatic Medicine, 50,* 165–174.

Contrada, R. J., & Krantz, D. S. (1988). Stress, reactivity, and Type A behavior: Current status and future directions. *Annals of Behavioral Medicine, 10,* 64–70.

Costa, P. T., Jr., McCrae, R., R., & Dembroski, T. (1989). Agreeableness versus antagonism: Explication of a potential risk factor for CHD. In A. Siegman & T. Dembroski (Eds.), *In search of coronary-prone behavior: Beyond Type A* (pp. 41–63). Hillsdale, NJ: Erlbaum.

Dembroski, T. M., & Costa, P. T. (1987). Coronary-prone behavior: Components of the Type A pattern and hostility. *Journal of Personality, 55,* 211–236.

Dembroski, T. M., & Costa, P. T., Jr. (1988). Assessment of coronary-prone behavior: A current overview. *Annals of Behavioral Medicine, 10,* 60–63.

Derogatis, L. R. (1977). *SCL-90 (Revised) Version Manuel-1.* Baltimore, MD: John Hopkins Press.

Dimsdale, J. E. (1988). A perspective on Type A behavior and coronary disease. *New England Journal of Medicine, 318,* 110–112.

Epstein, S. (1983). The unconscious, the preconscious, and the self-concept. In J. Suls & A. G. Greenwald (Eds.), *Psychological perspectives on the self* (Vol. 2, pp. 219–247). Hillsdale, NJ: Erlbaum.

Friedman, H. S., & Booth-Kewley, S. (1987). The "disease-prone personality." *American Psychologist, 42,* 534–555.

Friedman, M., & Rosenman, R. H. (1959). Association of a specific overt behavior pattern with increases in blood cholesterol, blood clotting time, incidence of arcus senilis and clinical coronary artery disease. *Journal of the American Medical Association, 169,* 1286–1296.

Friedman, M., Thoresen, C., Gill, J., Ulmer, D., Powell, L., Price, V., Brown, B., Thompson, L., Rabin, D., Breall, W., Bourg, E., Levy, R., & Dixon, T. (1986). Alternation of Type A behavior and its effect on cardiac recurrences in post-myocardial infarction patients: Summary results of the Recurrent Coronary Prevention Project. *American Heart Journal, 11,* 653–665.

Gastorf, J. W., Suls, J., & Sanders, G. S. (1980). Type A coronary-prone behavior pattern and social facilitation. *Journal of Personality and Social Psychology, 38,* 773–780.

Glass, D. C. (1977). *Behavior patterns, stress, and coronary disease.* Hillsdale, JN: Erlbaum.

Glass, D. C., & Singer, J. E. (1972). *Urban stress.* New York: Academic Press.

Gotlib, I. H. (1984). Depression and general psychopathology in university students. *Journal of Abnormal Psychology 93,* 19–30.

Gough, H. H., & Heilbrun, A. B. (1975). *The Adjective Checklist.* Palo Alto, CA: Consulting Psychologists Press.

Hackett, T., Cassem, N., & Wishnie, H. (1968). The coronary care unit: An appraisal of its psychological hazards. *New England Journal of Medicine, 279,* 1365-1370.

Harbin, T. J. (1989). The relationship between the Type A behavior pattern and physiological responsivity: A quantitative review. *Psychophysiology, 26,* 110-119.

Haynes, S., Feinleib, M., & Kannel, W. (1980). The relationship of psychosocial factors to coronary heart disease in the Framingham Study: 3. Eight-year incidence of coronary heart disease. *American Journal of Epidemiology, 111,* 37-58.

Hedges, L., & Olkin, I. (1985). *Statistical methods for meta-analysis.* Orlando, FL: Academic Press.

Houston, B. K. (1988). Cardiovascular and neuroendocrine reactivity, global Type A, and components of Type A behavior. In B. K. Houston & C. R. Snyder (Eds.), *Type A behavior pattern* (pp. 212-252). New York: Wiley.

Jenkins, C. D., Rosenman, R. H., & Friedman, M. (1967). Development of an objective psychological test for the determination of the coronary-prone behavior pattern in employed men. *Journal of Chronic Diseases, 20,* 371-379.

Kelly, G. A. (1955). *The psychology of personal constructs* (Vols. 1-2). New York: Norton.

Krantz, D. S., Contrada, R. J., LaRiccia, P., Anderson, J., Durel, L., Dembroski, T. M., & Weiss, T. (1987). Effects of beta-adrenergic stimulation and blockage on cardiovascular reactivity, affect, and Type A behavior. *Psychosomatic Medicine, 49,* 146-158.

Lazarus, R. (1983). The costs and benefits of denial. In S. Bresnitz (Ed.), *Denial of stress* (pp. 1-30). New York: International Universities Press.

Lecky, P. (1945). *Self-consistency: A theory of personality.* New York: Island Press.

Margolis, L., McLeroy, K., Runyan, C., & Kaplan, B. (1983). Type A behavior: An ecological approach. *Journal of Behavioral Medicine, 6,* 245-258.

Matthews, K. A. (1977). Caregiver-child interactions and the Type A coronary-prone behavior pattern. *Child Development, 48,* 1752-1756.

Matthews, K. A. (1982). Psychological perspectives on the Type A behavior pattern. *Psychological Bulletin, 91,* 293-323.

Matthews, K. A. (1988). Coronary heart disease and Type A behaviors: Update on and alternative to the Booth-Kewley and Friedman (1987) quantitative review. *Psychological Bulletin, 104,* 373-380.

Matthews, K. A., Glass, D. C., Rosenman, R. H., & Bortner, R. (1977). Competitive drive, pattern A, and coronary heart disease: A further analysis of some data from the Western Collaborative Group Study. *Journal of Chronic Diseases, 30,* 489-498.

Matthews, K. A., Krantz, D. S., Dembroski, T., & MacDougall, J. (1982). Unique and common variance in Structured Interview and Jenkins Activity Survey assessments of the Type A behavior pattern. *Journal of Personality and Social Psychology, 42,* 303-313.

Matthews, K. A., Rosenman, R. H., Dembroski, T. M., MacDougall, J. M., & Harris, E. (1984). Familial resemblance in components of the Type A behavior pattern: A reanalysis of the California Type A twin study. *Psychosomatic Medicine, 46,* 512-522.

Matthews, K. A., & Siegal, J. M. (1982). The Type A behavior pattern in children and adolescents: Assessment, development, and associated coronary-risk. In A. Baum & J. Singer (Eds.), *Handbook of psychology and health* (Vol. 2). Hillsdale, NJ: Erlbaum.

Matthews, K. A., Siegel, J. M., Kuller, L., Thompson, M., & Varat, M. (1983). Determinants of decisions to seek medical treatment by patients with acute myocardial infarction symptoms. *Journal of Personality and Social Psychology, 44,* 1144-1156.

Musante, L., MacDougall, J. M., Dembroski, T., & Costa, P. T., Jr. (1989). Potential for hostility and dimensions of anger. *Health Psychology, 8,* 343-354.

Myers, A., & Dewar, H. A. (1975). Circumstances attending 10 sudden deaths from coronary artery disease with coroner's necropsies. *British Heart Journal, 37,* 1133-1143.

Osler, W. (1892). *Lectures on angina pectoris and allied states.* New York: Appleton.

Pittner, M. S., & Houston, B. K. (1980). Response to stress, cognitive coping strategies, and the Type A behavior pattern. *Journal of Personality and Social Psychology, 36,* 147-157.

Price, V. A. (1982). What is Type A? A cognitive social learning model. *Journal of Occupational Behavior, 3,* 109-129.

Rabkin, J., & Struening, E. L. (1976). Life events, stress, and illness, *Science, 194,* 1013-1020.

Ragland, D. R., & Brand, R. J. (1988). Coronary heart disease mortality in the Western Collaborative Group Study. *American Journal of Epidemiology, 127,* 462-475.

Rahe, R. H., Hervig, L., & Rosenman, R. H. (1978). Heritability of Type A behavior. *Psychosomatic Medicine, 40*, 478–486.

Rosenman, R. H. (1978a). The interview method of assessment of the coronary-prone behavior pattern. In T. Dembroski, S. Weiss, J. Shields, S. Haynes, & M. Feinleib (Eds.), *Coronary-prone behavior* (pp. 55–70). New York: Springer-Verlag.

Rosenman, R. H. (1978b). Introduction. In T. Dembroski, S. Weiss, J. Shields, S. Haynes, & M. Feinleib (Eds.), *Coronary-prone behavior* (pp. xiii–xvi). New York: Springer-Verlag.

Rosenman, R. H. (in press). Type A behavior pattern: A personal overview. *Journal of Social Behavior and Personality.*

Rosenman, R. H., Brand, R. J., Jenkins, C. D., Friedman, M., Straus, R., & Wurm, M. (1975). Coronary heart disease in the Western Collaborative Group Study: Final follow-up experience of 8 1/2 years. *Journal of the American Medical Association, 233*, 872–877.

Rosenman, R. H., & Ward, M. (1988). The changing concept of cardiovascular reactivity. *Stress Medicine, 4*, 241–251.

Rosenthal, R. (1984). *Meta-analytic procedures for social research.* Beverly Hills, CA: Sage.

Roth, S., & Cohen, L. (1986). Approach, avoidance, and coping with stress. *American Psychologist, 41*, 813–819.

Schlegel, R. P., Wellwood, J., Copps, B., Gruchow, W., & Sharratt, M. (1980). The relationship between perceived challenge in daily symptom reporting in Type A vs. Type B postinfarct subjects. *Journal of Behavioral Medicine, 3*, 191–204.

Schwartz, G. E. (1983). Disregulation theory and disease: Applications to the repression/cerebral disconnection/cardiovascular disorder hypothesis. *International Review of Applied Psychology, 32*, 95–118.

Shekelle, R. B., Hulley, S., Neaton, J., Billings, J., et al. (1985). The MRFIT behavior pattern study II: Type A behavior and incidence of coronary heart disease. *American Journal of Epidemiology, 56*, 559–570.

Shekelle, R. B., Schoenberger, J. A., & Stamler, J. (1976). Correlates of the JAS Type A behavior pattern score. *Journal of Chronic Diseases, 29*, 381–394.

Siegman, A. W. (1989). The role of hostility, neuroticism, and speech style in coronary artery disease. In A. W. Siegman & T. Dembroski (Eds.), *In search of coronary-prone behavior: Beyond Type A* (pp. 65–89). Hillsdale, NJ: Erlbaum.

Siegman, A. W., Dembroski, T., & Ringel, N. (1987). Components of hostility and the severity of coronary artery disease. *Psychosomatic Medicine, 49*, 127–134.

Steinberg, L. (1985). Early temperamental antecedents of adult Type A behaviors. *Developmental Psychology, 21*, 1171–1180.

Strube, M. J. (1987). A self-appraisal model of the Type A behavior pattern. In R. Hogan & W. Jones (Eds.), *Perspectives in personality theory* (Vol. 2, pp. 201–250). Greenwich, CT: JAI Press.

Suls, J., Becker, M., & Mullen, B. (1981). Coronary-prone behavior, social insecurity, and stress among college-aged adults. *Journal of Human Stress, 7*, 27–34.

Suls, J., & Fletcher, B. (1985). The relative efficacy of avoidant and nonavoidant coping strategies: A meta-analysis. *Health Psychology, 4*, 249–288.

Suls, J., & Sanders, G. S. (1988). Type A behavior as a risk factor for physical disorder. *Journal of Behavioral Medicine, 11*, 201–226.

Suls, J., & Sanders, G. S. (1989). Why do some behavioral styles increase coronary risk? In A. Siegman & T. M. Dembroski (Eds.), *In search of coronary-prone behavior: Beyond Type A* (pp. 1–20). Hillsdale, NJ: Erlbaum.

Suls, J., & Wan, C. K. (1989). The relationship between Type A behavior pattern and chronic emotional distress: A meta-analysis. *Journal of Personality and Social Psychology, 57*, 503–512.

Thurstone, L. L. (1949). *Thurstone Temperament Schedule.* Chicago: Science Research Associates.

Van Egeren, L. F. (in press). A "success trap" theory of Type A behavior: 1. Historical background. *Journal of Social Behavior and Personality.*

Watson, D., & Clark, L. A. (1984). Negative affectivity: The disposition to experience aversive states. *Psychological Bulletin, 96*, 465–490.

Weidner, G., & Matthews, K. A. (1978). Reported physical symptoms elicited by unpredictable events and the Type A coronary-prone behavior pattern. *Journal of Personality and Social Psychology, 36*, 1213–1220.

Williams, R. B., Barefoot, J., & Shekelle, R. B. (1985). The health consequences of hostility. In M. Chesney & R. H. Rosenman (Eds.), *Anger and hostility in cardiovascular and behavioral disorders* (pp. 173–186). Washington, DC: Hemisphere.

Zyzanski, S. J. (1978). Coronary-prone behavior pattern and coronary heart disease: Epidemiological evidence. In T. Dembroski, S. Weiss, S. Shields, S. Haynes, & M. Feinleib (Eds.), *Coronary-prone behavior* (pp. 25–40). New York: Springer-Verlag.

12

Anxiety and Mitral Valve Prolapse

Stephen R. Dager and David L. Dunner

PATHOPHYSIOLOGY

The mitral valve separates the left ventricle from the left atrium in the heart. Mitral valve prolapse (MVP) refers to a condition in which the two mitral leaflets sag back into the left atrium during systole (see Figure 1). The presumed anatomical basis for this leaflet prolapse appears to be an increase or redundancy in valvular area causing a folding of the leaflets (Waller et al., 1982). Anatomical features of MVP may consist of segmental or generalized enlargement of the mitral leaflets, which has been described as "hooding" or "billowing" (Davies, Moore, & Brainbridge, 1978). Typically the posterior leaflet is involved, and rarely is the anterior leaflet involved in the absence of posterior leaflet deformity. Myxomatous degeneration of the mitral leaflets, the progressive replacement of collagen tissue by mucopolysaccharide deposits, is a histological finding often associated with MVP (King, Clark, Baba, Kilman, & Wooley, 1982). This finding is not thought to be the sine qua non of MVP. It is only variably found on postmortem examination and is not specific to MVP (Davies et al., 1978; Kerns & Tucher, 1972). As will be further discussed, it is likely that different forms of MVP exist that encompass both anatomical and functional or state-dependent types (Wynne, 1986).

Certain auscultatory findings that are commonly associated with MVP help characterize the condition (Jeresaty, 1979). A sudden tension on the submitral attachments (Chordae tendineae) that connect the papilllary muscles with the mitral leaflets is thought to result in audible, nonejection clicks during mid to late systole as the leaflets sag. More specifically associated with MVP is the late systolic murmur of mitral regurgitation. This can occur as the leaflets prolapse back into other atrium and the force of the blood during ventricular contraction pushes them further apart rather than tighter together, as would normally occur. A leaky seal is created, allowing back flow of blood.

MVP was initially diagnosed on the basis of auscultatory findings. However, auscultatory signs are variably present even on serial examinations of the same patient (Jeresaty, 1979; Markiewicz, Stoner, London, Hunts, & Popp, 1976; Savage, Devereux et al., 1983), suggesting that the underlying pathophysiological basis for the clicks and systolic murmur may be absent or state-dependent in some individuals with MVP. Consistent with this has been the demonstration that auscultatory findings can be brought out by maneuvers designed to decrease ventricular filling, such as having the patient squat or perform a Valsalva maneuver (Fontana, Wooley, Leighton, & Lewis, 1975; Jeresaty, 1979). Abnormal coaptation of the leaflets also can be acutely

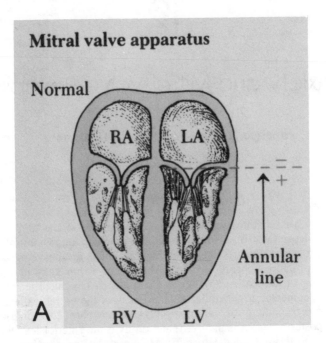

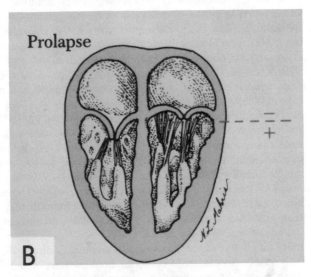

Figure 1   (a) Normal closure of the mitral leaflets on the
ventricular side of the annular line. (b) Prolapse of the
mitral leaflets into the left atrium. Courtesy of CPC
Communications.

provoked by decreasing ventricular filling in presumably normal humans during amyl nitrite inhalation (Gavin et al., 1983). Physiological increases in blood volume during pregnancy can instead resolve evidence of MVP (Lutas, Devereux, Spitzer, & Kramer-Fox, 1984), again, suggesting that at least some cases of MVP may be functional in nature.

EPIDEMIOLOGY

MVP has become the most frequently diagnosed cardiac valvular condition among the general population (Markiewicz et al., 1976; Procacci, Savran, Schreiter, et al., 1976; Savage, Garrison et al., 1983; Wann, Grove, & Hess, 1983). Whites, Blacks, and Asians all appear to have the same relative prevalence rates for MVP. The Framingham study, the largest population-based cardiac risk factor survey to date, reported a 5% overall prevalence rate for MVP using M-mode echocardiographic techniques for diagnosis (Savage, Garrison et al., 1983). Men had an age-independent prevalence of 4%, whereas women had an age-dependent prevalence rate ranging from 17% for those between the ages of 20 to 29 to less than 2% for women over 70. Other studies have also reported a prevalence of up to 21% in asymptomatic young women (Markiewicz et al., 1976).

The basis for an increased prevalence of MVP found in women and the declining prevalence among older women is not clearly understood. It is possible that this finding may reflect the existence of a particular form of MVP that is capable of resolving itself over time. This could be due to the progressive thickening of the mitral leaflets or from myxomatous changes, causing them to be stiffer and less prone to prolapse. Alternatively, alterations in left ventricular volume or relative increases in blood volume may mask echocardiographic evidence of MVP among older women. The declining prevalence is not due to an increased rate of mortality associated with the condition (Nichimura et al., 1985).

ETIOLOGY

Historically, a cardiac syndrome that was most commonly recognized in soldiers was frequently related to factors such as wearing overly tight uniforms or excessive exercise (Hartshorn, 1864; Skerritt, 1983). Following World War I, investigators began to link associated symptoms including chest pain, palpitations, tachycardia, arrhythmia, dyspnea, light headedness, fatigue, and nervousness with life events or stress (Cohen, White, & Johnson, 1948). Not until the 1960s was it established by angiography that clinical features of a click or systolic murmur frequently associated with this constellation of symptoms were due to abnormal displacement of the two mitral valve leaflets into the left atrium during systole (Barlow, Bosman, Pocock et al., 1968; Reid, 1961). Subsequently, this condition has commonly been referred to as the MVP syndrome, although more recent work would suggest that individuals with MVP are typically asymptomatic and associated symptoms are nonspecific for the condition (Markiewicz et al., 1976; Savage, Devereux et al., 1983; Uretsky, 1982).

It is recognized that MVP may be a common feature in a number of heritable connected tissue disorders including Marfan's syndrome (Pyeritz, 1983), Ehlers-Danlos syndrome (Jaffe, Geltman, Rodey, & Uitto, 1981), and osteogenesis imperfecta (Schwarz & Gotsman, 1981). These conditions, however, are extremely rare in the general population and are thus not significant contributing factors for the overall prevalence of MVP (Levy & Savage, 1987). Similarly, although rheumatic fever may be responsible for some cases of MVP (de Moor, Lachman, & Human, 1986) this cause of MVP is extremely uncommon in most developed countries. Cases of MVP associated with these rare conditions may comprise a particularly severe subtype of MVP with specific prognostic implications such as an increased risk for rupture of the chordae tendineae (Davies et al., 1978).

MVP may be a manifestation of some underlying hyperadrenergic state or autonomic dysregulation (Gaffney et al., 1979). Supportive of this, MVP has been associated with autonomic arousal or increased sympathetic nervous system activity among symptomatic MVP patients (Boudoulas, Reynolds, Mazzaferi, & Wooley, 1980; DeCarvalho, Messerli, & Frohlich, 1979; Gaffney, 1983; Gaffney et al., 1979; Pasternac et al., 1982; Puddu et al., 1983). However, by selecting for study a subgroup of MVP patients who experience symptoms indistinguishable from those associated with anxiety or adrenergic arousal, it should not be surprising that peripheral measures of autonomic dysregulation correlate best with the severity of anxiety symptoms among these patients (Boudoulas et al., 1980). In fact, when asymptomatic MVP patients are studied, findings of autonomic arousal or plasma catecholamine levels at rest and in response to cardiovascular challenge are no different from those for control subjects (Chesler, Weir, Braatz, & Francis, 1985).

When distinguished by the presence or absence of MVP, differences among anxious patients have not been observed for findings of autonomic arousal, including resting heart rate or blood pressure (Dager, Khan, Comess, Raisys, & Dunner, 1987). Along this same line of investigation, urinary 3-methoxy, 4-hydroxy phenyl glycol, or plasma monoamine oxidase activity also do not appear to be different (Dager, Khan et al., 1987), and urinary catecholamine levels appear to be the same or even higher among anxious control subjects without MVP (Nesse et al., 1985). Although unproven, symptoms may reflect the presence of hyperadrenergic states among panic patients (Charney, Heninger, & Breier, 1984; Nesse, Cameron, & Curtis, 1984). Evidence to date, however, does not support a specific relation between hyperadrenergic states or autonomic hyperactivity and the phenomena of MVP independent of symptoms commonly related to anxiety states.

Recent work has suggested that a "super coupling" among symptomatic patients with MVP may occur because of hypersensitive beta-2 adrenergic receptors (Davies, Mares, Pool, & Taylor, 1987). This has yet to be studied in symptomatic patients without MVP or asymptomatic individuals with MVP. Thus it is not possible at this time to establish whether MVP per se may prove to be a particular marker for beta-2 adrenergic receptor hypersensitivity.

At one time MVP was considered to be the cause of symptoms now commonly ascribed to the anxiety disorders (Pariser, Jones, Pinter, Young, & Fontana, 1979; Pariser, Pinta, & Jones, 1978; Wooley, 1976). A more current view is that MVP associated with panic disorder may instead be a consequence of panic attacks (Dager, Comess, & Dunner, 1986; Klein & Gorman, 1984). As was previously mentioned, acute changes in ventricular filling, such as those caused by inhalation of amyl nitrite, can produce state-dependent MVP during two-dimensional echocardiography (Gavin et al., 1983). Thus repeated hemodynamic changes during panic attacks could conceivably result in MVP. It has even been suggested that echocardiographic evidence of MVP in panic patients can normalize following successful treatment of panic attacks (Gorman, Fyer, Glicklich, King, & Klein, 1981). This is a difficult hypothesis to adequately test because of problems with the validity and reliability of echocardio-graphic techniques, as will be further discussed.

Because many patients with panic attacks have no evidence of MVP, a simple relation between panic attacks and the provocation of MVP probably does not exist. It is thought that at least some forms of MVP are heritable through an autosomal domi-nant pattern of transmission (Devereux, Brown, Kramer-Fox, & Sachs, 1982). Panic attacks also appear to be familial or have a genetic basis (Crowe, 1984; Torgersen, 1983). Inconsistent with a shared genetic diathesis, investigation of MVP's relation to panic attacks in families of patients with MVP suggests that the two conditions segre-gate independently (Crowe, Gaffney, & Kerber, 1982). This does not, however, pre-clude the possible involvement of some common third factor.

Although physical characteristics including thoracic bony abnormalities such as pectus excavatum, low body weight, elevated palate, raised arches, small breast mass, and asthetic body habitus are not specific to MVP, they are frequently associ-ated with the condition (Read, Thal, & Wendt, 1965; Rosenberg, Derman, Grubb, & Buda, 1983). It has been suggested, but remains unproven, that this type of body habitus in conjunction with MVP may reflect the presence of a particular type of connective tissue rich in elastin fibers. This so-called forme fruste or incomplete expression of Marfan's syndrome may cause the mitral leaflets to be more susceptible to prolapsing (Read et al., 1965). Panic patients who also exhibit a similar asthetic body habitus could conceivably share a similar type of connective tissue and thus more elastic mitral leaflets. In the presence of possible hemodynamic alterations occurring during repeated panic attacks, these individuals might be more prone to stretching or elongation of the mitral leaflets. Physical characteristics of panic pa-tients differentiated by findings of MVP may indirectly address this hypothesis. More definitive confirmation awaits actual study of connective tissue composition, a costly and difficult endeavor.

DIAGNOSIS

MVP was initially diagnosed clinically on the basis of isolated or multiple clicks and mid to late systolic murmur heard on auscultation (Jeresaty, 1979). Presenting symptoms including chest pain, palpitations, tachycardia, dypsnea, dizziness, and anxiety were often thought by the clinician to corroborate a diagnosis of MVP. As has been mentioned, it became increasingly apparent that in the examination of the symp-tomatic individual, auscultatory findings were often not present or were variably present on serial examinations and that asymptomatic individuals might exhibit char-acteristic auscultatory findings. For these reasons, it was felt necessary to develop more specific and sensitive diagnostic tests to detect the presence of MVP.

Echocardiography, a type of ultrasound, became generally available in the early 1970s as a method to characterize the mitral valve apparatus. M-mode, the first widely available type of echocardiography, has been the technique most widely used to investigate MVP. This modality provides a very limited view of the mitral appa-ratus, which is depicted as a one-dimensional representation of leaflet motion (Morganroth & Pohost, 1980). A number of methodologic problems pertaining to the use of this technique have become apparent. Incorrect beam angulation and the lim-ited visualization possible of the mitral apparatus have long been recognized to in-crease the likelihood of both false positive and false negative diagnoses (Abbasi, DeCristofaro, Anabtawi, & Irwin, 1983; DeMaria, King, Bogren, Lies, & Mason,

1974; Markiewicz, London, & Popp, 1978). Of greater concern, findings necessary to establish the diagnosis of MVP are actively disputed and open to interpretation among raters.

Recent work suggests that diagnosis of MVP based on M-mode echocardiography may be invalid due to unacceptably low interrater and intrarater reliability. In one study, two senior echocardiologists, each using his own diagnostic criteria, read the same 15 preselected M-mode echocardiograms with one diagnosing 60% and the other 0% as having MVP (Gorman, Shear, Devereux, King, & Klein, 1986). A prospective study identified serious problems with both interrater and intrarater reliability when widely accepted M-mode criteria for the diagnosis of MVP were used (Dager et al., 1989). Two well-trained and experienced echocardiologists, each reading the same 50 consecutive M-mode tracings, demonstrated interrater agreement of 44% with diagnostic reliability at the level of chance as indicated by a kappa score of 0.11. When a subset of 35 M-mode tracings was reread by each rater 10 months later, better intrarater reliability was obtained with agreement for each rater of 63%, which, however, was still considered unacceptable with kappa scores of .41 and .45, respectively. These findings suggest that M-mode criteria used to establish a diagnosis of MVP can be ambiguous and open to interpretation.

Because of the need for better echocardiographic techniques that could provide anatomical definition of leaflet position, two-dimensional echocardiography was developed. This technique allows observation of leaflet motion in relation to valvular anatomy from different perspectives during "real" time (Morganroth & Pohost, 1980). Additionally, this technique has been used in an attempt to provide nonhistological evidence of myxomatous changes of the leaflets as determined by the thickening of leaflets in comparison with the septal wall (Morganroth, Jones, Chen, & Naito, 1980). As will be further discussed, this finding has been proposed to have clinical implications.

Certain problems arise, however, with the use of two-dimensional echocardiography, partly because of the topography of the mitral apparatus. Because the valve is not planer, but instead has a characteristic saddle-like conformation, certain views, such as the apical four-chamber view, may present a false picture of prolapse (Levine, Triulzi, Harrigan, & Weyman, 1986). Further limitation of the clinical utility of two-dimensional echocardiography has been the lack of consensus regarding the extent of leaflet sagging that is necessary to establish a diagnosis of MVP (Levine & Weyman, 1984; Shah, 1984). Although it is now generally considered to be a normal variant, flat closure of the leaflets at the level of the annulus would be diagnosed by some cardiologists as MVP.

In addition, the utility of two-dimensional echocardiography for reliably detecting myxomatous changes of the leaflets has not been determined. It is also not at all clear the echocardiographic techniques actually define anatomical prolapse. This latter point is illustrated by findings that echocardiographic evidence of MVP associated with certain conditions, including anorexia nervosa (Meyers, Starke, Pearson, & Wilken, 1986) and panic disorder (Gorman, Fyer, Glicklich, King, & Klein, 1981a), may resolve with successful treatment of the conditions. It should be emphasized, however, that over and beyond concerns raised regarding the reliability for rereading the same tracings, test–retest reliability of echocardiography has not been adequately tested.

Because of the problems inherent in deriving an anatomical definition of MVP, recent work has focused on the use of Doppler echocardiography to study cardiac function. Doppler studies provide a dynamic model of blood flow and are sensitive enough to pick up even trivial amounts of mitral regurgitation (Adhar, Abbasi, & Nanda, 1985). Again, it is difficult to define what is abnormal because a large proportion of a presumably normal population exhibits trace regurgitation on Doppler examination (Hutle & Agnelsen, 1985; York, Schnittger, & Popp, 1984). Thus, although the technique appears to be a very sensitive indicator of regurgitation associated with abnormal coaptation of the mitral leaflets, trace regurgitation may be too nonspecific a finding to establish a diagnosis of MVP.

Because a "gold standard" does not exist for the diagnosis of MVP, it is imperative that a general consensus be reached between centers for defining what constitutes a diagnosis of MVP (Levine & Weyman, 1984; Perloff, Child, & Edwards, 1987; Shah, 1984). Such an approach must taken into consideration our increasing awareness of the wide spectrum of normal variation in mitral leaflet motion along with the likelihood that both state-dependent and anatomical forms of MVP exist. It is too early to determine whether attempts to develop a systematic approach, analogous to that of the Jones criteria for rheumatic heart disease, which may encompass auscultatory findings, stricter and combined (M-mode, two-dimensional, and Doppler) echocardiographic features, and associated features such as body habitus and family history (Krivokapich, Child, Dadourian, & Perloff, 1988; Perloff, Child, & Edwards, 1986; Perloff et al., 1987), adequately determine a pathological condition. Although echocardiographic evidence of leaflet thickening or redundancy as an indicator of myxomatous degeneration has been proposed to have specific prognostic value (MacMahon et al, 1987; Nichimura et al., 1985), both the reliability and validity of this finding await confirmation. These problems, which appear to be inherent difficulties in establishing a definition of MVP, highlight our changing concepts of MVP as a disease entity and the confusion surrounding what constitutes a pathological condition (Levine & Weyman, 1984).

ANXIETY DISORDERS AND MITRAL VALVE PROLAPSE

The anxiety disorders have been commonly divided into two particular types of anxiety disorder, generalized anxiety disorder (GAD) and panic disorder. GAD refers to a chronic condition characterized by a variety of autonomic nervous system complaints such as weakness, fatigue, headaches, sweating, palpitations, sighing, stomach distress, muscular tension, and anxiety and worries. Criteria for diagnosis include symptoms from three of four categories, including motor tension, autonomic hyperactivity, apprehensive expectation, and vigilance and scanning. This entity, created with the revision of the psychiatric nomenclature (i.e., in the American Psychiatric Association's *Diagnostic and Statistical Manual of Mental Disorders*—DSM-III) in 1980, has not been well studied. Some feel, in fact, that GAD is not an actual condition but should instead by viewed as a residual condition.

In contrast, panic disorder is a well-defined condition characterized by the presence of panic attacks. Panic attacks are acute short-lived occurrences often resembling heart attacks and characterized by a grouping of symptoms including dyspnea, palpitations, chest pain, dizziness, choking sensations, feelings of unreality, parasthesias, hot and cold flashes, sweating, faintness, trembling, nausea, fears of dying, going crazy or doing something uncontrolled, and anxiety. The occurrence of such attacks may be infrequent or multiple during the day. Panic attacks are frequently complicated by GAD, phobic avoidance (or agoraphobia), and depression (Dealy,

Ishiki, Avery, & Dunner, 1981; Klein, 1964). Several lines of investigation suggest a biological basis for panic attacks, and some suggest a familial or genetic transmission (Crowe, 1984; Torgersen, 1983) and the ability to model panic attacks among susceptible individuals in the laboratory by the infusion of agents such as sodium lactate (Dager, Cowley, & Dunner, 1987).

A number of medical conditions may be confused with the anxiety disorders. These would include pheochromocytoma, caffeinism, hyper- or hypothyroidism, epilepsy, and drug withdrawal states (Rosenbaum, 1979). At one time, MVP was also considered to produce symptoms mimicking the anxiety disorders (Pariser et al., 1979; Wooley, 1976). This was based on the common association made by clinicians between MVP and symptoms of autonomic arousal. In addition, because many of the symptoms experienced by the anxious patient were attributable to the heart, a cardiac cause was sought. Thus the presence of MVP was commonly investigated among anxious populations.

Reviewing the available literature, we and our colleagues evaluated the results of research to find a possible association between MVP and panic disorder (Dager, Comess, Saal, & Dunner, 1986; Dager, Saal, Comess, & Dunner, 1988). Overall, the findings have been both contradictory and confusing with various studies reporting prevalence rates of MVP among anxious patients ranging anywhere from 0% to 59%. In 8 of 16 studies in which researchers evaluated 301 patients who predominantly had panic disorder, a significant relation between panic attacks and MVP was found. In another study, an increased prevalence of MVP was found, across a range of diagnostic criteria, among patients with panic attacks as compared to those with GAD (Dager, Comess, & Dunner, 1986). Those data suggested that MVP was more specifically associated with the phenomena of panic attacks rather than anxiety per se. However, eight other studies comprising a total population of 256 patients with panic or anxiety disorders failed to demonstrate a significant relation between anxiety disorders and MVP (Dager, Comess, Saal, & Dunner, 1986; Dager, Saal et al., 1988).

Several methodological problems, including differences in psychiatric populations studied, cardiac diagnostic criteria used for establishing the prevalence of MVP, and an inadequate appreciation of problems with ascertainment bias make it difficult to generalize conclusions based on these diverse findings (Dager, Comess, Saal, & Dunner, 1986; Dager, Saal et al., 1988; Margraf, Ehlers, & Roth, 1988). More troublesome has been the failure of most studies to include anonymous comparison populations. This may, in part, reflect a widespread lack of appreciation regarding the poor diagnostic reliability of echocardiographic techniques used to define the condition and the fact that MVP is not a discrete entity, either present or not present. Only three of the studies previously summarized that reported a significant relation between MVP and panic attacks (and none of those that did not) used control populations. Because of serious problems with diagnostic inconsistency between echocardiologists, the widespread use of hypothetical general population prevalence rates or unmatched clinic populations used for comparison as a basis by which to draw conclusions regarding the association or prevalence of MVP is clearly unacceptable.

Controlled studies indicate that echocardiographically defined MVP is more common among individuals who experience panic attacks (Dager, Comess, & Dunner, 1986; Kantor, Zitrin, & Zeldis, 1980; Venkatesh et al., 1980). It appears that at least one-third or more of those individuals have echocardiographic evidence of MVP. The actual prevalence of MVP among panic patients, however, remains poorly defined because of the difficulties involved in quantifying a condition that exists along a continuum. As an example, according to one report, the prevalence of MVP among patients experiencing panic attacks was 34% as compared to 15% among GAD patients for a diagnosis of definite prolapse based on two-dimensional echocardiographic documentation from two views (apical four-chamber and parasternal long axis) of mitral valve leaflet buckling below the level of the annular plane (Dager, Comess, & Dunner, 1986). The prevalence of MVP among these patient groups increased to 59% and 30%, respectively, when diagnostic criteria were broadened to include flat closure of the mitral leaflets. It is also difficult to establish prevalence rates of MVP among individuals who experience panic attacks because MVP is typically a silent or asymptomatic condition detected by routine examination in the primary care setting (Markiewicz et al., 1976; Savage, Devereux et al., 1983). In fact, a majority of studies comparing the prevalence of anxiety symptoms among individuals with MVP have failed to demonstrate an increase in incidence of psychiatric symptoms, particularly when these individuals were compared with other medically ill control populations (Dager, Comess, Saal, & Dunner, 1986; Dager, Saal et al., 1988).

Although MVP has been studied as a possible marker for differentiating a subpopulation of patients with anxiety disorders, thus far this approach has not proven to be clinically useful. The range or clinical severity of presenting symptoms (Dager, Cowley, & Dunner, 1987), specific biological abnormalities (Dager, Khan et al., 1987; Nesse et al., 1985), or treatment outcome (Dager, Cowley & Dunner, 1987; Gorman et al., 1981a) do not appear to be specifically related to findings of MVP. At one time, it was considered that presumed cardiac symptoms associated with MVP might be the cause of anxiety among this population. Although this would be consistent with the James–Lange theory of anxiety, in which panic could result from central interpretation of peripheral symptoms that are due to an underlying cardiac condition, evidence demonstrating that MVP is typically an asymptomatic condition is not consistent with this position. In our own studies, we have demonstrated that patients with MVP do not differ in presenting symptoms, or severity of presenting symptoms, as compared to other anxiety patients (Dager, Cowley, & Dunner, 1987). Thus MVP does not appear to be responsible for a specific symptom complex different from panic or anxiety symptoms.

Studies of MVP among patients with anxiety disorders also support the notion that individuals with MVP exhibit biological features similar to those of other anxiety patients. This has been demonstrated in studies evaluating sensitivity to lactate-induced panic among panic patients differentiated by MVP findings (Dager, Cowley, & Dunner, 1987; Gorman et al., 1981b). It appears that lactate-induced panic is mostly specific for the phenomenon of panic attacks regardless of associate findings of MVP. This suggests that some biological mechanism other than MVP is responsible for the production of panic. In previous investigations of the relation between MVP and the anxiety disorders, we viewed MVP as a potential marker that might define a more pure subpopulation of panic patients having a specific biological basis for their illness. Studying autonomic arousal as a possible mechanism for the expression of anxiety in patients differentiated by findings of MVP, no differences in urinary 3-methoxy, 4-hydroxy phenyl glycol excretion, or resting heart rate or blood pressure were found (Dager, Khan et al., 1987). This finding also held when attempts were made to quantify the degree of MVP.

A similar line of reasoning led us to evaluate treatment response to pharmaceutical intervention as a means of testing the hypothesis that patients with MVP would have a more specific response to medication. In a double-blind study, we found that anxiety patients with MVP did no better on alprazolam or diazepam when compared to a group of anxiety patients with normal cardiac status (Dager, Cowley, & Dunner, 1987). Interestingly, we found that the anxiety patients with MVP had a significantly increased placebo response, a finding that we are unable to explain. Other investigators have also demonstrated a similar response to imipramine for these two groups of anxious patients (Gorman et al., 1981). Although further investigation is warranted, MVP does not presently appear to be a useful marker for distinguishing a specific subpopulation of anxious patients based on the available data.

MEDICAL INTERVENTION

The presence of MVP has been related to a number of serious medical conditions including sudden cardiac death (Pocock, Bosman, Chesler, Barlow, & Edwards, 1984), cerebral emboli (Barnett et al., 1980), ventricular and supraventricular arrhythmias (DeMaria, Amsterdam, Vismara, Neuman, & Mason, 1976; Winkel et al., 1982), chordae tendineae rupture (Jeresaty, Edwards, & Chawla, 1985), infective endocarditis (Clemens, Horwitz, Jaffe, Feinstein, & Stanton, 1982), and progressive mitral regurgitation (Kolibash et al., 1986; Nishimura et al., 1985). Medical opinion regarding the clinical significance of MVP, however, has substantially changed in more recent years, and most clinicians now consider the condition to be, in general, benign (Appelblatt, Willis, Lenhart, Shulman, & Walton, 1977; Jeresaty, 1985; Leatham & Brigden, 1980; Levine & Weyman, 1984; Mills, Rose, Hollingsworth, Amara, & Craige, 1977; Shah, 1984).

Several factors may have contributed to the confusion surrounding the clinical significance and prognosis of the condition. Influential studies reporting on the medical risk of MVP generally used M-mode echocardiographic techniques to establish a diagnosis of MVP and in many instances were uncontrolled or nonblinded studies (Dager, Comess, Saal, & Dunner, 1987). A further problem has been a poor appreciation of the high prevalence of MVP found among the general population. This has been compounded by the use of increasingly sensitive diagnostic modalities that may have led to the overinclusion of normal variants among populations defined as having MVP (Leatham & Brigden, 1980; Levine & Weyman, 1984; Shah, 1984). Methodologic problems caused by ascertainment bias (Motulsky, 1978) or comorbidity, the increased likelihood that two conditions may coexist, probably have led to the overascription of cause and effect relationships between MVP and other medical conditions.

Symptoms commonly associated with MVP are difficult to relate to a cardiac origin (Jeresaty, 1979). Chest pain is usually not exertional in contrast to what might be expected with angina. Symptoms of palpitations or dizziness do not correspond to the presence of concurrent arrhythmias. Problems with dyspnea or fatigue do not progress and are not associated with hemodynamic impairment. When ambulatory monitoring techniques became available, researchers evaluating the medical significance of MVP studied the occurrence of arrythmias among symptomatic patients (Winkel et al., 1982). Large numbers of ectopic beats were recorded during ambulatory monitoring for periods of 24 hours or longer. Based largely on poorly controlled or uncontrolled study designs, these findings were thought to be specific to MVP. However, studies such as the Framingham cardiac risk-factor study, which was population-based, subsequently showed that these clinically insignificant arrythmias were common among the general population as a whole and failed to confirm a specific association to MVP (Savage, Levy et al., 1983).

Although associated with MVP, the risk of infective endocarditis among the total population with MVP is extremely low (Jeresaty, 1985; MacMahon et al., 1987). There is no evidence to date demonstrating an increased risk for infective endocarditis among patients with an isolated click on physical examination or in patients with MVP diagnosed on the basis of echocardiography alone (MacMahon et al., 1987). There is evidence to suggest, however, that patients with auscultatory findings of a systolic murmur may be at some increased risk for infective endocarditis, particularly in men over the age of 45. Attempts to associate echocardiographic findings of leaflet thickening to an increased risk for infective carcioditis await further confirmation of echocardiographic criteria necessary to reliably establish the diagnosis.

Patients who have sustained cerebral vascular accidents are often sent for echocardiographic evaluation because a purported causal relationship exists with MVP. This may help explain inconsistencies among studies evaluating the relation between cerebral embolic phenomena and MVP. An increased prevalence of MVP has been found only retrospectively in patients under the age of 45 who had sustained a cerebral vascular event (Barnett et al., 1980). In comparison with the general population, individuals with MVP do not appear to be at increased risk for the occurrence of cerebral vascular events (Cheitlin, 1979; Leatham & Brigden, 1980).

Cases of sudden cardiac death related to MVP are quite rare, and it is unclear whether such cases are a chance association due to the high prevalence of MVP in the general population. Earlier reports associating MVP with the "long QT syndrome" (Schwartz, Periti, & Malliani, 1975) as a possible risk factor for sudden cardiac death have not been substantiated (Levy & Savage, 1987). Although an increased risk for cardiovascular mortality has been related to the panic disorders, this has not been studied with respect to associated findings of MVP (Coryell, Noyes, & Clancy, 1982; Coryell, Noyes, & House, 1986). It has also not been adequately established that panic attacks are a particular risk factor for cardiovascular mortality (Dager, Roy-Byrne, & Dunner, 1988). Overall, the average life span of individuals diagnosed as having MVP does not appear to be different from that of the general population, and there is no substantial evidence establishing MVP as a risk factor for sudden cardiac death among panic or anxiety patients.

Although MVP is now generally considered a benign condition, contradictory findings concerning the long-term prognosis of MVP continue to be reported. In one recent study, among 237 patients with MVP diagnosed by M-mode echocardiography (greater than 3 mm late or holosystolic bowing below the annular line) followed up after an average of 6 years, only 4.2% had MVP-associated medical complications (Nichimura et al., 1985). With the exception of an increased risk for progressive mitral regurgitation, outcome was no different from that of an actuarial-derived general population comparison group.

In contrast, in a recent study that followed 300 patients over the same average period, with MVP initially documented by either cardiac catheterization, M-mode echocardiography, or two-dimensional echocardiography in association with auscultatory findings, found that 50% developed complications that were considered to be serious in 33% of the patients (Duren, Becker, & Dunning, 1988). In that study, MVP was related to an increased risk for sudden cardiac death, ventricular tachycardia, infectious endocarditis, progressive mitral regurgitation, and cerebral vascular accidents. Although a companion editorial has enumerated a number of concerns regarding the latter study (Kessler, 1988), the continued publication of contradictory findings furthers the confusion regarding prognostic implications of MVP. Greater attention directed to defining possible subtypes of MVP that could encompass functional and anatomical distinctions may improve prognostication (Wynne, 1986). More generally, the lack of a reliable definition of MVP and problems in obtaining diagnostic consensus will continue to confound efforts to establish whether or not medical risks are actually associated with the condition.

TREATMENT OF MITRAL VALVE PROLAPSE

It has become apparent that MVP is typically an asymptomatic condition often found during routine evaluation by the practitioner. Symptoms commonly associated with MVP appear to be mostly nonspecific and more consistent with a diagnosis of panic disorder, which should be considered the primary diagnosis. Thus medications useful for the treatment of panic attacks should be considered the primary intervention in symptomatic individuals with findings of MVP. Anti-arrhythmic agents, such as the beta-blockers, should be reserved for patients with documented clinically significant arrythmias. These agents do not appear to be an effective treatment and may, in fact, exacerbate panic symptoms (Katon, 1984; Levinson & Acquaviva, 1988).

Antibiotic prophylaxis for infective endocarditis does not appear to be warranted in cases of echocardiographically defined MVP without associated auscultatory findings of a systolic murmur (MacMahon et al., 1987). There is also no scientific basis at this time for recommending antibiotics in the presence of isolated echocardiographic findings of leaflet thickening. In the case of patients with a systolic flow murmur, particularly men over the age of 45, there is evidence to suggest that prophylactic treatment with antibiotics may be useful. However, the lack of data establishing situations in which antibiotic prophylaxis is appropriate for infective endocarditis is troublesome. As an example, studies have demonstrated that tooth brushing can be as likely to produce a bacteremia as are dental procedures (Guntheroth, 1984).

The presence of MVP is not predictive of future cerebral vascular events and prophylactic treatments are not recommended regardless of whether diagnosis is based on auscultatory findings or echocardiographic features (Cheitlin, 1979). In the case of patients with MVP, who have previously sustained cerebral embolic events, the use of anti-platelet agents such as aspirin or dipyridamole should be considered, as they would be regardless of the associated presence of MVP.

SUMMARY

Controlled studies suggest that the prevalence of MVP is increased in patients who experience panic attacks. At one time thought to be the cause of symptoms mimicking anxiety, MVP in many instances is an asymptomatic condition found incidentally on routine examination. More current theories suggest that, instead, MVP can result from panic attacks, particularly in those individuals who may also have more elastic connective tissue. This hypothesis, however, remains to be tested.

The diagnosis of MVP has not been shown to identify a clinically distinct subpopulation of anxious patients. MVP does not appear to predict severity of symptoms or clinical course among this population. Although possible medical complications associated with the anxiety and panic disorders have not been assessed in relation to echocardiographic findings, it is not yet established that this population is at greater risk for cardiovascular-related events. It is now generally believed that MVP per se is not a significant risk factor. Associated findings of mitral regurgitation, however, may have prognostic implications, particularly in older men.

Research applications of echocardiography are of heuristic interest; however, the general clinical use of echocardiography to establish a diagnosis of MVP does not appear to be particularly helpful for the clinical management of anxious patients. Of greater clinical utility, auscultation by someone skilled in detecting systolic murmurs would provide more useful information and certainly be less expensive for the patient. A diagnosis of MVP may greatly exaggerate hypochondriacal fears often present among anxious patients, particularly if great care is not taken to reassure them of the generally benign nature of the condition.

REFERENCES

Abbasi, A., DeCristofaro, D., Anabtawi, J., & Irwin, L. (1983). Mitral valve prolapse: Comparative value of M-mode, two-dimensional, and doppler echocardiography. *Journal of the American College of Cardiology, 2,* 1219–1223.

Adhar, C. G., Abbasi, A., & Nanda, N. C. (1985). Doppler echocardiography in the assessment of mitral regurgitation and mitral valve prolapse. In N. C. Nanda (Ed.), *Doppler echocardiography* (pp. 188–210). New York: Iyaku-Shoin.

Appelblatt, N. H., Willis, P. W., Lenhart, J. A., Shulman, J., & Walton, J. A. (1975). Ten- to 4-year follow-up of 69 patients with systolic click with or without late systolic murmur. *American Journal of Cardiology, 35,* 119.

Barlow, J. B., Bosma, C. K., Pocock, W. A., Marehand, P., & Denny, M. (1968). Late systolic murmurs and non-ejection (mid-late) systolic clicks: An analysis of 90 patients. *British Heart Journal, 30,* 203–218.

Barnett, H. J. M., Boughner, D., Taylor, D. W., Cooper, P., Kostuk, W., & Nichol, P. (1980). Further evidence relating mitral valve prolapse to cerebral ischemic events. *New England Journal of Medicine, 102,* 139–144.

Boudoulas, H., Reynolds, J., Mazzaferi, E., & Wooley, C. (1980). Metabolic studies in mitral valve prolapse syndrome. *Circulation, 61,* 1200–1205.

Charney, D. S., Heninger, G. R., & Breier, A. (1984). Noradrenergic function in panic anxiety. *Archives of General Psychiatry, 41,* 751–763.

Cheitlin, M. D. (1979). Thromboembolic studies in the patient with the prolapsed mitral valve (Has Salome dropped another veil?). *Circulation 60*(1), 46–47.

Chesler, E., Weir, E. K., Braatz, G. A., & Francis, G. (1985). Normal catecholamine and hemodynamic responses to orthostatic tilt in subjects with mitral valve prolapse. *American Journal of Medicine, 78,* 754–760.

Clemens, J. D., Horwitz, R. I., Jaffe, C. C., Feinstein, A., & Stanton, B. (1982). A controlled evaluation of the risk of bacterial endocarditis in persons with mitral valve prolapse. *New England Journal of Medicine, 307,* 776–781.

Cohen, M. E., White, P. D., & Johnson, R. E. (1948). Neurocirculatory asthenia: Anxiety neurosis or the effort syndrome. *Archives of Internal Medicine, 81,* 260–261.

Coryell, W., Noyes, R., & Clancy, J. (1982). Excess mortality in panic disorder. *Archives of General Psychiatry, 39,* 701–703.

Coryell, W., Noyes, R., & House, J. D. (1986). Mortality among outpatients with panic disorder. *American Journal of Psychiatry, 143,* 508–510.

Crowe, R. (1984). The role of genetics in the etiology of panic disorder. In L. Grinspoon (Ed.), *Psychiatry Update, Vol. III.* Washington, DC: American Psychiatric Press.

Crowe, R. R., Gaffney, G., Kerber, R. (1982). Panic attacks in families of patients with mitral valve prolapse. *Journal of Affective Disorder, 4,* 121–125.

Dager, S. R., Comess, K. A., & Dunner, D. L. (1986). Differentiation of anxious patients by two-dimensional echocardiographic evaluation of the mitral valve. *American Journal of Psychiatry, 143,* 533–535.

Dager, S., Comess, K. A., Saal, A. K., & Dunner, D. L. (1986). Mitral valve prolapse in a psychiatric setting: Diagnostic assessment, research, and clinical implications. *Integr Psychiatry, 4,* 211–223.

Dager, S. R., Comess, K. A., Saal, A. K., Sisk, E. J., Beach, K. W., Dunner, D. L. (1989). Diagnostic reliability of M-mode echocardiography for detecting mitral valve prolapse in 50 consecutive panic patients. *Comprehensive Psychiatry, 30,* 369–375.

Dager, S. R., Cowley, D. S., & Dunner, D. L. (1987). Biological markers in panic states: Lactate-induced panic and mitral valve prolapse. *Biological Psychiatry, 22,* 339–359.

Dager, S., Khan, A., Comess, K. A., Raisys, V., & Dunner, D. L. (1987). Mitral valve abnormalities and catecholamine activity in anxious patients. *Psychiatry Research, 20,* 13–18.

Dager, S. R., Roy-Byrne, P., & Dunner, D. L. (1988). Stress, anxiety, and the cardiovascular system. In R. Noyes, M. Roth, & G. D. Burrows (Eds.), *Handbook of anxiety* (pp. 399–429). Amsterdam: Elsevier.

Dager, S. R., Saal, A. K., Comess, K. A., & Dunner, D. L. (1988). Mitral valve prolapse and the anxiety disorders. *Hospital and Community Psychiatry, 39,* 517–527.

Davies, A. O., Mares, A., Pool, J. L., & Taylor, A. A. (1987). Mitral valve prolapse with symptoms of beta-adrenergic hypersensitivity. *American Journal of Medicine, 82,* 193–201.

Davies, J. M., Moore, B. P., & Brainbridge, M. V. (1978). The floppy mitral valve: Study of incidence, pathology, and complications in surgical, necropsy, and forensic material. *British Heart Journal, 40,* 468–481.

Dealy, R. S., Ishiki, D. M., Avery, D. H., & Dunner, D. L. (1981). Secondary depression in anxiety disorders. *Comprehensive Psychiatry, 22,* 612–618.

DeCarvalho, J. G. R., Messerli, F. H., & Frohlich, E. D. (1979). Mitral valve prolapse and borderline hypertension. *Hypertension, 1,* 518.

DeMaria, A. N., Amsterdam, E. Z., Vismara, L. A., Neuman, A., & Mason, D. T. (1976). Arrhythmias in the mitral valve prolapse syndrome. *Annals of Internal Medicine, 84,* 656–660.

DeMaria, A. N., King, J. F., Bogren, H. G., Lies, J., & Mason, D. (1974). The variable spectrum of echocardiographic manifestations of the mitral valve prolapse syndrome. *Circulation, 50,* 33–41.

de Moor, M. M. A., Lachman, P. I., & Human, D. G. (1986). Rupture of tendinous chords during acute rheumatic carditis in young children. *International Journal of Cardiology, 12,* 363–367.

Devereux, R. B., Brown, W. T., Kramer-Fox, R., & Sachs, I. (1982). Inheritance of mitral valve prolapse: Effect of age and sex on gene expression. *Annals of Internal Medicine, 97,* 826–832.

Duren, D. R., Becker, A. E., & Dunning, A. J. (1988). Long-term follow-up of idiopathic mitral valve prolapse in 300 patients: A prospective study. *Journal of the American College of Cardiology, 2,* 42–47.

Fontana, M. E., Wooley, C. F., Leighton, R. F., & Lewis, R. P. (1975). Postural changes in left ventricular and mitral valvular dynamics in the systolic click-late systolic murmur syndrome. *Circulation, 51,* 165–173.

Gaffney, F. A. (1983). Abnormal cardiovascular regulation in the mitral valve prolapse syndrome. *American Journal of Cardiology, 52,* 316–320.

Gaffney, F. A., Karlsson, E. S., Campbell, W. G., Schutte, J., Nixon, J., Willerson, J., & Blomqvist, C. (1979). Autonomic dysfunction in women with mitral valve prolapse syndrome. *Circulation, 59,* 894–901.

Gavin, W. A., Pearlman, A. S., Saal, A. K., Scoblionko, D. P., Janko, C. L., Bolson, E. L., & Dodge, H. T. (1983). Abnormal mitral leaflet coaptation: A nonspecific 2-D echo finding. *Circulation, 68*(Suppl. 2), 111–365.

Gorman, J. M., Fyer, A. F., Glicklich, J., King, D. L., & Klein, D. F. (1981a). Effects of imipramine on prolapsed mitral valves of patients with panic disorder. *American Journal of Psychiatry, 138,* 977–978.

Gorman, J. M., Fyer, A., F., Glicklich, J., King, D. L., & Klein, D. F. (1981b). Effects of sodium lactate on patients with panic disorder and mitral valve prolapse. *American Journal of Psychiatry, 138,* 247–249.

Gorman, J., Shear, K. Devereux, R., King, M., & Klein, D. (1986). Prevalence of MVP in panic disorder: Effect of echocardiographic criteria. *Psychosomatic Medicine, 48,* 167–171.

Guntheroth, W. (1984). How important are dental procedures in the etiology of infectious endocarditis? *American Journal of Cardiology, 54,* 797–801.

Hartshorn, H. (1864). On heart disease in the army. *American Journal of Medical Sciences, 48,* 89–92.

Hutle, L., & Agnelsen, B. (1985). *Doppler ultrasound, in cardiology: Physical principles and clinical applications* (2nd ed.). Philadelphia: Lea & Febiger.

Jaffe, A. S., Geltman, E. M., Rodey, G .E., & Uitto, J. (1981). Mitral valve prolapse: A consistent manifestation of type IV Ehlers-Danlos syndrome. The pathogenetic role of the abnormal production of type III collagen. *Circulation, 64,* 121–125.

Jeresaty, R. M. (1979). *Mitral valve prolapse*. New York: Raven Press.

Jeresaty, R. M. (1985). Mitral valve prolapse: An update. *Journal of the American Medical Association,* 254, 793–795.

Jeresaty, R. M., Edwards, J. E., & Chawla, S. K. (1985). Mitral valve prolapse and ruptured chordae tendinae. *American Journal of Cardiology, 55,* 138–142.

Kantor, J. S., Zitrin, C. M., & Zeldis, S. M. (1980). Mitral valve prolapse syndrome in agoraphobic patients. *American Journal of Psychiatry, 137,* 467–469.

Katon, W. (1984). Panic disorder and somatization. *American Journal of Medicine, 77,* 101–106.

Kern, W. H., & Tucher, B. L. (1972). Myxoid changes in cardiac valves: Pathologic, clinical, and ultra-structural studies. *American Heart Journal, 84,* 294–301.

Kessler, K. M. (1988). Prolapse paranoia. *Journal of the American College of Cardiology, 1,* 48–49.

King, B. D., Clark, M. A., Baba, N., Kilman, J. W., & Wooley, C. F. (1982). "Myxomatous" mitral valves: Collagen dissolution as the primary defect. *Circulation, 66* 288–296.

Klein, D. F. (1964). Delineation of two drug-responsive anxiety syndromes. *Psychopharmacologia, 5,* 397–408.

Klein, D. F. (1984). Psychopharmacological treatment of panic disorder. *Psychosomatics, 25,* 32–36.

Klein, D. F., & Gorman, J. M. (1984). Panic disorder and mitral valve prolapse. *Journal of Clinical Psychiatry, 2,* 14–17.

Kolibash, A., Kilman, J. W., Bush, C. A., Ryan, J. M., Fontana, M. E.., & Wooley, C. F. (1986). Evidence of progression from mild to severe mitral regurgitation in mitral valve prolapse. *American Journal of Cardiology, 58,* 762–767.

Krivokapich, J., Child, J. S., Dadourian, B. J., & Perloff, J. K. (1988). Reassessment of echocardio-graphic criteria for diagnosis of mitral valve prolapse. *American Journal of Cardiology, 61,* 131–135.

Leatham, A., & Brigden, W. (1980). Mild mitral regurgitation and the mitral prolapse fiasco. *American Heart Journal, 99,* 659–664.

Levine, R. A., Triulzi, M. O., Harrigan, P. H., & Weyman, A. (1986). In vivo validation of non-planer mitral annular shape: Implications for the diagnosis of mitral valve prolapse. *Journal of the American College of Cardiology, 7,* 7A.

Levine, R. A., & Weyman, A. (1984). Mitral valve prolapse: A disease in search of or created by its definition. *Echocardiography, 1,* 3–14.

Levinson, D. F., & Acquaviva, J. (1988). Exacerbation of panic disorder during propranolol therapy. *Journal of Clinical Psychiatry, 8*(3), 193–195.

Levy, D., & Savage, D. (1987). Prevalence and clinical features of mitral valve prolapse. *American Heart Journal, 113,* 1281–1288.

Lutas, E. M., Devereux, R. B., Spitzer, M. C., & Kramer-Fox, R. (1984). Disappearance of mitral valve prolapse during pregnancy. *Journal of Cardiovascular Ultrasonography, 3,* 183–186.

MacMahon, S. W., Roberts, J. K., Kramer-Fox, R., Zucker, D., Roberts, R., & Devereux, R. B. (1987). Mitral valve prolapse and infective endocarditis. *American Heart Journal, 113,* 1291–1298.

Margraf, J., Ehlers, A., & Roth, W. (1988). Mitral valve prolapse and panic disorder: A review of their relationship. *Psychosomatic Medicine, 50,* 93–113.

Markiewicz, W., London, E., & Popp, R. L. (1978). Effect of transducer placement on echocardiographic mitral valve motion. *American Heart Journal, 6,* 555–556.

Markiewicz, W., Stoner, J., London, E., Hunts, S., & Popp, R. L. (1976). Mitral valve prolapse in one hundred presumably healthy young females. *Circulation, 53,* 464–473.

Meyers, D. G., Starke, H., Pearson, P. H., & Wilken, M. K. (1986). Mitral valve prolapse in anorexia nervosa. *Annals of Internal Medicine, 105,* 384–386.

Mills, P., Rose, J., Hollingsworth, J., Amara, I., & Craige, E. (1977). Long-term prognosis of mitral valve prolapse. *New England Journal of Medicine, 297,* 13–18.

Morganroth, J., Jones, R. H., Chen, C. C., & Naito, M. (1980). Two dimensional echocardiography in mitral, aortic and tricuspid valve prolapse: The clinical problem, cardiac nuclear imaging consider-ations and a proposed standard for diagnosis. *American Journal of Cardiology, 46,* 1164–1177.

Morganroth, J., & Pohost, G. (1980). Noninvasive approaches to cardiac imaging: Comparisons and contrasts. *American Journal of Cardiology, 46,* 1093–1096.

Motulsky, A. G. (1978). Biased ascertainment and the natural history of diseases. *New England Journal of Medicine, 198,* 1196–1197.

Nesse, R. M., Cameron, O. G., & Curtis, G. C. (1984). Adrenergic function in patients with panic disorder. *Archives of General Psychiatry, 41,* 771–776.

Nesse, R. M., Cameron, O. G., Buda, A., McCann, D., Curtis, G., & Huber-Smith, M. (1985). Urinary catecholamines and mitral valve prolapse in panic-anxiety patients. *Psychiatry Research, 14,* 67–74.

Nichimura, R. A., McGoon, M. D., Shub, C., Miller, F., Ilstrup, D., & Tajik, A. (1985). Echocardiographically documented mitral valve prolapse: Long-term follow-up of 237 patients. *New England Journal of Medicine, 313*, 1305–1309.

Pariser, S. F., Jones, B., Pinta, E., Young, E., & Fontana, M. (1979). Panic attacks: Diagnostic evaluation of 17 patients. *American Journal of Psychiatry, 136*, 105–106.

Pariser, S. F., Pinta, E. R., & Jones, B. A. (1978). Mitral valve prolapse syndrome and anxiety neurosis/panic disorder. *American Journal of Psychiatry, 135*, 246–247.

Pasternac, A., Tubau, J., Puddu, P., Krol, R., Farley, L., & de Champlain, J. (1982). Increased plasma catecholamine levels in patients with symptomatic mitral valve prolapse. *American Journal of Medicine, 73*, 783–790.

Perloff, J. K., Child, J. S., & Edwards, J. E. (1986). New guidelines for the clinical diagnosis of mitral valve prolapse. *American Journal of Cardiology, 57*, 1124–1129.

Perloff, J. K., Child, J. S., & Edwards, J. E. (1987). Clinical and epidemiologic issues in mitral valve prolapse: Overview and perspective. *American Heart Journal, 113*, 1324–1332.

Pocock, W. A., Bosman, C. K., Chesler, E., Barlow, J., & Edwards, J. (1984). Sudden death in primary mitral valve prolapse. *American Heart Journal, 107*, 387–382.

Procacci, P. M., Savran, S. V., Schreiter, S. L., & Byrson, A. L. (1976). Prevalence of clinical mitral valve prolapse in 1,169 young women. *New England Journal of Medicine, 294*, 1086–1088.

Puddu, P. E., Pasternac, A., Tubau, J. F., Krol, R., Farley, L., & de Champlain, J. (1983). Q-T interval prolongation and increased plasma catecholamine levels in patients with mitral valve prolapse. *American Heart Journal, 105*, 422–428.

Pyeritz, R. E. (1983). Cardiovascular manifestations of heritable disorders of connective tissue. *Prog Med Genet, 5*, 191–202.

Read, R. C., Thal, A. P., & Wendt, V. E. (1965). Symptomatic valvular myxomatous transformation (the floppy valve syndrome): A possible "forme fruste" of the Marfan syndrome. *Circulation, 32*, 897–910.

Reid, J. (1961). Midsystolic clicks. *South Africa Medical Journal, 135*, 353–355.

Rosenbaum, J. F. (1979). Anxiety. In A. Lazare (Ed.), *Outpatient psychiatry: Diagnosis and treatment* (pp. 252–256). Baltimore: Williams and Wilkins.

Rosenberg, C., Derman, G., Grubb, W., & Buda, A. (1983). Hypomastia and mitral valve prolapse. *New England Journal of Medicine, 309*, 1230–1232.

Savage, D. D., Devereux, R. B., Garrison, R. J., Castelli, W., Anderson, S., Levy, D., Thomas, H., Kannel, W., & Feinleib, M. (1983). Mitral valve prolapse in the general population: 1. Clinical features: The Framingham study. *American Heart Journal, 106*, 577–581.

Savage, D. D., Garrison, R. J., Devereux, R. B., Castelli, W., Anderson, S., Levy, D., McNamara, P., Stokes, J., Kannel, W., & Feinleib, M. (1983). Mitral valve prolapse in the general population: 2. Epidemiological features: The Framingham study. *American Heart Journal, 106*, 571–576.

Savage, D. D., Levy, D., Garrison, R. J., Castelli, W. P., Kligfield, P., Devereux, R. B., Anderson, S. S., Kannel, W. B., & Feinleib, M. (1983). Mitral valve prolapse in the general population: 3. Dysthythmias: The Framingham study. *American Heart Journal, 106*, 582–586.

Schwartz, P. H., Periti, M., & Malliani, A. (1975). The long Q-T syndrome. *American Heart Journal, 89*, 378–390.

Schwarz, T., & Gotsman, M. S. (1981). Mitral valve prolapse in osteogenesis imperfecta. *Isr Med Sci, 17*, 1087–1088.

Shah, P. (1984). Update of mitral valve prolapse syndrome: When is echo prolapse a pathological prolapse? *Echocardiology, 1*, 1219–1223.

Skerritt, P. W. (1983). Anxiety and the heart: A historical review. *Psychological Medicine, 13*, 17–25.

Torgersen, S. (1983). Genetic factors in anxiety disorders. *Archives of General Psychiatry, 40*, 1085–1089.

Uretsky, B. (1982). Does MVP cause non-specific symptoms? *International Journal of Cardiology, 1*, 435–442.

Venkatesh, A., Pauls, D. L., Crowe, R., Noyes, R., Van Valkenburg, C., Martins, J. B., & Kerber, R. (1980). Mitral valve prolapse in anxiety neurosis (panic disorder). *American Heart Journal, 100*, 302–305.

Waller, B. F., Morrow, A. G., Maron, B. J., Del Negro, A., Kent, K., McGrath, F., Wallace, R., McIntosh, C., & Roberts, W. (1982). Etiology of clinically isolated, severe, chronic pure mitral regurgitation: Analysis of 97 patients over 30 years of age having mitral valve replacement. *American Heart Journal, 104*, 276–288.

Wann, L. S., Grove, J. R., & Hess, T. R. (1983). Prevalence of mitral prolapse by two-dimensional echocardiography in healthy young women. *British Heart Journal, 49*, 334–340.

Winkel, R. A., Lopes, M. G., Fitzgerald, J. W., Goodman, D. J., Schroeder, J. S., & Harrison, D. C. (1982). Arrhythmias in patients with mitral valve prolapse. *New England Journal of Medicine, 307,* 776–781.

Wooley, C. F. (1976). Where are the diseases of yesteryear? *Circulation, 53,* 749.

Wynne, J. (1986). Mitral valve prolapse. *New England Journal of Medicine, 314,* 577–578.

York, P. G., Schnittger, I., & Popp, R. L. (1984). Is continuous wave Doppler too sensitive in diagnosing pathologic valvular regurgitation? *Circulation, 70*(2), 38.

13

Pathogenesis of Mitral Valve Prolapse and Its Relationship to Anxiety

Ray H. Rosenman

VARIANTS OF MITRAL VALVE PROLAPSE

Mitral valve prolapse (MVP) refers to the invagination or herniation of one or both valve leaflets superiorly or backwards into the left atrium during left ventricular systole. Although sometimes considered to be a specific syndrome (Barlow & Pocock, 1979; Jeresaty, 1971; Naggar, 1979), the variability of findings in subjects with MVP (Devereux, Perloff, Reichek, & Josephson, 1976; Jeresaty, 1979; Malcolm, 1985) indicates that it has diverse predisposing mechanisms (Barlow, Bosman, Marchard, & Denny, 1968; Barlow & Pocock, 1985; Devereux, 1982; Pocock & Barlow, 1971). Various classifications have been used to separate these heterogeneous disorders (Wooley & Boudoulas, 1985). MVP describes the anatomic leaflet displacement, whereas mitral valve prolapse syndrome (MVPS) designates subjects with anatomic prolapse associated with a symptom complex (Wooley, 1983; Wooley & Boudoulas, 1988) that is generally ascribed to states of autonomic dysfunction or imbalance (Boudoulas, Kolibash, & Wooley, 1986; Boudoulas, Reynolds, Mazzaferri, & Wooley, 1980; Coghlan, 1979; Gaffney et al., 1979; Wooley, 1983). The term primary or idiopathic MVP has been used to describe anatomic prolapse purportedly resulting from myxomatous changes in valve leaflets, and secondary MVP to designate anatomic prolapse that results from abnormalities of other components of the mitral valve apparatus or disorders of left ventricular contractility (Naggar & Aretz, 1984). Minor and major MVP are used to distinguish normal variants from pathologic states (Perloff, Child, & Edwards, 1986), although functional MVP might preferably be used to describe such normal variants.

Anatomic Mitral Valve Prolapse

The mitral valve apparatus is a complex structure, the normal function of which depends on the integrity of components that include the valve leaflets, mitral annulus fibrosus, chordae tendinae, left atrium, and papillary muscles and their basal supporting structures in the left ventricle (Bryhn & Garding, 1986; Naggar & Aretz, 1984). Abnormality of any component can lead to a failure of apposition or coaptation of the valve leaflets and their prolapse (Naggar & Aretz, 1984). Normally the papillary muscles, chordae tendinae, and leaflet structure prevent prolapse of leaflets during the rapid rise of left ventricular systolic pressure (Falk & Hood, 1981). The chordae tendinae have an important functional role in normal leaflet apposition (Van der Bel-Kahn, Duren, & Becker, 1985) because the forces that arise from chordae and papillary muscles play an integral role in the genesis of mitral valve semidiastolic equilibrium during absent transmittal blood flow and in governing diastolic leaflet motion (Binkley, Bonagura, Olson, Boudoulas, & Wooley, 1987). Mitral valve leaflets are normally displaced superiorly into the left atrium during left ventricular systole. Under the burden of systolic contraction, the cusps can stretch and become convex toward the left atrium, with resulting leaflet prolapse and increased tugging effects on the chordae tendinae that lead to their attenuation and elongation (Dean, 1985).

Continued hemodynamic stress can eventuate in a ballooning, billowing, or floppy valve (Barlow & Pocock, 1985). The annulus can enlarge (Bryhn & Garding, 1986; Dean, 1985) and contribute to further failure of leaflet coaptation and valve regurgitation (Naggar, 1979). A floppy valve also can result from a separation between the junction of the valve with the left atrial wall and ventricular attachment and allow hypermobility of the valve apparatus. Anatomic variations of normal annulus morphology may occasionally cause such disjunction (Hutchins, Moore, & Skoog, 1986). Prolapse of the posterior, and occasionally both leaflets, occurs during the early and middle phase of left ventricular systole. If there is a failure to close the line of coaptation-apposition, mitral regurgitation can occur during middle and late systole and become holosystolic from increased valve deformation and stress-induced elongation of the chordae tendinae or when the mitral annulus dilates.

Secondary Mitral Valve Prolapse

In view of the fact that failure of leaflet apposition is the keystone condition leading to MVP (Barlow & Pocock, 1985), it is not surprising that a variety of cardiovascular disorders can induce anatomic prolapse. Dyskinesis of the left ventricle beneath papillary muscles can alter contractile tension on leaflets and prevent normal apposition (Godley, Wann, Rogers, Feigenbaum, & Weyman, 1981; Waller, Fanning, & Barker, 1985) or cause relative displacement of papillary muscles toward the mitral orifice (Tei et al., 1983). MVP can thus occur with ischemia or infarction of papillary muscles or their sites of attachment in the left ventricle (Cebelin & Hirsch, 1980). Abnormal diastolic configuration of the left ventricle can interfere with the predictable relationship between valve closure and onset of left ventricular systole (Smalcelj & Gibson, 1985) and cause disordered left ventricular contractility (DeMaria, Takeda, & Mason, 1981). MVP can thus occur in patients with myocardial infarction, ischemic cardiomyopathies, or ventricular aneurysms (Crawford, 1977; Godley et al., 1981; Makino & Al-Sadir, 1983; O'Rourke & Crawford, 1976; Tei et al., 1983). However, it occurs infrequently with acute myocardial infarction, and its prevalence in chronic ischemic heart disease also appears to be low (Peller, Devereux, & Schreiber, 1988).

The size of the mitral valve apparatus and length of chordae tendinae are fixed, and leaflet prolapse can occur with a variety of disorders that cause a mismatch between a relatively smaller size of the left ventricle and larger mitral orifice (Byrhn & Garding, 1986). A reduction of left ventricular size therefore predisposes to MVP, and an increased left ventricular mass leads to a smaller intracavity size that cannot accommodate normal leaflet motion and apposition (Panidis, McAllister, Ross, &

Mintz, 1986). Prolapse thus can occur in patients with congestive, hypertrophic, idiopathic, or other cardiomyopathies (Chandraratna, Tolentino, Mutucumarana, Lopi, & Gomez, 1977; Davies, Moore, & Bainbridge, 1978; Dean, 1985; Gooch, Vicencio, Maranhao, & Goldberg, 1972; Haikal, Alpert, Whiting, & Kelly, 1982), with secundum type of interatrial septal defects (Devereux, 1982), and with severe pulmonary hypertension, which also may be associated with tricuspid valve prolapse (Waller et al., 1986). However, it is significant that, in the absence of myocardial infarction, MVP occurs infrequently in patients with hypertension (Devereux et al., 1982; Gaffney, Bastian, & Lane, 1983; Holgado & Prakash, 1987; Holgado, Prakash, Kaushik, Sarma, & Marks, 1986; Pasternac et al., 1986). This may be due to hypertrophy of papillary muscles that pull chordae down and leaflets away from the left atrium during left ventricular systole and thereby prevent their eversion or prolapse (Holgado et al., 1986).

Primary Mitral Valve Prolapse

MVP is commonly found in patients with a wide variety of heritable mucopolysaccharidoses, connective tissue disorders, and muscle dystrophies such as Hunter's syndrome, Hurler's syndrome, Ehlers-Danlos syndrome, Fabry's disease, Hurler's-Hunter-Sanfillippo syndrome, Sandhoff's diseases, pseudoxanthoma elasticum, osteogenesis imperfecta, Marfan's syndrome, lupus erythematosus, Down's syndrome, von Willebrand's disease, psoriatic arthritis, muscle dystrophies such as myotonic and Duchenne's, and sickle cell anemia (Alpert et al., 1983; Depace, Segal, Fischl, & Farry, 1981; Devereux, 1982; Goldhaber et al., 1986; Goldman, Cantor, Schwartz, Baker, & Desnick, 1986; Greenwood, 1986; Haywood, 1987; Hortop, Tsipouras, Hanley, Maron, & Shapiro, 1981; Naggar & Aretz, 1984; Perloff, Stevenson, Roberts, Cabeen, & Weiss, 1984). There also is high prevalence of MVP in otherwise normal people with thoracic skeletal deformities such as scoliosis and kyphoscoliosis, and particularly in those with pectus excavatum and straight back syndromes (Chan, Chen, Wang, & Chow, 1983; Darsee, Mikolich, Nicoloff, & Lesser, 1979; Schutte, Gaffney, Blend, & Blomqvist, 1981; Tomaso & Gardin, 1980; Zema, Chiaramida, DeFilipp, Goldman, & Pizzarello, 1982). In one study, MVP was found in 58% of subjects with straight back syndromes and pectus excavatum (Ansari, 1985).

PATHOLOGIC FINDINGS IN MVP

The normal mitral leaflet is composed of three layers (Shrivastava, Guthrie, & Edwards, 1977). The atrial layer or atrialis is rich in elastin. The central collagenous structure is called the fibrosa. There is loose connective tissue in the spongy layer or spongiosa on the atrial aspect of the fibrous core, containing proteoglycans, elastic fibers, and connective tissue cells. The ventricular fibroelastic layer or ventricularis has denser elastic bundles than does the atrial layer (Angelini, Becker, Anderson, & Davies, 1988). The chordae tendinae are composed of dense collagen. The principal histopathologic finding in prolapsed mitral valve leaflets that are obtained at surgery or autopsy is a replacement of the dense fibrous core by infiltration of glycosaminoglycans that leads to a myxomatous transformation (Van der Bel-Kahn et al., 1985). Normal mitral valves contain several types of collagen, and one type is increased in myxomatous leaflets (Cole, Chan, & Hickey, 1984), suggesting that increased production of this collagen and of aminoglycans accompanies a proliferation of cells that is part of a repair process in myxomatous valves (Angelini et al., 1988).

Historically, the proteoglycan accumulation has been believed to be the primary lesion (Davies et al., 1978; Shrivastava et al., 1977), but others hypothesize that the initial lesion is collagen dissolution (King, Clark, Baba, Kilman, & Wooley, 1982). Collagen bundles are disrupted and fragmented in prolapsed valves, and the normal connective tissue structure is variably replaced by a secondary proliferation of myxomatous tissue that is rich in acid mucopolysaccharides (Davies et al., 1978; Devereux, 1985; King et al., 1982). Similar myxomatous changes and cystic necrosis can occur in chordae tendinae (Tomaso & Gardin, 1980), leading to their attenuation, elongation, and occasional spontaneous rupture (Aronson, Hoffman, Algueti-Margulis, & Yust, 1987; Hickey, Wilcken, Wright, & Warren, 1985; Jeresaty, 1973; Naggar, Pearson, & Seljan, 1986). The myxomatous transformation of leaflets and chordae is associated with a weakened structure and elongation that makes the valve cusps redundant relative to left ventricular cavity size and allows them to prolapse backwards into the left atrium as left ventricular systole shrinks its cavity size below a critical level (Angelini et al., 1988; Devereux et al., 1976).

Continued hemodynamic stress can lead to a billowing or floppy valve (Barlow & Pocock, 1985) and to enlargement of the mitral annulus and papillary muscle dysfunction (Waller et al., 1985) with associated valve regurgitation. The importance of hemodynamic factors (Angelini et al., 1988) is shown by the fact that, in the absence of underlying rheumatic mitral disease, the myxomatous transformation is not accompanied by any inflammatory reaction (Chopra et al., 1983; Tomaru et al., 1987). Superficial leaflet fibrosis and thickening can probably be ascribed to secondary wear and tear phenomena.

The infiltration of glycosaminoglycans and myxomatous transformation are often believed to occur as part of heritable mucopolysaccharidoses and other generalized connective tissue disorders. A traditional concept views the proteoglycan accumulation as the initial lesion in MVP, even when it occurs in the absence of heritable mucopolysaccharidoses (Angelini et al., 1988; Davies et al., 1978; Devereux, 1985; Naggar & Aretz, 1984; Shrivastava et al., 1977). Support for this belief is given by the frequent occurrence of MVP in subjects with thoracic skeletal disorders (Ansari, 1985; Chan et al., 1983; Zema et al., 1982). The mesenchymal primordia of the mitral valve undergoes embryologic differentiation during the sixth week of gestation, at a time when the vertebral column and thoracic rib cage develop their shape and form through chondrification (Ansari, 1985; Rosenberg, Derman, Grabb, & Buda, 1983; Savage, Devereux, & Garrison, 1983), possibly linking MVP to a congenital abnormality of mesenchymal tissue (Rosenberg et al., 1983). The myxomatous transformation in the mitral valve could be ascribed to a genetic DNA disorder, and the characteristic dissolution or dysgenesis of collagen bundles in mitral leaflets to a block in enzyme synthesis leading to an accumulation of procollagen and faulty mesenchymal tissue (Dean, 1985).

In the following discussion, except as otherwise indicated, the term MVP will be used to designate anatomic prolapse that occurs idiopathically in the absence of connective tissue disorders or other myocardial diseases. Myxomatous valve transformation occurring as part of generalized connective tissue disorders predisposes to anatomic MVP by rendering the leaflets less well supported. However, in most other instances, the changes observed in postmortem specimens and in severely prolapsed and billowing or flail valves that are surgically excised (Davies et al., 1978; Van der Bel-Kahn et al., 1985) do not indicate the pathogenesis of the myxomatous leaflet transformation or deviations of chordal architecture (Malcolm, 1985). With the exception of primary mucopolysaccharidoses and generalized connective tissue disorders, the histopathologic changes observed in more severely prolapsed valves can be secondary to the prolapse. Similar histologic changes are thus found in severely prolapsed leaflets of patients without connective tissue disorders (Van der Bel-Kahn et al., 1985) and, although differing in extent, are similar whether prolapse is of mild or more severe degree (Jeresaty, 1985). Moreover, although dissolution and disruption of normal collagen bundles are characteristic of severely prolapsed leaflets, the histologic changes are similar to those that occur in valve leaflets that are not prolapsed (Wooley, 1983).

The appearance of myxomatous tissue is nonspecific and is initiated by any process that leads to undue stress on connective tissue of the valve apparatus, and similar changes are seen at many diverse sites in the body where supportive tissue is damaged (Van der Bel-Kahn et al., 1985). The infiltration of glycosaminoglycans and increased collagen production may thus be part of a repair process in myxomatous valves (Angelini et al., 1988). Heart valves may normally produce a factor that accelerates degradation of intercellular matrix (Decker & Dingle, 1982; Devereux et al., 1982). Constant neuroaminal stimulation of the valve apparatus contributes to direct hemodynamic stress on the leaflet structure (Gorman, Fyer, Glicklich, King, & Klein, 1981b), as well as stimulating left ventricular contractility, with increased tugging effects on chordae tendinae that may pull down posterior leaflets and lead to prolapse. An abnormally stressed valve can develop the same abnormalities that occur in primary MVP (Levine & Weyman, 1984). The mitral myxomatous transformation can thus occur in a valve that was initially normal, because the prolapse induced an increased stress on the apparatus and caused the collagen disruption and eventual myxomatous changes (Malcolm, 1985).

The motion of the anterior leaflet is restricted because it abuts against the interventricular septum during diastole, and the leaflets are normally displaced posteriorly into the left atrium during ventricular systole. Therefore, the predilection for prolapse to involve the middle third of the posterior leaflet and, when the anterior leaflet is involved, its posteromedial half (Shrivastava et al., 1977), emphasizes the important role of hemodynamic stress. The myxomatous transformation in mitral leaflets therefore does not explain the pathogenesis of idiopathic MVP. Age-related changes that occur in prolapsed valves are consistent with a response-to-injury hypothesis and fit with the finding that MVP is infrequent before the growth spurt of adolescence (Wilcken & Hickey, 1986). Finally, biochemical studies of excised valves (Cole et al., 1984) indicate that the processes of ongoing injury and repair in the leaflets are the final common pathway for occurrence of the observed lesions (Wilcken & Hickey, 1988).

Demographics

Idiopathic MVP is the most common valvular disorder in adults in the United States (Jeresaty, 1986) and is estimated to occur in about 5% to 8% of its general population (Brown, Kloster, & DeMots, 1975; Darsee et al., 1979; Markiewicz, Stoner, London, Hunt, & Popp, 1976; Procacci, Savran, Schreiter, & Bryson, 1976). Differences in reported prevalence can be ascribed to ascertainment bias and different methods used for diagnosis (Gorman, Shear, Devereux, King, & Klein, 1986; Wann et al., 1983). In an unselected, free-living, population-based sample in the

Framingham heart study that was evaluated by echocardiography, MVP was found in 5% of subjects, with a prevalence of 3% in an older age group, and 7% in younger offspring. A higher prevalence of 17% was found in women in the third age decade, with decreased prevalence after age 40, declining to 1% in the ninth age decade. A prevalence of 2% to 4% in men remained unchanged across all age decades (Savage, 1982). In other large populations of healthy young women, MVP was found in 6% to 10% of subjects (Markiewicz et al., 1976; Procacci et al., 1976). However, MVP may occur at all ages (Criley, Lewis, Humphries, & Ross, 1966; Khandheria, Tajik, Naessens, Shub, & Seward, 1987; Kolibash et al., 1983; Savage, 1982; Tresch, Siegel, Keelan, Gross, & Brooks, 1979).

A much higher prevalence of MVP has consistently been found in women compared to men, with the highest prevalence in the third age decade and decreasing progressively after age 40 (Criley et al., 1966; Khandheria et al., 1987; Savage, 1982). In one large study of unselected subjects, MVP was found by two-dimensional echocardiography in 14.5% of the population, of whom 60% were women (Khandheria et al., 1987). There is a high familial occurrence of MVP, and the preponderance in women also prevails in its distribution in first-degree relatives of index subjects with MVP (Devereux, 1985). MVP is reported to occur in about 6% of neonates (Chandraratna, Vlahovich, Kong, & Wilson, 1979; Devereux, 1985) and in about 5% of the pediatric population in both sexes (Greenwood, 1986), often in association with connective tissue disorders, muscle dystropies, or thoracic skeletal deformities.

MVP apparently occurs in all populations and races, although usually in lower prevalence than that reported in white subjects in the United States. A high prevalence found in Black subjects in one study in the United States (Savage et al., 1982) was not confirmed elsewhere (McLaren et al., 1976). A prevalence of 2.5% was found in adult Korean subjects (Lee, Sheikh, & Lee, 1985), who were generally under age 30 and almost invariably exhibited straight back syndromes (Ansari, 1985). Low prevalences of .33% were found in a large Italian population of female students (Rizzon, Biasco, & Brondicci, 1973), of 1.4% in 12,500 South African schoolchildren (McLaren et al., 1976), and of 1.03% in young Japanese schoolchildren (Sakamoto, 1982), although increasing in older children (Sakamoto, 1988).

Echocardiography

Echocardiography is well suited to confirm the presence of MVP (Procacci et al., 1976). The M-mode is a specific method for detecting the presence of mitral regurgitation in subjects with MVP (Waller & Roberts, 1983). However, the principal finding of a fairly abrupt posterior motion of valve apparatus in middle or late systole is not sensitive enough to detect prolapse that occurs in the absence of valve regurgitation, and the two-dimensional mode may improve the specificity of diagnosis (Cohen, 1987). However, there is a continuum from normal to abnormal, and the variance of interpretation is such that up to half of subjects with auscultatory signs of MVP may have negative two-dimensional findings. Using this method, there may be a spontaneous development of high posterior wall dyskinesis in the upright position that is not observed in the supine position (Krafchek, Shaw, & Kisslo, 1985), which is a normal finding (Levine, Stathogiannis, Finkelstein, & Weyman, 1987; Perloff et al., 1986) that is related to orthostatic decreases of ventricular preload and left ventricular cavity size. Thus, superior systolic displacement of mitral leaflets cannot necessarily be considered to be abnormal (Levine et al., 1987; Perloff et al., 1986).

Echocardiography is actually of limited value for diagnosis (Levine, Triulzi, Harrigan, & Weyman, 1987) because there is a wide variety of leaflet motion in asymptomatic young subjects, with no cut-off point to define the degree of abnormal leaflet motion, and diagnostic criteria remain controversial (Dager, Comess, & Dunner, 1986; Kriwisky, Froom, Gross, Ribak, & Lewis, 1987). Moreover, there is a poor correlation with findings and clinical features when MVP is defined by echocardiography (Cohen, 1987; Savage, Levy et al., 1983). Because the degree of leaflet motion is a continuous variable, with a wide spectrum of motion in healthy individuals and without a definite cut-off point to define abnormality (Kriwisky et al., 1987), true leaflet displacement is required to distinguish normal leaflet motion from abnormal prolapse, and mild to moderate superior systolic displacement of the anterior or both mitral leaflets is considered to be within the normal physiological range of mitral valve motion (Perloff et al., 1986). The high prevalence of MVP that is found in some studies may be far lower when echocardiographic criteria are stringently applied (Bashore, Grines, Utlak, Boudoulas, & Wooley, 1985; Devereux, Hawkins & Kramer-Fox, 1986; Rogers, Boudoulas, & Wooley, 1984b), with an adult prevalence of about 3% when diagnosis is based on a billowing of the leaflets across the correctly defined plane of the mitral annulus (Hickey & Wilcken, 1986).

The two-dimensional method is generally superior for diagnosis (Wann et al., 1983) and better for defining a subset of patients with redundant leaflets who are at higher risk for complications (Chandraratna et al., 1977) or who exhibit mitral regurgitation caused by a disproportionate mitral annulus enlargement (Cohen, 1987). The presence of mitral regurgitation can be diagnosed and quantified by combined echocardiography and pulsed Doppler study (Blumlein et al., 1986; Panidis et al., 1986). The initial enthusiasm about echocardiographic diagnosis has waned with the recognition that echocardiography, cineangiography, and Doppler ultrasound findings may be normal in many subjects who exhibit a failure of leaflet coaptation in the absence of significant prolapse or valve regurgitation, and this has increasingly led to a return to auscultatory manifestations as the basis for diagnosis (Barlow, 1987; Barlow & Pocock, 1985).

Physical Findings in Mitral Valve Prolapse

The hallmark finding in subjects with MVP is the presence of one or more midsystolic, nonejection clicks over the cardiac apex, sometimes followed by a crescendo or high-pitched murmur that occupies middle and late systole (Jeresaty, 1986). The murmur may become holosystolic with the advent of more severe mitral regurgitation, and an aortic diastolic murmur may occasionally be heard (Wei & Fortuin, 1981). The midsystolic click has been ascribed to a chordal snap that results from sudden stretch on the chordae tendinae as the posterior mitral leaflet bulges or prolapses into the left atrium during ventricular systole (Reid, 1961). The click can be increased or decreased by maneuvers that alter ventricular size and contractility (DeMaria et al., 1981; Tomaso & Gardin, 1980), and subjects with suspected MVP should always be examined in seated, upright, and left lateral decubitus positions.

The redundancy of mitral leaflets is reduced by an increase of left ventricular volume, because this pulls the papillary muscles further away from the leaflets. Maneuvers such as squatting, inducing bradycardia, and administering beta-blockers or pressor agents enlarge left ventricular dimensions and advance the click and onset of murmurs to later in systole. Conversely, standing, sitting forward, inducing tachycardia, inhaling amyl nitrate, and release from the Valsalva maneuver will reduce left ventricular volume and move the onset of prolapse and the click and murmur to earlier in systole. Maneuvers that increase systolic pressure, such as squatting, isometric handgrip, or administering pressor agents will increase the intensity of the murmur, whereas systolic pressure is lessened by maneuvers that decrease systolic blood pressure (Dean, 1985; Tomaso & Gardin, 1980). The striking changes that can occur in these dynamic auscultatory sounds and their evanescence and rapid changes over time have long been emphasized (Dean, 1985; Falk & Hood, 1981; Wooley, 1983). It is interesting to note that Osler had observed that the "remarkable way in which the murmur appears and disappears is the most puzzling and singular feature" (Osler, 1880).

Assumption of the orthostatic position rapidly sifts 500 to 1,000 ml of blood into the venous reservoir below heart level (Malcolm, 1985; Tifft & Chobanian, 1985), with decrease of preload filling pressure, systolic and diastolic blood pressures, and stroke volume (Boudoulas, Barrington, Olson, Bashore, & Wooley, 1985). The sympathetic nervous system is activated, with changes in left ventricular contractility and dimensions (Boudoulas et al., 1985) and the spontaneous development of an associated high posterior wall motion that is not observed in the supine position (Krafchek et al., 1985). An orthostatic decrease of cardiac index and stroke volume diminishes left ventricular end-volumes, increases the degree of valve prolapse, and stimulates adrenergic activity that can cause symptoms in patients with MVP (Santos, Mathew, Hilal, & Wallace, 1981).

The orthostatic decrease of end-diastolic and stroke volumes causes clicks and murmur to become more intense in subjects with supine clicks and, in others, to appear only when they are upright. The relationship of prolapse and decreased left ventricular size is confirmed by the finding that clicks can transiently be induced in healthy people when intracavity size and volume are decreased when people are placed in the Trendelenburg position, when tourniquets or negative body pressure is applied to lower extremities, and when isosorbide (Harris & Crawford, 1985) or orthostatic stress (Beattie, Blomqvist, & Gaffney, 1985) is administered.

MVP tends to occur in tall, thin people of both sexes. In comparison with control subjects, MVP is strongly associated with a distinctive anthropometric habitus that is characterized by a relatively low weight for height, thin arms, a high arched palate, and a thoracic skeletal configuration of narrow anteroposterior chest diameter, straight back, and pectus excavatum (Chan et al., 1983; Devereux et al., 1982; Jeresaty, 1979; King, Boudoulas, Fontana, & Wooley, 1980; Markiewicz et al., 1976; Salomon, Shah, & Heinle, 1975; Savage, Devereux, & Garrison, 1983; Schutte et al., 1981; Zema et al., 1982). One study showed that almost half of a group of ballet dancers had MVP (Cohen, Austin, Segal, Millman, & Kim, 1987). It also was reported anecdotally by the former physician of a well-known Los Angeles basketball team that at least half of the tall players had evidence of MVP. The ballet dancers had small, bony diameters and body circumferences, but only the ponderal index was predictive of MVP in both the dancers and control subjects, further confirming the association of MVP with relative low body weight that was found in many groups, including the population-based Framingham heart study in which MVP was diagnosed by echocardiography (Savage, Levy et al., 1983). A strong association of leanness and MVP also is found in young children (Arfken et al., 1986).

Compared to control groups, subjects with MVP have low systolic and diastolic blood pressures (Devereux et al., 1982; Savage, Devereux, & Garrison, 1983), with an orthostatic hypotensive response (Coghlan, 1979; Fontana, Wooley, Leighton, & Lewis, 1975; Santos et al., 1981; Weissman, Shear, Kramer-Fox, & Devereux, 1987) and lower rise of diastolic blood pressure during isometric exercise (Lenders, Fast, Blankers, Lemmens, & Thien, 1986). The relative hypotension may be related to hypovolemia (Devereux et al., 1982). The orthostatic fall of blood pressure can be associated with occurrence of symptoms in patients with MVPS (Depace et al., 1981; Santos et al., 1981), particularly lightheadedness, dizziness, and even syncope (Santos et al., 1981).

There is an association of MVP with hypomastia in females. The breast and mitral valve are of mesenchymal origin and undergo embryologic differentiation and primordial development during the sixth week of fetal life, and this has been offered in support of both being due to a congenital mesenchymal abnormality (Rosenberg et al., 1983). However, female subjects with MVP are usually thin. Hypomastia may merely be related to their ectomorphic habitus and a lean weight that provides less adipose tissue to the breast (Devereux, Lutas, Kramer-Fox, & Brown, 1984).

Clinical Symptoms and Complications

There is a marked heterogeneity of clinical features in subjects with MVP (Dean, 1985; DeMaria et al., 1981; Savage, Devereux, & Garrison, 1983; Fontana, 1970; Jeresaty, 1979, 1985; Wooley, 1983). A variety of symptoms may be present, and these generally occur more frequently in women (Boudoulas, Wooley, & King, 1984). They include chest pains or discomfort, exertional dyspnea, palpitations, orthostatic intolerance with faintness, dizziness, lightheadedness, unsteady feelings or syncope, fatigue, poor exercise tolerance, cold distal extremities, pallor, and sweats, and some patients may exhibit panic attacks or other manifestations of anxiety disorders (Wooley, 1983).

Palpitations are particularly common and tend to occur as initial manifestations more often in women (Boudoulas et al., 1984). Chest pains may occur (Natarajan et al., 1975) and more often be an initial manifestation in men (Boudoulas et al., 1984). They can be described as sharp or stabbing sensations that occur transiently over the cardiac apex, or as burning sensations or prolonged, aching discomfort over the precordial and upper-left chest areas (Engel, Baile, Costa, Brimlow, & Brinker, 1985; Tomaso & Gardin, 1980). Sharp apical pains may be due to cardiac ectopy or tachyarrhythmias (Gooch et al., 1972), and more prolonged precordial aches are ascribed to musculoskeletal sources. Some central chest pain may be due to esophageal spasm or motility dysfunction (Day, Koch, Davidson, & Spears, 1987; Spears, Koch, & Day, 1986). Chest pains also have been ascribed to papillary muscle ischemia caused by increased tension and stretching of chordae tendinae by prolapsed leaflets during ventricular systole (Swartz & Dack, 1982), and even to magnesium deficiency (Cohen et al., 1985).

Exertional dyspnea is common in symptomatic patients (Engel et al., 1985; Tomaso & Gardin, 1980) and is associated with lightheadedness and presyncopal symptoms that may in part be due to hyperventilation and orthostatic hypotension (Freeman & Nixon, 1985a,b; Grossman, 1983; Santos et al., 1981). Hyperventilation leads to hypocapneic respiratory alkalosis, with alkaline circulatory change that induces augmented affinity of hemoglobin for oxygen, and can also induce coronary vasoconstriction or spasm (Freeman & Nixon, 1985a, 1985b; Fujii et al., 1988). It reduces myocardial perfusion, with a subnormal release of oxygen from the coronary circulation that further contributes to myocardial hypoxia (Freeman & Nixon, 1985). Nonspecific repolarization changes can be seen in ST segments of resting electrocardiograms and are more prone to occur in a subset of younger female patients with MVP who exhibit ischemic ST-T responses during forced hyperventilation (Gardin, Isner, Ronan, & Fox, 1980; Tomaso & Gardin, 1980).

Some patients exhibit false positive responses in stress tests (Tebbe et al., 1985), although these tend to disappear when tests are repeated after administration of beta-adrenergic blockers (Abinader, 1983). The symptoms and false positive stress test responses may bring many patients to coronary angiography (Engel et al., 1985; Freeman & Nixon, 1985a,b). Fatigability is another common complaint. Symptomatic patients usually exhibit less physical strength and less endurance on stress tests (Boudoulas & Wooley, 1986; Gaffney et al., 1983; Holmgren et al., 1957; Tomaso & Gardin, 1980; Wooley, 1983). This is more common in women and occurs particularly when physical exertion is performed in the upright position (Bashore et al., 1985, 1988; Boudoulas et al., 1986; Tomaso & Gardin, 1980).

MVP may be associated with atrial and ventricular arrhythmias (Alpert, 1984; Campbell, 1982; DeMaria, Amsterdam, Vismara, Neumann, & Mason, 1976; Kramer, Kligfield, & Devereux, 1984; Savage, Levy et al., 1983; Winkle et al., 1975), complex ventricular arrhythmias (Hochreiter et al., 1983; Kligfield et al. 1985) and bradyarrhythmias (Leichtman, Nelson, & Fraderick, 1976; Mason, Lee, Chan, & DeMaria, 1984), but sudden cardiac death is rare (Abinader, 1983; Davies et al., 1978; Kligfield et al., 1985; Mason et al., 1984). Although the prevalence of ectopic and complex arrhythmias is low except in subjects with mitral regurgitation (Abinader, 1983; Ansari, 1985; Davies et al., 1978; Kramer et al., 1984; Savage, Levy et al., 1983), it may be high in subjects with hemodynamically significant regurgitation (Hochreiter et al., 1983; Kligfield et al., 1985).

Although MVP is generally a benign condition, long-term follow-up studies show an increased rate of complications with passage of time (Duren, Becker, & Dunning, 1988; Koch & Hancock, 1976). There is a marked heterogeneity for the risk of complications (Devereux et al., 1986; MacMahon et al., 1987; Pini, Greppi, Kramer-Fox, Roman, & Devereux, 1988; Shrivastava et al., 1977), with disproportionate occurrence in older patients and particularly in men (Clemens, Horwitz, Jaffe, & Feinstein, 1982; Devereux et al., 1983; Kolibash, Kilman, Bush, Ryan, Fontana & Wooley, 1986; Kolibash, 1988; Lachman, Bramwell-Jones, & Lazier, 1973; MacMahon et al., 1987; Nishimura et al., 1985; Tresch et al., 1979; Wilcken & Hickey, 1986, 1988). These include infective endocarditis, arrhythmias, syncope, ruptured chordae tendinae, progressive mitral regurgitation, and congestive heart failure. Such complications particularly occur in patients with thickened (Tak, Gamage, Lin, Rahimtoola, & Chandraratna, 1987) or redundant valve leaflets (Salomon et al., 1975) and associated mitral regurgitation. Neurologic manifestations include migraine headaches, transient ischemic attacks, and other cerebral thromboembolic and ischemic events. These occur at younger ages, more often in women (Barnett, 1982; Barnett, Jones, Boughner, & Kostuk, 1976; Barnett, Roughner, Taylor, & Cooper, 1980; Broughner, 1986; Kelley, Pina, & Lee, 1988), and may result from adherence of platelets to valve leaflets (Swartz & Dack, 1982; Tomaso & Gardin, 1980) due to an increased aggregability and activation that is ascribed to adrenergic stimulation (Pasternac, Latour, Kouz, Gauthier et al., 1986; Walsh et al., 1981). Some neurologic manifestations in symptomatic patients may be due to hyperventilation syndromes (Perkin & Joseph, 1986).

Patients with MVP may exhibit some symptoms when they have billowing or flail valves or more severe mitral regurgitation (Barlow & Pocock, 1985). However, the presence of most symptoms other than minor palpitations generally suggests that MVPS is present, and the symptomatic manifestations of MVPS closely resemble those associated with anxiety and panic disorders (Thase, 1983). They are generally ascribed to adrenergic hyperactivity (Boudoulas & Reynolds, 1983; Coghlan, 1979; Gaffney & Blomqvist, 1981; Gaffney et al., 1979; Wooley, 1983) and may be confusing to physicians because of the coexistence of MVP and anxiety disorders. Patients may present initially to psychiatrists because of manifestations related to their anxiety state, panicogenic disorder, or hyperventilation syndrome, or to general physicians, internists, or cardiologists because of functional cardiovascular symptoms (Lader, 1984).

The highest prevalence of midsystolic clicks due to MVP occurs in young women, but the majority are either asymptomatic or have minor palpitations due to cardiac ectopy and generally not noticed (Darsee et al., 1979; Devereux, Kramer-Fox et al., 1986; Kramer et al., 1984; Procacci et al., 1976; Savage, Devereux, & Garrison, 1983; Thase, 1983). The high prevalence of reported symptoms probably reflects a selection bias, because usually only patients with MVPS who seek medical attention or are hospitalized because of their symptoms are studied. Among unselected patients, only palpitations appear to be related to MVP (Devereux et al., 1986), and the prolapse itself is not the cause of other nonspecific symptoms (Boudoulas et al., 1986; Retchin, Fletcher, Earp, Lamson, & Waugh, 1986). Among relatives of index probands with MVP, those with MVP symptomatically note only palpitations in comparison with relatives without MVP (Devereux et al., 1986). Chest pains, dyspnea, electrocardiographic abnormalities, and other manifestations of anxiety disorders are similar in relatives with and without MVP, although occurring in much higher frequency in younger females (Cheitlin & Byrd, 1981; Devereux, Kramer-Fox, 1986; Thase, 1983). A relation between nonspecific symptoms and MVP has not been established either in a free-living, population-based adult sample (Savage et al., 1982) or in children with auscultatory manifestations (Arfken et al., 1986). A high proportion of subjects with nonejection systolic clicks are thus entirely asymptomatic (Brown et al., 1975; Darsee et al., 1979; Lee et al., 1985; Markiewicz et al., 1976; Thase, 1983).

IDIOPATHIC MITRAL VALVE PROLAPSE: A NORMAL VARIANT

It is probable that most instances of idiopathic MVP occur as a normal variant for functional reasons. This is particularly true of mild prolapse incidentally found by echocardiography or nonejection, midsystolic clicks in patients who are asymptomatic (Barlow & Pocock, 1985; Jeresaty, 1985). Anatomic MVP is a common occurrence that should probably be considered to be abnormal in only a small proportion of subjects (Malcolm, 1985). The advent of more sensitive echocardiographic methods has led to the inclusion of normal variants into the diagnosis of MVPS, despite the fact that the pattern of superior mitral leaflet displacement is a continuous one (Dager et al., 1986; Kriwisky et al., 1987) that cannot be dichotomized into normal and abnormal (Perloff et al., 1986; Wynne, 1984). The current high prevalence of MVP in the United States is partly based on the fact that diagnoses are often only variants of normal diagnoses (Cohen et al., 1987; Salomon et al., 1975). Many subjects thus have a disorder created by definition, because it was assumed that certain auscultatory and echocardiographic evidence implied the same anatomic abnormality whenever it was present in the general population (Levine, 1988), and despite the discrepancy between occurrence of midsystolic clicks and echocardiographic findings (Savage, Devereux, & Garrison, 1983).

Consideration of idiopathic MVP as a normal functional variant in most subjects in whom it is found is supported by the fact that the proportion of young children with nonejection, midsystolic clicks is much less than expected from its higher prevalence in young adults (Arfken et al., 1986), and that even echocardiographic MVP is a transient occurrence at certain stages of life, at least in females (Savage, Devereux, & Garrison, 1983). The functional basis also is demonstrated by the fact that prolapse can transiently occur solely as the result of left ventricular loading conditions (Beattie et al., 1985; Malcolm, 1985), with spontaneous development of high posterior wall dyskinesis and leaflet displacement in the upright position (Krafchek et al., 1985). This is a normal finding (Levine, Stathogiannis et al., 1987; Perloff et al., 1986) that is related to orthostatic changes in ventricular dimensions that subject the chordae tendinae to greater tension and induce a failure of leaflet apposition in healthy, asymptomatic subjects (Barlow & Pocock, 1985). The functional mechanism is further shown by the fact that auscultatory manifestations come and go in an unpredictable manner and are often evanescent and rapidly changing over time (Barlow, 1987; Dean, 1985; Falk & Hood, 1981; Wooley, 1983), being strongly influenced by changes in body position and other factors that alter left ventricular dimensions and contractility (Chesler, Weir, Braatz, & Francis, 1985; Tomaso & Gardin, 1980). It is particularly relevant that MVP can be transiently induced in normal people by maneuvers that reduce left ventricular size (Beattie et al., 1985; Gavin, Pearlman, & Saal, 1983; Harris & Crawford, 1985).

It is therefore not surprising that most subjects with idiopathic MVP are asymptomatic (Brown et al., 1975; Darsee et al., 1979; Devereux, Kramer-Fox et al., 1986; Kramer et al., 1984; Lee et al., 1985; Markiewicz et al., 1976; Procacci et al., 1976; Savage, Devereux, & Garrison, 1983; Thase, 1983) and that unselected populations with and without nonejection, midsystolic clicks or echocardiographic evidence of prolapse do not differ in the frequency of palpitations, chest pains, fatigability, and other symptoms often found in subjects with MVPS (Procacci et al., 1976; Savage, Devereux, & Garrison, 1983). The major association of anatomic prolapse is with an anthropometric habitus that is characterized by leanness for height and an associated thoracic skeletal configuration characterized by straight back and tendency to pectus excavatum (Bon Tempo, Ronana, de Leon, & Twigg, 1975; Chan et al., 1983; Cohen et al., 1987; Devereux et al., 1982; Devereux, Kramer-Fox et al., 1986; Jeresaty, 1979; King et al., 1980; Markiewicz et al., 1976; Roman, Devereux, Kramer-Fox, & Spitzer, 1989, Salomon et al., 1975; Savage, Devereux, & Garrison, 1983; Schutte et al., 1981; Zema et al., 1982), whether in adults (Savage, Devereux, & Garrison, 1983) or young children (Arfken et al., 1986).

The histopathologic changes in prolapsed leaflets occur in initially normal valves, because the prolapse causes an increased stress on the apparatus that disrupts collagen and is secondarily followed by myxomatous transformation (Malcolm, 1985). The complications of MVP are largely caused by the development of mitral regurgitation (Kessler, 1988; Leatham & Brigden, 1980; Salomon et al., 1975; Tak et al., 1987) and the symptoms sometimes associated with MVP by the presence of anxiety disorders and associated adrenergic dysfunction. The variability of MVP prevalence in different populations is therefore not surprising (Lee et al., 1985; Rizzon et al., 1973; Savage, Devereux, & Garrison, 1983), and an apparent low prevalence among Blacks (McLaren et al., 1976) may be ascribed to their expanded blood volume (Wright, 1988).

THE ASSOCIATION BETWEEN MITRAL VALVE PROLAPSE AND UNDERLYING CONDITIONS

Left Ventricular Dimensions and Blood Volume

It has been well demonstrated that a mismatch between left ventricular and mitral valve dimensions can lead to prolapse of the valve leaflets in the absence of pathological features in either leaflets or chordae tendinae (Malcolm, 1985), usually because of a relatively smaller cavity size (Criley & Kissel, 1975). The higher prevalence of anatomic MVP in females, compared to males, is in part due to their larger mitral leaflets and annulus relative to body size. The internal dimensions of the left ventricular cavity are larger in normal males than in females, but the valve dimensions are the same in both sexes. Thus the ratio of valve dimensions to body surface area and cavity size is larger in females than in males (Devereux, Lutas, & Casale, 1984; Pini et al., 1988; Triulzi, Gillam, Gentile, Newell, & Weymann, 1984; Valdez, Rotta, & London, 1979).

Any factor that decreases left ventricular cavity size can cause a mismatch and induce a failure of leaflet coaptation and functional prolapse (Chesler et al., 1985; Harris & Crawford, 1985; Naggar & Aretz, 1984; Tomaso & Gardin, 1980). However, even in connective tissue disorders such as Marfan's syndrome there is a close inverse relationship between the prevalence of MVP and cavity size, and prolapse appears and disappears with respective decrease and increase of cavity dimensions (Lima, Lima, Pyeritz, & Weiss, 1985). The same relationship of MVP to reduced left ventricular cavity size can be seen in patients with atrial septal defects (Angel, Soler-Soler, del Castillo, Anivarro, & Batelle-Diaz, 1980).

As was already noted, functional prolapse can be induced by a variety of physical and pharmacological maneuvers that involve transient reduction of cavity size and thereby cause increased systolic displacement of the leaflets superiorly in relation to the annular plane (Beattie et al., 1985; Gavin et al., 1983; Harris & Crawford, 1985). This can occur when left ventricular cavity size is diminished by a reduce filling pressure (Lavine, Campbell, & Gunther, 1986). Heart rate is one determinant of filling pressure (Nishiwaka et al., 1986). Even within the physiologic range, an increased heart rate can decrease the internal dimensions of the left ventricular cavity (Kenny, Plappert, Doubilet, Salzman, & St. John Sutton, 1987) and thereby predispose people to anatomic prolapse, and subjects with MVP commonly exhibit orthostatic tachycardiac responses.

Another variable is left ventricular preload filling, and prolapse can occur when this is decreased (Beattie et al., 1985; Malcolm, 1985). The functional occurrence of prolapse in the upright position (Krafchek et al., 1985) is related to orthostatic changes that reduce ventricular preload (Barlow & Pocock, 1985; Boudoulas et al., 1985) caused by the pooling of blood below heart level (Malcolm, 1985; Tifft & Chobanian, 1985), and this form of prolapse diminishes end-systolic and diastolic volumes (Fontana et al., 1975). The relationship of prolapse and left ventricular cavity size is confirmed by its high prevalence in normal valves in anorexic females (Devereux et al., 1976; Meyers, 1986; Meyers, Starke, Pearson, Wilken, & Ferrell, 1987). This is ascribable to a starvation-induced depletion of intravascular volume that reduces left ventricular preload filling and internal dimensions (Devereux et al., 1976). The prolapse often disappears after refeeding and weight gain (Meyers et al., 1987).

The strongest relationship of MVP is with the somatotype that is characterized by the low body weight for height and reduced blood volume that subjects with MVP often exhibit (Bashore et al., 1985; Coghlan, 1988; Devereux et al., 1982; Gaffney & Blomqvist, 1981; Gaffney, Bastian, & Lane, 1983; Pasternac et al., 1986). The important role of intravascular volume is shown by the finding that MVP resolves during pregnancy in association with a physiologically increased blood volume (Lutas, Devereux, Spitzer, & Kramer-Fox, 1984). Hypovolemia may be greatest in patients with increased atrial natriuretic factor (ANF). An increased ANF was found in 44% of subjects with MVPS, that was possibly due to ANF stimulation caused by the bulging of leaflets into the left atrium (Pasternac, Kouz et al., 1986). A relationship of lower body positive pressure to atrial dimensions and plasma ANF (Wilkins et al., 1986) may underlie a hemodynamic role of ANF in functional MVP.

Left ventricular contractility related to specific anthropometric features also may be an important factor in occurrence of functional prolapse (Cohen et al., 1987). Subjects with MVP commonly exhibit increased left ventricular contractility (Boudoulas et al., 1980), asynergy, contractile (Colle et al., 1986; Iskandrian, Heo, Hakki, & Mandler, 1986) and other wall motion, and ventriculographic abnormalities (Gooch et al., 1972; Tebbe et al., 1985). It is of interest that these are similar to abnormalities that occur with myocardial hypoxia (Natarajan et al., 1975) and increased lactate production (Hattori et al., 1985). Left ventricular function and contractility are related to end-systolic volume and pressure (Mehmel et al., 1981; Sagawa, 1981). The hypovolemia that is present in many subjects with MVP stimulates autonomic neural activity (Gaffney & Blomqvist, 1981), with increased myocardial contractility and peripheral vaso- and venoconstriction that in turn further contracts intravascular volume and reduces left ventricular preload filling (Gaffney et al., 1983).

The subset of taller, lean females with hypovolemia and increased left ventricular contractility in particular exhibit symptoms associated with adrenergic dysfunction. The relation between prevalence and age in females (Savage et al., 1983) is probably in part a function of the more vigorous left ventricular contractility present at younger ages (Lee et al., 1985). Subjects with MVP tend to have ectomorphic habitus, with hearts that are suspended vertically in their narrower thoracic cavity. It can be visualized that, under beta-adrenergic stimulation, such hearts may respond with more vigorous systolic contractions than occur in heavier individuals with hearts that lie more horizontally in the thoracic cavity.

Physical Endurance

Subjects with MVP often have less muscular development, physical strength, and endurance on stress tests compared to normal subjects (Boudoulas et al., 1986; Fontana et al., 1975; Gaffney, Bastian, & Lane, 1983; Holmgren et al., 1957; Tomaso & Gardin, 1980; Wooley, 1983). This is particularly found in females (Iskandrian et al., 1986) and often can historically be traced to onset in late adolescence. The reduced work capacity is associated with low resting A-V oxygen difference both at rest and during physical work. This may be related to high sympathetic neural tone (Holmgren et al., 1957), and symptomatic patients may have an abnormal sympathetic neural and RAA system response to their intravascular volume depletion (Gaffney et al., 1981; Rogers, Boudoulas, Malarkey, & Wooley, 1983).

Decreased exercise tolerance and abnormal hemodynamic responses in patients with MVPS particularly occur in the upright position (Bashore et al., 1988; Gaffney et al., 1983; Pasternac, Tubau, Puddu, Krol, & DeChamplain, 1982; Puddu et al., 1983) and may be associated with dyspnea, dizziness, syncope, hypotension, tachycardia, and arrhythmias (Santos et al., 1981; Wooley, 1983). This orthostatic intolerance appears to be causally related to hypovolemia and postural left ventricular volume changes (Bashore et al., 1985; Boudoulas & Wooley, 1987; Coghlan, 1988). There may be no differences between patients with MVPS and normal control subjects in the supine position, but those with MVPS often fail to increase end-diastolic volume during upright exercise and are therefore unable to increase stroke volume appropriately at all levels of exertion (Bashore et al., 1988; Chesler et al., 1985; Gaffney, Bastian, & Lane, 1983). Thus there is a failure of venous return to augment during upright exercise. Increased venous capacitance might contribute to this, but data based on reduced lower body negative pressure fail to reveal such abnormal venous pooling, and the response to such negative pressure with increased forearm conductance suggests that increased basal alpha-adrenergic tone is present, with a reduction in the venous reservoir (Coghlan, 1988; Gaffney et al., 1983). Moreover, blood reservoirs contribute surprisingly little to the neurogenically increased cardiac output that normally occurs with exercise (Konstam et al., 1982).

Intravascular volume and sympathetic nervous system activity are inversely correlated (Dustan, Tarazi, Bravo, & Dart, 1973; Finnerty, Buchholz, & Gillaudeu, 1958). Assumption of the upright position stimulates release of norepinephrine as well as of renin and arginine vasopressin, the latter stimulating release of antidiuretic hormone via brainstem neurons and vagal connections. Diminished circulatory perfusion of arterial baroreceptors therefore simultaneously activates the three major vasoconstrictor systems (Schrier, 1988). The activation of cardiac sympathetic and inhibition of parasympathetic nervous systems release catecholamines and increase heart rate (Bashore et al., 1988), and vagal mechanisms play an important role in mediating retention or excretion of sodium and water in response to volume changes (Manders, Knight, & Vatner, 1986).

Alpha-adrenergic tone is increased in the basal state (Coghlan, 1988; Gaffney & Blomqvist, 1981; Gaffney, Bastian, & Lane, 1983). Exercise stimulates sympathetic and decreases parasympathetic traffic to the heart, with increased catecholamines, heart rate, and left ventricular contractility (Jones & Campbell, 1982). Exercise initially increases cardiac output by increasing both stroke volume and heart rate, but later heart rate plays a greater role that is more apparent in upright than in supine activity. Exercise also leads to a metabolic and epinephrine-induced vasodilatation in the muscle bed (Stratton, Halter, Hallstrom, Caldwell, & Ritchie, 1983; Stratton, Pfeifer, Ritchie, & Halter, 1985) and provides a stimulus for alpha-1 adrenergic activity to maintain blood pressure in the upright position.

The latter also induces venoconstriction in order to increase venous return, but thereby reduces the venous reservoir (Bryhn & Persson, 1984). Increased vaso- and venoconstriction further contribute to hypovolemia and enhanced sympathetic neural stimulation in MVPS (Bashore et al., 1985, 1988; Boudoulas et al., 1986; Coghlan,

1988; Gaffney et al., 1983; Pasternac et al., 1982; Puddu et al., 1983; Tomaso & Gardin, 1980), as occur in patients with pheochromocytomas (Brunjes, Johns, & Crane, 1960; Holland, 1980). MVPS and idiopathic orthostatic hypotension share a reduced blood volume (Newman, Gibbons, & Jones, 1981) and venous return during upright exercise that contribute to exertional intolerance and stimulate autonomic responses that aggravate the abnormal venous return. Patients with MVPS are particularly susceptible to clinical settings of dehydration and diuretics as well as vigorous physical exercise (Gaffney et al., 1983; Coghlan, 1988; Coghlan et al., 1986).

Normally during quiet standing there is little increase in plasma epinephrine (Robertson et al., 1979; Sever, 1983). However, it may markedly increase in patients with MVPS (Coghlan, 1988), possibly in a homeostatic attempt to augment stroke volume in the upright position (Stratton et al., 1985). Patients with MVPS often exhibit resting tachycardia (Gaffney, Bastian, & Lane, 1983), in association with increased supine plasma norepinephrine (Coghlan, 1988). However, this is not caused by adrenergic overactivity and a hyperkinetic circulatory state, but is a normal response to inadequate intravascular volume (Coghlan, 1988; Gaffney & Blomqvist, 1988). Beta-blockers improve peripheral symptoms and benefit patients with orthostatic hypotension, showing that responses to orthostasis are not hyperkinetic but only appropriate beta-adrenergic responses to orthostatic shifts of intravascular volume and decreased stroke volume. The orthostatic responses are related to beta-adrenergic stimulation; the benefits are similar whether lipo- or hydrophilic blockers are used. During orthostatic stress, tachycardia is used to maintain blood pressure in the face of subnormal cardiac output responses (Coghlan, 1988; Gaffney et al., 1983).

The highest heart rates occur in subjects with the highest plasma norepinephrine during quiet standing (Boudoulas & Reynolds, 1983; Gaffney et al., 1979, 1983), and those with relatively slower heart rates are less symptomatic (Coghlan, 1979, 1988; Gaffney & Blomqvist, 1988). Patients with hypotensive and high tachycardia responses to upright exercise exhibit exaggerated reduction of left ventricular end-diastolic volume (Liedtke, Gault, Leaman, & Blumenthal, 1973). Clonidine has been shown to interrupt the vicious cycle of orthostatic hypotension, chronic vasoconstriction, and hypovolemia in patients with MVPS, thus proving that excessive norepinephrine is responsible for many of the symptoms and hemodynamic findings in MVPS (Fouad, Tadena-Thome, Bravo, & Tarazi, 1986; Gaffney et al., 1983).

Subnormal ejection fraction and cardiac output responses to upright exercise occur particularly in females (Konstam et al., 1982), although these phenomena are not invariably found (Higgenbotham, Morris, Coleman, & Cobb, 1981). Inadequate left ventricular filling in these patients during upright exercise may be a function of poor venous return due to reduction of intravascular volume, in part caused by inadequate noradrenergic responses to appropriate stimuli. These patients may thus have a relative autonomic insufficiency (Coghlan, 1988; Gaffney, Bastian, & Lane, 1983; Santos et al., 1981).

However, factors that regulate blood volume are of primary importance and underlie abnormal cardiovascular regulation (Weissman et al., 1987), and the combination of hypovolemia, increased sympathetic stimulation, and chronic vasoconstriction explains orthostatic hypotension, upright exercise intolerance, and manifestations such as palpitations and arrhythmias (Abildskov, 1975; Coghlan et al., 1986; Gaffney & Blomqvist, 1988; Hageman, Goldberg, Armour, & Randall, 1973; Hageman, Randall, & Armour, 1975; Pasternac et al., 1982; Puddu et al., 1983; Santos et al., 1981; Weissman et al., 1987). Chronic hypovolemia magnifies the reduction of stroke volume that normally occurs during orthostatic stress, with a vicious cycle when more vasoconstriction is needed to maintain the arterial blood pressure (Gaffney & Blomqvist, 1988). Volume expansion fails to suppress plasma catecholamines both in the supine and upright positions, and particularly when orthostatic stress is prolonged (Rogers et al., 1983). Increased alpha-adrenergic drive is an appropriate response to reduced intravascular volume, and the inability to suppress plasma norepinephrine after volume expansion in MVPS suggests an abnormal regulation of intravascular volume (Boudoulas & Wooley, 1988).

Females exhibit a lower functional left ventricular reserve compared to males, and this is particularly reduced in patients with MVPS who exhibit exercise intolerance (Nemiah, 1980). Many of their symptoms are engendered by physical exertion (Cohen & White, 1950). Lactate is the end product of anaerobic glycogenolysis, the process by which cells break down glucose or its glycogen storage form and extract energy from it. Working muscle cells convert glycogen to lactate, most of which diffuses into the circulation and is eventually resynthesized into glucose in the liver. The anaerobic threshold is the point at which increased lactate is due to anaerobic glycogenolysis and dyspnea occurs (Mizock, 1987), and the onset of lactate accumulation in plasma corresponds to lactate accumulation in working muscles. The workload at which it accumulates is related to exercise performance and endurance (Fontana et al., 1975), and tolerance for work is diminished when it is performed at higher lactate loads. In the absence of acidosis, hyperlactatemia occurs in the setting of hypermetabolic conditions (Mizock, 1987).

Exercise stimulates autonomic neural activity (Stratton et al., 1983), with release of epinephrine that, in turn, increases lactate production (Caruso, Orszulak, & Miles, 1987; Pitts & McClure, 1967) by acting on metabolic receptor sites on cell surfaces to activate intracellular glycolytic enzyme systems. Epinephrine displaces a calcium molecule from receptor sites by a chelation process, thereby initiating a series of biochemical steps that result in increased heart rate; stroke volume; ejection fraction; cardiac output; systolic blood pressure; splanchnic vasoconstriction; vasodilatation in the skin, brain, and muscle beds; and activation of the Emden-Meyerhoff anaerobic pathway that increases lactate production by muscles and other tissues. Patients with MVPS produce more lactate per unit of work during exertion (Holmgren et al., 1957; Pitts & McClure, 1967). Those people with poor exercise tolerance and marked fatigability develop abnormal plasma lactate levels during submaximal exercise, and at much lower workload levels than do control subjects or the subjects described by Holmgren et al. (1957). The crucial factor of abnormal venous tone (Shepherd, 1981) may be a key factor in the abnormal circulatory control of the patients with poor exercise tolerance.

Anxiety stimulates release of epinephrine, and chronic overproduction of epinephrine by patients with MVPS (Coghlan, 1988) can induce a deficit in the normal ratio of aerobic to anaerobic metabolism in working muscles. A resulting enhanced rise of plasma lactate during exercise (Caruso et al., 1987) can be associated with increased anxiety (Pitts & McClure, 1967) and stimulate attacks of panic in patients with panic disorder. It is significant that administration of the beta-agonist, isoproterenol, can cause extreme fatigue, as well as other typical symptoms in a dose-related manner in subjects with MVPS (Boudoulas & Wooley, 1987).

Exercise training may benefit patients with symptomatic MVP (Wooley, 1983). Fitness increases the use of fatty acids and decreases the use of glycogen for the source of energy in working muscles. It thus increases the ability of muscles to extract oxygen, thereby diminishing anaerobic metabolism and lactate production by working muscles. There also is a strong correlation between left ventricular end-diastolic dimensions and stroke volume (Martin, Coyle, Bloomfield, & Ehsani, 1986), and exercise conditioning augments end-diastolic volume (Merino, Alegria, Castello, & Martinez-Caro, 1988). Moreover, endurance training for upright exercise is associated with a greater stroke volume during exercise in the upright position, because of augmented preload. However, this adaptation can be rapidly lost after periods of inactivity (Martin et al., 1986).

Genetic Predisposition

It would be possible for anatomic prolapse to occur as the result of an inherited defect of the leaflet or valve apparatus or of other factors that are associated with occurrence of MVP, and for MVPS to occur as the result of an inherited defect of autonomic neural regulation. MVP can occur secondarily as a phenotypic feature of a number of connective tissue disorders that have an autosomal dominant pattern of inheritance (Devereux & Brown, 1989; Leier, Call, Fulkerson, & Wooley, 1980; Pyeritz & McKusick, 1979). There also are strong genetic relationships for idiopathic MVP, and its transmission exhibits an autosomal dominant pattern of inheritance, with age- and sex-linked expressions (Chen, Chan, Wong, & Chew, 1983; Devereux, 1982; Jeresaty, 1979; Schutte et al., 1981; Strahan, Murphy, Fortuin, Humphries, & Come, 1983; Weiss, Mimbs, Ludbrook, & Sobel, 1975). There is high familial aggregation of MVP (Chen et al., 1983; Jeresaty, 1979; Pocock & Barlow, 1971; Rizzon et al., 1973; Scheele, Allen, Kraus, & Rubin, 1976; Strahan et al., 1983; Weiss et al., 1975), although of smaller magnitude in some studies (Devereux, 1982; Devereux et al., 1987).

Further evidence for an autosomal dominant pattern of transmission resides in a high concordance of MVP in twins (Jeresaty, 1979; Rotmensch, Ayzenberg, Jacobi, & Laniado, 1980). However, there is incomplete penetration of the autosomal dominant inheritance pattern, because females are affected far more frequently than males (Kramer-Fox, Devereux, Brown, Hartman, & Elston, 1984; Savage, 1982). The preponderance of MVP among females prevails in its familial distribution in first-degree relatives of index subjects (Devereux, 1982; Weiss et al., 1975) and is the same whether or not the proband has acoustic or echocardiographic abnormalities, adrenergically related symptoms, or other manifestations (Devereux, 1982; Gooch et al., 1972).

A classic concept that ascribes MVP to inherited structural defects in connective tissue that enlarge leaflets and lead to their billowing into the left atrium during ventricular systole is probably based on studies of patients in whom mitral regurgitation has complicated the prolapse (Cohen, Shah, & Spindola-Franco, 1979; Criley et al., 1966; Gilbert, Schatz, von Ramm, Behar, & Kisslo, 1976; Ranganathan et al., 1973). Nor is there any strong basis to hypothesize (Pini et al., 1986) that an inherited connective tissue defect provides the mechanism for echocardiographic prolapse in subjects with functional MVP. The concept that idiopathic MVP is a forme fruste of Marfan's syndrome (Read, Thal, & Wendt, 1965) is not supported by the evidence that indicates that the two conditions differ in all major skeletal and cardiovascular features (Roman et al., 1989).

It seems doubtful that idiopathic MVP is directly inherited. In the first place, there is no demonstrated chromosomal abnormality for MVP, and the substantial majority of involved subjects do not exhibit any other congenital or hereditary abnormalities, aside from those of the thoracic skeletal configuration (Ansari, 1985; Naggar & Aretz, 1984). Moreover, the concordance for MVP in twins is only slightly higher in mono- than in dizygotic twin pairs (Brauman et al., 1985). The age distribution also fails to indicate direct heritability. About 6% of neonates exhibit echocardiographic evidence of MVP (Chandraratna et al., 1979), but this is at a time when the left ventricle is relatively underdeveloped, owing to the predominant role of the right ventricle in the fetal circulation.

As the left ventricle develops in childhood, prevalence decreases to about 2% (Devereux et al., 1982; McLaren et al., 1976) and increases in later adolescence and early adult life. The proportion of young children with MVP (Arfken et al., 1986) is much lower than would be expected from higher prevalence found in young adults (Savage et al., 1983). Prevalence progressively declines in females, particularly after 40 to 50 years of age (Hickey & Wilcken, 1986; Savage, 1982; Strahan et al., 1983). This cannot be ascribed to complications, because the same low prevalence occurs in males in all age groups (Savage, 1982; Savage, Devereux, & Garrison, 1983), and most complications of MVP occur in older males in association with hemodynamically significant mitral regurgitation. A reduced prevalence also is found after age 50 in first-degree relatives (Strahan et al., 1983).

There is a powerful association of MVP with low blood pressure and distinctive body habitus that is characterized by low body weight for height, straight back, narrow anteroposterior chest diameter, and pectus excavatum (Devereux et al., 1982). Moreover, the biologic differences that exist between relatives with and without MVP are particularly those of low blood pressure and weight for height and the distinctive thoracic skeletal configuration. Abnormalities of the bony thorax can be found in more than half of subjects with clinically recognized MVP (Bon Tempo et al., 1975; Devereux, Kramer-Fox et al., 1986; Lee et al., 1985; Salomon et al., 1975; Zema et al., 1982). An autosomal dominant pattern of inheritance also prevails for these anthropometric and biological measures, suggesting that MVP is a common condition that is systematically associated with specific factors that have strong genetic relationships. However, its prevalence in family studies is the same, regardless of the presence or absence of these thoracic skeletal abnormalities in the probands (Devereux, 1982). It may be that the thoracic skeletal configuration associated with MVP is merely that which often occurs in people who are tall and thin.

The changing prevalence of MVP at different ages in females indicates that there is a need to look beyond the valve to etiological factors such as blood volume and left ventricular size and contractility. The relationship of MVP to orthostatic stress, blood volume, left ventricular filling and contractility, and the evanescent and changing nature of echocardiographic and auscultatory manifestations strongly suggest that MVP is due to functional mechanisms rather than being a directly inherited disease condition. Moreover, the ability to induce anatomic prolapse by a variety of suitable maneuvers does not support the concept of a heritable disorder of the mitral valve but rather that there are genetic relationships for specific factors that may be associated with functional MVP.

An autosomal dominant pattern of inheritance is found in symptomatic MVP and other anxiety disorders (Cohen, Badal, & Kilpatrick, 1951; Devereux, 1982; Strahan et al., 1983; Weiss et al., 1975). In comparing unselected MVP and normal control subjects, adrenergically related symptoms are equally prevalent in the same clinical setting (Retchin et al., 1986; Uretsky, 1982), regardless of whether the presence or absence of MVP is determined by echocardiography (Devereux, Kramer-Fox et al., 1986). Similar findings prevail in comparisons of affected first-degree relatives and control subjects (Devereux, Kramer-Fox et al., 1986). Moreover, no association of MVP is found with chest pain, anxiety, panic attacks, or ECG abnormalities in studies of unselected subjects (Devereux et al., 1986; Savage et al., 1983). Those with symptomatic MVP are significantly more likely to exhibit orthostatic hypotension than are individuals who have similar symptoms but no prolapse (Santos et al., 1981). In comparing families with and without MVP, there is similar morbidity for panic disorder in both sexes and in all classes of relatives. Thus, panic disorder and MVP are independently transmitted, and panic disorder patients with prolapse are not a separate subgroup.

Some postulate that MVP is a marker for a general developmental defect that affects midbrain control of the circulatory system and structure of the heart valve and that midbrain centers fail to appropriately interpret messages from cardiac receptors or to maintain a proper balance between sympathetic and parasympathetic nervous systems (Coghlan, 1979). Boudoulas and Wooley (1988) have continued to regard MVPS as a constitutional neuroendocrine process with genetic relationships for MVP and for central or peripherally mediated states of autonomic dysfunction or imbalance. However, it seems unlikely that there is an inherited central nervous system abnormality in subjects with MVPS. The fact that their increased catecholamine release primarily occurs in the daytime (Boudoulas et al., 1980; Wooley, 1983) in the upright position (Boudoulas & Reynolds, 1983; Coghlan, 1979; Gaffney, Bastian, & Lane et al., 1983) shows that this is an appropriate response to abnormalities of blood volume, orthostatic changes, and related factors (Pasternac et al., 1982; Puddu et al., 1983).

Autonomic Nervous System Dysfunction

There is widespread belief that the symptoms occurring in patients with MVPS are the result of autonomic dysfunction, with a hyperadrenergic state and metabolic disturbance in which the heart and cardiovascular system are targets (Boudoulas & Reynolds, 1983; Boudoulas et al., 1980; Coghlan, 1979; Davies, Mares, Pool, & Taylor, 1987; Gaffney et al., 1979). It is interesting to note that Crile (1934) found that denervation of the adrenal glands provided striking symptomatic benefit to the majority of patients with MVPS. Many researchers have found that MVPS patients, in comparison with control groups, exhibit higher baseline plasma levels and 24-hour urinary excretion of catecholamines (Boudoulas et al., 1980, 1984, 1985; Coghlan, 1979; Gaffney et al., 1979; King et al., 1980; Pasternac et al., 1982; Puddu et al., 1983). A pattern of increased noradrenergic activity and vagal tone remained stable in one group of patients over a period of six years (Pasternac, Latour et al., 1986).

Although additional evidence supports the belief that MVPS is associated with hyperbeta-adrenergic activity (Boudoulas & Wooley, 1987; Boudoulas et al., 1984), there is disagreement about this (Blomqvist, 1986; Chesler et al., 1985; Lenders et al., 1986; Nesse et al., 1985), as well as whether this primarily involves beta- or alpha-adrenergic systems or both (Gaffney et al., 1979). Clearly, adrenergic overactivity is not systematically associated with MVP (Weissman et al., 1987). Sympathetic discharge is highly differentiated, and neural traffic to a given target organ may be poorly reflected in pooled venous samples (Brown, Jenner, Allison, & Dollers, 1981; Esler et al., 1988), which may account for some conflicting findings.

The human left ventricle has a high proportion of beta-2 receptors located on myocardial cells, and their stimulation causes increased ventricular contractility (Levine & Leenan, 1989). The primary endogenous beta-1 receptor agonist is norepinephrine and the beta-2 receptor agonist is mainly epinephrine (Epstein & Lefkowitz, 1986). The increased left ventricular contractility found in patients with MVPS (Pasternac et al., 1982) is probably related to beta-adrenergic stimulation, and administration of epinephrine also increases state anxiety (Mathew & Wilson, 1986) and decreases left ventricular preload filling and cavity dimensions. Even relatively low levels of arterial plasma epinephrine cause cardiac stimulation and induce peripheral vasodilatation. Although there are chronotropic beta-2 receptors in the human heart (Levine & Leenen, 1989), tachycardia is not a prominent part of the response to epinephrine or its effects on stroke volume (Freyschuss, Hjemdahl, Jamlin-Dannfelt, & Linde, 1986). Beta-adrenergic stimulation also causes venoconstriction, further reducing intravascular volume and stimulating myocardial contractility (Boudoulas et al., 1980).

Some believe that MVPS patients have a dual dysfunction that involves both the sympathetic and parasympathetic systems (Gaffney et al., 1979; Pasternac, Latour et al., 1982, 1986). Although there may be evidence of poor parasympathetic control (Coghlan, 1979), there is disagreement on whether vagal activity is decreased (Kramer et al., 1984), increased (Coghlan, 1979; Gaffney et al., 1979; Pasternac, Latour et al., 1982, 1986; Weissman et al., 1987), or unchanged (Gaffney, 1986; Gaffney et al., 1979). There also is disagreement on whether increased adrenergic activity is due to central sympathetic neural stimulation or to increased peripheral beta-receptor sensitivity (Liedtke et al., 1973) and thus whether autonomic nervous system dysfunction in MVPS is due to a disorder of central or peripheral regulation. Some investigators have found that sensitivity to beta-agonists is increased (Boudoulas & Reynolds, 1983; Boudoulas et al., 1984; Davies et al., 1987; De Carvalho, Messerli, & Frohlich, 1979; Frolich, Tarazi, & Dustan, 1969; Gaffney et al., 1979), whereas others found no abnormality or peripheral beta-receptor density, affinity (Coghlan, 1979), or sensitivity (Gaffney, 1986; Gaffney et al., 1979).

There is evidence that only patients with high-resting plasma catecholamine levels are hypersensitive to beta-agonists (Boudoulas & Reynolds, 1983). Receptor theory states that the number of active receptors should be low in the presence of elevated catecholamines (Lefkowitz, Caron, & Stiles, 1984). A downregulation of beta-receptors would thus be anticipated in MVPS (Boudoulas & Reynolds, 1983; Boudoulas & Wooley, 1987), whereas the finding of hyperresponsiveness to beta-agonists suggests increased beta-receptor function. However, the number of active beta-receptors increases with short-term infusion of isoproterenol, whereas longer infusions decrease receptor density (Tohmeh & Cryer, 1980).

The finding of increased beta-receptor responsiveness thus suggests that symptomatic subjects only have transient, inappropriate releases of catecholamines that occur throughout the daytime in association with physical activity, postural changes, stress responses (Boudoulas & Reynolds, 1983; Boudoulas & Wooley, 1987; Combs, Shah, Klorman, Klorman, & Sylvester, 1980; Wooley, 1983), and dysautonomic responses to various maneuvers (Pasternac, Latour et al., 1982, 1986; Rogers et al., 1983). The increased plasma and urinary catecholamines in symptomatic patients may be ascribed to these transient daytime secretory peaks that stimulate beta-adrenergic receptors, albeit not sustained long enough to downregulate and reduce their density (Boudoulas et al., 1984; McMurray, Seidelin, Balfour, & Struthers, 1988). A parallelism may be found in patients with panic disorder where stimulation of brain noradrenergic activity may be too brief to affect levels of its metabolites (Woods, 1987). However, it was recently found that patients with MVPS who exhibit higher than normal orthostatic rise of norepinephrine also exhibit increased cyclic AMP production in response to beta-agonists, thus having beta-adrenergic sensitivity that is due to biochemical supercoupling (Davies et al., 1987) rather than to increased density of beta-adrenergic receptors.

Some investigators believe that the disordered catecholamine regulation (Boudoulas et al., 1984; Pasternac, Kouz et al., 1986) and cardiovascular instability (Coghlan, 1979; Gaffney et al., 1979) in patients with MVPS are due to an abnormal central modulation of baroreflexes that underlies their dysautonomic responses (Coghlan, 1979) and failure to exhibit the fine, graded responses that make the autonomic nervous system function in a smooth and stable fashion (Gaffney, 1986). Cardiovascular instability is greater in subjects who exhibit tachycardia and is less in those with relative bradycardia (Coghlan, 1979; Gaffney et al., 1979). Those with highest orthostatic heart rates have the highest plasma norepinephrine levels, albeit diminished cardiac output (Boudoulas & Reynolds, 1983), showing that they use tachycardia to maintain the blood pressure during orthostatic stress (Gaffney, Bastian, & Lane, 1983).

It is relevant that the aortic baroreflex is an important regulator of efferent sympathetic responses during acute hypotension in normal humans (Sanders, Mark, & Ferguson, 1989). The presence of psychiatric symptoms and sleep disorders in patients with MVPS and the ability of beta-agonists to induce multiple symptoms and even panic attacks in patients with MVPS (Boudoulas & Wooley, 1987) also suggest an abnormality in central autonomic regulatory mechanisms, with complex neuroendocrine cardiovascular relationships (Pasternac et al., 1986). Patients with MVPS are believed to have a central hyperadrenergic overactivity (Ko, Ellsworth, & Roth, 1983; Weissman et al., 1987), with normal or down-regulated peripheral responses (Nesse, Cameron, Curtis, McCann, & Huber-Smith, 1984). However, the autonomic dysfunction in many patients may only reflect orthostatic decline of systolic blood pressure with accompanying tachycardia (Coghlan, 1979; Pasternac et al., 1982; Santos et al., 1981; Schatz, 1986), with accompanying symptoms of dizziness, palpitations, and fatigue (Schatz, 1986)

Autonomic dysfunction is primarily exhibited in the upright position (Boudoulas & Reynolds, 1983; Coghlan, 1979; Gaffney et al., 1983; Pasternac et al., 1982; Puddu et al., 1983) in response to hypovolemia (Coghlan, 1979), and patients with MVPS commonly exhibit orthostatic hypotension (Brown et al., 1975; Coghlan, 1979) that may be a major cause of adrenergically related symptoms (Boudoulas et al., 1984; Depace et al., 1981; Gaffney & Blomqvist, 1988; Santos, 1981). Some patients exhibit postural decreases of left ventricular and stroke volumes that so markedly stimulate sympathetic nervous system activity (Gaffney et al., 1979) that chronic vasoconstriction occurs and can rarely even lead to sustained hypertension (Gaffney et al., 1983; Blomqvist, 1986). However, despite this chronic peripheral vasoconstriction, hypertension is an exception in subjects with MVPS (Gaffney et al., 1979, 1983, 1988), possibly because of hypovolemia (Devereux et al., 1982).

Orthostatic hypotension with marked tachycardia is a sympathicotonic response caused by peripheral effects. It is characterized by normal baseline norepinephrine levels but decreased alpha-adrenergic responses to infusion of norepinephrine, low supine mean blood pressure, and orthostatic tachycardia caused by excessive beta-adrenergic receptor stimulation (Polinsky, 1983). Norepinephrine levels in such patients markedly increase in the upright position as a homeostatic response to peripheral receptors that are not normally activated by postural changes (Polinsky, 1983). This excessive norepinephrine response during quiet standing also occurs in females with MVPS who exhibit this sympathotonic type of hypotensive response to orthostatic stress (Davies et al., 1987). They may not have a hyperkinetic circulatory system (DeCarvalho et al., 1979; Frolich et al., 1969; Gaffney et al., 1979; Guazzi, 1984) but merely exhibit homeostatically appropriate responses to a cycle of orthostatic decreases of intravascular and stroke volumes, vasoconstriction, and tachycardia (Gaffney & Blomqvist, 1988; Gaffney et al., 1979, 1983).

In support of this belief is the fact that catecholamine excretion is considerably reduced in the supine position at night in patients with MVPS (Boudoulas et al., 1980; Coghlan, 1979; Gaffney et al., 1983; Wooley, 1983). Although there may be a hyperdynamic circulation (DeCarvalho et al., 1979; Frolich et al., 1969), responses to passive upright tilting, Valsalva maneuver, and isometric handgrip are normal (Chesler et al., 1985; DeCarvalho et al., 1979). Stress-mediated or activated biochemical mechanisms are what alter adrenergic tone (Dimsdale, Young, Moore, & Strauss, 1987) and provide the basis for symptoms in patients with MVPS (Coghlan, 1988; Gaffney & Blomqvist, 1988). In control subjects, beta-agonists cause only palpitations, but in patients with MVPS they cause multiple symptoms and even panic attacks in a dose-related manner (Boudoulas & Wooley, 1987). Decrease of hyperadrenergic manifestations with aging in patients with MVPS may be due to neuroendocrine changes that are marked by increases in plasma norepinephrine and decreased responsiveness to hormones and their metabolites (Everitt, 1988). There also are age-related cardiovascular changes that are characterized by increase of heart size and decrease of myocardial contractility (Merino et al., 1988).

The validity of considering MVPS to be a true condition has been increasingly questioned (Kjeldsen et al., 1986; Leatham & Brigden, 1980; Lenders et al., 1986; Leor & Markiewicz, 1982; Mazza, Martin, & Spacavento, 1986; Pollack, 1987). The finding of autonomic dysfunction in patients with MVPS may only indicate that hyperadrenergic manifestations are part of an anxiety disorder (Leatham & Brigden, 1980) that is associated with such dysfunction (Nesse et al., 1984). Although anatomic prolapse may be a marker for the constitutional neuroendocrine process that is called MVPS (Boudoulas et al., 1980), the prolapse and adrenergically mediated symptoms are independent and may merely be the coincidence of two conditions that are commonly found in clinical practice (Chesler et al., 1985; Uretsky, 1982). It is relevant to determine whether MVP can be related only to peripheral autonomic factors, as appears to be the case in hyperthyroid patients.

Hyperthyroidism

There is an increased prevalence of MVP in hyperthyroid patients (Amidi, 1984; Aronson et al., 1987; Brauman et al., 1985; Channick et al., 1981; Denenberg, Channick, & Spann, 1983), estimated to be as high as 43% (Thompson & Levine, 1935), although the prevalence rates may be subject to ascertainment bias (Brauman et al., 1985; Zullo, Devereux, Kramer-Fox, Lutas, & Brown, 1985). Prolapse disappears after resumption of the euthyroid state, suggesting that its occurrence in hyperthyroid patients is not due to structural alterations in the valve apparatus (Thompson & Levine, 1935), but that prolapse is a functional disorder that can be ascribed to transient effects on cardiac function. Loss of weight in hyperthyroid patients probably plays a contributing role. Thyroid hormone has direct inotropic and chronotropic effects on the heart, and all factors involved in left ventricular performance are affected, including preload, afterload, heart rate, and myocardial fiber and left ventricular shortening (Feldman, Borow, Sarne, Neuman, & Lang, 1986; Hammond et al., 1985; Wilkin, 1983). However, left ventricular contractility appears to be responsible for ventricular shortening, rather than altered loading or chronotropic effects (Feldman et al., 1986). Systolic blood pressure is increased and peripheral vascular resistance is decreased (Feldman et al., 1986; Goldman & Morkin, 1983).

The enhanced contractility of hyperthyroid patients cannot be ascribed to an increase of central sympathetic neural activity, circulating catecholamines, or increased receptor sensitivity (Wilkin, 1983). Thus hyperthyroidism is not associated with increased central sympathetic stimulation or increased plasma catecholamines or their metabolites (Goldman & Morkin, 1983; Iskandrian, Rose, Hakki, Segal, & Kane, 1983; Skelton, 1982; Wilkin, 1983). However, thyroid hormone stimulates upregulation of myocardial receptors, with enhanced beta-adrenergic responsiveness and normal sympathetic stimulation (Amidi, 1984; Hammond et al., 1985; Levey & Levey, 1985; Wilkin, 1983; Williams, Lefkowitz, Watanabe, Hathaway, & Besch, 1977). The increased receptor density is associated with an increased contractility (Van de Schoot & Moran, 1965) that augments left ventricular shortening (Cohen, 1988; Feldman et al., 1985, 1986). The peripheral nature of the hyperbeta-adrenergic responsiveness probably accounts for the failure of beta-adrenergic blocking drugs to improve symptoms in hyperthyroid patients (Amidi, 1984). Their left ventricular reserve is normal at rest but diminished during exercise (Cohen, 1988; Iskandrian et al., 1983; Smallridge, Goldman, Raines, Jones, & Van Nostrand, 1987; Wilkin, 1983). This probably is a physiologic response to the hyperdynamic, hemodynamic state that is already present before exercise, and during which the left ventricular is operating at or near its functional capacity (Goldman & Morkin, 1983), although it may partly be due to the cardiomyopathy that can occur after prolonged hyperthyroidism (Wilkin, 1983).

The hyperkinetic cardiac effects of thyroid hormone are due to augmented contractility, but its inotropic effects are partly independent of beta-adrenergic function (Buccino, Spann, Pool, Sonnenblick, & Braunwald, 1967; Cohen, 1988). Thyroid hormone has a molecular basis for increasing contractility. It binds to specific nucleus receptors in myofibrils and increases DNA and RNA synthesis, leading to more rapid synthesis of specific structural proteins and enzymes (Levey & Levey, 1985). It thus alters protein synthesis at the level of the cell nuclear (Cohen, 1988) and changes the distribution of myosin isoenzymes (Goldman & Morkin, 1983), with synthesis of a new myosin that has a higher level of the ATPase activity (Skelton, 1982) that controls the speed of myocardial contraction. Thyroid hormone thus directly stimulates myocardial cell growth and increases muscle mass (Amidi, 1984; Cohen, 1988; Gay et al., 1986; Skelton, 1982). It also increases calcium uptake by sarcoplasmic reticulum during excitation-coupling (Cohen, 1988), and the enhanced accumulation and release of calcium augment ventricular shortening characteristics and enhances contractility (Amidi, 1984; Feldman et al., 1986; Skelton, 1982). Hyperthyroid patients thus have an increased left ventricular contractility that increases the tugging effects of chordae tendinae that can pull down the posterior mitral leaflet of histologically normal valves and cause a failed coaptation and functional prolapse that disappears after restoration of the euthyroid state.

ANXIETY AND MITRAL VALVE PROLAPSE SYNDROME

History

Interrelationships between anxiety and the cardiovascular system have long been of unique interest in clinical medicine, and the association of anxiety disorders and MVP may be a paradigm of the interaction of physical and psychological variables (Thase, 1983). The history of this interaction provides a fascinating scenario that was first documented by Wooley in 1976 and recently summarized (Wooley & Boudoulas, 1988). The early literature on "nervous heart" was traced by Bedford (1977), and the functional nature of nervous palpitation was emphasized in a classical text published in 1836 (Williams, 1836). Much of the literature described in the following paragraphs was concerned with the occurrence of various aspects of MVPS in military personnel during wartime experiences.

Hartshorne described "cardiac muscular exhaustion" in 1864. The experience in British soldiers was described in 1867 (MacLean, 1867) and further elaborated in 1870 (Myers, 1870). DaCosta published his first observations on "irritable heart syndrome" in Civil War soldiers (1871), later known as DaCosta's syndrome. DaCosta recognized that this syndrome was not specifically caused by military life; he noted that many soldiers had exhibited it prior to entering the service and also that it was present in many civilians. He considered its familial nature by describing occurrence in a pair of twins. Osler had a continuing interest in this syndrome, calling attention to the evanescent nature of a systolic murmur in a young woman (1880), and recognizing that the complex of palpitation, chest pain, exertional dyspnea, and neurasthenia occurred in women as well as in soldiers (1887). International use of the influential term *neurasthenia* had followed its introduction in 1867 (Beard, 1867).

Leading British cardiologists, such as Clifford Allbutt, Sir Thomas Lewis, John Parkinson, and James MacKenzie revived interest in the syndrome during World War I. Lewis (1919) perceived the clinical manifestations as exaggerated physiologic responses to exercise, calling the condition the effort syndrome, and he noted the high prevalence of thoracic skeletal abnormalities in soldiers with this syndrome. MacKenzie preferred to call the syndrome "soldier's heart." Concurrent interest in the United States by Paul White, Samuel Levine, and Frank Wilson led to the designation "neurocirculatory asthenia." Interest revived during World War II, and Paul Wood collaborated with a psychiatrist, Aubrey Lewis. They emphasized psychosomatic and psychiatric aspects, with emergence of terms such as battle fatigue and anxiety neurosis. The military surgeon, Alfred Stille, provided the first written description of anxiety in 1863, using the term *prolapse* (Criley et al., 1966). Hancock (1966) proposed the term *palpitation of the heart*, and Freud had introduced the term *anxiety neurosis* in 1895 (see Paul, 1987; Wooley, 1976). Wood (1941) rejected the concept of Lewis (1919) and considered the syndrome to be a cardiac neurosis.

The occurrence of systolic clicks was recognized by Laennec, Austin Flint, and DaCosta, and the gallop rhythm that it caused was well described (Cuffer, 1887; Galavardin, 1913; Griffith, 1892). In the late 19th century, Potain had ascribed these clicks to pericardial adhesions, and the concept of an extracardiac mechanism prevailed well into the 20th century (Humphries & McKusick, 1962; Luisada & Alimurung, 1949; Thompson & Levine, 1935). Griffith (1892) believed that the systolic murmur was due to mitral regurgitation, and this was ascribed independently by Hall to a "yielding" of the mitral valve that explained its timing in the cardiac cycle (Wooley & Boudoulas, 1988). However, belief that systolic murmurs are nonorganic long prevailed.

Reid (1961) and Barlow and associates (Barlow, Pocock, Marchand, & Denny, 1963) demonstrated that the nonejection systolic clicks and mid- and late-systolic murmur originated at the mitral valve and were associated with its prolapse into the left atrium during left ventricular systole. Criley and associates clarified these associations and introduced the term, *midsystolic click–late mitral murmur syndrome*, and drew attention to the constellation of symptoms in young women with these cardiac sounds. Other designations followed, including the electrocardiographic auscultatory syndrome (Humphries & McKusick, 1962), floppy valve syndrome (Read et al., 1965), mitral valve prolapse syndrome (Engle, 1969), systolic click–late systolic murmur syndrome (Fontana, 1970), billowing posterior mitral leaflet syndrome (Pocock & Barlow, 1970), prolapsing mitral leaflet syndrome (Scampardonis, Yanag, Maranhao, Goldberg, & Gooch, 1973), and billowing mitral leaflet syndrome (Barlow & Pocock, 1975). The prolapse or herniation of mitral leaflets into the left atrium was well shown to be the cause of mitral regurgitation and the associated mid- and late-systolic murmur (Barlow et al., 1968). The designation MVP is now widely used, regardless of whether valve dysfunction is mild, can be confirmed by echocardiography, or is clinically silent. Barlow and Pocock (1984, 1985) have properly differentiated valve anomalies such as prolapse, billowing, and floppy and flail valves, and Wooley and Boudoulas (1988) have continued to emphasize the difference between anatomic prolapse and MVPS.

It seems probable that many patients diagnosed as having irritable heart syndrome and allied disorders in the past were suffering from a biological anxiety disorder that is associated with a high incidence of MVP. The symptomatic manifestations that occur in some patients with idiopathic MVP closely resemble those in subjects with anxiety disorders (Thase, 1983) and are widely ascribed to adrenergic hyperactivity (Boudoulas & Reynolds, 1983; Coghlan, 1979; Gaffney et al., 1979; Gaffney & Blomqvist, 1981; Wooley, 1983; Wooley & Boudoulas, 1988). Cannon (1929) described beta-adrenergic relationships to anxiety. Wearn and Sturgis (1919) found that administration of epinephrine reproduced symptoms in patients with anxiety and functional cardiac symptoms, and Tompkins, Sturgis, and Wearn (1919) found that it exacerbated the anxiety of soldiers with irritable heart syndrome. Mendlowitz and associates later found that an exacerbation of anxiety could be induced in patients with a history of anxiety disorder by administration of epinephrine, but not norepinephrine (Vlachakis, DeGuta, Mendlowitz, Antram, & Wolf, 1974). Administration of epinephrine or of the pure beta-agonist, isoproterenol, was found to induce hysteria in patients with anxiety disorders (Frolich et al., 1969; Lindemann & Finesinger, 1938, 1940); exacerbate anxiety in patients with panic disorder (Easton & Sherman, 1976); and cause anxiety, panic, and chest pains in patients with MVPS (Boudoulas et al., 1984). Lindemann and Finesinger (1938) ascribed this to beta-adrenergic hypersensitivity, and Frohlich and associates considered MVPS to be a hyperdynamic beta-adrenergic circulatory state with an increased receptor site responsiveness to beta-agonists (DeCarvalho et al., 1979; Frolich et al., 1969). Similar effects of epinephrine and isoprotenol were not induced in control subjects in the aforementioned studies.

Generalized Anxiety Disorder and Panic Disorder

Anxiety disorders have been separated into two prototypic types, generalized anxiety disorders (GAD) and panic disorder. Panic disorder is considered by some to be a reflection of core endogenous anxiety that can evolve into GAD (Sheehan, 1982; Sheehan, Ballenger, & Jacobsen, 1980), but consensus favors an official classification in the third edition of the *Diagnostic and Statistical Manual of Mental Disorders* (American Psychiatric Association, 1980), into two distinct subgroups (Gorman et al., 1981b; Jeresaty, 1986; Klein, Zitrin, & Woerner, 1978; Klerman, 1985; Wooley, 1976). Whereas GAD is not a well-studied condition with proven or fully accepted status (Shuckit, 1987), panic disorder appears to be defined and accepted (Dager, Cowley, & Dunner, 1987; Dunner, 1985; Gorman et al., 1981b; Jefferson, 1987; Klein et al., 1978; Klerman, 1985; Wooley, 1976). Panic attacks have been biologically precipitated by the administration of agents that include lactate, caffeine, an alpha-2-adrenergic agonist such as yohimbine, beta-agonists such as isoproterenol and epinephrine, and inhalation of 5% carbon dioxide (Dager et al., 1987; Easton & Sherman, 1976; Frolich et al., 1969; Pitts & McClure, 1967; Pyke & Greenberg, 1986).

Lactate infusion can also induce panic attacks in many subjects with panic disorder (Liebowitz, Gorman, & Fyer, 1985; Yeragani et al., 1987), and with more regularity than isoproterenol (Pyke & Greenberg, 1986). It is believed that panic attacks induced by lactate infusion are due to release of epinephrine, and the vulnerability to lactate is related to higher baseline levels of plasma epinephrine (Pitts & McClure, 1967). Patients with panic disorder produce more lactate during exercise than do paired control subjects (Cohen et al., 1951; Jones & Mellersh, 1946). Between attacks of panic, patients with panic disorder may resemble those with GAD (Dager et al., 1987).

There is considerable support for considering panic disorder to be a separate entity (Gorman et al., 1981b; Klein et al., 1978; Klerman, 1985; Wooley, 1976) that is not associated with other psychiatric disease. There is an increased risk for panic disorder (Crowe, Pauls, Slymen, & Noyes, 1980) but not for GAD (Klerman, 1985) in families of patients with panic disorder, and an apparent genetic dimension for anxiety (Sheehan, 1982) prevails for panic disorder but not for GAD. Thus mono- and dizygotic twin pairs have similar concordance for GAD, but the frequency of panic disorder is much higher in monozygotic twins (Devereux & Brown, 1989). Panic disorder has a significantly higher prevalence in females, an onset in late adolescence and early adult life, and, in familiar relationships, is transmitted in an autosomal dominant pattern of inheritance (Cohen et al., 1951; Crowe et al., 1980, 1982; Sheehan, 1982; Torgerson, 1983). However, there is no known method of transmission.

Panic attacks are characterized by central alpha-adrenergic discharge involving the locus coeruleus, and the vulnerability to lactate administration in patients with panic disorder is related to high baseline levels of epinephrine (Liebowitz et al., 1985). Although patients with panic disorder do not continuously exhibit high heart rates, tachycardia occurs during panic attacks (Freedman, Ianni, Ettedgui, & Puthezbath, 1985; Margraf, Taylor, Ehlers, Roth, & Agras, 1987; Taylor, Telch, & Haavik, 1983; Taylor et al., 1986). The locus coeruleus is the major norepinephrine-containing brain nuclei and is strongly involved in anxiety (Redmond, 1979; Redmond & Huang, 1979; Uhde et al., 1984). Application of epinephrine, norepinephrine, or clonidine to the locus coeruleus reduces neuronal activity and anxiety responses, whereas yohimbine and piperoxane increase locus coeruleus noradrenergic activity and anxiety responses (Charney, Heninger, & Breier, 1984; Tyrer, 1986).

It is significant that high trait anxiety is associated with high noradrenergic response to moderate exercise (Fontana et al., 1975). Drugs that benefit patients with panic disorder alter central noradrenergic function, and the effects of these drugs relate to whether they stimulate or inhibit the locus coeruleus. Drugs that stimulate it arouse anxiety, whereas clonidine and other drugs that reduce brain noradrenergic activity are able to diminish panic disorder and psychological symptoms (Beckett, Fishman, & Rosenbaum, 1986; Hoehn-Saric, 1981; Kramer-Fox et al., 1984; Tyrer, 1986) and improve dysautonomia in MVPS (Gaffney, Lane, Pettinger, & Blomqvist, 1983).

There is some evidence that patients with panic disorder have autonomic dysfunction (Nesse et al., 1984; Weissman et al., 1987). However they exhibit normal cardiovascular responses to supine and orthostatic positions, deep breathing, and Valsalva maneuver (Crowe, Pauls, Kerber, & Noyes, 1981), thus differing from subjects with MVP or borderline hypertension (Harshfield, Shear, Polan, Frances, & Pickering, 1984). They may exhibit either high or low blood pressure (Fontaine & Boisvert, 1982), whereas subjects with MVP usually have relative hypotension. There is no evidence of increased cardiovascular reactivity in patients with panic disorder (Levine, 1988) or that a reactive or labile autonomic nervous system triggers panic attacks (Harshfield et al., 1984), and such attacks appear to be precipitated by biologic factors rather than psychologic events. Response to lactate infusion particularly has strong specificity in patients with panic disorder (Appleby, Klein, Sachar, & Levitt, 1981; Bonn, Harrison, & Rees, 1981; Grosz & Farmer, 1969; Haslam, 1973; Kelly, Mitchell-Heggs, & Sherman, 1971; Lapierre, Knott, & Gray, 1984; Pitts & McClure, 1967; Rainey et al., 1984).

Panic attacks are prevalent in patients with MVPS (Boudoulas et al., 1984; Chesler et al., 1985; Hartman, Kramer, Brown, & Devereux, 1982; Lenders et al., 1986; Pasternac et al., 1982). Conversely, an increased prevalence of MVP occurs in patients with anxiety and particularly with panic disorder (Ballenger, Gibson, Peterson, & Laraia, 1988; Chan, Hibbert, & Watkins, 1984; Crowe et al., 1982; Crowe, 1985; Dunner, 1985; Gorman et al., 1986, 1988; Grunhaus, Gloger, & Lewis, 1982; Kantor, Zitrin, & Zeldis, 1980; Klerman, 1985; Mazza, Martin, Spacevento, Jacobsen, & Gibbs, 1986; Pariser, Pinta, & Jones, 1978; Pitts & McClure, 1967; Sprafkin, McCroskery, Lantinga, & Hills, 1984; Thase, 1981; Venkatesh et al., 1980; Weinstein, Allen, & Ford, 1982), although sometimes MVP is found to be only slightly higher in patients with anxiety than in the general population (Shear, Devereux, Kramer-Fox, Mann, & Frances, 1984). A careful review found marked differences in observed prevalences (Margraf, Ehlers, & Roth, 1988), showing the influences of ascertainment bias (Levine, 1988) and of criteria used for diagnosis (Gorman et al., 1986).

Panic disorder and MVP may not be strongly associated with each other or linked by a common etiology (Hartman et al., 1982; Hickey et al., 1983; Mazza et al., 1986; Shear et al., 1984; Weissman et al., 1987), but the prevalence of MVP is higher in patients with panic disorder than in those with GAD or other anxiety disorders (Davies et al., 1987; Dunner, 1985; Margraf et al., 1988). Although perhaps not closely linked (Crowe et al., 1980; Min & Lee, 1986), the evidence indicates that patients with panic disorder have an increased prevalence of anatomic prolapse, albeit of minor consequence (Gorman et al., 1986, 1988; Gaffney et al., 1979; Panidis et al., 1986). The functional nature of this anatomic prolapse (Gaffney et al., 1979) also is shown by the fact that it can resolve in patients who have sustained improvement on anti-panic drug therapy (Gorman et al., 1981b), similar to its resolution in anorexic patients after refeeding (Meyers, 1986). However, this resolution occurred only in subjects with high plasma norepinephrine levels prior to treatment (Ballenger et al., 1988; Gorman et al., 1981b).

Anxiety is higher in patients with panic disorder (Weissman et al., 1987) and tends to be more prevalent in subjects with MVP (Criley et al., 1966; Hancock & Cohn, 1966; Klerman, 1985; Thase, 1983; Wooley, 1976), but a causal relationship may not exist (Coghlan, 1979; Procacci et al., 1976). Sympathetic nervous system stimulation may be associated with cardiac awareness (Callaway & Thompson, 1953; Jones, Jones, Rou, Scott, & Caldwell, 1987; Margraf, Ehlers, & Roth, 1987; Tyrer, 1976) that induces anxiety in some individuals, similar to that which can occur in patients with pheochromocytomas. Anxiety can cause adrenergic dysregulation (Cameron, Smith, Lee, & Curtis, 1987) and a cycle of positive feedback loop can occur when excitability stimulates sympathetic neural activity that in turn enhances excitability (Callaway & Thompson, 1953), and feedback perception can induce panic attacks and anxiety (Margraf et al., 1987).

However, there is considerable disbelief about whether an hyperadrenergic state can arouse significant anxiety (Hartman et al., 1982; Hickey et al., 1983; Mavissakalian, Salerni, & Thompson, 1983; Shear et al., 1984). Anxiety is probably not the cause of an hyperadrenergic state in MVPS; the latter is stable over many years (Pasternac et al., 1986) and there are no specific psychophysiological consequences of MVP (Dager et al., 1987). Many of the clinical findings in MVPS can be explained by hemodynamic factors such as hypovolemia, increased sympathetic neural responses, and chronic veno- and vasoconstriction, rather than by cardiovascular manifestations of chronic anxiety (Gaffney & Blomqvist, 1988). These include orthostatic intolerance, palpitations, arrhythmias, cold digits, and low exercise tolerance.

The familial morbidity for panic disorder is high but is independent of MVP in index cases (Crowe et al., 1980), and there is no specific association of MVP and panic disorder relatives of patients with MVPS in the general population (Coghlan, 1979; Hartman et al., 1982). Although panic disorder is common in patients with MVPS, there is no increased prevalence of it in subjects with anatomic prolapse, compared to matched control subjects (Margraf et al., 1988; Uretsky, 1982). Panic disorder is the same, regardless of the presence or absence of MVP, and patients with echocardiographically defined MVP do not generally exhibit more anxiety than control subjects without MVP (Hickey et al., 1983). Moreover, the presence of MVP does not alter the responses of patients with panic disorder to either biological triggers of panic attacks or anti-panic drugs (Gorman et al., 1981b; Grunhaus et al., 1982). It has therefore become apparent that MVP is neither the cause of panic disorder (Kantor et al., 1980; Pariser, Jones, & Pinta, 1979; Shappel, Orr, & Gunn, 1974), its symptoms (Arfken et al., 1986; Boudoulas & Wooley, 1987; Boudoulas et al., 1986; Devereux et al., 1986; Pollack, 1987; Retchin et al., 1986; Savage et al., 1983), or panic attacks.

Patients with panic disorder and MVPS have many similarities (Crowe, 1985), including genetic relationships and the same pattern of inheritance (Crowe et al., 1981); exercise intolerance (Crowe et al., 1981; Thase, 1983); electrocardiogram abnormalities (Tyrer, 1986); adrenergic hyperactivity; and difficulties with anxiety

(Boudoulas et al., 1980; Thase, 1981) even prior to identification of MVP (Venkatesh et al., 1980). However, MVP per se is not associated with anxiety (Chesler et al., 1985; Hickey et al., 1983), which is present only in a subset of patients with MVPS (Gitter, Lyons, & Talano, 1986). Plasma catecholamines are often increased in MVPS but not in subjects with anxiety disorders or in all panic disorder patients (Dager, 1988; Nesse et al., 1984; Weissman et al., 1987). Downregulation of beta-receptors occurs with panic disorder (Nesse et al., 1984) due to adrenergic stimulation, and patients with panic disorder do not exhibit hyperresponsiveness to beta-agonists. They have higher baseline plasma catecholamines and heart rates than do patients with MVPS, and higher nocturnal catecholamine excretion in the absence of MVP (Nesse et al., 1985). During quiet standing, patients with MVPS have more hypotension and less increase of heart rate and mean blood pressure, compared to those with panic disorder. Both conditions may be associated with autonomic dysfunction, but the abnormal patterns are different. Thus panic disorder is associated with heightened cardiovascular responses to positive intrathoracic pressure and postural stresses, whereas MVPS is associated with decreased effectiveness of responses to orthostatic stress, abnormal vagal tone, and lower excretion of catecholamines (Weissman et al., 1987).

Although panic disorder and MVPS appear to be independent entities and their interaction only coincidental and unrelated (Weinstein et al., 1982), the increased prevalence of anatomic MVP in anxiety disorders needs to be explained. Such MVP is only of functional nature (Gaffney & Blomqvist, 1988). It is apparent that certain hemodynamic conditions can produce functional MVP in normal mitral valves of healthy individuals and that there is no progression over time in such people (Sanfillippo et al., 1989). The common denominator is the pathophysiology of self-sustaining hypovolemia, orthostatic intolerance, chronic hyperadrenergic activity, and veno- and vasoconstriction (Gaffney & Blomqvist, 1988). Chronic anxiety enhances adrenergic activity (Weissman et al., 1987) and thereby induces vasoconstriction (Galosy & Gaebelein, 1977; Turkkan, Brady, & Harris, 1986), hypovolemia, and increased left ventricular contractility. These combine to decrease left ventricular preload and cavity size and induce functional MVP. A contributing factor is the tachycardia induced by sympathetic neural stimulation in patients with panic disorder (Gorman et al., 1988), particularly during panic attacks and in responses to specific stressors (Albus, Braune, Hohn, & Scheiber, 1988). The role of tachycardia in functional MVP is well recognized (Ballenger, 1986; Ballenger et al., 1988; Rosenthal et al., 1985).

THE POSSIBLE DOMINANT ROLE OF SALT

Sodium is the critical substance in the regulation of the body's fluid volume. Because one common denominator of functional MVP and of MVPS is the hypovolemia that underlies orthostatic intolerance and chronic hyperadrenergic activity in a self-sustaining manner, regulation of intravascular volume is particularly important. Sodium depletion may be of primary importance in the pathogenesis of functional MVP in many subjects predisposed by their anthropometric habitus. It may also play a major role in the fatigability and other symptoms and clinical manifestations that are related to their chronic hyperadrenergic activity engendered by hypovolemia and orthostatic intolerance, rather to cardiovascular manifestations of chronic anxiety (Gaffney & Blomqvist, 1988).

The primary integrator of volume regulation and of interrelationships between cardiac output and peripheral vascular resistance is baroreceptor activation of the sympathetic nervous system. When lowered blood pressure is sensed by arterial baroreceptors, a sequence occurs that stimulates effector sympathetic neural tone to increase peripheral vasoconstriction and activate the renin–angiotensin system and arginine vasopressin, thus stimulating the three major vasoconstrictor systems (Schrier, 1988). Autoregulatory mechanisms normally maintain a rather precise balance between sodium intake and excretion, regardless of load size. Changes in extracellular fluid volume are detected by volume sensors in the cardiopulmonary areas, vascular system, kidney, and other organs. The perception of a change in the normal relationship between intravascular volume and circulatory capacity activates mechanisms that effect physiologically appropriate changes of renal sodium excretion. This adjusts extracellular fluid volume to a quantity that is appropriate for the vascular capacitance in order to maintain circulatory function. Proper functioning of the system relies on a neural mechanism for regulation that parallels a classic reflex neural arc.

Dietary sodium intake and urinary catecholamine excretion are inversely correlated (Henry, Luft, Weinberger, Fineberg, & Grim, 1980; Lilavivathana & Campbell, 1980; Nicholls et al., 1980). Thus sympathetic nervous system activity is inversely related to sodium intake (Luft et al., 1979), and salt restriction and sodium depletion stimulate such activity (Folkow & Ely, 1987; Kjeldsen et al., 1988; Romoff et al., 1979; Stene et al., 1980; Watson, Esler, & Leonard, 1984), particularly during short-term restriction (Kjeldsen et al., 1986). Dietary sodium restriction not only markedly stimulates central noradrenergic activity (Brosnahan, Szilagyi, & Ferrario, 1981) but also influences peripheral adrenoreceptor density and function (Skrabal, Kotanko, Meister, Doll, & Gruber, 1986).

Although chronic restriction also stimulates release of myocardial norepinephrine, it may not always increase contractility because of induced dysfunction at the receptor level (Nii, Fouad-Tarazi, Ferrario, Bravo, & Czerska, 1987). Furthermore, chronic restriction causes sustained increase of plasma renin activity, which plays an important role in maintaining homeostasis during restricted sodium intake (Volpe, Lembo, Morganti, Condorelli, & Trimarco, 1988), and in the blood pressure response (Silman, Mitchell, & Locke, 1983). Within a physiologic range, noradrenergic activity can decrease sodium excretion by enhancing renal antinatriuresis. Thus renal sympathetic nervous system activity is an important regulator of sodium excretion (Boudoulas & Wooley, 1986; DiBona, 1983).

The quantity of sodium determines extracellular fluid volume and steady-state urinary sodium excretion is closely matched to dietary intake to ensure its near-constancy for optimal circulatory performance (Skorecki & Brenner, 1981). However, individual sensitivity to sodium loading and restriction varies widely and is closely related to sympathetic nervous system activity. Salt-sensitive people have higher resting plasma norepinephrine levels, although their pressor responses are poorly influenced by altered sodium intake, and release of norepinephrine is decreased in subjects who are less sensitive to sodium alterations (Koolen & van Brummelen, 1984). Sodium-sensitive subjects have increased forearm vascular resistance during high sodium intake, which is associated with decreased responsiveness of the renin–angiotensin system during sodium depletion (Sullivan & Ratts, 1988). Sodium sensitivity in younger people may partly be due to higher adrenergic venous tone, which serves to increase cardiac output and release a plasma Na^+K^+ pump inhibitor (Krzesinski & Rorive, 1986).

Dietary sodium restriction is commonly used for treatment of hypertension, although it is not universally applicable (Laragh & Pecker, 1983; Omvik & Lund-Johansen, 1987) because only salt-sensitive patients are benefited (Holden, Ostfeld & Freeman, 1983). Moreover, dietary sodium restriction does not augment effects of all antihypertensive drugs (Kimura et al., 1988), and much of the reported lowering of blood pressure may be due only to a regression toward the mean effect (Silman et al., 1983). Dietary restriction may lower blood pressure by reducing cardiac preload, output, and ejection fraction, but it does not correct the increased peripheral vascular resistance that is the basic abnormality in hypertension (Nii et al., 1987; Omvik & Lund-Johansen, 1986).

Guyton has pointed out that the level to which arterial blood pressure is controlled is the system's set point, that this can be increased as the result of pathophysiological change in renal function or from increased salt and volume intake, but that hypertension does not result from a primary increase in peripheral vascular resistance without some concurrent abnormality that affects renal function. In the person who develops hypertension because of high cardiac output, eventual increase of peripheral resistance is a secondary result of hypertension itself rather than its primary cause (Guyton, 1982). Borderline hypertensives have an abnormality in neurohumoral control of the renal circulation. This can be unmasked by a high sodium intake, which produces a greater decrease in renal blood flow and enhanced renal vasoconstriction and water retention in the upright position (Lawton, Sinkey, Fitz, & Mark, 1988). Renin-angiotensin and sympathetic nervous system overactivity play a role in this response (Fujita, Noda, & Ando, 1984).

A higher sodium content enhances vascular smooth muscle responsiveness to neurogenic stimulation (Dzau, Packer, & Lily, 1984), and hypertensives have increased peripheral vascular resistance (Egan & Schmouder, 1988; Messerli, 1988) and vasoconstrictor sensitivity to both norepinephrine and angiotensin II (Genest, 1983). The sensitivity of adrenergic responsiveness to high salt intake is also found in SHR (Gradin, Dahlof, & Persson, 1986; Koepke, Jones, & DiBona, 1988) and is associated with noradrenergic overactivity (Gavras, 1988). Hypertensives often have altered cellular sodium ion transport with enhanced tubular sodium reabsorption and increased intracellular sodium concentration in the vessel wall. An increased Na + Li + countertransport activity in smooth muscle cells may be important for this (de la Sierra, Coca, Aguilera, & Urbano-Marquez, 1986). Weight is the most frequently reported correlate of the countertransport mechanism (Trevisan et al., 1981), although it may not be related to body mass index (de la Sierra et al., 1986).

Although dietary restriction is useful alone or as an adjunct in treatment of hypertension in salt-sensitive subjects, there has arisen a widespread misunderstanding that ignores the fundamental role of sodium in homeostasis, cardiovascular functioning, and the normal body economy. The pejorative belief has often led to inappropriate rigid dietary salt restriction as well as its near elimination from many prepared foodstuffs. Urinary sodium excretion is inversely correlated with sympathetic neural activity in patients with MVPS (Boudoulas & Wooley, 1986). Many have reduced 24-hour urinary sodium excretion (Boudoulas & Reynolds, 1983; Pasternac et al., 1982; Puddu et al., 1983). Their diet history may show a long and rigid reduction of salt intake based on the popular belief that salt is always injurious to people with heart problems (Gaffney & Blomqvist, 1988).

Moreover, particularly younger females may chronically restrict their salt intake and add diuretics for weight control to achieve slimness, which may signal an eating problem or affective disorder (Mitchell, Pomeroy, Seppala, & Huber, 1988). Sodium restriction in hypertensives with undetected sodium-resistance imposes a risk, because the resistance can cause the blood pressure to rise when dietary intake is rigidly reduced. Sensitivity to sodium is genetically related to anthropometric variables that include height, weight, and body surface area and to noradrenergic activity and response to salt infusion (Luft, Miller, Cohen, Fineberg, & Weinberger, 1988). Subjects with MVPS exhibit leanness for height, poor muscular development, hypovolemia, reduced cardiac output and relative hypotension and thus are at the opposite end of the spectrum that characterizes subjects prone to hypertension. Rigid salt restriction, particularly when combined with diuretics, can cause orthostatic hypotension in hypertensive patients (Frohlich, 1987). Salt sensitivity may underlie the predisposition to anatomic prolapse. When such individuals restrict dietary sodium, this predisposition is enhanced and engenders high noradrenergic activity and chronic vasoconstriction found in MVPS in the face of appropriate beta-adrenergic responsiveness. It augments their hypovolemia, orthostatic intolerance, and plausibly causes the complex central and peripheral cardiovascular dysregulation (Takashita & Ferrario, 1982) and increased platelet activity and catecholamine release (Kjeldsen et al., 1988) that are often found in patients with MVPS.

Repletion of salt in MVPS serves to expand intravascular volume and cardiac preload, enlarge left ventricular cavity size, reduce orthostatic sympathetic nervous system stimulation, and thereby decrease beta-adrenergic responses and diminish central noraderenergic activity. When successful, such repletion can normalize resting blood pressure levels and have marked benefits for exercise tolerance and fatigability, cardiac ectopy, and cold extremities. Nonejection, mid-systolic clicks tend to disappear and there may be salutary benefits for anxiety and associated hyperadrenergic manifestations. However, such responses to salt-loading are successful only when it expands intravascular volume, and this may not be possible until chronic vasoconstriction can be effectively interrupted (Gaffney & Blomqvist, 1988).

Normally saline volume expansion suppresses sympathetic nervous system activity both in the supine and upright positions, but this may not occur in patients with MVPS (Boudoulas & Wooley, 1987), possibly because of diminished baroreflex sensitivity (DiBona, 1983). The hypovolemia in MVPS may be associated with a subnormal increase of plasma renin activity due to defective recognition of reduced intrasvascular volume by renin receptors (Boudoulas & Wooley, 1988). These responses suggested that MVPS is associated with a disorder of catecholamine regulation (Krishna, Danovitch, & Sowers, 1983; Rogers et al., 1983; Wigle, Rakowski, & Ranganathan, 1976). However, it has been shown that saline-volume expansion can successfully be accomplished when it is combined with administration of clonidine to reduce noradrenergic activity and associated peripheral vasoconstriction (Gaffney & Blomqvist, 1988).

CONCLUSION

The variability of findings in subjects with anatomic MVP indicates that MVP is associated with diverse underlying disorders. However, these disorders have in common an ability to cause a mismatch between the size of the left ventricle and mitral valve orifice. It is a reduction of left ventricular cavity size relative to the mitral orifice that induces anatomic leaflet prolapse. Moreover, the size of the left ventricle appears to be of dominant importance, whether the prolapse is idiopathic or occurs in so-called primary MVP or MVP that is secondary to many other cardiovascular disorders.

The myxomatous transformation that can occur in mitral leaflets and chordae tendinae does not explain the pathogenesis of prolapse. Age-related changes are consistent with the belief that processes of ongoing injury and repair are the final common pathway for the observed histopathologic changes. Continuing neuroaminal and hemodynamic trauma underlie the development of mitral regurgitation, leaflet billowing, and other complications that largely occur with aging in patients with thickened or redundant leaflets and associated progressive mitral regurgitation.

A large proportion of subjects with nonejection, mid-systolic clicks are asymptomatic and have normal mitral valves. They have anatomic variants or minor prolapse due to specific hemodynamic factors. The hemodynamic basis for such functional prolapse is shown by the fact that it can transiently be induced by a variety of experimental conditions that reduce left ventricular preload filling and cause a smaller left ventricle cavity size relative to the mitral orifice, thereby inducing a failure of leaflet coaptation. Specific hemodynamic factors that are causally related to idiopathic MVP include hypovolemia, orthostatic intolerance, and chronic hyperadrenergic stimulation. These induce increased left ventricular contractility, veno- and vasoconstriction, and tachycardia in a self-sustaining vicious cycle.

The presence of symptoms other than minor palpitations suggests the presence of MVPS, generally ascribed to adrenergic overactivity and with clinical manifestations that closely resemble those of chronic anxiety disorders and panicogenic syndromes. Symptomatic patients with MVPS exhibit hypovolemia, orthostatic hypotension, postural exercise intolerance, and hyperadrenergic neural activity. However, they do not have a hyperkinetic circulatory system, but they exhibit homeostatically appropriate adrenergic responses to hypovolemia and a cycle of orthostatic decrease of intravascular and stroke volumes and chronic vasoconstriction. Many patients with MVPS thus exhibit clinical and adrenergic manifestations that are explained by hemodynamic factors rather than cardiovascular manifestations of chronic anxiety.

The validity of assuming MVPS to be a true condition is increasingly questioned. Chronic hyperadrenergic activity can be viewed as appropriate autonomic neural responses to specific hemodynamic abnormalities, with lack of valid evidence to substantiate a belief that MVPS is a constitutional neuroendocrine disorder due to a genetically determined abnormality of central autonomic regulation that targets the cardiovascular system. The evidence suggests that neither MVP nor MVPS is a directly inherited condition and that genetic relationships prevail only for anthropometric variables that may predispose people to MVP. Thus functional MVP is strongly related to a body habitus that is characterized by leanness for height, narrow anteroposterior chest diameter, and straight back, with accompanying tendency to pectus excavatum.

Chronic anxiety stimulates adrenergic activity, hypovolemia, tachycardia, and left ventricular contractility, which combine to cause a high prevalence of functional MVP in people with anxiety and panic disorders. It is the factors that regulate blood volume that may be of primary importance and that underlie cardiovascular dysregulation. The role of sodium has not been adequately considered, although it may have dominant importance in the pathogenesis of functional MVP in many predisposed subjects and causal relevance for the clinical manifestations of MVPS and anxiety disorders.

REFERENCES

Abildskov, J. (1975). The nervous system and cardiac arrhythmias. *Circulation, 51*, 16–19.

Abinader, E. G. (1983). Clinical considerations in interpretation of the exercise electrocardiogram in the patient with mitral valve prolapse. *Practical Cardiology, 9*, 172–190.

Albus, M., Braune, S., Hohn, T., & Scheiber, G. (1988). Do anxiety patients with or without frequent panic attacks differ in their response to stress? *Stress Medicine, 4*, 189–194.

Alpert, J. S. (1984). Association between arrhythmias and mitral valve prolapse. *Archives of Internal Medicine, 144*, 2333–2334.

Alpert, M. A., Goldberg, S. H., Singsen, B. H., Durham, J. B., Sharp, G. C., Ahmad, M., Madigan, N. P., Hurst, D. P., & Sullivan, W. D. (1983). Cardiovascular manifestations of mixed connective tissue disease in adults. *Circulation, 68*, 1182–1193.

American Psychiatric Association. (1980). *Diagnostic and statistical manual of mental disorders* (3rd ed). Washington, DC: Author.

Amidi, M. (1984). Hyperthyroid heart disease. *Cardiovascular Reviews and Reports, 5*, 833–838.

Angel, J., Soler-Soler, J., del Castillo, G., Anivarro, I., & Batelle-Diaz, J. (1980). The role of reduced left ventricular end-diastolic volume in the apparently high prevalence of mitral valve prolapse in atrial septal defect. *European Journal of Cardiology, 11*, 341–355.

Angelini, A., Becker, A. E., Anderson, R. H., & Davies, M. J. (1988). Mitral valve morphology: Normal and mitral valve prolapse. In H. Boudoulas & C. F. Wooley (Eds.), *Mitral valve prolapse and the mitral valve prolapse syndrome* (pp. 13–54). Mount Kisco, NY: Futura.

Ansari, A. (1985). The "straight back" syndrome: Current perspective more often associated with valvular heart disease than pseudo disease: A prospective clinical, electrocardiographic, roentgenographic, echocardiographic study of 50 patients. *Clinical Cardiology, 8*, 290–305.

Appleby, I., Klein, D., Sachar, E., & Levitt, M. (1981). Biochemical indices of lactate-induced panic: A preliminary report. In D. Klein & J. Rabkin (Eds.), *Anxiety: New research and changing concepts* (pp. 411–423). New York: Raven Press.

Arfken, C. L., Lachman, A. S., Schulman, P., Farrish, G. C. M., Slowik, D. S., & McLaren, M. J. (1986). Auscultatory mitral valve prolapse in children (Abstract). *Journal of the American College of Cardiology, 7*, 1A.

Aronson, R. J., Hoffman, M., Algueti-Margulis, A., & Yust, I. (1987). Spontaneous rupture of mitral chordae tendinae in hyperthyroidism. *American Journal of Cardiology, 59*, 475–476.

Ballenger, J. C. (1986). Biological aspects of panic disorder (Editorial). *American Journal of Psychiatry, 143*, 516–518.

Ballenger, J. C., Gibson, R., Peterson, G. A., & Laraia, M. T. (1988, May 10). "Functional" MVP in agoraphobia/panic disorder. *CME Syllabus*. Washington, DC: American Psychiatric Association.

Barlow, J. B., (1987). *Perspectives on the mitral valve*. Philadelphia: F. A. Davis.

Barlow, J. B., Bosman, C. K., Marchard, P., & Denny, M. (1968). Late systolic murmurs and nonejectional ("mid-late") systolic clicks: An analysis of 90 patients. *British Heart Journal, 30*, 203–218.

Barlow, J. B., & Pocock, W. A. (1975). The problem of nonejection systolic clicks and associated mitral systolic murmurs: Emphasis on the billowing mitral leaflet syndrome. *American Heart Journal, 90*, 636–655.

Barlow, J. B., & Pocock, W. A. (1979). Mitral valve prolapse: The specific billowing mitral leaflet syndrome, or an insignificant nonejection systolic click. *American Heart Journal, 97*, 277–285.

Barlow, J. B., & Pocock, W. A. (1984). The mitral valve prolapse enigma—two decades later. *Modern Concepts of Cardiovascular Disease, 53*, 13–17.

Barlow, J. B., & Pocock, W. A. (1985). Billowing, floppy, prolapsed or flail mitral valves. *American Heart Journal, 55*, 501–502.

Barlow, J. B., Pocock, W. A., Marchand, P., & Denny, M. (1963). The significance of late systolic murmurs. *American Heart Journal, 66*, 443–452.

Barnett, H. J. M. (1982). Embolism in mitral valve prolapse. *Annual Review of Medicine, 33*, 489–507.

Barnett, H. J. M., Roughner, D. R., Taylor, D. W., & Cooper, P. E. (1980). Further evidence relating mitral valve prolapse to cerebral ischemic events. *New England Journal of Medicine, 302*, 139–144.

Barnett, R. J., Jones, M. W., Boughner, D. R., & Kostuk, W. T. (1976). Cerebral ischemic events associated with prolapsing mitral valve. *Archives of Neurology, 33*, 777–782.

Bashore, T. M., Grines, C., Utlak, D., Boudoulas, H., & Wooley, C. F. (1985). Mitral valve prolapse: Postural exercise response reflects a volume disorder. *Journal of American College of Cardiology, 5,* 504.

Bashore, T. M., Grines, C. L., Utlak, D., Boudoulas, H., & Wooley, C. F. (1988). Postural exercise abnormalities in symptomatic patients with MVP. *Journal of American College of Cardiology, 11,* 499–507.

Beard, G. (1867). Neurasthenia or nervous exhaustion. *Boston Medical and Surgery Journal, 53,* 217–221.

Beattie, J. M., Blomqvist, C. G., & Gaffney, F. A. (1985). Mitral valve prolapse in normal subjects during orthostatic stress. *Journal of the American College of Cardiology, 5,* 404.

Beckett, A., Fishman, S. M., & Rosenbaum, J. F. (1986). Clonazepam blockade of spontaneous CO^2 inhalation-provoked panic in a patient with panic disorder. *Journal of Clinical Psychiatry, 47,* 475–476.

Bedford, E. (1977). *Evan Bedford Library of Cardiology catalogue of books, pamphlets and journals* (p. 196). London: Royal College of Physicians.

Binkley, P. F., Bonagura, J. D., Olson, S. M., Boudoulas, H., & Wooley, C. F. (1987). The equilibrium position of the mitral valve: An accurate model of mitral valve motion in humans. *American Journal of Cardiology, 59,* 109–113.

Blomqvist, C. G. (1986). Orthostatic hypotension. *Hypertension, 8,* 722–731.

Blumlein, S., Bouchard, A., Schiller, N. B., Dae, M., B. F., Ports, T., & Botvinick, E. H. (1986). Quantitation of mitral regurgitation by Doppler echocardiography. *Circulation, 74,* 306–314.

Bonn, J., Harrison, J., & Rees, W. (1981). Lactate-induced anxiety: Therapeutic applications. *British Journal of Psychiatry, 119,* 468–471.

BonTempo, C. P., Ronan, J. A., deLeon, A. C., & Twigg, H. L. (1975). Radiographic appearance of the thorax in systolic-click late systolic murmur syndrome. *American Journal of Cardiology, 36,* 27–31.

Boudoulas, H., Barrington, W., Olson, W. M., Bashore, T. M., & Wooley, C. F. (1985). Effect of acute standing and prolonged upright activity on left ventricular hemodynamics, systolic and diastolic intervals, and QT-QS2 relationship. *American Heart Journal, 110,* 623–630.

Boudoulas, H., Kolibash, A. J., & Wooley, C. F. (1986). Anatomic mitral valve prolapse and the mitral valve prolapse syndrome: A diagnostic classification (Abstract). *Circulation Supplement, 74,* II-299.

Boudoulas, H., & Reynolds, J. C. (1983). Mitral valve prolapse syndrome: The effect of adrenergic stimulation. *Journal of the American College of Cardiology, 2,* 638–644.

Boudoulas, H., Reynolds, J. C., Mazzaferri, E., & Wooley, C. F. (1980). Metabolic studies in mitral valve prolapse syndrome: A neuroendocrine–cardiovascular process. *Circulation, 61,* 1200–1205.

Boudoulas, H., & Wooley, C. F. (1986). Mitral valve prolapse and the mitral valve prolapse syndrome. In P. N. Yu & J. F. Goodwin (Eds.), *Progress in Cardiology*. Philadelphia: Lea & Febiger, 14, 275–309.

Boudoulas, H., & Wooley, C. F. (1987, May). Mitral valve prolapse syndrome: Hyperresponse to adrenergic stimulation. *Primary Cardiology,* 119–128.

Boudoulas, H., & Wooley, C. F. (1988). Hyperadrenergic state, autonomic dysfunction, and pathogenesis of symptoms in mitral valve prolapse syndrome. In H. Boudoulas & C. F. Wooley (Eds.), *Mitral valve prolapse and the mitral valve prolapse syndrome* (pp. 479–510). Mount Kisco, NY: Futura.

Boudoulas, H., Wooley, C. F., & King, B. D. (1984). Mitral valve prolapse: A marker for anxiety or an overlapping phenomenon? *Psychopathology, 17*(Suppl. 1), 98–106.

Brauman, A., Algom, M., Gilboa, Y., Ramot, Y., Golik, A., & Stryjer, D. (1985). Mitral valve prolapse in hyperthyroidism of two different origins. *British Heart Journal, 53,* 374–377.

Brosnahan, K. B., Szilagyi, J. E., & Ferrario, C. M. (1981). Effect of chronic sodium depletion on cerebrospinal fluid and spinal catecholamines. *Hypertension, 3,* 233–239.

Broughner, D. R. (1986). Risk of vascular complications in patients with mitral valve prolapse. *Practical Cardiology, 12,* 89–94.

Brown, M. J., Jenner, D. A., Alison, D. J., & Dollers, C. T. (1981). Variation in individual organ release of noradrenaline measured by an improved radioenzymatic technique: Limitations of peripheral venous measurements in assessment of sympathetic nervous activity. *Clinical Science, 61,* 585–590.

Brown, O. R., Kloster, F. E., & DeMots, H. (1975). Incidence of mitral valve prolapse in the asymptomatic normal. *Circulation, 52*(Suppl. 2), 77.

Brunjes, S., Johns, V. J., & Crane, M. G. (1960). Pheochromocytoma: Postoperative shock and blood volume. *New England Journal of Medicine, 262,* 393–396.

Bryhn, M., & Garding, L. (1986). The mitral valve mechanism with normal and prolapsed leaflets in the light of a dynamic model. *Clinical Cardiology, 9,* 483–486.

Bryhn, M., & Persson, S. (1984). The prevalence of mitral valve prolapse in healthy men and women in Sweden. *Acta Medica Scandinavica, 215,* 157–160.

Buccino, R. A., Spann, J. R., Pool, P. E., Sonnenblick, E. H., & Braunwald, E. (1967). Influence of the thyroid state on the intrinsic contractile properties and energy stores of the myocardium. *Journal of Clinical Investigation, 46*, 1669-1682.

Callaway, E., & Thompson, S. V. (1953). Sympathetic activity and perception. *Psychosomatic Medicine, 5*, 443-453.

Cameron, O. B., Smith, C. B., Lee, M. A., & Curtis, G. C. (1987). Adrenergic dysfunction in anxiety (Abstract). *Psychosomatic Medicine, 49*, 208.

Campbell, R. W. F. (1982). Arrhythmias in mitral valve prolapse. *Practical Cardiology, 8*, 124-135.

Cannon, W. (1929). *Bodily changes in pain, hunger, fear, and rage.* New York: Appleton Century Crofts.

Caruso, M., Orszulak, T. A., & Miles, J. M. (1987). Lactate acidosis and insulin resistance associated with epinephrine administration in a patient with noninsulin-dependent diabetes mellitus. *Archives of Internal Medicine, 147*, 1422-1424.

Cebelin, M. S., & Hirsch, C. S. (1980). Human stress cardiomyopathy: Myocardial lesions of homicidal assaults without internal injuries. *Human Pathology, 2*, 123-132.

Chan, F. L., Chen, W. C. C., Wang, P. Y. C., & Chow, J. S. F. (1983). Skeletal abnormalities in mitral valve prolapse. *Clinical Radiology, 34*, 2207-2213.

Chan, M. P., Hibbert, G. A., & Watkins, J. (1984). Mitral valve prolapse and anxiety disorders. *British Journal of Psychiatry, 145*, 216-217.

Chandraratna, P., Tolentino, A. O., Mutucumarana, W., Lopi, L., & Gomez, A. (1977). Echocardiographic observations on the association between mitral valve prolapse and asymmetric septal hypertrophy. *Circulation, 55*, 622-626.

Chandraratna, P. A. N., Vlahovich, G., Kong, Y., & Wilson, D. (1979). Incidence of mitral valve prolapse in one hundred clinically stable newborn baby girls: An echocardiographic study. *American Heart Journal, 98*, 312-314.

Channick, B. J., Adlin, E. V., Marks, A. D., Denenberg, B. S., Chakko, C., & Spann, J. F. (1981). Hyperthyroidism and mitral valve prolapse. *New England Journal of Medicine, 305*, 497-499.

Charney, D. S., Heninger, G. R., & Breier, A. (1984). Noradrenergic function in panic anxiety: Effects of yohimbine in healthy subjects and patients with agoraphobia and panic disorder. *Archives of General Psychiatry, 41*, 751-763.

Cheitlin, M. D., & Byrd, R. C. (1981). The click-murmur syndrome: A clinical problem in diagnosis and treatment. *Journal of the American Medical Association, 245*, 1357-1361.

Chen, W. W. C., Chan, F. L., Wong, P. H. C., & Chew, J. S. F. (1983). Familial occurrence of mitral valve prolapse: Is this related to the straight back syndrome? *British Heart Journal, 50*, 97-100.

Chesler, E., Weir, E. K., Braatz, G. A., & Francis, G. S. (1985). Normal catecholamine and hemodynamic responses to orthostatic tilt in subjects with mitral valve prolapse. *American Journal of Medicine, 78*, 754-760.

Chopra, F., Haricharan, D. T., Raizada, V., Gopinath, N., Butler, C., & Williams, R. C. (1983). Comparative studies of mitral valves in rheumatic heart disease. *Archives of Internal Medicine, 143*, 661-666.

Clemens, J. D., Horwitz, R. I., Jaffe, C. C., & Feinstein, A. R. (1982). A controlled evaluation of the risk of bacterial endocarditis in persons with mitral valve prolapse. *New England Journal of Medicine, 307*, 776-781.

Coghlan, H. C. (1979). Dysautonomia in mitral valve prolapse. *American Journal of Medicine, 67*, 236-244.

Coghlan, H. C. (1988). Autonomic dysfunction in the mitral valve prolapse syndrome: The brain–heat connection and interaction. In H. Boudoulas & C. F. Wooley (Eds.), *Mitral valve prolapse and the mitral valve prolapse syndrome* (pp. 389-426). Mount Kisco, NY: Futura.

Coghlan, H. C., Carranza, C., Hsiung, M. C., Alliende, I., Mee-Nin, K., & Nanda, N. C. (1986). Abnormal left ventricular volume response during upright exercise in symptomatic mitral prolapse patients. *Tenth World Congress of Cardiology*, in abstract book, 120.

Cohen, I. S. (1987). Two-dimensional echocardiographic mitral valve prolapse: Evidence for a relationship of echocardiographic morphology to clinical findings and to mitral annual size. *American Heart Journal, 113*, 859-865.

Cohen, J. L., Austin, S. M., Segal, K. R., Millman, A. E., & Kim, C. S. (1987). Echocardiographic mitral valve prolapse in ballet dancers: A function of leanness. *American Heart Journal, 113*, 341-344.

Cohen, L., Bitterman, H., Grenadier, E., Laor, A., Lahat, N., & Palant, A. (1985). Idiopathic magnesium deficiency in mitral valve prolapse. *American Journal of Cardiology, 57*, 486-487.

Cohen, M. E., Badal, D. W., & Kilpatrick, A. (1951). The high familial prevalence of neurocirculatory asthenia (anxiety neurosis, effort syndrome). *American Journal of Human Genetics, 3*, 126-158.

Cohen, M. E., & White, P. D. (1950). Life situations, emotions, and neurocirculatory asthenia (anxiety neurosis, neurasthenia, effort syndrome). *Proceedings of Association of Research in Nervous and Mental Diseases, 29*, 832–869.

Cohen, M. V. (1988). Thyrogenic heart disease: An overview (Part 1). *Cardiology Illustrated, 3*, 17–25.

Cohen, M. V., Shah, P. K., & Spindola-Franco, H. (1979). Angiographic–echocardiographic correlation in mitral valve prolapse. *American Heart Journal, 97*, 43–52.

Cole, W. G., Chan, D., & Hickey, A. J. (1984). Collagen composition of normal and myxomatous human mitral valves. *Biochemical Journal, 219*, 451–460.

Colle, J. P., LeGoff, G., Ohayon, J., Bonnet, J., Bricaud, H., & Besse, P. (1986). Quantitative frame analysis of regional contraction and lengthening on left ventricular angiograms: Applications to the study of normal left ventricles and left ventricles with mitral valve prolapse. *Clinical Cardiology, 9*, 43–51.

Combs, R., Shah, P. M., Klorman, R. S., Klorman, R., & Sylvester, L. (1980). Effects of induced psychological stress on click and rhythm in mitral valve prolapse. *American Heart Journal, 99*, 714–721.

Crawford, M. H. (1977). Mitral valve prolapse due to coronary artery disease. *American Journal of Medicine, 62*, 447–451.

Crile, G. (1934). Indications for and end-results in 308 denervations of the adrenal glands. *American Journal of Surgery, 24*, 378–385.

Criley, J. M., & Kissel, G. L. (1975). Prolapse of the mitral valve—the click and late systolic murmur syndrome. *Progress in Cardiology, 4*, 213–241.

Criley, J. M., Lewis, K. B., Humphries, J. O., & Ross, R. S. (1966). Prolapse of the mitral valve: Clinical and cineangiographic findings. *British Heart Journal, 28*, 488–496.

Crowe, R. R. (1985). Mitral valve prolapse and panic disorder. *Psychiatric Clinics of North America, 8*, 63–71.

Crowe, R. R., Gaffney, G., & Kerber, R. (1982). Panic attacks in families of patients with mitral valve prolapse. *Journal of Affective Discord, 4*, 121–125.

Crowe, R. R., Pauls, D. L., Kerber, R. L., & Noyes, R. (1981). Panic disorder and mitral valve prolapse. In D. F. Klein & J. Rabkin (Eds.), *Anxiety: New research and changing concepts*. New York: Raven Press.

Crowe, R. R., Pauls, D. L., Slymen, D. J., & Noyes, R. (1980). A family study of anxiety neurosis. *Archives of General Psychiatry, 37*, 77–79.

Cuffer, B. (1887). Nouvelles recherches sur le bruit de galop cardiaque: Memoires originaux. *Archives of General Medicine, 1*, 129–149.

DaCosta, J. M. (1871). On irritable heart: A clinical study of a functional cardiac disorder and its consequences. *American Journal of Medical Science, 61*, 17–52.

Dager, S. R. (1988). Mitral valve abnormalities and catecholamine activity in anxious patients. *Psychiatry Research, 20*, 13–18.

Dager, S. R., Comess, K. A., & Dunner, D. L. (1986). Differentiation of anxious patients by two-dimensional echocardiographic evaluation of the mitral valve. *American Journal of Psychiatry, 143*, 532–535.

Dager, S. R., Cowley, D. S., & Dunner, D. L. (1987). Biological markers in panic states: Lactate-induced panic and mitral valve prolapse. *Biological Psychiatry, 22*, 339–359.

Darsee, J. R., Mikolich, J. R., Nicoloff, N. B., & Lesser, L. E. (1979). Prevalence of mitral valve prolapse in presumably healthy young men. *Circulation, 59*, 619–622.

Davies, A. O., Mares, A., Pool, J. L., & Taylor, A. A. (1987). Mitral valve prolapse with symptoms of beta-adrenergic hypersensitivity: Beta-2 adrenergic receptor supercoupling with desensitization on isoproterenol exposure. *American Journal of Medicine, 82*, 193–201.

Davies, J. M., Moore, B. P., & Bainbridge, M. V. (1978). The floppy mitral valve: Study of incidence, pathology, and commplications in surigical, necropsy, and forensic material. *British Heart Journal, 40*, 468–481.

Day, F. P., Koch, K. L., Davidson, W. R., & Spears, P. M. (1987). Etiology of chest pain in patients with mitral valve prolapse (Abstract). *Journal of the American College of Cardiology, 9*(Suppl. A), 9.

Dean, G. A. (1985). Mitral valve prolapse. *Hospital Practice, 20*, 75–82.

De Carvalho, J. G. R., Messerli, F. H., & Frohlich, E. D. (1979). Mitral valve prolapse and borderline hypertension. *Hypertension, 1*, 518–522.

Decker, R. S. & Dingle, J. T. (1982). Cardiac, catabolic factors: The degradation of heart valve intercellular matrix. *Science, 235*, 987–989.

de la Sierra, A., Coca, A., Aguilera, M. T., & Urbano-Marquez, A. (1986). NA + Li + countertransport in essential hypertension. *Journal of Hypertension, 6*, 931–937.

De Maria, A. N., Amsterdam, E. A., Vismara, L. A., Neumann, A., & Mason, D. T. (1976). Arrhythmias in the mitral valve prolapse syndrome: Prevalence, nature and frequency. *Annals of Internal Medicine, 84*, 656–660.

De Maria, A. N., Takeda, P., & Mason, D. T. (1981). Mitral valve prolapse syndrome. *Cardiac Impulse, 2*, 1–6.

Denenberg, B., Channick, B. J., & Spann, J. F. (1983, October). Hyperthyroidism and mitral valve prolapse. *Primary Cardiology*, 73–84.

Depace, N., Segal, B. L., Fischl, S. J., & Farry, J. P. (1981). Mitral valve prolapse and orthostatic hypotension. *Practical Cardiology, 7*, 160–162.

Devereux, R. B. (1982). Inheritance of mitral valve prolapse: Effect of age and sex on gene expression. *Annals of Internal Medicine, 97*, 826–832.

Devereux, R. B. (1985). Mitral valve prolapse. *Cardiology in Practice*, 81–89.

Devereux, R. B., & Brown, W. T. (1989). Structural heart disease. In R. A. King, J. I. Rotter, & A. G. Motulsky (Eds.), *The genetic basis of common disease.* New York: Oxford University Press.

Devereux, R. B., Brown, W. T., Lutas, E. M., Kramer-Fox, R., & Laragh, J. H. (1982). Association of mitral valve prolapse with low body-weight and low blood pressure. *Lancet, 2*, 792–795.

Devereux, R. B., Hawkins, I., & Kramer-Fox, R. (1986). Complications of mitral valve prolapse: Disproportionate occurrence in men and older patients. *American Journal of Medicine, 81*, 751–758.

Devereux, R. B., Kramer-Fox, R., Brown, W. T., Shear, K. M., Hartman, N., Kligfield, P., Lutas, E. M., Spitzer, M. C., & Litwin, S. D. (1986). Relation between clinical features of mitral prolapse syndrome and echocardiographically documented mitral valve prolapse. *Journal of the American College of Cardiology, 8*, 763–772.

Devereux, R. B., Kramer-Fox, R., Shear, M. K., Kligfield, P., Pini, R., & Savage, D. D. (1987). Diagnosis and classification of severity of mitral valve prolapse: Methodologic, biologic and prognostic considerations. *American Heart Journal, 113*, 1265–1280.

Devereux, R. B., Lutas, E. M., & Casale, P. N. (1984). Standardization of M-mode echocardiographic left ventricular anatomic measurements. *Journal of the American College of Cardiology, 4*, 1222–1230.

Devereux, R. B., Lutas, E. M., Kramer-Fox, R., & Brown, W. T. (1984). Hypomastia and mitral valve prolapse (Letter to the editor). *New England Journal of Medicine, 310*, 1053–1054.

Devereux, R. B., Perloff, J. K., Reichek, N., & Josephson, M. E. (1976). Mitral valve prolapse. *Circulation, 54*, 3–14.

DiBona, G. F. (1983). Neural mechanisms of volume regulation. *Annals of Internal Medicine, 98*, 750–752.

Dimsdale, J. E., Young, D., Moore, R., & Strauss, H. W. (1987). Do plasma norepinephrine levels reflect behavioral stress? *Psychosomatic Medicine, 49*, 375–382.

Dunner, D. L. (1985). Anxiety and panic: Relationship to depression and cardiac disorders. *Psychosomatics, 26*, 18–21.

Duren, D. R., Becker, A. E., & Dunning, A. J. (1988). Long-term follow-up of idiopathic mitral valve prolapse in 300 patients: A prospective study. *Journal of the American College of Cardiology, 11*, 42–47.

Dustan, H. P., Tarazi, R. C., Bravo, E. L., & Dart, R. A. (1973). Plasma and extracellular fluid volumes in hypertension. *Circulation Research, 33*(Suppl. 1), 73–83.

Dzau, V. J., Packer, M., & Lily, L. S. (1984). Prostaglandins in severe congestive heart failure: Relation to activation of the renin-angiotensin system and hyponatremia. *New England Journal of Medicine, 310*, 347–352.

Easton, J., & Sherman, D. (1976). Somatic anxiety attacks and propranolol. *Archives of Neurology, 33*, 689–691.

Egan, B., & Schmouder, R. (1988). The importance of hemodynamic considerations in essential hypertension. *American Heart Journal, 116*, 594–599.

Engel, B. T., Baile, W. F., Costa, P. T., Brimlow, D. L., & Brinker, J. A. (1985). A behavioral analysis of chest pain in patients suspected of having coronary artery disease. *Psychosomatic Medicine, 47*, 274–278.

Engle, M. A. (1969). The syndrome of apical systolic click, late systolic murmur, and abnormal T waves. *Circulation, 39*, 12.

Epstein, S. E., & Lefkowitz, R. J. (1986). A symposium: Clinical applications of nonselective beta-blockers (Introduction). *American Journal of Cardiology, 57*, 1F.

Esler, M., Jennings, G., Korner, P., Willett, I., Dudley, F., Hasking, G., Anderson, W., & Lambert, G. (1988). Assessment of human sympathetic nervous system activity from measurement of norepinephrine turnover. *Hypertension, 11*, 3–20.

Everitt, A. V. (1988). Changes in neuroendocrine function with age. *Geriatric Medicine Today.*

Falk, R. H., & Hood, W. B. (1981). Mitral valve prolapse: Striking a therapeutic balance. *Drug Therapy,* 2, 125–134.

Feldman, T., Borow, K. M., Neuman, A., Sarne, D. H., Lang, R. M., & DeGroot, L. J. (1985). What are the factors influencing augmented left ventricular shortening in hyperthyroidism? (Abstract). *Journal of the American College of Cardiology,* 5, 535.

Feldman, T., Borow, K. M., Sarne, D. H., Neuman, A., & Lang, R. M. (1986). Myocardial mechanics in hyperthyroidism: Importance of left ventricular loading conditions, heart rate and contractile state. *Journal of the American College of Cardiology,* 7, 967–974.

Finnerty, F. A., Buchholz, J. H., & Guillaudeu, R. L. (1958). The blood volumes and plasma protein during levarterenol induced hypertension. *Journal of Clinical Investigation,* 37, 427–429.

Folkow, B., & Ely, D. L. (1987). Dietary sodium effects on cardiovascular and sympathetic neuroeffector functions as studied in various rat models (Editorial review). *Hypertension,* 5, 383–395.

Fontaine, R., & Boisvert, D. (1982). Psychophysiological disorders in anxious patients: Hypertension and hypotension. *Psychosomatic Medicine,* 38, 165–172.

Fontana, M. B. (1970). The varying clinical spectrum of the systolic click in late-systolic murmur syndrome. *Circulation,* 41, 807–816.

Fontana, M. E., Wooley, C. F., Leighton, R. F., & Lewis, R. P. (1975). Postural changes to left ventricular and mitral valvular dynamics in the systolic click–late systolic murmur syndrome. *Circulation,* 51, 165–173.

Fouad, F. M., Tadena-Thome, L., Bravo, E. L., & Tarazi, R. C. (1986). Idiopathic hypovolemia. *Annals of Internal Medicine,* 104, 298–303.

Freedman, R. B., Ianni, P., Ettedgui, E., & Puthezbath, N. (1985). Ambulatory monitoring of panic disorder. *Archives of General Psychiatry,* 42, 244–246.

Freeman, L. J., & Nixon, P. G. F. (1985a). Are coronary artery spasms and progressive damage to the heart associated with the hyperventilation syndrome? *British Journal of Cardiology,* 291, 851–852.

Freeman, L. J., & Nixon, P. G. F. (1985b). Chest pain and the hyperventilation syndome: Some aetiological considerations. *Postgraduate Medical Journal,* 61, 957–961.

Freyschuss, U., Hjemdahl, P., Jamlin-Dannfelt, A., & Linde, B. (1986). Cardiovascular and metabolic responses to low dose adrenaline infusion: An invasive study in humans. *Clinical Science,* 70, 199–206.

Frohlich, E. D. (1987). Diuretics in hypertension. *Journal of Hypertension,* 5(Suppl. 5), 43–49.

Frolich, E. D., Tarazi, R. C., & Dustan, H. P. (1969). Hyperdynamic beta-adrenergic circulatory state. *Archives of Internal Medicine,* 123, 1–7.

Fujii, H., Yasue, H., Okumura, K., Matsuyama, K., Morkami, Y., Miyagi, H., & Ogawa, H. (1988). Hyperventilation-induced simultaneous multivessel coronary spasm in patients with variant angina: An echocardiographic and arteriographic study. *Journal of the American College of Cardiology,* 12 1184–1192.

Fujita, T., Noda, H., & Ando, K. (1984). Sodium susceptibility and potassium effects in young patients with borderline hypertension. *Circulation,* 69, 468–476.

Gaffney, D. (1986). *Mitral valve prolapse syndrome.* Paper presented at symposium on Panic Disorders: Current Perspectives (Abstract). Tufts University School of Medicine, 15–17.

Gaffney, F. A., Bastian, B. C., & Lane, L. B. (1983). Abnormal cardiovascular regulation in the mitral valve prolapse syndrome. *American Journal of Cardiology,* 52, 316–320.

Gaffney, F. A., & Blomqvist, C. G. (1981). Mitral valve prolapse syndrome: Autonomic dysfunction. *Primary Cardiology,* 132–145.

Gaffney, F. A., & Blomqvist, C. G. (1988). Mitral valve prolapse and autonomic nervous system dysfunction: A pathophysiological link. In M. Boudoulas & C. F. Wooley (Eds.), *Mitral valve prolapse and the mitral valve prolapse syndrome* (pp. 427–444). Mount Kisco, NY: Futura.

Gaffney, F. A., Huxley, R.L., Nicod, P., Blend, L. B., Corbet, J. R., Lewis, S. E., Pettinger, W. A., Willerson, J. T., & Blomqvist, C. G. (1981). Abnormal cardiovascular regulation in mitral valve prolapse during exercise (Abstract). *Circulation,* 64(Suppl. 4), 248.

Gaffney, F. A., Karlsson, E. S., Campbell, W., Schutte, J. E., Nixon, J. V., Willerson, J. T., & Blomqvist, C. G. (1979). Autonomic dysfunction in women with mitral valve prolapse. *Circulation,* 59, 894–901.

Gaffney, F. A., Lane, L. B., Pettinger, W., & Blomqvist, C. G. (1983). Effects of long-term clonidine administration on the hemodynamic and neuroendocrine postural responses of patients with dysautonomia. *Chest,* 2(Suppl.), 436–438.

Galavardin, L. (1913). Pseudo-dedoublement du deuxieme bruit de coeur simulant le dedoublement mitral. *Lyon Medicine, 121,* 409–422.

Galosy, R. A., & Gaebelein, C. J. (1977). Cardiovascular adaptation to environmental stress: Its role in the development of hypertension, responsible mechanisms, and hypotheses. *Biobehavioral Review, 1,* 165–175.

Gardin, J. M., Isner, J. M., Ronan, J. A., & Fox, S. M. (1980). Pseudoischemic "false positive" S-T segment changes induced by hyperventilation in patients with mitral valve prolapse. *American Journal of Cardiology, 45,* 952–958.

Gavin, W. A., Pearlman, A. S., & Saal, A. K. (1983). Abnormal mitral leaflet coaptation: A nonspecific 2-D echocardiographic finding. *Circulation,* (Suppl. 2), 365.

Gavras, H. (1988). Effect of sodium on central alpha-2-adrenergic receptors (Letter to the editor). *Hypertension, 12,* 525.

Gay, R. G., Rays, T. E., Lancaster, L. D., Moffett, C., Morkin, E., & Goldman, S. (1986). Left ventricular function in hypothyroid and hyperthyroid rats (Abstract). *Circulation, 74*(Suppl. 2), 442.

Genest, J. (1983). Volume hormones and blood pressure. *Annals of Internal Medicine, 98*(Part 2), 744–749.

Gilbert, B. W., Schatz, R. A., von Ramm, O. T., Behar, V. S., & Kisslo, J. A. (1976). Mitral valve prolapse: Two-dimensional echocardiographic and angiographic correlation. *Circulation, 54,* 716–723.

Gitter, H. T., Lyons, J., & Talano, J. V. (1986). Psychological heterogeneity in mitral valve prolapse. *Circulation, 74*(Suppl. 2), 453.

Godley, R. W., Wann, L. S., Rogers, E. W., Feigenbaum, H., & Weyman, A. E. (1981). Incomplete mitral valve closure in patients with papillary dysfunction. *Circulation, 63,* 565–571.

Goldhaber, S. Z., Rubin, I. L., Brown, W., Robertson, N., Stubblefield, F., & Sloss, L. J. (1986). Valvular heart disease (aortic regurgitation and mitral valve prolapse) among institutionalized adults with Down's Syndrome. *American Journal of Cardiology, 57,* 278–281.

Goldman, M. E., Cantor, R., Schwartz, M. F., Baker, M., & Desnick, R. G. (1986). Echocardiographic abnormalities and the disease severity in Fabry's disease. *Journal of the American College of Cardiology, 7,* 1157–1161.

Goldman, S., & Morkin, E. (1983). Cardiomyopathy in hyperthyroidism (Letter to the editor). *New England Journal of Medicine, 308,* 780.

Gooch, A. S., Vicencio, F., Maranhao, V., & Goldberg, H. (1972). Arrhythmias and left ventricular asynergy in the prolapsing mitral leaflet syndrome. *American Journal of Cardiology, 29,* 611–620.

Gorman, J. M., Fyer, A. F., Glicklich, J., King, D., & Klein, D. F. (1981a). Effects of sodium lactate on patients with panic disorder and mitral valve prolapse. *American Journal of Psychiatry, 138,* 247–249.

Gorman, J. M., Fyer, A. F., Glicklich, J., King, D. L., & Klein, D. F. (1981b). Mitral valve prolapse and panic disorders: Effect of imimipramine. In D. F. Klein & J. Rabkin (Eds.) *Anxiety: New research and changing concepts.* New York: Raven Press.

Gorman, J. M., Shear, M. K., Devereux, R. B., King, D. L., & Klein, D. F. (1986). Prevalence of mitral valve prolapse in panic disorder: Effect of echocardiographic criteria. *Psychosomatic Medicine, 48,* 167–171.

Gorman, J. M., Goetz, R. R., Fyer, M., King, D. L., Fyer, A. J., Liebowitz, M. R., & Klein, D. F. (1988). The mitral valve prolapse-panic disorder connection. *Psychosomatic Medicine, 50,* 114–122.

Gradin, K., Dahlof, C., & Persson, B. (1986). Neuronal release of noradrenaline and blood pressure in SHR maintained on a low or high sodium diet. *Journal of Hypertension, 6,* 285–286.

Greenwood, R. D. (1986). Mitral valve prolapse in children. *Western Journal of Medicine, 144,* 375–376.

Griffith, J. P. C. (1892). Mid-systolic and late systolic mitral murmurs. *American Journal of Medical Science, 104,* 285–294.

Grossman, P. (1983). Respiration, stress, and cardiovascular function. *Psychophysiology, 20,* 284–300.

Grosz, H. J., & Farmer, B. S. (1969). Blood lactate in the development of anxiety symptoms. *Archives of General Psychiatry, 21,* 611–619.

Grunhaus, L., Gloger, S., & Lewis, B. S. (1982). Mitral valve prolapse and panic attacks. *Israel Journal of Medical Science, 18,* 221–223.

Guazzi, M. D. (1984, July). Hyperkinetic heart syndrome. *Primary Cardiology,* 94–102.

Guyton, A. C. (1982). Essential cardiovascular regulation: The control linkages between bodily needs and circulatory function. In C. J. Dickinson & J. Marks (Eds.), *Developments in cardiovascular medicine.* Baltimore: University Park Press.

Hageman, G. R., Goldberg, J. M., Armour, J. A., & Randall, W. C. (1973). Cardiac dysrhythmias induced by autonomic nerve stimulation. *American Journal of Cardiology, 32,* 823–830.

Hageman, G. R., Randall, W. C., & Armour, J. A. (1975). Direct and reflex cardiac bradydysrhythmias from small vagal nerve stimulations. *American Heart Journal, 89*, 338–348.

Haikal, M., Alpert, M. A., Whiting, R. B., & Kelly, D. (1982). Increased left ventricular mass in idiopathic mitral valve prolapse. *Chest, 82*, 329–333.

Hammond, H. K., White, F. C., Buxton, I. L. Saltzstein, P., Brunton, L. L., & Longhurst, J. C. (1985). The hyperthyroid pig: Myocardial beta-receptor changes are associated with a physiological response "in vivo." *Circulation, 72*(Suppl. 3), 332.

Hancock, E. W. (1966). The ejection sound in aortic stenosis. *American Journal of Medicine, 40*, 569–577.

Hancock, E. W., & Cohn, K. (1966). The syndrome associated with mid-systolic click and late systolic murmur. *American Journal of Medicine, 41*, 183–196.

Harris, S. L., & Crawford, H. (1985). Mitral leaflet/left ventricular cavity size disproportion: Can it cause prolapse of normal mitral valves? (Abstract). *Journal of the American College of Cardiology, 5*, 404.

Harshfield, G. A., Shear, M. K., Polan, J., Frances, A. J., & Pickering, T. G. (1984, May). The cardiovascular functioning of panic disorder patients during a normal day. *Behavioral Medicine Society.*

Hartman, M., Kramer, R., Brown, W., & Devereux, R. B. (1982). Panic disorder in patients with MVP. *American Journal of Psychiatry, 139*, 669–670.

Haslam, M. (1973). The relationship between the effect of lactate infusion on anxiety states, and their amelioration by carbon dioxide inhalation. *British Journal of Psychiatry, 125*, 88–90.

Hattori, R., Takatsu, Y., Yui, Y., Sakaguchi, K., Susawa, T., Murakami, T., Tamaki, S., & Kawai, C. (1985). Lactate metabolism in acute myocardial infarction and its relation to regional ventricular performance. *Journal of the American College of Cardiology, 5*, 1283–1291.

Haywood, L. J. (1987). Cardiovascular findings in sickle cell anemia. *Internal Medicine, 8*, 84–89.

Henry, D. P., Luft, F. C., Weinberger, M. H., Fineberg, N. S., & Grim, C. E. (1980). Norepinephrine in urine and plasma following provocative maneuvers in normal and hypertensive subjects. *Hypertension, 2*, 20–28.

Hickey, A. J., Andrews, G., & Wilken, D. E. (1983). Independence of mitral valve prolapse and neurosis. *British Heart Journal, 50* 333–336.

Hickey, A. J., & Wilcken, D. E. L. (1986). Age and the clinical profile of idiopathic mitral valve prolapse. *British Heart Journal, 55*, 582–586.

Hickey, A. J., Wilcken, D. E. L., Wright, J. S., & Warren, B. A. (1985). Primary (spontaneous) chordal rupture: Relation to myxomatous valve disease and mitral valve prolapse. *Journal of the American College of Cardiology, 5*, 1341–1346.

Higgenbotham, M. B., Morris, K. G., Coleman, R. E., & Cobb, F. R. (1984). Sex-related differences in normal cardiac response to upright exercise. *Circulation, 70*, 357–366.

Hochreiter, C., Kramer, H. M., Kligfield, P., Kramer-Fox, M. A., Devereux, R. B., & Borer, J. S. (1983). Arrhythmias in mitral valve prolapse: Effect of additional mitral regurgitation (Abstract). *Journal of the American College of Cardiology, 1*(2), 607.

Hoehn-Saric, R. (1981). Characteristics of chronic anxiety patients. In D. Klein & J. Rabkin (Eds.), *Anxiety: New research and changing concepts.* New York: Raven Press.

Holden, H. A., Ostfeld, A. M., & Freeman, D. H. (1983). Hypertension: Perhaps only the salt-sensitive need reduce NA+ intake. *Journal of the American Medical Association, 250*, 366–369.

Holgado, G. M., & Prakash, R. (1987). Prevalence of mitral valve prolapse in hypertension. *Journal of the National Medical Association, 79*, 966–968.

Holgado, G. M., Prakash, R., Kaushik, V. W., Sarma, R., & Marks, G. (1986). Mitral valve prolapse in hypertension: Echocardiographic comparison, between 133 hypertensive and 230 normotensive cardiac patients (Abstract). *Journal of the American College of Cardiology, 7*, 186.

Holland, O. B. (1980). Pheochromocytoma. In K. J. Isselbacher, R. D. Adams, E. Braunwald, R. G. Petersdorf, & J. D. Wilson (Eds.), *Harrison's principles of internal medicine.* New York: McGraw Hill.

Holmgren, A., Jonsson, B., Levander, M., Linderholm, H., Sjostrand, T., & Strom, G. (1957). Low physical working capacity in suspected heart cases due to inadequate adjustment of peripheral blood flow (vasoregulatory asthenia). *Acta Medica Scandinavica, 158*, 413–436.

Hortop, J., Tsipouras, P., Hanley, J. A., Maron, B. J., & Shapiro, J. R. (1986). Cardiovascular involvement in osteogenesis imperfecta. *Circulation, 73*, 54–61.

Humphries, J. O. & McKusick, V. A. (1962). The differentiation of organic and "innocent" systolic murmurs. *Progress in Cardiovascular Diseases, 5*, 152–171.

Hutchins, G. M., Moore, W., & Skoog, D. K. (1986). The association of floppy mitral valve with disjunction of the mitral annulus fibrosus. *New England Journal of Medicine, 314*, 535–540.

Iskandrian, A. S., Heo, J., Hakki, A., & Mandler, J. M. (1986). Age- and gender-related changes in exercise left ventricular function in mitral valve prolapse. *American Journal of Cardiology, 58*, 117–120.

Iskandrian, A. S., Rose, L., Hakki, A.-H., Segal, B. L., & Kane, S. A. (1983). Cardiac performance in thyrotoxicosis: Analysis of 10 untreated patients. *American Journal of Cardiology, 51*, 349–352.

Jefferson, J. S. (1987). Anxiety and the aching heart. *Stress Medicine, 3*, 33–39.

Jeresaty, R. M. (1971). The syndrome associated with midsystolic click and/or late-systolic murmur: Analysis of 32 cases. *Chest, 59*, 643–647.

Jeresaty, R. M. (1973). Mitral valve prolapse and ruptured chordae tendinae. *Progress in Cardiovascular Diseases, 15*, 623–652.

Jeresaty, R. M. (1979). *Mitral valve prolapse*. New York: Raven Press.

Jeresaty, R. M. (1985). Mitral valve prolapse: An update. *Journal of the American Medical Association, 254*, 793–795.

Jeresaty, R. M. (1986). Mitral valve prolapse: Complications, prognosis, and treatment. *Practical Cardiology, 12*, 136–149.

Jones, G. E., Jones, K. R., Rou, C. H., Scott, D. M., & Caldwell, J. A. (1987). The effect of body position on the perception of cardiac sensations: An experiment and theoretical implications. *Psychophysiology, 24*, 300–311.

Jones, M., & Mellersh, V. (1946). Comparison of exercise response in anxiety states and normal controls. *Psychosomatic Medicine, 8*, 180–187.

Jones, N. L., & Campbell, E. J. M. (1982). The heart in work and exercise. In N. L. Jones & E. J. M. Campbell (Eds.), *Clinical exercise testing*. Philadelphia: Saunders.

Kantor, J. S., Zitrin, C. M., & Zeldis, S. M. (1980). Mitral valve prolapse syndrome in agoraphobic patients. *American Journal of Psychiatry, 137*, 467–470.

Kelley, R. E., Pina, I., & Lee, S. C. (1988). Cerebral ischemia and mitral valve prolapse case-control study of associated factors. *Stroke, 49*, 443–446.

Kelly, D., Mitchell-Heggs, N., & Sherman, D. (1971). Anxiety and the effect of sodium lactate assessed clinically and physiologically. *British Journal of Psychiatry, 119*, 129–141.

Kenny, J., Plappert, T., Doubilet, P., Salzman, D., & St. John Sutton, M. G. (1987). Effects of heart rate on ventricular size, stroke volume, and output in the normal human fetus: A prospective Doppler echocardiographic study. *Circulation, 76*, 52–58.

Kessler, K. M. (1988). Prolapse paranoia. *Journal of the American College of Cardiology, 11*, 48–49.

Khandheria, B., Tajik, J., Naessens, J. M., Shub, C., & Seward, J. B. (1987). Prevalence of mitral valve prolapse by two-dimensional echocardiography: A population-based study (Abstract). *Journal of the American College of Cardiology, 8*(Suppl. A), 77.

Kimura, G., Deguchi, F., Kojima, S., Ashida, T., Yoshimi, H., Abe, H., Kawano, Y., Yoshida, K., Imanishi, M., Kawamura, M., Kuramochi, M., & Omae, T. (1988). Anti-hypertensive drugs and sodium restriction. *American Journal of Hypertension, 1*, 372–379.

King, B. D., Boudoulas, H., Fontana, M. E., & Wooley, C. F. (1980). Mitral valve prolapse syndrome: Anthropometric, sexual and clinical features (Abstract). *American Journal of Cardiology, 45*, 443.

King, B. D., Clark, M. A., Baba, N., Kilman, J. W., & Wooley, C. F. (1982). "Myxomatous" mitral valve. Collagen dissolution as the primary defect. *Circulation, 66*, 288–296.

Kjeldsen, S. E., Os, I., Beckman, S. L., Westheim, A., Hjermann, I., Leren, P., & Eide, I. (1986). Decreased noradrenergic sympathetic tone during controlled long-term low sodium treatment of mild essential hypertension. *Journal of Hypertension, 6*, 200–202.

Kjeldsen, S. E., Westheim, A., Lande, K., Gjesdal, K., Leren, P., Enger, E., & Eide, I.K. (1988). Sodium depletion increases platelet and plasma catecholamines in hypertensive men. *Hypertension, 11*, 477–482.

Klein, D. F., Zitrin, C. M., & Woerner, M. (1978). Antidepressants, anxiety, panic and phobias. In M. A. Lipton, A. DiMascio & K. F. Killam (Eds.), *Psychopharmacology: A generation of progress*. New York: Raven Press.

Klerman, G. L. (1985). Understanding anxiety: Normal emotion, symptom, and clinical disorder (Special Issue). *Internal Medicine, 6*, 3–12.

Kligfield, P., Hochreiter, C., Kramer, H., Devereux, R. B., Niles, N., Kramer-Fox, R., & Borer, J. S. (1985). Complex arrhythmias in mitral regurgitation with and without mitral valve prolapse: Contrast to arrhythmias in mitral valve prolapse without mitral regurgitation. *American Journal of Cardiology, 55*, 1545–1549.

Ko, G. N., Elsworth, J., D., & Roth, R. H. (1983). Panic-induced elevation of plasma MHPG levels in phobic-anxious patients. *Archives of General Psychiatry, 40*, 425–430.

Koch, F. H., & Hancock, E. W. (1976). Ten-year follow-up of 40 patients with the midsystolic click/late-systolic murmur syndrome. *American Journal of Cardiology, 37*, 149.

Koepke, J. P., Jones, S., & DiBona, G. F. (1988). Sodium responsiveness of central alpha-2-adrenergic receptors in spontaneously hypertensive rats. *Hypertension, 11*, 326–333.

Kolibash, A. J. (1988). Natural history of mitral valve prolapse. In H. Boudoulas & C. F. Wooley (Eds.), *Mitral valve prolapse and the mitral valve prolapse syndrome* (pp. 257–274). Mount Kisco, NY: Futura.

Kolibash, A. J., Bush, C. A., Fontana, M. B., Ryan, J. M., Kilman, J., & Wooley, C. F. (1983). Mitral valve prolapse syndrome: Analysis of 62 patients aged 60 years and older. *American Journal of Cardiology, 52*, 534–539.

Kolibash, A. J., Kilman, J. W., Bush, C. A., Ryan, J. M., Fontana, M. E., & Wooley, C. F. (1986). Evidence for progression from mild to severe mitral regurgitation in mitral valve prolapse. *American Journal of Cardiology, 58*, 762–767.

Konstam, M. A., Tomeh, S., Wayne, J., Beck, J. B., Kozlowski, J., & Holman, B. L. (1982). Effect of exercise on erythrocyte count and blood activity concentration after technetium-99m in vivo red blood cell labeling. *Circulation, 66*, 638–642.

Koolen, M. I., & van Brummelen, P. (1984). Adrenergic activity and peripheral hemodynamics in relation to sodium sensitivity in patients with essential hypertension. *Hypertension, 6*, 820–825.

Krafchek, J., Shaw, M., & Kisslo, J. (1985). Upright paradoxical posterior wall movement in mitral valve prolapse. *American Journal of Cardiology, 56*, 804–806.

Kramer, H. M., Kligfield, P., & Devereux, R. B. (1984). Arrhythmias in mitral valve prolapse: Effect of selection bias. *Archives of Internal Medicine, 144*, 2360–2364.

Kramer-Fox, R., Devereux, R. B., Brown, W. T., Hartman, N., & Elston, R. C. (1984). Lack of association between dermal arches and mitral prolapse: Relation to anxiety. *American Journal of Cardiology, 53*, 148–152.

Krishna, G. G., Danovitch, G. M., & Sowers, J. R. (1983). Catecholamine responses to central volume expansion produced by head-out water immersion and saline infusion. *Circulation, 56*, 998–1002.

Kriwisky, M., Froom, P., Gross, M., Ribak, J., & Lewis, B. S. (1987). Usefulness of echocardiographically determined mitral leaflet motion for diagnosis of mitral valve prolapse in 17- and 18-year-old men. *American Journal of Cardiology, 59*, 1149–1151.

Krzesinski, J. M., & Rorive, G. L. (1986). Is the decrease of central venous compliance the factor responsible for salt sensitivity? *Journal of Hypertension, 6*, 68–70.

Lachman, A. S., Bramwell-Jones, D. M., & Lazier, J. B. (1973). Infective endocarditis in the billowing mitral leaflet syndrome. *British Heart Journal, 37*, 326–330.

Lader, M. (1984). Neurotransmitters and anxiety: Overview. *Psychopathology, 17*(Suppl. 3), 3–7.

Lapierre, Y., Knott, V., & Gray, R. (1984). Psychophysiological correlates of sodium lactate. *Psychopharmacology Bulletin, 20*, 50–57.

Laragh, J. H., & Pecker, M. S. (1983). Dietary sodium and essential hypertension: Some myths, hopes, and truths. *Annals of Internal Medicine, 98*, 735–743.

Lavine, S. J., Campbell, C., & Gunther, S. J. (1986). Effect of increased left ventricular size and filling pressure on diastolic filling. *Circulation, 74*(Part 2), 148.

Lawton, W. J., Sinkey, C. A., Fitz, A. E., & Mark, A. L. (1988). Dietary salt produces abnormal renal vasoconstriction responses to upright posture in borderline hypertensive subjects. *Hypertension, 11*, 529–536.

Leatham, A., & Brigden, W. (1980). Mild mitral regurgitation and the mitral prolapse fiasco. *American Heart Journal, 99*, 659–664.

Lee, W. R., Sheikh, M. U., & Lee, K .J. (1985). Prevalence of mitral valve prolapse in presumably healthy Korean adults. *Clinical Cardiology, 8*, 356–358.

Lefkowitz, R. J., Caron, M. G., & Stiles, G. L. (1984). Mechanisms of membrane–receptor regulation. *New England Journal of Medicine, 310*, 1570–1579.

Leichtman, D., Nelson, R., & Fraderick, L. G. (1976). Bradycardia with mitral valve prolapse: A potential mechanism of sudden death. *Annals of Internal Medicine, 85*, 453–457.

Leier, C. V., Call, T. D., Fulkerson, P. K., & Wooley, C. F. (1980). The spectrum of cardiac defects in the Ehlers-Danlos syndrome types I and III. *Annals of Internal Medicine, 91*, 171–178.

Lenders, J. W. M., Fast, J. H., Blankers, J., Lemmens, W. A. J., & Thien, T. H. (1986). Normal sympathetic neural activity in patients with mitral valve prolapse. *Clinical Cardiology, 9*, 177–182.

Leor, R., & Markiewicz, W. (1982). Neurocirculatory asthenia and mitral valve prolapse: Two unrelated entities. *Israel Journal of Medical Science, 17,* 1137-1139.

Levey, G. S., & Levey, B. A. (1985). Cardiovascular effects of thyroid disease. *Hospital Medicine, 21,* 147-158.

Levine, M. A. H., & Leenen, F. H. H. (1989). Role of beta-1-receptors and vagal tone in cardiac inotropic and chronotropic response to a beta-2-agonist in humans. *Circulation, 79,* 107-119.

Levine, R. A. (1988). Mitral valve prolapse: Who has the disease? *Cardio,* 85-89.

Levine, R. A., Stathogiannis, E., Finkelstein, D., & Weyman, A. E. (1987). Mitral valve prolapse: Additional support for the "normality" of displacement in the apical 4-chamber view only (Abstract). *Journal of the American College of Cardiology, 9*(Suppl. A), 9A.

Levine, R. A., Triulzi, M. O., Harrigan, P., & Weyman, A. E. (1987). The relationship of mitral annular shape to the diagnosis of mitral valve prolapse (Abstract). *Circulation, 75,* 756.

Levine, R. A., & Weyman, A. E. (1984). Mitral valve prolapse: A disease in search of, or created by its definition. *Echocardiography, 10,* 3-14.

Lewis, T. (1919). *The soldier's heart and the effort syndrome.* New York: Paul B. Hoeber.

Liebowitz, M. F., Gorman, J. M., & Fyer, A. J. (1985). Lactate provocation of panic attacks: Biochemical and physiological findings. *Archives of General Psychiatry, 42,* 709-719.

Liedtke, A. J., Gault, J. H., Leaman, D. M., & Blumenthal, M. S. (1973). Geometry of left ventricular contraction in the systolic click syndrome: Characterization of a segmental myocardial abnormality. *Circulation, 47,* 27.

Lilavivathana, U., & Campbell, R. G. (1980). The influence of sodium restriction on orthostatic nervous activity. *Archives of Internal Medicine, 140,* 1485-1489.

Lima, S. D., Lima, J. A. C., Pyeritz, R. E., & Weiss, J. L. (1985). Relation of mitral valve prolapse to left ventricular size in Marfan's syndrome. *American Journal of Cardiology, 55,* 739-743.

Lindemann, E., & Finesinger, J. (1938). The effect of adrenaline and mecholyl in states of anxiety in psychoneurotic patients. *American Journal of Psychiatry, 95,* 353-370.

Lindemann, E., & Finesinger, J. (1940). The subjective response of psychoneurotic patients to adrenaline and mecholyl. *Psychosomatic Medicine, 2,* 231-248.

Luft, F. C., Miller, J. Z., Cohen, S. J., Fineberg, N. S., & Weinberger, M. H. (1988). Heritable aspects of salt sensitivity. *American Journal of Cardiology, 61,* 1H-6H.

Luft, F. C., Rankin, L. I., Henry, D. P., Bloch, R., Grim, C. E., Weyman, A. E., Murray, R. H., & Weinberger, M. H. (1979). Plasma and urinary norepinephrine values at extremes of sodium intake in normal man. *Hypertension, 1,* 261-266.

Luisada, A. A., & Alimurung, N. M. (1949). The systolic gallop rhythm. *Acta Cardiologica, 4,* 309-323.

Lutas, E. M., Devereux, R. B., Spitzer, M. C., & Kramer-Fox, R. (1984). Disappearance of mitral valve prolapse during pregnancy. *Journal of Cardiovascular Ultrasonography, 3,* 183-2186.

MacLean, W. C. (1867). Disease of the heart in the British army: The cause and the remedy. *British Medical Journal, 1,* 161-164.

MacMahon, S. W., Roberts, J. K., Kramer-Fox, R., Zucker, D. M., Roberts, R. B., & Devereux, R. B. (1987). Mitral valve prolapse and infective endocarditis. *American Heart Journal, 113,* 1291-1298.

Makino, H., & Al-Sadir, J. (1983). Myocardial infarction in patients with mitral valve prolapse and normal coronary arteries. *Journal of the American College of Cardiology, 1,* 661.

Malcolm, A. D. (1985). Mitral valve prolapse associated with other disorders: Casual coincidence, common links, or fundamental genetic disturbance? *British Heart Journal, 53,* 353-362.

Manders, W. T., Knight, D. R., & Vatner, S. F. (1986). Vagal mechanism mediating excretion of water and sodium in response to volume expansion in conscious primates (Abstract). *Hypertension, 72*(Part 2), 243.

Margraf, J., Ehlers, A., & Roth, W. T. (1987). Panic attack associated with perceived heart rate acceleration: A case report. *Behavioral Therapy, 18,* 84-89.

Margraf, J., Ehlers, A., & Roth, W. T. (1988). Mitral valve prolapse and panic disorder: A review of their relationship. *Psychosomatic Medicine, 50,* 93-113.

Margraf, J., Taylor, C. B., Ehlers, A., Roth, W. T., & Agras, W. S. (1987). Panic attacks in the natural environment. *Journal of Mental Disorders, 175,* 558-565.

Markiewicz, W., Stoner, J., London, E., Hunt, S. A., & Popp, R. L. (1976). Mitral valve prolapse in one hundred presumably healthy young females. *Circulation, 53,* 464-473.

Martin, W. H., Coyle, E. F., Bloomfield, S. A., & Ehsani, A. A. (1986). Effects of physical deconditioning after intense endurance training on left ventricular dimensions and stroke volume. *Journal of the American College of Cardiology, 7,* 982-989.

Mason, D. T., Lee, G., Chan, M. C., & DeMaria, A. N. (1984). Arrhythmias in patients with mitral valve prolapse: Types, evaluation, and therapy. *Medical Clinics of North America, 68*, 1039–1048.

Mathew, R. J., & Wilson, W. H. (1986). Hematocrit and anxiety. *Journal of Psychosomatic Research, 30*, 307–311.

Mavissakalian, M., Salerni, R., & Thompson, M. E. (1983). Mitral valve prolapse and agoraphobia. *American Journal of Psychiatry, 140*, 1612–1614.

Mazza, D. L., Martin, K. D., & Spacavento, L. (1986). Mitral valve prolapse: Disease or illness? *American Journal of Psychiatry, 142*, 349–352.

Mazza, D. L., Martin, D., Spacevento, L., Jacobsen, J., & Gibbs, H. (1986). Prevalence of anxiety disorders in patients with mitral valve prolapse. *American Journal of Psychiatry, 143*, 349–352.

McLaren, M. J., Hawkins, D. M., Lachman, A. S., Lakier, J. B., Pocock, W. A., & Barlow, J. B. (1976). Non-ejection systolic clicks and mitral systolic murmurs in black schoolchildren of Soweto, Johannesburg. *British Heart Journal, 38*, 718–714.

McMurray, J. J., Seidelin, P. H., Balfour, D. J. K., & Struthers, A. D. (1988). Physiological increases in circulating noradrenaline are antinatriuretic in man. *Journal of Hypertension, 6*, 757–761.

Mehmel, H. C., Stockins, B., Ruffmann, K., Olshausen, K. V., Schuler, G., & Kubler, W. (1981). The linearity of the end-systolic pressure-volume relationship in man and its sensitivity for assessment of left ventricular function. *Circulation, 63*, 1216–1223.

Merino, A., Alegria, E., Castello, R., & Martinez-Caro, D. (1988). Influence of age on left ventricular contractility. *American Journal of Cardiology, 62*, 1103–1108.

Messerli, F. H. (1988). The heterogeneity of essential hypertension: Hemodynamic aspects. *American Heart Journal, 116*, 590–596.

Meyers, D. (1986). Mitral valve prolapse in anorexia nervosa. *Annals of Internal Medicine, 105*, 384–384.

Meyers, D. G., Starke, H., Pearson, P. H., Wilkin, M. K., & Ferrell, J. R. (1987). Leaflet to left ventricular size disproportion and prolapse of structurally normal mitral valve in anorexia nervosa. *American Journal of Cardiology, 60*, 911–914.

Min, S. K., & Lee, H. Y. (1986). No mitral prolapse in Korean patients with panic attacks. *American Journal of Psychiatry, 143*, 943–944.

Mitchell, J. E., Pomeroy, C., Seppala, M., & Huber, M. (1988). Diuretic use as a marker for eating problems and affective disorders among women. *Journal of Clinical Psychiatry, 49*, 267–270.

Mizock, B. A. (1987). Controversies in lactic acidosis; Implications in critically ill patients. *Journal of the American Medical Association, 258*, 497–501.

Myers, A. B. R. (1870). *On the etiology and prevalence of diseases of the heart among soldiers.* London: J. Churchill.

Naggar, C. A, (1979). The mitral valve prolapse syndrome: Spectrum and therapy. *Medical Clinics of North America, 63*, 337–353.

Naggar, C. Z., & Aretz, H. T. (1984). Pathogenesis of mitral valve prolapse. *Medical Times, 112*, 27–35.

Naggar, C. Z., Pearson, W. N., & Seljan, M. P. (1986). Frequency of complications of mitral valve prolapse in subjects aged 60 years and older. *American Journal of Cardiology, 58*, 1209–1212.

Natarajan, G., Nakhjavan, F. K., Kahn, D., Yazdanfar, S., Sahibrada, W., Khawaja, F., & Goldberg, H. (1975). Myocardial metabolic studies in prolapsing mitral leaflet syndrome. *Circulation, 52*, 1105–1110.

Nemiah, J. C. (1980). Anxiety state (anxiety neurosis). In A. M. Freedman & B. J. Sadock (Eds.), *Comprehensive textbook of psychiatry* (3rd ed., pp. 1483–1493). Baltimore: Williams & Willkins.

Nesse, R. M., Cameron, O. G., Buda, A. J., McCann, D. S., Curtis, G. C., & Huber-Smith, M. J. (1985). Urinary catecholamines and mitral valve prolapse in panic–anxiety patients. *Psychiatry Research, 14*, 67–75.

Nesse, R., Cameron, O. G., Curtis, G., McCann, D., & Huber-Smith, M. (1984). Adrenergic function in panic anxiety patients. *Archives of General Psychiatry, 41*, 771–776.

Newman, G. E., Gibbons, R. J., & Jones, R. H. (1981). Cardiac function during rest and exercise in patients with mitral valve prolapse. *American Journal of Cardiology, 47*, 14–19.

Nicholls, M. G., Kiowski, W., Zweifler, A. J., Julius, S., Schork, M. A., & Greenhouse, J. (1980). Plasma norepinephrine variations with dietary sodium intake. *Hypertension, 2*, 29–32.

Nii, T., Fouad-Tarazi, F. M., Ferrario, C. M., Bravo, E. L., & Czerska, B. (1987). Changes in hemodynamics and myocardial contractility during chronic sodium depletion in conscious dogs. *Hypertension, 9*, (Suppl. 3), 176–180.

Nishimura, R. A., McGoon, M. D., Shub, C., Miller, F. A., Ilstrup, D. M., & Tajik, A. J. (1985). Echocardiographically documented mitral valve prolapse. *New England Journal of Medicine, 313*, 1305–1309.

Nishiwaka, T., Akaishi, M., Hokozuka, H., Ikegawa, T., Handa, S., & Nakamura, Y. (1986). Left ventricular diastolic mechanics determinants of filling volume (Abstract). *Circulation, 74*(Part 2), 441.

Omvik, P., & Lund-Johansen, P. (1986). Moderate low-salt diet does not normalize central hemodynamics in mild essential hypertension. *Journal of Hypertension, 6*, 651–653.

Omvik, P., & Lund-Johansen, P. (1987). Is sodium restriction effective treatment of borderline and mild essential hypertension? A long-term hemodynamic study at rest and during exercise. *British Journal of Hypertension, 4*, 535–541.

O'Rourke, R. A., & Crawford, M. H. (1976). The systolic click-murmur syndrome: Clinical recognition and management. *Current Problems in Cardiology, 1*, 1–60.

Osler, W. (1880). On a remarkable heart murmur, heard at a distance from the chest wall. *Medical Times and Gazette, 2*, 432–436.

Osler, W. (1887). The irritable heart of civil life. *Canadian Practitioner, 12*, 156–157.

Panidis, I. P., McAllister, M., Ross, J., & Mintz. G. S. (1986). Prevalence and severity of mitral regurgitation in the mitral valve prolapse syndrome: A Doppler echocardiographic study of 80 patients. *Journal of the American College of Cardiology, 7*, 975–981.

Pariser, S. F., Jones, B. A., & Pinta, E. R. (1979). Panic attacks: Diagnostic evaluations of 17 patients. *American Journal of Psychiatry, 136*, 105–106.

Pariser, S. F., Pinta, E. R., & Jones, B. A. (1978). Mitral valve prolapse syndrome and anxiety neurosis panic disorder. *American Journal of Psychiatry, 135*, 246–247.

Pasternac, A., Kouz, S., Gutkowska, J., Petitclerc, R., Taillefer, R., Cequier, A., DeChamplain, J., & Cantin, M. (1986). Atrial natriuretic factor: A possible link between left atrium, plasma volume, adrenergic control and renin-aldosterone in the mitral valve prolapse syndrome. *Journal of Hypertension, 4*(Suppl. 5), 76–79.

Pasternac, A., Latour, J. G., Kouz, S., Gauthier, C., Petitclerc, R., DeChamplain, J., Vellas, B., & Goulet, C. (1986). Increased platelet products and aggregation in symptomatic mitral valve prolapse. *Journal of the American College of Cardiology, 7*, 28A.

Pasternac, A., Latour, J. G., Kouz, S. Petitclerc, R., Vellas, B., DeChamplain, J., & Goulet, C. (1986). Stability of hyperadrenergic state in symptomatic patients with mitral valve prolapse: A six-year follow-up (Abstract). *Circulation, 74* (Part 2), 299.

Pasternac, A., Tubau, J. F., Puddu, P. E., Krol, R. B., & DeChamplain, J. (1982). Increased plasma catecholamine levels in patients with symptomatic mitral valve prolapse. *American Journal of Medical Science, 73*, 783–789.

Peller, O. G., Devereux, R. B., & Schreiber, T. L. (1988). Lack of association between acute myocardial infarction and mitral valve prolapse. *American Journal of Cardiology, 62*, 1297.

Perkin, G. D., & Joseph, R. (1986). Neurological manifestations of the hyperventilation syndrome. *Journal of the Royal Society of Medicine, 79*, 448–450.

Perloff, J. K., Child, J. S., & Edwards, J. E. (1986). New guidelines for the clinical diagnosis of mitral valve prolapse. *American Journal of Cardiology, 57*, 1124–1129.

Perloff, J. K., Stevenson, W. G., Roberts, N. K., Cabeen, W., & Weiss, J. (1984). Cardiac involvement in myotonic muscular dystrophy (Steinert's disease): A prospective study of 25 patients. *American Journal of Cardiology, 54*, 1074–1081.

Pini, R., Greppi, B., Devereux, R. B., Erlebacher, J., Spitzer, M., Kramer-Fox, R., & Brown, W. T. (1986). Phenotypic heterogeneity in mitral valve prolapse: Relation of mitral valve abnormalities to body weight and blood pressure. *Journal of the American College of Cardiology, 7*, 7A.

Pini, R., Greppi, B., Kramer-Fox, R., Roman, M. J., & Devereux, R. B. (1988). Mitral valve dimensions and motion and familial transmission of mitral valve prolapse with and without mitral leaflet billowing. *Journal of the American College of Cardiology, 12*, 1423–1431.

Pitts, F., & McClure, J. (1967). Lactate metabolism in anxiety neurosis. *New England Journal of Medicine, 277*, 1329–1336.

Pocock, W. A., & Barlow, J. B. (1970). Postexercise arrhythmias in the billowing posterior mitral leaflet syndrome. *American Heart Journal, 80*, 740–745.

Pocock, W. A., & Barlow, J. B. (1971). Etiology and electrocardiographic features of the billowing posterior mitral leaflet syndrome: Analysis of a further 130 patients with a late systolic murmur or nonejection systolic clicks. *American Journal of Medicine, 57*, 731–739.

Polinsky, R. J. (1983). Neurogenic orthostatic hypotension: Concepts in diagnosis and management. *Internal Medicine, 4*, 120–137.

Pollack, R. D. (1987). Mitral valve prolapse syndrome: Myth or reality? *Western Journal of Medicine, 146*, 381–382.

Procacci, P. M., Savran, S. V., Schreiter, S. L., & Bryson, A. L. (1976). Prevalence of clinical mitral valve prolapse in 1169 young women. *New England Journal of Medicine, 294*, 1086-1088.

Puddu, P. E., Pasternac, A., Tubau, J. F., Krol, R., Farley, L., & DeChamplain, J. (1983). QT prolongation and increased plasma catecholamine levels in patients with mitral valve prolapse. *American Heart Journal, 105*, 422-428.

Pyeritz, R. E., & McKusick, V. A. (1979). The Marfan syndrome: Diagnosis and management. *New England Journal of Medicine, 300*, 772-777.

Pyke, R. E., & Greenberg, H. S. (1986). Norepinephrine challenges in panic patients. *Journal of Clinical Psychopharmacology, 6*, 279-285.

Rainey, J., Frohman, C., Freedman, R., Phl, R., Ettedgui, E., & Williams, M. (1984). Specificity of lactate infusion as a model of anxiety. *Psychopharmacology Bulletin, 20*, 45-49.

Ranganathan, N., Silver, M. D., Robinson, T. I., Kostuk, W. J., Felderhof, C. H., Patt, N. L., Wilson, J. K., & Wigle, E. D. (1973). Angiographic-morphologic correlation in patients with severe mitral regurgitation due to prolapse of the posterior mitral valve leaflet. *Circulation, 48*, 514-518.

Read, R. C., Thal, A. P., & Wendt, V. E.. (1965). Symptomatic valvular myxomatous transformation (the floppy valve syndrome): A possible fruste of the Marfan syndrome. *Circulation, 32*, 897-910.

Redmond, D. E. (1979). New and old evidence for the involvement of a brain norepinephrine system in anxiety. In W. E. Fann & L. Kokracan (Eds.), *Phenomenology and treatment of anxiety* (pp. 153-203). New York: Spectrum.

Redmond, D. E., & Huang, Y. H. (1979). New evidence for a locus coeruleus-norepinephrine connection with anxiety. *Life Sciences, 25*, 2149-2162

Reid, J. V. (1961). Mid-systolic clicks. *South African Medical Journal, 35*, 353-355.

Retchin, S. M., Fletcher, R. H., Earp, J., Lamson, N., & Waugh, R. A. (1986). Mitral valve prolapse: Disease or illness? *Archives of Internal Medicine, 146*, 1081-1084.

Rizzon, P., Biasco, G., & Brondicci, G. (1973). Familial syndrome of midsystolic click and late systolic murmur. *British Heart Journal, 35*, 245-259.

Robertson, D., Johnson, G. A., Robertson, R. M., Nies, A. S., Shand, D. G., & Oates, J. A. (1979). Comparative assessment of stimuli that release neuronal and adrenomedullary catecholamines in man. *Circulation, 59*, 637-643.

Rogers, J. M., Boudoulas, H., Malarkey, W. B., & Wooley, C. F. (1983). Mitral valve prolapse: Disordered catecholamine regulation with intravascular volume maneuvers. *Circulation, 68*(Suppl. 3), 111.

Rogers, J. M., Boudoulas, H. M., & Wooley, C. F. (1984b). Mitral valve prolapse: Evidence of baroreflex abnormality with intravascular volume maneuvers (Abstract). *Journal of the American College of Cardiology, 3*, 559.

Rogers, J. M., Boudoulas, H. M., & Wooley, C. F. (1984a). Abnormal renin-aldosterone response to volume depletion in mitral valve prolapse (Abstract). *Circulation, 70*(Suppl. 2), 336.

Roman, M. J., Devereux, R. B., Kramer-Fox, R., & Spitzer, M. C. (1989). Comparison of cardiovascular and skeletal features of primary mitral valve prolapse and Marfan syndrome. *American Journal of Cardiology, 63*, 317, 321.

Romoff, M. S., Keusch, G., Campese, V. M., Wang, M. S., Friedler, R. M., Weidmann, P., & Massry, S. G. (1979). Effect of sodium intake on plasma catecholamines in normal subjects. *Journal of Clinical Endocrinology and Metabolism, 48*, 26-31.

Rosenberg, C. A., Derman, G. H., Grabb, W. C., & Buda, A. J. (1983). Hypomastia and mitral valve prolapse: Evidence of a linked embryologic and mesenchymal dysplasia. *New England Journal of Medicine, 309* 1230-1232.

Rosenthal, M. E., Hamer, A., Gang, E. S., Oseran, D. S., Mandel, W. J., & Peter. T. (1985). The yield of programmed ventricular stimulation of mitral valve prolapse patients with ventricular arrhythmias. *American Heart Journal, 220*, 970-976.

Rotmensch, H. H., Ayzenberg, O., Jacobi, J. J., & Laniado, S. (1980). Mitral valve prolapse in identical twins (Letter). *Archives of Internal Medicine, 140*, 1249

Sagawa, K. (1981). The end-systolic pressure-volume relation of the ventricle: Definition, modifications and clinical use (Editorial). *Circulation, 63*, 1223-1226.

Sakamoto, T. (1982). Prospective phonocardiographic study of mitral valve prolapse. In E. D. Dietrich (Ed.), *Noninvasive assessment of the cardiovascular system* (pp. 153-157). Bristol, England: John Wright.

Sakamoto, T. (1988). Mitral valve prolapse: Contributions of Japanese investigators. In C. F. Wooley & H. Boudoulas (Eds.), *Mitral valve prolapse and the mitral valve prolapse syndrome* (pp. 633-650). Mount Kisco, NY: Futura.

Salomon, J., Shah, P. M., & Heinle, R. A. (1975). Thoracic skeletal abnormalities in mitral valve prolapse. *American Journal of Cardiology, 36*, 32–36.

Sanders, J. S., Mark, A. L., & Ferguson, D. W. (1989). Importance of aortic baroreflex in regulation of
sympathetic responses during hypotension. *Circulation, 79*, 83–92.

Sanfillippo, A. J., Popovic, A. D., Harrigan, P. H., Handschumacher, M. D., Weyman, A. E., & Levine,
R. A. (1989). Two to five year echocardiographic follow-up of patients with mitral valve prolapse: Is
apical four-chamber view displacement a precursor of abnormality? (Abstract). *Journal of the American College of Cardiology, 13*, 226A.

Santos, A. D., Mathew, P. K., Hilal, A., & Wallace, W. A. (1981). Orthostatic hypotension: A commonly
unrecognized cause of symptoms in mitral valve prolapse. *American Journal of Medicine, 71*, 746–
750.

Savage, D. D. (1982). Mitral valve prolapse in the general population: 1. Epidemiologic features: The
Framingham study. *American Heart Journal, 106*, 571–586.

Savage, D. D., Devereux, R. B., Donahue, R., Joiner, G., Anderson, S. J., Rosen, R. A., Wilson, J.,
Kramer, R., Brown, W., Garrison, R., & Feinleib, M. (1982). Mitral valve prolapse in blacks. *Journal
of the National Medical Association, 74*, 895–900.

Savage, D. D., Devereux, R. B., & Garrison, R. J. (1983). Mitral valve prolapse in the general population: 2. Clinical features: The Framingham study. *American Heart Journal, 106*, 577–581.

Savage, D. D., Levy, D., Garrison, R. J., Castelli, W. P., Kligfield, P., Devereux, R. B., Anderson, S. J.,
Kannel, W. B., & Feinleib, M. (1983). Mitral valve prolapse in the general population: 3. Dysrhythmias: The Framingham study. *American Heart Journal, 106*, 582–586.

Scampardonis, G., Yang, S. S., Maranhao, V., Goldberg, H., & Gooch, A. S. (1973). Left ventricular
abnormalities in prolapsed mitral leaflet syndrome: Review of 87 cases. *Circulation, 48*, 287–297.

Schatz, I. J. (1986). *Orthostatic hypotension*. Philadelphia: F. A. Davis.

Scheele, W., Allen, H. N., Kraus, R., & Rubin, P. G. (1976). Familial prevalence and genetic transmission of mitral valve prolapse. *Circulation, 54*(Suppl. 3), 11.

Schrier, R. W. (1988). Pathogenesis of water and sodium retention in high-output and low-output cardiac
failure, nephrotic syndrome, cirrhosis and pregnancy. *New England Journal of Medicine, 319*, 1065–
1072.

Schutte, J. E., Gaffney, F. A., Blend, L., & Blomqvist, C. G. (1981). Distinctive anthropometric characteristics of women with mitral valve prolapse. *American Journal of Medicine, 71*, 533–538.

Sever, P. S. (1983). Plasma noradrenaline in autonomic failure. In R. Bannister (Ed.), *Autonomic failure*
(pp. 155–173). London: Oxford University Press.

Shappel, S. D., Orr, W., & Gunn, C. G. (1974). The ballooning posterior leaflet syndrome: Minnesota
Multiphasic Personality Inventory profiles in symptomatic and asymptomatic groups. *Chest, 66*, 690–
692.

Shear, M. K., Devereux, R. B., Kramer-Fox, R., Mann, J. J., & Frances, A. (1984). Low prevalence of
mitral valve prolapse in patients with panic disorder. *American Journal of Psychiatry, 141*, 302–303.

Sheehan, D. V. (1982). Panic and phobic disorders. *New England Journal of Medicine, 307*, 156–158.

Sheehan, D. V., Ballenger, J., & Jacobsen, G. (1980). Treatment of endogenous anxiety with phobic,
hysterical, and hypochondriacal symptoms. *Archives of General Psychiatry, 37*, 51–59.

Shepherd, J. T. (1981). Reflex control of the venous system in man. In A. G. B. Kovach, P. Sander, M., &
Kollai (Eds.), *Advances in physiological sciences: Cardiovascular physiology, neural control mechanisms* (pp. 247–252). New York: Pergamon Press.

Shrivastava, S., Guthrie, R. B., & Edwards, J. E. (1977). Prolapse of the mitral valve. *Modern Concepts
of Cardiovascular Disease, 46*, 57–62.

Shuckit, M. A. (1987). The diagnosis of generalized anxiety disorder and the hidden risk of treatment: An
overview. *Modern Medicine, 55*, 32–36.

Silman, A., J., Mitchell, P., & Locke, C. (1983). Hypertensive diet Rx: Is it the NA+ restriction that
actually lowers BP? *Lancet, 1*, 1179–1182.

Skelton, C. L. (1982). The heart and hyperthyroidism. *New England Journal of Medicine, 307*, 1206–
1207.

Skorecki, K. L. & Brenner, B. M. (1981). Body fluid homeostasis in man. *American Journal of Medicine,
70*, 77–88.

Skrabal, F., Kotanko, P., Meister, B., Doll, P., & Gruber, G. (1986). Up-regulation of alpha-2 adrenoreceptors and down-regulation of beta-2 adrenoreceptors by high-salt diet in normotensive men: Enhanced up-regulation of operative (alpha-2: beta-2) adrenoreceptor ratio predicts salt sensitivity. *Journal of Hypertension, 6*, 196–199.

Smalcelj, A., & Gibson, D. G. (1985). Relation between mitral valve closure and early systolic function of the left ventricle. *British Heart Journal, 53*, 436–442.

Smallridge, R. C., Goldman, M. H., Raines, K., Jones, S., & Van Nostrand, D. (1987). Rest and exercise left ventricular ejection fraction before and after therapy in young adults with hyperthyroidism and hypothyroidism. *American Journal of Cardiology, 60*, 929.

Spears, P. F., Koch, K. L., & Day, F. P. (1986). Chest pain associated with mitral valve prolapse. *Archives of Internal Medicine, 146*, 796–797.

Sprafkin, R. P., McCroskery, J. H., Lantinga, L. J., & Hills, N. (1984). Cardiovascular and psychological characteristics of patients with chest pain. *Behavioral Medicine Update, 6*, 11.

Stene, M., Panagiotis, N., Tuck, M. L., Sowers, J. R., Mayers, D., & Berg, G. (1980). Plasma norepinephrine levels are influenced by sodium intake, glucocorticoid administration, and circadian changes in normal man. *Journal of Clinical Endocrinology and Metabolism, 51*, 1340–1345.

Strahan, N. V., Murphy, E. A., Fortuin, N. J., Humphries, O., & Come, P. C. (1983). Inheritance of the mitral valve prolapse syndrome: Discussion of a three-dimensional penetrance model. *American Journal of Medicine, 74*, 967–973.

Stratton, J. R., Halter, J. B., Hallstrom, A. P., Caldwell, J. H., & Ritchie, J. L. (1983). Comparative plasma catecholamine and hemodynamic responses to handgrip, cold pressor and supine bicycle exercise testing in normal subjects. *Journal of the American College of Cardiology, 2*, 93–104.

Stratton, J. R., Preifer, M. A., Ritchie, J. E., & Halter, J. B. (1985). Hemodynamic effects of epinephrine: Concentration-effect study in humans. *Journal of Applied Physiology, 58*, 1199–1206.

Sullivan, J. M., & Ratts, T. E. (1988). Sodium sensitivity in human subjects: Hemodynamic and hormonal correlates. *Hypertension, 11*, 717–723.

Swartz, M. H., & Dack, S. (1982). Mitral valve prolapse syndrome. *Hospital Medicine, 11*, 49–64.

Tak, T., Gamage, N., Lin, S., Rahimtoola, S. H., & Chandraratna, P. A. N. (1987). Identification of textural differences of the mitral leaflets in subsets of patients with mitral valve prolapse. *American Journal of Cardiology, 60*, 917–919.

Takashita, S., & Ferrario, C. M. (1982). Altered neural control of cardiovascular function in sodium-depleted dogs. *Hypertension, 4*(Suppl. 4), 175–181.

Taylor, C. B., Telch, M. J., & Haavik, D. (1983). Ambulatory heart rate changes during panic attacks. *Journal of Psychiatric Research, 17*, 261–266.

Taylor, C. B., Skeikh, J., Agras, W. S., Roth, W. T., Margraf, J., Ehlers, A., Maddock, R. J., & Gossard, D. (1986). Ambulatory heart rate changes in patients with panic attacks. *American Journal of Psychiatry, 143*, 478–482.

Tebbe, U., Schicha, H., Neumann, P., Voth, E., Emrich, D., Neuhaus, K. L., & Kreuzer, H. (1985). Mitral valve prolapse in the ventriculogram: Scintigraphic, electrocardiographic and hemodynamic abnormalities. *Clinical Cardiology, 8*, 341–347.

Tei, C., Sakamaki, T., Shah, P. M., Meerbaum, S., Kondo, S., Shimoura, K., & Corday, E. (1983). Mitral valve prolapse in short-term experimental coronary occlusion: A possible mechanism of ischemic mitral regurgitation. *Circulation, 68*, 183–189.

Thase, M. E. (1981). The click-murmur syndrome and anxiety disorder (Letter to the editor). *Journal of the American Medical Association, 246*, 2156.

Thase, M. E. (1983, October–November). Mitral valve prolapse and anxiety. *CVP, 74*–78.

Thompson, W. P., & Levine, S. A. (1935). Systolic gallop rhythm: A clinical study. *New England Journal of Medicine, 213*, 1021–1025.

Tifft, C. P., & Chobanian, A. V. (1985). Evaluation and treatment of orthostatic hypotension. *Practical Cardiology, 11*, 103–117.

Tomaru, T., Uchida, Y., Mohri, N., Mori, W., Furuse, A., & Asano, K. (1987). Postinflammatory mitral and aortic valve prolapse: A clinical and pathological study. *Circulation, 76*, 68–76.

Tomaso, C. L., & Gardin, J. M. (1980). Mitral valve prolapse: Clinical perspectives. *Primary Cardiology, 6*, 65–69.

Tohmeh, J. F., & Cryer, P. E. (1980). Biphasic adrenergic modulation of beta adrenergic receptors in man: Agonist-induced early increment and late decrement in beta-adrenergic receptor number. *Journal of Clinical Investigation, 65*, 836–840.

Tompkins, E. H., Sturgis, C. C., & Wearn, J. T. (1919). Studies in epinephrine: 2. *Archives of Internal Medicine, 24*, 247–265.

Torgerson, S. (1983). Genetic factors in anxiety disorders. *Archives of General Psychiatry, 40*, 1085–1089.

Tresch, D. D., Siegel, R., Keelan, M. H., Gross, C. M., & Brooks, H. L. (1979). Mitral valve prolapse in the elderly patient. *Journal of the American Geriatric Society, 27*, 421–424.

Trevisan, M., Ostrow, D., Cooper, R., Liu, K., Sparks, S., Okonek, A., Stevens, E., Marquardt, J., & Stamler, J. (1981). Abnormal red blood cell ion transport and hypertension: The people's gas company study. *Hypertension, 5*, 363–367.

Triulzi, M., Gillam, L. D., Gentile, F., Newell, J. B., & Weymann, A. E. (1984). Normal adult cross-sectional echocardiographic values: Linear dimensions and chamber areas. *Echocardiography, 1*, 403–426.

Turkkan, J. S., Brady, J. V., & Harris, A. H. (1986). Animal studies of stressful interactions: A behavioral–physiological overview. In L. Goldberger & S. Breznitz (Eds.), *Handbook of stress: Theoretical and clinical aspects* (pp. 153–180). New York: Macmillan.

Tyrer, P. (1976). *The role of bodily feelings in anxiety*. London: Oxford University Press.

Tyrer, P. (1986). Central mechanisms in pathological anxiety. *Stress Medicine, 2*, 97–99.

Uhde, T. W., Boulenger, J. P., Post, R. M., Siever, L. J., Vittone, B. J., Jimerson, D. C., & Roy-Byrne, P. P. (1984). Fear and anxiety: Relationship to noradrenergic function. *Psychopathology, 17*(Suppl. 3), 8–23.

Uretsky, B. (1982). Does MVP cause nonspecific symptoms? *International Journal of Cardiology, 1*, 435–442.

Valdez, R. S., Rotta, J. A., & London, E. (1979). Evaluation of the echocardiogram as an epidemiology tool in an asymptomatic population. *Circulation, 60*, 921–929.

Van der Bel-Kahn, J., Duren, D. R., & Becker, A. E. (1985). Isolated mitral valve prolapse: Chordal architecture as an anatomic basis in older patients. *Journal of the American College of Cardiology, 5*, 1335–1340.

Van der Schoot, J. B., & Moran, N. C. (1965). An experimental evaluation of the reputed influence of thyroxine on the cardiovascular effects of catecholamines. *Journal of Pharmacological and Experimental Therapy, 149*, 336–345.

Venkatesh, A., Pauls, D. L., Crow, R., Noyes, R., Van Valkenburg, C., Martins, J. B., & Kerber, R. E. (1980). Mitral valve prolapse in anxiety neurosis (panic disorder). *American Heart Journal, 100*, 302–305.

Vlachakis, N. D., DeGuta, D., Mendlowitz, M., Antram, S., & Wolf, R. L. (1974). Hypertension and anxiety: A trial with epinephrine and norepinephrine infusion. *Mt. Sinai Journal of Medicine, 41*, 1615–1625.

Volpe, M., Lembo, G., Morganti, A., Condorelli, M., & Trimarco, B. (1988). Contribution of the renin-angiotensin system and of the sympathetic nervous system to blood pressure homeostasis during chronic restriction of sodium intake. *American Journal of Hypertension, 1*, 353–358.

Waller, B. F., Fanning, T. V., & Barker, B. (1985) Morphologic evidence in support of papillary muscle dysfunction as an element of mitral regurgitation in patients with floppy mitral valves: Morphologic analysis of 17 study patients and 15 control patients. *Journal of the American College of Cardiology, 5*, 504.

Waller, B. F., Moriarty, A. T., Eble, J. N., Davey, D. M., Hawley, D. A., & Pless, J. E. (1986). Etiology of pure tricuspid regurgitation based on annular circumference and leaflet area: Analysis of 45 necropsy patients with clinical and morphologic evidence of pure tricuspid regurgitation. *Journal of the American College of Cardiology, 7*, 1063–1074.

Waller, B. F., & Roberts, W. C. (1983). A high sensitivity and specificity of the M-mode echocardiogram in predicting mitral valve prolapse as the cause of pure mitral regurgitation: Analysis of 60 patients with operatively-excised floppy mitral valves. *Journal of the American College of Cardiology, 1*(Part 2), 608.

Walsh, P. N., Kansu, T. A., Corbett, J. J., Savino, P. J., Goldburgh, W. P், & Schatz, N. J. (1981). Platelets, thromboembolism and mitral valve prolapse. *Circulation, 63*, 552–559.

Wann, I. S., Grove, J. R., Hess, T. R., Glisch, L., Ptacin, M. J., Hughes, C. V., & Gross, C. M. (1983). Prevalence of mitral prolapse by two dimensional echocardiography in healthy young women. *British Heart Journal, 49*, 334–340.

Watson, R. D. S., Esler, M. D., & Leonard, P. (1984). Influence of variations in dietary sodium intake on biochemical indices of sympathetic activity in normal man. *Clinical Experimental Pharmacology and Physiology, 11*, 163–170.

Wearn, J., & Sturgis, C. (1919). Studies on epinephrine: Effects of the injection of epinephrine in soldiers with "irritable heart." *Archives of Internal Medicine, 24*, 247–268.

Wei, J. Y., & Fortuin, N. J. (1981). Diastolic sounds and murmurs associated with mitral valve prolapse. *Circulation, 63*, 559–564.

Weinstein, G., Allen, G., & Ford, C. V. (1982). Anxiety and mitral valve prolapse syndrome. *Journal of Clinical Psychiatry, 43*, 33–34.

Weiss, A. N., Mimbs, J. W., Ludbrook, P. A., & Sobel, B. E. (1975). Echocardiographic detection of mitral valve prolapse: Exclusion of false positive diagnosis and determination of inheritance. *Circulation, 52,* 1091–1096.

Weissman, N., Shear, M. K., Kramer-Fox, R., & Devereux, R. B. (1987). Contrasting patterns of autonomic dysfunction in patients with mitral valve prolapse and panic attacks. *American Journal of Medicine, 82,* 880–888.

Wigle, E. D., Rakowski, H., & Ranganathan, N. (1976). Mitral valve prolapse. *Annual Review of Medicine, 17,* 165–180.

Wilcken, D. E. L., & Hickey, A. J. (1986). The lifetime risk of mitral valve prolapse developing severe mitral regurgitation. *Circulation, 74*(Part 2), 453.

Wilcken, D. E. L., & Hickey, A. J. (1988). Lifetime risk for patients with mitral valve prolapse of developing severe valve regurgitation requiring surgery. *Circulation, 78,* 10–14.

Wilkin, T. (1983). Hyperthyroidism and the heart. *British Medical Journal, 281,* 1459–1460.

Wilkins, M. R., Gammage, M. D., Bun Tan, L., Kendall, M. J., Lote, C. J., Weissberg, P. L., & Littler, W. A. (1986). Effect of lower-body positive pressure on atrial dimension and plasma atrial natriuretic peptide concentration. *Journal of Hypertension, 4*(Suppl. 6), 500–502.

Williams, J. C. (1836). *Practical observations on nervous and sympathetic palpitation of the heart.* London: Lingman, Rees, Orme, Browne.

Williams, L. T., Lefkowitz, R. J., Watanabe, A. M., Hathaway, D. R., & Besch, J. R. (1977). Thyroid hormone regulation of β-adrenergic receptor number. *Journal of Biological Chemistry, 252,* 2787–2789.

Winkle, R. A., Lopes, M. G., Fitzgerald, J. W., Goodman, D. J., Schroeder, J. S., & Harrison, D. C. (1975). Arrhythmias in patients with mitral valve prolapse. *Circulation, 52,* 73–81.

Wood, P. (1941). DaCosta's syndrome. *British Medical Journal, 1,* 767–772.

Woods, S. W. (1987). Situational panic attacks: Behavioral physiologic, and biochemical characterization. *Archives of General Psychiatry, 44,* 365–375.

Wooley, C. F. (1976). Where are the diseases of yesteryear? DaCosta's syndrome, soldiers's heart, the effort syndrome? *Circulation, 53,* 749–751.

Wooley, C. F. (1983). The mitral valve prolapse syndrome. *Hospital Practice, 18,* 163–174.

Wooley, C. F., & Boudoulas, H. (1985). Mitral valve prolapse: A basis for diagnostic classification. In J. V. Harris & R. P. Lewis (Eds.), *Diagnostic procedures in cardiology: A clinician's guide* (p. 437). Chicago: Year Book Medical Publishers.

Wooley, C. F., & Boudoulas, H. (1988). Mitral valve prolapse: A classification, In H. Boudoulas & C. F. Wooley (Eds.), *Mitral valve prolapse and the mitral valve prolapse syndrome.* Mount Kisco, NY: Futura.

Wright, J. T., (1988). Profile of systemic hypertension in black patients. *American Journal of Cardiology, 61,* 41H–45H.

Wynne, J. (1984). Mitral valve prolapse. *New England Journal of Medicine, 214,* 577–578.

Yeragani, V. K., Pohl, R., Balon, R., Weinberg, P., Berchou, R., & Rainey, J. M. (1987). Preinfusion anxiety predicts lactate-induced panic attacks in normal controls. *Psychosomatic Medicine, 49,* 383–389.

Zema, M. J., Chiaramida, S., DeFilipp, G. J., Goldman, M. A., & Pizzarello, R. A. (1982). Somatotype and idiopathic mitral valve prolapse. *Cathet Cardiovascular Diagnosis, 8,* 105–111.

Zullo, M. A., Devereux, R. B., Kramer-Fox, R., Lutas, E. M., & Brown, T. (1985). Mitral valve prolapse and hyperthyroidism: Effect of patient selection. *American Heart Journal, 110,* 977–982.

14

The Relationship of Anxiety and Cardiovascular Reactivity

Marcia M. Ward

Anxiety is presumed by many to be reliably related to cardiovascular reactivity. It is widely assumed that individuals who are anxious have elevated blood pressure and heart rate levels at rest in addition to increased cardiovascular reactivity to stressful or challenging situations. The purpose of this chapter is to examine these widely held beliefs. To do so I review the studies of the relationship between anxiety and cardiovascular reactivity in normal subjects and in patients with anxiety disorders. Unfortunately, much of this literature suffers from methodological weaknesses. Only studies that employed adequate control groups are described, and the most pervasive difficulties in these studies are discussed. Finally, the conclusions that can be drawn from this body of research are presented.

DEFINITIONS

Anxiety

In chapter 1 of this volume, McReynolds defines anxiety as an emotion characterized by intense inner feelings of distress and anguish, and by associated behavioral and physiological features. The experience of anxiety varies widely. Anxiety may be a momentary discomfort in anticipation of a physically or psychologically uncomfortable situation, such as waiting for a dental appointment. At the other end of the continuum, anxiety can be pathologic in intensity and lead to disabling behavior, such as severe agoraphobia in which the afflicted individual refuses to leave home. The diagnostic criteria of pathologic anxiety are presented in a later section, and the terms used to describe more normal types of anxiety are covered here.

It is important to distinguish between episodic bouts of anxiety and a chronic anxiety condition. According to a widely accepted classification, these two kinds of anxiety are called state and trait anxiety (see chap. 4). In general terms, state anxiety is the level of anxiety at a given point in time, whereas trait anxiety is an individual's general level of anxiety. More specifically, state anxiety captures the concept of changing levels of anxiety. Anxiety levels can change frequently, even momentarily, as a function of changing circumstances. State anxiety includes the notion of "reac-

Preparation of this chapter was supported by Grant HL41635 from the National Heart, Lung, and Blood Institute.

tive" anxiety, an emotional state that results from a specific stimulus or environmental cue, such as being evaluated or encountering a new situation. Measures of state anxiety are expected to vary over time.

Trait anxiety is the relatively stable tendency of an individual to manifest anxiety in a range of stressful situations. An individual with elevated trait anxiety is likely to experience greater than normal state anxiety in a broad range of situations, especially those involving the possibility of failure and loss of self-esteem. Thus trait anxiety is conceptualized both as a summary of past states and as a reflection of anxiety proneness to current and future situations.

Cardiovascular Reactivity

Cardiovascular reactivity has received considerable attention lately because it is thought by some to be related to coronary heart disease, hypertension, and the development or progression of atherosclerosis (Clarkson, Manuck, & Kaplan, 1986; Manuck & Krantz, 1986). However, cardiovascular reactivity usually represents normal homeostatic adaptations to challenge (Rosenman & Ward, 1988). Cardiovascular reactivity is most frequently measured in terms of changes in heart rate, blood pressure, and peripheral blood flow. Reactivity is defined as the deviation of a physiological response parameter from a comparison or control value that results from an individual's response to a discrete, environmental stimulus. It is measured in terms of absolute change from baseline or changes adjusted for baseline (Krantz & Manuck, 1984).

STUDIES OF ANXIETY AND CARDIOVASCULAR REACTIVITY IN NORMAL SUBJECTS

Studies of the relationship between anxiety and cardiovascular reactivity in normal subjects fall into two categories—those evaluating state anxiety responses to laboratory challenges and those evaluating the relationship between the magnitude of cardiovascular response and the degree of trait anxiety. State anxiety is assessed in the laboratory through the presentation of stimuli called *stressors*. These stressors may be psychologically, cognitively, or physically challenging. Common psychological stressors include presenting a speech on an ego-threatening topic or being interviewed about an area of intrapersonal conflict. Typical cognitive stressors involve arithmetic calculations, pattern recognition, or anagram solution. Physical stressors frequently presented in the laboratory include handgrip, cold pressor, or treadmill testing.

Originally it was believed that any challenge to the organism was met with arousal and increases in all cardiovascular measures. Ax (1953) was one of the first who attempted to differentiate the cardiovascular response to different emotional states. He conducted a classic experiment provoking fear and anger in subjects and found that increased diastolic blood pressure and decreased heart rate were more likely to occur during anger than during fear. More recent research has shown that certain measures, particularly heart rate and blood flow, show a differentiation of responses determined by stimulus characteristics. Lacey's (1967) pioneering work differentiated heart rate responses by showing that environmental intake (attention to external events) produces decreases in heart rate, whereas sensory rejection (involvement in mental work) produces increases in heart rate. Lacey and colleagues (Lacey, Bateman, & VanLehn, 1953) also introduced the concept of response specificity, according to which individuals have a specific response pattern that is consistent across time and across situations. For example, the predominant response pattern under challenge would define some individuals as heart rate responders and others as electrodermal responders.

There is an overwhelming body of literature on cardiovascular responses to laboratory stressors. It is often assumed that these laboratory stressors increase state anxiety, but this assumption is rarely verified. In these studies state anxiety is conceptualized to be synonymous with stress and arousal rather than being viewed as a distinct emotion. Because of the complexity of cardiovascular responses and homeostatic mechanisms, and the lack of specificity of the concept of state anxiety, it is impossible to define one pattern of cardiovascular responses that is indicative of state anxiety.

A more fruitful approach is to examine the relationship between trait anxiety and cardiovascular reactivity. Trait anxiety studied in this manner constitutes an "individual difference." Numerous individual differences have been related to the degree of cardiovascular reactivity, including gender, age, anthropometry, and family history of hypertension. Individual differences are identified and studied as sources of variability in a response pattern. As an individual difference, anxiety's relationship to cardiovascular reactivity is most frequently studied in one of three ways. One way is to compare patients with anxiety disorders to a control group of normal individuals. A second way is to administer a measure of general or trait anxiety to normal individuals and then use either a median split or extreme scores to construct two groups—those who have high anxiety scores and those who have low anxiety scores. The third way is to do a correlational study of anxiety and reactivity to investigate whether the degree of cardiovascular reactivity is related to an anxiety scale score.

Studies Using Measures of General Trait Anxiety

Three studies using the correlational approach failed to find a relationship between trait anxiety and any measure of cardiovascular reactivity. In particular, trait anxiety, as defined by the State–Trait Anxiety Inventory (STAI), was not related to heart rate during digit recall under threat of shock or no shock (Houston, 1977); to heart rate change immediately after three minutes of isometric handgrip exercise (Sullivan et al., 1981); or to blood pressure reactivity to the Stroop color–word task, a video game, or a distressing movie (Steptoe, Melville, & Ross, 1984). The same conclusion—that cardiovascular reactivity is not related to trait anxiety—can be drawn from studies using group analysis to compare cardiovascular responses in subjects who score high versus those who score low on a measure of general anxiety.

Glass and colleagues (Glass, Lake, Contrada, Kehoe, & Erlanger, 1983) did not find a relationship between general anxiety, as measured by the Cattell 16-PF Questionnaire, and cardiovascular responses across a mental arithmetic task and a modified Stroop task. Balshan (1962) did not find a difference between subjects with high and low anxiety, as defined by the Freeman Manifest Anxiety Scale and the Taylor Manifest Anxiety Scale, and heart rate responses to a white noise. A relationship between general anxiety, as measured by the Taylor Manifest Anxiety Scale, and heart rate responses during a difficult task following ego-threatening instructions shock threat instructions, or neutral instructions was not found (Hodges, 1968). Likewise, Smith, Houston, and Zurawski (1984) did not find a relationship between trait anxiety, as measured by the STAI, and heart rate or finger pulse volume responses either in anticipation of or during verbal responses to videotaped questions under either evaluative threat or nonthreat conditions.

In contrast to these findings, Dykman, Ackerman, Galbrecht, and Reese (1963) found that highly anxious subjects, as defined by the Taylor Manifest Anxiety Scale, by self-report, or by a modified Taylor scale that ruled out defensiveness, showed less heart rate reactivity to a series of tasks, a digit-recall exercise, and a series of questions. Stamps, Fehr, and Lewis (1979) found that both high- and low-anxious subjects exhibited heart rate acceleration followed by deceleration, but low-anxious subjects, as defined by the STAI, showed a shorter latency deceleration and maintained heart rate deceleration over a longer period following the warning signal and showed a dramatic decelerative swing following response during a warned reaction time task. Matthews, Manuck, and Saab (1986) found that high-anxious adolescents, as defined by the STAI, showed higher levels of systolic blood pressure prior to giving a public speech and higher levels of heart rate prior to and after giving a public speech than did low-anxious adolescents. No group differences in diastolic blood pressure were found. In summary, the study by Matthews et al. (1986) using a real-life stressor, is the only study to convincingly demonstrate differences between high- and low-trait anxious individuals in cardiovascular reactivity.

Studies Using Anxiety-Specific Trait Measures

A number of studies have investigated the relationship between anxiety and cardio-vascular reactivity in subjects who are anxious in specific situations. For example, a typical paradigm tests subjects who score high and low on a measure of social anxiety during a social situation such as giving a speech to a live audience. The most frequently studied situation-specific anxieties are test anxiety, social anxiety, performance anxiety, and specific phobias.

Test Anxiety

Glass et al. (1983) found a relationship between anxiety, as measured by the Mandler-Sarason Test Anxiety Questionnaire, and systolic blood pressure, diastolic blood pressure, and heart rate responses to a mental arithmetic task and a modified Stroop task. Judson and Gelber (1965) found that subjects judged to have high test anxiety by the Mandler-Sarason Test Anxiety Questionnaire showed higher heart rate upon initial exposure to a learning task. Harleston, Smith, and Arey (1965) found that subjects with high test anxiety showed greater heart rate increases in response to an anagram-solving task than did subjects with low test anxiety. Beidel (1988) found that children with high test anxiety (measured by the Test Anxiety Scale for Children) showed greater increases in heart rate, but not systolic or diastolic blood pressure, during two social-evaluation tasks (vocabulary test and oral reading). Although both groups showed an initial heart rate acceleration to the tasks, the highly anxious children maintained the higher heart rate level during the seven-minute task, whereas the low-anxious children showed rapid heart rate habituation that declined to baseline levels by the end of the task. In a study by Montgomery (1977), during a problem-solving task under evaluative stress conditions, highly anxious subjects, as defined by the Test Anxiety Scale, showed greater and longer periods of heart rate acceleration and less deceleration than did low-anxious subjects.

In contrast to these positive findings, Holroyd, Westbrook, Wolf, and Badhorn (1978) tested subjects both high and low in test anxiety (as defined by the Test

Anxiety Scale) and found no differences between groups in heart rate responses to a modified Stroop test or difficult anagrams. Smith et al. (1984) did not find a relationship between Fear of Negative Evaluation Scale scores and heart rate or finger pulse volume responses either in anticipation of or during verbal responses to videotaped questions under either evaluative threatening or nonthreatening conditions. Orlebeke and Van Doornen (1977) found no difference between high- and low-anxious subjects, as defined by the Mandler–Sarason Test Anxiety Questionnaire and the Maudsley Personality Inventory, in the heart rate level preceding either warned or unwarned unpleasant tones, although there was a trend for decreased initial acceleration in the high-anxious subjects.

Social Anxiety

Lykken, Macindoe, and Tellegen (1972) presented a series of warned and unwarned shocks to high- and low-anxious subjects who were identified by the Activity Preference Questionnaire. When unwarned, high-anxious subjects showed higher heart rate levels during the shock. When warned, low-anxious subjects showed a larger anticipatory heart rate acceleration and a smaller post-shock acceleration. The researchers suggested that low-anxious subjects may be better able to use cardiac acceleration adaptively to inhibit sensory input. Knight and Borden (1979) found a relationship between social anxiety (as measured by the Activity Preference Questionnaire) and finger pulse volume response in anticipation of a verbal task involving social evaluation. However, they found no relationship between social anxiety and finger pulse volume response during instructions or during the task, or for heart rate during any phase of the study.

Turner, Beidel, and Larkin (1986) found that socially anxious individuals recruited either from a clinic or through a questionnaire showed significantly higher systolic blood pressure levels than did normal individuals during an impromptu speech, but not during two role playing interactions. There were no differences in diastolic blood pressure or heart rate. Borkovek, Stone, O'Brien, and Kaloupek (1974) found that socially anxious men exhibited higher heart rate during instruction, anticipation, and interaction with a female confederate. Beidel, Turner, and Dancu (1985) found that socially anxious subjects, as defined by the Social Avoidance and Distress Scale, the Fear of Negative Evaluation Scale, and the STAI, showed greater increases in systolic blood pressure and heart rate during an opposite-sex social interaction and greater systolic blood pressure responses during an impromptu speech than did subjects who were not socially anxious. No differences between groups were observed for diastolic blood pressure or during a same-sex social interaction, possibly because of the subject's prior contact with the same-sex confederate. These studies each give partial support for a relationship between cardiovascular reactivity and social anxiety, but the finding of a specific stimulus for eliciting exaggerated responses in highly anxious individuals is unreliable.

Performance Anxiety

Dimberg, Fredrikson, and Lundquist (1986) found that high-anxious subjects, as identified by the Public Report of Confidence as a Speaker Questionnaire, showed greater heart rate deceleration at the first presentation of social stimuli (i.e., a picture of people's faces) than did low-anxious subjects, but the groups did not differ in heart rate response across 20 visual presentations of either social stimuli or neutral stimuli. Giesen and McGlynn (1977) found that high-anxious subjects, also identified by the

Public Report of Confidence as a Speaker Questionnaire, showed greater heart rate reactivity in response to imagining a neutral scene and imagining giving a speech. However, in contrast to expectations, high-anxious subjects responded more to imagining the neutral scene, and low-anxious subjects responded more to imagining giving a speech.

Tremayne and Barry (1988) studied elite gymnasts and found that high-anxious subjects, as defined by the Sports Competition Anxiety Test and the Marlow-Crowne Social Desirability Scale, showed greater initial heart rate deceleration followed by greater heart rate acceleration to imagery (i.e., mentally rehearsing their competitive routine) than did low-anxious subjects. These results are interpreted to mean that high-anxious gymnasts initially register and then cognitively process the stimuli more than do low-anxious gymnasts.

Specific Phobias

In several studies individuals who did not have elevated anxiety, except for phobic anxiety to a specific stimulus, were tested. For example, Hare (1973) and Hare and Blevings (1975) found that spider phobics responded to spider slides with defense responses, whereas subjects without the phobia did not. The defense response is elicited at higher levels of stimulus intensity than is the orienting response and is thought to represent decreased processing or motivated inattention to stimuli. The defense response is characterized by an initial heart rate acceleration, followed by a deceleration and then another acceleration, all within 10 to 15 seconds. Unlike the orienting response, the defense response exhibits little habituation and may even increase with repeated exposure.

Klorman, Wiesenfeld, and Austin (1975) showed slides of people that were neutral, incongruous, or mutilated to subjects who scored high and low in fear on the Mutilation Questionnaire. The high-scoring group showed heart rate acceleration (indicative of a defense response) to the mutilation slides, whereas the low-scoring group showed heart rate deceleration (indicative of an orienting response). The groups did not differ in heart rate responses to the other slides; both groups showed deceleration to the incongruous slides and, unexpectedly, acceleration to the neutral slides. Thus increased cardiovascular reactivity in stimulus-specific anxious individuals occurs periodically but unreliably to laboratory stressors that mimic the specific anxiety-triggering stimulus.

STUDIES OF CARDIOVASCULAR REACTIVITY IN PATIENTS WITH GENERALIZED ANXIETY DISORDER

Classification of Anxiety Disorders

Psychiatry employs a carefully defined system of diagnosis of psychopathologies, which is laid out in a reference book entitled the *Diagnostic and Statistical Manual of Mental Disorders* (DSM-III-R), which is currently in its third edition (American Psychiatric Association, 1987). The DSM-III classifies anxiety disorders into phobic disorders, panic disorder, generalized anxiety disorder (GAD), obsessive–compulsive disorder, and posttraumatic stress disorder. A brief summary of the DSM-III-R descriptions of each of these clinical disorders follows.

Phobic disorders feature a persistent and irrational fear of a specific object, activity, or situation. This fear leads to a compelling desire to avoid certain situations, and this desire interferes with normal functioning. The phobic disorders are subdivided into three types: agoraphobia, social phobia, and simple phobia. Agoraphobia is a marked fear of being alone or in public places from which escape might be difficult or help not available. Social phobia is a marked fear of situations in which the individual is exposed to possible scrutiny by others and fears embarrassment. Simple phobia is a marked fear other than agoraphobia or social phobia, such as fear of insects, spiders, snakes, heights, and closed spaces.

Panic disorder is manifested by the sudden onset of intense apprehension, fear, or terror, and feelings of impending doom. The symptoms include dizziness, faintness, tingling, sweating, trembling, smothering sensations, chest pains, palpitations, and fear of dying or doom. GAD is marked by a generalized, persistent anxiety manifested by motor tension, autonomic hyperactivity, and vigilance and scanning. Obsessive–compulsive disorders feature either recurrent, persistent thoughts that invade consciousness (obsessive) or repetitive, ritualistic behaviors that are senseless but do provide a release of tension (compulsions).

Finally, posttraumatic stress disorder features symptoms such as reexperiencing the traumatic events and numbing of responsiveness to the outside world that follow a traumatic and unusual event (e.g., rape, war, earthquake, or plane crash).

Baseline Levels of Cardiovascular Reactivity and the Orienting Response

Researchers have not agreed on whether normal control subjects and patients with GAD differ in baseline levels of cardiovascular measures. Anxiety patients have been found to exhibit significantly elevated heart rate levels (Bond, James & Lader, 1974; Kelly, 1966, 1980; Kelly, Brown, & Shaffer, 1970; Tan, 1964; White & Gildea, 1937; Wing, 1964), blood pressure levels (Goldstein, 1964; Kelly, 1980), forearm blood flow levels (Brierley, 1969; Kelly, 1966, 1980; Kelly et al., 1970; Kelly & Walter, 1969), and decreased pulse volume (Ackner, 1956) in a number of studies, whereas other researchers have not found any differences (Harper, Gurney, Savage, & Roth, 1965; Hart, 1974; Mathew, Ho, Francis, Taylor, & Weinman, 1982; Mathew & Wilson, 1986).

The orienting response paradigm has been frequently employed in psychophysiological assessments of patient populations. In normal individuals, the orienting response is a highly consistent pattern of central and autonomic nervous system changes. It is elicited by the presentation of an attention-arousing novel stimulus, such as a loud tone. In addition to the response to the first presentation, the habituation of responses to subsequent presentations is of interest. A few researchers have examined the cardiovascular component of the orienting response in patients with GAD and compared it to that found in normal individuals. The typical pattern for normal individuals is a marked, momentary decrease in heart rate that occurs for the first few stimulus presentations. The heart rate deceleration quickly habituates if the stimulus has no signal value—meaning that the subject recognizes that he or she is not required to respond in any way.

Hart (1974) found that anxious patients did not show an initial decelerative pattern in the heart rate response to a series of low-intensity tones that was evident for normal control subjects. Thus the anxious subjects appeared to be more prone to respond with a heart rate pattern characteristic of the defense response. However, Tan (1964) found no differences between a mixed group of anxious patients and normal control subjects in the occurrence or habituation of the heart rate orienting response. Goldstein (1964) found no differences between anxious patients and control subjects in heart rate or blood pressure responses to the single presentation of white noise.

Although there are few studies of cardiovascular measures, a sizable body of studies of the orienting response in patients with GAD across other central and autonomic response systems generally indicate that these patients show a pattern that includes a decreased response to the initial stimulus presentations and a decreased habituation rate to later presentations. Lader and Mathews (1968) have developed a theory of anxiety states based on the idea that patients with GAD show impaired ability to habituate. They hypothesize that if an individual who has a slow habituation rate (supposedly a genetic trait) is exposed to repeated environmental stimuli, the inability to habituate will lead to a continuous state of activation.

Reactions to Stress

It has been hypothesized that patients with GAD show an exaggerated response to stress. However, there have been few studies that adequately test this hypothesis. White and Gildea (1937) found that patients with GAD had larger heart rate responses to the cold pressor test than did normal control subjects. Malmo and Shagass (1952) found that patients with GAD showed increased cardiovascular reactivity to thermal pain, visual discrimination, and mirror drawing and that this response continued to increase when habituation was shown by normal control subjects. In contrast, Wing (1964) found that patients with GAD and normal control subjects did not differ in cardiovascular reactivity to a color naming task. Brierley (1969) found that agoraphobics showed no forearm blood flow response to loud sounds, whereas normal control subjects showed a large response that rapidly habituated. Harper et al. (1965) found no difference in forearm blood flow responses to mental arithmetic between patients with GAD and normal control subjects.

Kelly and colleagues (Kelly, 1966, 1980; Kelly et al., 1970; Kelly & Walter, 1969) showed in a number of studies that patients with GAD exhibited decreased heart rate, blood pressure, and forearm blood flow reactivity to a mental arithmetic task. No correction was made for large differences in baseline levels between patients with GAD and control subjects in the earlier studies (Kelly, 1966; Kelly & Walter, 1969), but similar results were found when cardiovascular reactivity was adjusted for baseline levels in a later study (Kelly et al., 1970). Kelly et al. suggested that the state of persistent physiological arousal in the patients with GAD produced continuously elevated baseline levels even at rest so that the additional stress of mental arithmetic had less effect on them than on relaxed normal control subjects.

One tremendous difficulty in conducting studies of reactivity with patients who have GAD is eliminating the arousal induced by the testing situation. The typical psychophysiological laboratory testing situation produces fears of evaluation, test anxiety, and damage to ego strength, along with fear that one is trapped and cannot escape. The discomfort produced by the laboratory setting may be so great that, in comparison, most typical psychophysiological tasks (i.e., the orienting response paradigm, reaction-time tasks, and various cognitive performance tests) meant to be challenging or stressful are relatively benign. It is conceivable that studies of stress reactions in these situations could produce such elevated baseline levels that ceiling effects would produce diminished cardiovascular responses compared to those of control subjects.

STUDIES OF CARDIOVASCULAR REACTIVITY IN PATIENTS WITH PANIC DISORDER

Panic disorder has been intensively studied over the past few years as a result of the discovery by Pitts and McClure (1967) that lactate infusion provoked panic attacks in susceptible individuals. This laboratory model of panic attack permitted a wide range of physiological and biochemical effects of panic attack to be documented. The cardiovascular responses to lactate infusion and other panic-inducing drugs, strictly speaking, is a form of cardiovascular reactivity. However, because the nature of the stimulus is unlike that used in any other studies of anxiety and cardiovascular reactivity, this body of research is not reviewed in detail here. Instead, the reader is referred to Margraf, Ehlers, and Roth (1986) and to chapter 3 of this volume for a review of panicogenic syndrome.

Baseline Levels of Cardiovascular Reactivity

A number of researchers have investigated whether patients with panic disorder differ from normal control subjects in baseline levels of blood pressure and heart rate. Unfortunately, in most of these studies resting cardiovascular measures were collected immediately preceding infusion of lactate or some other substance known to trigger panic attack. These studies have shown patients with panic disorder to have elevated heart rate (Gorman et al., 1988; Kelly, Mitchell-Heggs, & Sherman, 1971; Liebowitz et al., 1983; Rainey et al., 1984), blood pressure (Cowley, Hyde, Dager, & Dunner, 1987; Gorman et al., 1988; Liebowitz et al., 1983), and forearm blood flow (Kelly et al., 1971).

However, Ehlers et al. (1986) discussed the methodological weakness of lactate infusion studies and questioned whether resting cardiovascular measures were significantly elevated immediately preceding infusion because the subjects were aware that the infused substance was known to produce panic attacks. They hypothesized that patients with panic disorder may have anticipated the discomfort of an induced panic attack and thus showed anticipatory increases in heart rate and blood pressure. In fact, patients experienced significantly higher heart rate and lower skin temperature before or while being infused with placebo (Freedman, Ianni, Ettedgui, Pohl, & Rainey, 1984) or clonidine (Charney & Heninger, 1986), and heart rate differences between patients and control subjects, although present, were less marked when patients were certain they would not receive lactate infusions (Liebowitz et al., 1985). Ehlers et al. (1986) controlled for expectancy by having subjects participate in a baseline session 4 days prior to lactate infusion. However, even under these controlled conditions, patients had nearly significantly higher systolic blood pressure and heart rate than did normal control subjects.

Cameron, Lee, Curtis, and McCann (1987) found no differences between patients with panic disorder and normal control subjects in systolic blood pressure, diastolic blood pressure, or heart rate measured every 4 hours during a day-long clinic bed rest. And Freedman, Ianni, Ettedgui, and Puthezhath (1985), using ambulatory monitoring, found no difference between patients and control subjects in average daytime levels of finger temperature or heart rate or patterns of variation. In summary, these studies generally indicate that baseline cardiovascular measures are elevated in patients with panic disorder prior to infusion with a panicogenic substance. But patients appear to have normal baseline blood pressure and heart rate levels when the resting measures are taken in a manner that eliminates anticipatory anxiety.

Reactions to Laboratory Stressors

Panic disorder patients and normal controls have been compared on cardiovascular responses to a number of laboratory challenges and the majority of studies have shown no differences between these two groups. In particular, Nesse, Cameron, Curtis, McCann, and Huber-Smith (1984) found no difference between patients and control subjects in blood pressure and heart rate reactivity to standing. Roth et al. (1986) found no differences between the two groups in heart rate reactivity to an orienting sequence. Kelly et al. (1971) found no difference between groups in heart rate or forearm blood flow values during mental arithmetic following a lactate infusion. Grunhaus, Gloger, Birmacher, Palmer, and Ben-David (1983) found no differences in systolic blood pressure or diastolic blood pressure reactivity to the cold pressor test in patients with panic disorder and control subjects. Taylor and colleagues (Taylor et al., 1986) found no difference between groups in baseline or maximum heart rate during a treadmill test.

In contrast, Ehlers, Margraf, Roth, Taylor, and Birbaumer et al. (1988) found that normal control subjects showed a significant decrease in systolic blood pressure, diastolic blood pressure, and heart rate during false heart rate feedback, but panic disorder patients showed no change. And Gaffney, Fenton, Lane, and Lake (1988) found that patients with panic disorder had significantly lower maximal heart rate and significantly higher mean systolic blood pressure in response to maximal exercise. However, rather than being a test of reactivity to a physical stressor, this challenge indicated that patients with panic disorder have a significantly lower level of fitness. Thus, taken together, these studies reliably failed to uncover differences between patients with panic disorder and normal control subjects in cardiovascular responses across a range of laboratory challenges.

Reactivity to Phobic Situations

In addition to studies of cardiovascular reactivity to standard laboratory stressors, blood pressure and heart rate responses have been evaluated while panic disorder patients were exposed to phobic situations. Most studies have been conducted on agoraphobics who typically experienced panic disorders while in public places, such as supermarkets, cafeterias, and shopping malls. Both Roth et al. (1986) and Holden and Barlow (1986) found that agoraphobics with panic disorder showed significantly higher heart rate levels than did control subjects at baseline and during a walk through a public place, but their degree of heart rate reactivity did not differ from normal control subjects. In contrast, Woods, Charney, McPherson, Gradman, and Heninger (1987) found that panic disorder patients showed significantly greater heart rate reactivity, but not systolic blood pressure or diastolic blood pressure reactivity, than did normal control subjects during exposure to a phobic situation.

PROBLEMS IN STUDIES OF ANXIETY
AND CARDIOVASCULAR REACTIVITY

The reviews of studies of the relationship of trait anxiety to cardiovascular reactivity in normal subjects, psychiatric populations, and patients with panic disorder do not lead to easy conclusions. The relationship between a characteristic such as anxiety and cardiovascular reactivity is rarely straightforward. Many factors are at play in the relationship, including the context of testing (particularly how threatening it is) and the interaction of cognitive and physiological variables (particularly how attentive the subject is to cardiovascular responses). Individual difference variables, such as anxiety, need to be studied in great detail. Unfortunately, the body of studies on the relationship of anxiety to cardiovascular reactivity is wrought with theoretical and methodological problems.

Gale and Edwards (1986) provided a scathing review of such studies. They stated that most of these studies "merely select an 'off-the-rack' self-report measure of trait anxiety, choose an equally 'off-the-rack' physiological index, and subject the experimental population to an 'off-the-rack' and ecologically meaningless laboratory test" (p. 468). The difficulties with this body of research fall into several general categories. These include problems in the diagnosis of clinic populations, problems with self-report measures of anxiety, problems in the subject's ability to recognize physiological correlates of anxiety, problems in choosing the correct test situation, and problems in obtaining resting baseline measures.

Diagnosing Clinical Populations

Although the DSM-III-R is immensely helpful in providing a common diagnostic scheme for clinical disorders, it is not infallible when used as a research tool. For example, Zahn (1986) pointed out that the DSM-III criteria for diagnosing GAD recognizes that increased cardiovascular reactivity is not always a measure of anxiety. The DSM-III did so by giving four categories of symptoms for this disorder but requiring that only three of the symptom categories be met. The DSM-III lists 18 symptoms and requires that at least 6 be present. Consequently, in both cases a positive diagnosis of GAD can be made whether autonomic hyperactivity is present or not. This presents a problem in reviewing the studies of cardiovascular reactivity in patients with these disorders, because some samples may include a high percentage of patients with heightened cardiovascular arousal, whereas other samples have few such individuals. An even greater problem exists in the older studies that predated the DSM classification scheme. These early studies identified patients in a number of ways, and it is unclear how homogeneous the patient groups are. In particular, no mention is made of the presence of concomitant psychoses in some studies, and others included patients who were predominantly anxious but who also showed considerable depression.

Self-Report Measures of Anxiety

Lamb (1978) pointed out that self-report measures of trait anxiety have been criticized because their questions have different meanings to different people, they are affected by the individual's response set, and individuals have difficulty accurately reporting how they feel. Sarason (1960) suggested that anxiety scales may be measuring a number of individual characteristics other than anxiety, such as the extent to which individuals (a) are willing to admit to certain feelings; (b) attribute "bad" characteristics to themselves; (c) are frank and open; or (d) are particularly perceptive of their own reactions. Sarason (1960) pointed out that several anxiety scales correlate very highly and negatively with test-taking attitude, measures of defensiveness, and social desirability tendencies.

Measures of general anxiety do not distinguish subgroups of anxiety-prone individuals, such as those who experience test anxiety, or fear of physical harm, or fear of other people. Thus studies that use a general measure of trait anxiety will identify high-scoring groups of subjects, but the predominant type of anxiety represented in these groups may vary from study to study. Measures of situation-specific anxiety are better predictors of cardiovascular reactivity for specific situations than are more general measures. For example, Glass et al. (1983) did not find a relationship between general anxiety as measured by the Cattell 16-PF Questionnaire and cardiovascular responses during two cognitive tasks, but they did find a relationship between situation-specific anxiety as measured by the Test Anxiety Questionnaire and blood pressure and heart rate responses to these two tasks.

Awareness of Physiological Correlates of Anxiety

Anxiety, by definition, is associated with numerous autonomic and somatic changes. However, there are marked individual differences in the pattern of these physiological concomitants of anxiety, in their magnitude, and to what extent individuals are aware of these physiological changes. In chapter 1 of this volume, McReynolds points out that "felt anxiety" is associated with numerous autonomic and somatic changes. Individuals with felt anxiety who are aware of these autonomic and somatic changes may feel threatened by these physiological sensations and thus experience increased anxiety. However, other individuals may experience these autonomic and somatic changes but at the same time deny any feeling of anxiety. These individuals with "unfelt anxiety" are not likely to endorse items that would be scored as anxiety on an anxiety questionnaire. Thus they would be labeled as low-anxious even though they were experiencing physiological changes. It is easy to see how these mislabeled individuals could muddle the results of studies comparing high- and low-anxiety groups on cardiovascular reactivity.

Two studies have successfully identified these individuals with unfelt anxiety and have labeled them "repressors." Weinberger, Schwartz, and Davidson (1979) and Asendorpf and Scherer (1983) combined a measure of general anxiety with a measure of defensiveness to identify three groups: truly low-anxious individuals, defensive individuals who underreported anxiety (i.e., repressors), and high-anxious individuals. High-anxious subjects and repressors showed greater heart rate reactivity to a free association task than did low-anxious subjects. Both studies clearly show that measures of self-reported trait anxiety are not sufficient to distinguish between subjects who are truly low-anxious and subjects who show repressive coping with anxiety.

In addition, these studies indicate that interindividual differences in autonomic correlates of anxiety can be reliably predicted by paper and pencil trait anxiety measures if defensive tendencies are taken into account and if the laboratory challenge is conceptually linked to the measure of anxiety. Asendorpf and Scherer (1983) stated that they would expect to find similar autonomic responses in low-anxious subjects and repressors to tasks that elicit a fairly stereotyped anxiety response, such as fear of electric shock. But they would expect low-anxious subjects and repressors to differ in autonomic responses to tasks that are relevant to the repressor's idealized self-concept.

Choosing the Test Situation and Obtaining Baseline Measures

Studies of situation-specific anxiety must use laboratory stressors that closely mimic the specific anxiety-producing stimulus. For example, three of the four studies of social anxiety found increased cardiovascular reactivity to some components of tasks involving social interactions, but not to others (Beidel et al., 1985; Knight & Borden, 1979; Turner et al., 1986). Turner et al. (1986) suggested that in socially anxious individuals there is a need to assess physiological responses in a variety of interpersonal situations.

Researchers attempting to investigate the relationship of anxiety to cardiovascular reactivity have employed a range of test situations to either measure performance or induce anxiety states. What they tend to ignore is the anxiety-arousing effect of the laboratory itself. Before the first stressful task is introduced, the individual is subjected to a laboratory filled with bizarre looking electronic equipment, the application of electrodes to various parts of his or her anatomy, and the presence of an experimenter who makes permanent recordings of the subject's responses. Once the electrodes are attached, the subject is instructed to relax during baseline measurements. Cardiovascular measurements during this initial baseline period are then subtracted from levels during the experimental tasks as an index of reactivity.

It is unlikely that the baseline measurements capture the subject's true resting state. This baseline is probably elevated in all high-anxious subjects, and particularly in those subjects who are claustrophobic or who fear evaluation. This methodological weakness has been particularly problematic in the investigation of panic disorder. Baseline differences in cardiovascular and other measures are generally found when the patient anticipates a lactate infusion that can induce panic attacks. The expectation effect is so strong that up to a third of patients with panic disorder experience panic attacks to placebo infusion. Giesen and McGlynn (1977) have shown that different conclusions are reached if the effects of baseline levels are removed or not removed from measures of reactivity.

CONCLUSIONS

To summarize the literature reviewed in this chapter, in normal individuals trait measures of general anxiety have rarely been found to relate to cardiovascular reactivity. Studies using either a correlational approach (Houston, 1977; Steptoe et al., 1984; Sullivan et al., 1981) or group comparisons (Balshan, 1962; Glass et al., 1983; Hodges, 1968; Smith et al., 1984) have failed to find significant relationships between trait anxiety—as measured by the STAI, the Taylor Manifest Anxiety Scale, the Freeman Manifest Anxiety Scale, or the Cattell 16-PF Questionnaire—and cardiovascular reactivity. These studies have used a vast array of cognitive, physical, and psychological laboratory stressors, including white noise, isometric handgrip, mental arithmetic, video games, the Stroop color–word task, a distressing movie, an interview under evaluation threat, and tasks under ego-threatening or shock threat instructions.

Two important caveats need to be mentioned. First, Matthews et al. (1986) measured adolescents before, during, and after giving a speech in the presence of their peers for a grade in English class, and found that high-anxious subjects showed larger cardiovascular responses. Thus, if the challenge is salient enough, such as this real-life stressor, a trait measure of general anxiety is a useful individual difference index of reactivity. Second, a relationship between general anxiety and cardiovascular reactivity appears to surface when defensive underreporting of anxiety is taken into account (Asendorpf & Scherer, 1983; Weinberger et al., 1979).

Lamb (1978), Martin (1961), and others have pointed out that the concept of response specificity (Lacey et al., 1953) can account for the discrepancies in studies of the relationship between trait anxiety and cardiovascular reactivity. Lacey et al. (1953) found that different subjects had different patterns of autonomic responses that were reproducible over time and across stressors. This pattern was called response specificity. Some anxious subjects may express maximal responses with changes in cardiovascular measures, whereas other equally anxious subjects favor electrodermal responses. Thus response specificity in heterogeneous samples tends to dilute the stimulus-specific response patterns to anxiety-producing stimuli and accounts for different findings, especially in studies that do not make multiple physiological measurements.

In contrast to the lack of significant relationships between cardiovascular reactivity and general trait anxiety, a partial relationship has been found for anxiety-specific trait measures. These include studies of test anxiety, social anxiety, performance anxiety, and specific phobias. Test anxiety has been related to cardiovascular reactivity in a number of studies involving various test-like stimuli. These include mental arithmetic and the Stroop test (Glass et al., 1983), difficult anagrams (Harleston et al., 1965), a learning task (Judson & Gelber, 1965), oral reading and a vocabulary test (Beidel, 1988), and a problem-solving task (Montgomery, 1977). Three studies failed to find a relationship between test anxiety and cardiovascular reactivity. Orlebeke and Van Doornen (1977) employed a task that is unrelated to test anxiety. The other two studies (Holroyd et al., 19878; Smith et al., 1984), however, employed laboratory stressors that should have produced test anxiety. This suggests that the effect is not completely reliable.

Social anxiety has been related to cardiovascular reactivity during social interactions with an opposite-sex confederate (Beidel et al., 1985; Borkovec et al., 1974), an impromptu speech (Turner et al., 1986), and anticipation of a verbal task involving social evaluation (Knight & Borden, 1979). However, some studies have employed social interactions in the laboratory that failed to elicit group differences (Beidel et al., 1985; Knight & Borden, 1979; Turner et al., 1986). Thus, as with test anxiety, the effect is not completely reliable.

Performance anxiety has been related to greater initial heart rate deceleration to the presentation of pictures of people's faces (Dimberg et al., 1986) and to mentally rehearsing a competitive routine in gymnastics (Tremayne & Barry, 1988). Individuals with normal levels of anxiety but specific phobias have been found to show a defense response when presented with the phobia-specific stimuli, whereas normal control subjects show an orienting response (Hare, 1973; Hare & Blevings, 1975; Klorman et al., 1975).

To summarize, in most studies of subjects who have stimulus-specific anxiety increased cardiovascular reactivity has been found when the laboratory task mimics the anxiety producing stimuli. However, a number of published studies failed to find a relationship, even when the laboratory task should have produced stimulus-specific anxiety. Thus increased cardiovascular reactivity in stimulus-specific anxious individuals to certain stimuli in the laboratory occurs periodically but not consistently.

The topic of cardiovascular reactivity in psychiatric populations has been well investigated in patients with panic disorder, especially over the past ten years. Unfortunately, the literature for other anxiety psychopathologies is very limited, quite dated, and difficult to interpret in light of present-day methodological standards. The two largest methodologic problems are unclear diagnostic criteria and large baseline differences between anxiety patients and control subjects.

The limited literature on patients with GAD indicates that they exhibit a defense response instead of an orienting response in a standard orienting sequence (Hart, 1974), and increased cardiovascular responses to the cold pressor test (White & Gildea, 1937) and to thermal pain, visual discrimination, and mirror drawing (Malmo & Shagass, 1952). In contrast, patients and control subjects have not been found to differ in cardiovascular responses to a color naming task (Wing, 1964), or in orienting responses (Goldstein, 1964; Tan, 1964), and showed decreased cardiovascular reactivity to loud sounds (Brierley, 1969) and a mental arithmetic task (Kelly, 1966; Kelly et al., 1970; Kelly & Walter, 1969). However, some of these studies have shown large differences between patients and control subjects on resting baseline measures that were not considered in the analyses.

It is not clear from the literature whether anxiety patients do (Ackner, 1956; Bond et al., 1974; Brierley, 1969; Goldstein, 1964; Kelly, 1966; Kelly et al., 1970; Kelly & Walter, 1969; Tan, 1964; White & Gildea, 1937; Wing, 1964) or do not (Harper et al., 1965; Hart, 1974; Mathew et al., 1982; Mathew & Wilson, 1986) exhibit chronically elevated resting cardiovascular measures, or whether the increased baseline levels occurred because of the patient's reactivity to the laboratory setting. Ambulatory monitoring in the natural environment would be very helpful, as it has been for patients with panic disorder, in investigating resting levels of heart rate and blood pressure.

In contrast to the patients with GAD, patients with panic disorder have been well studied recently, and a number of studies have found no difference between patients and normal control subjects in cardiovascular reactivity to a range of laboratory tasks, including standing (Nesse et al., 1984), an orienting sequence (Roth et al., 1986), mental arithmetic (Kelly et al., 1971), cold pressor (Grunhaus et al., 1983), or treadmill test (Taylor et al., 1986). Like the relatively normal subjects with stimulus-specific anxiety, panic disorder patients have shown elevated heart rate when confronted with exposure to phobic situations (Woods et al., 1987). However, other studies using the same approach (Holden & Barlow, 1986; Roth et al., 1986) have failed to find increased reactivity to panic-producing situations when elevated baseline levels are accounted for. These studies, using ambulatory monitoring during exposure to phobic situations in the natural environment, are an excellent way to investigate this question. This approach could easily be applied in normal subjects with stimulus-specific anxieties during exposure to specific stimuli (i.e., test taking) in the natural environment.

Unlike other researchers, Matthews et al. (1986) found increased cardiovascular reactivity in subjects with high general anxiety, presumably because subjects were tested in their usual environment during a potent natural stressor. Although the presence of stimulus-specific anxieties (e.g., speech performance anxiety) was not ruled out in these subjects, this methodology appears to be a valuable approach to help clarify whether individuals with high general anxiety show any increased cardiovascular reactivity.

The available literature generally does not indicate that anxious individuals show dramatically increased cardiovascular reactivity. However, the presence of increased cardiovascular reactivity to certain stimuli in susceptible individuals, in combination with numerous methodologic problems in this literature, makes this conclusion, at this point, tentative. Ambulatory monitoring during real-life challenges would be an excellent means to investigate this question.

REFERENCES

Ackner, B. (1956). The relationship between anxiety and the level of peripheral vasomotor activity: An experimental study. *Journal of Psychosomatic Research, 1,* 21–48.

American Psychiatric Association. (1987). *Diagnostic and statistical manual of mental disorders* (3rd ed., Rev.). Washington, DC: Author.

Asendorpf, J. B., & Scherer, K. R. (1983). The discrepant repressor: Differentiation between low anxiety, high anxiety, and repression of anxiety by autonomic-facial-verbal patterns of behavior. *Journal of Personality and Social Psychology, 45,* 1334–1346.

Ax, A. F. (1953). The physiological differentiation between fear and anger in humans. *Psychosomatic Medicine, 15,* 433–442.

Balshan, I. D. (1962). Muscle tension and personality in women: A factorial study. *Archives of General Psychiatry, 7,* 436–448.

Beidel, D. C. (1988). Psychophysiological assessment of anxious emotional states of children. *Journal of Abnormal Psychology, 97,* 80–82.

Beidel, D. C., Turner, S. M., & Dancu, C. V. (1985). Physiological, cognitive and behavioral aspects of social anxiety. *Behavioral Research Therapy, 23,* 109–117.

Bond, A. J., James, D. C., & Lader, M. H. (1974). Physiological and psychological measures in anxious patients. *Psychological Medicine, 4,* 364–373.

Borkovek, T. D., Stone, N. M., O'Brien, G. T., & Kaloupek, D. G. (1974). Evaluation of a clinically relevant target behavior for analog outcome research. *Behavior Therapy, 5,* 503–513.

Brierley, H. (1969). The habituation of forearm muscle blood flow in phobic subjects. *Journal of Neurology, Neurosurgery, and Psychiatry, 32,* 15–20.

Cameron, O. G., Lee, M. A., Curtis, G. C., & McCann, D. S. (1987). Endocrine and physiological changes during "spontaneous" panic attacks. *Psychoneuroendocrinology, 12,* 321–331.

Cattell, R. B. (1972). *Manuel for the 16-PF.* Champaign, IL: Institute for Personality and Ability Testing.

Charney, D. S., & Heninger, G. R. (1986). Abnormal regulation of noradrenergic function in panic disorders. *Archives of General Psychiatry, 43,* 1042–1054.

Clarkson, T. B., Manuck, S. B., & Kaplan, J. R. (1986). Potential role of cardiovascular reactivity in atherogenesis. In K. A. Matthews, S. M. Weiss, T. Detre, T. M. Dembroski, B. Falkner, S. B. Manuck, & R. B. Williams (Eds.), *Handbook of stress, reactivity, and cardiovascular disease* (pp. 35–47). New York: Wiley.

Cowley, D. S., Hyde, T. S., Dager, S. R., & Dunner, D. L. (1987). Lactate infusions: The role of baseline anxiety. *Psychiatry Research, 21,* 169–179.

Crowne, D. P., & Marlowe, D. (1964). *The approval motive: Studies in evaluative dependence.* New York: Wiley.

Dimberg, U., Fredrikson, M., & Lundquist, O. (1986). Autonomic reactions to social and neutral stimuli in subjects high and low in public speaking fear. *Biological Psychology, 23,* 223–233.

Dykman, R. A., Ackerman, P. T., Galbrecht, C. R., & Reese, W. G. (1963). Physiological reactivity to different stressors and methods of evaluation. *Psychosomatic Medicine, 25,* 37–59.

Ehlers, A., Margraf, J., Roth, W., Taylor, C. B., Maddock, R. J., Sheikh, J., Kopell, M. L., McClenahan, K. L., Gossard, D., Blowers, G. H., Agras, W. S., & Kopell, B. S. (1986). Lactate infusions and panic attacks: Do patients and controls respond differently? *Psychiatry Research, 17,* 295–308.

Ehlers, A., Margraf, J., Roth, W. T., Taylor, C. B., & Birbaumer, N. (1988). Anxiety induced by false heart rate feedback in patients with panic disorder. *Behavioral Research Therapy, 26,* 1–11.

Freedman, R. R., Ianni, P., Ettedgui, E., & Puthezhath, N. (1985). Ambulatory monitoring of panic disorder. *Archives of General Psychiatry, 42,* 244–248.

Freedman, R. R., Ianni, P., Ettedgui, E., Pohl, R., & Rainey, J. M. (1984). Psychophysiological factors in panic disorder. *Psychopathology, 17,* 66–73.

Freeman, M. J. (1953). The development of a test for the measurement of anxiety: A study of its reliability and validity. *Psychological Monographs, 67,* 1–19.

Gaffney, F. A., Fenton, B. J., Lane, L. D., & Lake, C. R. (1988). Hemodynamic, ventilatory, and biochemical responses of panic patients and normal controls with sodium lactate infusion and spontaneous panic attacks. *Archives of General Psychiatry, 45,* 53–60.

Gale, A., & Edwards, J. A. (1986). Individual differences. In M. G. H. Coles, E. Donchin, & S. W. Porges (Eds.), *Psychophysiology: Systems, processes, and applications* (pp. 431–507). New York: Guilford Press.

Giesen, J. M., & McGlynn, D. (1977). Skin conductance and heart-rate responsivity to public speaking imagery among students with high and low self-reported fear: A comparative analysis of "response" definitions. *Journal of Clinical Psychology, 33,* 68–76.

Glass, D. C., Lake, C. R., Contrada, R. J., Kehoe, K., & Erlanger, L. R. (1983). Stability of individual differences in physiological responses to stress. *Health Psychology, 2,* 317–341.

Goldstein, I. B. (1964). Physiological responses in anxious women patients: A study of autonomic activity and muscle tension. *Archives of General Psychiatry, 10,* 382–388.

Gorman, J. M., Fyer, M. R., Goetz, R., Askanazi, J., Liebowitz, M. R., Fyer, A. J., Kinney, J., & Klein, D. F. (1988). Ventilatory physiology of patients with panic disorder. *Archives of General Psychiatry, 45,* 31–39.

Grunhaus, L., Gloger, S., Birmacher, B., Palmer, C., & Ben-David, M. (1983). Prolactin response to the cold pressor test in patients with panic attacks. *Psychiatry Research, 8,* 171–177.

Hare, R. D. (1973). Orienting and defensive responses to visual stimuli. *Psychophysiology, 10,* 453–464.

Hare, R. D., & Blevings, G. (1975). Conditioned orienting and defensive responses. *Psychophysiology, 12,* 289–297.

Harleston, B. W., Smith, M. G., & Arey, D. (1965). Test-anxiety level, heart rate, and anagram problem solving. *Journal of Personality and Social Psychology, 6,* 551–557.

Harper, M., Gurney, C., Savage, D., & Roth, M. (1965). Forearm blood flow in normal subjects and patients with phobic anxiety states. *British Journal of Psychiatry, 3,* 725–731.

Hart, J. D. (1974). Physiological responses of anxious and normal subjects to simple signal and non-signal auditory stimuli. *Psychophysiology, 11* 443–451.

Hodges, W. F. (1968). Effects of ego threat and threat of pain on state anxiety. *Journal of Personality and Social Psychology, 8,* 364–372.

Holden, A. E., & Barlow, D. H. (1986). Heart rate and heart rate variability recorded in vivo in agoraphobics and nonphobics. *Behavior Therapy, 17,* 26–42.

Holroyd, K. A., Westbrook, T., Wolf, M., & Badhorn, E. (1978). Performance, cognition, and physiological responding in test anxiety. *Journal of Abnormal Psychology, 87,* 442–451.

Houston, B. K. (1977). Dispositional anxiety and the effectiveness of cognitive coping strategies in stressful laboratory and classroom situations. In C. D. Spielberger & I. G. Sarason (Eds.), *Stress and anxiety* (Vol. 4, pp. 205–226). New York: Wiley.

Judson, A. J., & Gelber, G. (1965). Test anxiety, pulse rate and learning. *Psychonomic Science, 3,* 397–398.

Kelly, D. H. W. (1966). Measurement of anxiety of forearm blood flow. *British Journal of Psychiatry, 112,* 789–798.

Kelly, D. (1980). *Anxiety and emotions: Physiological basis and treatment* (pp. 121–180). Springfield, IL: Charles C Thomas.

Kelly, D., Brown, C. C., & Shaffer, J. W. (1970). A comparison of physiological and psychological measurements on anxious patients and normal controls. *Psychophysiology, 6,* 429–441.

Kelly, D., Mitchell-Heggs, N., & Sherman, D. (1971). Anxiety and the effects of sodium lactate assessed clinically and physiologically. *British Journal of Psychiatry, 119,* 129–141.

Kelly, D., & Walter, C. J. S. (1969). A clinical and physiological relationship between anxiety and depression. *British Journal of Psychiatry, 115,* 401–406.

Klorman, R., Hastings, J. E., Weerts, T. C., Melamed, B. G., & Lang, P. J. (1974). Psychometric description of some specific-fear questionnaires. *Behavior Therapy, 5,* 401–409.

Klorman, R., Wiesenfeld, A. R., & Austin, M. L. (1975). Autonomic responses to affective visual stimuli. *Psychophysiology, 12,* 553–560.

Knight, M. L., & Borden, R. J. (1979). Autonomic and affective reactions of high and low socially-anxious individuals awaiting public performance. *Psychophysiology, 16,* 209–213.

Krantz, D. S., & Manuck, S. B. (1984). Acute psychophysiologic reactivity and risk of cardiovascular disease: A review and methodologic critique. *Psychological Bulletin, 96,* 435–464.

Lacey, J. I. (1967). Somatic response patterning and stress: Some revisions of activation theory. In M. H. Appley & R. Trumbull (Eds.), *Psychological stress: Issues in research (pp. 14–37).* New York: Appleton-Century-Crofts.

Lacey, J. I., Bateman, D. E., & VanLehn, R. (1953). Autonomic response specificity: An experimental study. *Psychosomatic Medicine, 15,* 8–21.

Lader, M. H., & Mathews, A. M. (1968). A physiological model of phobic anxiety and desensitization. *Behavioral Research and Therapy, 6,* 411–421.

Lamb, D. H. (1978). Anxiety. In H. London & J. E. Exner (Eds.), *Dimensions of personality* (pp. 37–83). New York: Wiley.

Liebowitz, M. R., Fyer, A. J., Appleby, I., Levitt, M., Gorman, J., Dillon, D., Levy, G., Anderson, S., Davies, S. O., Palij, M., & Klein, D. F. (1983). Lactate provocation of panic attacks. *Psychopharmacology Bulletin, 19,* 476–478.

Liebowitz, M. R., Gorman, J. M., Fyer, A. J., Levitt, M., Dillon, D., Levy, G., Appleby, I. L., Anderson, S., Palij, M., Davies, S. O., & Klein, D. F. (1985). Lactate provocation of panic attacks: 2. Biochemical and physiological findings. *Archives of General Psychiatry, 42,* 709–719.

Lykken, D. T., & Katzenmeyer, C. G. (1969). *Manual for the Activity Preference Questionnaire (Rep. No. PR-68-3).* Minneapolis: Department of Psychiatry, University of Minnesota.

Lykken, D. T., Macindoe, I., & Tellegen, A. (1972). Preception: Autonomic response to shock as a function of predictability in time and locus. *Psychophysiology, 9,* 318–333.

Malmo, R. B., & Shagass, C. (1952). Studies of blood pressure in psychiatric patients under stress. *Psychosomatic Medicine, 14,* 82–93.

Mandler, G., & Sarason, S. B. (1952). A study of anxiety and learning. *Journal of Abnormal and Social Psychology, 47,* 166–173.

Manuck, S. B., & Krantz, D. S. (1986). Psychophysiologic reactivity in coronary heart disease and essential hypertension. In K. A. Matthews, S. M. Weiss, T. Detre, T. M. Dembroski, B. Falkner, S. B. Manuck, & R. B. Williams (Eds.), *Handbook of stress, reactivity and cardiovascular disease* (pp. 11–34). New York: Wiley.

Margraf, J., Ehlers, A., & Roth, W. T. (1986). Sodium lactate infusions and panic attacks: A review and critique. *Psychosomatic Medicine, 48,* 23–51.

Martens, R. (1977). *Sports Competition Anxiety Test.* Champaign, IL: Human Kinetics.

Martin, B. (1961). The assessment of anxiety by physiological behavioral measures. *Psychological Bulletin, 58,* 234–255.

Mathew, R. J., Ho, B. T., Francis, D. J., Taylor, D. L., & Weinman, M. L. (1982). Catecholamines and anxiety. *Acta Psychiatrica Scandinavica, 65,* 142–147.

Mathew, R. J., & Wilson, W. H. (1986). Hematocrit and anxiety. *Journal of Psychosomatic Research, 30,* 307–311.

Matthews, K. A., Manuck, S. B., & Saab, P. G. (1986). Cardiovascular responses of adolescents during a naturally occurring stressor and their behavioral and psychophysiological predictors. *Psychophysiology, 23,* 198–209.

Montgomery, G. K. (1977). Effects of performance evaluation and anxiety on cardiac response in anticipation of difficult problem solving. *Psychophysiology, 14,* 251–257.

Nesse, R. M., Cameron, O. G., Curtis, G. C., McCann, D. S., & Huber-Smith, M. J. (1984). Adrenergic function in patients with panic anxiety. *Archives of General Psychiatry, 41,* 771–776.

Orlebeke, J. F., & Van Doornen, L. J. P. (1977). Perception (UCR diminution) in normal and neurotic subjects. *Biological Psychology, 5,* 15–22.

Paul, G. L. (1966). *Insight versus desensitization in psychotherapy.* Stanford, CA: Stanford University Press.

Pitts, F. N., & McClure, J. H. (1967). Lactate metabolism in anxiety neurosis. *New England Journal of Medicine, 277,* 1329–1336.

Rainey, J. M., Frohman, C. E., Freedman, R. R., Pohl, R. B., Ettedgui, E., & Williams, M. (1984). Specificity of lactate infusion as a model of anxiety. *Psychopharmacology Bulletin, 20,* 45–49.

Rosenman, R. H., & Ward, M. M. (1988). The changing concept of cardiovascular reactivity. *Stress Medicine, 4,* 241–251.

Roth, W. T., Telch, M. J., Taylor, C. B., Sachitano, J. A., Gallen, C. C., Kopell, M. L., McClenahan, K.

L., Agras, S., & Pfefferbaum, A. (1986). Autonomic characteristics of agoraphobia with panic attacks. *Biological Psychiatry, 21,* 1133–1154.

Sarason, I. G. (1960). Empirical findings and theoretical problems in the use of anxiety scales. *Psychological Bulletin, 57,* 403–415.

Sarason, I. G. (1972). Experimental approaches to test anxiety: Attention and the uses of information. In C. D. Spielberger (Ed.), *Anxiety and behavior* (Vol. 2). New York: Academic Press.

Sarason, S. B., Davidson, K. S., Lighthall, F. F., & Waite, R. (1958). A test anxiety scale for children. *Child Development, 29,* 105–113.

Smith, T. W., Houston, B. K., & Zurawski, R. M. (1984). Irrational beliefs and the arousal of emotional distress. *Journal of Counseling Psychology, 31,* 190–201.

Spielberger, C. D., Gorsuch, R. L., & Lushene, R. E. (1970). *Manual for the State-Trait Anxiety Inventory (Self-Evaluation Questionnaire).* Palo Alto, CA: Consultant Psychologists Press.

Stamps, L. E., Fehr, L. A., & Lewis, R. A. (1979). Differential effects of state and trait anxiety on heart rate responses and reaction time. *Biological Psychology, 8,* 265–272.

Steptoe, A., Melville, D., & Ross, A. (1984). Behavioral response demands, cardiovascular reactivity, and essential hypertension. *Psychosomatic Medicine, 46,* 33;ne48.

Sullivan, P., Schoentgen, S., DeQuattro, V., Procci, W., Levine, D., Van der Meulen, J., & Bornheimer, J. (1981). Anxiety, anger, and neurogenic tone at rest and in stress in patients with primary hypertension. *Hypertension, 3,* 119–123.

Tan, B. K. (1964, February). Physiological correlates of anxiety: A preliminary investigation of the orienting reflex. *Canadian Psychiatric Journal,* 63–71.

Taylor, C. B., Sheikh, J., Agras, W. S., Roth, W. T., Margraf, J., Ehlers, A., Maddock, R. J., & Gossard, D. (1986). Ambulatory heart rate ranges in patients with panic attacks. *American Journal of Psychiatry, 143,* 478–482.

Taylor, J. A. (1952). A personality scale of manifest anxiety. *Journal of Abnormal and Social Psychology, 48,* 285–290.

Tremayne, P., & Barry, R. J. (1988). An application of psychophysiology in sports psychology: Heart rate responses to relevant and irrelevant stimuli as a function of anxiety and defensiveness in elite gymnasts. *International Journal of Psychophysiology, 6,* 1–8.

Turner, S. M., Beidel, D. C., & Larkin, K. T. (1986). Situational determinants of social anxiety in clinic and nonclinic samples: Physiological and cognitive correlates. *Journal of Consulting and Clinical Psychology, 54,* 523–527.

Watson, D., & Friend, R. (1969). Measurement of social-evaluative anxiety. *Journal of Consulting and Clinical Psychology, 33,* 448–457.

Weinberger, D. A., Schwartz, G. E., & Davidson, R. J. (1979). Low-anxious, high-anxious, and repressive coping styles: Psychometric patterns and behavioral and physiological responses to stress. *Journal of Abnormal Psychology, 88,* 369–380.

White, B. V., & Gildea, E. F. (1937). "Cold pressor test" in tension and anxiety: A cardiochronographic study. *Archives of Neurology and Psychiatry, 38,* 964–984.

Wing, L. (1964). Physiological effects of performing a difficult task in patients with anxiety states. *Journal of Psychosomatic Research, 7,* 283–294.

Woods, S. W., Charney, D. S., McPherson, C. A., Gradman, A. H., & Heninger, G. R. (1987). Situational panic attacks. *Archives of General Psychiatry, 44,* 365–375.

Zahn, T. P. (1986). Psychophysiological approaches to psychopathology. In M. G. H. Coles, E. Donchin, & S. W. Porges (Eds.), *Psychophysiology, systems, processes, and applications* (pp. 508–610). New York: Guilford Press.

IV

RESPONSES TO CARDIOVASCULAR ILLNESS AND PATIENT MANAGEMENT

15

Psychological Aspects of Outcomes and Interventions Following Heart Attack

D. G. Byrne

INTRODUCTION

The experience of heart attack is typically sudden, frequently without forewarning, often dramatic, usually distressing, and almost always life-threatening. Although mortality data vary cross-nationally and between studies, heart disease appears to account for between 30% and 35% of all deaths yearly, at least in Western, urbanized societies. It is not surprising, therefore, that heart disease figures prominently both as a focus of epidemiological and biological investigation, and as a source of concern for health in the general population.

Heart disease, of course, encompasses a wide range of pathophysiological states. Most epidemiological studies have, however, concerned themselves with one particular sequence of pathoclinical events, this being the development of coronary heart disease, which come about through the process of coronary atherosclerosis and, in some individuals, proceeds via coronary occlusion (through thrombus formation, subintimal hemorrhage, or coronary vasospasm) to acute myocardial infarction or coronary heart disease. Myocardial infarction and coronary heart disease are often used interchangeably in reports on the epidemiology of heart attack, and this discussion will refer to all clinical events involving coronary occlusion and subsequent infarction as coronary heart disease. I discuss only studies in which this illness event defines the primary clinical sample.

Life crises inevitably produce emotional consequences. The experience of myocardial infarction is a major crisis for most individuals and, in the short term, the most typically observed response to this event will be emotional distress in one of its various forms. Myocardial infarction assumes different cognitive meanings for different people (Byrne & Whyte, 1978); however, the observable characteristics of the illness experience are essentially invariant. First, it is an experience that, in some individuals, will initiate thoughts, attitudes, and even preoccupation about the nearness of death (Cay, Vetter, Philip, & Dugard, 1972). Second, the onset of symptoms will herald the beginning of a potentially long period of recovery, and rehabilitation and will imply, for some, the possibility of protracted disability (Finlayson & McEwen, 1977). Third, the acute phase of myocardial infarction may bring a period of

A version of this chapter was presented at a symposium "Anxiety and the Heart," 9th World Congress of the International College of Psychosomatic Medicine, Sydney, August 30 to September 4, 1987.

pain and physical discomfort and an unavoidable dependence on the attentions of others (Byrne & Whyte, 1979). Finally, enforced occupation of a coronary care unit, with its necessary but mysterious technology and with the potential to witness medical emergencies in other victims of the same illness, will constitute, for a significant minority of people, what has been called a psychological hazard (Hackett, Cassem, & Wishnie, 1968).

The collective actions of these factors—although they might be mediated by a range of influences including individual patterns of personality, past experience with myocardial infarction either personal or vicarious, the degree of information communicated by physician to patient about the nature of the illness, the sociocultural expectations regarding myocardial infarction inherent in a given society and levels of simultaneous life stress and social support—will act to produce a range of affective and behavioral responses that can bear an immediate progress during the stages of medical recovery and that will most likely influence the long-term outcome for any individual patient. These responses can be discussed at two levels. They will certainly reflect emotional distress, perhaps intense but essentially time-limited, which represents a recognition of the presence of serious illness. Emotional distress may, however, achieve an intensity and duration out of proportion to the threat occasioned by the myocardial infarction and may produce patterns of thought and behavior at odds with adaptation to the demands of the illness event.

PATTERNS OF OUTCOME
AFTER MYOCARDIAL INFARCTION

The clinical importance attached to understanding the progress and process of outcome for patients who survive myocardial infarction is clearly reflected in the volume of work addressing this area. Comprehensive overviews of this work may be found in recent reviews (Byrne, 1987; Doehrman, 1977), and it would be redundant to repeat that material here. Because the focus of the chapter is, however, on outcomes, a brief specification of those variables constituting accepted end-points in studies of outcome will help to establish boundaries for later discussion. Recurrent myocardial infarction, whether survived or not, has been taken as the most common end-point both in studies documenting unassisted outcome and in those evaluating programs of active intervention. Illness events provide convenient, concrete, and well-recognized end-points in a clinicopathological process and are subject to ready confirmation by medical record and death certificate data.

Moreover, as survival rates have increased, with a progressively more favorable ratio of morbidity to mortality over time, attention has turned to the speed and success of return to work without loss of position or earning power as an index of outcome after myocardial infarction. Like reinfarction, return to work provides a clear-cut index of outcome amenable to objective assessment, and it has accompanied reinfarction as a standard outcome measure in most recent studies. Return to work may, however, be short-lived, and to consolidate this index as a stable reflection of outcome, some assurance of permanence must be incorporated into the measure.

Whereas most studies have settled on reinfarction and return to work as exclusive indices of outcome, both Doehrman (1977) and Mayou (1979) have foreshadowed the need to combine measures of psychosocial disability with these more concrete end-points, in order to cover the full range of possible outcomes after heart attack. Mayou

Table 1 Data from selected studies illustrating morbidity and mortality rates following survived
myocardial infarction

Source	Follow-up interval	Morbidity rate	Mortality rate
Cay et al. (1973)	12 months	—	18.0%[a]
Pole et al. (1976)	12 months	—	14.5%[a]
	5 years	—	33.0%[c]
	9 years	—	48.0%[a,c]
Finlayson & McEwen (1977)	12 months	—	14.5%[a]
Croog & Levine (1977)	12 months	14.9%[b]	4.5%[b]
Kallio et al. (1979)	3 years	—	29.4%[b]
Byrne & Whyte (1980)	8 months	19.6%[b]	6.9%[b]
Byrne (1982)	2 years	25%[b,d]	
Jellinek et al. (1982)	6 months	3.4%[b]	2.7%[b]
	12 months	8.2%[b]	4.5%[b]
	3 years	18.5%[b]	7.3%[b]
Takeuchi (1983)	5 years	—	14.7%[b]

[a]Mortality from all causes.
[b]Mortality or morbidity from subsequent myocardial infarction only.
[c]Cumulative rate.
[d]Morbidity and mortality combined.

(1979) reported data revealing that protracted psychological and social impairment after myocardial infarction represented a substantial but hitherto unrecognized area of concern for patients recovering from heart attack. Measures of psychosocial disability pose difficulties both in conceptualization and measurement and constitute so-called soft variables in epidemiology, and for this reason they have often been rejected as a suitable focus of study in cardiovascular disease. The work of Mayou and his colleagues would suggest that despite this, psychosocial disability as an end-point cannot be ignored if the study of outcomes is to be complete.

With these categories in mind, the evidence reveals wide variation in patterns of outcome following survival, most likely indicating little more than equally wide variation between studies in the nature of the samples examined, the duration of follow-up periods, and the criteria by which outcome was assessed. Table 1 shows data from selected studies reflecting the pattern of morbidity and mortality after an initially survived myocardial infarction. Three features of these data deserve comment: (a) mortality rates from all causes exceed those where death only from subsequent infarction was considered, (b) both morbidity and mortality increase with the length of follow-up, and (c) those studies showing highest rates of recurrent infarction were typically those in which no age restrictions were placed on sample selection. (A closer consideration of these data may be found in Byrne, 1987.)

Examination of the data on return to work indicates, as Table 2 shows, an even greater variability in results between studies. Once more, a number of general comments may be made about these data, in particular: (a) Rates of return to work are generally encouraging, (b) return to work increases with time after infarction, (c) studies showing poorer rates of return to work are generally those in which no age limits have been placed on the samples, and (d) there is a suggestion that rates of

Table 2 Data from selected studies illustrating rates of return to work following survived myocardial infarction

Source	Follow-up interval	Return rate
Crain & Missal (1956)	—	82%
Morris (1959)	—	65%[a]
		33%[b]
Pell & D'Alonzo (1963)	12 months	80%[c]
		70%[d]
Weinblatt et al. (1966)	18 months	95%[c]
		85%[d]
Johnson (1966)	12 months	85%
Cay et al. (1973)	4 months	36%
	12 months	77%
Mulcahy (1976)	3 months	76%
Croog & Levine (1977)	12 months	76%
Finlayson & McEwen (1977)	6 months	77%
Byrne & Whyte (1980)	8 months	85%

[a]Mild infarction.
[b]Severe infarction.
[c]White-collar jobs.
[d]Blue-collar jobs.

return to work are better where there are less physical demands involved in the job. (These data, too, were examined more closely in Byrne, 1987.)

Perhaps for the reasons just outlined, measures of psychosocial outcome are conspicuously absent from most studies examining survivors of myocardial infarction. Doehrman's (1977) review noted, however, that for most people myocardial infarction results in a temporary disruption of normal psychological and social functioning, whereas for a "significant minority" it produces protracted distress. Finlayson and McEwen (1977) reported that almost half of their sample of male survivors of a first infarction experienced a decrease in premorbid social functioning for up to four years after the event, whereas Mayou (1979) found that 66% of his sample of men felt compelled to make moderate to major changes in their levels of leisure and social activity afterward. Some 23% of one sample of survivors (Byrne, 1982) complained of a decrease in social activity eight months after infarction. On the basis of a growing body of evidence such as this, Mayou (1984) concluded not only that psychosocial disability after infarction constituted a substantial problem but also that it was largely unrelated to the cardiologically identified severity of the infarct.

Outcome cannot, therefore, be viewed as a simple or unitary phenomenon. It is defined by multiple end-points, and attention to each of these is necessary if a complete assessment of outcome is to be claimed. Moreover, the time course of outcome is both protracted and variable. Whereas recovery from the acute physiological insult may be complete within a short period of time, the process of occupational rehabilitation clearly extends over a far longer span. Moreover, as Finlayson and McEwen (1977) reported, social readjustment following the trauma of heart attack may be incomplete even four years after the event. In this context, tying outcome to whether or not the patient survives the first weeks after infarction clearly imposes unrealistic constraints on the assessment of a patently complex patho-clinical process.

AFFECTIVE AND BEHAVIORAL RESPONSES TO MYOCARDIAL INFARCTION

The experience of affective symptoms of substantial proportions is not uncommon as an immediate response to myocardial infarction (Cay, Vetter, Philip, & Dugard, 1973), and in some patients, sufficiently large in number to be of clinical importance, these can be both prolonged and disabling (Doehrman, 1977). Estimates of the prevalence of severe affective reactions vary, although a recent study employing a structured psychiatric interview indicated that 35% of a consecutive series of 100 male survivors of infarction exhibited conspicuous psychiatric morbidity within the first week after admission to hospital (Lloyd & Cawley, 1982).

In a series of comprehensive reports, Cay and her colleagues examined the nature and course of symptoms of affective disturbance evident in survivors. Overall prevalence rate for emotional disturbance was similar to that reported by Lloyd and Cawley (1982), although disturbance was detected by means of a self-reported questionnaire. Using this technique it was found that 43% of patients who had suffered a first infarction and 27% of patients who had suffered a subsequent infarction reported borderline symptoms of overt affective disorder. A closer examination of these symptoms suggested a roughly even division between features of anxiety and depression. In first-time survivors approximately 55% of patients with affective symptoms were anxious and 37% were depressed. Among patients experiencing more than one infarction, 42% reported anxiety. However, 58% exhibited symptoms of overt depressive disorder (Cay et al., 1972). It has been suggested (Cay, Philip, & Aitken, 1976) that anxiety after myocardial infarction, if it is sufficiently longstanding, can transform into symptoms of depression. The preponderance of depressive symptoms over those of anxiety in the sample of patients with second or subsequent infarction might, therefore, reflect a continuation of emotional disturbance after the initial episode of illness, such that patients with a second episode are likely to be predisposed this time to the experience of depression.

The distinction between depression and anxiety in response to myocardial infarction is also reflected in results reported by Mayou, Foster, and Williamson (1978). A study of 100 survivors of a first infarction revealed 32% with moderate affective distress and 32% with distress within two months of the onset of illness. Of these patients, rather more than half reported either tension or situational anxiety, whereas less than half were troubled by depression. Moreover, depression would seem to be most evident later rather than earlier in the process of recovery (Segers & Mertens, 1975). Therefore, although both anxiety and depression occur with notable frequency after myocardial infarction (Cay et al., 1972; Dreyfuss, Dasberg, & Assael, 1969; Mayou et al., 1978), the latter is most likely to be of clinical prominence in the later stages of the illness when the patient has had sufficient time to comprehend the reality of the threat to life and the potential for future incapacity (Degre-Coustry & Grevisse, 1982). Anxiety, however, is probably the most common immediate emotional response (Groen, 1976), and this would seem to be consistent with a wealth of evidence on emotional responses to all serious physical illness (Lipowski, 1975). Whereas denial is common among those predisposed to that defense mechanism (Soloff, 1978), there is little doubt that in the acute phase anxiety predominates the pattern of emotional responses.

Psychometric scales of anxiety were administered to a sample of 286 men with acute symptoms who were admitted to a coronary care unit. These measures were subsequently given to the same patients 4, 7, and 10 days, and 4 months after admission to the hospital (Dellipiani et al., 1976). During the early stages of illness, anxiety was high relative to normal population data. However, it fell rapidly between the fourth and seventh days when most patients were transferred from the coronary care unit to a general medical ward. At this point, anxiety in survivors was no greater than that in other patients with medical conditions in general wards. Anxiety rose again as patients approached the end of their stay in the hospital and contemplated the post-hospital phase of their illness; but at four months after admission, anxiety had once more fallen and was again equivalent to levels found in the general population.

Measures of anxiety taken serially over time allowed the natural history of the affective response to be gauged. It is interesting to note that the fluctuations observed in anxiety levels over time were consistent with the perceived seriousness of the challenge being faced by patients at particular points in the progress of their illness. Thus it is entirely sensible that anxiety should be high soon after symptom onset when threat to life is greatest, and then again when patients are reminded that they must soon relinquish constant medical attention and face a possibly lengthy period of rehabilitation, but that anxiety should fall to normal or near-normal levels once more when patients are able to reevaluate the threat of death or disability in the light of post-hospital experience. In a similar study (Vetter, Cay, Philip, & Strange, 1977), anxiety among patients admitted to a coronary care unit was found to be no higher than that among patients admitted for medical emergencies to other hospital wards. Women showed higher levels of anxiety in response to myocardial infarction than did men. Moreover, patients with the less critical condition of myocardial ischemia but with symptoms mimicking those of infarction, responded with greater anxiety than did patients who were aware that they had sustained an infarction. One possible explanation for this hinges on the proposition that the certainty associated with an unequivocal diagnosis of myocardial infarction may actually limit experienced anxiety, whereas the relative uncertainty of a diagnosis of myocardial ischemia may enhance the fear associated with admission to coronary care.

Wrzesniewski (1977) investigated levels of anxiety in a consecutive series of 105 male survivors of a first myocardial infarction. Both state and trait anxiety were measured 15 days after, and these data were compared with anxiety in a group of healthy men free from coronary disease and in a group of outpatients with rheumatic disease. Both state and trait anxiety were markedly elevated in patients with myocardial infarction relative to both comparison groups; however, this anxiety dissipated with time and was consonant with levels of anxiety in the comparison groups at around four months after admission to the hospital. There was a significant correlation between measures of state and trait anxiety, and this finding has also emerged in later studies (Byrne, 1979).

Both state anxiety and trait anxiety were assessed in a sample of 120 survivors of myocardial infarction and in a comparison group of 40 patients who were admitted to a coronary care unit with the appearance of infarction but were discharged from that facility within 48 hours of admission, with a confirmed diagnosis of some (less serious) illness (Byrne, 1979). Some of these patients suffered chest pain of ischemic origin, some had pericarditis, and others had contracted pulmonary infections, although all were aware that they had not sustained a heart attack. The two groups of patients were not differentiated by the measure of trait anxiety, indicating, perhaps, that both groups entered the hospital with the same average tendency to respond to life crises with emotional distress. Measures of state anxiety did differentiate between the two patient groups, with those suffering from infarction reporting higher levels of state anxiety than did those for whom a lesser diagnosis was given. It was found, moreover, that measures of state and trait anxiety were significantly intercorrelated for both groups of patients. When patients with infarction were grouped according to sex, it was evident that female patients exhibited generally higher levels of state anxiety than did male subjects, although this did not hold for measures of trait anxiety.

Segers and Mertens (1977a, 1977b) examined anxiety in samples of survivors of acute infarction, in symptom-free subjects who had been found positive for coronary risk factors, and in healthy volunteers in whom there was no evidence of cardiac disease. Psychometric measures of anxiety failed to distinguish between the three groups, although this was attributed to higher standard deviations found for self-ratings of anxiety for coronary patients. Evidence of both denial and defensiveness was, however, to be seen in survivors, accounting perhaps for their apparent lack of anxiety.

The collective data on affective distress after infarction are not, therefore, in complete agreement. The finding that patients with myocardial infarction experienced higher levels of anxiety than did those with a less serious medical diagnosis (Byrne, 1979) does not precisely accord with the results of Vetter et al. (1977) that patients with the uncertain diagnosis of myocardial ischemia were more highly anxious than were patients with definite infarction. This disparity may, however, be viewed in the light of the relative certainty or otherwise of diagnoses. In the former study, patients in the noninfarction group were sure that at worst, they had received a warning of cardiac problems, whereas in the latter, they appear to have been faced with a rather less definite explanation of their symptom. This aside, the bulk of the literature supports the contention that anxiety, at least, is a characteristic accompaniment to the early phases of recovery.

Significant relationships between measures of state and trait anxiety have consistently emerged in the literature (Byrne, 1979; Wrzesniewski, 1977). These relationships give support to the more general suggestion of Cay et al. (1976) that those patients with a preexisting neurotic disposition will respond with the greatest emotional disturbance to the crisis of myocardial infarction and are very much in accord with the notion that the intensity of an affective response to any challenge (state anxiety) is modulated by an individual predisposition to neuroticism (trait anxiety; Spielberger, 1972).

The evidence is also clear that different kinds of people express anxiety in response to infarction in different ways and to different degrees. For example, women report greater state anxiety than do men (Byrne, 1979; Vetter et al., 1977), although this result cannot be explained in terms of a stronger neurotic predisposition to anxiety responses among these women patients (Byrne, 1979). This sex difference reflects a more generalized phenomenon related to sex differences in affective behavior in response to the challenge of illness (Brown & Rawlinson, 1977; Haney, 1977). The issue of sex differences in the presentation of affective distress is a controversial one (Byrne, 1981; Phillips & Segal, 1969), and such differences in psychological responses to illness need to be interpreted with some caution. The fact that these appear in the absence of sex differences in predisposing neurotic traits does, however, indicate the finding to be a real rather than an apparent one.

Socio-occupational class, too, appears to influence affective reactions, although the evidence is not consistent on the direction of this influence. Blue-collar workers have been shown to exhibit higher levels of state anxiety in response to myocardial infarction than did white-collar workers (Byrne, 1981). Croog and Levine (1977) and Dominian and Dobson (1969) found that people of lower social class experience more difficulties in the hospital after infarction than do people of higher social class, the reasons for this relating either to the patient's faulty communications with the physician or failure to interpret the hospital environment in a reassuring way. In reporting on similar findings, Hackett and Cassem (1976) suggested that patients of higher social class probably enjoyed a greater exchange of information with their physicians than did patients of lower social class, reflecting, presumably, the benefits of educational, social, and financial compatibility between higher social status patients and their physicians. This finding may, however, also reflect a greater readiness by educated and articulate patients of higher social status to actively seek information from physicians and others regarding their cardiac conditions.

The clinical importance of affective distress is now receiving considerable recognition (Byrne, 1979; Vetter et al., 1977). Some years ago, Mather, Pearson, and Read (1971) noted an increased mortality among patients with myocardial infarction who were treated in the hospital relative to those who were treated at home (the two groups being presumably unselected for severity of infarction) and speculated that this might be due to the additional anxiety generated by the coronary care unit atmosphere. There is a growing body of comment that the technology and setting of the coronary care unit, necessary as these are, produce a range of subjective responses to the experience (Geersten, Ford, & Castle, 1976) and that anxiety and apprehension predominate among these responses. Lee and Ball (1975) were led to comment, "When a patient is totally dependent on strangers and mysterious machines, conditions are right for psychological trauma" (p. 1498). There is some speculation then, that at least part of the affective distress occurring in the short-term after myocardial infarction may be attributed to the experience of the coronary care unit.

Razin (1982), however, pointed out that there is by no means universal agreement with this view. For some patients at least, the medical environment and the presence of equipment for cardiac monitoring and resuscitation acted as a reassurance that medical care was rapidly available in case of complications, thus alleviating some of the anxiety associated with hospitalization. There is now, in fact, evidence that release from the coronary care unit into a general medical ward and away from the environment of intensive medial scrutiny acts to increase anxiety in some patients (Klein, Kliner, Zipes, Troyer, & Wallace, 1968) and may even enhance physiological vulnerability to cardiological complications unless the patient is suitably prepared for the experience.

The time course for affective distress following myocardial infarction is extremely variable. Some patients will experience fear immediately on recognition of the symptoms of heart attack, leading in some instances to denial of the significance of these and delay in seeking medical care (Surwit, Williams, & Shapiro, 1982). For others, the symptom at onset will be of sufficient intensity that clouding or loss of consciousness may occur, so that any recognition of the real implications of the situation will be delayed until some days after admission to the hospital. Others still will be able to mobilize denial sufficiently rapidly that emotional distress never becomes manifest;

however, although there is little doubt that denial is widely seen following myocardial infarction (Croog, Shapiro, & Levine, 1971), its real extent has been challenged (Soloff, 1978).

Many studies of emotional distress after heart attack have limited their inquiry to the period of hospitalization. It is important to recognize that the patient does not revert to normality immediately upon discharge but may continue to experience both anxiety and depression well into the period of recovery and rehabilitation. There is little doubt that anxiety is elevated in most if not all survivors of myocardial infarction at some time during recovery, in response both to the illness itself with its myriad personal and psychosocial implications for the individual patient and to the unfamiliar atmosphere of the coronary care unit. The evidence indicates that at least part of the intensity of this anxiety may be explained in terms of a predisposing neurotic trait toward anxiety in the face of crisis. There is a great danger, however, that discharge from the hospital is taken as an indication of a resumption of psychological and affective normality. This is by no means true, and attention to psychological needs may be demanded past the time when cardiological recovery is complete.

THE INFLUENCE OF AFFECT
AND BEHAVIOR ON OUTCOME

Outcomes after myocardial infarction are not chance events but are determined by a diversity of factors that are, at least in principle, both identifiable and measurable. Although the certain prediction of outcome in individual cases is not possible, the medical pronouncement of individual prognosis is both scientifically feasible and routine in clinical practice. From the cardiological perspective, two groups of factors are preeminent. One group derives from the identification and quantification of the degree of compromise suffered by the myocardium as a result of infarction (Humphries, 1977) and is best exemplified by the so-called cardiac prognostic indicators (Norris, Caughey, Deeming, Mercer, & Scott, 1970; Peel, Semple, Wang, Lancaster, & Dall, 1960). Recent work (Marmor, Geltman, Schechtman, Sobel, & Roberts, 1982; Marmor, Sobel, & Roberts, 1981; Martin, Thompson, Armstrong, Hobbs, & De Clerk, 1983) has confirmed the usefulness of variables on which prognostic indices have been based. The other group consists of standard risk factors for coronary heart disease that have been shown in epidemiological studies to predict first episodes of infarction, and that, if they persist after this clinical event, may also influence the rate of recurrent infarction (Kornitzer et al., 1983; Multiple Risk Factor, Intervention Research Group, 1981; Rose, Tunstall-Pedoe, & Heller, 1983). It was foreshadowed earlier in this chapter, however, that intense and prolonged affective distress might itself create conditions that further challenge a vulnerable myocardium leaving it open to recurrent insult, or might lead to patterns of thought and behavior at odds with those necessary for an uncomplicated recovery. Evidence supporting such a role for affect and behavior is currently growing.

Anxiety and depression reported by patients recovering from myocardial infarction can be expected to influence outcome on two general levels. First, as Lown, Desilva, Reich, and Murawski (1980) have pointed out, the higher nervous system modifies the electrical activity of the heart, and the neurophysiological correlates of intense affect may act to trigger ventricular arrhythmias resulting in reinfarction or sudden death. The liberation of catecholamines into the myocardium during times of affective distress (Frankenhaeuser, 1979) might also be seen as a pathway of influence between emotions and cardiovascular functioning. Both these factors can be seen as potential determinants of cardiological outcome, and because the evidence on the time course of severe affective distress places this in the first few days or weeks after infarction, its effects are most likely to be seen sooner rather than later in the course of recovery when the myocardium is vulnerable to insult from challenges of a physiological or chemical nature.

Second, affective distress, if prolonged, may also act to influence occupational rehabilitation, either by generating uncertainty regarding the ability of the cardiovascular system to withstand the demands of the occupational situation (Byrne, 1979) or, if depression predominates, by producing a situation of demoralization, hopelessness, and low motivation (Cay et al., 1976). The influence of psychological distress on occupational outcome is most likely to be seen later rather than sooner in the course of recovery, because successful return to work as an index of outcome does not typically occur for some weeks or months following the onset of illness.

Evidence relating psychological distress to outcome following myocardial infarction can be drawn from a number of studies. Ruberman, Weinblatt, Goldberg, and Chaudhary (1984) undertook a prospective investigation of 2,320 male survivors of acute infarction for whom extensive psychosocial data were available at the time of initial hospitalization. Follow-up of these men revealed that those socially isolated within peer groups and experiencing unduly high levels of life stress after illness had more than four times the risk of sudden cardiac death in the period immediately after infarction than did those with low levels of stress and appropriate social integration. High levels of stress and social isolation were most prevalent amongst the least educated men (Ruberman, Weinblatt, Goldberg, & Chaudhary, 1983). This risk was independent of the presence of premature ventricular beats reported during the initial hospitalization.

A multivariate study of predictors of outcome in a smaller cohort of patients (Philip, Cay, Stuckey, & Vetter, 1981; Philip, Cay, Vetter, & Stuckey, 1979) ventured more widely in its consideration of outcomes than the simple index of recurrent coronary morbidity or mortality. Predictor variables consisted of measures of psychological distress obtained during the first few days of hospitalization, and these were related, by means of a multivariate predictive equation, to outcome variables assessed one year after the initial hospitalization. Psychological distress evident soon after infarction significantly predicted a range of outcomes; however, these were predominantly to do with the persistence of distress into the year following infarction and the emergence of self-perceived difficulties related to incomplete rehabilitation and adjustment. Outcome, as measured by cardiovascular complication, reinfarction, or failure to return to work was not successfully predicted by psychological state immediately following heart attack. Similar results have been found in other studies (e.g., Mayou, 1984). By contrast, Mulcahy (1976) and Diederiks, van der Sluijs, Weeda, and Schobre (1983) found failure to return to work to be more strongly related to psychological distress following myocardial infarction than to scores on a prognostic index reflecting the severity of the infarction.

A broadly based, prospective examination of the psychological determinants of outcome conceptualized within the framework of illness behavior has been reported (Byrne, Whyte, & Butler, 1981). The independent variables in this study consisted of eight descriptive factors representing a broad range of cognitive, behavioral, and affective responses to myocardial infarction (Byrne & Whyte, 1978). These factors are as follows.

1. somatic concern
2. psychosocial precipitants
3. affective disruption
4. affective inhibition
5. illness recognition
6. subjective tension
7. sick role acceptance
8. trust in the doctor

Prospective analyses of the data were undertaken so as to establish associations between patterns of illness behavior evident soon after infarction and indices of outcome evident at periods 8 and 24 months after the clinical event. The three outcome categories of cardiologic, occupational, and social were dealt with independently. Significant associations were evident for all indices of outcome 8 months after infarction, although the same pattern did not hold for outcome at 24 months. Patients experiencing an unsatisfactory cardiological outcome had shown, soon after infarction, significantly higher levels on the illness behavior dimensions representing anxious concern with somatic functioning and recognition of the presence of areas of life stress than had patients experiencing a cardiologically uneventful outcome at 8 months. When nonroutine medical consultations were taken as the measure of 8-month outcome, the same pattern of significant associations with illness behavior emerged.

Failure to return to work was related to three aspects of illness behavior evident soon after infarction. Patients failing to return to work had, soon after infarction, significantly higher levels of affective inhibition and subjective tension, and a greater readiness to accept the sick role, than had patients returning to active employment during the 8-month follow-up period. Two aspects of social outcome at 8 months, those of subjective satisfaction with progress toward rehabilitation and of return to an active social life, were associated with illness behavior evident soon after infarction. Patients dissatisfied with progress during the 8-month follow-up period reported a greater recognition of the presence of areas of life stress than did patients who viewed their rehabilitation in a more optimistic light. Patients who found themselves unable to resume a satisfactory social life in the 8 months since infarction reported, soon after the clinical event, significantly higher levels of anxious concern with somatic functioning and significantly higher levels of affective disruption (affective distress that interferes with interpersonal relationships) than did those patients whose social functioning was unimpaired by the event. These data are summarized in Table 3.

Patterns of illness behavior evident soon after myocardial infarction were not significantly associated either with cardiological outcome or occupational outcome 24 months after the clinical event. There were, however, significant associations between illness behavior soon after and subjective satisfaction with progress 24 months later. Patients who were, on the whole, satisfied with their progress during the 24-month period had reported, soon after the event, significantly lower levels of affective disruption and significantly higher levels of illness recognition, sick role acceptance, and trust in the doctor than had those patients who viewed their 24-month progress in a less optimistic light.

Of course, not all aspects of illness behavior in response to infarction will necessarily be noxious; some may indeed be adaptive. Furthermore, because this study examined illness behavior only in the acute phase of illness, the possibility exists that some aspects of illness behavior may change with time. Finally, the potentially nox-

Table 3 Illness behavior and outcome eight months after myocardial infarction

Illness behavior factor	Outcome measure	t
Somatic concern	Recurrent infarction vs. no further infarction	1.82*
	Excessive vs. routine follow-up care	1.78*
	Normal vs. deteriorated social life	2.09**
Psychosocial	Recurrent infarction vs. no further infarction	2.08**
Precipitants	Excessive vs. routine follow-up care	3.83***
	Satisfaction vs. dissatisfaction with progress	3.54***
Affective disruption	Normal vs. deteriorated social life	4.10***
Affective inhibition	Return to work vs. inability	1.88*
Subjective tension	Return to work vs. inability	1.92*
Sick role acceptance	Return to work vs. inability	2.55**

*$p < 0.1$.
**$p < 0.05$.
***$p < 0.01$.

ious effects of some aspects of illness behavior may change with time. The physiologically arousing effects of anxiety for example, may prove threatening to a vulnerable myocardium in the early stages of illness, but provide a useful motivating influence on compliance with therapeutic directions later in the course of recovery and rehabilitation.

Associations, when they emerge, are more apparent at 8 months than at 24 months after infarction. This is not surprising, because it is to be expected that the temporal proximity of events to one another would bear on the strength of associations between them. Significant associations between illness behavior and outcome occur most prominently when measures of the former represent responses of an affective kind. Such dimensions of illness behavior as somatic concern, psychosocial precipitants, affective disruption, and subjective tension figure largely in these associations. Once more, there is little surprise in these findings; it has been speculated (Byrne, 1987) that affective responses, particularly if they are prolonged, portend unsatisfactory outcomes.

The proposition that both affect and behavior can influence the process of recovery and rehabilitation after myocardial infarction begs consideration of the role played by the Type A behavior pattern in determining outcome. Those persons with the behavior pattern appear to have about twice the risk of coronary heart disease, all other risk factors being accounted for, as those for whom Type A behavior is absent, and as Razin (1982) has so succinctly put it, there is "ample reason to believe that the Type A Behavior Pattern does not stop at the door of the coronary care unit." One might therefore expect the possession of Type A behavior to be as relevant a determinant of recurrent infarction as of the initial event. Somewhat surprisingly, then, few studies have addressed this issue.

In a prospective investigation of 3,000 participants in the Western Collaborative Group Study, it was found that scores on a self-reported scale of the Type A behavior pattern distinguished between men with single and men with recurrent myocardial infarctions, with scores for those with recurrent illness being significantly higher than those recorded by their single infarction counterparts (Jenkins, Zyzanski, Rosenman, & Cleveland, 1971). These results were confirmed in a later examination of the same cohort of subject (Jenkins, Zyzanski, & Rosenman, 1976). In this report, the Type A behavior pattern was shown to be an independent predictor of recurrent infarction unrelated to the presence of serum cholesterol, cigarette smoking, or blood pressure. The strength of association between Type A behavior and recurrent infarction was, in fact, stronger than that for either serum cholesterol levels or cigarette smoking.

These data build on similar results reported by Rosenman, Friedman, and Jenkins (1967) and have encouraged the development of a "recurrence scale" (Jenkins, 1978) in which items from one self-report scale of the Type A behavior pattern (the Jenkins Activity Survey) are being examined in an attempt to predict risk of recurrent infarction among those who have survived an initial event. Such data have also encouraged the initiation of large scale attempts to modify Type A behavior following infarction in an attempt to reduce the risk of secondary occurrence (Powell, Friedman, Thoresen, Gill, & Ulmer, 1984).

Not all studies of the role of Type A behavior in recurrent infarction have, however, been equally positive. Case, Heller, and Shamai (1983) failed to find any association between the two. The major evidence, albeit from the one cohort of subjects (the Western Collaborative Group Study) does, however, support a causal role for this behavior pattern in predicting secondary heart attack.

The evidence linking affect and behavior with outcome is, therefore, by no means unequivocal. Although it is clear that most survivors of myocardial infarction respond to illness with some form of affective distress, it is less clear with what strength or by which means these responses might influence the process of recovery and rehabilitation. Simple measures of affect evident at the time of illness do not appear to be useful predictors of outcome, although when viewed in conjunction with patterns of behavior, outcome is more clearly related to the diverse collection of psychological responses to infarction. Mechanisms mediating this relationship have yet to be fully explored and remain, at present, in the area of speculation. The most fruitful and unifying approach, however, is most likely to arise from the suggestion of Lown and his colleagues (Lown et al., 1980) that the process of regulation exerted on the cardiovascular system by the central nervous system will figure prominently in future investigations.

PSYCHOLOGICAL INTERVENTION

The psychological management of survivors of myocardial infarction is a contentious issue for at least three reasons. First, data on behavior, affect, and outcome require considerable clarification; second, there is no single theory to guide empirical research; and third, the work that is available for review is frequently unsystematic, largely uncontrolled, and often marred by design faults. Nonetheless, there now exists a growing concern among those charged with both the short- and long-term care of survivors of heart attack that attention only to the biological integrity of the heart and circulation falls somewhat short of complete patient care (Razin, 1982).

Survivors are more and more commonly advised to adopt a less stressful pattern of life upon leaving the hospital, cardiologists are more frequently inviting the participation of psychiatrists and clinical psychologists in the care of difficult patients in coronary care units, and systematic programs of psychological counseling and support are being routinely offered in growing numbers of hospitals. In many European centers, it is customary for patients in the rehabilitation stages to spend time in a specifically designated rehabilitation center as an inpatient, and although the programs in such places have typically been based on exercise retraining, psychological and behavioral procedures such as relaxation therapy and life-style planning are assuming a growing importance.

Systematic studies on psychological intervention are not plentiful. They have ranged in magnitude from those involving a single, brief visit from a psychologist or social worker to inquire about the experience and disruption of affective distress, to a long series of psychoanalytically oriented interviews with a psychiatrist. Programs have been developed and evaluated both for individual and group interventions and have variously used both specialist-trained mental health professionals (psychiatrists and clinical psychologists) and generalist-trained medical and paramedical people (medial registrars, interns, and nurses). Doehrman's (1977) review of 36 published accounts of largely uncontrolled attempts at psychological intervention after infarction revealed that 60% were conducted directly by medically qualified persons, whereas the remaining 40% were undertaken by nurses, occupational therapists, and social workers. The bulk of these (around 70%) focused on the acute phase immediately after illness. Although none of the accounts presented what could pass for empirical evaluation, the consensus of opinion was that psychological interventions acted to the general advantage of the patient, both in terms of occupational and psychosocial adjustment and (rather more tenuously) in terms of a reduction in subsequent coronary risk.

The degree of interest now being expressed in the behavioral and psychological management of the survivor of myocardial infarction is evident in the volume of work, both speculative and empirical, that has been produced in the past decade (Byrne, 1987). A definitive statement on the usefulness of this work, however, awaits the accumulation of more and better evidence, and this, in turn, may require a clear theoretical statement to guide the process and evaluation of intervention. Much of the literature of psychological intervention after myocardial infarction has been anecdotal—not based on systematic examinations of particular forms of intervention but relying heavily on clinical experience and intuition to guide the important and sometimes delicate process of behavioral, emotional, and cognitive change following this life-threatening event. Although there is much clinical wisdom contained in many of the published accounts in this area, in this chapter I will deal no more with the exhortatory material than to acknowledge its existence and encourage its exploration by the individual reader. The systematic evidence is somewhat smaller in volume and may be divided into two sections: one focusing on acute phase interventions (while the patient remains in the hospital, sometimes even in intensive care) and the other dealing with the somewhat protracted period after leaving the hospital but typically prior to returning to work.

Systematic Acute Phase Interventions

Although there is a large observational and clinical literature on psychological interventions directed at the resolution of intrapsychic, emotional, and social difficulties associated with myocardial infarction, there has been an apparent reluctance to commence structured interventions directed toward the long-term recovery and rehabilitation of cardiac patients while the patient remains within the intensive care unit or the inpatient hospital environment. Perhaps this is due to the fact that the patient remains acutely and sometimes dangerously ill, and the initiation of any activity other than that aimed directly at the protection of the cardiovascular system is seen as superfluous and unwarranted. It may be due also to the fact that the already crowded coronary care unit environment is unable to tolerate the routine presence of yet another caregiver. Still, the patient's emotional and psychological state during the acute phase of recovery can have both immediate and long-term influences on ultimate outcome. Lynch, Thomas, Mills, Malinow, and Katcher (1974) showed that a range of emotional and social circumstances such as adverse psychological responses to illness or family visits could precipitate potentially dangerous cardiac arrhythmias among at least some cardiac patients. The potential consequences of failure to initiate psychological intervention in the early stages of recovery are, therefore, clear, and the need for early psychological intervention following myocardial infarction would appear to be self-evident.

Stein, Murdaugh, and MacLeod (1969) offered brief supportive psychotherapy to a small number of patients experiencing pronounced emotional reactions to infarction on the grounds that such emotional reactions might prove noxious to the patient's cardiac state. The focus of the investigation was on the experience of undue emotional stress during the acute phase of recovery. Although psychotherapy varied according to the needs of individual patients and the study was uncontrolled, the authors reported that patients experienced both cardiological and psychological benefits from intervention at this early stage in their illness. The interpretation of data such as these does, however, pose difficulties, because the unsystematic presentation of psychotherapy does not allow a differential evaluation of its active elements, and the absence of control groups limits inferences that can be drawn from the data. Moreover, failure to make therapy consistent across patients muddies interpretation even further and precludes replication.

A much more extensive and well-controlled investigation into the effects of psychological intervention following infarction was reported by Gruen (1975). Patients in this study comprised those who had experienced a first occurrence and were in the age range of 40 to 69 years. Patients with conspicuous psychological disorder under treatment were excluded from investigation. Eligible patients were seen in the first few days of admission to a coronary care unit and were randomly assigned either to an intervention or a control group until 35 patients had accumulated in each. Comparisons of a number of demographic and medical variables at the conclusion of the study indicated that the samples were matched for age, sex, marital status, and social class. They were also matched for severity and location of myocardial infarction. Patients in the intervention group were contacted either on the first or second day in the coronary care unit and, after agreement to participate in the study, this was followed by regular half-hour sessions on five or six days per week until release from the hospital. Psychological intervention, although essentially open-ended, attempted to systematically introduce a series of therapeutic strategies that were considered to be important both for the resolution of emotional distress following infarction and in the facilitation of adaptive behavior during the rehabilitation phase, leading to reintegration into work and society.

Control and intervention subjects were then compared both at discharge from the hospital and after a short follow-up period on a range of measures of cardiological, social, and emotional outcomes. The results indicated that distinct and significant outcome benefits arising from intervention were to be gained in a number of respects.

Patients in the intervention group spent significantly fewer days in the hospital, significantly fewer days in intensive care, and significantly fewer days on cardiac monitoring equipment than did patients in the control group. Moreover, there were significantly fewer patients in the intervention group who experienced congestive heart failure as compared with those in the control group. Patients receiving psychological intervention also appeared to experience gains in the emotional sphere and reported significantly less anxiety and depression than did their control colleagues. These emotional benefits were carried through to the follow-up period.

This study is important in at least three respects. First, psychological intervention was initiated early in the course of the patient's recovery. Second, the study was methodologically well conducted and represents a serious scientific attempt to evaluate the effectiveness of early psychological intervention on outcome following infarction. The presentation of empirical data underscores the scientific credibility of the study. Third, the results are encouraging and indicate that a range of cardiological and emotional benefits are to be gained by early psychological intervention.

Drawing on Gruen's pioneering work, Oldenburg and Perkins (1984) examined the influence of brief hospital-based psychological intervention among survivors of first infarction, beginning within a day or two of admission to intensive care and extending over the following 7 to 10 days. Intervention was based on two assumptions, the first being that it should be offered early in the acute phase and the second that it should serve the functions of support, education, and life-style change. All patients were seen individually, and direct educational advice and relaxation instructions used in intervention were reinforced by the use of prerecorded, audiocassette tapes. Patients were encouraged to retain these tapes following discharge from the hospital, to continue relaxation exercises, and to involve their families both in relaxation and education.

A range of outcomes for intervention relative to control patients (who received only medical treatment) were assessed at the point of discharge from the hospital. Patients for whom intervention was provided received no noticeable benefits in terms of days spent in the hospital relative to control patients. Nor were any benefits evident in terms of days spent in the intensive care unit. Intervention patients did, however, score significantly lower on two composite indices of chest pain than did control patients, and those receiving both counseling and education experienced significantly fewer cardiac complications during hospitalization than did either patients who received only education or control patients. This pattern was also reflected in a measure of state anxiety. Thus, although the results of the study were not quite so encouraging as those reported by Gruen (1975) and the numbers of patients examined were appreciably smaller, this study once more presents empirical evidence in support of a range of benefits to be gained by early psychological intervention following myocardial infarction.

The mechanisms through which early intervention exerts its influence seem likely to be related in complex ways to the modification of a variety of maladaptive responses to myocardial infarction of the kind discussed in earlier chapters. Gruen (1975), for example, suggested that benefits arising from early psychological intervention came about either because they produced a decrease in the overall level of arousal or because they facilitated the use of active coping resources in the face of crisis. Both of these suggestions ultimately reduce to the notion that rapid intervention decreases cardiovascular activation in the short term and might act to attenuate disproportionate cardiovascular responses to a challenging environment in the long-term. As a consequence, feelings of psychological well-being appear to be enhanced and the cardiovascular system as a whole may be given a degree of protection from further damage. Because the myocardium is both compromised and vulnerable to the effects of excessive demand after infarction (Frankenhaeuser, 1976; Razin, 1982), it is logical to assume that strategies aimed at arousal reduction will decrease the risk of cardiovascular incidents during the acute phase following infarction. Moreover, the characteristic enhancement of psychological well-being associated with arousal reduction, together with a decrease in the experience of cardiovascular complications and distress, may produce in the patient a more optimistic attitude toward the future and, therefore, a greater readiness for social reintegration and return to work.

The Post-Hospital Phase

The post-hospital phase following myocardial infarction has produced a useful number of well-conducted studies evaluating the effectiveness of psychological and behavioral intervention. Once more, one might speculate on the reasons for this. Whereas the patients in the intensive care unit constitute a captive population for intervention, the convenience of initiating this intervention, particularly in groups, is clearly greater once the patient has left the hospital. Moreover, the real or implied risk of cardiovascular complications that exists during the acute phase decreases by the time of discharge from the hospital. Intervention may, therefore, be initiated with a greater degree of security that a more stable cardiovascular system will not respond adversely to the strategies being used. It has also been suggested that anxiety peaks and depression begins to develop around the time of hospital discharge (Byrne, 1979; Cassem & Hackett, 1971), presenting, perhaps, an opportune time for the emotional management of the cardiac patient. Finally, the patient's emotional state, together with the recognition of the fact that reentry into social and family roles and active employment is now a distinct possibility, may act to increase the patient's compliance with the various behavioral strategies involved in post-hospital intervention.

Thockloth, Ho, Wright, and Seldon (1973) examined the effects on outcome of psychological intervention with 50 randomly selected men who had survived a first infarction and related this to clinical outcomes of a control group. The intervention was offered on an individual basis and involved regular weekly contact beginning during the final stages of hospitalization and extending over three months after discharge from the hospital. The primary emphasis of intervention was on counseling to deal with the resolution of social, emotional, and financial problems following myocardial infarction. A long-term follow-up of all patients demonstrated a range of advantages to be gained from intervention, even when it was simply directed at practical issues. Although intervention did not result in a more rapid return to work, a greater number of intervention than control patients returned to work during an optimal period of time, which the authors defined as two to four months following infarction. Intervention patients were also more compliant with medical advice and instructions than were control patients and reported less emotional distress than did patients whose only contact was with their physicians.

A similar emphasis was taken by Adsett and Bruhn (1968); however, patients (all male) were, in this instance, specifically selected for the fact that they were experiencing substantial psychological problems following infarction. These patients were treated in a group, and their wives received simultaneous group therapy that was undertaken separately but organized along similar lines. A control group consisted of male patients who had survived infarction and who were matched on demographic characteristics to those in the intervention group but who received nothing other than routine medical care. Intervention involved regular outpatient contacts extending over 10 sessions and was concerned with supportive but exploratory psychotherapy aimed at the resolution of specific problems raised by individual patients within the group.

The therapeutic program appeared to be well accepted by the intervention patients, but they experienced little additional advantage relative to control patients either on measures indicating relief from psychological distress or in terms risk of subsequent cardiac events. Patients with psychological problems who refused to participate in the intervention group (although not control patients) appeared to suffer a higher frequency of subsequent cardiac events; however, the small numbers involved strongly limited the inferences that could be drawn from this. Bruhn, Wolf, and Philips (1971) followed the long-term outcomes of these same patients over several years after psychotherapeutic intervention. This provision appeared to confer no real advantages with regard to long-term relief from psychological distress. However, there was a trend among patients in the intervention group to show rates of long-term survival in excess of those patients in the control group.

The first extensive and controlled study of post-hospital psychological intervention in survivors of myocardial infarction was reported by Ibrahim and his colleagues (Ibrahim et al., 1974). Subjects were both male and female patients between 35 and 65 years of age, who had been admitted to an intensive care unit with a confirmed infarction. They were approached shortly after discharge from the hospital and the first 12 eligible and consenting patients were assigned to an intervention group. The second 12 patients were assigned to a control group, and this procedure was repeated until five intervention and five control groups were achieved.

Patients in the intervention groups were given one and a half hours of group therapy on a weekly basis for a total of 50 weeks. The aim of this therapy was to provide an atmosphere in which problems and solutions common to cardiac patients could be shared. The therapists (experienced clinical psychologists) served primarily to encourage exploration of emotion and attitudes surrounding the infarction and avoided, so far as possible, any educative role with regard to exercise, diet, and medication. Patients were encouraged to raise these issues with their physicians as the most appropriate providers of such information. Although patients appeared comfortable in discussing the relatively pragmatic and concrete issues of resumption of leisure and social activity and return to active employment, there was an observed tendency among them to redirect discussions away from issues of emotional response and self-exploration of difficulties. Therapists were encouraged to counteract this tendency, so far as they were able. Patients in the control groups were offered routine follow-up contact with their physicians. No attempt was made to provide anything other than normal medical care as indicated by individual patient's conditions.

At discharge from the hospital, both intervention and control patients were found to be closely similar on a quantitative prognostic index of outcome. Follow-up examinations were made on all intervention patients completing the program and all control patients at 6, 12, and 18 months after discharge from the hospital. Intervention subjects showed a high level of compliance with the activity of group therapy, although 10 failed to complete the course. Although there was no difference between intervention and control patients in rates of re-hospitalization during the follow-up period, the mean duration of re-hospitalization for intervention patients was significantly shorter than that for control patients.

Although follow-up examinations suggested that intervention patients achieved no greater benefits in terms of reductions of levels of emotional distress and coronary risk factors than did those in control groups, the study produced one very important result. This was that at 18-month follow-up, intervention patients (who had been matched on all important prognostic variables with control patients) showed a 10% lower mortality rate from subsequent infarction than did their colleagues in the control groups. The importance of this finding is that it demonstrates the long-term survival benefits that can be gained by psychological intervention following infarction. However, it should be remembered that intervention patients participated in group therapy in a medical setting over the course of 50 weeks, and this may have sensitized them to seek help for perceived cardiac irregularities sooner than did the control patients.

A novel approach to the psychological management of the cardiac patient was reported by Prince and Miranda (1977). This was based on the notion that at least part of the recurrence rate following myocardial infarction could be explained in terms of the experience of a surfeit of distressing life events in the recovery phase. Thirty-seven survivors of a first infarction were enlisted into the study one week after discharge from the hospital. At this point, all patients were interviewed by telephone, and a 20-item self-report scale of psychological distress was administered. All patients were then followed up by telephone at monthly intervals over a period of seven months, and the same scale was given at each follow-up point. Whenever a patient scored 5 or more on the questionnaire (a common cut-off point indicating a potentially high level of psychological distress), a nurse was notified, and she made another telephone call to arrange a home visit. Patients almost always agreed to this.

A retrospective view of the experience reported by Prince and Miranda (1977) identified three primary areas of difficulty for which intervention was indicated. The first related to the simple provision of information concerning myocardial infarction and its medical treatment, and literature was prepared for distribution to assist patients in understanding this process. The second related to difficulties reported in social, economic, and interpersonal areas experienced by patients, and this resulted either in referral to social workers or back to the physician. Finally, some patients required periodic emotional support and reassurance, which was provided by the nurse. Occasionally, referral for psychiatric attention was necessary.

There was a significant correlation between levels of emotional and life stress following infarction and the probability of re-hospitalization. Moreover, when intervention was indicated by scores on the questionnaire but was unable to be initiated for one reason or another, the rates of re-hospitalization and subsequent cardiac death were greater than when intervention was either not indicated or was indicated and given. Although this study is small and was not designed as a prospective outcome study, its value is that it presents the novel approach of monitoring an individual patient's needs and of offering intervention on this needs basis. As such, it appears to have been both economical and, to the extent that evaluation could take place, effective in reducing both emotional distress and, possibly, further coronary events.

An extensive study by Naismith, Robinson, Shaw, and MacIntire (1979) once more focused attention on male patients under 60 years of age who had survived a first infarction. A consecutive series of such patients were randomly allocated either to intensive intervention or control groups resulting in 76 in the former and 77 in the latter. The initial contact was made on the third day after hospital admission while the patient was still in the intensive care unit, and regular contacts with a nurse (and a medical practitioner when necessary) were then initiated over a six-month post-hospital period. Patients were seen individually, both as outpatients and in their home, and wives were actively encouraged to participate in the intervention. The intervention procedure was open-ended and involved counseling directed toward the achievement of maximum social independence and medical advice with regard to secondary preventive measures. Regular follow-up for outcome evaluation was made at 6 weeks, 12 weeks, and 6 months after infarction. Patients allocated to the control group received routine medical care and printed educational material relating to risk factors for subsequent occurrence of infarction. They received no other active rehabilitation but were followed-up six months after discharge from the hospital to assess their outcome experience.

Patients in the intervention group were substantially more effective in achieving social independence over the follow-up period than were control patients. Moreover, the former group returned to work in a significantly shorter period of time than did the latter group. When patients in the intervention group were divided according to their levels of neuroticism, those with high levels of this attribute were more likely than others to achieve benefits from psychological intervention. Although this might indicate, paradoxically, that outcome is facilitated to an extent by the patient's neurotic state, there was no change over the follow-up period in neuroticism scores for either patient group. A more likely explanation might, therefore, rest with the facilitation of therapeutic compliance among patients with elevated levels of psychological arousal accompanying a neurotic state. Interestingly, the initial severity of the infarction had little bearing either on psychological or occupational outcomes. These results add to the encouraging evidence that psychological intervention following myocardial infarction can produce outcome benefits. The point of overriding importance for Naismith and her colleagues appeared to be that psychological intervention can be both open-ended and conducted relatively economically using nursing staff as the primary facilitators of behavioral change.

The primary focus of a study by Rahe and his colleagues (Rahe, O'Neil, Hagan, & Arthur, 1975; Rahe, Ward, & Hayes, 1979) was the provision of group therapy in the rehabilitation of survivors of myocardial infarction. Initial intake involved the random allocation of half a consecutive series of admitted patients to an intervention group and the other half to a control group, resulting in equal group sizes of 22 patients each. The early success of the program produced, however, an enthusiasm for the group psychotherapeutic approach among both prospective patients and staff, so that an additional 17 patients who met the admission criteria were allocated to psychological intervention. Both intervention samples and the control sample were matched on a variety of sociodemographic variables and on a quantitative index of the severity of the infarction. Patients allocated to intervention groups were scheduled to commence these approximately one month after hospital discharge. Groups consisted of approximately four patients and one psychiatrically trained therapist (sometimes with a co-therapist) and involved six sessions of 90 minutes each, held once every two weeks. Patients were expected to attend all six sessions, and spouses were invited to participate in the second session, which covered the role of physical and psychological risk factors in the genesis of coronary heart disease. All other sessions were closed.

Attendance averaged greater than 70%. Although there was no adherence to a strict therapeutic program, the six sessions covered the areas of (a) life stress and the onset of myocardial infarction, (b) the distribution of physical and psychological risk factors to coronary heart disease, (c) the coronary-prone behavior pattern, (d) home problems, and (e) problems associated with return to work after heart attack. The major approach to group sessions was an educational one. Groups were problem oriented, and an active discussion of problems encountered by patients was encouraged. Occasionally, specific behavioral prescriptions were given to individual patients in an effort to modify coronary-prone behaviors. However, this was the exception rather than the rule and was used only when patients demonstrated a high potential to benefit from such an exercise. Control subjects received no active rehabilitation procedures of a psychological kind but were given routine follow-up medical care.

Follow-up examinations were conducted at intervals of 6 months, 18 months, 36 months, and 48 months after infarction. The study demonstrated a range of benefits to be gained from the psychological intervention. A significantly greater number of control subjects than intervention subjects were hospitalized for coronary insufficiency during the first six months of follow-up, although this trend was not maintained over the total four-year follow-up period. Patients in the intervention group did, however, experience significantly fewer re-infarctions over the four-year follow-up period than did patients in the control group. In the period between 7 and 18 months following infarction, a significantly greater number of coronary artery bypass operations were performed in control patients relative to those involved in group therapy. These benefits to cardiological outcome did not, however, spill over into measures of coronary mortality, and long-term survival rates did not appear to be influenced by psychological intervention.

In addition to the apparent cardiovascular benefits to be gained by intervention, patients who participated in group therapy were more likely to return to full-time work during the follow-up period than were control patients. Although there was considerable variability in patients' levels of affect (depression and anxiety) over the course of the follow-up period, psychological intervention appeared to confer no consistent benefit on emotional outcome following infarction. This is surprising in view of the nature of the intervention (its psychological orientation) and of the accumulating evidence supporting the potential benefits of psychological intervention on affective distress after infarction. Neither was there a consistent influence of psychological intervention on a variety of physical risk factors (body weight, cigarette smoking, or serum cholesterol) or on the presence of the coronary-prone behavior pattern over the course of intervention. The importance of this study lies not only in its positive outcomes but also with the fact that its therapeutic elements were not open-ended but well specified and clearly described. This imparts the study with replicability and allows for an integration of the intervention strategy into routine clinical practice.

A modest study by Fielding (1980) was the first to specifically address the issue of problem-oriented behavior modification following infarction. Intervention rested on the assumption that a variety of behaviors commonly observed in response to infarction—notably anxiety, depression, and tension—might act to increase the risk of subsequent cardiac events by producing elevations in levels of psychophysiological arousal. Fielding's study was based on a consistent speculation (Cay et al., 1973; Nagle, Gangola, & Picton-Robinson, 1971) that outcomes such as social integration and return to work are more a function of the emotional and behavioral adjustments that patients make than of the severity of the infarction itself.

Ten male patients under 60 years of age and representing a consecutive series of admissions to an intensive care unit with a diagnosis of first infarction were randomly allocated either to an intervention or a control group. The five subjects in the intervention group were offered 10 sessions of group intervention each lasting 90 minutes, extending over 10 weeks and commencing shortly after discharge from the hospital. The first hour of each session was devoted to the resolution of difficulties and adjustment problems following infarction and adopted a problem-solving approach drawing on a variety of behavioral strategies. One session was given over entirely to education regarding the physical mechanisms and risk factors for myocardial infarction, and the remaining sessions conducted were devoted to progressive muscle relaxation. Patients in the control group were given routine medical care during this 10-week period. Both groups were matched with respect to age, social class, and severity of infarction.

Both self-report and psychophysiological assessments of emotional arousal were made on intake into the study and following the 10-week intervention and control period. Intervention subjects showed a significant reduction in muscle tension levels (as measured electromyographically) over the course of therapy, and this result was paralleled by self-reported measures of anxiety. No such temporal changes were observed for control subjects. Moreover, a significantly greater number of intervention than control subjects were able to return to work over this 10-week period. No outcome data were collected on subsequent coronary events. This study was limited in scope and involved only 10 patients who were followed up over a short period of time. Nonetheless, the encouraging results together with an emphasis on replicable behavioral strategies make it a potential model for the development of standardized behavioral intervention packages following myocardial infarction.

The trend from open-ended programs of psychological intervention and toward programs using more defined and circumscribed behavioral strategies is exemplified in a study by Langosch et al. (1982). Patients for this study were male survivors of a first infarction under the age of 60 years. Although these patients had been discharged from the hospital, all were inpatients in a cardiac rehabilitation center at the time of the study. Participation was voluntary, and, in contrast to other studies, approximately 40% of patients were reluctant to take part in any psychological program of rehabilitation.

The study compared two strategies of behavioral management, the first involving stress management and the second focusing specifically on progressive muscle relaxation. Participation in these two groups was according to personal preference, with the former group attracting 32 patients and the latter attracting 28. A random allocation procedure resulted in a further 30 subjects being assigned to a control group. Consistent with previous studies, the patients in these three groups were matched with respect to age, social class, and indices of the severity of infarction.

Intervention was conducted in groups and was intensively applied. It consisted of eight sessions, each lasting one hour and extending over the entire two-week period of the patient's rehabilitation hospitalization. Both intervention groups emphasized learned sensitivity so as to recognize early cues of tension and on doing so, to engage in coping behaviors to reduce the consequent arousal. The relaxation group followed a program involving a modified version of Jacobson's progressive muscle relaxation, which went on to emphasize the use of regular breathing exercises as an aid to relaxation. This was followed by autogenic training exercise centered on perceptions of "heaviness' and "warmth." At the termination of the relaxation exercises, patients were encouraged to generalize these to situations outside the rehabilitation hospital.

Patients in the control group received routine medial care but no direct psychological intervention.

A six-month follow-up of patients discharged from the rehabilitation hospital was also undertaken to assess outcome. No measure of either cardiological status or of social, demographic, or occupational variables distinguished either of the intervention groups, or the control group, on intake into the study. At the termination of the program, patients in the relaxation group reported a significantly reduced frequency of cardiac complications relative to patients in either the stress management or control groups. By contrast, patients in the self-management group reported decreased work stress and increased assertiveness in the occupational situation relative to both the other groups. At six-month follow-up, both intervention groups appeared to have an advantage in terms of return to work relative to the control group. Patients in the stress management group experienced significantly less difficulty in this respect than did patients in the relaxation group. Advantages that were manifest in terms of decreases in symptoms of cardiac distress and increases in levels of social and emotional adjustment, evident at the termination of program, appeared by and large to be maintained over the follow-up period, regardless of intervention group.

While acknowledging the limitations of the study, Langosch and his colleagues concluded that both treatment procedures produced improvements in psychological and occupational adjustment not evident in the control group. Benefits were most evident in terms of modifications of assertiveness and achievement-oriented behavior and social anxiety, and those modifications that were evident also appeared to be maintained over time. Moreover, there was evidence that the coping skills learned during intervention generalized to everyday life situations and were maintained following the termination of the intervention program.

The effects of behavioral self-management and relaxation were by no means identical. Behavioral self-management appeared to persuade patients that they were able to invoke the use of coping mechanisms in the face of stressful life experiences following discharge from the hospital. This program acted to improve patients' abilities to recognize and discriminate aspects of a stressful environmental situation as cues emerged from it, and to initiate activity from a repertoire of coping mechanisms in order to deal with this stress. The primary recommendation arising from the study is that the combination of behavioral self-management and relaxation into an intervention package should serve to enlarge the patient's coping repertoire and improve discrimination abilities in the face of life stress so as to enhance capacity for self-control over stressful conditions in daily life.

A study by Van Dixhoorn, De Loos, and Duivenvoorden (1983) looked specifically at the effects of progressive muscle relaxation training on outcomes following infarction. The rationale underlying this specific focus rested on three assumptions: (a) relaxation is a technique effective at a psychophysiological level both in reducing arousal and promoting a sense of psychological well-being; (b) it provides the individual with direct feedback and, therefore, a sensitivity to adequately estimate present emotional and physical states; and (c) it can be taught and practiced conveniently in most rehabilitation settings after only a small amount of training. Subjects were drawn from patients applying to join a coronary rehabilitation program who satisfied the criteria that they had suffered a well-documented myocardial infarction, were physically able to join a program involving exercise, and had been discharged from the hospital for a period of less than three weeks. All subjects were assessed for subjective perceptions of cardiac symptoms, immediate psychological state, sleep quality, and unpleasant bodily experiences. Following this, they were randomly assigned to one of two groups, the first involving relaxation training and the second being a control group and focusing only on exercising retraining.

The relaxation procedure involved the use of electromyographic biofeedback from the frontalis muscle, together with instructions and guidance about diaphragmatic breathing. Patients were also given instructions for passive relaxation so that they could generalize the procedure to situations outside of the clinic. Relaxation instructions were given individually, in sessions averaging one hour's duration occurring weekly over six weeks. Patients in this group were also given exercise retraining using a standard bicycle ergometer, adjusted to allow peak loads of 80% of maximal heart rate. Patients in the control group received only exercise retraining and were placed on a five-week program of daily training on the bicycle ergometer, once more directed toward the attainment of peak loads of 80% of maximal heart rate. Exercise retraining was accomplished in groups of four patients. A repeat evaluation of all intake variables was given to all patients immediately upon termination of the intervention procedures.

Relaxation training conferred no outcome benefits additional to exercise retraining on measures of anxiety, sleep quality, or somatic stress. Patients in the relaxation group did, however, report significantly higher scores on a scale of subjective well-being and significantly lower scores on a scale reflecting perceived invalidity than did subjects in the exercise-only group. The strength of these differences led the authors to conclude that the addition of relaxation training made a positive and substantial contribution to the well-being of patients following myocardial infarction. Regrettably, the outcome measures were restricted to those of subjective experience immediately upon termination of the intervention program, and follow-up was not undertaken for a sufficiently long period of time to examine the influence of relaxation training on measures of occupational rehabilitation and subsequent coronary morbidity and mortality. The short-term benefits of this program seem, nonetheless, to be very worthwhile, and long-term studies of the intervention strategies would appear to be indicated.

Clinical Implications

This overview of studies on psychological intervention after myocardial infarction is not exhaustive but is representative of the efforts undertaken to employ psychological and behavioral techniques in the management of patients who have survived this life-threatening event. In common with many areas assessing the usefulness of such interventions in medical management, the methodologies of many studies limit to a serious degree the inferences that may be drawn from the results. Issues of inadequate sample sizes, poor selection of both patient and control groups (the absence of true control groups in some cases), scant attention to measurement, inadequate description of intervention strategies (so limiting the ability of independent groups to replicate either clinically or empirically), failure to demonstrate specific versus nonspecific effects of intervention, and poor regard for the importance of follow-up periods have all presented themselves for consideration.

These issues, however, do not negate the potential importance of psychological intervention following infarction but point to the need for well-controlled research guided by sound theoretical principles. There is sufficient evidence to support at least a nonspecific effect of psychological intervention on aspects of well-being and psychological comfort after myocardial infarction. Moreover, there is a definite trend toward an effect of psychological intervention on occupational rehabilitation and return to work. There is not, however, sufficiently compelling or even very suggestive evidence on the role of psychological intervention in cardiological outcome. This is not to say the potential is not there; the theoretical basis for such a possibility certainly exists. The design of a definitive study would be, however, inordinately difficult. Given the interest currently pervading the area, there is little doubt that the definitive study, or something closely approximating it, will eventually be done. Until then, however, we must remain content to regard the area as having clinical promise.

REFERENCES

Adsett, C. A., & Bruhn, J. G. (1968). Short-term group psychotherapy with post-myocardial infarction patients and their wives. *Canadian Medical Association Journal, 99* 577-584.

Brown, J. S., & Rawlinson, M. E. (1977). Sex differences in sick role rejection and in work performance following cardiac surgery. *Journal of Health and Social Behavior, 18,* 276-292.

Bruhn, J. G., Wolf, S., & Philips, B. U. (1971). A psychosocial study of surviving male coronary patients and controls followed over nine years. *Journal of Psychosomatic Research, 15,* 305-313.

Byrne, D. G. (1979). Anxiety as state and trait in survived myocardial infarction. *British Journal of Social and Clinical Psychology, 18,* 417-423.

Byrne, D. G. (1981). Sex differences in the reporting of symptoms of depression in the general population. *British Journal of Clinical Psychology, 20,* 83-92.

Byrne, D. G. (1982). Psychological responses to illness and outcome after heart attack. *Journal of Psychosomatic Research, 26,* 105-112.

Byrne, D. G. (1987). *The behavioral management of the cardiac patient.* Norwood, NJ: Ablex.

Byrne, D. G., & Whyte, H. M. (1978). Dimensions of illness behavior in survivors of myocardial infarction. *Journal of Psychosomatic Research, 22,* 485-491.

Byrne, D. G., & Whyte, H. M. (1979). Severity of illness and illness behavior: A comparative study of coronary care patients. *Journal of Psychosomatic Research, 23,* 57-61.

Byrne, D. G., & Whyte, H. M. (1980). Life events and myocardial infarction revisited: The role of measures of individual impact. *Psychosomatic Medicine, 42,* 1-10.

Byrne, D. G., Whyte, H. M., & Butler, K. L. (1981). Illness behavior and outcome following survived myocardial infarction: A prospective study. *Journal of Psychosomatic Research, 25,* 97-107.

Case, R. B., Heller, S. S., & Shamai, E. (1983). Type A behavior and survival after myocardial infarction. *Circulation, 68*(29), Suppl. 3.

Cassem, N. H., & Hackett, T. P. (1971). Psychiatric consultation in a coronary unit. *Annals of Internal Medicine, 75,* 9-14.

Cay, E. L., Philip, A. E., & Aitken, C. B. (1976). Psychological aspects of cardiac rehabilitation. In O. Hill (Ed.), *Modern trends in psychosomatic medicine* (pp. 330-348). London: Butterworth.

Cay, E. L., Vetter, N., Philip, A. E., & Dugard, P. (1972). Psychological reactions to coronary care unit. *Journal of Psychosomatic Research, 16,* 437-447.

Cay, E. L., Vetter, N., Philip, A. E., & Dugard, P. (1973). Return to work after a heart attack. *Journal of Psychosomatic Research, 17,* 231-243.

Crain, R. B., & Missal, M. E. (1956). The industrial employee with myocardial infarction and his ability to return to work: Follow-up report. *New England Journal of Medicine, 56,* 2238-2244.

Croog, S. H., & Levine, S. (1977). *The heart patient recovers.* New York: Human Science Press.

Croog, S. H., Shapiro, D. S., & Levine, S. (1971). Denial among heart patients. *Psychosomatic Medicine, 33,* 385-392.

Degre-Coustry, C., & Grevisse, M. (1982). Psychological problems in rehabilitation after myocardial infarction. *Advances in Cardiology, 29,* 126-131.

Dellipiani, A. W., Cay, E. L., Philip, A. E., Vetter, N. J., Colling, W. A., Donaldson, R. J., & McCormick, P. (1976). Anxiety after a heart attack. *British Heart Journal, 38,* 752-757.

Diederiks, J. P., van der Sluijs, H., Weeda, H. W., & Schobre, M. G. (1983). Predictors of physical activity one year after myocardial infarction. *Scandinavian Journal of Rehabilitation Medicine, 15,* 103-107.

Doerhman, S. R. (1977). Psychosocial aspects of recovery from coronary heart disease: A review. *Social Science and Medicine, 11,* 199-218.

Dominian, J., & Dobson, M. (1969). Psychological attitudes to a coronary care unit. *British Medical Journal, 4,* 705–799.

Dreyfuss, F., Dasberg, H., & Assael, M. I. (1969). The relationship of myocardial infarction to depressive illness. *Psychotherapy and Psychosomatics, 17,* 73–81.

Fielding, R. (1980). A note on behavioral treatment in the rehabilitation of myocardial infarction patients. *British Journal of Social and Clinical Psychology, 19,* 157–161.

Finlayson, A., & McEwen, J. (1977). *Coronary heart disease and patterns of living.* London: Croom Helm.

Frankenhaeuser, M. (1976). Experimental approaches to the study of catecholamines and emotion. In L. Levi (Ed.), *Emotions: Their parameters and measurement* (pp. 209–234). New York: Raven Press.

Frankenhaeuser, M. (1979). Psychoneuroendocrine approaches to the study of emotion as related to stress and coping. In H. E. Howe & R. A. Dienstbier (Eds.), *Nebraska symposium on motivation* (pp. 123–161). Lincoln: University of Nebraska Press.

Geersten, H. R., Ford, M., & Castle, C. M. (1976). The subjective aspects of coronary care. *Nursing Research, 25,* 211–215.

Groen, J. J. (1976). Psychosomatic aspects of ischemic (coronary) heart disease. In O. Hill (Ed.), *Modern trends in psychosomatic medicine* (pp. 288–329). London: Butterworth.

Gruen, W. (1975). Effects of brief psychotherapy during the hospitalization period on the recovery process in heart attacks. *Journal of Consulting and Clinical Psychology, 43,* 223–232.

Hackett, T. P., & Cassem, N. H. (1976). White and blue collar responses to heart attack. *Journal of Psychosomatic Research, 20,* 85–95.

Hackett, T. P., Cassem, N. H., & Wishnie, H. A. (1968). The coronary care unit: An appraisal of psychological hazards. *New England Journal of Medicine, 279,* 1365.

Haney, C. A. (1977). Illness behavior and psychosocial correlates of cancer. *Social Science and Medicine, 11,* 223–228.

Humphries, J. O. (1977). Survival after myocardial infarction: Prognosis and management. *Modern Concepts of Cardiovascular Disease, 46,* 51–56.

Ibrahim, M. A., Feldman, J. G., Sultz, H. A., Staiman, M. G., Young, L. J., & Dean, D. (1974). Management after myocardial infarction: A controlled trial of the effect of group psychotherapy. *International Journal of Psychiatry in Medicine, 5,* 253–268.

Jellinek, V. M., McDonald, I. G., Ryan, W. F., Ziffer, R. W., Clemens, A., & Gerloff, J. (1982). Assessment of cardiac risk 10 days after uncomplicated myocardial infarction. *British Medical Journal, 284,* 227–230.

Jenkins, C. D. (1978). A comparative review of the interview and questionnaire methods in the assessment of the coronary-prone behavior pattern. In T. M. Dembroski, S. M. Weiss, J. L. Shields, S. G. Haynes, & M. Feinlieb (Eds.), *Coronary-prone behavior* (pp. 71–86). New York: Springer-Verlag.

Jenkins, C. D., Zyzanski, S. J., & Rosenman, R. H. (1976). Risk of new myocardial infarction in middle-aged men with manifest coronary heart disease. *Circulation, 53,* 342–347.

Jenkins, C. D., Zyzanski, S. J., Rosenman, R. H., & Cleveland, G. L. (1971). Association of coronary-prone behavior scores with recurrence of coronary heart disease. *Journal of Chronic Diseases, 24,* 601–611.

Johnson, W. L. (1966). *A study of family adjustment to the crisis of cardiac disease.* New York: American Nurses Foundation.

Kallio, V., Hamalainen, H., Hakkila, J., & Luurila, O. J. (1979). Reduction in sudden deaths by a multifactorial intervention program after acute myocardial infarction. *Lancet, 2,* 1091–1094.

Klein, R. F., Kliner, V. A., Zipes, D. P., Troyer, W. G., & Wallace, A. G.. (1968). Transfer from a coronary care unit. *Archives of Internal Medicine, 122,* 104–108.

Kornitzer, M., De Backer, G., Dramaix, M., Kittel, F., Thilly, C., Graffar, K., & Vuylsteek, K. (1983). Belgian heart disease prevention project: Incidence and mortality results. *Lancet, 1,* 1066–1070.

Langosch, W., Seer, P., Brodner, G., Kallinke, D., Kulick, B., & Heim, F. (1982). Behavior therapy with coronary heart disease patients: Results of a comparative study. *Journal of Psychosomatic Research, 26,* 475–484.

Lee, R. L., & Ball, P. A. (1975). Some thought on the psychology of the coronary care unit patient. *American Journal of Nursing, 75,* 1498–1501.

Lipowski, Z. J. (1975). Physical illness, the patient and his environment. In S. Arieti (Ed.), *American handbook of psychiatry* (pp. 3–42). New York: Basic Books.

Lloyd, G. G., & Cawley, R. H. (1982). Psychiatric morbidity after myocardial infarction. *Quarterly Journal of Medicine, 51,* 33–42.

Lown, B., DeSilva, R. A., Reich, P., & Murawski, B. J. (1980). Psychophysiologic factors in sudden cardiac death. *American Journal of Psychiatry, 137,* 1325–1335.

Lynch, J. J., Thomas, S. J., Mills, M. E., Malinow, K., & Katcher, A. H. (1974). The effects of human contact on cardiac arrthymia in coronary care patients. *Journal of Nervous and Mental Diseases, 158,* 83–89.

Marmor, A., Geltman, E. M., Schechtman, K., Sobel, B. E., & Roberts, R. (1982). Recurrent myocardial infarction: Clinical predictors and prognostic implications. *Circulation, 66,* 415–421.

Marmor, A., Sobel, B. E., & Roberts, R. (1981). Factors presaging early recurrent myocardial infarction (extension). *American Journal of Cardiology, 48,* 603–610.

Martin, C. A., Thompson, D. L., Armstrong, B. K., Hobbs, M. S. T., & De Clerk, N. (1983). Long-term prognosis after recovery from myocardial infarction: A nine-year follow-up of the Perth coronary register. *Circulation, 68,* 961–969.

Mather, H. G., Pearson, N. G., & Read, K. L. O. (1971). Acute myocardial infarction: Home and hospital treatment. *British Medical Journal, 3,* 334.

Mayou, R. (1979). The course and determinants of reactions to myocardial infarction. *British Journal of Psychiatry, 134,* 588–594.

Mayou, R. (1984). Predition of emotional and social outcome after a heart attack. *Journal of Psychosomatic Research, 28,* 17–25.

Mayou, R., Foster, A., & Williamson, B. (1978). Psychosocial adjustments in patients one year after myocardial infarction. *Journal of Psychosomatic Research, 22,* 447–453.

Morris, J. W. (1959). Occupation and coronary heart disease. *Archives of Internal Medicine, 104,* 903–907.

Mulcahy, R. (1976). The rehabilitation of patients with coronary heart disease: A clinician's view. In U. Stockmeier (Ed.), *Psychological approach to the rehabilitation of coronary patients* (pp. 52–61). Berlin: Springer.

Multiple Risk Factor Intervention Trial Research Group. (1981). Multiple risk factor intervention trial: Risk factor changes and mortality results. *Journal of the American Medical Association, 248,* 1465–1477.

Nagle, R., Gangola, R., & Picton-Robinson, I. (1971). Factors influencing return to work after a myocardial infarction. *Lancet, 2,* 454–455.

Naismith, L. D., Robinson, J. R., Shaw, G. B., & MacIntire, M. M. J. (1979). Psychological rehabilitation after myocardial infarction. *British Medical Journal, 1,* 439–442.

Norris, D. E., Caughey, D. E., Deeming, L. W., Mercer, C. J., & Scott, P. J. (1970). Coronary prognostic index for predicting survival after recovery from acute myocardial infarction. *Lancet, 2,* 485–488.

Oldenburg, B., & Perkins, R. (1984). *Psychological intervention in myocardial infarction.* Unpublished manuscript, Prince Henry Hospital, Department of Psychiatry, Sydney, Australia.

Peel, A. A. F., Semple, T., Wang, I., Lancaster, W. M., & Dall, J. L. G. (1960). A coronary prognostic index for grading the severity of infarction. *British Heart Journal, 24,* 743–760.

Pell, S., & D'Alonzo, C. A. (1963). Acute myocardial infarction in a large industrial population: Report of a 6-year study of 1,356 cases. *Journal of the American Medical Association, 185,* 831–838.

Phillips, D. L., & Segal, B. E. (1969). Sexual status and psychiatric symptoms. *American Sociological Review, 34,* 58–72.

Philip, A. E., Cay, E. L., Stuckey, N. A., & Vetter, N. J. (1981). Multiple predictors and multiple outcomes after myocardial infarction. *Journal of Psychosomatic Research, 25,* 137–141.

Philip, A. E., Cay, E. L., Vetter, N. J., & Stuckey, N. A. (1979). Personal traits and the physical, psychiatric and social state of patients one year after myocardial infarction. *International Journal of Rehabilitation Research, 2,* 479–487.

Pole, D. J., McCall, M. G., Reader, R., & Woodings, T. (1977). Incidence and mortality of acute myocardial infarction in Perth, Western Australia. *Journal of Chronic Diseases, 30,* 19–27.

Powell, L. H., Friedman, M., Thoresen, C. E., Gill, J. J., & Ulmer, D. K. (1984). Can the Type A behavior pattern be altered after myocardial infarction? A second year report from the recurrent coronary prevention project. *Psychosomatic Medicine, 26,* 293–313.

Prince, R., & Miranda, L. (1977). Monitoring life stress to prevent recurrence of coronary heart disease episodes: Report of a feasibility study. *Canadian Psychiatric Association Journal, 22,* 161–169.

Rahe, R. H., O'Neil, T., Hagan, A., & Arthur, R. J. (1975). Brief group therapy following myocardial infarction: Eighteen-month follow-up of a controlled trial. *International Journal of Psychiatry in Medicine, 6,* 349–358.

Rahe, R. H., Ward, H. W., & Hayes, V. (1979). Brief group therapy in myocardial infarction rehabilitation: Three- to four-year follow-up of a controlled trial. *Psychosomatic Medicine, 41,* 229–242.

Razin, A. M. (1982). Psychosocial intervention in coronary artery disease: A review. *Psychosomatic Medicine, 44,* 363–387.

Rose, G., Tunstall-Pedoe, H. D., & Heller, R. F. (1983). United Kingdom heart disease prevention project: Incidence and mortality results. *Lancet, 1*, 1062-1065.

Rosenman, R. H., Friedman, M., & Jenkins, C. D. (1967). Recurring and fatal myocardial infarction in the Western Collaborative Group Study. *American Journal of Cardiology, 19*, 771-789.

Ruberman, W., Weinblatt, E., Goldberg, J. D., & Chaudhary, B. S. (1983). Education, psychosocial stress and sudden cardiac death. *Journal of Chronic Diseases, 36*, 151-160.

Ruberman, W., Weinblatt, E., Goldberg, J. D., & Chaudhary, B. S. (1984). Psychosocial influences on mortality after myocardial infarction. *New England Journal of Medicine, 311*, 552-559.

Segers, M. J., & Mertens, C. (1975). Relationship between anxiety, depression, self-ratings and cardiac heart disease risk factors among obese, normal and lean individuals. *Journal of Psychosomatic Research, 20*, 25-35.

Segers, M. J., & Mertens, C. (1977a). Personality aspects of cardiac heart disease related behavior. *Journal of Psychosomatic Research, 21*, 79-85.

Segers, M. J., & Mertens, C. (1977b). Preventive behavior and awareness of myocardial infarction: A factorial definition of anxiety. *Journal of Psychosomatic Research, 21*, 213-223.

Soloff, P. H. (1978). Denial and rehabilitation of the post-infarction patient. *International Journal of Psychiatry in Medicine, 8*, 125-132.

Spielberger, C. D. (1972). *Anxiety: Current trends in theory and research.* New York: Academic Press.

Stein, E. H., Murdaugh, J., & MacLeod, J. A. (1969). Brief psychotherapy for psychiatric reactions to physical illness. *American Journal of Psychiatry, 8*, 1040-1047.

Surwit, R. S., Williams, R. B., & Shapiro, D. (1982). *Behavioral approaches to cardiovascular disease.* New York: Academic Press.

Takeuchi, M. (1983). In-hospital rehabilitation at the recovery phase after acute myocardial infarction. *Japanese Circulation Journal, 47*, 744-751.

Thockloth, R. M., Ho, S. C., Wright, H., & Seldon, W. A. (1973). Is cardiac rehabilitation really necessary. *Medical Journal of Australia, 2*, 669-674.

Van Dixhoorn, J., De Loos, J., & Duivenvoorden, H. J. (1983). Contribution of relaxation technique to the rehabilitation of myocardial infarction patients. *Psychotherapy and Psychosomatics, 40*, 137-147.

Vetter, N. J., Cay, E. L., Philip, A. E., & Strange, R. C. (1977). Anxiety on admission to a coronary care unit. *Journal of Psychosomatic Research, 21*, 73-78.

Weinblatt, E., Shapiro, S., Frank, C. W., & Sager, R. V. (1966). Return to work and work status following first myocardial infarction. *American Journal of Public Health, 56*, 169-185.

Wrzesniewski, K. (1977). Anxiety and rehabilitation after myocardial infarction. *Psychotherapy and Psychosomatics, 27*, 41-46.

16

Psychological and Pharmacologic Treatment of Anxiety, Generalized Anxiety Disorder, Social Phobia, and Panic Disorder

James W. Jefferson and John H. Greist

Many of the anxiety cases confronting clinicians fall outside the formal diagnostic criteria of the *Diagnostic and Statistical Manual of Mental Disorders* (DSM-III-R— American Psychiatric Association, 1987) and may be associated with other psychiatric and nonpsychiatric medical disorders. Anxiety as a reaction to myriad psychosocial or physical stressors may not meet the "maladaptive" criterion for an adjustment disorder yet may still be a cause of discomfort and impairment. When and how to treat anxiety is a matter of clinical judgment. Few would contest the need to find relief for someone experiencing Darwin's description of fear:

> *The frightened man first stands like a statue motionless and breathless . . . the heart beats quickly and violently . . . the skin instantly becomes pale . . . perspiration immediately exudes from the skin and as the surface is then cold [we have what is termed] a cold sweat . . . the hairs also on the skin stand erect and superficial muscles shiver . . . in connection with the disturbed action of the heart, the breathing is hurried . . . the mouth becomes dry . . . one of the best marked symptoms is trembling of all the muscles of the body and this is often first seen in the lips. (cited in Marks, 1978, p. 7)*

As this symptom complex intensified still further it was called terror:

> *The heart beats wildly or may fail to act and faintness ensues; there is a death-like pallor; the breathing is labored; the wings of the nostrils are widely dilated . . . there is a gulping of the throat, protruding eyeballs . . . dilated pupils, rigid muscles. [In the final stages] as fear rises to an extreme pitch, the dreadful scream of terror is heard. Great beads of sweat stand on the skin. All the muscles of the body are relaxed, utter prostration soon follows, and the mental powers fail. The intestines are affected. The sphincter muscles cease to act, and no longer retain the contents of the body. (cited in Marks, 1978, p. 7)*

Unless it is brief, self-limiting, and nonrecurrent, anxiety of this magnitude is most deserving of treatment. On a lesser scale, however, what constitutes abnormal anxiety may be a source of disagreement between patient and clinician or among clinicians themselves. It is also important to recognize that although anxiety may be normal, it may nonetheless be of sufficient severity and duration to require treatment.

DIAGNOSIS, THE CORNERSTONE OF TREATMENT

Anxiety and Medical Disorders

Several years ago our psychiatric consultation service was asked to evaluate and treat the anxiety of an orthopedic patient. During the evaluation, however, the patient steadfastly denied feeling anxious but, instead, acknowledged a long-standing problem with his "nerves." When asked to explain, he extended his arms to reveal a fine tremor that was readily diagnosed as essential tremor. The psychiatric consultant found no psychopathology, advised against the use of anti-anxiety drugs, and pointed out that a beta-blocker was the indicated treatment for essential tremor. This case illustrates the pitfalls that await clinicians who jump to unwarranted linguistic conclusions.

Whereas anxiety that occurs in association with a medical illness may be due to an independent, coexisting anxiety disorder, it is more likely to be either a psychological reaction to the medical illness or an intrinsic component of that illness (Jefferson & Marshall, 1981). Except in those whose ability to deny is of gargantuan proportion, anxiety almost always accompanies the symptoms of or the diagnosis of a major medical illness. The discovered but not yet biopsied breast lump or the exercise-induced crushing chest pain are but two examples. Medical illness carries with it the threat of death, disability, suffering, and fears of the unknown. A number of medical disorders have anxiety symptoms as an intrinsic part of the disorder. To list all of these conditions would be burdensome; suffice it to say that some of the better known are hyperthyroidism, hypoglycemia, pheochromocytoma, and hyperadrenalism. Treating anxiety without recognizing the underlying conditions could have grave clinical consequences.

The unfortunate tendency for some clinicians to "fire before aiming" is illustrated by the case of the hyperventilating soldier. A young military recruit was returning to camp following a visit home over the Christmas holidays. On the way to the airport he became anxious and began hyperventilating. Following a cursory evaluation at a local emergency room, he was diagnosed as having "separation anxiety," treated with diazepam, and sent back to the airport. His symptoms worsened, however, necessitating a return to the emergency room. When a more extensive history was obtained, it was learned that the soldier enjoyed the military and was looking forward to returning to camp—an attitude inconsistent with a diagnosis of separation anxiety. A more extensive medical evaluation ensued and led to the recognition of a massive pneumomediastinum and pneumopericardium (hardly a psychiatric anxiety disorder). To cite another example, a 52-year-old woman with a three-day history of panic attacks, palpitations, and breathlessness received the diagnosis of "hysterical hyperventilation" and was treated with diazepam and a psychiatric referral (Treasure, Fowler, Millington, & Wise, 1987). When she returned to the emergency room several days later, the correct diagnosis of diabetic ketoacidosis was made—not a condition that could be expected to respond favorably to diazepam and psychiatric referral.

Anxiety Associated with Other Psychiatric Disorders

In nonpsychiatric medical settings, more patients with major depression are (inappropriately) treated with anti-anxiety drugs than with antidepressants. Because conventional anxiolytics are generally not effective antidepressants (alprazolam may be an exception), failure to recognize anxiety as a manifestation of an underlying depressive disorder can only delay appropriate treatment. Incidentally, there is growing evidence that antidepressant drugs also have anti-anxiety properties. The effectiveness of heterocyclic and monoamine oxidase inhibitor antidepressants in the treatment of panic disorder (even in the absence of associated depression) is a well-established example.

Delirium is another condition commonly misidentified as a primary anxiety problem. Before the more classic manifestations of memory impairment, disorientation, and hallucinations appear, anxiety may be the predominant symptom. The use of conventional anxiolytics may aggravate the delirium by further impairing cognition. Anxiety is frequently associated with substance use and withdrawal. The list of potential offenders is extensive, but a few examples should suffice. Akathisia is a common neurological side effect of antipsychotic drugs that is often mistaken for anxiety that is not drug related. Symptoms of akathisia include restlessness and the inability to sit still. Although benzodiazepine anxiolytics can be useful in the treatment of akathisia, alternative treatments may be more practical and more effective. These include reducing or discontinuing the antipsychotic or the addition of an anticholinergic or beta-receptor blocking drug.

Excessive caffeine use is another cause of anxiety symptoms, the treatment of which should be intake reduction rather than the use of an anti-anxiety drug. In addition to mimicking anxiety disorders, caffeinism may aggravate coexisting anxiety disorders and may also counteract the effectiveness of appropriately prescribed anti-anxiety drugs. Because caffeine is such an integral part of our society, it is not often considered to be a drug, and its role as an anxiogenic agent remains unrecognized. Other drug classes that commonly generate anxiety-type symptoms include bronchodilators, sympathomimetics, and steroids. A careful drug use history should be an integral part of every anxiety evaluation.

Substance withdrawal is another important, often unrecognized, cause of anxiety symptoms, with anti-anxiety drugs themselves being major offenders. Although the intensity and duration of withdrawal syndromes vary both with drug and dosage, most medications with anti-anxiety activity should be assumed to have anxiety as a withdrawal-related symptom (a possible exception is the anxiolytic, buspirone). Adrenergic rebound associated with discontinuation of beta-blockers and clonidine may also present as anxiety. Alcohol withdrawal is a well-recognized cause of anxiety, although denial on the part of the patient often obscures the diagnosis. Fortunately, this is one condition for which benzodiazepine anxiolytics are beneficial.

It should be obvious that embarking on the treatment of anxiety without scrupulous attention to diagnosis would be folly. In many situations, a specific diagnosis will lead to a specific treatment. From the examples given, it should be apparent that anxiety associated with diabetic ketoacidosis requires quite different treatment from caffeine-induced anxiety, the anxiety of a major depression, or a primary anxiety disorder. With this in mind, we now focus on general and then more specific treatment approaches to anxiety, generalized anxiety disorder (GAD), social phobia, and panic disorder.

TREATMENT APPROACHES

Education, support, and reassurance are (or should be) essential components of all psychotherapies. They may be, in fact, the vital ingredients in the success of many therapies that have evolved into elegant, formalized, yet relatively invalidated structures. Most anxiety is treated outside professional settings by relatives, friends, neighbors, or others with a sense of empathy and understanding. People who have anxiety as a psychological reaction to a medical disorder often respond well to the ministrations of a sensitive primary care physician. Unfortunately, the dazzle of technology has seduced many physicians into treating patients inanimately like automobiles with malfunctioning carburetors or clogged fuel lines. It would be well to heed the words of Peabody (1927, cited in Strauss, 1968): "The treatment of disease may be entirely impersonal, the care of the patient must be completely personal." In many cases, the success of a mental health professional is due to this person-oriented approach to treatment.

There is little scientific evidence that people with anxiety disorders respond to or should be solely treated with psychoanalysis or psychoanalytically oriented psychotherapy. This is not to say that these modalities are without value for certain individuals but merely to point out that the rate of return from other therapies is likely to be considerably greater. Richard Asher, addressing the British Psychological Society in 1955, said it well:

> Psychiatry seems to me to differ from medicine in having a closer resemblance to religion. Beliefs and dogmas are promulgated by certain masters—Freud, Adler, Jung, and so on—and these ideas are believed more from reverence of their originator than from repeated experimental observation.
> Secondly, the language of psychiatry, like that of religion, is often . . . esoteric and concerns itself with concepts and abstractions whose exact meaning is less precisely comprehended than are the majority of medical concepts . . . Although much wisdom is written by psychiatrists, the nature of the subject and its language make it hard for the ordinary doctor (and patient) to distinguish the profound from the profuse. (cited in Greist, Jefferson, & Marks, 1986, p. 119)

In general, the psychotherapies that have been most effective or promising for treating anxiety, GAD, and panic disorder are cognitive and behavioral therapies. Their specific applications to these disorders are discussed more extensively in the next section. In brief, cognitive therapy is directed at changing unrealistically negative cognitions held by patients about themselves, the world, and the future. Although a number of well-conducted studies have shown cognitive therapy to be of benefit in treating certain types of depression, studies of its effectiveness in treating anxiety and anxiety disorders are just beginning.

Behavior therapies have well-established effectiveness in the treatment of some, but not all, anxiety disorders. Broadly defined, behavioral principles include education, support, and reassurance, but, they also involve more specific techniques. People with agoraphobia, which may occur as a complication of recurrent panic attacks or exist as a separate entity, are especially amenable to treatment with exposure therapy. There is growing evidence that people who have panic attacks may be effectively treated both acutely and in a preventive fashion by behavioral techniques. Patients with GAD, however, have not been particularly responsive to behavior therapy, perhaps, because it is difficult to find a specific area on which to focus exposure therapy. Relaxation and biofeedback are often used to treat people with GAD, but the studies necessary to validate their efficacy have not been done.

Patients with anxiety may not require treatment with medication. When they do, they may respond better to antidepressants (even in the absence of depression) than to conventional anti-anxiety drugs such as benzodiazepines. The precise role of the various classes of drugs with anxiolytic properties is constantly evolving as more scientific testing is done and as newer agents are introduced. Whether anxiolytics are overprescribed or underprescribed continues to be a matter of debate. There is also convincing evidence that anxiety and anxiety disorders are underdiagnosed and, consequently, undertreated. At the same time, the millions of annual prescriptions for these drugs and their apparent haphazard use in patient populations suggest both overuse and misuse. The truth must lie somewhere between these two extremes.

> Whatever treatment is used, it is important for each patient to understand the reasons that particular treatment was selected, what to expect in terms of improvement and side effects, and what to do if treatment does not proceed as expected. Selecting the best treatment for each patient requires knowledge, experience, skills, and—frankly—sometimes luck. When one treatment is ineffective, another may yet be successful. Optimism that a successful treatment will be found, persistence in pursuit of a successful treatment, and flexibility in matching a patient with the best treatment are hallmarks of good therapy. (Greist et al., 1986, p. 105)

Treatments should be selected "on the basis of their scientifically demonstrated effectiveness, efficacy of administration, cost, patient preference, and availability of capable therapists" (Greist et al., 1986, p. 103). Finally, prior to elaborating on the psychological and pharmacological approaches to treatment, it would be well to once again heed the words of Richard Asher, who said "Just as we swallow food because we like it and not because of its nutritional content, so do we swallow ideas because we like them and not because of the rational content" (cited in Jones, 1972).

PSYCHOTHERAPY

All psychotherapies share certain nonspecific features "such as warmth, empathy, positive regard, encouragement, reassurance, forgiveness, simply attending sessions, belief in treatment, and expectation of success" (Greist et al., 1986, p. 117). Psychotherapies differ in their theoretical underpinnings and the amount of support for their effectiveness and safety based on controlled research findings. There are now more than 200 psychotherapies with common nonspecific factors but different theoretical explanations for their claimed benefits. Often the theoretical differences are but sophistical nuances of psychoanalytic theory, and it is surprising how few psychotherapies have been subjected to scientific scrutiny. Most psychotherapies are more akin to religions than to treatments based on scientific studies, and their advocacy depends more on belief than on knowledge. Behavioral and cognitive psychotherapies are exceptions to this general observation. Although their theoretical bases are as sophisticated as those of dynamic psychotherapies, both have been the subject of many controlled studies, and their relative strengths and limitations are better defined.

Dynamic Psychotherapies

> Dynamic psychotherapies assume that behavior is determined by genetic endowment, present realities, and past experience. Conflictual parts of past experience may be hidden as "unconscious" yet be quite important in determining present situations and functioning. Psychoanalysis is the grand-daddy of dynamic psychotherapies, and other dynamic therapies also seek to understand unresolved unconscious conflicts that may lead to Anxiety Disorders. Interpretation of dreams, free association, and exploration of the past as it relates to present problems are important techniques of psychoanalytic psychotherapy. Other psychodynamic psychotherapists may use the same techniques but focus more on present relationships and role functioning. Using these techniques, attempts are made to understand the possible roles that less conscious conflicts play in Anxiety Disorders and to find new ways of dealing with people, thoughts, and feelings. (Greist et al., 1986, p. 120)

Some present-day dynamic psychotherapists are either unaware of or have forgotten Sigmund Freud's statements about the ineffectiveness of psychoanalysis in treating phobia:

> One can hardly ever master a phobia if one waits till the patient lets the analysis influence him to give up. . . . One succeeds only when one can induce them through the influence of the analysis to . . . go about alone and struggle with the anxiety while they make the attempt. (cited in Greist et al., 1986, p. 120)

There is surprisingly little evidence that dynamic psychotherapies are effective in the treatment of panic disorder. In fact, their ineffectiveness is documented by the past experience of patients and practitioners who have worked long and hard but unsuccessfully to find and treat conflicts causing the eruptions of anxiety called panic. As effective drug treatments emerged, many psychiatrists who practice dynamic psychotherapy have embraced medications for treatment of panic disorder. A similar picture has emerged with regard to the use of benzodiazepines for panic disorder and, more recently, buspirone for the treatment of GAD, although there is more persistence in the use of dynamic psychotherapeutic approaches for this problem. Free-floating anxiety, unassociated with specific fears or symptoms, remains the legitimate domain of dynamic psychotherapies. Tradition supports this use of psychotherapies, but problems of accurately defining free-floating anxiety and the effective elements of dynamic psychotherapies have precluded careful study of the efficacy and safety of psychotherapies for this indication.

Cognitive Therapy

Cognitive therapists work from the perspective that changing negative thoughts or cognitions will lead to changes in unpleasant feelings and maladaptive (often avoidance) behaviors. By contrast, behavior therapists believe that reductions in avoidance will be followed by improvements in cognitions and affects, although a delay of a few weeks or months is commonly seen (cognitive or affective lag). Because both approaches seek improvement on these three dimensions (cognitions, affects, and behaviors), measures of these parameters are relevant in studies of the efficacy of both treatments.

Virtually all cognitive therapies include a behavioral component at some point. At the least, patients are asked to practice their cognitive techniques in situations that evoke anxiety. This is a form of exposure therapy, and most cognitive therapists emphasize the importance of exposure so that cognitive therapy is often called cognitive–behavior therapy. For their part, behavior therapists frequently provide a corrective rationale for the pathological thoughts or cognitions patients have developed. Consequently, because both kinds of therapists appear to use elements of both cognitive and behavioral treatments, the relative effectiveness of cognitive and behavioral components is an important issue.

Cognitive therapy focuses on and attempts to help patients change unrealistically negative thoughts or cognitions regarding themselves, their world, and their future. Whereas negative thoughts about the self reduce self-esteem, excessive caution is the consequence of negative cognitions about the world, and pessimism, hopelessness, and anxiety result from negative cognitions about the future. "Negative thoughts about normal but unpleasant bodily sensations (sweating, palpitations, shortness of breath with exercise, etc.) may lead to exaggerated and inappropriate anxiety (catastrophizing), which then progresses to panic'' (Greist et al., 1986, pp. 121–122).

Some cognitive therapies, such as rational emotive therapy (Ellis, 1962), challenge irrational ideas and attempt a cognitive or rational restructuring (Goldfried, Decentenceo, & Weinberg, 1974). Other workers have emphasized changing self-statements to modify the patient's internal dialogue (Meichenbaum, 1977). These and other techniques have been variously combined and emphasized in cognitive therapy for anxiety disorders as described by Beck and Emery (1985, p. 487). Marks has reviewed the controlled trials of cognitive therapy for the treatment of patients with anxiety disorders and found discouraging results (Marks, 1987, pp. 487–492). For agoraphobia there were no positive studies and 6 negative ones; for social anxiety, 2 positive studies, 6 equivocal studies, and 12 negative studies; and for specific phobias, there were 1 positive study, 1 slightly positive study, and 4 negative studies. The results of these studies indicate that cognitive therapy had little effect alone and, when combined with exposure, enhanced neither the speed nor the amount of improvement. In explaining the comparative failure of cognitive therapies to alleviate anxiety disorders, Marks offered the following:

> At first sight it seems obvious that attitudes and thoughts affect behavior, and that modifying them should change behavior. But it is hard to conquer race prejudice, for instance, by extended rational discussion. It seems to yield more readily when bigots come into prolonged, intimate contact on an equal footing with many people from the race they dislike, so allowing the development of close interracial relations. That strategy is performance-based exposure. (Marks, 1987, p. 492)

There is an additional point. Piano teachers often teach their pupils that before playing a piece of music, they should think carefully about its structure, work out exactly what they want to achieve, and only then start playing. Similarly, many pole vaulters, shotputters, and other athletes think a long time about what they are aiming at before carrying out their actions. This type of action-oriented thought, or behavioral rehearsal, is not a feature of cognitive therapy, except insofar as it involves exposure.

There is no evidence that a decrease in negative thoughts precedes the reduction of fear, although this should be seen if cognitive methods worked in the way they are often assumed to do. It has been shown that negative thoughts and attitudes improved as fear fell after exposure without cognitive therapy (Stravynski, Marks, & Yule, 1982; Watson & Marks, 1971), and in the only study to report on the detailed timing of change, loss of negative thoughts occurred later than the reduction in some other signs of fear (Mavissakalian & Michelson, 1983). Cognitive therapy needs to become action oriented. It needs to help clients work out what they are striving for and the detailed steps needed to attain that end, and then to practice those steps covertly as well as overtly. But that would be behavior therapy— problem definition, breaking down the solution into manageable pieces, and rehearsing those steps covertly and overtly, first in the training situation and then in the natural environment. Such skills training (of which social skills training is one type) and programmed practice (of which exposure is an example) are helpful. But challenging irrational beliefs, cognitive or rational restructuring, and current types of self-statement rehearsal are largely redundant for the relief of phobic or obsessive–compulsive problems.

Behavior Therapy

Marks defined the elements of behavior therapy as follows: "Problem definition, breaking down the solution into manageable pieces, and rehearsing those steps covertly and overtly, first in the training situation and then in the natural environment" (I. M. Marks, personal communication). More simply, *exposure therapy,* the active component in many behavior therapies, may be conveyed to patients with the simple instructions, "Seek and find the things you fear and avoid and remain in contact with them until your anxiety falls. Repeat and repeat this practice until your anxiety subsides and you no longer experience the urge to avoid."

The key to designing a behavior therapy treatment program is identifying the things that the patient avoids. For anxieties unassociated with avoidance (and they are few if one includes avoiding thoughts of unpleasant situations), behavioral treatment has no specific techniques to offer. In this realm, the general behavioral strategies of activity rather than passivity and confrontation rather than avoidance may be personalized for each patient with phrases of encouragement such as, "work instead of worrying" and "it feels good to function." These can be employed whenever the barriers of fear emerge in the guise of "what if" and "yes—but."

Many clinicians fail to use behavior therapy because they think that they have not been trained in its principles and techniques and because they think that they will need to accompany patients into feared settings, thus disrupting their office-based practice. Neither of these concerns is correct: Straightforward exposure therapy can be taught in simple terms and conducted in the office setting. Patients are given an explanation for their anxiety disorder and the behavioral rationale for overcoming it. Basically, this includes a statement that avoidance propagates anxiety, whereas exposure reduces it through mechanisms of habituation or extinction. Next comes a specific behavioral prescription with exposure session targets negotiated between patient and clinician. The targets should be feasible in the patient's mind, and the clinician recommends coping tactics to sustain the patient should anxiety mount during exposure sessions (Greist et al., 1986, p. 138).

Patients carry out the treatment prescription using live self-exposure when possible and fantasy exposure when that approach is the only one available. The patient keeps accurate written records of the amount of time spent doing exposure assignments as well as the levels of anxiety and distress encountered and any coping tactics employed. A family member or friend may be enlisted as a co-therapist if necessary. The patient returns to the clinician's office at regular intervals for review of the written records that he or she has kept, preparation of a new exposure treatment prescription, and management of any other issues. Brief office visits are the rule. By contrast, long exposure sessions are better than short ones, and the common question, "How long should an exposure session last?" is answered, "Until your anxiety declines significantly."

At times, the clinician may set an example for the patient with a behavioral technique known as modeling. Modeling and its companion, role playing, are especially useful for social phobia but seldom needed for GAD or panic disorder. For pure panic disorder (where no avoidance occurs—this disorder is much less common than panic disorder with agoraphobia), exposure in fantasy to the frightening symptoms of panic can be helpful. Thus patients who experience tachycardia, dyspnea, paresthesias, and feelings of faintness can be asked to image this constellation of symptoms as well as any more extreme outcome such as actual fainting, being conveyed unconscious to an emergency room, or even dying.

Hyperventilation is a frequent component of panic disorder, and instructions to breathe "slow and shallow" or other approaches to diaphragmatic or belly breathing can easily be taught in the office setting. A hyperventilation challenge may be helpful by initiating some symptoms of panic and then demonstrating the beneficial effects of normal respiratory rate and excursion. Several studies (Bonn, Readhead, & Timmons, 1984; Clark, Salkovskis, & Chalkley, 1985; Lum, 1981) have shown significant decreases in frequency and intensity of panic attacks as well as avoidance in patients who were taught respiratory control. Many patients are able to plan and carry out behavioral therapy independently after reading the self-help chapter in *Anxiety and Its Treatment: Help is Available* (Greist et al., 1986, pp. 127-153). Patients who used this chapter in controlled trial were able to reduce avoidance and anxiety symptoms as much as those treated by a clinician, and they maintained their gains for at least six months.

Behavior therapy has been shown to be very effective in the treatment of phobic and obsessive–compulsive disorders. Although its use in the treatment of panic disorder has not been studied as thoroughly, a number of controlled trials have demonstrated its benefit in this disorder as well (Barlow & Cermy, 1988). Behavioral techniques for treating patients with GAD have not been developed beyond the general admonition that most people and patients are better served by dealing directly with identifiable problems than by avoiding them, and when specific causes of anxiety cannot be identified, continuing life's important routines will prevent secondary dysfunction and distress. Benefits of behavior therapy typically last for years, perhaps because patients learn the exposure technique and can apply it repeatedly if relapse occurs.

PHARMACOLOGIC TREATMENT

Anti-anxiety drugs (anxiolytics) and the pharmacologic treatment of anxiety disorders are overlapping but not synonymous topics. To restrict the discussion to those drugs conventionally classified as anxiolytics would omit the antidepressants, antipsychotics, and beta-blockers, all of which have documented anti-anxiety effects. The effectiveness of antidepressants in treating people with panic disorders is established and considered by many to be a cornerstone of treatment. Antidepressants have also been of value in treating people with GAD (Hoehn-Saric, McLeod, & Zimmerli, 1988; Tyrer, Murphy, & Kingdon et al., 1988). Although antipsychotics do not occupy center stage in the anxiety disorder arena, the current package insert for trifluoperazine (Stelazine) suggests approval by the Food and Drug Administration (FDA): "Stelazine is indicated for the management of manifestations of psychotic disorders as well as the short-term treatment of nonpsychotic anxiety, where it is considered second-line therapy" (*Physicians' Desk Reference*, 1989). The following discussion deals with the conventional anxiolytics, the less conventional anxiolytics, and the antidepressant anxiolytics, and then with the pharmacologic approaches to treating people with situational anxiety, GAD, social phobia, and panic disorder.

Conventional Anxiolytics

Drugs within this broad class are prescribed to millions of individuals every year. Most receiving these drugs do not have a formal DSM-III-R anxiety disorder diagnosis but rather have relatively short-lived anxiety reactions to psychosocial or physical stressors. Although anxiety of this type may not meet rigid diagnostic criteria, it is often of sufficient magnitude to warrant treatment intervention (whether pharmacologic or psychological therapies are most appropriate is a matter of preference for both patient and physician). The DSM-III-R diagnosis of adjustment disorder with anxious mood is frequently used to label such individuals, although it is often questionable whether the anxiety reaction is truly maladaptive.

Barbiturates

The availability of safer and better tolerated medications has rendered this class of drugs archaic with regard to treating anxiety. These drugs are quite toxic in overdose, are potent respiratory depressants, have great abuse potential, and are potent inducers of hepatic enzymes. Although phenobarbital is still widely used in the treatment of epilepsy, the barbiturates are of only historical interest with regard to treating anxiety.

Meprobamate

Under labels such as Equanil and Miltown, meprobamate was initially viewed as an improvement on and replacement for the barbiturates in the treatment of anxiety. Following its introduction as an anti-anxiety agent in 1955, "There was a phenomenal and immediate acceptance of meprobamate, and there developed both a medical and popular craze for the drug" (Harvey, 1980, p. 365). In more recent years, the use of meprobamate has decreased substantially for several reasons: introduction of the benzodiazepines; its resemblance to placebo in a number of controlled studies; and an adverse effect, abuse, and toxicity profile similar to that of the barbiturates. Although still marketed in the United States both alone and in combination with other drugs (meprobamate plus benactyzine, meprobamate plus aspirin, meprobamate plus conjugated estrogens), the continued use of this drug is more likely to reflect outmoded prescription patterns than appropriate clinical indications.

Benzodiazepines

Drugs in this class are major advances over the barbiturates and meprobamate for the treatment of anxiety. Since the early 1960s many have been marketed, yet none has established superior effectiveness for treating patients with anxiety. There is no question that these drugs have been misused (for inappropriate indications, in inappropriate doses, and for inappropriate lengths of time), overprescribed, and abused. Unfortunately, the risks of using these drugs are sometimes overestimated. There are real risks, but they are of far less magnitude than many professionals and lay persons believe.

These drugs can cause physical dependence—as is evidenced by a withdrawal syndrome that occurs when they are abruptly discontinued. There is growing recognition that a withdrawal reaction occurs in many, but not all, patients treated with benzodiazepines for moderate to long periods of time (Noyes, Garvey, Cook, & Perry, 1988). Although the withdrawal syndrome associated with discontinuation of therapeutic doses tends to be mild, it is nonetheless real and can have clinical consequences (Busto, Sellers, & Naranjo et al., 1986). Unfortunately, the presence of a pharmacologic withdrawal reaction has been equated by some to represent addiction in the full antisocial meaning of the term. The abuse of benzodiazepines is more likely to occur in a substance abuse-prone population, and concern that the carefully monitored prescription of these drugs for appropriate indications will create a nation of junkies is unfounded (Uhlenhuth, DeWit, Balter, Johanson, & Mellinger, 1988).

It is generally agreed that benzodiazepines should be prescribed for short periods of time in moderate dosages, but some patients appear to benefit from long-term use and do not demonstrate tolerance to the anti-anxiety effect, or escalate dosage, or misuse the drugs in other ways. No patient, however, should be treated indefinitely with a benzodiazepine without periodic attempts to gradually taper and discontinue the medication (Rickels, Schweizer, & Csanatosi et al., 1988). Working with patients to help them develop alternative, nonpharmacologic coping techniques will facilitate drug withdrawal.

When benzodiazepines are discontinued, five possibilities must be considered (Noyes, Garvey et al., 1988). Because real-life circumstances are rarely adaptable to rigid classification, it should be noted that there may be overlap among these possibilities. First and ideally, drug discontinuation will be uneventful and not associated with any of the other four possibilities. Second, the underlying condition may return in the way that elevated blood pressure returns when antihypertensive medication is discontinued. Third, drug withdrawal may be associated with a symptomatic rebound lasting for a week or two during which the symptoms of the underlying condition are exaggerated. Rebound is important to recognize so that patients are not restarted on medication that otherwise might not be necessary once a true baseline is reached. Fourth, patients may experience a true pharmacologic withdrawal reaction. Although severe withdrawal may occur, especially with abrupt discontinuation of high dosages, and be associated with seizures or psychoses, more subtle withdrawal symptoms are the rule. These may be difficult to distinguish from recurrence of the underlying anxiety disorder. Fifth, patients may experience pseudowithdrawal, which reflects psychological but not pharmacologic dependence on medication, and which is best dealt with by the use of ancillary, nonpharmacologic therapies during withdrawal.

There are currently eight benzodiazepine drugs marketed in the United States for the treatment of anxiety. Although they are not identical, they share more similarities than differences (other benzodiazepines that may be used to treat anxiety include the anticonvulsant, clonazepam, and the hypnotics, flurazepam, temazepam, and triazolam).

All have demonstrated short-term effectiveness in the treatment of anxiety, and no drug has been shown to be more effective than another. It is important to realize, however, that a particular drug may be more effective or better tolerated in a given individual. These drugs also have a similar spectrum of side effects, and all have the potential for causing tolerance, dependence, habituation, and withdrawal symptoms. Because higher benzodiazepine doses are often used for panic, the risk of dependency and subsequent withdrawal symptoms is increased. (Greist et al., 1986, p. 103)

There are differences among some of these drugs with regard to speed of onset of action, duration of action, potential for interaction with other drugs, and availability of parenteral forms.

The fact that these drugs vary in milligram potency should not be misconstrued to mean they vary in effectiveness. For example, alprazolam is roughly ten times more potent than diazepam, and clonazepam is roughly twice as potent as alprazolam.

Therefore, an equivalent therapeutic effect might be expected from a daiiy dose of 10 mg of diazepam, 1 mg of alprazolam, and 0.5 mg of clonazepam.

Although all benzodiazepines have the potential for dependency, withdrawal symptoms, and abuse, certain generalizations can be made. Drugs with shorter half-lives tend to have more severe withdrawal symptoms that appear sooner following discontinuation. Drugs with higher lipid solubility (diazepam, alprazolam, and lorazepam) have more rapid onsets of action and, in some susceptible individuals, may be more likely to be abused. Drugs with shorter half-lives may require more frequent daily dosing. Failure to dose frequently enough may be associated with a phenomenon known as interdose anxiety. One advantage of the benzodiazepines is that they work rapidly. This is in contrast to the anxiolytic effect of buspirone and the anti-panic effect of tricyclic and monoamine oxidase inhibitor antidepressants. During the treatment of situational anxiety, benzodiazepines may be taken on a scheduled or an as-needed basis. Conditions such as GAD and panic disorder, however, tend to require scheduled dosing to maximize the effectiveness of these drugs.

As a group, the benzodiazepines share similar side effects, the occurrence of which tends to depend much more on the dose than on the specific drug. Sedation is the most common side effect and, fortunately, is one to which many patients become tolerant with continued use of the drug. Other side effects include incoordination, impaired memory, and paradoxical restlessness, agitation, and hostility. In recent years, it has become more obvious that relatively low doses of these drugs cause subtle impairment in memory and psychomotor performance that may compromise a patient without being readily recognized. On the other hand, the benzodiazepines are essentially devoid of clinically important cardiovascular effects, have no anticholinergic activity, and do not cause extrapyramidal side effects. They are quite safe in overdose if taken alone, although the risk of death is increased in the presence of other drugs such as alcohol.

Buspirone

Buspirone is an azospirodecanedione anxiolytic that is unrelated to the benzodiazepines (Goa & Ward, 1986). It does not bind to the benzodiazepine receptor and does not have anticonvulsant, muscle relaxant, or sedative effects. It does not appear to interact adversely with alcohol, has no withdrawal syndrome, and has no abuse potential (when tested in a substance-abusing population, the drug was given a street value equivalent to that of placebo). Unlike the benzodiazepines, the side-effect profile of buspirone consists of gastrointestinal upset, dizziness, headache, and dysphoria. It also differs in having a gradual onset of action so that full therapeutic benefits may not occur until after several weeks of treatment.

Because there is no cross-tolerance with the benzodiazepines, buspirone will not block the benzodiazepine withdrawal syndrome and cannot be abruptly substituted for a benzodiazepine. There have been some reports of increased blood pressure occurring when buspirone was given to patients taking monoamine oxidase inhibitors and, consequently, the combination is not advised. Preliminary studies have shown buspirone to be ineffective in the treatment of panic disorder (Schweizer & Rickels, 1988) and, given its gradual onset of action, it would be inappropriate to use it for situational anxiety. Buspirone's primary indication, therefore, appears to be generalized, persistent anxiety (which may or may not be formally diagnosed as GAD).

Less Conventional Anxiolytics

Antihistamines

Antihistamines such as diphenhydramine and hydroxyzine have anti-anxiety, sedative effects. Unlike the benzodiazepines, they are not subject to the Controlled Substances Act of 1970 and are not associated with the risk of tolerance or dependency. They have not been studied for the treatment of GAD or panic disorder but rather are used for the intermittent, short-term treatment of nonspecific anxiety. Overall, these drugs are not as well tolerated as the benzodiazepines, in part because they have anticholinergic effects, but also because many patients find them too sedating in relationship to their anxiolytic activity.

AntiPsychotics

The antipsychotics have not been extensively studied for the treatment of nonpsychotic anxiety (Chou & Sussman, 1988). Recently, trifluoperazine was shown to be more effective than placebo for the short-term treatment (four-week maximum) of GAD (Mendels, Krajewski, & Huffer et al., 1986). How effective these drugs would be compared to benzodiazepines is not known. Because the long-term use of antipsychotic drugs is associated with the risk of tardive dyskinesia, their role in the chronic treatment of anxiety should be minimized.

Beta-Blockers

Beta-adrenergic receptor-blocking drugs have been used in psychiatry for many years for the treatment of certain anxiety conditions. Currently, none of these drugs have FDA labeling approval for any anxiety indication. Conventionally, beta-blockers are thought to be more useful for anxiety conditions characterized by somatic symptoms, although Lader (1988) has pointed out that research studies have been inconsistent. Overall, these drugs are less effective than benzodiazepines both for GAD and panic disorder.

The condition for which beta-blockers show the most promise is performance anxiety (specific social phobia) in which double-blind studies have shown that a single dose taken before an anxiety-provoking situation such as public speaking or musical performance may be quite effective. When used in such circumstances, it is advisable that the patient take a trial dose at a time unrelated to the stressful situation to be sure that there are no unanticipated side effects. It should also be recognized that behavior therapy is a very effective treatment for social phobia.

Although propranolol has been the most extensively studied beta-blocker, there is currently no support that it is unique among this class of drugs. The beta-blockers do vary in lipid solubility (ease of entry into the central nervous system), receptor specificity, membrane stabilizing effect, and intrinsic sympathomimetic activity, and it is possible that these properties could influence anxiolytic activity. Although studies have shown beta-blockers to be less effective than benzodiazepines in the treatment of panic disorder (Noyes, Anderson, & Clancy et al., 1984), clinicians sometimes find the combination to be effective in treatment-resistant cases. If beta-blockers are used, it should be noted that they have neuropsychiatric side effects including fatigue, lethargy, depression, vivid dreaming, and a hyperadrenergic withdrawal syndrome.

Antidepressants

Anxiety and depressive symptoms often coexist, making it difficult to determine which, if either, represents the underlying disorder and which the secondary complication. The evidence that at least some heterocyclic and monoamine oxidase inhibitor antidepressants are effective in the long-term treatment of panic disorder, even in the absence of depression, is rather convincing, although not without controversy (Lydiard, Roy-Byrne, & Ballenger, 1988). Despite overwhelming clinical preference for using benzodiazepines to treat non-panic anxiety, there is growing evidence that antidepressants may also be useful for treating conditions such as GAD. For example, Kahn, McNair, and Lipman et al. (1986) found imipramine to be more effective than both chlordiazepoxide and placebo in the treatment of anxiety symptoms. These researchers were convinced that the effectiveness of imipramine was not due to misdiagnosing depression as anxiety or to "the inadvertent inclusion of imipramine-responsive agoraphobics in the anxiety group" (Kahn et al., 1986).

In the Nottingham Study of Neurotic Disorder (Tyrer et al., 1988), patients with GAD, panic disorder, and dysthymic disorder were treated with either diazepam, dothiepin (a tricyclic antidepressant), placebo, cognitive and behavior therapy, or self-help. Diazepam was found to be less effective than the other three active treatments, leading the researchers to suggest that when drug treatment is used for these disorders, an antidepressant would be preferable to a benzodiazepine. These conclusions were not universally accepted, as is evidenced by Klein's criticisms: "This study encompasses almost every feature likely to produce a type II error (false negative)—i.e. the use of unproven drugs, low dose, short duration, and a low power design with small cell size" (1988).

When Hoehn-Saric et al. (1988) studied the differential effects of a benzodiazepine and a tricyclic antidepressant in patients with GAD, they found both alprazolam and imipramine to be effective. Although alprazolam had an earlier onset of action, by two weeks both drugs were "equally effective by measures that contained psychic and somatic items" although alprazolam appeared more effective for somatic symptoms and imipramine more effective for psychic symptoms. Overall, the anti-anxiety properties of antidepressant drugs appear to have been underestimated, although the more acceptable side effect profile of anxiolytics may also favor their more extensive use for non-panic anxiety conditions. The tricyclic antidepressants have both anticholinergic and cardiovascular side effects not shared by the benzodiazepines (they also do not share the same propensity for both tolerance and withdrawal).

PHARMACOLOGIC EFFECTS
ON SPECIFIC ANXIETY DISORDERS

Situational Anxiety

Anxiety of this type is quite common and is usually self-limited. Nonpharmacologic interventions are often quite effective, but if medication is used, the benzodiazepine anxiolytics are the preferred drugs. As contrasted to both buspirone and antidepressants, the benzodiazepines have a relatively rapid onset of action. A scheduled rather than as-needed pattern of treatment is often preferred until symptom control is obtained. Once the situational stressors have been favorably modified, the drug should be tapered and discontinued. Under certain circumstances, the benefits of benzodiazepines may involve more than merely reducing anxiety. These drugs have been shown to attenuate the rise of both catecholamines and cortisol that occurs in response to stress, and also to inhibit platelet activating factor. Although these properties suggest that benzodiazepines may be particularly valuable in patients following a myocardial infarction, confirmatory studies have not yet been done.

Generalized Anxiety Disorder

By definition, generalized anxiety disorder is a chronic condition. On the other hand, most drug studies of its treatment have been relatively short-term. Benzodiazepines, buspirone, antidepressants, and antipsychotics have all been shown to be beneficial over the short-term. In a six-month study comparing the benzodiazepine clorazepate with buspirone in anxiety patients (134 with generalized anxiety disorder and 16 with panic disorder), a long-term beneficial effect was noted with both drugs. While the benzodiazepine was better tolerated (fewer dropouts), a withdrawal syndrome was noted in 72% following abrupt, double-blind switch to placebo. About a quarter of the patients on both drugs noted a gradual return of underlying anxiety over a several week period following drug discontinuation. These findings suggest that some patients will require long-term treatment for chronic anxiety while others may maintain improvement despite drug discontinuation (Rickels et al., 1988). Most clinicians agree that there is a subgroup of patients in whom the long-term use of benzodiazepines is both beneficial and safe. Rickels et al. concluded:

> There may exist a small group of patients, however, which is in need, just as is the diabetic patient, of continuous uninterrupted benzodiazepine therapy. However, the features identifying this patient group have not yet been identified. Until we can predict with some certainty which patients will clearly benefit from prolonged therapy, only trial and error will allow us to treat chronically anxious patients appropriately, yet conservatively and in the safest and medically most acceptable manner. (Rickels, Case, Downing, & Winokur, 1985)

Preferably, long-term use should be intermittent rather than continuous since it does appear that following gradual taper and discontinuation some patients do not have recurrences that would warrant additional drug treatment.

Social Phobia

Social phobias can be circumscribed (specific) or generalized. The anxiety associated with circumscribed social phobia is restricted to specific situations such as public speaking, the use of public lavatories, eating in the presence of others, or musical performances. Circumscribed social phobias can be effectively treated with non-pharmacologic behavioral therapy but beta-blocking drugs have also been used successfully (Lader, 1988).

Recent studies of the scheduled use of both beta-blockers (Gorman, Liebowitz, & Fyer et al., 1985), and monoamine oxidase inhibitors (Liebowitz, Fyer, & Gorman, et al., 1986; Versiani, Mundim, Nardi, & Liebowitz, 1988) have shown favorable results in the treatment of social phobia. At present, the monoamine oxidase inhibitor antidepressants appear to be the most promising drugs for the long-term treatment of generalized social phobia. As reviewed by Lydiard et al. (1988), while case reports have ascribed benefit to tricyclic antidepressants, benzodiazepines, and clonidine, convincing studies are lacking. The benzodiazepines have been used extensively to treat social phobic symptoms, yet their efficacy has not been clearly established in research studies. It should be recognized that social phobics may abuse both alcohol and benzodiazepines in a misguided attempt to relieve symptoms.

Panic Disorder

Panic disorder may occur alone or with varying degrees of phobic avoidance (agoraphobia). Although some would deny it, agoraphobia may also occur without a history of panic disorder; indeed, the National Institute of Mental Health Epidemiologic Catchment Area (ECA) study found agoraphobia to be more prevalent than panic disorder (Myers, Weissman, & Tischler et al., 1984). Whether the presence of so-called "limited symptom attacks" in agoraphobic patients represents a variant of panic disorder is still open to question.

The primary goal of pharmacologic treatment of panic disorder is to prevent the recurrence of panic attacks. Additional benefits may involve attenuation of anticipatory anxiety and reduction of avoidance behavior. Since individual attacks tend to remit spontaneously over relatively brief periods of time, treatment focuses on long-term prevention. Some patients do, however, benefit from the availability of a benzodiazepine anxiolytic to deal with anticipatory anxiety or to take at the time of a panic attack. Unless these drugs are used sparingly, they may actually interfere with the effectiveness of behavior therapy.

Both antidepressants and benzodiazepine anxiolytics can effectively block the recurrence of panic attacks (Levin & Liebowitz, 1987; Lydiard, 1988; Lydiard et al., 1988; Sheehan & Soto, 1987). Because there is no clearly established drug of choice for the treatment of panic disorder, treatment preference must take into consideration onset of action, side-effect profile, abuse potential, past treatment response, patient characteristics and preferences, and the attitude of the physician. In general, the benzodiazepines have a front-end advantage of a more rapid onset of action (within the first week) and a better tolerated side effect profile. However, discontinuation of benzodiazepines may be more problematic because they have a more troublesome withdrawal syndrome. If the panic disorder patient is also depressed, antidepressants might be preferable to benzodiazepines. Relapse following discontinuation occurs in well over 50% of patients regardless of the drug used, and whether a more favorable relapse rate is associated with a particular drug has not been firmly established.

Benzodiazepines

Without question, alprazolam is the most extensively studied benzodiazepine with regard to the treatment of panic disorder. The Cross-National Collaborative Panic Study first-phase results were recently published (Ballenger, Burrows, & DuPont et al., 1988; Noyes, DuPont & Pecknold et al., 1988; Pecknold, Swinson, Kuch, & Lewis, 1988) and showed alprazolam to be both effective and well tolerated. Patients on placebo were much more likely to withdraw prematurely from the study, whereas typical benzodiazepine side effects such as sedation, fatigue, ataxia, slurred speech, and amnesia were more common in patients taking alprazolam. The second phase of the study in which alprazolam was compared to both imipramine and placebo has been completed and the results will soon be published.

At first alprazolam was thought to have unique anti-panic effects (attributed to its triazolo ring); subsequent studies have shown other benzodiazepines (clonazepam, diazepam, and lorazepam) to also be of benefit. The effectiveness of benzodiazepines in the treatment of patients with panic disorder appears to depend more on dose than on drug specificity. Although many patients respond to doses within the accepted anti-anxiety dose range, studies tend to show that average doses are usually higher than those conventionally used for the treatment of anxiety. When used to treat panic disorder, benzodiazepines are started at conservative anti-anxiety doses (e.g., alprazolam 0.25 or 0.5 mg three times daily) and increased as tolerated until the panic attacks no longer occur. The rate of dose increase is limited primarily by excessive sedation.

Given the extensive studies of alprazolam, many would use it as the benzodiazepine of choice, although concern has been expressed about its relatively short duration of action, which may be associated with the emergence of anxiety symptoms prior to the next scheduled dose. This problem can be dealt with either by more frequent dosing of alprazolam or by substituting a longer half-life drug such as clonazepam (Herman, Rosenbaum, & Brotman, 1987). When being discontinued, benzodiazepine doses should be lowered quite gradually to minimize or prevent a withdrawal syndrome. Withdrawal programs vary with regard to rate of dosage decrease, whether alternative medications are used, and the use of nonpharmacological management techniques (Higgitt, Lader, & Fonagy, 1985).

Heterocyclic Antidepressants

Imipramine is the most extensively studied antidepressant drug, and most studies have shown it to have anti-panic effectiveness. Less extensively studied drugs such as clomipramine, desipramine, nortriptyline, amitriptyline, doxepin, fluoxetine, and fluvoxamine also appear to have similar activity. Trazodone is more controversial in terms of whether it is less effective or as effective as the other medications. Bupropion, amoxapine, and maprotiline are not held in high regard for treating non-depressed patients with panic disorder.

With antidepressants, the time course for onset of anti-panic effectiveness parallels that seen in depression. Consequently, patients may not benefit until after several weeks of treatment. This disadvantage has led some clinicians to begin some patients on both a benzodiazepine and an antidepressant with the intent of tapering and discontinuing the former when the latter's effectiveness has become established. When antidepressants are used, the starting dose should be lower than for depression because a substantial number of patients experience a jittery, dysphoric reaction early in the course of treatment. This phenomenon has been observed in approximately 20% of patients treated with imipramine and 50% of those treated with desipramine. The appearance of this syndrome does not predict eventual response, and the symptoms tend to remit with continued use of medication. It is best dealt with by educating the patient and starting with a low dose.

Monoamine Oxidase Inhibitors

Whereas phenelzine has been the most extensively studied of these drugs, both tranylcypromine and isocarboxazid also appear to have anti-panic activity. Although not firmly established, some clinicians think that this class of drugs is somewhat more effective than both the heterocyclic antidepressants and the benzodiazepines. Nonetheless, the need for dietary and drug proscriptions makes monoamine oxidase inhibitors somewhat more difficult to use and, hence, they are generally reserved for patients who do not respond adequately to the other drug classes. As with other antidepressants, the effective anti-panic dose appears to be similar to that used in the treatment of depression. These drugs also have a relatively slow onset of action.

Beta-Blockers and Other Drugs

Beta-blockers have not been extensively studied in the treatment of patients with panic disorder. When compared with diazepam in patients with panic disorder and agoraphobia, propranolol was considerably less effective (Noyes et al., 1984). Although some clinicians have reported success with the combination of a benzodiazepine and beta-blocker, these findings remain in the realm of clinical anecdote. Preliminary studies of buspirone, carbamazepine, clonidine, and verapamil have not been encouraging with regard to anti-panic effectiveness (Bond, 1986; Lydiard et al., 1988).

CONCLUSION

Effective treatments are available for patients with anxiety, GAD, social phobia, and panic disorder. It is imperative that patients not be lost in the debates about the relative merits of psychological and pharmacological interventions. Proponents of one form of treatment should not be oblivious to the merits of the other. Clinicians able to implement both forms of treatment will be able to develop individualized treatment programs that have the greatest likelihood of success (Greist & Jefferson, 1988; Greist et al., 1986). As one patient stated:

> I certainly enjoyed hearing "both sides of the story," but I couldn't help thinking that I'd probably have dropped out of both "Doctor Behavior Therapy's" and "Doctor Drug Therapy's" programs. Thanks to a fine blend of both that you used, I'm happy and grateful to be listed among the treatment successes and not the failures. (Greist et al., 1986, p. 165)

REFERENCES

American Psychiatric Association. (1987). *Diagnostic and statistical mannual of mental disorders* (3rd ed., rev.). Washington, DC: Author.

Ballenger, J. C., Burrows, G. D., & DuPont, R. L., et al. (1988). Alprazolam in panic disorder and agoraphobia: Results from a multicenter study: 1. Efficacy in short-term treatment. *Archives of General Psychiatry, 45*, 413–422.

Barlow, O. H., & Cermy, J. A. (1988). *Psychological treatment of panic*. New York: Guilford Press.

Beck, A. T., & Emery, G. (1985). *Anxiety disorders and phobias: A cognitive perspective*. New York: Basic Books.

Bond. W. S. (1986). Psychiatric indications for clonidine: The neuropharmacologic and clinical basis. *Journal of Clinical Psychopharmacology, 6*, 81–87.

Bonn, J. A., Readhead, C. P. A., & Timmons, B. H. (1984). Enhanced adaptive behavioral response in agoraphobic patients pretreated with breathing retraining. *Lancet, 2*, 665–669.

Busto, U., Sellers, E. M., Naranjo, C. A., et al., (1986). Withdrawal reaction after long-term therapeutic use of benzodiazepines. *New England Journal of Medicine, 315*, 854–859.

Chou, J. C. Y., & Sussman, N. (1988). Neuroleptics in anxiety. *Psychiatric Annals, 18*, 172–175.

Clark, D. M., Salkovskis, P. M., & Chalkley, A. J. (1985). Respiratory control as a treatment for panic attacks. *Journal of Behavior Therapy and Experimental Psychiatry, 16*, 23–30.

Ellis, A. (1962). *Reason and emotion in psychotherapy.* New York: Lyle-Stuart.

Goa, K. L., & Ward, A. (1986). Buspirone: A preliminary review of its pharmacological properties and therapeutic efficacy as an anxiolytic. *Drugs, 32*, 114–129.

Goldfried, M. R., Decentenceo, E. T., & Weinberg, L. (1974). Systematic rational restructuring as a self-control technique. *Journal of Behavior Therapy, 5*, 247–254.

Gorman, J. M., Liebowitz, M. R., & Fyer, A. J., et al. (1985). Treatment of social phobia with atenolol. *Journal of Clinical Psychopharmacology, 5*, 298–301.

Greist, J. H., & Jefferson, J. W. (1988). Anxiety disorders. In H. H. Goldman (Ed.), *Review of general psychiatry* (pp. 349–364). Norwalk, CT: Appleton and Lange.

Greist, J. H., Jefferson, J. W., & Marks, I. A. (1986). *Anxiety and its treatment: Help is available.* Washington, DC: American Psychiatric Press.

Harvey, S. C. (1980). Hypnotics and sedatives. In A. G. Gilman, L. S. Goodman, & A. Gilman (Eds.), *The pharmacological basis of therapeutics* (pp. 339–375). New York: Macmillan.

Herman, J. B., Rosenbaum, J. F., & Brotman, A. W. (1987). The alprazolam to clonazepam switch for the treatment of panic disorder. *Journal of Clinical Psychopharmacology, 7,* 175–178.

Higgitt, A. C., Lader, M. H., & Fonagy, P. (1985). Clinical management of benzodiazepine dependence. *British Medical Journal, 291,* 688–690.

Hoehn-Saric, R., McLeod, D. R., & Zimmerli, W. D. (1988). Differential effects of alprazolam and imipramine in generalized anxiety disorder: Somatic versus psychic symptoms. *Journal of Clinical Psychiatry, 49,* 293–301.

Jefferson, J. W., & Marshall, J. R. (1981). *Neuropsychiatric features of medical disorders.* New York: Plenum Press.

Jones, F. A. (Ed.). (1972). *Richard Asher talking sense.* London: Pitman.

Kahn, R. J., McNair, D. M., & Lipman, R. S., et al. (1986). Imipramine and chlordiazepoxide in depressive and anxiety disorders: 2. Efficacy in anxious outpatients. *Archives of General Psychiatry, 43,* 79–85.

Klein, D. F. (1988). Nottingham study of neurotic disorder. *Lancet, 2,* 1015.

Lader, M. (1988). β-adrenoreceptor antagonists in neuropsychiatry: An update. *Journal of Clinical Psychiatry, 49,* 213–223.

Levin, A. P., & Liebowitz, M. R. (1987). Drug treatment of phobias: Efficacy and optimum use. *Drugs, 34,* 504–514.

Liebowitz, M. R., Fyer, A. J., & Gorman, J. M., et al. (1986). Phenelzine on social phobia. *Journal of Clinical Psychopharmacology, 6,* 93–98.

Lum, L. C. (1981). Hyperventilation and anxiety state. *Journal of the Royal Society of Medicine, 74,* 1–4.

Lydiard, R. B. (1988). Pharmacologic treatment. *Psychiatric Annals, 18,* 468–472.

Lydiard, R. B., Roy-Byrne, P. P., & Ballenger, J. C. (1988). Recent advances in the psychopharmacological treatment of anxiety disorders. *Hospital and Community Psychiatry, 39,* 1157–1165.

Marks, I. M. (1978). *Living with fear.* New York: McGraw-Hill.

Marks, I. M. (1987). *Fears, phobias, and rituals.* New York: Oxford University Press.

Mavissakalian, M., & Michelson, L. (1983). Self-directed in vivo exposure practice in behavioral and drug treatments of agoraphobia. *Journal of Behavior Therapy, 14,* 505–519.

Meichenbaum, D. (1977). *Cognitive behavior modification.* New York: Plenum Press.

Mendels, J., Krajewski, T. F., & Huffer, V., et al. (1986) Effective short-term treatment of generalized anxiety disorder with trifluoperazine. *Journal of Clinical Psychiatry, 47,* 170–174.

Myers, J. K., Weissman, M. M., & Tischler, G. L., et al. (1984). Six-month prevalence of psychiatric disorders in three communities. *Archives of General Psychiatry, 41,* 959–967.

Noyes, R., Anderson, D. J., & Clancy, J., et al. (1984). Diazepam and propranolol in panic disorder and agoraphobia. *Archives of General Psychiatry, 41,* 287–292.

Noyes, R., DuPont, R. L., & Pecknold, J. C., et al. (1988). Alprazolam in panic disorder and agoraphobia: Results from a multicenter trial: 2. Patient acceptance, side effects, and safety. *Archives of General Psychiatry, 45,* 423–428.

Noyes, R., Garvey, M. J., Cook, B. L., & Perry, P. J. (1988). Benzodiazepine withdrawal: A review of the evidence. *Journal of Clinical Psychiatry, 49,* 382–389.

Pecknold, J. C., Swinson, R. P., Kuch, K., & Lewis, C. P. (1988). Alprazolam in panic disorder and agoraphobia: Results from a multicenter trial: 3. Discontinuation effects. *Archives of General Psychiatry, 45,* 429–436.

Physicians desk reference. (43rd ed.). (1989). Oradell, NJ: Medical Economics Co.

Rickels, K., Case, W. G., Downing, R. W., & Winokur, A. (1985). Indications and contraindications for chronic anxiolytic treatment: Is there tolerance to the anxiolytic effect? *Advanced Biochemistry of Psychopharmacology, 40,* 193–204.

Rickels, K., Schweizer, E., & Csanatosi, I., et al. (1988). Long-term treatment of anxiety and risk of withdrawal. *Archives of General Psychiatry, 45,* 444–450.

Schweizer, E., & Rickels, K. (1988). Buspirone in the treatment of panic disorder: A controlled pilot comparison with clorazepate. *Journal of Clinical Psychopharmacology, 8,* 303.

Sheehan, D. V., & Soto, S. (1987). Recent developments in the treatment of panic disorder. *Acta Psychiatrica Scandinavica, 76,* (Suppl. 335), 75–83.

Strauss, M. B. (Ed.). (1968). *Familiar medical quotations.* Boston: Little, Brown.
Stravynski, A., Marks, I. M., & Yule, W. (1982). Social skills problems in neurotic outpatients. *Archives of General Psychiatry, 39,* 1378-1385.
Treasure, R. A. R., Fowler, P. B. S., Millington, H. T., & Wise, P. H. (1987). Misdiagnosis of diabetic ketoacidosis as hyperventilation syndrome. *British Medical Journal, 294,* 630.
Tyrer, P., Murphy, S., & Kingdon, D., et al. (1988). The Nottingham study of neurotic disorder: Comparison of drug and psychological treatment. *Lancet, 2,* 235-240.
Uhlenhuth, E. H., DeWit, H., Balter, M. B., Johanson, C. E., & Mellinger, G. D. (1988). Risks and benefits of long-term benzodiazepine use. *Journal of Clinical Psychopharmacology, 8,* 161-167.
Versiani, M., Mundim, F. D., Nardi, A. E., & Liebowitz, M. R. (1988). Tranylcypromine in social phobia. *Journal of Clinical Psychopharmacology, 8,* 279-283.
Watson, J. P., & Marks, I. M. (1971)., Relevant and irrelevant fear in flooding: A crossover study of phobic patients. *Journal of Behavior Therapy, 2,* 275-293.

17

Psychological and Pharmacological Management of Anxiety in Patients with Coronary Heart Disease

Theodore A. Stern

Coronary artery disease and myocardial infarction have both physical and emotional manifestations. Therefore, clinicians need to be cognizant of the relationship between psychiatry and cardiology so that patients receive timely and effective treatment. Anxiety, one of the most common psychiatric symptoms, often leads individuals to seek, or to delay, medical attention. The manifestations of anxiety may complicate the treatment of an underlying cardiac condition and prompt a referral for psychiatric care. In this chapter I review the features of anxiety and place them in the context of their relationship to the cardiovascular system. In addition, I provide a rational approach to the psychopharmacologic treatment of the cardiac patient.

Anxiety can be defined as the subjective experience of dread and foreboding that occurs in association with a variety of autonomic signs and symptoms (Rosenbaum, 1982). It can be distinguished from fear in that fear is the subjective experience of dread and autonomic arousal that typically occurs in the presence of an external and threatening event (Geringer & Stern, 1988). Anxiety can be a normal and adaptive response that facilitates coping (Rosenbaum & Pollack, 1987). It is deemed to be pathologic when normal functioning of the individual is impaired by ineffective coping mechanisms, when its intensity becomes so severe that physicians insist on its treatment, or when it appears to have a life of its own (Rosenbaum & Pollack, 1987).

Anxiety has been categorized in a variety of ways. It can be acute (i.e., a state disturbance), or chronic (i.e., a trait disturbance), or occur only in the presence of specific stimuli, as in a phobia (Geringer & Stern, 1988). Moreover, anxiety may be termed primary (when it is the sole manifestation of a problem) or secondary (as a result of another medical condition such as hyperthyroidism). Unfortunately for clinicians, the signs and symptoms of anxiety are varied (e.g., chest pain, diaphoresis, dizziness, dyspnea, hyperventilation, palpitations, tachycardia, and tremulousness) and reflect the interplay between anxiety and the cardiovascular system. Patients who have these symptoms, and the clinicians who treat them, often become confused as to whether or not the signs and symptoms of anxiety are primary or secondary (Stern & Tesar, 1988).

PSYCHIATRIC DISORDERS AND CARDIAC SYMPTOMS

Physicians have known for decades that patients often attribute symptoms to their hearts in the absence of significant or identifiable cardiac pathology. Anxiety, as well as other psychiatric conditions, commonly heralds medical illness (Cameron, 1985; Cavanaugh & Wettstein, 1984; Hoffman, 1982; Rosenbaum & Pollack, 1987). Anxiety disorders have been diagnosed in 5% to 14% of general medical outpatients and in 5% to 20% of medical inpatients (Strain, Liebowitz, & Klein, 1981). Unfortunately, failure to recognize an individual's psychopathology may result in inappropriate diagnostic and therapeutic maneuvers that are costly and potentially harmful to the patient.

Several psychiatric disorders manifest anxiety-like symptoms and lead patients to seek medical attention. These include anxiety disorders, affective disorders, somatoform disorders, factitious illness, and complex partial seizures. Each of these disorders is common among patients who complain of chest pain in the absence of significant coronary artery disease (Bass & Wade, 1984; Channer et al., 1985; McLaurin, Raft, & Tate, 1977; Ostfield et al., 1964, Wielgosz et al., 1984). Between 10% and 14% of visits to a cardiologist's office for complaints of chest pain (in the absence of significant disease) have an anxiety-based complaint (Rosenbaum & Pollack, 1987).

A high score on the hypochondriasis subscale of the Minnesota Multiphasic Personality Inventory (MMPI) has been associated in patients with the complaint of frequent chest pain in the absence of, or with minimal coronary artery disease (Wielgosz et al., 1984). In another study, patients who complained of chest pain had high levels of anxiety and depression and had a tendency to have a higher rate of normal treadmill exercise tests as compared with those patients without symptoms of anxiety and depression (Channer et al., 1985). Patients with continuous chest pain continued to use anti-anginal medication, had moderate to severe limitation of activity, and had reduced their work schedule 12 to 18 months after their initial evaluation (Pasternak et al., 1980).

Anxiety Disorders

Epidemiologic studies demonstrate a 2% to 4% incidence of prominent anxiety in the general population (Marks & Lader, 1973). Appropriate treatment of those patients with anxiety disorders and coronary artery disease depends on accurate diagnosis. Once the diagnosis has been made, the same general principles of treatment that apply to the treatment of anxiety disorders in patients without disease can and should be applied to the cardiac patient with only a few exceptions. In general, it can be assumed that the psychiatric disorder in question (e.g., panic disorder with or without agoraphobia, agoraphobia, obsessive–compulsive disorder, generalized anxiety disorder [GAD], and posttraumatic stress disorder [PTSD]) antedated the diagnosis of coronary artery disease. However, symptoms of PTSD may be stimulated by the trauma of illness (e.g., myocardial infarction), and each of the anxiety disorders may be exacerbated by the stress of medical illness. Anxiety is the predominant symptom in GAD and panic disorder, whereas avoidance characterizes behavior when agoraphobia or phobias occur. In phobic disorders, anxiety typically increases when the patient confronts a feared object or situation, whereas in obsessive–compulsive disorder it increases during attempts to resist giving in to an obsession or compulsion.

Historically, a variety of terms have been used to characterize patients with cardiovascular symptoms in the absence of known cardiovascular disease. These have included DaCosta's syndrome, soldier's heart, neurocirculatory asthenia, and irritable heart (Cameron, 1985; Crowe, 1985); many of these patients have been further labeled as "cardiac cripples." More recently, many of the patients that had previously received these diagnoses have been shown to meet criteria for panic disorder.

Panic Disorder

This syndrome, the hallmark of which is the presence of recurrent panic attacks, that is, discrete episodes of intense fear or anxiety, also involves at least four of the following symptoms: dyspnea, choking, palpitations, sweating, faintness or lightheadedness, unsteadiness or vertigo, gastrointestinal distress (nausea, vomiting, diarrhea), depersonalization or derealization, paresthesias, flushing or chills, trembling or shaking, and chest pain or discomfort. Typically, panic attacks last for several minutes; only rarely do they persist for several hours. Anticipatory anxiety (the fear of recurrent episodes) develops rapidly and may contribute to the development of agoraphobia (American Psychiatric Association, 1980).

The disorder commonly begins during the third decade and may last for several years with varying periods of remission. During these phases, limited symptom panic attacks (those attacks with fewer than four symptoms) may occur. Predisposing factors may include separation anxiety of childhood, a sudden loss of personal supports, or interruption of current interpersonal relationships (American Psychiatric Association, 1987).

Panic disorder is thought to result from abnormal noradrenergic function (Charney, Heninger, & Breier, 1984; Redmond & Huang, 1979). The pathophysiology of panic attacks is thought to depend on an altered sensitivity of noradrenergic receptors in the locus ceruleus, a midbrain nucleus that contains 60% to 70% of the brain's noradrenergic neuron cell bodies. The locus ceruleus sends axons to the regions in the limbic system responsible for the experience of anxiety.

Fortunately, recent advances in psychopharmacologic (Liebowitz, 1985; Sheehan, 1985) and behavioral techniques (Marks, 1985) have made this a readily treatable condition. Because of the severity of panic symptoms, many patients self-medicate with alcohol or anxiolytics and refer themselves for evaluation by a physician. Standard treatments of panic disorder include use of certain antidepressants (employed at usual antidepressant dosages), benzodiazepines, and behavior therapy. The most intensively studied tricyclic antidepressant (TCA), imipramine (usually in doses exceeding 150 mg/d), and the monoamine oxidase (MAO) inhibitor, phenelzine (typically used in dosages approaching 15 mg/kg/d), usually result in abolition of panic attacks after two to four weeks of treatment (Sheehan, Ballenger, & Jacobson, 1980). More recently, high potency benzodiazepines (e.g., alprazolam and clonazepam) have been found to effectively treat panic attacks when used either alone or in combination with antidepressants. The triazolobenzodiazepine alprazolam commonly is effective at doses of 2–6 mg/d, whereas clonazepam, the benzodiazepine with the highest affinity for central nervous system benzodiazepine receptors, typically works at doses of 2–4 mg/d (Chouinard et al., 1983; Spier et al., 1986). Unlike the TCAs or MAO inhibitors, the benzodiazepines tend to produce therapeutic effects within hours to days of administration (Sheehan et al., 1984).

Beta-adrenergic blockers can benefit some patients as an adjunctive treatment or second line treatment of panic attacks (Schuckit, 1981). Their blockade of peripheral manifestations of anxiety may increase the level of comfort and secondarily increase the patient's confidence. Behavioral treatment, which involves the technique of desensitization, progressively increases one's exposure to a given anxiety-provoking situation in order that mastery over anxiety may be achieved (Marks, 1985).

Generalized Anxiety Disorder

Patients with GAD manifest a chronically anxious mood, worry about two or more life circumstances, have physical signs and symptoms of motor tension and sympathetic arousal (e.g., tachycardia, hyperventilation, tremulousness, or diaphoresis), and have heightened vigilance (e.g., irritability, exaggerated startle response, or feeling on edge). Treatment focuses on the judicious use of anxiolytic medication and use of behavioral and psychotherapeutic strategies that promote relaxation (e.g., relaxation response, relaxation tapes, or psychotherapy) and reduce anxiety.

Affective Disorders

This diagnostic category includes disorders of mood, namely major depression and manic-depressive illness, as well as adjustment disorder with depressed features. Patients with these disorders frequently have physical complaints. Depressed patients tend to focus on and amplify bodily symptoms (e.g., fatigue and chest pain) that may result in their seeking evaluation by an internist or cardiologist. It is important to remember that the diagnoses of depression and anxiety are not mutually exclusive. Not uncommonly, such patients, even when symptomatic, will deny feelings of depression, leading to a diagnosis of masked depression.

Somatoform Disorders

Patients having somatoform disorders (somatization disorder, hypochondriasis, or psychogenic pain disorder) often seek medical attention because of their physical complaints and anxiety-like symptoms. These disorders may either coexist with coronary artery disease or suggest its diagnosis. The essential features of this group of disorders are physical symptoms that suggest a physical disorder in the absence of demonstrable organic findings or known physiologic mechanisms, and for which there is evidence or presumption of an underlying psychologic conflict. Although there is no diagnostic test to prove that a patient has a somatoform disorder, the MMPI is a useful test that can help to identify patients who suffer from these disorders. The MMPI can also document patterns of responses so that referral for psychiatric help can be facilitated, especially among those individuals who deny or reject a psychologic basis for their complaints. Successful treatment usually depends on the recognition of the patient's dilemma, supportive care, and regular follow-up. Without a doubt, diagnostic and management problems are greatest in those patients for whom somatoform disorders coexist with organic pathology (e.g., coronary artery disease).

Somatization Disorder

Diagnosis of this relatively uncommon disorder depends on the presence of multiple, chronic, and often dramatic somatic symptoms (more than 12 symptoms in men, and more than 14 symptoms in women) that may vary from one exam to the next. Individuals with this disorder typically seek evaluation and treatment from many physicians and are subject to numerous, and often unnecessary, diagnostic tests and procedures.

Hypochondriasis

The essential features of this disorder include an unrealistic interpretation of physical signs and symptoms as abnormal, a fear of disease, a conviction that one is sick, a preoccupation with one's body, and a persistent and insatiable pursuit of medical care despite reassurance and negative work-ups. Among cardiac patients this constellation of symptoms constitute what has been termed *cardiac neurosis*. High scores on the hypochondriasis and hysteria subscales of the MMPI have been associated with complaints of atypical chest pain (Ostfield et al., 1964; Wielgosz et al., 1984).

Although the diagnosis is essential to treatment, an understanding and supportive approach helps patients to contain the disorder. Challenging the patient's belief system rarely leads to a cure. Because hypochondriasis may coexist with, and be exacerbated by, other psychiatric conditions, the presence of other primary psychiatric conditions needs to be determined.

Psychogenic Pain Disorder

This disorder is manifest by the singular complaint of pain in the absence of adequate physical findings and a suspicion of a psychologic etiology. A temporal relationship can often be detected between a psychologic stressor and a psychologic conflict, or by the appearance of secondary gain (e.g., support a patient may receive because of the complaint). Patients with this disorder can have cardiac complaints. It is important to perform a thorough medical work-up and not assume that the distress is merely psychologic. Patient management is even more difficult if the physician is unaware of, or fails to attend to, the psychologic findings. Attention paid to the emotional conflict may be helpful. Unfortunately, many patients with its disorder are unable or unwilling to perceive psychologic factors.

Factitious Disorders

Although listed in many texts of psychiatry and cardiology as uncommon, most practitioners of medicine have been faced by patients with this disorder. Commonly known as Munchausen's syndrome, when cardiac symptoms (e.g., chest pain or rhythm disturbance) have been involved, the term *cardiopathica fantastica* is used (Pitt & Pitt, 1984). These patients typically present with detailed and grandiose stories, lack social supports, report extensive travel, and have personality disorders manifest by hostility, masochism, and poor impulse control (Stern, 1980). A history of coronary artery disease, prior myocardial infarction, or cardiac surgery does not preclude the diagnosis of factitious disorder.

Complex Partial Seizures

Complex partial seizures, a neuropsychiatric diagnosis, account for only a small percentage of patients with anxiety-like symptoms and cardiac complaints. However, patients with complex partial seizures may have cardiovascular phenomena including chest pain, tachyarrhythmias, and syncope secondary or bradycardia or sinus arrest (Devinsky, Price, & Cohen, 1986; Kiok et al., 1986). The diagnosis of complex partial seizures is a clinical one, but it may be confirmed by electrodiagnostic studies (e.g., an abnormal electroencephalogram [EEG], but without electrocardiographic evidence of myocardial ischemia) and a therapeutic response to anticonvulsants but not anti-anginal medications. Not uncommonly, patients with complex partial seizures have normal EEGs because the origin of the electrical abnormality resides in deep limbic structures that escape detection by surface electrodes.

PSYCHIATRIC RISK FACTORS FOR CARDIAC DISEASE: THE ROLE OF STRESS AND THE TYPE A BEHAVIOR PATTERN

Practitioners of internal medicine and psychiatry have long recognized that cardiac patients exhibit certain characteristic emotions and patterns of coping, for example, worry (Osler, 1910), suppression of anger (Menninger & Menninger, 1936), and joyless striving (Wolf, 1969). In addition, both acute and chronic psychologic stress have been noted to precede myocardial infarction (Weiss et al., 1957), cardiac arrhythmias (Fricchione & Vlay, 1986; Harvey & Levine, 1952), and sudden cardiac death (DeSilva, 1982; Engel, 1971). As a result of these observations, clinicians and researchers have sought to delineate other psychologic risk factors for cardiac disease. An accumulation of stressful life events (Eliot & Buell, 1983), bereavement (Parkes, Benjamin, & Fitzgerald, 1969; Rees & Lutkins, 1967), and a lack of social support have been identified as such factors.

Acute and Chronic Stress

Physiologic changes that accompany stressful events involve arousal of the sympathetic nervous system. Acute reactions to stress stimulate elevations in catecholamines that in turn will lead to increases in heart rate, myocardial contractility, cardiac output, peripheral resistance, and systolic and diastolic blood pressures; the threshold for ventricular fibrillation will decrease. Chronic stressors will activate the pituitary–adrenal cortical system and lead to increases in platelet mass, blood pressure, potassium excretion, and cholesterol, as well as a sensitivity to catecholamines (Eliot & Buell, 1983).

Type A Behavior Pattern

The hypothesis that a specific behavior pattern, the Type A behavior pattern, was an independent risk factor for the genesis of coronary artery disease was first proposed by Friedman and Rosenman in 1959. Defined as an action–emotion complex found in both sexes (Matthews & Haynes, 1986), it is manifested primarily by competitiveness, excessive drive, an enhanced sense of time urgency, and unexpressed hostility. More recent research suggests that the unexpressed hostility may be the critical factor for increased risk of coronary artery disease (Dembroski et al., 1985; Matthews, Glass, Rosenman, & Bortner, 1977; Matthews & Haynes, 1986). Although few physicians would disagree with the existence of the Type A behavior pattern as a risk factor, controversy rages as to its potency (Dimsdale, 1988).

Hostility in the Type A individual may not be immediately apparent to the untrained observer. Some angry individuals have learned to channel their anger into their work (sublimation) and can disguise their internal reactions. Therefore, a person who appears calm on the surface should not be assumed to be calm underneath. Type A individuals exhibit more vigorous cardiovascular and neuroendocrine responses to stress, for example, mental work (Glass et al., 1980; Lane, White, & Williams,

1984; Williams et al., 1982) which may lead to increases in epinephrine, norepinephrine, heart rate, blood pressure (Eliot & Buell, 1983), and cholesterol (Dimsdale, Herd, & Hartley, 1983), and a tendency to lower the threshold for ventricular fibrillation (Verrier & Lown, 1984).

If one holds that the Type A behavior pattern is an important risk factor for the development of coronary artery disease, then its treatment should be expected to decrease the morbidity and mortality associated with cardiovascular disease. Several prospective studies have shown that the pattern can be modified and that such a modification is associated with a significant reduction in recurrent myocardial infarction (Friedman et al., 1982, 1984, 1986). Anecdotal reports have also suggested that these psychological interventions reduce the risk of ventricular arrhythmias (Reich & Gold, 1983; Verrier & Lown, 1984). Pharmacologic agents that treat arrhythmias and the symptoms of coronary artery disease (e.g., beta-blockers and calcium channel blockers) may reduce the physiologic effects of stress. Use of propranolol in one study was associated with a reduction in some features of the Type A pattern (Krantz et al., 1982). A high potency benzodiazepine, alprazolam, has been shown to reduce the levels of circulating catecholamines (Stratton & Halter, 1985) as well as blood pressure and cortisol responses to mental stress in Type A men (Williams & Schanberg, 1986).

PSYCHIATRIC SYMPTOMATOLOGY AND MYOCARDIAL INFARCTION

Although several discrete cardiac conditions and disorders (e.g., myocardial infarction, ventricular tachyarrhythmias, cardiac surgery, mitral valve prolapse, and silent ischemia) have been associated with psychiatric symptomatology, the focus of this section is on psychiatric symptomatology associated with acute coronary events. Although most individuals adjust well to their illness, a substantial number develop anxiety, depression, behavioral abnormalities, and delirium.

Each year several hundred thousand individuals suffer from myocardial infarction (Hillis & Braunwald, 1977). Most deaths (55%–80%) secondary to myocardial infarction occur during the first four hours as a result of arrhythmias or pump failure (Wallace & Yu, 1975). A factor that contributes to this mortality is the delay between the onset of chest pain and arrival at the hospital (Hackett & Cassem, 1969) where antiarrhythmics or devices such as the intraaortic balloon pump can be initiated. Hackett and Cassem (1969) found that this mean delay time was 3.9 hours. One-third of patients still had not arrived for medical attention six hours after the onset of chest pain. No relationship has been found between delaying arrival for medical attention and educational level, socioeconomic class, sex, prior history of myocardial infarction, acquaintance with individuals who had angina or coronary artery disease, or those who had been educated about the nature of the disease (Moss & Goldstein, 1970; Simon, Feinleib, & Thompson, 1972).

Such delays it seems are in large part the result of denial—"the conscious or unconscious repudiation of all or part of the total available meaning of an event to allay fear, anxiety, or other unpleasant affects" (Weisman & Hackett, 1961). Fortunately, delays are decreased as an individual's symptoms increase, and when attended to by an interested, nonrelated person (Hackett & Cassem, 1969). Therefore, one might expect that programs directed at the education of patient contacts on the signs

and symptoms of myocardial infarction would help overcome patient denial and facilitate rapid transport of symptomatic patients to the hospital.

Initial Evaluation and the Coronary Care Unit Stay

Once a patient has arrived in the emergency ward, even those familiar with the
practice of medicine are faced with an often disturbing sequence of events. Anxiety
and fear are common emotions because of the fear of death, ongoing chest pain and
shortness of breath, the recollections of previous hospital stays after similar symptoms, the onslaught of medical personnel subjecting the patient to uncomfortable
procedures (e.g., arterial line placement) and making preparations for a trip to the
catheterization suite (Stern, 1985). Anxiety in some patients during this stage is
heightened more by being left alone (when their imagination runs wild) than it is by
the experience of high technology care. In many cases, busy emergency room personnel are unable to provide explanations or reassurance, though indicated, and avoid the
use of anxiolytic medications. Early in the evaluation, family members are often left
uninformed, a factor that contributes to their sense of anxiety and dread. When family
members finally meet the patient, they typically transmit their anxiety. Brief, limited
explanations about one's condition, reassurance, and the administration of anxiolytics
should begin in the emergency room.

During the coronary care unit (CCU) stay, the most common psychiatric conditions include anxiety, depression, delirium, and manifestations of premorbid character states (Cassem & Hackett, 1971). Each has a tendency to develop along characteristic time frames. Anxiety, the most frequent psychiatric problem following
myocardial infarction, is responsible for the greatest number of psychiatric consultations on the first two days in the CCU (Cassem & Hackett, 1971). Sources of anxiety
in the CCU include the threat of death, the threat of disability, the initiation of
invasive cardiac procedures, the opportunity to witness someone else's cardiac arrest
(Hackett & Cassem, 1974), and the physician's bedside rounds (Jarvinen, 1955).
Many patients have misconceptions about resuscitation after cardiac arrest, which
leads to a superficial sense of security (Hackett, Cassem, & Wishnie, 1968). However, all patients in one study who had witnessed a cardiac arrest would choose a
single-bed room if they were to be readmitted to the hospital to avoid having another
such opportunity (Hackett & Cassem, 1974).

A statistically significant increase in peri-infarction complications was noted in one
Scandinavian CCU during the one hour surrounding morning attending rounds (Jarvinen, 1955). Although not measured, a surge in serum catecholamines that coincided
with a patient's normal diurnal elevation in catecholamines and with the anticipation
that accompanies a physician's decisions (or pronouncements of prognosis), was
probably responsible for the result. This effect may be negated by forewarning patients about the routine nature of daily attending rounds, thereby minimizing the
impact of these rounds on patients.

Although prior to one's admission to the hospital denial may be a liability because
it leads the patient to delay receiving medical attention, after one is already in a CCU
denial may serve some protective function. Individuals who minimize the impact of
their illness, deny fear, and appear calm have been found to survive their CCU stay
more often than those who worry incessantly (Froese et al., 1974; Hackett et al.,
1968). However, when denial becomes excessive and patients either refuse life-saving
treatment, attempt to sign out against medical advice, or insist on demonstrating the

fitness of their heart by showing off athletic prowess in the CCU, then denial may be dangerous. This degree of pathologic denial must be overcome to protect the patient.

Treatment of Anxiety

Treatment of anxiety in the CCU depends on accurate diagnosis and then application of psychotherapeutic or pharmacologic treatments. Patients with only mild apprehension will usually benefit from receiving information about their clinical status (Hackett et al., 1968; Tesar & Hackett, 1985). However, when anxiety increases, patients often become inattentive and this information may need to be repeated several times. Appropriate information, clarification, and the opportunity for emotional ventilation helps to reduce anxiety (Cassem & Hackett, 1971; Hackett et al., 1968; Lynch, 1974; Stern, 1985). Not everyone wants to hear about the details of his or her situation. The clinician in charge needs to decide what information is needed, and when to make it available to the patient. Drawings by patients can be useful to generate hypotheses about a patient's character, emotional state, and level of understanding of their illness (Stern, 1985).

Although most CCU patients are anxious, many go through their entire CCU stay without any anti-anxiety medication (Hackett & Cassem, 1976; Hackett, Cassem, & Wishnie, 1969). In one study at the Massachusetts General Hospital (Stern, Caplan, & Cassem, 1987), only two-thirds of all CCU patients had any hypnotic or anxiolytic medication prescribed. When prescribed, a majority of the orders were written as PRN, rather than on fixed-dose schedules. Only 15% of prn and 82% of fixed-dose medication was administered to the patient. Even when administered, the doses employed were in general inadequate to treat the patient's anxiety. Reasons for underprescription of anxiolytics included failure by staff to detect anxiety in their patients, fear by patients and physicians that drug dependency would ensue, and inadequate knowledge by staff of the pharmacokinetics and pharmacodynamics of anxiolytics prescribed. Undue sedation limits administration of anxiolytics in only a small minority of cases (Hackett & Cassem, 1975).

The goals of anxiolytic treatment include reduction of circulating catecholamines (thereby reducing the potential for arrhythmias in those with ischemic and injured myocardium), reduction of emotional reactivity (e.g., autonomic response) to fear and conflict, and improvement in disrupted sleep patterns. In addition, benzodiazepines (e.g., intravenous diazepam) have been shown to have a nitroglycerin-like action on the coronary and systemic circulation that results in decreases in myocardial oxygen consumption without modification of either coronary blood flow or coronary vascular resistance (Cote, Gueret, & Bourassa, 1974). Intravenous diazepam and midazolam (Marty et al., 1986) and oral alprazolam (Stratton & Halter, 1985) also decrease sympathetic tone. This may be helpful in patients with acute myocardial infarction or congested heart failure, conditions that show elevations in circulating catecholamines (Goldstein, 1984). Benzodiazepine-mediated reductions in sympathetic tone could be problematic in hypovolemic patients receiving a combination of benzodiazepine and morphine treatment (Hoar et al., 1981).

Benzodiazepines have become the therapeutic drugs of choice to treat anxiety because of their high degree of efficacy and low side-effect profile (Greenblatt, Shader, & Abernathy, 1983). Because all benzodiazepines are capable of alleviating anxiety, rational prescribing of these agents depends on knowledge of their therapeutic effects and side effects. Differences are found in their potency, rapidity of action, duration of action, locus of metabolism and excretion, and level of sedation (see Table

Table 1 Profile of commonly used benzodiazepines

Drug	t¹/₂ (hours)	Dose equivalent (mg)	Onset	Level of sedation	Primary site of metabolism and excretion
Oxazepam	5–15	15.0	Slow	+	Kidney
Lorazepam	10–20	1.0	Intermediate	+ + +	Kidney
Alprazolam	12–15	0.5	Intermediate	+	Liver
Diazepam	20–100	5.0	Fast	+ + +	Liver
Chlordiazepoxide	5–30	10.0	Intermediate	+ +	Liver
Clorazepate	30–200	7.5	Fast	+ +	Liver
Flurazepam	40–140	5.0	Fast	+ + +	Liver
Clonazepam	20–120	0.25	Fast	+ + +	Liver

+ = Low; + + = moderate; + + + = high.

1). Rather than using one agent for all anxious patients in the CCU, it makes more sense to tailor the choice of agent to the pharmacokinetic properties and clinical situation. Diazepam, 5–10 mg TID to QID (or another benzodiazepine when given in similar equivalents) is usually effective in routine circumstances. Its rapid onset, sedation, and long half-life provides rapid and sustained relief.

However, in the elderly, or in those with impaired renal or hepatic metabolism, lower doses are generally required. Use of agents with shorter half-lives, and minor or no active metabolism (e.g., alprazolam, 0.25–1.0 mg TID to QID; lorazepam, 0.5–1.0 mg TID to QID; and oxazepam, 10–30 mg QID) is reasonable. Hypnotic doses are in general equivalent to twice the anxiolytic dose. Alprazolam may be a benzodiazepine with special benefits to patients with coronary artery disease because it has been shown to inhibit platelet-activating factor-induced aggregation of human platelets (Kornecki, Ehrlich, & Lenox, 1984).

Treatment of Depression

Depression, like anxiety, is fueled by limitations on activity, by weakness, and by fear. Fears of disability tend to arise on the third and fourth days of the CCU stay as the psychological defense of denial fades. Not uncommonly, depressive feelings and anxiety coexist. Although fears, misconceptions about future function, and injury to one's self-esteem are important, one needs to manifest more than depressed mood in order to qualify for a diagnosis of major depression. A neurovegetative symptom complex with four or more symptoms lasting for a duration of two weeks is required (American Psychiatric Association, 1980) and includes a disturbance of mood with (a) disturbed sleep, (b) loss of normal interest or motivation, (c) feelings of guilt or excessive rumination, (d) loss of energy, (e) impaired concentration, (f) disturbed appetite, (g) psychomotor retardation or agitation, and (h) suicide ideation or thoughts of death. A majority of CCU patients have some of these criteria, but only a few will meet criteria for major depression.

For most patients with depressive reactions in the CCU, supportive psychotherapy, reassurance, the provision of information, and the beginning of cardiac rehabilitation are sufficient. When psychotropic medication is considered, knowledge of the side effect profile of antidepressants is required. Conservative practitioners delay initiation of treatment with polycyclic antidepressants until 4 to 6 weeks following myocardial infarction (Stern, 1985). The rationale behind this delay is that cardiovascular side effects (i.e., orthostatic hypotension, conduction system disturbances, and tachycardia) of the polycyclic antidepressants are most likely to interfere with patient care during this time period. This is a time during which scar formation and healing of myocardium occurs. Tachycardia, as well as orthostatic hypotension, may place patients with myocardial infarction at risk for congestive heart failure, chest pain, and reinfarction. Conduction system disturbances, already common in the acute phases of myocardial infarction, may be exacerbated by the type IA, quinidine-like effects of the polycyclic antidepressants. However, alprazolam, which has been purported to have both anxiolytic and antidepressant properties (Fabre & McLendon, 1980; Feighner et al., 1983) is safe and particularly useful in the group of patients with both anxiety and depression because it appears to be devoid of adverse cardiovascular side effects.

Evaluation of Coping Factors

Inappropriate and disruptive behavior generally arises after the third day in the CCU (Cassem & Hackett, 1971). The most difficult of these problems for CCU staff are presented by demanding, regressed, or exhibitionistic patients. When these problems are understood in the context of the underlying character style, these stress reactions can be managed more easily.

Seven distinct personality styles—hysterical, obsessive, narcissistic, oral, masochistic, schizoidal, and paranoid—have been identified (Bibring & Kahana, 1968) and each has a characteristic reaction to illness. These styles reflect an individual's methods of coping with stress. When management of these styles is inadequate, anxiety and regressive and maladaptive behavior will be the result. It is important to remember that an individual need not demonstrate a pathologic degree of any of these styles, and an individual may manifest more than one of these traits (Stern, 1985).

Patients with a hysterical style tend to be dramatic and anxious and react as if their masculinity or femininity were being attacked. Their anxiety can usually be controlled when they are provided with support, allowed to ventilate their fears, and praised for their courage. Anxiety fails to resolve with detailed, scientific explanations.

Obsessive characters tend to be meticulous, intense, and anxious. For them, illness is a punishment for their letting things get out of control. They may feel guilty ("I know this heart attack is all my fault. I should have exercised to 80% of my maximal heart rate three times a week"). They do well with detailed explanations that make them feel as though they were in control. These patients often manage numbers and ideas better than they do feelings.

Narcissistic or self-involved individuals see myocardial infarction as an attack on their sense of perfection. Unless their sense of self is supported, they will act in a condescending manner and manifest inappropriate anger toward staff. The oral character tends to be demanding, dependent, and clingy, with a need for attention that at times seems boundless. Their greatest fear is of being abandoned, an issue that is rekindled by the infarction. Management is facilitated by an approach that supports patients and sets limits on their neediness.

Masochists often display a long-suffering depressed appearance. They usually believe that the infarction is a well-deserved punishment for their worthlessness. Reassurance about their improvement is of little effect. Instead, an approach that respects the patient's courage and ability to withstand suffering is more acceptable.

The schizoidal individual, often remote and uninvolved, tends to see care as an invasion of their privacy. Anxiety increases when one cares too much for them or gets too close to their emotional life. Respecting their need for privacy will help control their anxiety. Individuals with a paranoid personality tend to be suspicious and accusatory. Intensive CCU care with multiple caregivers reaffirms their sense of danger. In order to minimize their terror, clear, often-repeated explanations about their illness and care are required.

When communication appropriate to an individual's character style and situation is insufficient to reduce anxiety and regression, anxiolytics are useful. However, when the patient's behavior becomes disruptive, threatening, or dangerous, use of physical restraint or neuroleptic agents may be required to ensure adequate care and prevent harm to both the patient and the staff (Tesar & Stern, 1986).

When psychiatric consultation is requested for patients, an attempt is made to recognize the existence of personality traits; diagnose anxiety, depression, and delirium; and assess the level of denial manifested by a patient. Attempts to discover how individuals have coped with stressful life experiences in the past often provides clues as to how an individual will respond to myocardial infarction. When physician and patient can share a common language then useful metaphors can be employed to explain the nature and treatment of coronary artery disease and myocardial infarction in order that treatment adherence may be enhanced (Stern, 1985). For example, speaking to a plumber about clogged pipes enables one to discuss treatments (e.g., Roto-Rooter; angioplasty: liquid drain cleaner; tissue plasminogen activator).

Treatment of Delirium

Delirium is a reversible organic mental syndrome that when mild is often confused with anxiety. It has been reported to occur in 2% to 12% of CCU patients (Hackett et al., 1968; Parker & Hodge, 1967). The hallmarks of delirium are a clouded consciousness, disorientation, memory impairment, perceptual disturbances (e.g., hallucinations and illusions), incoherent speech, an increase or decrease in psychomotor activity, and a disturbance of the sleep–wake cycle (American Psychiatric Association, 1980; Lipowski, 1967; Murray, 1978; Romano & Engel, 1944). The clinical features characteristically fluctuate over time and may go unrecognized for brief periods. Delirium commonly occurs in those with serious medical illness and can occur during any part of the CCU stay (Cassem & Hackett, 1971). Typically, patients with delirium are restless and pick at the bedsheets and intravenous tubing. Restlessness may proceed to violent agitation, especially when the patient's movement is restricted by devices such as the intraaortic balloon pump, pulmonary artery and arterial line monitoring equipment, or mechanical ventilator (Tesar, Murray, & Cassem, 1985; Tesar & Stern, 1986).

A wide range of clinical conditions, medications (e.g., antiarrhythmics, H_2 blockers, narcotics, and sedative agents), and metabolic states have been implicated as potential precipitants of delirium (Fox, Topel, & Huckman, 1975; Jacobs et al., 1977; Murray, 1978; Tesar & Stern, 1986). Factors commonly responsible for delirium in myocardial infarction patients include central nervous system dysfunction following cardiac arrest; low cardiac output; hypotension; toxicity of antiarrhythmic drugs, especially lidocaine in intravenous doses ≥ 2–4 mg/min (Cassem, 1984; Tesar &

Stern, 1986); hypoxia; electrolyte imbalance; and anticholinergic excess. Drug and alcohol withdrawal must also be considered because emergency admission may have led to sudden discontinuation of the agent in question. EEGs of delirious patients indicate that delirium is the result of acute brain dysfunction (Adams, 1984; Adams, Fernandez, & Andersson, 1986; Engel & Romano, 1959). Although sleep depriva-.tion has been considered to be an etiologic factor, disturbed sleep, common among CCU patients, is more likely to be an associated feature than a specific cause of delirium (Adams et al., 1986).

Appropriate treatment of delirium depends on the identification of the etiologic agent. If left untreated, it can interfere with a patient's medical therapy and result in chronic neurologic sequelae or death (Adams et al., 1986; Lipowski, 1980, 1983). While the search for a precipitating factor proceeds, a combination of common sense (i.e., orientation and comfort measures) and neuroleptic medication is administered. Behavioral control is essential to prevent a patient from self-injury (e.g., exsanguina-tion after pulling out the balloon pump or arterial line).

The neuroleptic used most often to treat delirium (i.e., agitation and confusion) is haloperidol. Whether administered orally or parenterally (Cameron, 1978; Dobson et al., 1971; Dudley, Rowlett, & Loebel, 1979; Settle & Ayd, 1983), as it is at the Massachusetts General Hospital, even in extremely high doses (Tesar et al., 1985; Sos & Cassem, 1980a, 1980b; Stern, 1985) it has only minimal effects on heart rate, blood pressure, and respiration, unlike agents such as barbiturates, benzodiazepines, and narcotics (Sos & Cassem, 1980a, 1980b). When used intravenously it is rapidly acting (mean onset of action is 11 minutes), and potent (50 times as potent in equal dosages as chlorpromazine (Sos & Cassem, 1980b). By using haloperidol intraven-ously, painful intramuscular injections that can elevate creative kinase levels can be avoided. Commonly, delirious patients require less than 20 mg per day of intravenous haloperidol to adequately control specific target symptoms. Intravenous haloperidol injection must be preceded by flushing the intravenous line with saline because halo-peridol precipitates with phenytoin and heparin, if these drugs are present.

Dosing begins at 1–2 mg for mildly agitated patients, at 5 mg for moderate degrees of agitation, and at 10 mg for severely agitated patients. Doses are doubled every 15 to 20 minutes until target symptoms are successfully treated (Tesar & Stern, 1986). Repeated intravenous boluses of 40 mg/hour have been used in unusual cases for several days (Tesar et al., 1985) and doses as high as 150 mg every 2 hours and 975 mg in a 24-hour period (Stern, 1985) have been required to control severe agitation in a man with cardiogenic shock on the intraaortic balloon pump. At present, haloperi-dol is not approved by the Food and Drug Administration (FDA) for intravenous use; therefore, it seems advisable to inform the hospital pharmacy before prescribing intravenous haloperidol. Intravenous lorazepam, which has little effect on respiratory or hemodynamic indices (Paulson, Becker, & Way, 1983), appears to have a synergis-tic effect with intravenous haloperidol (Adams, 1984; Adams et al., 1986). If the agitated, delirious patient cannot be adequately controlled with benzodiazepines, nar-cotics, or neuroleptics, then use of a paralytic agent (e.g., metocurine iodide or pancuronium bromide) may be necessary (Tesar & Stern, 1986).

The Step-Down Unit

Despite the fact that transfer from the CCU to a step-down unit is a sign of progress, many patients become anxious upon transfer. Some individuals become anxious because they will no longer have the around-the-clock observation provided for them in the CCU by trained staff and cardiac monitoring devices. In one study (Klein et al., 1968) this anxiety resulted in an increase in 24-hour urinary catechol-amine production and was associated with an increase in peri-infarction complications. When patients were forewarned of transfer and introduced to the routines and person-nel on the step-down unit, urinary catecholamines remained normal and posttransfer peri-infarction complications were absent. This study reinforces the benefits of in-forming the patient about upcoming transfers and placing them in the context of the patient's improvement and reduced need for continuous monitoring and care.

Even after transfer from the CCU, sleep patterns remain abnormal for several days. During the step-down unit stay, the use of sedative–hypnotic agents will help ensure that the patient gets the rest needed for continued improvement. Prior to discharge, educating patients about the convalescence from myocardial infarction should be a focus of the staff's attention. The patient should understand the nature and timing of his or her medications. Explicit instructions should be given to the patient and the spouse regarding daily activities (e.g., exercise, sexual relations, travel, and work). Vague instructions such as "Do what you think you're able to do" only generate more anxiety. Follow-up appointments should be provided, and, if available, contact with a cardiac rehabilitation program should be made.

Post-Hospital Course

Problems with anxiety and depression are still common in post-infarct patients. However, whereas family problems were often left in the background during the patient's CCU stay, now these issues should be dealt with to minimize psychologic, as well as cardiovascular, complications. Management of anxiety during the recovery phase requires identification of the nature and extent of the problem and then initiat-ing the appropriate treatment. For some, anxiety in this phase is merely an extension of a psychiatric disorder that existed prior to infarction. For others, it is a prolonged manifestation of fear and apprehension stimulated by the infarction. Frequently, reas-surance, information, and the enrollment in a cardiac rehabilitation program help patients to decrease anxiety. In one study, improved cardiovascular functioning, im-proved compliance with treatment recommendations, more positive self-perception, and better psychological functioning were reported (Rovarios, Holmes, & Holmes-tein, 1984). Benzodiazepines may still be helpful to reduce undue anxiety and pro-mote sleep. Fears of patients and physicians about dependency or addiction to anx-iolytic agents are usually excessive; however, potentially addictive medications should be used cautiously, or avoided, in those patients known to have abused, or been dependent on, drugs (e.g., alcohol or benzodiazepines) in the past. Additional benefit may be achieved by the support and education provided in groups for patients (Bilodeau & Hackett, 1971; Ibrahim et al., 1974; Rahe, Ward, & Hayes, 1978). In a minority of cases, individual psychiatric care may be necessary to help patients man-age or resolve conflicts that are contributing to distress.

Post-infarct patients commonly enter the recovery phase with a sense of loss and depression that may increase upon return home (Cassem & Hackett, 1973; Wishnie, Hackett, & Cassem, 1971). Called the "home-coming depression" (Hackett & Cas-sem, 1982), this state frequently reflects the extent to which an individual sees him-self or herself as disabled. This perception is often promoted by the patient's feeling weak, a result of enforced inactivity or bed rest in the hospital that has led to muscle atrophy and a corresponding loss of strength. Therefore, physical reconditioning is an important aspect of one's psychological recovery (Cassem & Hackett, 1973; Stern, Pascale, & Ackerman, 1977).

Specific recommendations on physical exertion can be based on the quantification of physical activity in mets (metabolic units), defined as the energy expenditure per kilogram of body weight per minute for an average person sitting quietly in a chair (approximately 1.4 calories/min or 3.5 to 4 ml oxygen/min (Cassem & Hackett, 1973). A typical middle-aged man is capable of performing at 8–9 mets following an uncomplicated myocardial infarction. When ordinary activities (e.g., using a bed pan or playing golf) produce cardiac symptoms, one's performance capacity may be closer to 4 mets (Cassem & Hackett, 1973).

A patient's sexual activity should be discussed with the patient despite the reluctance of many patients and physicians. Prior experience of chest pain during intercourse, sexual difficulty prior to myocardial infarction, and the patient's and spouse's understanding of when to resume sexual activity (Scalzi, 1982) should be covered. One common method to assess a patient's cardiovascular capacity to resume sexual activity is to assess the patient's ability to asymptomatically climb 20 steps in 10 seconds (Siewicki & Mansfield, 1977). It has been estimated that at maximal heart rate during coitus, 5 mets are required (Hellerstein & Friedman, 1970; Scalzi, 1982).

Spouses and children of patients also are subject to uncertainty, concern, and fear (Papadopoulos et al., 1980). Adolescent children, in particular, may be at risk for extreme emotional reactions such as depression, guilt, and impaired school and social performance (Wishnie, Hackett, & Cassem, 1976). Once identified, specific treatment recommendations can be offered.

Treatment of Depression

If depressive symptomatology persists for several weeks following myocardial infarction, most clinicians would find it reasonable to consider treatment of depression with antidepressant medications (Stern, 1985). Several varieties of antidepressants (tricyclics, second generation antidepressants, psychostimulants, MAO inhibitors, and lithium) are in general effective in treating depressive symptomatology; therefore, their use in cardiac patients is often determined by their side-effect profile (See Table 2). Although their mechanism of action has yet to be firmly established, they have central and peripheral adrenergic, cholinergic, histaminergic, and serotonergic activity. These actions are responsible for their principle cardiac (i.e., tachycardia, orthostatic hypotension, conduction system abnormalities, and pro- and antiarrhythmic) effects (Cassem, 1982; Jefferson, 1985; Kaufmann et al., 1984; Stern, 1987).

Tricyclic antidepressants. Doxepin, amitriptyline, imipramine, nortriptyline, desipramine, protriptyline, and other tricyclics can be used to treat people with depressive disorders as well as certain anxiety disorders (e.g., panic attacks). They can be either sedating or stimulating. If sedation is desired, then a serotonergic-enhancing tertiary amine (e.g., doxepine or amitriptyline) is reasonable. If stimulation is needed to treat an individual with psychomotor retardation, then a more energizing secondary amine (e.g., desipramine or protriptyline) can be used.

In general, the propensity of a given tricyclic to cause postural hypotension is correlated with its ability to cause sedation. Orthostatic hypotension is severe enough in 6% to 24% of cases to result in modification or discontinuation of the tricyclic (Glassman et al., 1979; Muller, Goodman, & Bellet, 1961; Nelson et al., 1982; Tesar

Table 2 Profile of commonly used antidepressants

	Neurotransmitter			Hypotensive properties	Anti-cholinergic properties	Sedative effects	Cardiac conduction effects
Drug	5-HT	NE	DA				
Tricyclics							
Doxepin	+ + +	0	0	+ + +	+ +	High	Yes
Amitriptyline	+ + +	0	0	+ + + +	+ + + + + +	High	Yes
Imipramine	+ + +	+ +	0	+ + + +	+ +	Medium	Yes
Nortriptyline	+ +	+ +	0	+ +	+ +	Low	Yes
Desipramine	0	+ + + +	0	+	+	Low	Yes
Protriptyline	0	+ + + +	0	+	+	Low	Yes
Second generation antidepressants							
Trazodone	+ + +	0	0	+ + +	0	High	Yes
Maprotiline	0	+ +	0	+	+	Medium	Yes
Amoxapine	+ +	+ +	+ +	+	+	Low	Yes
Fluoxetine	+ + +	0	0	0	0	0	Rare
Bupropion	0	0	+ +	+	+	Low	Rare
Stimulants							
Dextro-amphetamine	0	+ +	+	0	0	0	Rare
Methylphenidate	0	+	+ +	0	0	0	Rare
MAO inhibitors							
Phenelzine	+ +	0	0	+ + + +	? +	0	Rare
Tranylcypromine	+ +	0	0	+ + +	? +	0	Rare
Alprazolam	0	0	0	0	0	Medium	No

Abbreviations: 5-HT, serotonin; NE, norepinephrine; DA, dopamine.

0 = None; + = low; + +, medium; + + + = high; + + + + = very high; + + + + + = extremely high.

et al., 1987). It occurs more commonly in those patients taking other medications that lower blood pressure (Glassman, 1984; Glassman & Bigger, 1981; Tesar et al., 1987) and in whom there was a pretreatment blood pressure drop in systolic blood pressure of > 10 mm Hg (Glassman et al., 1979). Clinical experience suggests that gradual increases in the dose minimize these orthostatic effects. Of the tricyclics, imipramine is probably most likely to cause hypotension (Cassem, 1982).

Tricyclics also have the ability to increase heart rate by virtue of their anticholinergic effects. This elevation in heart rate, on average 10–15 beats/min, is usually clinically insignificant; however, it can be problematic in patients with marginally compensated CHF or unstable angina. Desipramine is the tricyclic with the least anticholinergic potency. Their effect on the cardiac conduction system is similar to that of the type IA antiarrhythmic drugs such as quinidine. Each of the tricyclics slows cardiac conduction through the His–ventricular pathway; the severity of slowing correlates with dosage and plasma levels. Prolongation of the QRS segment, and PR and QT intervals can occur during the routine administration of tricyclics. Preexisting conduction defects increase the likelihood of tricyclic-induced high grade heart block (Glassman, 1984; Glassman & Bigger, 1981). In general, these drugs also decrease ventricular ectopy. However, as often as 10% of the time they may, like quinidine, increase ventricular ectopy. When tricyclics are used in combination with type IA drugs, their effects will be additive. Fortunately, tricyclics do not significantly impair mechanical functioning of the heart, whether left ventricular function is normal (Thorsand, 1976) or abnormal (Glassman et al., 1983; Roose et al., 1986; Veith et al., 1982).

Second generation antidepressants. Like the tricyclics, these agents have been used to treat both depressive and anxiety disorders. Although this group of drugs (including trazodone, maprotiline, amoxapine, bupropion, fluoxetine, and alprazolam) have been purported to be less cardiotoxic than the traditional tricyclics, their use has not been subjected to the same intensive scrutiny as the tricyclics have. Trazodone has been suggested as a useful drug for the elderly depressed person, because it is sedating but not anticholinergic. It has been associated with orthostatic hypotension (Hames, Burgess, & George, 1982) and with a tendency to aggravate cardiac arrhythmias (Janowsky et al., 1983; Pellettier & Bartolucci, 1984; Vlay & Friedling, 1983).

The tetracyclic maprotiline has cardiovascular effects similar to those of desipramine (Cassem, 1982). However, it has been reported to cause torsades de pointes (Cassem, 1982) and seizures (Ramrize, 1983) at high therapeutic doses. Amoxapine has dopamine-blocking effects that may result in extrapyramidal side effects (e.g., akathisia) and in anticholinergic effects and has been reported to cause atrial arrhythmias and conduction abnormalities (Pi & Simpson, 1985). Bupropion is an energizing antidepressant. Although it is apparently without anticholinergic effects, it has been reported to cause seizures at slightly toxic doses (Peck, Stern, & Watkinson, 1983).

Fluoxetine, the newest antidepressant on the market, is another energizing, serotonergic-enhancing agent without apparent anticholinergic or cardiotoxic effects. Alprazolam, a high-potency anxiolytic benzodiazepine has also been noted to have mild antidepressant properties (Fabre & McLendon, 1980; Feighner et al., 1983); it appears to be devoid of cardiac side effects. This may make it a suitable agent for those cardiac patients with a mixture of anxiety and depressive reactions.

Psychostimulants. This class of drugs, which includes dextroamphetamine and methylphenidate, has been safely and effectively used to treat depression in geriatric patients (Clark & Mankikar, 1979; Lazarus & Hagens, 1968), in those with medical illness (Katon & Raskind, 1980; Kaufmann & Murray, 1982; Woods et al., 1986) and in patients recovering from cardiac surgery (Kaufmann et al., 1984). Psychostimulants are not indicated for the treatment of anxiety states. They differ from TCAs in their rapid onset of action, absence of anticholinergic effects, and failure to produce orthostatic hypotension. Cardiovascular side effects infrequently occur with their use (e.g., tachycardia, coronary spasm, arrhythmias, and hypertension) at doses generally used to treat depressed cardiac patients (5–20 mg/day p.o.). Possible contraindications to their use include clinically significant hypertension, and concomitant use of MAO inhibitors.

Monoamine oxidase inhibitors. The MAO inhibitors (phenelzine, tranylcypromine, and isocarboxizide) are generally used as a second-line treatment of depression and panic attacks. Many physicians have been reluctant to prescribe MAO inhibitors because of the hypertensive crisis that may arise when tyramine-containing foods or stimulant medications are ingested by patients taking these agents. In addition, strict dietary restrictions may have prevented others from realizing the benefits of MAO inhibitors (Sullivan & Shulman, 1984). A common, clinically relevant, side effect with routine use of these medications in patients with ischemic heart disease is orthostatic hypotension (Kronig et al., 1983; Tesar et al., 1987).

Lithium carbonate. Although not specifically an antidepressant, lithium is useful in the treatment of mood disorders, and manic-depressive illness in particular. It is not in general prescribed for anxiety disorders. Although serious cardiotoxicity secondary to lithium is rare, benign EKG changes such as T-wave flattening (Lydiard & Gelenberg, 1982), sinus node dysfunction (Roose et al., 1979; Schou, 1963), reversible first-degree atrioventricular block (Jaffe, 1977), and ventricular arrhythmias (Schou, 1963; Worthley, 1974) have been reported. Reduced glomeruler filtration, use of thiazide diuretics, and sodium restriction each contribute to elevated serum lithium levels and may predispose to lithium toxicity. Reduction of the lithium level by approximately 25% may be necessary in those conditions to maintain therapeutic lithium levels.

CONCLUSION

Recognition of the spectrum of symptoms associated with anxiety disorders will lead to more effective treatment of the anxious patient with coronary artery disease. Knowledge about the assortment of psychiatric disorders that are manifest by cardiac symptoms and a host of cardiac conditions and medications that generate, or are associated with, anxiety-like symptoms will help physicians apply appropriate pharmacologic and nonpharmacologic interventions. The appropriate use of this knowledge should lead to a decrease in morbidity and mortality among these patients.

REFERENCES

Adams, F. (1984). Neuropsychiatric evaluation and treatment of delirium in the critically ill cancer patient. *Cancer Bulletin, 36,* 156–160.

Adams, F., Fernandez, F., & Andersson, B. S. (1986). Emergency pharmacotherapy of delirium in the critically ill cancer patient. *Psychosomatics, 27* (Suppl. 1), 33–37.

American Psychiatric Association. (1980). *Diagnostic and statistical manual of mental disorders* (3rd ed.). Washington, DC.

American Psychiatric Association. (1987). *Diagnostic and statistical manual of mental disorders* (3rd ed. rev.) Washington, DC: American Psychiatric Press.

Bass, C., & Wade, C. (1984). Chest paint with normal coronary arteries: A comparative study of psychiatric and social morbidity. *Psychological Medicine, 14,* 51–61.

Bibring, G. L., & Kahana, R. J. (1968). *Lectures in medical psychology: An introduction to the care of patients.* New York: International Universities Press.

Bilodeau, C. B., & Hackett, T. P. (1971). Issues raised in a group setting by patients recovering from myocardial infarction. *American Journal of Psychiatry, 128,* 105–110.

Cameron, O. G. (1978). Safe use of haloperidol in a patient with cardiac dysrrhythmia. *American Journal of Psychiatry, 135,* 1244.

Cameron, O. G. (1985). The differential diagnosis of anxiety: Psychiatric and medical disorders. *Psychiatric Clinics of North America, 8*(1), 3–23.

Cassem, N. H. (1982). Cardiovascular effects of antidepressants. *Journal of Clinical Psychiatry, 43*(11), 22–28.

Cassem, N. H. (1984). Critical care psychiatry. In W. C. Shoemaker, W. L. Thompson, & P. R. Holbrook (Eds.), *Textbook of critical care* (pp. 981–989). Philadelphia: W. B. Saunders.

Cassem, N. H., & Hackett, T. P. (1971). Psychiatric consultation in a coronary care unit. *Annals of Internal Medicine, 75,* 9–14.

Cassem, N. H., & Hackett, T. P. (1973). Psychological rehabilitation of myocardial infarction patients in the acute phase. *Heart Lung, 2,* 382–388.

Cavanaugh, S., & Wettstein, R. M. (1984). Prevalence of psychiatric morbidity in medical populations. In L. Grinspoon (Ed.), *Psychiatric update* (Vol. 3). Washington, DC: American Psychiatric Press.

Channer, K. S., James, M. A., Papouchado, M., et al. (1985). Anxiety and depression in patients with chest pain referred for exercise testing. *Lancet, 2,* 820–823.

Charney, D. S., Heninger, G. R., & Breier, A. (1984). Noradrenergic function in panic anxiety. *Archives of General Psychiatry, 41,* 751–763.

Chouinard, G., Labonte, A., Fontaine, R., et al. (1983). New concepts in benzodiazepine therapy: Rebound anxiety and new indications for the more potent benzodiazepines. *Prog Neuropsychopharmacol and Biol Psychiatry, 7*, 669–672.

Clark, A. N. G., & Mankikar, G. D. (1979). D-amphetamine in elderly patients refractory to rehabilitation procedures. *Journal of The American Geriatric Society, 27*, 174–177.

Cote, P., Gueret, P., & Bourassa, M. G. (1974). Systemic and coronary hemodynamic effects of diazepam in patients with normal and diseased coronary arteries. *Circulation, 50*, 1210–1216.

Crowe, R. R. (1985). Mitral valve prolapse and panic disorder. *Psychiatric Clinics of North America, 8*, 63–71.

Dembroski, T. M., MacDougall, J. M., Williams, R. D., et al. (1985). Components of type A, hostility and anger in relationship to angiographic findings. *Psychosomatic Medicine, 47*, 219–233.

DeSilva, R. A. (1982). Central nervous system risk factors for sudden cardiac death. *Annals of the New York Academy of Science, 382*, 143–161.

Devinsky, O., Price, B. H., & Cohen, S. I. (1986). Cardiac manifestations of complex partial seizures. *American Journal of Medicine, 80*, 195–202.

Dimsdale, J. E. (1988). A perspective on type A behavior and coronary disease. *New England Journal of Medicine, 318*, 110–112.

Dimsdale, J. E., Herd, J. A., & Hartley, L. H. (1983). Epinephrine mediated increases in plasma cholesterol. *Psychosomatic Medicine, 45*, 227–232.

Dobson, M., Tattersfield, A. E., Adler, M. W., et al. (1971). Attitudes and long-term adjustment of patients surviving cardiac arrest. *British Medical Journal, 3*, 207–212.

Dudley, D. L., Rowlett, D. B., & Loebel, P. J. (1979). Emergency use of intravenous haloperidol. *General Hospital Psychiatry, 1*, 240–246.

Eliot, R. S., & Buell, J. C. (1983). The role of the CNS in cardiovascular disorders. *Hospital Pract, 5*, 189–199.

Engel, G. L. (1971). Sudden and rapid death during psychologic stress: Folklore or folk wisdom? *Annals of Internal Medicine, 74*, 771–782.

Engel, G. L., & Romano, J. (1959). Delirium: A syndrome of cerebral insufficiency. *Journal of Chronic Diseases, 9*, 260–277.

Fabre, L. F., & McLendon, D. M. (1980). A double-blind study comparing the efficacy and safety of alprazolam with imipramine and placebo in primary depression. *Current Therapeutic Research, 27*, 474–482.

Feighner, J. P., Aden, G. C., Fabre, L. F., et al. (1983). Comparison of alprazolam, imipramine and placebo in the treatment of depression. *Journal of The American Medical Association, 249*, 3057–3064.

Fox J. H., Topel, J. L., & Huckman, M. J. (1975). Dementia in the elderly: A search for treatable illnesses. *Journal of Gerontology, 30*, 557–564.

Fricchione, G. L., & Vlay, S. C. (1986). Psychiatric aspects of patients with malignant ventricular arrhythmias. *American Journal of Psychiatry, 143*, 1518–1526.

Friedman, M., & Rosenman, R. H. (1959). Association of specific overt behavior pattern with blood and cardiovascular findings. *Journal of the American Medical Association, 169*, 1286–1295.

Friedman, M., Thoresen, C. E., Gill, J. J., et al. (1982). Feasibility of altering type A behavior pattern after myocardial infarction. *Circulation, 66*, 83–92.

Friedman, M., Thoresen, C. E., Gill, J. J., et al. (1984). Alteration of type A behavior and reduction in cardiac recurrences in postmyocardial infarction patients. *American Heart Journal, 108*, 237–248.

Friedman, M., Thoresen, C. E., Gill, J. J., et al. (1986). Alteration of type A behavior and its effect on cardiac recurrences in post myocardial infarction patients: Summary results of the recurrent coronary prevention project. *American Heart Journal, 112*, 653–665.

Froese, A., Hackett, T. P., Cassem, N. H., et al. (1974). Trajectories of anxiety and depression in denying and non-denying acute myocardial infarction patients during hospitalization. *Journal of Psychosomatic Medicine, 18*, 413–420.

Geringer, E. S., & Stern, T. A. (1988). Anxiety and depression in the critically ill. *Prob Critical Care, 2*(1), 35–46.

Glass, D. C., Krakoff, L. R., Contrada, R., et al. (1980). Effect of harrassment and competition upon cardiovascular and plasma catecholamine responses in type A and type B individuals. *Psychophysiology, 17*, 453–463.

Glassman, A. H. (1984). Cardiovascular effects of tricyclic antidepressants. *Annual Review of Medicine, 35*, 503–511.

Glassman, A. H., & Bigger, J. T. (1981). Cardiovascular effects of therapeutic doses of tricyclic antidepressants: A review. *Archives of General Psychiatry, 38*, 815–820.

Glassman, A. H., Bigger, J. T., Giardina, E. V., et al. (1979). Clinical characteristics of imipramine-induced orthostatic hypotension. *Lancet, 1,* 468–472.

Glassman, A. H., Johnson, L. L., Giardina, E. G. V., et al. (1983). The use of imipramine in depressed patients with congestive heart failure. *Journal of the American Medical Association, 250,* 1997–2001.

Goldstein, D. S. Plasma catecholamines in clinical studies of cardiovascular diseases. *Acta Physiologica Scandinavica, 527* (Suppl.), 39–41.

Greenblatt, D. J., Shader, R. I., & Abernathy, D. R. (1983). Current status of benzodiazepines (Part 1). *New England Journal of Medicine, 309,* 354–358.

Hackett, T. P., & Cassem, N. H. (1969). Factors contributing to delay in responding to the signs and symptoms of acute myocardial infarction. *American Journal of Cardiology, 24,* 651–658.

Hackett, T. P., & Cassem, N. H. (1974). The impact of myocardial infarction. *Rhode Island Medical Journal, 57,* 327–331.

Hackett, T. P., & Cassem, N. H. (1975). In *Coronary care: Patient psychology* (pp. 1–19). Washington, DC: American Heart Association.

Hackett, T. P., & Cassem, N. H. (1976). White-collar and blue-collar responses to heart attack. *Journal of Psychosomatic Research, 20,* 85–95.

Hackett, T. P., & Cassem, N. H. (1982). Coping with cardiac disease. *Advances in Cardiology, 31,* 212–217.

Hackett, T. P., Cassem, N. H., & Wishnie, H. A. (1968). The coronary-care unit: An appraisal of its psychological hazards. *New England Journal of Medicine, 279,* 1365–1370.

Hackett, T. P., Cassem, N. H., & Wishnie, H. (1969). Detection and treatment of anxiety in the coronary care unit. *American Heart Journal, 78,* 727–730.

Hames, T. K., Burgess, C. D. & George, C. F. (1982). Hemodynamic responses of trazodone and imipramine. *Clinical Pharmacology, 12,* 497–502.

Harvey, W. P., & Levine, S. A. (1952). Paroxysmal ventricular tachycardia due to emotion. *Journal of the American Medical Association, 150,* 479–480.

Hellerstein, H. K., & Friedman, E. H. (1970). Sexual activity and the postcoronary patient. *Archives of Internal Medicine, 125,* 987–999.

Hillis, L. D., & Braunwald, E. (1977). Myocardial ischemia (Part 1). *New England Journal of Medicine, 296,* 971–978.

Hoar, P. F., Nelson, N. T., Mangano, D. T., et al. (1981). Adrenergic response to morphine–diazepam anesthesia for myocardial revascularization. *Anesthesia and Analgesia, 60,* 406–411.

Hoffman, R. S. (1982). Diagnostic errors in the evaluation of behavioral disorders. *Journal of the American Medical Association, 248,* 964–967.

Ibrahim, M. A., Feldman, J. G., Sultz, H. A., Staiman, M. G., Young, L. J., & Dean, D. (1974). Management after myocardial infarction: A controlled trial of the effect of group psychotherapy. *International Journal of Psychiatric Medicine, 5,* 253–268.

Jacobs, J. W., Bernhard, M. R., Delgado, A., et al. (1977). Screening for organic mental syndromes in the medically ill. *Annals of Internal Medicine, 86,* 40–46.

Jaffe, C. M. (1977). First-degree atrioventricular block during lithium carbonate treatment. *American Journal of Psychiatry, 134,* 88–89.

Janowsky, D., Curtis, G., Zisook, S., et al. (1983). Ventricular arrhythmias possibly aggravated by trazodone. *American Journal of Psychiatry, 140,* 796–797.

Jarvinen, K. A. J. (1955). Can ward rounds be a danger to patients with myocardial infarction? *British Medical Journal, 2,* 318–320.

Jefferson, J. W. (1985). Biologic treatment of depression in cardiac patients. *Psychosomatics, 26*(11), 32–37.

Katon, W., & Raskind, M. (1980). Treatment of depression in the medically ill elderly with methylphenidate. *American Journal of Psychiatry, 137,* 963–965.

Kaufmann, M. W., & Murray, G. B. (1982). The use of d-amphetamine in medically ill depressed patients. *Journal of Clinical Psychiatry, 43,* 463–464.

Kaufmann, M. W., Cassem, N. H., Murray, G. B., et al. (1984). The use of methylphenidate in depressed patients after cardiac surgery. *Journal of Clinical Psychiatry, 45,* 82–84.

Kiok, M. C., Terrence, C. F., Fromm, G. H., et al. (1986). Sinus arrest in epilepsy. *Neurology, 36,* 115–116.

Klein, R. F., Liner, V. A., Sipes, D. P., et al. (1968). Transfer from a coronary unit. *Archives of Internal Medicine, 122,* 104–108.

Kornecki, E., Ehrlich, Y. H., & Lenox, R. H. (1984). Platelet-activating factor-induced aggregation of human platelets specifically inhibited by triazolobenzodiazepines. *Science, 226,* 1454–1456.

Krantz, D. S., Durel, L. A., David, J. E., et al. (1982). Propranolol medication among coronary patients: Relationship to type A behavior and cardiovascular response. *Journal of Human Stress, 4,* 4–12.

Kronig, M. H., Roose, S. P., Walsh, B. T., et al. (1983). Blood pressure effects of phenelzine. *Journal of Clinical Psychopharmacology, 3,* 307–310.

Lane, J. D., White, A. D., & Williams, R. B. (1984). Cardiovascular effects of mental arithmetic in type A and type B females. *Psychophysiology, 21,* 39–46.

Lazarus, H. R., & Hagens, J. H. (1968). Prevention of psychosis following open-heart surgery. *American Journal of Psychiatry, 124,* 1190–1195.

Liebowitz, M. R. (1985). Imipramine in the treatment of panic disorder and its complications. *Psychiatric Clinics of North America, 8,* 37–47.

Lipowski, Z. J. (1967). Delirium, clouding of consciousness, and confusion, *Journal of Nervous and Mental Disease, 145,* 227–255.

Lipowski, Z. J. (1980). *Delirium: Acute brain failure in man.* Springfield, IL: Charles C. Thomas.

Lipowski, Z. J. (1983). Transient cognitive disorders (delirium, acute confusional states) in the elderly. *American Journal of Psychiatry, 140,* 1426–1436.

Lydiard, R. B., & Gelenberg, A. J. (1982). Hazards and adverse effects of lithium. *Annual Review of Medicine, 33,* 327–344.

Lynch, J. J. (1974). The effect of human contact on cardiac rhythm in coronary care patients. *Journal of Nervous and Mental Diseases, 158,* 88–99.

Marks, I. (1985). Behavioral psychotherapy for anxiety disorders. *Psychiatric Clinics of North America, 8,* 25–35.

Marks, I., & Lader, M. (1973). Anxiety states (anxiety neurosis): A review. *Journal of Nervous and Mental Disease, 156,* 3–18.

Marty, J., Gauzit, R., Lefevre, P., et al. (1986). Effects of diazepam and midazolam on baroreflex control of heart rate and on sympathetic activity in humans. *Anesthesia and Analgesia, 65,* 113–119.

Matthews, K. A., Glass, D. C., Rosenman, R. H., & Bortner, R. (1977). Competitive drive, pattern A, and coronary heart disease: A further analysis of some data from the Western Collaborative Group Study. *Journal of Chronic Diseases, 30,* 489–498.

Matthews, K. A., & Haynes, S. G. (1986). Type A behavior pattern and coronary disease risk: Update and critical evaluation. *American Journal of Epidemiology, 123,* 923–960.

McLaurin, L. P., Raft, D., & Tate, S. C. (1977). Chest pain with normal coronaries: A psychosomatic illness? *Circulation, 56*(Suppl. 3), 174.

Menninger, K. A., & Menninger, W. C. (1936). Psychoanalytic observations in cardiac disorders. *American Heart Journal, 11,* 10–21.

Moss, A. J., & Goldstein, S. (1970). The pre-hospital phase of acute myocardial infarction. *Circulation, 41,* 737–742.

Muller, O. F., Goodman, N., & Bellet, S. (1961). The hypotensive effect of imipramine hydrochloride in patients with cardiovascular disease. *Clinical Pharmacology and Therapeutics, 2,* 300–307.

Murray, G. B. (1978). Confusion, delirium, and dementia. In T. P. Hackett & N. H. Cassem (Eds.), *Massachusetts General Hospital handbook of general hospital psychiatry* (pp. 93–116). St. Louis: Mosby.

Nelson, J. C., Jatlow, P. I., Bock. J., et al. (1982). Major adverse reactions during desipramine treatment. *Archives of General Psychiatry, 39,* 1055–1061.

Ostfield, A. M., Lebovits, B. Z., Shekelle, R. B., et al. (1964). A prospective study of the relationship between personality and coronary heart disease. *Journal of Chronic Diseases, 17,* 265–276.

Papadopoulos, C., Larrimore, P., Cardia, S., et al. (1980). Sexual concerns and needs of the post-coronary patient's wife. *Archives of Internal Medicine, 140,* 38–41.

Parker, D. L., & Hodge, J. R. (1967). Delirium in a coronary care unit. *Journal of the American Medical Association, 201,* 702–703.

Parkes, C. M., Benjamin, S., & Fitzgerald, R. G. (1969). Broken heart: A statistical study of increased mortality among widowers. *British Medical Journal, 1,* 740–743.

Pasternak, R. C., Thibault, G. E., Savoia, M., et al. (1980). Chest pain with angiographically insignificant coronary arterial obstruction *American Journal of Medicine, 68,* 813–817.

Paulson, B. A., Becker, L. D., & Way, W. L. (1983). The effects of intravenous lorazepam alone and with meperidine on ventilation in man. *Acta Anaesthesiologica Scandinavica, 27,* 400–402.

Peck, A. W., Stern, W. C., & Watkinson, C. (1983). Incidence of seizures during treatment with tricyclic antidepressants and bupropion. *Journal of Clinical Psychiatry, 44,* 197–201.

Pellettier, J. R., & Bartolucci, G. (1984). Trazodone and cardiovascular side effects. *Journal of Clinical Psychopharmacology, 4,* 119.

Pi, E. H., & Simpson, G. M. (1985). New antidepressants: A review. *Hosp Formul, 20,* 580–588.

Pitt, E., & Pitt, B. (1984). Cardiopathica fantastica. *American Heart Journal, 108,* 137–141.

Rahe, R. H., Ward, H. W., & Hayes, V. (1978). Brief group therapy in myocardial infarction rehabilitation: Three to four years follow-up of a controlled trial. *Psychosomatic Medicine, 41,* 229–241.

Ramrize, A. L. (1983). Seizures associated with maprotiline. *American Journal of Psychiatry, 140,* 509–510.

Redmond, D. E., & Huang, Y. H. (1979). New evidence for a locus coeruleus–norepinephrine connection with anxiety. *Life Sciences, 25,* 2149–2162.

Rees, W. D., & Lutkins, S. G. (1967). Mortality of bereavement. *British Medical Journal, 4,* 13–16.

Reich, P., & Gold, P. W. (1983). Interruption of recurrent ventricular fibrillation by psychiatric intervention. *General Hospital Psychiatry, 5,* 255–257.

Romano, J., & Engel, G. L. (1944). Physiologic and psychologic considerations of delirium. *Medical Clinics of North America, 28,* 629–638.

Roose, S. P., Glassman, A. H., Giardina, E. G. V., et al. (1986). Nortriptyline in depressed patients with left ventricular impairment. *Journal of the American Medical Association, 256,* 3253–3257.

Roose, S. P., Nurnberger, J. I., Dunner, D. L., et al. (1979). Cardiac sinus node dysfunction during lithium treatment. *American Journal of Psychiatry, 136,* 804–806.

Rosenbaum, J. F. (1982). Current concepts in psychiatry: The drug treatment of anxiety. *New England Journal of Medicine, 306,* 401–404.

Rosenbaum, J. F., & Pollack, M. H. (1987). Anxiety. In T. P. Hackett & N. H. Cassem (Eds.), *Massachusetts General Hospital handbook of general hospital psychiatry* (pp. 154–183). Littleton, MA: PSG.

Rovarios, S., Holmes, D. S., & Holmstein, R. D. (1984). Influence of a cardiac rehabilitation program on the cardiovascular, psychological, and social functioning of cardiac patients *Journal of Behavioral Medicine, 7,* 61–81.

Scalzi, C. C. (1982). Sexual counseling and sexual therapy for patients after myocardial infarction. *Journal of Cardiovascular Nursing, 18,* 13–17.

Schou, M. (1963). Electrocardiographic changes during treatment with lithium and with drugs of the imipramine-type. *Acta Psychiatrica Scandinavica, 39,* (Suppl. 169), 258–259.

Schuckit, M. A. (1981). Current therapeutic options in the management of typical anxiety. *Journal of Clinical Psychiatry, 42,* 15–24.

Settle, E. C., & Ayd, F. J. (1983). Haloperidol: A quarter century of experience. *Journal of Clinical Psychiatry, 44,* 440–448.

Sheehan, D. V. (1985) Monoamine oxidase inhibitors and alprazolam in the treatment of panic disorder and agoraphobia. *Psychiatric Clinics of North America, 8,* 49–62.

Sheehan, D. V., Ballenger, J., & Jacobson, G. (1980). Treatment of endogenous anxiety with phobic, hysterical, and hypochondriacal symptoms. *Archives of General Psychiatry, 37,* 51–59.

Sheehan, D. V., Coleman, J., Greenblatt, D., et al. (1984). Some biochemical correlates of panic attacks with agoraphobia and their responses to a new treatment. *Journal of Clinical Psychopharmacology, 4,* 66–75.

Siewicki, B. J., & Mansfield, L. W. (1977). Determining readiness to resume sexual activity. *American Journal of Nursing, 77,* 604.

Simon, A. B., Feinleib, M., & Thompson, H. K. (1972). Components of delay in the pre-hospital phase of acute myocardial infarction. *American Journal of Cardiology, 30,* 476–482.

Sos, J., & Cassem, N. H. (1980a). The intravenous use of haloperidol for acute delirium intensive care settings. In H. Speidel & G. Rodewald (Eds.), *Psychic and neurologic dysfunctions after open heart surgery.* Stuttgart: George Thieme Verlag.

Sos, J., & Cassem, N. H. (1980b). Managing postoperative agitation. *Drug Therapy, 10,* 103–106.

Spier, S. A., Tesar, G. E., Rosenbaum, J. F., et al. (1986). Clonazepam in the treatment of panic disorder and agoraphobia. *Journal of Clinical Psychiatry, 47,* 238–242.

Stern, M. J., Pascale, L., & Ackerman, A. (1977). Life adjustment postmyocardial infarction. *Archives of Internal Medicine, 137,* 1680–1685.

Stern, T. A. (1980). Munchausen's syndrome revisited. *Psychosomatics, 21,* 329–336.

Stern, T. A. (1985). The management of depression and anxiety following myocardial infarction. *Mt. Sinai Journal of Medicine, 52,*(8) 623–633.

Stern, T. A. (1987). Psychiatric management of acute myocardial infarction in the coronary care unit. *American Journal of Cardiology, 60,* 59J–67J.

Stern, T. A., Caplan, R. A., & Cassem, N. H. (1987). Use of benzodiazepines in a coronary care unit. *Psychosomatics, 28,* 19–23.

Stern, T. A., & Tesar, G. E. (1988). Anxiety and the cardiovascular system. *Mt. Sinai Journal of Medicine, 55*(3), 230–239.

Strain, J. J., Liebowitz, M. R., & Klein, D. F. (1981). Anxiety and panic attacks in the medically ill. *Psychiatric Clincis of North America, 4*(2), 333–350.

Stratton, J. R., & Halter, J. B. (1985). Effect of benzodiazepine (alprazolam) on plasma epinephrine and norepinephrine levels during exercise stress. *American Journal of Cardiology, 56,* 136–139.

Sullivan, E. A., & Shulman, K. I. (1984). Diet and monoamine oxidase inhibitors: A reexamination. *Canadian Journal of Psychiatry, 29,* 707–711.

Tesar, G. E., & Hackett, T. P. (1985). Psychiatric management of the hospitalized cardiac patient. *Journal of Cardiopulmonary Rehabilitation, 5,* 219–225.

Tesar, G. E., Murray, G. B., & Cassem, N. H. (1985) Use of high-dose intravenous haloperidol in the treatment of agitated cardiac patients. *Journal of Clinical Psychopharmacology, 5/6,* 344–347.

Tesar, G. E., Rosenbaum, J. F., et al. (1987). Orthostatic hypotension and antidepressant pharmacotherapy. *Psychopharmacological Bulletin, 23,* 182–186.

Tesar, G. E., & Stern, T. A. (1986). Evaluation and treatment of agitation in the intensive care unit. *Journal of Intensive Care Medicine, 1,* 137–148.

Thorstrand, C. (1976). Clinical features in poisonings by tricyclic antidepressants with special reference to the ECG. *Acta Medica Scandinavica, 199,* 337–344.

Veith, R. C., Raskind, M. A., Caldwell, J. H., et al. (1982). Cardiovascular effects of tricyclic antidepressants in depressed patients with chronic heart disease. *New England Journal of Medicine, 306,* 954–959.

Verrier, R. L., & Lown, B. (1984). Behavioral stress and cardiac arrhythmias. *Review of Physiology, 46,* 155–176.

Vlay, S. C., & Friedling, S. (1983). Trazodone exacerbation of VT. *American Heart Journal, 106,* 604.

Wallace, W. A., & Yu, P. N. (1975). Sudden death and the prehospital phase of acute myocardial infarction. *Annual Review of Medicine, 26,* 1–7.

Weisman, A. D., & Hackett, T. P. (1961). Predilection to death: Death and dying as a psychiatric problem. *Psychosomatic Medicine, 23,* 232–257.

Weiss, E., Dlin, B., Rullin, H. R., et al. (1957). Emotional factors in coronary occlusion. *Archives of Internal Medicine, 99,* 628–641.

Wielgosz, A. T., Fletcher, R. H., McCants, C. B., et al. (1984). Unimproved chest pain in patients with minimal or no coronary disease: A behavioral phenomenon. *American Heart Journal, 108,* 67–72.

Williams, R. B., Lane, J. D., Kuhn, C. M., et al. (1982). Type A behavior and elevated physiological and neuroendocrine responses to cognitive tasks. *Science, 218,* 483–485.

Williams, R. B., & Schanberg, S. M. (1986). *Influence of alprazolam on neuroendocrine and cardiovascular responses to stress in type A men and patients with panic disorder (abstract-protocol 4006).* Panic Disorder Biological Workshop, Washington, DC.

Wishnie, H. A., Hackett, T. P., & Cassem, N. H. (1971). Psychological hazards of convalescence following myocardial infarction. *Journal of the American Medical Association, 215,* 1292–1296.

Wishnie, H., Hackett, T. P., & Cassem, N. H. (1976). Response of adolescent children to myocardial infarction in their fathers. *McLean Hospital Journal, 1,*(4), 190–208.

Wolf, S. (1969). Psychosocial forces in myocardial infarction and sudden death. *Circulation, 40,* 74–81.

Woods, S. W., Tesar, G. E., Murray, G. B., et al. (1986). Psychostimulant treatment of depressive disorders secondary to medical illness. *Journal of Clinical Psychiatry, 47,* 12–15.

Worthley, L. I. C. (1974). Lithium toxicity and refractory cardiac arrhythmia treated with intravenous magnesium. *Anesthesia and Intensive Care, 2,* 357–360.

18

Psychological and Behavioral Treatment of Hypertension

Chandra Patel

INTRODUCTION

The control of hypertension in the community is a major challenge to public health today. Hypertension affects as much as a quarter of the adult population in industrialized countries (Joint National Committee, 1984; Office of Health Economics, 1971). Benefits of treating severe or moderately severe hypertension by means of antihypertension drugs have been demonstrated (Hamilton, Thompson, & Wisniewski, 1964; Veterans Administration, 1967), but the results of mild hypertension trials show that reduction in blood pressure achieved by means of antihypertension drugs may not reduce coronary heart disease or save lives, whereas the rate of undesirable side effects may be quite high (Medical Research Council, 1981, 1985). However, lowering mild hypertension is important because it has been shown that two-thirds of coronary heart disease and three-quarters of stroke mortality occurs in patients with mild hypertension (Rose, 1981). Three-quarters of all hypertensives are in the mild hypertension category, although the rate of complication in this group is low—approximately 1% per year (Hypertension Detection and Follow-up Program, 1979).

Thus, even if we have effective antihypertension drugs, a large proportion of the population has to be medicated for the rest of their lives to prevent a small number of complications. This creates a prevention paradox: "A measure that brings large benefits to the community offers little to each participating individual" (Patel, 1986; Rose, 1981). Nevertheless coronary heart disease remains a great burden on the community, and a great deal of attention is being paid to nonpharmacological measures. It is not surprising that the Joint National Committee on Detection, Evaluation, and Treatment of High Blood Pressure (1984) has recommended that in all patients with mild hypertension, nonpharmacological treatment should be tried first and antihypertension medication added only when other treatment fails to produce satisfactory control of blood pressure.

Despite enormous scientific advances and sophisticated technological innovations, the cause of essential or primary hypertension remains unknown. Approximately 90% to 95% of all hypertensives fall into this category, and as the cut-off point for defining hypertension for clinical purposes becomes lower, the proportion of hypertensives falling into the primary hypertension category becomes larger. Anxiety may cause temporary elevation of blood pressure (Rofe & Goldberg, 1983), but it has not been shown that anxious patients are more likely to suffer from chronic hypertension.

There is some evidence, however, that interaction between hereditary and environmental factors—stress, alcohol, sodium, obesity, and physical activity—is important. The contribution of stress factors is adequately discussed in this volume and elsewhere (e.g., Henry & Cassel, 1969; Steptoe, 1981, 1986). What is discussed in this chapter is the empirical evidence of the efficacy of relaxation-related therapies including anxiety management, which in a sense provides some direct evidence of the implications of psychosocial factors in essential hypertension.

Community screening for undiagnosed but treatable hypertension is becoming increasingly common and to some extent justifiable in view of the serious complications of uncontrolled hypertension. However, screening poses a moral dilemma. It is appropriate to tell those whose hypertension can be effectively treated by currently available antihypertension drug treatment that their blood pressure is high but can be beneficially controlled with treatment, but what should we tell those people whose blood pressure is in the borderline or mild hypertension range (however defined), for whom there is no effective antihypertension drug treatment available now? It would not be truthful to say that their blood pressure is normal, because borderline or mild hypertension is prognostically worse than normotension (however defined) and to disclose their prognosis would create unnecessary anxiety and would be a great disservice to those who participate in the screening program. Appropriate balance is a matter of clinical judgment. However, availability of safe, acceptable, cheap, effective, and probably nonpharmacological treatment would make this task easier and offer a tangible self-help to these individuals.

KINDS OF BEHAVIORAL
AND PSYCHOLOGICAL TECHNIQUES

There are no standardized behavioral or psychological techniques that have been consistently used in the control of hypertension. In fact, the term "behavioral or psychological techniques" has been used to denote a variety of techniques such as relaxation, biofeedback, counseling, cognitive therapy, coping techniques, and advice on nutritional measures or life-style changes. Each of these categories encompasses a variety of modes. For example, the relaxation may or may not be specified as progressive muscle relaxation, autogenic training, hypnosis, or yogic technique of breathing and relaxation posture (Shavasan). There are a number of meditation techniques that have been used either in their original form or have been adapted to suit Western culture or individual aptitudes and beliefs.

Through biofeedback, individuals are provided with information about one of their own physiological responses by means of an appropriate electronic instrument. The individual is then required to use this information to influence changes in his or her physiological function in the desired direction by means of volition. The instruments used vary from simple to elaborate, and the information fed to the patient may be specific or nonspecific. In hypertension control, for example, blood pressure feedback can be given, either by the constant-pressure cuff method, which gives intermittent feedback of either systolic or diastolic blood pressure (Tursky, Shapiro, & Schwartz, 1972) or by pulse wave velocity (time taken for the transmission of pulse wave between the heart and a peripheral artery), which measures blood pressure changes and offers continuous feedback (Steptoe, 1976). Sometimes patients are taught to measure their blood pressure and use a simple sphygmomanometer as a biofeedback instrument (Glasgow, Gaardner, & Engel, 1982). Among nonspecific methods, electronic instruments measuring galvanic skin resistance (GSR), or electromyography (EMG), or skin temperature (thermal) are used to enhance relaxation.

Counseling may range from cursory advice to stop smoking, handing out a diet sheet with or without an appropriate recipe booklet, advising the patient to take a holiday or change a job to a much deeper process in which a highly skilled counselor may not only unfold individual requirements using sophisticated psychological, behavioral and physiological diagnostic techniques but also bring about changes in the perception of stressful stimuli, in attitude to situations in life, in beliefs about one's own ability or in the ability of others to help, and in one's unrealistic expectations so that he or she is better able to deal with maladaptive behavior and make optimum use of coping resources. Such methods are variously described as counseling, behavior therapy, cognitive therapy, cognitive restructuring, insight therapy, or even health education or stress management. The words *counseling* or *cognitive therapy* often convey that intervention is taking place at the individual level, whereas *health education* often denotes intervention at the community level. The term *stress management* is frequently used when therapy is conducted in special groups of high-risk individuals, for example, in an occupational setting. However, the terms are interchangeable and often used to convey intervention at all levels.

Cultural differences often dictate the popularity and acceptance of certain terminology and the labels that comparable treatments may carry. For example, the use of term *psychotherapy* seems to be quite acceptable by hypertensive patients in the Soviet Union (Kchramelashville, personal communication), but it is not readily acceptable in Western Europe or North America where similar treatment may be called cognitive therapy. Evaluation of such complex therapies, shrouded under confused terminology, is difficult. Unfortunately this difficulty is compounded by scarce description of therapeutic methods used in the published literature. Often different combinations of techniques are used. Thus autogenic training and relaxation or meditation therapists often use biofeedback of different modality. Counseling may be described under different names—stress management, cognitive therapy, relaxation therapy, psychotherapy, or anxiety management—and similarly, biofeedback therapists often use some form of relaxation and opportunity to alter cognition. Even if direct efforts to change cognition are not made, relaxation itself can lead to changes in cognition (Peveler & Johnston, 1986).

Recently the term *biobehavioral treatment* is frequently being used to convey a treatment in which both behavioral and pharmacological treatments are combined. It must be realized that in a number of studies that are described as trials of behavioral of psychological interventions, the patients were already on antihypertension drugs. In some, the drugs were continued at the same dosage throughout the trial, but in others drugs were either reduced or eliminated.

Thus it is futile to separate studies into definite biofeedback, relaxation, or other categories. On the whole, a combination of some form of relaxation and stress management has been more successful than a single technique. In this chapter, therefore, I discuss preliminary studies of techniques that have been used predominantly. I analyze and tabulate only those studies that have included a control group for comparison and, preferably, have allocated patients randomly. I have selected both positive and negative studies for more detailed discussion to highlight important issues. As far as recommendations are concerned, even though objective data, as they are available, are taken into consideration, they are bound to be largely based on firsthand experience.

PRELIMINARY AND CONTROLLED STUDIES
OF THE EFFECTS OF THERAPY

A variety of techniques like yoga relaxation (Datey, Deshmukh, Dalvi, & Vinekar, 1969; Patel, 1973), biofeedback (Benson, Shapiro, Tursky, & Schwartz, 1971; Blanchard, Young, & Haynes, 1975; Elder & Eustis, 1975; Elder, Ruiz, Deabler, & Dillenkoffer, 1973; Goldman, Kleinman, Snow, Bidus, & Korol, 1975; Kristt & Engel, 1975; Miller, 1972; Richter-Heinrich, Knust, Muller, Schmidt, & Sprung, 1975; Surwitt & Shapiro, 1977; Walsh, Dale, & Anderson, 1977), progressive muscle relaxation (Brady, Luborsky, & Kron, 1974; Jacobson, 1939; Kallinke, Kullick, & Heim, 1982; Little et al., 1984), meditation and techniques derived from the principle of meditation (Benson, Rosner, & Marzetta, 1973; Benson, Rosner, Marzetta, & Klemchuk, 1974a, 1974b; Blackwell et al., 1976; Pollack, Case, Weber, & Laragh, 1977; Stone & De Leo, 1976), autogenic training (Klumbies & Eberhardt, 1966; Luther, 1969; Zaitsev et al., 1981), hypnosis (Deabler, Fidel, Dillenkoffer, & Elder, 1973; Friedman & Taub, 1977) have been reported to reduce blood pressure in hypertensive patients. These studies lacked the rigor of scientific experiments but they at least suggested that it was possible to develop a new behavioral mode of treatment in the management of hypertension.

Although it is not possible to carry out a double blind trial of behavior therapy, carefully executed, randomized, controlled trials, using a variety of relaxation techniques, with or without some form of biofeedback and often combined with stress management techniques, have now been published and have been succinctly reviewed (Johnston, 1987). Successful clinical trials require not only experimental vigor but also clinical flexibility. Resolving such competing demands is not easy in a single trial. However, the sheer number of trials, each with some deficiency but usually of a different kind, makes it possible to draw broad conclusions.

Because blood pressure is so readily affected by an array of nonspecific factors, it is essential to have a simultaneous control group that is similar in all respects to the treatment group except for receiving the treatment under evaluation. Simple, within-subject trials, irrespective of how much the investigators try to control confounding factors, are difficult to interpret and are unlikely to convince the scientific community. Fortunately there are a number of well-controlled trials with adequate sample sizes. They are tabulated in Table 1. Most of them have shown some reduction in subjects' blood pressure, and approximately half of them show statistically significant reduction in blood pressure in patients compared with control subjects.

After a randomized, controlled trial my colleague and I (Patel & North, 1975) reported a fall in mean blood pressure from 168/100 to 141/84 in the behavior modification group compared with a fall from 169/100 to 160/96 mm Hg in the control group. Control subjects attended the same number of sessions for the same length of time, and had the same number of measurements. Both groups were on antihypertension drugs with dosages that were kept constant. The fall in blood pressure was significant in both groups, but the drop in both systolic and diastolic blood pressure was significantly greater in the treatment group. This study was carried out on a one-to-one basis in a general practice setting.

My colleagues and I (Patel, Marmot, & Terry, 1981) carried out a study with 192 subjects who were identified as being at high risk for hypertension if two or more of the following factors were present: Subjects had blood pressure of 140/90 or more and were not on antihypertension medicine, exhibited plasma cholesterol of 6.3

Table 1 Summary of results of controlled trials of relaxation and stress management in hypertension

Source	Treatment	Number of subjects	Blood pressure (BP) reading			
			Initial	Posttrial reduction	Follow-up months	Follow-up change
Patel (1975)	Relaxation therapy	20	159/100	20/14[a]	12	14/13[a]
	Regular BP checks	20	163/99	1/2	12	+1/1
Richter-Heinrich et al. (1975)	Biofeedback of systolic BP	20	141/—	11	—	—
	False feedback	10	141/—	6	—	—
Patel & North (1975)	Relaxation, meditation, feedback, home practice	17	168/100	26/15[a]	6	21/13[a]
	Clinic attendance	17	160/101	9/5	—	—
Stone & De Leo (1976)	Meditation	14	147/97		6	15/13[a]
	Control	5			6	3/4
Friedman & Taub (1977)	Hypnosis, biofeedback	10		1/2	1	0/6
	Hypnosis only	13		15/9[a]	1	11/7
	Biofeedback of systolic BP	13		8/6	1	10/2
	BP check only	11		2/3	1	+2/2
Taylor et al. (1977)	Relaxation	10	150/96	14/5[a]	6	12/6
	Nonspecific support	10	141/92	3/2	6	4/4
Frankel et al. (1978)	Multiple forms of biofeedback and relaxation	7	148/99	3/1	—	—
	False BP feedback	7	150/99	+1/+2	—	—
	No treatment	7	151/99	4/2	—	—
Bali (1979)	Relaxation, meditation, biofeedback	9	149/97	12/9[a]	—	—
	Nonspecific support	9	150/99	0/1	—	—
Brauer et al. (1979)	Therapist-taught relaxation	10	153/93	11/6	6	18/10[a]
	Taped relaxation	9	150/95	5/1	6	+1/5
	Nonspecific support	10	145/93	9/5	6	2/11
Roberts & Forester (1979)	Meditation	22	136/84	8/4	—	—
	Health education	19	148/87	6/1	—	—
Seer & Raeburn (1980)	Transcendental meditation	14	152/104	5/6[a]	3	2/7
	Meditation without mantra	14	147/100	5/7[a]	3	8/12
	No treatment	13	150/102	+2/+2	—	—
Jorgenson et al. (1981)	Anxiety management	10	139/88	19/10[a]	1.5	28/18
	No treatment	8	136/85	2/1	—	—

(Table continues on next page)

Table 1   (continued)

Source	Treatment	Number of subjects	Initial	Posttrial reduction	Follow-up months	Follow-up change
				Blood pressure (BP) reading		
Glasgow et al.	Relaxation	15–20	—	7/6	—	—
(1982)	Feedback	15–20	—	5/6	—	—
	Relaxation, feedback	15–20	—	8/6	—	—
	Feedback, relaxation	15–20	—	14/10	—	—
Goldstein et al.	Feedback	9	149/97	4/4	—	—
(1982)	Relaxation	9	150/97	+3/+4	—	—
	Drugs	9	144/98	15/6	—	—
Hafner (1982)	Relaxation	7	146/103	15/14	13/15[a]	3
	Relaxation, feedback	7	160/107	22/15	12/15[a]	3
	No treatment	7	159/98	—	9/2	3
Luborsky et al.	Drugs	10	144/97	16/9	—	—
(1982)	Relaxation	16	142/93	7/4	—	—
	Exercise	11	137/95	3/2	—	—
	Feedback	14	138/90	5/5	—	—
Southam et al.	Relaxation	21	143/98	12/13[a]	15	12/14[a]
(1982)	No treatment	16	140/93	4/3	15	6/4
Crowther (1983)	Relaxation, stress management	12	155/98	24/12[a]	3	16/13[a]
	Relaxation	12	156/99	23/16[a]	3	20/15[a]
	No treatment	10	151/97	0/1	3	0/2
Wadden (1984)	Relaxation	16	136/91	6/5	7/8	5
	Relaxation (couples)	15	143/91	7/5	6/7	5
	Cognitive therapy (couples)	9	148/94	9/5	7/2	5
Goldstein et al.	Relaxation	13	144/99	5/4	—	—
(1984)	Relaxation, feedback	14	145/100	5/3	—	—
	Relaxation, no drugs	17	148/99	5/3	—	—
Charlesworth et al. (1984)	Stress management	22	131/83	6/3[a]	—	—
	No treatment	18	133/86	+1/0	—	—
Cottier et al.	Relaxation, placebo	17	130/90	2/3	—	—
(1984)	Placebo	9	130/90	+1/+2	—	—
Jacob et al. (1985)	Relaxation, salt and weight reduction	26	143/87	+3/+2	12	8/4
	No treatment	24	144/86	3/+1	12	10/4

(Table continues on next page)

Table 1 (*continued*)

| Source | Treatment | Number of subjects | Blood pressure (BP) reading | | | |
			Initial	Posttrial reduction	Follow-up months	Follow-up change
Hatch et al. (1985)	Feedback	13	135/87	9/7	3	6/6
	Relaxation	13	148/90	17/6	3	17/8
	Self-relaxation	13	136/87	5/3	3	6/3
	No treatment	13	136/88	7/5	3	6/6
Patel et al. (1985)	Relaxation, feedback	86	147/88	15/7	48	7/2
	No treatment	75	144/88	4/0	48	+2/+4
Irvine et al. (1986)	Relaxation	8	145/94	7/5[a]	3	7/3
	Relaxation (on drugs)	8	136/93	1/4[a]	3	6/6
	Mild exercise	8	148/94	+1/+5	3	+2/0
	Mild exercise (on drugs)	8	127/84	+1/+1	3	+3/+5
Chesney et al. (1987)	Relaxation, behavior therapy	118	138/95	7/5	12	9/5
	No treatment	40	139/94	9/6	12	12/6
Agras et al. (1987)	Relaxation	68	147/97	9/10[a]	30	8/10
	No treatment	69	145/99	3/6	30	7/10
Patel & Marmot (1988)	Relaxation, continue drugs, stop drugs, continue placebo, stop placebo	49	145/87	—	12	5/3[a]
	No relaxation, continue drug, or stop drug, or continue placebo, or stop placebo	53	136/85	—	12	+7/+3

[a]Reduction in either systolic or diastolic blood pressure or both was significantly greater in the treatment group compared with the control group.

mmol/l or more, and smoked 10 or more cigarettes a day. We then divided the subjects randomly into treatment and control groups. The goals of the study were to ensure that evidence of reduced blood pressure was not the result of increased compliance with antihypertension drugs, to discover whether the existence of prior established relationships between subjects and researchers (the subjects were my patients for some years) affected decreases in blood pressure, to ensure that efforts to make treatment more cost-effective did not affect blood pressure decreases, and to discover whether other risk factors for coronary heart disease could be altered by decreased blood pressure.

Both the groups were given health education leaflets advising them to stop smoking, to reduce animal fat in the diet, and to remain under the supervision of their own doctor. They were also issued with a booklet giving general information on blood pressure. The treatment group in addition received training in breathing exercise, relaxation, meditation, and stress management for 1 hour a week for 8 weeks, in groups of up to 10 subjects.

The results showed significantly a greater drop in blood pressure in the treatment group compared with the control group. In those with initial blood pressure of 140/ 90 or more, mean blood pressure fell from 166/101 to 143/89 in the treatment group compared with a fall from 160/98 to 159/97 mm Hg in the control group at an 8-month follow-up. Analysis of dietary diaries filled out over a period of 3 consecutive days at entry, after 8 weeks, and at 8 months showed modest changes in the diets consumed but did not reveal differences between the groups with regard to dietary fat, alcohol, or calories consumed. Their mean weight remained unchanged. Thus differences between the groups were unlikely to be due to any confounding factors.

At a 4-year follow-up (Patel et al., 1985) 18% of the treatment group and 20% of the control group were on antihypertension drugs. Despite the general tendency for blood pressure to rise over the 4 years, the differences between the groups were largely maintained. More people in the control group reported symptoms of angina, elicited by Rose's angina questionnaire (Rose & Blackburn, 1968), or checked one of the complications of hypertension listed in the questionnaire. We considered that such reports are subject to bias. Electrocardiograms (EKGs) were recorded in all patients at the 4-year follow-up, but recording the entry EKG was not a part of our original protocol. The medical department of the industry in which the subjects worked did, however, record EKG for most people to make the screening program more comprehensive. EKGs were available in only 69 out of 88 treatment group patients and 57 out of 83 control group subjects and were blindly coded using Minnesota code (Rose & Blackburn, 1968). There were five new events of coronary heart disease in the control group compared with one in the treatment group. In addition, there was one fatal myocardial infarction in the control group. Fisher's exact test for difference in this objective data was statistically significant ($p < .05$).

On the basis of traditional risk factor reduction, we estimated a 12% reduction in coronary heart disease incidence using multiple logistic function from the London Whitehall study. The observed reduction in incidence during this 4 years was greater than had been predicted. This could be due to chance variation, but it also suggests that relaxation-based psychological therapy may reduce coronary heart disease through pathways other than the established risk factors.

ASSESSING REDUCTIONS IN BLOOD PRESSURE

It is unlikely that observed reduction in blood pressure could be due to observer or subject bias, nonspecific placebo effects, or subjects being relaxed at the time of measurement. Even if blood pressure is genuinely low, it may be due to other unsuspected factors like reduction in body weight. It is unlikely that these factors can fully explain the observed changes. In several studies, control group patients attended training as many times as did the treatment group and had a similar number of blood pressure measurements made by observers who were unconnected with training (Brauer, Horlick, Nelson, Farquhar, & Agras, 1979; Crowther, 1983; Irvine, Johnston, Jenner, & Marie, 1986; Patel & North, 1975; Seer & Raeburn, 1980; Taylor, Farquhar, Nelson, & Agras, 1977) or made by random-zero sphygmomanometer (Benson et al., 1974; Patel et al., 1981; Patel & North, 1975).

Concomitant changes in serum cholesterol (Patel, 1976; Patel & Carruthers, 1976;

Patel et al., 1985), plasma renin activity, and plasma aldosterone (McGrady, Yonker, Tan, Fine, & Woewrner, 1981; Patel et al., 1981) also support the view that changes in blood pressure are likely to be real and not due to patients relaxing at the time of measurement. It can also be concluded from several studies that reduction in blood pressure is not likely to be due to changes in body weight (Irvine et al., 1986; Patel et al., 1981, 1985), consumption of less sodium (Stone & De Leo, 1976), or dietary fat (Patel et al., 1985). Increased compliance with current medication can explain further reductions, but equally beneficial effects have been observed in unmedicated patients (Bali, 1979; Patel et al., 1981).

The superiority of treatment over control procedures has been demonstrated even when the control procedure has been made equally plausible. Taylor et al. (1977) compared progressive muscle relaxation and home practice with nonspecific psychotherapy as well as continuing medication and found that relaxation produced significantly greater reductions in blood pressure than did either of the other two groups. These effects were maintained after six months, although the differences were no longer significant. The same team (Southam, Agras, Taylor, & Kraemer, 1982) later carried out a study in which patients had frequent blood pressure measurements made throughout the working day using a semi-automated ambulatory measuring system and found that the relaxation group had significantly greater reduction than did the control group at post-trial as well as at six-month follow-ups.

In another important study (Bali, 1979), 18 hypertensive patients were relegated randomly to treatment and control groups. The treatment consisted of a combination of relaxation, breathing exercise, meditation, EMG biofeedback, and daily home practice, whereas the control procedure consisted of supportive psychotherapy, impressive psychophysiological measurement in the laboratory, and advice to rest in bed for 20 minutes daily. Blood pressure was assessed weekly for 8 weeks before and after the treatment, and five measurements were made on each occasion. When averages of 30 measurements were compared, the relaxation group showed significantly greater reduction in blood pressure, which was maintained over a period of 12 months. The control group subjects did not show much change in blood pressure until after they were trained in relaxation therapy.

Irvine et al. (1986) used mild mobility exercise in control patients with the suggestion that it would improve their circulation and reduce blood pressure. The exercise schedules became increasingly complex each session. The patients were also connected to GSR biofeedback but were asked to hold the signal rather than reduce it, and they were asked to practice the exercise 15–20 minutes twice a day and also briefly through the day when triggered by drowsiness rather than a stress signal. Despite such elaborate control procedures, they showed relaxation therapy to be significantly better in reducing blood pressure.

POSSIBLE REASONS FOR NEGATIVE OUTCOME

Some studies have failed to show meaningful reductions in blood pressure with relaxation-based psychological treatments. These studies usually omitted some of the essential ingredients of the treatment, included inappropriate comparison groups, included patients with rather low initial blood pressure or had inflexible and demanding schedules. For example, Luborsky et al. (1982) studied 51 hypertensive patients, 20 of whom were on hypertension medication until three days before entering the trial. It is known that blood pressure may not revert back to its original level for several weeks or months after drug withdrawal (Medical Research Council, 1986), which can confound the true effect of any treatment that follows.

Frankel, Patel, Horwitz, Friedwald, and Gaardner (1978) described a remarkably complex form of treatment that included both continuous blood pressure and EMG biofeedback, autogenic training, and progressive muscle relaxation over 20 sessions and home practice of all components in rigidly specified schedules and compared it with no treatment or false biofeedback control. None of the groups showed much change in blood pressure. Such demanding and complex schedules interfere with adequate learning, which requires a more humanistic approach (see Henry, 1978). Crits-Christoph, Luborsky, Kron, and Fishman (1978) tested blood pressure responses to two periods of brief relaxation interspersed with two periods of sitting quietly and reading in a single session and failed to find difference in blood pressure between the two conditions. What is most disappointing and sometimes annoying is that such simplistic experiments lead both investigators and others to interpret relaxation as having no effect on hypertension, which is not only the subject of most importance to public health but also is so complex that no one yet knows exactly what causes primary hypertension in the first place.

Goldstein, Shapiro, Thananopavarn, and Sambhi (1982) also failed to find differences in blood pressure levels between relaxation and nonspecific control groups. They enlisted patients through a newspaper advertisement under the pretext of participating in a biofeedback experiment. The patients, therefore, must have been disappointed to be allocated to relaxation or control groups. There was not much difference in the treatment and control procedures. Patients in both groups rested in a comfortable chair, but the relaxation group was also asked to count breaths. With such a diluted procedure it is not surprising that no significant changes in blood pressure were found. In a later trial, however, the researchers introduced home practice and found modest reductions in blood pressure in relaxation groups compared with control groups (Goldstein, Shapiro, & Thananpavarn, 1984).

Surwit, Shapiro, and Good (1978) compared a combination of blood pressure and heart rate feedback with frontalis EMG feedback and brief relaxation training in mild hypertensives. The reductions in blood pressure were low, and there were no differences between the groups. The most feasible explanation that can be offered is that initial blood pressure was low in all groups, and it was not a controlled outcome study but a comparison of three different modalities. Drop in blood pressure does seem to be related to the levels of initial blood pressure: The higher the initial blood pressure, the larger the drop (Jacob, Kramer, & Agras, 1977; Tasto & Huebner, 1976). In many studies of behavioral therapy the initial blood pressure levels are not in the hypertensive range by the time baseline blood pressure is established, and it is unlikely that they will fall much further.

IMPORTANT THERAPEUTIC COMPONENTS

Not many studies have specifically or simultaneously tested for the differential effectiveness of various components of behavioral and psychological therapies. One study that stands out in this respect was carried out by Chesney, Black, and Ward (1987). They allocated 158 mild hypertensive patients with initial blood pressure of around 138/95 into six groups. One group received no treatment (the control group). The others received the following treatment components, respectively: relaxation; relaxation and biofeedback; relaxation and cognitive therapy; relaxation, cognitive therapy, and biofeedback; and relaxation, cognitive therapy, and health advice. Patients were followed up for 12 months.

Although the posttrial, mean, resting blood pressure level, taken in clinics, of all treatment groups combined was not significantly different from that of the control group (see Table 1), blood pressure readings taken at the work site showed that cognitive therapy combined with relaxation, with or without feedback or health advice, was significantly more influential in reducing blood pressure. Reductions in each of the six groups were as follows: no treatment, 2/3; relaxation, 4/0; relaxation and biofeedback, 1/5; relaxation and cognitive therapy, 8/5; relaxation, cognitive therapy, and biofeedback, 11/7; and relaxation, cognitive therapy, and health advice, 6/5. A combination of relaxation, cognitive therapy, and biofeedback, comparable to the combination my colleagues and I have used (Patel & Marmot, 1988a; Patel et al., 1985) turned out to be the best combination. Considering low initial blood pressure levels, a mean reduction of 11/7 in a sample of 24 patients is quite impressive. The cognitive component was the most important.

Wadden (1984) reported that relaxation training, given either to the patients on their own or together with their partners, was not different from cognitive therapy involving the couples. In view of these results, Wadden questioned the specificity of relaxation. Although his results are not doubtful, his interpretation seems to be. His study was more like a comparison of three treatments rather than a controlled trial of relaxation and it reveals that blood pressure may be lowered by more than one treatment rather than that all effects are nonspecific. Crowther (1983) did not find relaxation combined with stress management to be any better than relaxation alone at reducing blood pressure; however, her description of stress management was not clear and follow-up of patients was not long enough. My opinion is that relaxation is certainly very useful in lowering blood pressure acutely, but in the long-term, cognitive changes combined with subtle behavioral changes are important in maintaining lower blood pressure.

Meditation alone seems to produce very modest reductions in blood pressure, at least in the short-term, and if the principle components of meditation are included, it is not necessary to follow cult methods (Benson, 1975). The technique popularly known as transcendental meditation, taught by the followers of Maharishi Mahesh Yogi, involves chanting a secret word, called a mantra. It has been shown that meditation with or without the mantra is equally effective but superior to no treatment control procedure (Seer & Raeburn, 1980). Meditation was not found to be superior to health education by Roberts and Forrester (1979), although in this study the initial blood pressure levels in two groups were not comparable.

In a review article, Johnston (1982) discussed biofeedback studies quite extensively and came to the conclusion that practically all studies of conventional laboratory-based blood pressure biofeedback have been disappointing. The only exception is the study by Glasgow et al. (1982), which in fact is remarkably different from the rest. In this study 127 patients were taught to take their own blood pressure and recorded it three times a day at home for three months. Ninety patients who continued recording were randomly divided into three groups. One was a control group that continued self-measurement three times a day. The subjects of the second group, the biofeedback group (F), used their usual sphygmomanometer as a feedback instrument by inflating the cuff to just above systolic blood pressure in an effort to reduce blood pressure successfully 25% of the time before reducing the column by 2 mm Hg and trying again until no more reduction was possible. Later they learned to become aware of the feelings associated with reduction in blood pressure and practiced those feelings in daily life. The subjects in the third group, the relaxation group (R), were trained in progressive muscle relaxation, which they were later asked to generalize in daily life.

In the second phase, two treatment groups were further subdivided. One subgroup continued with its original treatment (RR or FF groups), whereas the other group was reversed (RF and FR) groups, so that the R group now received biofeedback and vice versa. The results showed that both relaxation and feedback were equally effective in lowering blood pressure moderately in phase 1. The greatest lowering occurred in the group in which biofeedback was followed by training in relaxation. They proposed the following steps: (a) supervised self-monitoring, (b) systolic feedback of the simplest type, and (c) relaxation training. If a patient achieves adequate control of blood pressure at any stage, he or she should not be enrolled in subsequent groups.

When patients can be motivated to measure their own blood pressure for many months, changes in cognition are likely and they can learn for themselves many therapeutic components. But which component is preferable? My colleagues and I have found that a comprehensive treatment program for groups for eight one-hour sessions is cost-effective, and it increases the quality of life, which may contribute a great deal to reducing complications. In addition to training patients in diaphragmatic breathing exercises, deep muscle relaxation, and simple meditation using GSR biofeedback in a group setting, one should also try to change their cognitions. The theoretical aspects of a training program such as this are outlined in Table 2.

CHARACTERISTICS OF THOSE LIKELY
TO RESPOND TO THERAPY

Some researchers have shown that neurotic individuals and those patients with a negative self-image seem to do less well with treatment (Richter-Heinrich et al., 1975, 1981; Shkhvatsabava, 1982) than do those with less neuroticism and a positive self-image. Eagan, Kogan, Garber, and Jarrett (1983) found that patients with current psychological distress and a higher life events score in months prior to relaxation therapy also seem to be resistant to therapy. These investigators did not find that level of compliance or expectation of success predicted outcome during a follow-up of 12 months. Agras, Horne, and Taylor (1982) found the opposite to be true. They told one group of patients to expect an immediate lowering of blood pressure and another group to expect a delayed lowering of blood pressure after relaxation therapy and found that reductions in systolic blood pressure for these two groups were 17.0 and 2.4 mm Hg, respectively ($p = .001$). Mean diastolic blood pressure did not differ. The training in relaxation was carried out over three sessions on a single day, which is not quite the same as long-term relaxation therapy.

For long-term efficacy, my colleagues and I found that belief in the therapy, availability of time, support from the family, and, most important, compliance, are essential factors (Patel & Marmot, 1988b; Steptoe, Patel, Marmot, & Hunt, 1987). It is not essential that the patient believe in the therapy from the outset. We have found that many of our patients, who are not volunteers but are recruited through screening programs, do have a healthy scepticism about the benefit of therapy until they see a reduction in blood pressure or experience a better quality of life. We thought that the

Table 2 Treatment plan for controlling hypertension

Session 1. Explain treatment plan, biofeedback concept, types of breathing in different states, and demonstrate diaphragmatic breathing. Handouts explaining some facts about high blood pressure and breathing exercises as well as relaxation instruction cassettes are distributed. The patients are asked to practice relaxation once a day or, if possible, twice a day. Questions are answered.

Session 2. The nature of stress and how it may strain health are explained. The importance of learning of stress management is pointed out. A film, *Understanding Stresses and Strains* (Disney), is shown. The Human Function Curve is explained. Creative imagery and its uses are explained. A handout listing biological, behavioral, and emotional signs of stress is distributed. Questions are answered.

Session 3. How stress response can be analyzed and how positive emotions and behaviors can be used to replace harmful or undesirable emotions and behaviors are explained. The how and why of meditation is explained, supported by a handout giving more details on the subject. Questions are answered.

Session 4. Figures and graphs showing beneficial effects of relaxation and meditation from other studies are shown to increase patients' belief in the methods used as well as to increase their motivation to comply with practice. Questions are answered.

Session 5. The ways of integrating relaxation into everyday life are discussed and the patient is asked to list ten situations he or she finds stressful and to practice one breath relaxation either during or before those situations. Management of emotions like anger, hostility, and aggression is discussed. A handout on how to develop effective communication skills is distributed. Questions are answered.

Session 6. Protective effects of social support and cultural and traditional aspects of life are pointed out. Questions are answered, and general discussion and supportive relationships within the group are encouraged.

Session 7. The coronary-prone personality, including Type A behavior, is discussed. Those who identify themselves as Type A are encouraged to change their behavior. Possible characteristics of resilient behavior are discussed.

Session 8. The whole course is summarized. General free discussion is encouraged. The importance of regular practice and integration of the new positive behavior is reemphasized without giving the impression that life is going to be regimented with do's and do not's. The emphasis is on making life more fulfilling and enjoyable.

best measure of their belief in therapy would be in their willingness to recommend it to other people with a similar condition. At a four-year follow-up we found that 75% of men and 91% of women were convinced of the benefits of our therapy and would without hesitation recommend it to others. Sympathetic support from the family members, without reminding the patient to do his or her relaxation practice, also predicted successful outcome.

When patients have been recruited through a screening program, not only do they represent hypertensive patients in the general population but also their response to therapy tends to be more satisfactory and predictable. My own experience as well as those of others suggests that such satisfactory outcomes may not be seen when patients are referred from hypertension clinics or by other physicians because their blood pressure is difficult to control or because they are generally problem patients. Patients who are poor compliers of drug therapy irrespective of side effects, those who have difficult home circumstances, those who stand to gain from their sick role, those who are too busy to give this slow-acting therapy an adequate chance to work, and those who are nihilistic are unlikely to benefit from this behavioral therapy and would probably require psychotherapy. Despite some of these observations, the characteristics of the patients who are likely to respond and those who are not likely to benefit much from behavioral therapy need to be investigated further.

LONG-TERM COMPLIANCE

Because hypertension is often asymptomatic, motivation to continue with time-consuming relaxation practice tends to be weak, and without compliance long-term benefits cannot be maintained. At a four-year follow-up of patients who had used relaxation therapy, my colleagues and I (Patel et al., 1985) were generally pleased with the results but were disappointed with the compliance rate and surprised at the apparent discrepancy. Further analysis clearly disclosed that the degree of success depended on the degree of compliance, as is shown in Table 3.

We had expected some reduction in the compliance rate over the long term and hence had taken some care to teach people to integrate relaxation in their daily lives, but we were puzzled to see that only 17% had admitted to relaxing regularly. They, of course, received the greatest benefit. Of the remaining patients those who had not given up relaxation practice altogether did better than did those who had abandoned the practice at least 18 months earlier. All was not lost, however. We probed deeper to see how often they were doing their mini, one-breath relaxation exercise and how often they used intellectual strategies to reappraise or redefine those situations as less threatening and told themselves to moderate their responses. Fortunately, 80%–90% of our patients had practiced both of these strategies often or sometimes, and these patients did retain considerable reductions in blood pressure compared to those who did not practice these strategies. On the whole we found that those who find it easier to fit relaxation into their daily schedule, whose life is unlikely to be disrupted by relaxation practices, those who develop a positive attitude to the therapy offered, whose family is generally supportive and those whose quality of life has generally improved are more likely to comply with one or other components of the therapy (Patel & Marmot, 1988b).

Table 3 Degree of compliance and change in subjects at a 4-year follow-up

Compliance characteristics of subjects	% of subjects	Mean change			
		Systolic BP	SEM	Diastolic BP	SEM
Relax regularly	17	−10.9	6.7	−7.0	3.2
Do not relax regularly	83	−6.3	3.0	−1.7	1.9
Last relaxed less than 18 months earlier	76	−10.8	3.7	−4.5	2.3
Last relaxed more than 18 months earlier	24	+2.2	4.4	+4.2	3.0
"Often or sometimes" integrates relaxation into daily life	83	−7.6	4.1	−2.3	2.5
"Never" integrates relaxation into daily life	17	−4.6	5.8	+4.4	3.6
"Often or sometimes" tells oneself to calm down	90	−7.9	3.9	−2.9	2.5
"Never" tells oneself to calm down	10	+6.1	8.7	0.00	3.5

Table 4 General effects associated with treatment and control conditions in the 4-year follow-up of a randomized controlled trial of relaxation

Aspect of life affected	Subject group	Percentage reporting improvement	X^2	p
Relationships at work	Treatment	27.1	6.03	.01
	Control	9.2		
General health	Treatment	36.7	6.67	.01
	Control	16.7		
Enjoyment of life	Treatment	35.4	4.04	.04
	Control	19.4		
Personal and family relationships	Treatment	27.84	5.62	.02
	Control	11.1		
General level of physical energy	Treatment	20.3	3.40	.07
	Control	8.3		
Sexual life	Treatment	11.8	2.95	.09
	Control	2.9		
Concentration at work	Treatment	26.8	2.72	.10
	Control	13.8		
Mental well-being	Treatment	30.8	1.98	.16
	Control	19.4		
Social life	Treatment	16.5	1.58	.21
	Control	8.3		

IMPROVING THE QUALITY
OF LIFE THROUGH THERAPY

Psychological and social functioning has been assessed in some studies of behavioral therapy of hypertension. The results have shown reduction in anxiety (Bali, 1979; Jorgensen, Housten, & Zurawski, 1981), anxiety and depression (Wadden, 1984), and a variety of psychosomatic symptoms, along with an increasing sense of well-being (Peters, Benson, & Peters, 1977). At a four-year follow-up my colleagues and I assessed the following aspects of life: relationships at work, general health, enjoyment of life, personal and family relationships, general level of physical energy, sexual life, concentration at work, mental well-being, and social life. As is shown in Table 4, in each of these aspects, a greater number of subjects in the treatment group reported improvements than did control group subjects, and for the first 4 aspects of life, the difference was statistically significant.

Among those who reported regular practice of relaxation, significant improvements ($p < .01$) occurred in six out of nine aspects of life: relationships at work, concentration at work, general health, enjoyment of life, personal and family relationships, and mental well-being (Patel & Marmot, 1987). In none of the studies mentioned earlier was there a correlation between improvement in various aspects of life and reduction in blood pressure. This could mean that such favorable psychological response is not associated with cardiovascular benefit, or that such positive effects may represent a different pathway through which relaxation could lead to a reduction in coronary heart disease.

USING BEHAVIORAL AND PSYCHOLOGICAL TECHNIQUES IN CLINICAL PRACTICE

Nonpharmacological measures are gaining popularity in the reduction of mildly elevated blood pressure. Their efficacy has been reported in a number of clinical trials. However, efficacy in a trial does not automatically ensure effectiveness in everyday clinical practice. There are two important questions. Can clinicians be successfully trained as relaxation and stress management therapists? Will patients make desirable behavioral changes and maintain them in the long term?

To see if we could effectively train general practitioners to successfully carry out training in relaxation and stress management, my colleagues and I conducted a study with 134 patients (Patel & Marmot, 1988a) who represented a subsample of phase 2 of the Medical Research Council (MRC) Treatment of Mild Hypertension Trial (Medical Research Council, 1986). In phase 1 some 18,000 patients with initial diastolic blood pressure of between 90 and 109 mm Hg had been receiving either an active drug or placebo for six years. In phase 2, a subsample of these patients were randomly allocated to either continue or to stop receiving the active drug or placebo. In another subsample we randomly allocated 134 patients, after full medical examination, to receive or not receive relaxation therapy (relaxation and stress management). This factorial design presented us with another opportunity to assess whether patients controlled on active drugs might have their blood pressure maintained once active drug treatment was stopped and to assess whether blood pressure may be further reduced by this therapy, in patients who had been receiving placebo tablets and regular medical attention for as long as six years.

I trained a group of general practitioners and their nurses, who were participating in the MRC Trial, in a weekend workshop and supplied them with a therapy manual and handouts for the patients. The protocol for therapy sessions was as described in Table 2. Follow-up examinations consisted of duplicate measurement of blood pressure using random zero sphygmomanometer after 8 weeks, 3 months, and 6 months and a full medical examination including EKG at 1 year. The analysis blood pressure of those seen at the 1-year follow-up is shown in Table 5. Blood pressure changes were more favorable in the treatment groups compared with the control groups. Despite randomization, initial blood pressure levels were not comparable in the two groups, so we carried out an analysis of covariance and showed an adjusted differ-

Table 5 Mean changes in systolic blood pressure (95% confidence intervals) in subjects with mild hypertension after one year of therapy conducted a general practitioner

Treatment group	Relaxation (n = 49)	Control (n = 54)	Difference	Confidence interval	p
All groups combined	−4.9	+7.1	−12.0	(6.2,18.0)	.0001
Continued drugs	−8.4	+3.9	−12.3	(1.1,23.5)	.032
Stopped drugs	0.0	+13.9	−13.9	(1.7,26.1)	.026
Continued placebo	−7.5	+7.3	−14.9	(−0.9,30.7)	.064
Stopped placebo	−6.0	+4.2	−10.2	(0.6,19.8)	.039

ence between the groups for systolic blood pressure to be 7.5 mm Hg (p = .007) and for diastolic blood pressure to be 2.2 (NS) mm Hg lower in the relaxation group.

The development of new cardiovascular events was assessed by reviewing documentation from the general practitioners and anonymously coded EKGs of the subjects. There were five new coronary events in the control group: one subject with angina, one with myocardial infarction, and three subjects with new EKG abnormalities suggesting significant ischemic changes. In the treatment group one patient who was selected randomly to stop taking propranolol had a stroke. Even though the number of cardiovascular events was small and although this study was not designed to study morbidity, when these results are taken in conjunction with our previous report of 6:1 events in control versus treatment group (Patel et al., 1985), the suggestion that this therapy may reduce coronary heart disease incidence becomes somewhat stronger. The conclusion that can be drawn from this study is that it is possible to train other medical colleagues relatively easily, and if the contents of the therapeutic program are sound, substantial benefits for patients can be expected.

THREE FACTORS NECESSARY FOR SUCCESSFUL OUTCOME

Efficacy of the Treatment Components

From the discussion so far it does seem that a more comprehensive program whereby considerable efforts are made to generalize the treatment components across everyday life is more likely to be successful. The underlying theoretical assumptions are that (a) people differ in their needs and in how different components of the treatment package appeal to them, (b) different strategies are required to cope with different situations that people may be exposed to in daily life, and (c) generalization of behavioral and cognitive techniques is necessary to maintain around-the-clock therapeutic benefits.

Characteristics of the Therapists

A therapist's commitment to the therapy, enthusiasm, beliefs about the therapy, previous experience, educational background, communication mode, and ability to form rapport with patients are some of the factors that can affect the results of therapy. In an ongoing study my colleagues and I used five therapists of different backgrounds and experience but with the same intervention protocol and a homogeneous group of patients (all civil servants) and found that three medically qualified therapists—a psychiatrist, a general practitioner, and I—were equally effective, whereas the patients treated by a clinical psychologist and a yoga teacher actually showed a rise in both systolic and diastolic blood pressure (Patel & Marmot, 1988b). Even in the study in which all therapists were general practitioners who trained their own patients using the same intervention protocol we found varying effectiveness.

The presence of a therapist does, however, seem to be necessary. Brauer et al. (1979) reported blood pressure reductions of 11/6 when relaxation was taught by a therapist compared with 5/1 when patients were supplied with relaxation tapes and were asked to practice them at home. The differences in posttrial blood pressure levels were not significant, but at a 6-month follow-up the therapist-taught patients showed a mean reduction in blood pressure of 18/10 compared with + 1/5 in the tape-taught patients. The differences between the groups were significant for diastolic blood pressure.

A good therapist is one who can motivate patients to comply with therapy in the long term. This requires tactful persuasion. The patients are also more likely to accept recommendations from a therapist whom they generally respect. Therefore it is not surprising that an experienced therapist with a wider educational background is more effective than a younger, inexperienced or nonmedical therapist. It is also important that contact with the therapist and a generally supportive relationship between the therapist and the patient is maintained over the long term if therapeutic effect is to continue. In hindsight my colleagues and I think that a contributing factor in the long-term success of the subjects in our study in industry (Patel et al., 1985) must have been the active participation of nurses from the occupational medical department who were available on daily basis if patients required counseling, just someone to talk to, or general reinforcement of the therapy.

Characteristics of the Patients

As has been discussed, initial level of blood pressure, willingness to comply, attitudes toward therapy, availability of time, support from family, benefits from ongoing therapy with respect to other aspects of life, degree of psychological distress, number of life events in the recent past, and personality of the patient are some of the important factors that affect the outcome of therapy. Even when the therapy has been successfully tried and tested before, the investigator may fail to replicate the results, because public awareness regarding risk factors and some of the nonpharmacological measures to alter them may increase and control group patients who feel deprived of an active therapy are likely to make every effort they can to change their health status for the better. Such changes were thought to play an important part in an inconclusive primary prevention trial of coronary heart disease (Multiple Risk Factor Intervention, 1982) and may have been partly responsible, along with poor compliance, for the disappearance of the differences between relaxation and control groups at a three-year follow-up (Agras, Taylor, Kraemer, Southam, & Schneider, 1987).

BEHAVIORAL CONTROL OF RISK FACTORS ASSOCIATED WITH HYPERTENSION

Epidemiological evidence suggests that behavioral factors such as obesity, high sodium and alcohol intake, and lack of physical activity are implicated in high blood pressure. Smoking may cause transient rises in blood pressure, but smokers do not have higher blood pressure compared with nonsmokers. However, smoking cessation is important, especially for hypertensive patients, because smoking and hypertension interact and the risk multiplies rather than becoming additive. Although Type A behavior is a risk factor for coronary heart disease, resting blood pressure levels of Type A individuals are not different from those of Type B individuals. Very little is known about the relation between social support and blood pressure status.

Obesity

Obesity is associated with both increased prevalence (Chiang, Perman, & Epstein, 1969; Kotchen & Havlik, 1980; Stamler, Stamler, Riedlinger, Algera, & Roberts,

1978) and incidence (Kannel, Brand, Skinner, Dawber, & McNamara, 1967; Miall, Bell, & Lovell, 1968; Tyroler, Hayden, & Hames, 1975; Svardsudd et al., 1980) of hypertension, whereas loss in weight leads to substantial reduction in blood pressure (Langford et al., 1985; MacMohan, MacDonald, Bernstein, Andrews, & Blackett, 1985; Maxwell, Kushiro, Dornfield, Tuck, & Haks, 1984; Stamler et al., 1980). It is thought that some of the reduction in blood pressure might be due to reduction of salt intake, but reduction in blood pressure was demonstrated even when salt intake was kept constant (Reisin et al., 1978). Not all studies have been positive, however (e.g., Haynes et al., 1984) and long-term maintenance seems to be disappointing.

Sodium Intake

Increased sodium intake has been known to be implicated in hypertension since 1904 (Ambard & Beaujard, 1904) and is associated with both increased prevalence and incidence in many cultures (Dahl, 1972; Lowenstein & Basle, 1961; Intersalt, 1988; Kesteloot, Huang, Li, Geboers, & Joosens, 1987; Oliver, Cohen, & Neel, 1975; Page, 1980; Sasaki, 1962; Watson, Langford, Abernethy, Barnes, & Watson, 1980), although it is uncertain how much a rise in blood pressure can be attributed to excess intake of sodium in view of other associated, and often profound, changes in social environments (Simpson, 1979; Swales, 1980). Some investigators did not find a relation between sodium intake and blood pressure but showed that potassium intake was negatively related to the level of blood pressure (Walker, Whelton, Saito, Russell, & Hemann, 1979), whereas others showed it was the sodium/potassium ratio that was important (Langford & Watson, 1975; Poulter et al., 1984).

Intervention studies have been few, and the results are conflicting (Beard, Cooke, Gray, & Barge, 1982; MacGregor et al., 1982; Morgan et al., 1978; Parijs, Joosens, Van de Lindens, & Amery, 1973; Richard et al., 1984; Watts, Edwards, Hart, Hart, & Walton, 1983). For example, MacGregor et al. (1982) found significant reduction in blood pressure in some but not in others, whereas Watts et al. (1983) did not find blood pressure decreases in low-salt subjects to be any greater than those in normal-salt control subjects. A salt-free diet would undoubtedly reduce blood pressure, but only a few people would find such a diet palatable, and the effects of a more modest reduction, even if maintained at a desired level, are at best only slight (Grobbee & Hofman, 1986). It is unlikely that salt reduction on its own without other intervention strategies is a viable proposal.

Alcohol Intake

The link between alcohol intake and level of blood pressure is becoming more apparent (Gyntelberg & Meyer, 1974; Klatsky, Friedman, Siegelaub, & Gerard, 1979; MacMohan, 1987; Pincherle & Robinson, 1974; Shaper et al., 1981), although in one longitudinal study alcohol did not turn out to be a major factor (Svardsudd et al., 1980) and it is still doubtful if alcohol-related hypertension is prognostically as serious as the hypertension of unknown origin (Beevers, 1988). Alcoholics show a reduction in blood pressure when they cease to drink and a relapse on resuming. For example, Saunders et al. (1981) studied 132 alcoholics whose daily consumption exceeded 80 g. They found a significant correlation between blood pressure and mean daily alcohol intake and also between the level of blood pressure and severity of alcohol withdrawal symptoms. In most patients blood pressure fell after abstinence and remained so for at least a year in those who continued to abstain, but rose in those who started to drink again. Such reduction in blood pressure following alcohol cessation has been shown in both hypertensives (Potters & Beevers, 1984) and normotensives (Puddey, Beilin, Vandongen, Rouse, & Rogers, 1985). No controlled trial of alcohol restriction has, however, been carried out.

Physical Activity

The relation between physical activity and blood pressure has been little studied in large population samples. In the Framingham study no significant relationship was detected (Dawber et al., 1967). In Gothenburg also no relation was found between blood pressure and either leisure time or occupational activity, and there was no association between change in activity level and change in blood pressure with time (Berglund & Wilhelmsen, 1975; Svardsudd & Wilhelmsen, 1980; Svardsudd et al., 1980). Intervention studies have been few and very small and most of them have not used randomized control groups that remained untrained in behavioral techniques. In general, physical activity appears to have little effect on blood pressure in normotensives, but among hypertensives some patients have shown a decrease, at least in diastolic blood pressure. Confounding factors such as body weight and other variables have not been sufficiently reported (Boyer & Kasch, 1970; Choquette & Ferguson, 1973; Krotkiewski et al., 1979).

EFFECTS OF LIFE-STYLE CHANGES

It has been argued that even a tiny shift to the left in the distribution curve of risk factors among the population is likely to lead to substantial reduction in the total number of people with disease as well as in mortality rates; the large number of people at slight risk for hypertension make the greatest contribution to the total number of cases (Epstein, 1979; Lewis, Nann, & Mancini, 1986; Rose, 1981). Unfortunately, shifting the distribution curve to the left is not easy. The dangers of smoking, obesity, excess alcohol, and physical inactivity have been widely known, yet risky behaviors largely remain unchanged. Even when patients have been successful in losing weight, the majority regain it within a year. Repeated relapses with smoking and alcohol behavior are widely known.

Because many of these behaviors are maintained by physical and social environments, it is only by changing social attitudes that we can expect changes in behavior. Successful outcome depends on increased public knowledge and understanding as well as individual counseling and support, which can lead to changes in attitudes and are necessary before changes in appropriate behavior and hence reduction in the risk factor can be expected. The efficacy of life-style changes is not questioned; however, such changes are difficult to effect in clinical practice. Handing out diet sheets or giving cursory advice to stop smoking or drinking is unlikely to lead to sustained reduction in weight or in blood pressure. In the long-term, proven behavioral principles will have to be used by clinicians who are involved in the care of hypertensive patients (Caggiula, Milas, & Wing, 1987).

Attempts to modify a single behavior have failed to show impressive results. However, a combined strategy of simultaneous reduction in several factors looks more promising. For example, in a controlled trial involving patients who were taken off antihypertension drugs, Stamler et al. (1978) found that with a program of reduction in weight as well as in the intake of salt and alcohol 33% of their subjects could stay off antihypertension drugs over a four-year period, compared with only 5% in a control group.

PHARMACOLOGICAL TREATMENT OF HYPERTENSION

The first generation of antihypertension drugs, namely, ganglion blockers, became available in the 1950s. Until then, hypertension was treated with an unpalatable salt-free diet. Occasionally sympathectomy or even adrenalectomy were carried out, and mortality, especially from malignant hypertension, used to be very high. In one study, it was shown that prior to drug treatment 80% of patients with malignant hypertension were dead within a year, whereas following the introduction of the drug hexamethonium, at least 50% of patients with malignant hypertension could be kept alive for a year or more (Dustan, Schneck, Corcoran, & Page, 1958; Farmer, Gifford, & Himes, 1963; Harrington, Kincaid-Smith, & McMichael, 1959). However, the side effects from drug treatment were so severe that treatment had to be restricted to severely afflicted, hospitalized patients.

A few years later, diuretics and the reserpine group of drugs became available, and treatment of moderately severe and severe hypertension became feasible for outpatients. Many other neuronal blockers and vasodilator drugs were soon introduced and, as a result, mortality from complications like uremia, strokes, and heart failure was drastically reduced (Hamilton et al., 1964; Veterans Administration, 1967, 1970). Thus we owe a great deal to the development of pharmacological agents for reducing morbidity and mortality from hypertension quite dramatically.

Unfortunately, mortality rates from coronary heart disease, the most common complication of hypertension, increased as those from other complications decreased (Breckenridge, Dollery, & Parry, 1970). Several reasons for this have been proposed. One, patients survive longer and thus long enough to eventually fall victim to coronary heart disease. Second, to prevent coronary heart disease, earlier intervention is needed to stop the atherosclerotic process before the critical point is reached. And third, the etiology of coronary heart disease is complex and merely lowering blood pressure is not adequate to prevent the disease. It became obvious that treatment has to be initiated when blood pressure is only mildly elevated. This temptation was increased even further when a new generation of drugs, such as beta-blockers, which were relatively free from side effects and were thought to be cardioprotective, were being introduced in large numbers. As a result, a number of studies of mild hypertension treatment were carried out. Most of the earlier studies did not show significant benefit, and it soon became apparent that clinical trials involving thousands, not hundreds, of patients were needed.

Recent Trials of Treatment of Mild Hypertension

In the Hypertension Detection and Follow-up Program (Hypertension Detection, 1979), 10,940 patients with diastolic blood pressure of 90 mm Hg or more, regardless of current antihypertension medication, were randomly grouped into stepped care groups (SC) or referred care groups (RC). Those allocated to the RC group were referred to their usual source of medical care, whereas those allocated to the SC group were treated in specialized centers, free of charge, and where a doctor was on duty 24 hours a day to deal with any medical problems. During the five years of

Table 6 Incidence of death among subjects in the Medical Research Council mild hypertension treatment trial

Cause of death	Number of subjects	
	Active drugs	Placebos
All causes	248	253
Cardiovascular	134	139
Noncardiovascular	114	114
Coronary	106	97
Cardiovascular accidents	60	109

follow-up, mortality from all causes was significantly lower in the SC group in stratum 1 (diastolic blood pressure 90–104 mm Hg), but, strangely, not in stratum 2 (diastolic blood pressure 105–114 mm Hg) or stratum 3 (diastolic blood pressure >115 mm Hg). The main criticism of the study was that it was not a placebo-controlled study but a comparison of good versus ordinary care, and because noncardiac deaths from diabetes, gastrointestinal and respiratory diseases, and cancer also occurred in the SC group, the results reflected the quality of care rather than value of antihypertension drugs.

The next study to be published was the Australian Trial (Management Committee, 1980). The subjects—3,931 men and women with diastolic blood pressure of 95 or systolic blood pressure of 200 mm Hg or higher—received either an active drug or a placebo. The investigators, following advice from an ethics committee, decided to stop the trial after four years because of a significantly higher number of cardiovascular deaths in the control group. The overall trend was a reduction in strokes and sudden cardiac deaths among subjects receiving drugs, but there was no evidence that incidence of coronary heart disease, which is the major cause of morbidity, was reduced. When both fatal and nonfatal myocardial infarctions were added together, the incidence was exactly the same (33 in each group) in both the control and treatment groups. It should also be noted that although mild hypertensives were included, the trial was not restricted to mild hypertension.

The largest placebo-controlled trial of mild hypertension treatment was carried out in England (Medical Research Council, 1985). In this study 17,354 men and women between the ages of 35 and 64 with phase 5 diastolic blood pressure 90–109 mm Hg were randomly selected to receive either an active drug (bendrofluazide or propranolol) or a comparable placebo. During the five years of follow-up, both systolic and diastolic blood pressure were significantly lower in the active drug group than in the placebo group, but overall results were very disappointing. Smokers as well as women came out particularly worse-off; both groups showed greater mortality on active drugs rather than on placebos. As can be seen from Table 6, for all causes of death incidence rates were similar for both groups. However, strokes were significantly lower in the active drug group ($p < .01$). It was calculated that 850 patients will have to be treated to reduce one person's stroke (not life).

Limitations on Pharmacological Treatment

The use of medication for treating mild hypertension has been limited for the following reasons:

1. The efficacy of hypertension in drugs saving lives or reducing coronary heart disease has not been proven in patients with mild hypertension.

2. Although drugs are more effective than therapy in reducing blood pressure, most of the advantage is counterbalanced by negative metabolic and other counterproductive effects. For example, most beta-blockers seem to raise lipid levels, and diuretics seem to raise blood sugar and serum uric acid and also lower the threshold for cardiac arrythmia.

3. There is no safe level of blood pressure according to the Framingham study investigators (Kannel, 1975), and mass medication of apparently healthy people for the rest of their lives is aesthetically, financially, and practically unattractive.

4. Even if physicians are ready to prescribe medications, many apparently healthy patients with mild hypertension are reluctant to swallow mediations for the rest of their lives. The level of side effects in relation to the degree of benefit is unacceptable. In the MRC study (Medical Research Council, 1981, 1985), more than 15% of the patients had to be withdrawn from their allocated active drugs because of unacceptable side-effects including diabetes, gout, impotence, headaches, lethargy, Raynaud's phenomena, dyspnoea, nausea or vomiting. In another study (IPPPSH Collaborative Group, 1985), beta-blockers did not fare better than non-beta-blockers in the amount of side effects or in the number of critical events induced.

CONCLUSION

I have reviewed literature on pharmacological and nonpharmacological, mainly psychological and behavioral measures, for reducing hypertension and associated risk factors. The majority of strokes and coronary heart disease occur in a large proportion of the middle-aged population who have mildly elevated blood pressure and other risk factors. Mass medication with currently available drugs is neither attractive nor shown to be safe or universally beneficial. Psychological or behavioral treatment is not an easy alternative. It requires time and commitment from both the clinicians and patients, and long-term compliance remains a major problem. Its benefits are not yet completely proven. However, the sheer number of positive studies point to its usefulness in the management of hypertension. It is remarkably free from undesirable side effects and may even enhance the quality of life. When delivered in group setting, training in relaxation-based behavioral treatment takes about one hour of an experienced clinician's time per patient. Thus in the long term it is cost-effective. Even when drugs have to be added, it is likely that a smaller dose would be sufficient to control blood pressure, thus reducing the negative effects of antihypertension drugs; there is also a strong indication that drugs may also reduce the risk of coronary heart disease. A sound policy would be to try nonpharmacological measures using behavior modification principles first and add hypertension drugs only when other measures fail to control blood pressure satisfactorily.

REFERENCES

Agras, W. S., Horne, M., & Taylor, C. B. (1982). Expectation and the blood pressure lowering effects of relaxation. *Psychosomatic Medicine, 44*, 389–395.

Agras, W. S., Taylor, C. B., Kramer, H. C., Southam, M. A., & Schneider, J. A. (1987). Relaxation training for essential hypertension at work site: 2. The poorly controlled hypertensive. *Psychosomatic Medicine, 49*, 264–273.

Ambard, L., & Beaujard, E. (1904). Causes de l'hypertension arterielle. *Archives of General Medicine, 1*, 520–533.

Bali, L. R. (1979). Long-term effect of relaxation on blood pressure and anxiety level in essential hypertensive males: A controlled study. *Psychosomatic Medicine, 41*, 637–646.

Beard, T. C., Cooke, H. M., Gray, W. R., & Barge, R. (1982). Randomized controlled trial of the no-added-sodium diet for mild hypertension. *Lancet, 2*, 455–458.

Beevers, D. G. (1988). Does alcohol cause hypertension or psuedohypertension? *Proceedings of the Nutrition Society, 47*, 31–34.

Benson, H. (1975). *Relaxation response.* New York: Morrow.

Benson, H., Rosner, J. F., Marzetta, B. R., & Klemchuk, H. D. (1974a). Decreased blood pressure in borderline hypertensive subjects who practiced meditation. *Journal of Chronic Diseases, 27*, 163–196.

Benson, H., Rosner, B. A., Marzetta, B. R., & Klemchuk, H. D. (1974b). Decreased blood pressure in pharmacologically treated hypertensive patients who regularly elicited the relaxation response. *Lancet, 1*, 287–291.

Benson, H., Shapiro, D., Tursky, B., & Schwartz, G. (1971). Decreased systolic blood pressure through operant conditioning techniques in patients with essential hypertension. *Science, 173*, 740–742.

Berglund, G., & Wilhelmsen, L. (1975). Factors related to blood pressure in a general population sample of Swedish men. *Acta Medica Scandinavica, 198*, 291.

Blackwell, B., Bloomfield, S., Gartside, P., Robinson, A., Hanenson, I., Magenheim, H., Nidith, S., & Zigler, R. (1976). Transcendental meditation in hypertension. *Lancet, 1*, 223–226.

Blanchard, E. B., Young, L. D., & Haynes, M. R. (1975). A simple feedback system for the treatment of elevated blood pressure. *Behavior Therapy, 6*, 241–245.

Boyer, J. L., & Kasch, F. W. (1970). Exercise therapy in hypertensive men. *Journal of the American Medical Association, 211*, 1668.

Brady, J. P., Luborsky, L., & Kron, R. E. (1974). Blood pressure reduction in patients with essential hypertension through metronome-conditioned relaxation: A preliminary report. *Behavior Therapy, 5*, 203–209.

Brauer, A., Horlick, L. F., Nelson, B., Farquhar, J. W., & Agras, W. S. (1979). Relaxation therapy for essential hypertension: A Veterans Administration out-patients study. *Journal of Behavioral Medicine, 2*, 21–29.

Breckenridge, A., Dollery, C. T., & Parry, E. H. O. (1970). Prognosis of treated hypertension. *Quarterly Journal of Medicine, 39*, 411–429.

Caggiula, A. W., Milas, C. N., & Wing, R. R. (1987). Optimal nutritional therapy in the treatment of hypertension. In M. D. Blaufox & H. G. Langford (Eds.), *Non-pharmacologic therapy hypertension.* Basel: Karger.

Charlesworth, E. A., Williams, B. J., & Baer, B. E. (1984). Stress management at work site for hypertension: Compliance, cost-benefit, health care and hypertension-related variables. *Psychosomatic Medicine, 46*, 387–397.

Chesney, M. A., Black, G. W., & Ward, M. M. (1987). Relaxation training for essential hypertension at the work site: 2. The untreated hypertensive. *Psychosomatic Medicine, 49*, 250–263.

Chiang, B. N., Perman, L. V., & Epstein, F. H. (1969). Overweight and hypertension: A review. *Circulation, 34*, 403–421.

Choquette, G., & Ferguson, R. J. (1973). Blood pressure redution in "borderline" hypertensives following physical training. *Canadian Medical Association Journal, 108*, 99.

Cottier, C., Shapiro, K., & Julius, S. (1984). Treatment of mild hypertension with progressive muscular relaxation: Predictive value of indexes of sympathetic tone. *Archives of Internal Medicine, 144*, 1954–1958.

Crits-Christoph, P., Luborsky, L., Kron, R., & Fishman, H. (1978). Blood pressure, heart rate and respiratory responses to a single session of relaxation: A partial replication. *Psychosomatic Research, 22*, 493–501.

Crowther, J. H. (1983). Stress management training and relaxation imagery in the treatment of essential hypertension. *Journal of Behavioral Medicine, 6*, 169–187.

Dahl, L. K. (1972). Salt and hypertension. *American Journal of Clinical Nutrition, 25*, 231–244.

Datey, K. K., Deshmukh, S. N., Dalvi, C. P., & Vinekar, M. D. (1969). "Shavasan," a yogic exercise in the management of hypertension. *Angiology, 20*, 325–333.

Dawber, T. R., Kannel, W. B., Kagan, A., Donabedian, R. K., McNamara, P. M., & Pearson, G. (1967). Environmental factors in hypertension. In J. Stamler et al. (Eds.), *The epidemiology of hypertension: Proceedings of an international symposium* (pp. 255–288). New York: Grune & Stratton.

Deabler, H. L., Fidel, E., Dillenkoffer, R., & Elder, S. T. (1973). The use of relaxation and hypnosis in lowering high blood pressure. *American Journal of Clinical Hypertension, 16*, 75–83.

Dustan, H. P., Schneck, R. E., Corcoran, A. C., & Page, I. H. (1958). The effectiveness of long-term treatment of malignant hypertension. *Circulation, 18*, 644–651.

Eagan, K. J., Kogan, H. N., Garber, A. G., & Jarrett, M. (1983). The impact of psychological distress on the control of hypertension. *Journal of Human Stress, 9*(4), 4–10.

Elder, S. T., & Eustis, N. K. (1975). Instrumental blood pressure conditioning of diastolic blood pressure in outpatient essential hypertension. *Behaviour Research and Therapy, 13*, 185–188.

Elder, S. T., Ruiz, R., Deabler, H. L., & Dillenkoffer, R. L. (1973). Instrumental conditioning of diastolic blood pressure in essential hypertensive patients. *Journal of Applied Behavioral Analysis, 6*, 377–382.

Epstein, F. H. (1979). Estimating the effect of preventing obesity on total mortality and hypertension. *International Journal of Obesity, 3*, 163–166.

Farmer, R. G., Gifford, R. W., & Himes, E. A. (1963). Effect of medical treatment of severe hypertension: A follow-up study of 161 patients with group 3 and group 4 hypertension. *Archives of Internal Medicine, 112*, 161–174.

Frankel, B. L., Patel. D. J., Horwitz, D., Friedwald, M. T., & Gaardner, K. P. (1978). Treatment of hypertension with biofeedback and relaxation techniques. *Psychosomatic Medicine, 40*, 276–293.

Friedman, H., & Taub, H. A. (1977). The use of hypnosis and biofeedback procedures for essential hypertension. *International Journal of Clinical and Experimental Hypnosis, 25*, 335–347.

Glasgow, M. S., Gaardner, K. R., & Engel, B. T. (1982). Behavioral treatment of high blood pressure: 2. Acute and sustained effects of relaxation and systolic blood pressure biofeedback. *Psychosomatic Medicine, 44*, 155–171.

Goldman, H., Kleinman, K. M., Snow, M., Bidus, D., & Korol, B. (1975). Relationship between essential hypertension and cognitive functioning: Effects of biofeedback. *Psychophysiology, 12*, 569–573.

Goldstein, I. B., Shapiro, D., & Thananpavarn, C. (1984). Home relaxation techniques for essential hypertension. *Psychosomatic Medicine, 46*, 399–414.

Goldstein, I. B., Shapiro, D., Thananopavarn, C., & Sambhi, M. P. (1982). Comparison of drug and behavioral treatment of essential hypertension. *Health Psychology, 1*, 7–26.

Grobbee, D. E., & Hofman, A. (1986). Does sodium restriction lower blood pressure? *British Medical Journal, 293*, 27–29.

Gyntelberg, F., & Meyer, J. (1974). Relationship between blood pressure and physical fitness, smoking and alcohol consumption on Copenhagen males aged 40–59. *Acta Medica Scandinavica, 195*, 375–.

Hafner, R. J. (1982). Psychological treatment of hypertension: A controlled comparison of meditation and meditation plus feedback. *Biofeedback and Self-Regulation, 7*, 305–316.

Hamilton, M., Thompson, E. N., & Wisniewski, T. K. M. (1964). The role of blood pressure control in preventing complications of hypertension. *Lancet, 1*, 235–238.

Hatch, J. J., Klatt, K. D., Supik, J. D., Rios, N., Fisher, J. G., Bauer, R. L., & Shimotsu, G. W. (1985). Combined behavioral and pharmacological treatment of hypertension. *Biofeedback and Self-Regulation, 10*, 119–138.

Harrington, M., Kincaid-Smith, P., & McMichael, J. (1959). Results of treatment of malignant hypertension: A seven-year experience in 94 cases. *British Medical Journal, 2*, 969–980.

Haynes, R. B., Harper, A. C., Costley, S. R., Johnston, M., Logan, A. G., Flanagan, P. T., & Sackett, D. L. (1984). Failure of weight reduction to reduce mildly elevated blood pressure: A randomized trial. *Journal of Hypertension, 2*, 535–539.

Henry, J. P., & Cassel, J. C. (1969). Psychosocial factors in essential hypertension: Recent epidemiological and animal experimental studies. *American Journal of Epidemiology, 90*(3), 171–200.

Hypertension Detection and Follow-Up Program Co-operative Group. (1979). Five-year findings of the hypertension detection and follow-up program. *Journal of the American Medical Association, 242*, 2562–2570.

Intersalt Co-operative Research Group. (1988). Intersalt: An international study of electrolyte excretion and blood pressure. Results of 24 hour urinary sodium and potassium excretion. *British Medical Journal, 297*, 319–328.

IPPPSH Collaborative Group. (1985). Cardiovascular risk and risk factors in a randomized trial of treatment based on the beta-blocker oxprenolol: The International Prospective Primary Prevention Study in Hypertension (IPPPSH). *Journal of Hypertension, 3*, 378–393.

Irvine, M. J., Johnston, D. W., Jenner, D. A., & Marie, G. V. (1986). Relaxation and stress management in the treatment of essential hypertension. *Journal of Psychosomatic Research, 30*, 437–450.

Jacob, R. G., Kramer, H. G., & Agras, W. S. (1977). Relaxation therapy in the treatment of hypertension. *Archives of General Psychiatry, 34*, 1417–1427.

Jacobson, E. (1939). Variation of blood pressure with skeletal muscle tension and relaxation. *Annals of Internal Medicine, 12*, 1194–1212.

Johnston, D. W. (1982). Behavioral treatment in the reduction of coronary risk factors: Type A behavior and blood pressure. *British Journal of Clinical Psychology, 21*(4), 281–294.

Johnston, D. W. (1987). Behavioral control of high blood pressure. *Current Psycho. Res. & Rev., 6*, 99–114.

Joint National Committee on Detection, Evaluation, and Treatment of High Blood Pressure. (1984). The 1984 report of the Joint National Committee on Detection, Evaluation, Treatment of High Blood Pressure. *Archives of Internal Medicine, 144*, 1045–1057.

Jorgensen, R. S., Housten, B. K., & Zurawski, R. M. (1981). Anxiety management training in the treatment of essential hypertension. *Behavior Research and Therapy, 19*, 467–474.

Kallinke, D., Kullick, B., & Heim, P. (1982). Behavior analysis and treatment of essential hypertension. *Journal of Psychosomatic Research, 26*, 541–549.

Kannel, W. B., Brand, N., Skinner, J., Dawber, T., & McNamara, P. (1967). The relation of adiposity to blood pressure and development of hypertension: The Framingham study. *Annals of Internal Medicine, 67*, 48–59.

Kesteloot, H., Huang, D. X., Li, Y. L., Geboers, J., & Joosens, J. B. (1987). The relationship between cations and blood pressure in the People's Republic of China. *Hypertension, 9*, 654–659.

Klatsky, A. L., Friedman, G. D., Siegelaub, A. B., & Gerard, M. J. (1977). Alcohol consumption and blood pressure. *New England Journal of Medicine, 296*, 1194.

Klumbies, G., & Eberhardt, G. (1966). Results of autogenic training in the treatment of hypertension. In J. J. Ibar (Ed.), *Int: Congress Series 117* (pp. 46–47). Amsterdam: Excerpta Medical Foundation.

Kotchen, T., & Havlik, R. (Eds.). (1980). High blood pressure in the young. *Hypertension, 2*(Suppl.), 1135.

Kristt, D. S., & Engel, B. T. (1975). Learned control of blood pressure in patients with high blood pressure. *Circulation, 51*, 370–378.

Krotkiewski, M., et al. (1979). Effects of long-term physical training on body fat, metabolism, and blood pressure in obesity. *Metabolism, 28*, 650.

Langford, H. G., Blaufox, M. D., Oberman, A., Hawkins, M., Curb, J. D., Cutter, G. R., Wassertheil-Smoller, S., Pressel, S., Babock, C., Abernethy, J. D., Hotchkiss, J., & Tyler, M. (1985). Dietary therapy slows the return of hypertension after stopping prolonged medication. *Journal of the American Medical Association, 253*, 657–664.

Langford, H. G., & Watson, R. L. (1975). Electrolytes and hypertension. In O. Paul (Ed.), *Epidemiology and control of hypertension* (pp. 119–130). New York: Grune & Stratton.

Lewis, B., Nann, J. I., & Mancini, M. (1986). Reducing the risk of coronary heart disease in individuals and in the population. *Lancet*, 956–959.

Little, B. E., Hayworth, J., Benson, P., Beard, R. W., Dewhurst, J., & Priest, R. G. (1984). Treatment of hypertension in pregnancy by relaxation and biofeedback. *Lancet, 1*, 865–867.

Lowenstein, F. W., & Basle, M. D. (1961). Blood pressure relaxation to age and sex in the tropics and subtropics: A review of the literature and investigation tw tribes of Brazil Indians. *Lancet, 1*, 389–392.

Luborsky, L., Crits-Christoph, P., Brady, J. P., Kron, R. E., Weiss, T., Cohen, M., & Levy, L. (1982). Behavioral vs. pharmacological treatment for essential hypertension: A needed comparison. *Psychosomatic Medicine, 44*, 203–214.

Luthe, W. (1969). *Autogenic therapy* (Vols. 1–6). New York: Grune & Stratton.

MacGregor, G. A., Markandu, N. D., Best, E. F., Elder, D. M., Cam, J. M., Sagnella, G. A., & Squires, M. (1982). Double-blind randomized crossover trial of moderate sodium restriction in essential hypertension. *Lancet, 1*, 352–354.

MacMohan, S. (1987). Alcohol consumption and hypertension. *Hypertension, 9*, 111–121.

MacMohan, S. W., MacDonald, G. J., Bernstein, D., Andrews, G., & Blackett, R. B. (1985). Comparison of weight reduction with metoprolol in the treatment of hypertension in young, overweight, hypertensive patients. *New England Journal of Medicine, 1*, 1233–1236.

Maxwell, M. H., Kushiro, T., Dornfield, L. P., Tuck, M. L., & Haks, A. U. (1984). Blood pressure changes in obese hypertensive subjects during rapid weight loss: Comparison of restricted vs. unchanged salt intake. *Archives of Internal Medicine, 144*, 1581–1584.

Management Committee. (1980). The Australian therapeutic trial in mild hypertension. *Lancet, 1*, 1261–1267.

McGrady, W. V., Yonker, R., Tan, S. Y., Fine, T. H., & Woewrner, M. (1981). The effect of biofeedback-assisted relaxation on blood pressure and selected biochemical parameters in patients with essential hypertension. *Biofeedback and Self-Regulation, 6*, 343–354.

Medical Research Council Working Party. (1985). MRC trial of treatment of mild hypertension: Principal results. *British Medical Journal, 291,* 97–104.

Medical Research Council Working Party on Mild Hypertension. (1986). Course of blood pressure in mild hypertensives: Withdrawal of long-term antihypertensive treatment. *British Medical Journal, 293,* 988–992.

Medical Research Council Working Party on Mild to Moderate Hypertension. (1981). Adverse reaction to bendrofluazide and propranolol in the treatment of mild hypertension. *Lancet, 2,* 543–563.

Miall, W. E., Bell, R. A., & Lovell, H. G. (1968). Relation between change in blood pressure and weight. *British Journal of Preventive and Social Medicine, 22,* 73–80.

Miller, N. E. (1972). Postscript. In D. Singh & C. T. Morgan (Eds.), *Current status of physiological psychology.* Monterey, CA: Brooks/Cole.

Morgan, T., Adam, H., Gillies, A., Wilson, N., Morgan, G., & Carney, S. (1978). Hypertension treated by salt restriction. *Lancet, 1,* 227–230.

Multiple Risk Factor Intervention Trial Research Group. (1982). Multiple risk factor intervention trial: Risk factor changes and mortality results. *Journal of the American Medical Association, 248,* 1465–1477.

Office of Health Economics. (1971). *Hypertension: A suitable case for treatment.* London: Office of Health Economics.

Oliver, H. J., Cohen, E. L., & Neel, J. V. (1975). Blood pressure and sodium intake and sodium related harmones in Yanomamo Indian: A no-salt culture. *Circulation, 52,* 146–151.

Parijs, S. J., Joosens, J. V., Van der Lindens, L., & Amery, A. K. P. C. (1973). Moderate sodium restriction and diuretics in the treatment of hypertension. *American Heart Journal, 85,* 22–34.

Patel, C. H. (1973). Yoga and biofeedback in the management of hypertension. *Lancet, 2,* 1053–1055.

Patel, C. (1975). 12-month follow-up of yoga and biofeedback in the management of hypertension. *Lancet, 1,* 62–65.

Patel, C. (1976). Reduction of serum cholesterol and blood pressure in hypertensive patients by behavioral modification. *Journal of the Royal College of General Practitioners, 26,* 211–215.

Patel, C. (1986). Prevention paradox in coronary heart disease. In T. Schmidt, T. Dembroski, & G. Blumchen (Eds.), *Biological and psychological factors in cardiovascular diseases* (pp. 533–549). Heidelberg: Springer-Verlag.

Patel, C., & Carruthers, M. (1977). Coronary risk factor reduction through biofeedback-aided relaxation and meditation. *Journal of the Royal College of General Practitioners, 27,* 401–405.

Patel, C., & Marmot, M. G. (1987). Stress management, blood pressure and quality of life. *Journal of Hypertension, 5*(Suppl. 1), 21–28.

Patel, C., & Marmot, M. G. (1988a). Can general practitioners use training in relaxation and management of stress to reduce mild hypertension? *British Medical Journal, 296,* 21–24.

Patel, C., & Marmot, M. G. (1988b). Efficacy versus effectiveness of behavioral therapy in reducing hypertension. *Stress Medicine, 4*(4).

Patel, C., Marmot, M. G., & Terry, D. J. (1981). Controlled trial of biofeedback-aided behavioral methods in reducing mild hypertension. *British Medical Journal, 282,* 2005–2008.

Patel, C., Marmot, M. G., Terry, D. J., Carruthers, M., Hunt, B., & Patel, M. (1985). Trial of relaxation in reducing coronary risk: Four-year follow-up. *British Medical Journal, 290,* 1103–1106.

Patel, C., & North, W. R. S. (1975). Randomized controlled trial of yoga and biofeedback in the management of hypertension. *Lancet, 2,* 92–95.

Peters, R. K., Benson, H., & Peters, D. (1977). Daily relaxation breaks in the working population: 1. Effects of self-reported measures of health, performance, and well-being. *American Journal of Public Health, 67,* 946–953.

Peveler, R., & Johnston, D. W. (1986). Subjective and cognitive effects of relaxation. *Behavior and Research Therapy, 24,* 413–420.

Pincherle, G., & Robinson, D. (1974). Mean blood pressure and its relation to other factors determined at a routine executive health examination. *Journal of Chronic Diseases, 27,* 245–###.

Pollack, A. A., Case, D. B., Weber, M. A., & Laragh, J. H. (1977). Limitation of transcendental meditation in the treatment of essential hypertension. *Lancet, 1,* 71–73.

Potters, J. F., & Beevers, D. J. (1984). Pressor effect of alcohol in hypertension. *Lancet, 1,* 119–122.

Poulter, N., Khow, K. T., Hopwood, B. E. C., Mugambi, M., Peart, W. S., Rose, G. A., & Sever, P. (1984). Blood pressure and associated factors in a rural Kenyan community. *Hypertension, 6,* 810–813.

Puddey, L. B., Beilin, L. J., Vandongen, R., Rouse, I. L., & Rogers, P. (1985). Evidence for a direct effect of alcohol consumption on blood pressure in normotensive men: A randomized controlled trial. *Hypertension, 7,* 703–713.

Reisin, E., Abel, R., Michaela, M., Silverberg, D. S., Eliahou, J. E., & Modan, B. (1978). Effects of weight loss without salt restriction on the reduction of blood pressure in overweight hypertensive patients. *New England Journal of Medicine, 298*, 1–6.

Richards, A. M., Nicholls, M. G., Espiner, E. A., Ikram, H., Maslowski, A. H., Hamilton, E. J., & Wells, J. E. (1984). Blood pressure response to moderate sodium restriction and to potassium supplementation in mild hypertension. *Lancet, 2*, 757–761.

Richter-Heinrich, E., Homouth, B., Heinrich, K., Schmidt, H., Wiedemann, R., & Gohlke, H. R. (1981). Long-term application of behavioral treatment in essential hypertensives. *Physiology and Behavior, 26*, 915–920.

Richter-Heinrich, E., Knust, U., Muller, W., Schmidt, K. H., & Sprung, M. (1975). Psychological investigation in essential hypertensives. *Journal of Psychosomatic Research, 19*, 251–158.

Roberts, B., & Forrester, W. E. (1979). Group relaxation: Acute and chronic effect on hypertension. *Cardiovascular Medicine, 1*, 375–380.

Rofe, Y., & Goldberg, J. (1983). Prolonged exposure to war environment and its effect on the blood pressure of pregnant women. *British Journal of Medical Psychology, 56*(4), 305–311.

Rose, G. A. (1981). A strategy for prevention: Lessons from cardiovascular disease. *British Medical Journal, 282*, 1847–1851.

Rose, G. A., & Blackburn, H. (1968). Cardiovascular survey methods. Geneva: World Health Organization.

Sasaki, N. (1962). High blood pressure and salt intake of the Japanese. *Japanese Heart Journal, 3*, 313.

Seer, P., & Raeburn, J. M. (1980). Meditation training and essential hypertension: A methodological study. *Journal of Behavioral Medicine, 3*, 59–73.

Shkhvatsabaya, I. K. (1982). Psychosocial factors and essential hypertension: Pathogenic and medical aspects. In *Hypertension: Biobehavioural epidemiology aspects* (NIH Publication No. 82-2115). Washington, DC: U.S. Government Printing Office.

Simpson, F. O. (1979). Salt and hypertension: A skeptical review of the evidence. *Clinical Science, 57*, 463–480.

Southam, M. A., Agras, W. S., Taylor, C. B., & Kraemer, H. C. (1982). Relaxation training: Blood pressure during the working day. *Archives of General Psychiatry, 39*, 715–717.

Stamler, J., Farino, E., Mojonnier, L. M., Hall, Y., Moss, D., & Stamler, R. (1980). Prevention and control of hypertension by nutritional hygienic means: Long-term experiments of the Chicago Coronary Prevention Evaluation Program. *Journal of the American Medical Association, 243*, 1819–1823.

Stamler, R., Stamler, J., Riedlinger, H., Algera, G., & Roberts, R. H. (1978). Weights and blood pressure: Findings in hypertension screening of 1 million Americans. *Journal of the American Medical Association, 240*, 1607–1610.

Steptoe, A. (1976). Blood pressure control: A comparison of feedback and instructions using pulse wave velocity measurements. *Psychophysiology, 13*, 528–536.

Steptoe, A. (1981). *Psychological factors in cardiovascular disorders*. London: Academic Press.

Steptoe, A. (1986). Stress mechanism in hypertension. *Postgraduate Medical Journal, 62*, 697–699.

Steptoe, A., Patel, C., Marmot, M. G., & Hunt, B. (1987). Frequency of relaxation practice, blood pressure reduction and the general effects of relaxation following a controlled trial of behavioral modification for reducing coronary risk. *Stress Medicine, 3*, 101–107.

Stone, R. A., & De Leo, J. (1976). Psychotherapeutic control of hypertension. *New England Journal of Medicine, 294*, 80–84.

Surwit, R., & Shapiro, D. (1977). Biofeedback and meditation in the treatment of borderline hypertension. In J. Beatty & H. Legewie (Eds.), *Biofeedback and behavior*. New York: Plenum Press.

Surwit, T. S., Shapiro, D., & Good, M. I. (1978). Comparison of cardiovascular biofeedback, neuromuscular biofeedback and meditation in the treatment of borderline hypertension. *Journal of Consulting and Clinical Psychology, 46*, 252–263.

Svardsudd, K. et al. (1980). Factors associated with the initial blood pressure level and with the subsequent blood pressure increase in a longitudinal population study: The study of men born in 1913. *European Heart Journal, 1*, 345–354.

Svardsudd, K., & Wilhelmsen, L. (1980). Change of blood pressure in relation to other variables and to development of hypertensive disease indices in a longitudinal population study: The study of men born in 1913. *European Heart Journal, 1*, 355.

Swales, J. D. (1980). Dietary salt and hypertension. *Lancet, 1*, 177.

Tasto, D. L., & Huebner, L. A. (1976). The effects of muscle relaxation and stress management on blood pressure levels of normotensives. *Behaviour Research and Therapy, 1*, 89–91.

Taylor, C. B., Farquhar, J. W., Nelson, E., & Agras, W. S. (1977). Relaxation therapy and high blood pressure. *Archives of General Psychiatry, 34*, 339–342.

Tursky, B., Shapiro, D., & Schwartz, G. E. (1972). Automated constant cuff-pressure system for measuring average systolic and diastolic blood pressure in man. *IEEE Trans Biomed. Eng., 19*, 271.

Tyroler, H. A., Hayden, S., & Hames, C. G. (1975). Weight and hypertension: Evans County Studies of Blacks and Whites. In O. Paul (Ed.), *Epidemiology and control of hypertension* (pp. 177–206). New York: Stratton.

Veterans Administration, Cooperative Group on Antihypertensive Agents. (1967). Effects of treatment on morbidity in hypertension: 1. Results in patients with diastolic blood pressures averaging 115 through 129 mm Hg. *Journal of the American Medical Association, 202*, 1028–1034.

Veterans Administration, Cooperative Group on Antihypertensive Agents. (1970). Effects of treatment on morbidity in hypertension: 2. Results in patients with diastolic blood pressure averaging 90 through 114 mm Hg. *Journal of the American Medical Association, 213*, 1143–1152.

Wadden, T. A. (1984). Relaxation treatment for essential hypertension: Specific or nonspecific effects. *Journal of Psychosomatic Research, 28*, 53–61.

Walker, W., Whelton, P., Saito, H., Russell, R., & Hemann, J. (1979). Relation between blood pressure and renin, renin substrate, angiotensin II, aldosterone and urinary sodium and potassium in ambulatory subjects. *Hypertension, 1*, 187–191.

Walsh, P., Dale, A., & Anderson, D. E. (1977). Comparison of biofeedback pulse wave velocity and progressive relaxation in essential hypertension. *Perception Motor Skills, 44*, 439–443.

Watson, R., Langford, H., Abernethy, J., Barnes, T., & Watson, M. (1980). Urinary electrolytes, body weight, and blood pressure: Pooled cross-sectional results among four groups of adolescent females. *Hypertension, 2*, 193–198.

Watts, G. C. M., Edwards, C., Hart, J. T., Hart, M., & Walton, P. (1983). Dietary sodium restriction for mild hypertension in general practice. *British Medical Journal, 286*, 433–436.

V

CONCLUSIONS

V

CONCLUSIONS

19

Anxiety and the Heart:
A Cardiological Perspective

Ray H. Rosenman

Anxiety serves a biologic function that enlists the individual for concerted action and probably involves many brain neurotransmitters that include gamma aminobutyric acid, serotonin, norepinephrine, and dopamine. However, a major brain dysfunction has not been identified for anxiety, an emotion that is part of a biologically useful reaction to danger that prepares the organism for fight or flight and enhances alertness and cardiac output (Klerman, 1985). Physiological changes that reflect autonomic activity are due to increased sympathetic discharge, particularly in the beta-adrenergic system, and reflect the secondary physiologic expression rather than pathology of anxiety (Klein, Zitrin, & Woerner, 1978). It is a universal emotion that has served as an evolutionary force, contributed to biological adaptation, and reinforced the processes of social bonding and communal living (Jeresaty, 1971). However, the factors that underly anxiety responses to exogenous situations (Sheehan & Soto, 1987) are now different from those in which the emotion evolved (Klerman, 1985), and older dangers have been replaced by new fears and anxieties that are more insidious and probably associated with heightened levels of anxiety in many people. Moreover, there also appears to be a high prevalence of individuals with anxiety disorders that are considered to be endogenous (Sheehan & Soto, 1987).

Anxiety disorders have largely been viewed in psychological terms that convey an image of hysteria, hypochondriasis, and overreaction of life stresses and give labels that infer neurosis. However, it is possible that anxiety and panic disorders may have a genetic alteration in benzodiazepine receptors or as yet unspecified ligands, or excessive amount of benzodiazepine receptor antagonists that bind receptors and make people too anxious, whether or not they are under stressful conditions (Braestrup & Nielsen, 1982). People with panic disorder may also have a biological defect within the brain stem redox-regulating apparatus; panic disorder may not be a psychiatric disturbance (Carr & Sheehan, 1984).

Panic disorder differs from day-to-day stress anxiety in normal humans because of familial clustering, age of onset, and its distribution between the sexes, and because it does not respond well to anxiolytic or phenothiazine drugs, improves with monoamine oxidase inhibitors and tricyclic antidepressants, and can be triggered by administration of lactate and other biological means (Gorman, Fyer, Glicklich, King, & Klein, 1981). It is therefore possible that there are inherited defects of endogenous biological mechanisms that are causally related to anxiety (Paul & Skolnick, 1981) and particularly to panic disorder (Gorman et al., 1981). This hypothesis is strengthened by the recent finding of a focal brain abnormality in the region of the parahippo-campal gyrus in patients with panic disorder (Reiman, Raichle, Butler, Herscovitch, & Robins, 1984). The sensitivity to lactate infusion is associated with this regional abnormality of cerebral blood flow in the limbic area that plays a role in central autonomic regulation.

As early as 200 B.C., Hippocrates (see Hackett & Rosenbaum, 1984) recognized a relationship between emotion and health when he advised "Let no one persuade you to cure the headache until he has first given you his soul to be cured. For this is the great error of our day in the treatment of the human body, that physicians separate the soul from the body." Interrelationships between emotions and the cardiovascular system have long been of unique interest in the history of clinical medicine, particularly for the effects of anxiety on cardiovascular function and symptoms. Physicians have long accepted a relationship between emotions and transient cardiovascular responses, as well as with symptoms related to cardiac dysfunction.

Harvey is credited with stating in 1628 that "every affection of the mind that is attended with either pain or pleasure, hope or fear, is the cause of an agitation whose influence extends to the heart." Williams (1836) emphasized the difference between nervous palpitations and organic disease in his classic text, and the functional nature of cardiovascular symptoms associated with anxiety was further emphasized by Da-Costa (1871) in Civil War soldiers in the United States and by MacLean (1867) in British soldiers in the Crimean War. Beard (1867) supported the concept of functional cardiovascular disorders when he introduced the term *neurasthenia*. Although physicians are perhaps still too prone to separate mind and body two millennia after Hippocrates, a dichotomy between emotions and somatic consequences is now less distinct.

A brain–heart dichotomy is partly the result of difficulties inherent in defining and quantifying emotions. Lader (1984) pointed out that subjective anxiety is difficult to define. In the United States one descriptive word is used, whereas most Europeans use two words, the main roots being derived from *angor*, a Latin reference to transitory physical symptoms, and *anxietas*, denoting a predisposition to mental disquiet, uncertainty, and fear. Interest in a role of anxiety in cardiovascular disorders has been stimulated by possible interrelationships with hypertension, cardiac arrhythmias, sudden cardiac death, and mitral valve prolapse. A different relationship between emotions, behaviors, and the cardiovascular system was recognized by Osler (1910) when he observed that his typical patient with ischemic heart disease was "a man whose engine is always set at full speed ahead." In the 1950s, evidence began to accumulate that such Type A behaviors might play an important role in the pathogenesis of ischemic heart disease (Rosenman, Swan, & Carmelli, 1988).

This chapter is not written to dispute any discussions that have been so well presented in this book, but rather to briefly review some areas in which anxiety has been considered to be relevant to cardiovascular disorders. Accordingly, there may some reiteration of data already discussed in earlier chapters. There is ample evidence that sympathetic traffic modulates development of cardiac arrhythmias (Lown, 1979). The final common pathway is via efferent vagal and sympathetic nerve fibers that act on electrophysiologic properties of the heart and autonomic interactions thus regulate myocardial electrical instability (MEI) in the conscious state (Lown & Verrier, 1976; Skinner, 1985). It is plausible that emotions such as anxiety may play a causal role in cardiac arrhythmias (Hageman, Goldberg, Armour, & Randall, 1973).

Autonomic nerves are driven by preganglionic sympathetic neurons in the spinal cord that are under control of descending brain pathways. A major source of background autonomic neural activity thus depends on the integrity of neurons that drive sympathetic nervous system centers that are part of contiguous adrenergic neurons. Central stimuli that increase sympathetic neural traffic and suppress baroreflex activity usually produce a rise of blood pressure and heart rate and increased release of epinephrine, whereas vagal nerve activity is diminished. During the post-stimulus period, the blood pressure usually remains elevated, baroreflexes are no longer inhibited, and vagal excitation occurs. It is in this vulnerable period of increased vagal tone and residual sympathetic neural drive, for example, that ventricular arrhythmias may occur after exercise (Lown, 1979), perhaps related to an associated acute decrease of serum potassium (Brown, 1985).

This is relevant for sudden cardiac death, which is commonly, if not invariably, due to ventricular fibrillation (Skinner, 1985). Its pathophysiology is not merely coronary artery disease (Lown, 1979), but is best comprehended in relation to MEI, which provides the substrate upon which a triggering factor such as adrenergic stimulation can precipitate ventricular fibrillation (Lown & Verrier, 1976). Both MEI and triggering catecholamine input are related to higher nervous system activity (Lown, 1979). Increased MEI in humans is induced by overt or silent myocardial ischemia, and higher neural traffic can thus precipitate arrhythmic sudden cardiac death in patients with coronary artery disease. Important triggering factors often relate to neurophysiologic activity that occurs in response to psychological stresses (Lown & Verrier, 1976; Skinner, 1985), and coronary artery vasospasm and platelet aggregation may play a role (Freeman & Nixon, 1985; Lee, Kimura, & DeQuattro, 1989; Rozanski et al., 1988).

There are many anecdotal reports that link sudden cardiac death with profound emotions. However, in successfully resuscitated patients, Reich, De Silva, Lown, and Murawski (1981) found that emotionally stressful events that caused major anxiety had occurred in proximate relationships to ventricular arrhythmias. The role of higher neural traffic in the genesis of lethal arrhythmias is now firmly based on evidence that links emotionally stressful events to sudden cardiac death in both animals and humans (Lown, 1979). Autonomic neural activity can induce ventricular ectopy and lower the threshold for ventricular fibrillation (Skinner, 1985). The relation to sudden cardiac death can be exemplified in several ways, among which is the fact that it occurs more frequently in males, plausibly related to their greater catecholamine response to stressors, compared to females (Frankenhaeuser, 1982). Moreover, in females who suffer sudden cardiac death there is often a history of smoking, psychiatric disorder, or taking psychotropic drugs (Talbott, Kuller, & Perper, 1981). In patients with myocardial ischemia, relatively minor physical or emotional stress can precipitate sudden cardiac death (Reich et al., 1981; Schwartz, 1984). Finally, long-term mortality in postinfarction patients is strongly related to psychosocial factors (Ruberman, Weinblatt, & Goldberg, 1984).

Anxiety may influence behaviors and habits that are relevant to cardiovascular disorders. For example, diet and weight are related to serum lipids, blood pressure, and ischemic heart disease. Alcohol has a more complex relationship. Considerable evidence confirms a relationship between moderate alcohol consumption and reduced incidence of ischemic heart disease in population-based, as well as prospective, studies (Marmot, 1984), despite its adverse effects on blood pressure in hypertensive (Klatzky, Friedman, Siegelman, & Gerard, 1977). There is good evidence for interactions between drinking habits and life events, and studies of inpatients who are being treated for alcohol detoxification indicate a high prevalence of anxiety disorders

(Weiss & Rosenberg, 1985). However, alcohol may play a biological stress-buffering role for some individuals (Neff, 1984; Strahlendorf & Strahlendorf, 1981). Cigarette smoking also may provide a buffer for anxiety in some, but for others may have synergistic effects with environmental stress on autonomic neural traffic and associated cardiovascular responses. Both caffeine and nicotine increase locus ceruleus function and may therefore be anxionic. The acute administration of caffeine can stimulate autonomic neural traffic and affect mood and sleep. However, its chronic ingestion probably has little effect on either autonomic traffic or cardiovascular responses and no confirmed effects on serum lipids or incidence of ischemic heart disease; the discrepancies in published data largely reflect differences in caffeine habituation among research and control subjects (Curatolo & Robertson, 1983). Anxiety may affect sleep patterns directly or via its influence on consumption of food, alcohol, caffeine, and nicotine. This is of importance in patients with ischemic heart disease because an acute coronary event can occur at times of sleep deprivation (Nixon, 1982).

A relationship between anxiety and hypertension remains unproven, despite widespread belief to the contrary. The central nervous system is critically involved in regulation of the blood pressure and integrates information from both the organism and the environment in order to provide neurohormonal adjustments that are essential to maintenance of the blood pressure. A common hypothesis suggests that environmental factors such as psychosocial stressors may stimulate autonomic overactivity that increases cardiovascular responses and elevates the blood pressure. This is based on accepted facts concerned with neurohormonal circulatory regulation. Thus blood pressure can be increased by activation of higher neural sites with neuroanatomic connections to the sympathetic nervous system, and these sites connect with higher centers involved in the perception of the environment. Considerable data indicate that external stressors are capable of elevating arterial blood pressure via neurohormonal mechanisms (Diamond, 1982), and animal studies support the hypothesis that certain types of stress can induce elevated blood pressure (Henry & Stephens, 1977). However, when the stressor is removed, sustained hypertension is the exception. In fact, a recent task force that was assigned to review this subject (Brody et al., 1987) concluded that there was inadequate evidence to support the common belief that stress alone can induce sustained hypertension in otherwise healthy animals.

Data concerning stress–blood pressure relationships in humans are even less significant. Stress can transiently elevate blood pressure but, as in animals, hypertension is infrequently sustained after the stressor is removed. Changing cultural norms from more primitive to more complex may be associated with rise of blood pressure (Salmond, Joseph, Prior, Stanley, & Wessen, 1985), but this probably involves interactions with dietary and other relevant variables. Predisposing genetic factors, excessive salt intake, or renal disease indeed appear necessary for the reliable expression of stress-induced hypertension in both animals and humans (Brody et al., 1987).

Evidence for a causal relationship of stress to hypertension is largely based on studies of acute responses that occur in some offspring of hypertensive parents (Falkner, Onesti, Angelakos, Fernandez, & Langman, 1979). It is difficult to find any strong evidence in the literature that hypertensives exhibit greater levels of anxiety than do normotensives, despite the old and still widespread belief that anxiety is causally related to hypertension. Many antihypertensive drugs and even the diagnosis of hypertension can induce anxiety and other behavioral responses. Moreover, hypertension can affect behavior at anatomic, physiologic, and emotional levels, and hypertensives have alterations of physiologic function that interact with behavioral factors (Elias & Streeten, 1980), further clouding any causal relationship between anxiety and hypertension.

Plasma catecholamine levels tend to be higher in many hypertensives (Esler et al., 1977), and heightened autonomic neural traffic may alter emotions and behaviors, particularly in younger borderline hypertensives. Enhanced pressor responses to psychological stressors that occur in some hypertensives and their offspring probably have a genetic basis that does not depend on cognitive perception. Young hyperreactors can evolve into people with sustained hypertension (Falkner, Onesti, & Hamstra, 1981), but established hypertensives are not consistently more reactive to stressors compared to normotensives. Subjects with Type A behavior generally respond to external stressors with enhanced cardiovascular reactivity, compared to Type B subjects (Rosenman & Chesney, 1982) but do not exhibit differences in prevalence of sustained hypertension (Rosenman, 1987).

Blood pressure variability in the daily milieu during ambulatory monitoring does not correlate with either severity or duration of hypertension, and there is no evidence of increased variability in young borderline hypertensives (Conway, 1983). Furthermore, ambulatory variability does not differ in subjects whose blood pressure is normal or mildly or markedly elevated (Pickering, Harshfield, Kleinert, Blank, & Laragh, 1982), and there are no population-based studies that show that hyperreactive normotensives exhibit an increased likelihood for sustained hypertension. There is therefore little evidence to indicate that transient, stress-induced rise of blood pressure is a causal precursor of sustained hypertension. Stress-induced cardiovascular responses may sometimes be a correlate or marker for the risk of developing hypertension, but not its cause (Julius, 1988). However, even this is probably not related to anxiety. Thus patients with chronic anxiety, such as those with mitral valve prolapse syndrome, do not exhibit increased reactivity to laboratory stressors (Mantysaari, Antila, & Peltonen, 1988), and they commonly exhibit hypotension (Devereux, Brown, Lutas, Kramer-Fox, & Laragh, 1982) and an unusually low prevalence of hypertension (see chap. 13).

It was therefore pointed out in a recent review (Rosenman & Ward, 1988) that cardiovascular responses to a wide variety of cognitive and physical stressors have long been measured in the laboratory, with the hypothesis that exaggerated reactivity plays a pathogenetic role in the development of essential hypertension. However, there are few data to support a belief that behavioral differences of cognitive perception of stressors account for observed differences of reactivity. With the possible exception of responses to cold pressor testing, cardiovascular reactivity in the laboratory setting is not found to predict hypertension or to account for differences of blood pressure variability in the natural environment. It is also relevant that antihypertensive therapy does not reduce cardiovascular stress responses either in laboratory tests or the natural environment, supporting a dual, largely independent regulation of the basal and reactive blood pressures (Reis & LeDoux, 1987).

It can be concluded (Rosenman & Ward, 1988) that there is little support for the use of cardiovascular reactivity tests to delineate either the pathogenesis of hypertension, the evaluation of hypertensive subjects, or the efficacy of antihypertensive therapy. An effect of anxiety on the blood pressure is transient, rather than having sustained effects or playing any causal role in the pathogenesis of essential hypertension. Relaxation-type therapies may provide some benefits, but I do not believe that such approaches are well directed at the pathogenesis of elevated blood pressure in most hypertensive patients. More important in this regard may be an association of the blood pressure level with hostility and anger dimensions. It appears that the blood pressure level and possibly the risk for hypertension are better correlated with ineffective anger management and expression than with the level of anxiety (Rosenman, 1985).

Relations between anxiety and cardiovascular disorders are exemplified in several types of patients. One primarily has an anxiety problem that is associated with somatic symptoms that suggest heart disease, as in mitral valve prolapse syndrome. A second is a patient who is healthy and not anxious but who develops symptoms that are interpreted as being due to heart disease and that can lead to iatrogenic disorders. A third is a patient with minor heart disease that is complicated by major anxiety. A fourth is one with major heart disease who develops secondary anxiety, as occurs with ischemic heart disease, in which a relation of anxiety to anginal symptoms is well known. In patients awaiting bypass graft surgery, for example, the frequency and severity of anginal symptoms are related far more to psychological and behavioral factors such as disturbed sleep, distress, and life dissatisfactions, and to hostile dimensions than they are to the severity of the coronary artery disease (Jenkins, Stanton, Klein, Savageau, & Harken, 1983).

An important link between anxiety and functional mitral valve prolapse is discussed in chapter 13 of this volume. A different link between anxiety and illness is well documented in postinfarct patients. Anxiety probably occurs in most and may often be more than mild. Most face difficult adjustments to loss of status, threat of dependency, changed family and vocational relationships, and fear of death. There is a predictable progression of the psychological responses to myocardial infarction that in many involves anxiety, depression, denial, and convalescence (Cassem & Hackett, 1977). Type A individuals appear to employ more denial and suppression of symptoms that enable them to endure stress at higher levels and for longer intervals, compared to Type Bs. Such denial may lead to delay in seeking medical care after onset of symptoms, with adverse consequences for immediate survival. However, denial is a coping mechanism that may be used to suppress anxiety (Gentry, Baider, & Oude-Weme, 1983) and might favorably influence long-term survival. It is possible that cognitive denial, by reducing anxiety, might diminish autonomic neural traffic that potentially has adverse consequences for occurrence of fatal and nonfatal coronary events (Rosenman, 1988).

Although it is apparent that ischemic heart disease may cause anxiety, it is unlikely that anxiety plays any causal role in the pathogenesis of coronary atherosclerosis. The fact that coronary atherosclerosis is infrequent in subjects with anxiety states (Bass, 1984; Blumenthal, Thompson, Williams, & Kong, 1979; Costa, 1981; DeMaria, Lee, Amsterdam, Low, & Mason, 1980; Schocken, Worden, Harrison, & Spielberger, 1984; Sprafkin, McCroskery, Lantinga, & Hills, 1984) strongly suggests that anxiety actually plays a protective role against coronary atherosclerosis, although for obscure reasons. The role of Type A behavior pattern in ischemic heart disease represents a different relationship of emotions to cardiovascular disease and occurs in contrast to the association of overt anxiety with various other cardiovascular disorders. Among component Type A behaviors, strong predictors of ischemic heart disease are competitiveness and hostility and anger dimensions (Rosenman et al., 1988). Montagu (1976) has pointed out that the drive for preservation of the species and the self leads to a type of competitiveness and aggression that is biologically adaptive, life-serving, and phylogenetically programmed and common to both animals and humans. However, other forms of aggression are not and may therefore be biologically maladaptive. They have not evolved but are exclusively found to have arisen out of the human experience.

Montagu also emphasized that the principal factor operating in animal evolution is cooperation, rather than the divisiveness and inappropriate aggression, competitiveness, and conflict that characterize the human experience and are exemplified by the coronary-prone facets of Type A behavior pattern. Type A behavior is a constellation of behaviors that are used to cope with the human experience. Although Type A behavior does not equate with anxiety, as is usually thought, it is possible that there is an underlying covert anxiety associated with the threat of failure and that this leads to Type A competitiveness, aggressiveness, accelerated pace of activities, impatience, and the hostile behaviors that are associated with an increased incidence of ischemic heart disease. At this juncture, I believe that a carefully concealed and deep-seated anxiety underlies an inappropriate competitiveness that confers coronary-proneness in Type As. This underlies the hostile and other behaviors that may only spuriously be related to ischemic heart disease.

The discussions in this book confirm an old belief that anxiety has many interrelationships with cardiovascular disorders. However, superb early observers appear to have been correct in their emphasis on relationships of anxiety to symptoms and functional disorders rather than to organic diseases. In particular, the widely held belief that anxiety, cardiovascular reactivity, and stress responses play causal roles in the pathogenesis of hypertension and coronary heart disease increasingly lacks validity.

REFERENCES

Bass, C. (1984). Mitral valve prolapse and anxiety disorders: No longer an enigma. *British Journal of Psychiatry, 145,* 447–448.

Beard, G. (1867). Neurasthenia or nervous exhaustion. *Boston Medical and Surgery Journal, 53,* 217–221.

Blumenthal, J. A., Thompson, L. W., Williams, R. B., & Kong, Y. (1979). Association of anxiety proneness and coronary heart disease. *Journal of Psychosomatic Research, 23,* 17–21.

Braestrup, C., & Nielsen, M. (1982). Anxiety. *Lancet, 74,* 1030–1034.

Brody, M. J., Natelson, B. H., Anderson, E., Folkow, B. U. G., Levy, M. N., Obrist, P. A., Reis, D. F., Rosenman, R. H., & Williams, R. B. (1987). Behavioral mechanisms in hypertension. *Circulation, 76,* (Part 2), 95–100.

Brown, M. J. (1985). Hypokalemia from beta-2-receptor stimulation by circulating epinephrine. *American Journal of Cardiology, 56,* 3D–9D.

Carr, D. B., & Sheehan, D. V. (1984). Panic anxiety: A new biological model. *Journal of Clinical Psychiatry, 45,* 323–330.

Cassem, N. H., & Hackett, T. P. (1977). Psychological aspects of myocardial infarction. *Medical Clinics of North America, 61,* 711–721.

Conway, J. (1983). Hemodynamic aspects of essential hypertension in humans. *Physiological Reviews, 63,* 617–660.

Costa, P. T. (1981). Neuroticism as a factor in the diagnosis of angina pectoris. *Behavioral Medicine Update, 3,* 18–20.

Curatolo, P. W., & Robertson, D. (1983). The health consequences of caffeine. *Annals of Internal Medicine, 98,* 641–653.

DaCosta, J. M. (1871). On irritable heart: A clinical study of functional cardiac disorder and its consequences. *American Journal of Medical Sciences, 61,* 17–521.

DeMaria, A. N., Lee, G., Amsterdam, E. A., Low, R., & Mason, D. T. (1980). The anginal syndrome with normal coronary arteries: Etiologic and prognostic considerations. *Journal of the American Medical Association, 244,* 826–828.

Devereux, R. B., Brown, W. T., Lutas, E. M., Kramer-Fox, R., & Laragh, J. H. (1982). Association of mitral valve prolapse with low body weight and low blood pressures. *Lancet, 2,* 792–794.

Diamond, E. L. (1982). The role of anger and hostility in essential hypertension and coronary heart disease. *Psychology Bulletin, 92,* 410–413.

Elias, M. F., & Streeten, D. H. P. (1980). *Hypertension and cognitive processes.* Mount Desert, ME: Beech-Hill.

Esler, M., Julius, S., Zweifler, A., Randall, O., Harburg, E., Gardiner, H., & DeQuattro, V. (1977). Mild high-renin essential hypertension: Neurogenic human hypertension? *New England Journal of Medicine, 296,* 405–411.

Falkner, B., Onesti, G., Angelakos, E. T., Fernandez, M., & Langman, C. (1979). Cardiovascular response to mental stress in normal adolescents with hypertensive parents. *Hypertension, 1,* 23–30.

Falkner, B., Onesti, G., & Hamstra, B. (1981). Stress response characteristics of adolescents with high genetic risk for essential hypertension: A five-year follow-up. *Clinical and Experimental Hypertension, 3,* 583–591.

Frankenhaeuser, M. (1982). The sympathetic–adrenal and pituitary–adrenal response to challenge: Comparison between the sexes. In T. M. Dembroski, T. H. Schmidt, & G. Blumchen (Eds.), *Biobehavioral bases of coronary heart disease* (pp. 91–105). Basel: Karger.

Freeman, L. J., & Nixon, P. G. F. (1985). Are coronary artery spasm and progressive damage to the heart associated with the hyperventilation syndrome? *British Journal of Cardiology, 291,* 851–852.

Gentry, W. D., Baider, L., & Oude-Weme, J. D. (1983). Type A/B differences in coping with acute myocardial infarction: Further considerations. *Heart and Lung, 12,* 212–214.

Gorman, J. M., Fyer, A. F., Glicklich, J., King, D. L., & Klein, D. F. (1981). Mitral valve prolapse and panic disorders: Effect of imipramine. In D. F. Klein & J. Rabkin (Eds.), *Anxiety: New research and changing concepts* (pp. 317–325). New York: Raven Press.

Hackett, T. P., & Rosenbaum, J. F. (1984). Emotional, psychiatric disorders and the heart. In E. Braunwald (Ed.), *Heart diesease* (pp. 1826–1946). Philadelphia: W.B. Saunders.

Hageman, G. R., Goldberg, J. M., Armour, J. A., & Randall, W. D. (1973). Cardiac dysrhythmias induced by autonomic nerve stimulation. *American Journal of Cardiology, 32,* 823–830.

Henry, J. P., & Stephens, P. M. (1977). In *Stress, health and social environment.* New York: Springer-Verlag.

Jenkins, C. D., Stanton, B. A., Klein, M. D., Savageau, J. A., & Harken, D. E. (1983). Correlates of angina pectoris among men awaiting coronary by-pass surgery. *Psychosomatic Medicine, 45,* 141–153.

Jeresaty, R. M. (1971). The syndrome associated with midsystolic click and/or late systolic murmur: Analysis of 32 cases. *Chest, 59,* 643–647.

Julius, S. (1988). The blood pressure seeking properties of the central nervous system. *Hypertension, 6,* 177–185.

Klatzky, A. L., Friedman, G. D., Siegelman, A. B., & Gerard, M. J. (1977). Alcohol consumption and blood pressure. *New England Journal of Medicine, 196,* 1194–1200.

Klein, D. F., Zitrin, C. M., & Woerner, M. (1978). Antidepressants, anxiety, panic and phobias. In M. A. Lipton, A. DiMascio, & K. F. Killam (Eds.), *Psychopharmacology: A generation of progress* (pp. 1401–1410). New York: Raven Press.

Klerman, G. L. (1985). Understanding anxiety: Normal emotion, symptoms, and clinical disorder (Special issue). *Internal Medicine, 6,* 3–12.

Lader, M. (1984). Neurotransmitters and anxiety: Overview. *Psychopathology, 17,* (Suppl. 3), 3–7.

Lee, D. D., Kimura, S., & DeQuattro, V. (1989). Noradrenergic activity and silent ischaemia in hypertensive patients with stable angina: Effect of metoprolol. *Lancet, 1,* 403–406.

Lown, B. (1979). Sudden cardiac death: The major challenge confronting contemporary cardiology. *American Journal of Cardiology, 43,* 313–328.

Lown, B., & Verrier, R. L. (1976). Neural activity and ventricular fibrillation. *New England Journal of Medicine, 294,* 1165–1170.

MacLean, W. C. (1867). Disease of the heart in the British Army: The cause and the remedy. *British Medical Journal, 1,* 161–164.

Mantysaari, M. J., Antila, K. J., & Peltonen, T. E. (1988). Blood pressure reactivity in patients with neurocirculatory asthenia. *American Journal of Hypertension, 1,* 132–139.

Marmot, M. G. (1984). Alcohol and coronary heart disease. *International Journal of Epidemiology, 13,* 160–167.

Montagu, A. (1976). *The nature of human aggression.* New York: Oxford University Press.

Neff, J. A. (1984). The stress-buffering role of alcohol consumption: The importance of symptom dimension. *Journal of Human Stress, 10,* 35–42.

Nixon, P. G. F. (1982). Are there clinically significant prodromal signs and symptoms of impending sudden death? *Practical Cardiology, 8,* 173–182.

Osler, W. (1910). The Lumleian lectures on angina pectoris. *Lancet, 1,* 829–844.

Paul, S. M., & Skolnick, P. (1981). Benzodiazepine receptors and psychopathological states: Toward a neurobiology of anxiety. In D. F. Klein & J. Rabkin (Eds.), *Anxiety: New research and changing concepts* (pp. 215–234). New York: Raven Press.

Pickering, T. G., Harshfield, G. A., Kleinert, H. D., Blank, S. B., & Laragh, J. H. (1982). Blood pressure during normal daily activities, sleep, and exercise: Comparison of values in normal and hypertensive subjects. *Journal of the American Medical Association, 247,* 992–996.

Reich, P. De Silva, R. A., Lown, B., & Murawski, J. (1981). Acute psychological disturbances preceding life-threatening ventricular arrhythmias. *Journal of the American Medical Association, 246,* 233–235.

Reiman, E. M., Raichle, M. E., Butler, F. K., Herscovitch, P., & Robins, E. (1984). A focal brain abnormality in panic disorder: A severe form of anxiety. *Nature, 310,* 683–685.

Reis, D. J., & Le Doux, J. E. (1987). Some central nervous mechanisms governing resting and behaviorally coupled control of blood pressure. *Circulation, 76*(Suppl.), 1–9.

Rosenman, R. H. (1985). Health consequences of anger and implications for treatment. In M. A. Chesney & R. H. Rosenman (Eds.), *Anger and hostility in cardiovascular and behavioral disorders.* Washington, DC: Hemisphere.

Rosenman, R. H. (1987). Type A behavior and hypertension. In S. Julius & D. R. Bassett (Eds.), *Handbook of hypertension: Vol. 9. Behavioral factors in hypertension* (pp. 147–149). Amsterdam: Elsevier.

Rosenman, R. H. (1988). The impact of certain emotions in cardiovascular disorders. In M. P. Janisse (Ed.), *Individual differences, stress, and health psychology* (pp. 1–23). New York: Springer-Verlag.

Rosenman, R. H., & Chesney, M. A. (1982). Stress, Type A behavior, and coronary disease. In L. Goldberger & S. Breznitz (Eds.), *Handbook of stress: Theoretical and clinical aspects* (pp. 547–565). New York: Free Press.

Rosenman, R. H., Swan, G. E., & Carmelli, D. (1988). Definition, assessment and evolution of the Type A behavior pattern. In B. K. Houston & C. R. Snyder (Eds.), *Type A behavior pattern: Research, theory, and intervention* (pp. 8–30). New York: Wiley.

Rosenman, R. H., & Ward, M. M. (1988). The changing concept of cardiovascular reactivity. *Stress Medicine, 4,* 241–251.

Rozanski, A., Bairey, C. N., Krantz, D. S., Friedman, J., Resser, K. J., Morell, M., Hilton-Chalfen, S., Hestrin, L., Bietendorf, J., & Berman, D. S. (1988). Mental stress and the induction of silent myocardial ischemia in patients with coronary artery disease. *New England Journal of Medicine, 318,* 1005–1012.

Ruberman, W., Weinblatt, E., & Goldberg, J. D. (1984). Psychosocial influences on mortality after myocardial infarction. *New England Journal of Medicine, 311,* 552–559.

Salmond, C. E., Joseph, J. G., Prior, I. A. M., Stanley, D. G., & Wessen, A. F. (1985). Longitudinal analysis of the relationship between blood pressure and migration: The Tokelau Island migrant study. *American Journal of Epidemiology, 122,* 291–301.

Schwartz, P. J. (1984). Stress and sudden cardiac death: The role of the autonomic nervous system. *Journal of Clinical Psychiatry Monograph, 2,* 7–13.

Sheehan, D. V., & Soto, S. (1987). Diagnosis and treatment of pathological anxiety. *Stress Medicine, 3,* 21–32.

Schocken, D. C., Worden, T. J., Harrison, E. E., & Spielberger, C. D. (1984). Anxiety differences in patients with angina pectoris, nonanginal chest pain, and coronary artery disease (Abstract). *Circulation, 70,* II-387.

Skinner, J. E. (1985). Psychosocial stress and sudden cardiac death: Brain mechanisms. In R. E. Beamish, P. K. Singal, & N. A. Dhalla (Eds.), *Stress and heart disease* (pp. 44–59). Boston: Martinus Nijhoff.

Sprafkin, R. P., McCroskery, J. H., Lantinga, L. J., & Hills, N. (1984). Cardiovascular and psychological characteristics of patients with chest pain. *Behavioral Medicine Update, 6,* 11.

Strahlendorf, J., & Strahlendorf, H. (1981). Response of locus coeruleus neurons to direct application of ethanol. *Society of Neuroscience Abstract, 104,* 7B.

Talbott, E., Kuller, L. H., & Perper, J. (1981). Sudden unexpected death in women: Biologic and psychosocial origins. *American Journal of Epidemiology, 114,* 671–682.

Weiss, K. J., & Rosenberg, D. J. (1985). Prevalence of anxiety disorder among alcoholics. *Journal of Clinical Psychology, 46,* 3–5.

Williams, J. C. (1836). *Practical observations on nervous and sympathetic-palpitation of the heart.* London: Lingman, Rees, Orme & Browne.

20

Anxiety and the Heart:
A Psychological Perspective

D. G. Byrne

Anxiety is one of the most fundamental of all psychological constructs. An understanding of its origins, forms, or functions is basic to the mastery of many discrete or interrelated areas of psychology, encompassing theories of learning and motivation, explanations of complex human cognitive and motor performance, and, of course, accounts of myriad kinds of behavioral and emotional disorders that are the province of abnormal psychology. Seen in a phylogenetic context, anxiety endows the individual with a degree of survival advantage, best illustrated in the form of the "flight or fight" response to threat or challenge. The arousal component of anxiety, which according to the classical James–Lange theory (James, 1890) constitutes the very essence of the emotion, relates positively to performance enhancement in a variety of cognitive and motor tasks up to a certain level of arousal, this effect being enshrined in the Yerkes–Dodson law (Yerkes & Dodson, 1908). Anxiety, therefore, would seem to be fundamental not just to psychology but to the biological integrity of the individual.

This assumes, however, that phylogenetic processes keep pace with environmental demands, and this assumption is not easily satisfied by the environmental conditions of the late 20th century. Patterns of response to threat or challenge, spurred on by heightened levels of sympathetic arousal, are constrained by cultural forces, social structures, and interpersonal expectations to a greater extent now than in the distant past (Mandler, 1984), and the degree to which sympathetic arousal may be dissipated by physical action (flight or fight) is limited by the demands and impositions of a modern society. The result, although simplistically conceived of, is the state of emotional distress to which we have attached the label "anxiety." From a clinical viewpoint, anxiety does not imply survival but rather the threat of suffering, incapacity, and serious disruption to most areas of human function. At the very least, the experience of anxiety signals the conscious recognition of an individual's inability to cope.

The experience of anxiety is seen and reported in most cultures and societies. Its ubiquity is nicely encapsulated in Rycroft's (1968) comment: "Anxiety is such a common experience that one would be disinclined to believe anyone who claimed to be immune to it" (p. 1). In many situations, and particularly those involving real or imagined threat, anxiety is the expected response. In such circumstances, its absence rather than its presence would be considered abnormal. McReynolds, in the introductory chapter of this book, conveys this message. In other circumstances, in which the experience of the emotional state of distress is out of proportion to the precipitating events in the individual's environment, or if in fact there are no identifiable events that can be seen to have warranted the response of anxiety, or, furthermore, if the response outlasts the presence or salience of such events, anxiety may be said to have entered the realm of the abnormal (as can be seen in chap. 2). Anxiety is, in other words, an essentially dimensional construct. It might be added, however, that although the notion of dimensionality reinforces the normality of the emotional experience, it may act to confuse the distinction that must, from time to time, be made between anxiety as an expected response and anxiety as a psychiatric condition.

Contemporary conceptualizations of clinical anxiety portray it both as a state, that is, the immediate experience and reporting of emotional distress, and as a trait, typically construed as a predisposition to respond with distress in the face of threat or challenge. Spielberger's approach to the measurement of anxiety, as set out in chapter 4, emphasizes this conjoined binary nature of the emotion. The notion of trait anxiety is similar in many ways to Eysenck's (1957) view of neuroticism, which was seen as a basic instability of personality leading to an incapacity to cope and a tendency to respond with emotional distress to life situations that presented a threat or challenge. The clinical and conceptual relations between neuroticism and neurosis as a psychiatric condition are widely debated (Henderson, Byrne, & Duncan-Jones, 1981), but it is widely accepted that anxiety forms the focal point of this area of discourse.

What is also agreed is that the experience of anxiety is both affectively and physically unpleasant. Reber (1985) defined anxiety as "a vague, unpleasant emotional state with qualities of apprehension, dread, distress and uneasiness" (p. 43). Sarason and Sarason (1987) added to this broad view the experience, variously, of symptoms of "rapid heart rate, shortness of breath, diarrhea, loss of appetite, fainting, dizziness, sweating, sleeplessness, frequent urination and tremors" (p. 145). Reference to any of the now abundant checklists and inventories of anxiety (McReynolds, 1968) reinforces the idea that anxiety is experienced both as affective and somatic pain (the James–Lange theory held that the affective experience was simply the perception of biological disequilibrium).

The crucial point to be drawn from this is that the experience of anxiety may be characterized by pronounced feelings of physical discomfort, and for many individuals and for many reasons (see chap. 3), these feelings may be perceived as, confused with, or consciously wished to be symptoms of physical illness. Equally important (see chap. 8), the experience of anxiety within the somatic domain mimics, to a large degree, the signs and symptoms of a variety of cardiovascular conditions. It is not surprising, then, that unsophisticated individuals might, having almost certainly themselves experienced anxiety, make the link between this emotional state and risk or onset of cardiovascular disease.

A good deal of highly sophisticated reasoning has led to the same conclusion with regard to the links between anxiety and illness broadly defined (Levi, 1971; Selye, 1976). Clear, causal pathways linking environmental events, often through the mediating effects of cognitive mechanisms, to the experience of both affective distress and somatic activation, have been postulated. In this respect, the work of Holmes and Rahe (1967) on life events, Lazarus (1982) on the role of cognitive interpretation, and Levi (1972) on the biology of the stress response is generally considered exemplary. Evidence deriving from this pioneering work, taken collectively, supports a sequential association between exposure to life events perceived as threatening or challenging and individual responses characterized by sympathetic activation and self-reported affective distress, the latter identical to or closely resembling anxiety (insofar as it is clinically described).

Taken thus far, the evidence, generally speaking, is not in serious dispute (Tennant, Langeluddecke, & Byrne, 1985). More particularly, it is clear that the activity of the cardiovascular system is regulated by way of a complex set of neurochemical mechanisms (see chap. 6) and in view of such fundamental neural involvement, one might expect direct and widespread psychological influences on cardiovascular activity. In the normal subject under controlled, laboratory conditions, these influences may be seen and measured (Steptoe, 1981). Subjects typically respond to a wide variety of environmental and cognitive challenges with cardiovascular activation (Surwit, Williams, & Shapiro, 1982), most frequently measured as variation in heart rate, diastolic or systolic blood pressure, limb blood flow, pulse volume, or pulse transit time (Greenfield & Sternbach, 1977). There is, moreover, good evidence that psychoneuroendocrine responses underlie visible alterations in cardiovascular activity (Frankenhaeuser, 1979).

Steptoe (1981) has warned, however, that not all hemodynamic indications of cardiovascular activation obtained by surface electrode technology may be trusted to reflect the direct influence of environmental or cognitive challenge (when these have been applied in a laboratory situation). A range of factors, including motor components of task responses, age, sex, the nature of the challenge and the context in which it is administered may all act to produce essentially artifactual variations in measured cardiovascular activation. Additionally, it may be seen in chapters 5 and 7 that the associations that are possible to establish in normal subjects become less clear-cut and replicable in subjects with either physical or psychological pathology.

Much of this evidence deriving from psychophysiological investigation, it must be said, relates specifically to the pathogenesis of hypertension. At the beginning of the decade, Steptoe (1981) was led by the available material to conclude that "normotensives who respond to demanding tasks with pronounced increases in heart rate and arterial pressure do not display generalized autonomic lability but may have a specific predisposition towards cardiovascular dysfunction" (p. 120). In a more recent review of the evidence, Rosenman and Ward (1988) arrived at the conclusion that "there is little support for the use of laboratory stress testing to delineate either the pathogenesis of hypertension, the evaluation of hypertensive subjects, or the efficacy of antihypertensive therapy" (p. 241). The progression from guarded optimism to an open negation of the hypothesis linking autonomic reactivity to cardiovascular disorder in the course of seven years recommends a cautious approach to the area. Despite a great deal of research effort directed toward the establishment of associations between autonomic reactivity and the Type A behavior pattern (see chap. 15) there is, moreover, no conclusive evidence to indicate a link, direct or otherwise, between cardiovascular reactivity to a wide range of environmental and cognitive challenges, and risk or incidence of coronary heart disease.

Failure to achieve consistent associations between autonomic reactivity measured under a variety of laboratory controlled circumstances and cardiovascular dysfunction in its various manifestations, and a consequent failure to discover the possible pathogenic pathways linking neural regulation of cardiovascular activity to disorders of that organ system, have been one of the more disappointing outcomes in this broad area. Reasons for this may be sought in several directions, including inaccuracies and inadequacies of psychophysiological measurement, inconsistencies in the selection and presentation of challenges designed to produce cardiovascular activation, and failure to take account of response variation attributable to intersubject differences. Most likely, however, failure to link autonomic reactivity in any clear and consistent way with cardiovascular disorder has arisen out of a simplistic view that there should be any montonic relation between discrete, cross-sectional, artificially induced variations in single parameters of cardiovascular activity and manifestations of cardiovascular pathology, the genesis of which are unbounded in their complexity.

Two additional sets of evidence must, however, be considered in any exploration of the relation between anxiety and the heart. These are, first, the extent to which affective distress acts to exacerbate the levels of established risk factors for coronary heart disease and, second, the epidemiological associations that may be found between environmental stressors, affective distress, and risk or incidence of coronary heart disease. Hopkins and Williams (1981) reported evidence implicating some 246 discrete risk factors, mostly metabolic or physiological, in the genesis of coronary heart disease. Of these, most emphasis has been given to just three: elevated levels of certain lipids in the blood, high arterial pressure (both diastolic and systolic), and present or immediate past cigarette smoking. The epidemiological evidence linking the presence of combinations of these factors with risk of coronary heart disease is readily available for consultation (although it is by no means uncontentious) and will not be further discussed. The supposed simplicity of these factors and their purported amenability to modification have made them the focus of innumerable programs of primary prevention of cardiovascular disease. More important, however, each factor is, in different ways, considered to be influenced by aspects of human behavior; cigarette smoking is itself a human behavior, serum lipid levels are influenced by the behavior of eating, and blood pressure is held to vary with a range of behavioral and psychological factors.

Although cigarette smoking is to a degree under conscious control (Byrne & Whyte, 1987), it is, above all, a habit based on both chemical and psychosocial addictions (Pechacek & McAlister, 1981). Its origins are to be found principally in peer pressure during adolescence (Pederson & Lefcoe, 1985), possibly mediated by personality (Cherry & Kiernan, 1976). There is some evidence that acute episodes of environmental stress may increase rates of cigarette consumption in already established smokers (O'Connor, 1980; Stanaway & Watson, 1980), but there is no evidence whatsoever that stress plays any role in the onset of smoking behavior among previously nonsmoking individuals. Moreover, increases in rates of cigarette consumption in established smokers secondary to the experience of stress quite rapidly return to baseline (preexisting levels of consumption) on cessation of stressor exposure. Smoking is therefore, likely to achieve tension reduction under some circumstances, and specific acts of cigarette consumption may be triggered by a variety of psychosocial conditions including boredom, interpersonal discomfort, and periods of negative affect, such as emotional distress (Joffe, Lowe, & Fisher, 1981).

Moreover, smoking cessation may be more difficult for individuals experiencing states of emotional distress (Byrne & Whyte, 1987). A somewhat diffuse collection of evidence therefore points to links between psychological and behavioral factors and rates of cigarette consumption, and insofar as smoking influences coronary risk, the presence of this nebulous collection of factors may accentuate this risk. The evidence is, however, neither uniform nor systematic, and it does not provide a simple behavioral pathway for the regulation of coronary risk. A recent suggestion (Dembroski & McDougall, 1986) that stress and smoking interact to constitute a synergistic risk factor for coronary heart disease presents a fascinating possibility but awaits further exploration.

The consumption of food, like the consumption of cigarettes, is also a complex human behavior. Its determinants, however, are to be found in individual metabolic needs as well as environmental precipitants. Hunger, unlike the acquisition of a smoking habit, is a basic human drive, and eating serves a tension reduction function (Hoyenga & Hoyenga, 1984). It is commonly believed that food consumption increases in times of environmental stress or emotional distress, although there is no systematic association between any index of stress and rates or types of food consumption.

Indeed, there is epidemiological evidence to the effect that those individuals who are overweight show lower levels of anxiety, depression, or environmental stress than do individuals of normal body weight (Crisp, 1986). It is unlikely, therefore, that environmental stress or emotional distress contributes significantly or systematically to food intake. Of course, even if such a relationship were established, there is growing doubt that dietary intake itself contributes substantially to levels of lipids in the blood (Flaim, Ferreri, Thye, Hill, & Ritchey, 1981; Hartung, Foreyt, Mitchell, & Vlasek, 1980). One would, therefore, be hard pressed to claim a link between anxiety or stress, dietary intake, and risk of coronary heart disease insofar as this link was mediated by dietary contributions to blood lipids.

From a different perspective, Dimsdale and Heid (1982) reviewed the results of more than 60 experimental and quasi-experimental studies examining associations between anxiety or stress, variously defined and measured, and serum levels of various lipid substances. They found consistent associations, although of widely varying magnitudes, suggesting that the experience of stress or anxiety may lead to elevations in serum lipid levels (in the short term), although the variability in the magnitude of associations gives some cause for concern. Thus, this is a potentially fruitful area for further investigation, but its value will depend on clarification of concepts, measures, and mechanisms of influence.

Associations between anxiety, stress, and blood pressure have been canvassed, to a large extent, earlier in the chapter. There is quite persuasive evidence that exposure to conditions of perceived threat or cognitive challenge, typically under laboratory control, can produce marked elevations in both diastolic and systolic blood pressure (Jones, 1985; Surwit, Williams, & Shapiro, 1982), but these changes are transient and return to baseline shortly after removal of the threat or challenge. The link between exposure to long-term environmental stressors and protracted elevations in blood pressure is evident in some studies, but the data are rather more equivocal (Surwit, Williams, & Shapiro, 1982). There is no evidence that such transient (or even longer term) changes in blood pressure translate into clinical hypertension (Rosenman & Ward, 1988). Any attempt to relate stress or anxiety to risk of coronary heart disease by way of chronic elevations in blood pressure must, therefore, be treated with very considerable caution.

The possibility, then, that stress or anxiety may influence risk of coronary heart disease through the secondary channel of established risk factors cannot be discounted entirely but also cannot be given overwhelming support. Evidence for short-term influences on both cigarette consumption and blood pressure does exist, but this cannot be translated into persuasive evidence for similar long-term effects. Once more, however, the expectation that such pathways of causal influence should exist may well rest on an oversimplification of the pathogenesis of coronary heart disease.

Finally, one must consider the evidence linking direct observations of environmental stressors or of clinical anxiety with the risk or incidence of coronary heart disease.
In this respect, the retrospective evidence is persuasive; clear links appear to exist
between accumulations of life events, again variously measured, and the experience
of coronary heart disease (Byrne & Whyte, 1980), although it must be kept in mind
that associations based on retrospective data are prone to measurement contamination
and do not allow causal inference. Studies attempting to eliminate measurement contamination have upheld the association (Connolly, 1976). There is still debate, however, as to whether any demonstrated pathogenicity of life events arises from their
objective nature or from the interpretations that individuals make of them (Byrne,
1983). Although retrospective studies of life event stress and coronary heart disease
have consistently supported an association (see chap. 8), the acceptance of the hypothesis rests, in part, on anecdotal or unsystematic evidence, and this must really be
discounted for its methodological frailty.

There is no good evidence that clinical anxiety, psychiatrically identified or
treated, constitutes a risk for coronary heart disease (Martin, Cloniger, Guze, &
Clayton, 1985), although it has been suggested that patients with schizophrenia do
have an increased risk of coronary mortality relative to the general population (Herman, Baldwin, & Christie, 1983). Moreover, the experience of coronary heart disease
does generate anxiety as a response (Byrne, 1979), and there is evidence that this
affective response may relate to patterns of outcome after survived myocardial infarction (Byrne, 1987). One of the areas with as yet untapped clinical potential would
seem to be that of psychological intervention following coronary heart disease (see
chap. 16).

The thrust of this evidence supports a relation between the experience of environ-
mentally originating stressors, or the interpretations that individuals make of them,
and incidence of coronary heart disease. The fact that most studies (and there are
many of them) are retrospective and case-control in design does, however, place
some considerable constraints on the degree to which the data allow conclusions
regarding anxiety, stress, and coronary heart disease. The need for prospective studies is self-evident, but their expense and methodological difficulty have so far impeded their conduct.

Overall, the conclusions that can be made about anxiety and the heart are as yet
limited. On the one hand, the hypotheses are attractive, persuasive, and logical; they
foretell a set of relationships that, to the layperson and scientist alike, might reasonably be expected to exist. The sheer volume of clinical reports, theoretical speculation, and empirical research attests to the attraction of the hypotheses. On the other
hand, the promise of one further explanation for the epidemic that is cardiovascular
disease remains to be completely realized; the empirical data quite simply do not form
consistent, interpretable patterns of results that lead to clear-cut causal inferences. A
great deal of the data do support an empirical relationship of some sort between
anxiety (loosely defined) and diseases of the heart and circulation, but closer inspec-
tion of these data reveal inadequacies of design, measurement, and conceptualization
that reduce their explanatory usefulness, sometimes marginally but occasionally to
nil. Moreover, even when well-collected data point to reliable associations, the mechanisms of influence are often obscure and unproven.

Some parts of the overall picture do give rise to an optimistic outlook. The largely
uniform support provided by studies of life events and coronary heart disease, although limited in interpretation by the retrospectivity of the data, fulfills the impor-

tant epidemiological criterion of consistency (see chap. 8). The establishment, in the laboratory, of possible neuroregulatory mechanisms of influence linking affective state or cognitive challenge with cardiovascular function (see chaps. 5 and 6) may, if extrapolated to the clinical situation, provide plausible explanations of the psychological and cardiovascular nexus. This evidence is strengthened by observed associations between anxiety and both silent myocardial ischemia (see chap. 9) and potentially fatal cardiac arrhythmias (see chap. 10).

The complete picture is, however, neither clear-cut in its pattern nor unconditionally supportive of the hypothesized link. Two broad issues emerge as crucial to an understanding of the failure to achieve more promising results. First, many studies are hindered by methodological problems of design, measurement, or conceptualization. This bears both on the interpretability of studies presenting generally supportive results and the reasons why other studies have been unable to support the hypothesis. Research relating stress and anxiety to illness is notoriously difficult to do well; it poses seemingly overwhelming problems in many respects, particularly if the data are to be relevant to clinical as opposed to theoretical concerns. Yet data from well-conducted, nontrivial studies are needed if the link between stress, anxiety, and coronary heart disease is ever to make the step from a reasonable hypothesis to a confirmed one. If psychology can make a contribution to this task, it will be in the areas of conceptualization and operationalization of key variables, the construction of measures to quantify these variables, and the design of studies of sufficient power to assess causal and uncontaminated associations between these variables.

Second, there appears to have been a view that relationships, if they exist, will be simple, bivariate, and montonic. This is hardly to be expected when one considers two areas, stress or anxiety and cardiovascular disease, both of which are patently complex in their origins, presentation, and outcomes. Subjects involving complex phenomena require sophisticated investigations, and it is no longer tenable to anticipate complete explanations of a pathological process as demonstrably complex as coronary heart disease by relating it statistically to limited fragments of an equally complex psychosocial process, often arbitrarily chosen, crudely measured, and examined at a single, random point in time.

As it stands, the evidence may be seen as a jigsaw puzzle; some of the pattern is discernable but many of the pieces still lie outside awaiting placement. Perhaps the complete pattern will never be apparent, but with care and perseverance in the job of biopsychosocial research, there is no reason to believe that a fuller understanding of anxiety and the heart cannot be achieved.

REFERENCES

Byrne, D. G. (1979). Anxiety as state and trait in survived myocardial infarction. *British Journal of Social and Clinical Psychology, 18,* 417–423.

Byrne, D. G. (1983). Personal determinants of life-events stress and myocardial infarction. *Psychotherapy and Psychosomatics, 40,* 106–114.

Byrne, D. G. (1987). *The behavioral management of the cardiac patient.* Norwood, NJ: Ablex.

Byrne, D. G., & Whyte, H. M. (1980). Life events and myocardial infarction revisited: The role of measures of individual impact. *Psychosomatic Medicine, 42,* 1–10.

Byrne, D. G., & Whyte, H. M. (1987). The efficacy of community based smoking cessation strategies: A long-term follow-up study. *International Journal of Addictions, 22,* 791–801.

Cherry, N., & Kiernan, N. (1976). Personality scores and smoking behavior. *British Journal of Preventative and Social Medicine, 30,* 123–131.

Connolly, J. (1976, December). Life events before myocardial infarction. *Journal of Human Stress,* 3–17.

Crisp, A. H. (1986). Some psychopathological aspects of obesity. In J. H. Lacey & D. A. Sturgeon (Eds.), *Psychosomatic research* (pp. 120–127). London: John Libbay.

Dembroski, T. M., & MacDougall, M. M. (1986). Stress and cigarette smoking: Implications for cardiovascular risk. In T. H. Schmidt, T. M. Dembroski, & G. Bluemchen (Eds.), *Biological and psychological factors in cardiovascular disease.* Berlin: Springer Verlag.

Dimsdale, J. E., & Heid, J. A. (1982). Variability of plasma lipids in response to emotional arousal. *Psychosomatic Medicine, 44,* 413–430.

Eysenck, H. J. (1957). *Dynamics of anxiety and hysteria.* London: Routledge & Kegan.

Flaim, E., Ferreri, L. F., Thye, F. W., Hill, J. E., & Ritchey, S. J. (1981). Plasma lipid and lipoprotein cholesterol concentrations in adult males consuming normal and high cholesterol diets under controlled conditions. *American Journal of Clinical Nutrition, 34,* 1103–1108.

Frankenhaeuser, M. (1979). Psychoneuroendocrine approaches to the study of emotion as related to stress and coping. In H. E. Howe & R. A. Dienstbier (Eds.), *Nebraska symposium on motivation.* Lincoln: University of Nebraska Press.

Greenfield, N. S., & Sternbach, R. A. (1977). *Handbook of psychophysiology.* New York: Holt, Rinehart & Winston.

Hartung, G. H., Foreyt, J. P., Mitchell, R. E., & Vlasek, I. (1980). Relation of diet to high density lipoprotein cholesterol in middle-aged marathon runners, joggers and inactive men. *New England Journal of Medicine, 302,* 358–361.

Henderson, A. S., Byrne, D. G., & Duncan-Jones, P. (1981). *Neurosis and the social environment.* Sydney: Academic Press.

Herman, H. E., Baldwin, J. A., & Christie, D. (1983). A record-linkage study of mortality and general hospital discharge in patients diagnosed as schizophrenic. *Psychological Medicine, 13,* 581–593.

Holmes, T. H., & Rahe, R. H. (1967). The social readjustment rating scale. *Journal of Psychosomatic Research, 11,* 213–218.

Hopkins, P. N., & Williams, R. R. (1981). A survey of 246 suggested coronary risk factors. *Atherosclerosis, 40,* 1–52.

Hoyenga, K. B., & Hoyenga, K. T. (1984). *Motivational explanations of behavior.* Monterey: Brooks/Cole.

James, W. (1890). *The principles of psychology* (Vols. 1–2). New York: Holt.

Joffe, R., Lowe, M. R., & Fisher, E. B. (1981). A validity test of the reasons of smoking scale. *Addictive Behaviors, 6,* 41–45.

Jones, K. V. (1985). The thrill of victory: Blood pressure variability and the Type A behavior pattern. *Journal of Behavioral Medicine, 8,* 277–285.

Lazarus, R. S. (1982). Thoughts on the relations between emotion and cognition. *American Psychologist, 36,* 1019–1024.

Levi, L. (Ed.). (1971). *Society, stress and disease* (Vol. 1). New York: Oxford University Press.

Levi, L. (1972). *Stress and distress in response to psychosocial stimuli.* Stockholm: Acta Medica Scandinavica.

Mandler, G. (1984). *Mind and body.* New York: Norton.

Martin, R. L., Cloniger, C. R., Guze, S. B., & Clayton, J. B. (1985). Mortality in a follow-up of 500 psychiatric outpatients: 1. Total mortality. *Archives of General Psychiatry, 42,* 47–54.

McReynolds, P. (1968). The assessment of anxiety: A survey of available techniques. In P. McReynolds (Ed.), *Advances in psychological assessment* (Vol. 1, pp. 244–264). Palo Alto, CA: Science and Behavior Books.

O'Connor, K. P. (1980). Individual differences in situational preference amongst smokers. *Personality and Individual Differences, 1,* 249–257.

Pechacek, T. F., & McAlister, A. L. (1981). Strategies for the modification of smoking behavior: Treatment and prevention. In J. M. Ferguson & C. B. Taylor (Eds.), *The comprehensive handbook of behavioral medicine* (pp. 257–298). New York: Spectrum.

Pederson, L. L., & Lefcoe, N. M. (1985). Cross-sectional analysis of variables related to cigarette smoking in late adolescence. *Journal of Drug Education, 15,* 225–240.

Reber, A. S. (1985). *Dictionary of psychology.* London: Penguin Books.

Rosenman, R. H., & Ward, M. M. (1988). The changing concept of cardiovascular reactivity. *Stress Medicine, 4,* 241–251.

Rycroft, C. (1968). *Anxiety and neurosis.* London: Penguin Books.

Sarason, I. G., & Sarason, B. R. (1987). *Abnormal psychology.* New Jersey: Prentice-Hall.

Selye, H. (1976). *Stress in health and disease.* Sydney: Butterworth.

Stanaway, R. G., & Watson, D. W. (1980). Smoking motivation: A factor analytic study. *Personality and Individual Differences, 1,* 371–380.

Steptoe, A. (1981). *Psychological factors in cardiovascular disorders*. London: Academic Press.

Surwit, R. S., Williams, R. B., & Shapiro, D. (1982). *Behavioral approaches to cardiovascular disease*. New York: Academic Press.

Tennant, C., Langeluddecke, P., & Byrne, D. G. (1985). The concept of stress. *Australian and New Zealand Journal of Psychiatry, 19*, 113–118.

Yerkes, R. M., & Dodson, J. D. (1908). The relation of strength of stimulus to rapidity of habit-formation. *Journal of Comparative and Neurological Psychology, 18*, 459–482.

Index